Matthew Helmke
with Andrew Hudson
and Paul Hudson

Ubuntu

UNLEASHED

2017 Edition

SAMS | 800 East 96th Street, Indianapolis, Indiana 46240 USA

Ubuntu Unleashed 2017 Edition

For information about buying this title in bulk quantities, or for special sales opportunities (which may include electronic versions; custom cover designs; and content particular to your business, training goals, marketing focus, or branding interests), please contact our corporate sales department at corpsales@pearsoned.com or (800) 382-3419.

For government sales inquiries, please contact governmentsales@pearsoned.com.

For questions about sales outside the U.S., please contact intlcs@pearson.com.

Visit us on the Web: informit.com/aw

ISBN-13: 978-0-13-451118-4

ISBN-10: 0-13-451118-2

Library of Congress Cataloging-in-Publication Data: 2016951091

Printed in the United States of America

Text printed in the United States on recycled paper at RR Donnelley, Crawfordsville, Indiana.

1   16

Editor-in-Chief
Mark Taub

Acquisitions Editor
Debra Williams Cauley

Managing Editor
Sandra Schroeder

Project Editor
Lori Lyons

Production Manager
Dhayanidhi

Proofreader
Sasirekha

Technical Editor
José Antonio Rey

Editorial Assistant
Kim Boedigheimer

Media Producer
Dan Scherf

Cover Designer
Chuti Prasertsith

Compositor
codeMantra

Contents at a Glance

> **NOTE**
>
> Chapters 45–47 can be accessed online at informit.com/title/9780134268118.

Table of Contents

NOTE

Chapters 45–47 can be accessed online at informit.com/title/9780134268118.

Bonus Chapters

About the Author

Matthew Helmke is an active member of the Ubuntu community. He served from 2006 to 2011 on the Ubuntu Forum Council, providing leadership and oversight of the Ubuntu Forums (www.ubuntuforums.org), and spent two years on the Ubuntu regional membership approval board for Europe, the Middle East, and Africa. He has written about Ubuntu for several magazines and websites, is a lead author of *The Official Ubuntu Book*, and coauthored *The VMware Cookbook*. He works as a technical writer for Canonical, Inc., documenting cloud- and DevOps-related software. Matthew first used Unix in 1987 while studying LISP on a VAX at the university. He has run a business using only free- and open-source software, has consulted, and has a master's degree in Information Resources and Library Science from the University of Arizona. You can find out more about Matthew at matthewhelmke.com or drop him a line with errata or suggestions at matthew@matthewhelmke.com.

Andrew Hudson is a freelance journalist who specializes in writing about Linux. He has significant experience in Red Hat- and Debian-based Linux distributions and deployments and can often be found sitting at his keyboard tweaking various settings and config files just for the hell of it. He lives in Wiltshire, which is a county of England, along with his wife, Bernice, and their son, John. Andrew does not like Emacs. He can be reached at andy.hudson@gmail.com.

Paul Hudson is a recognized expert in open source technologies. He is a professional developer and full-time journalist for Future Publishing. His articles have appeared in *MacFormat*, *PC Answers*, *PC Format*, *PC Plus*, and *Linux Format*. Paul is passionate about free software in all its forms and uses a mix of Linux and BSD to power his desktops and servers. Paul likes Emacs. Paul can be contacted through http://hudzilla.org.

Dedication

To Saralyn, Sedona, and Philip—the most amazing kids a guy could hope for; to Sandra and Evan, who are wonderful and welcome additions to our lives; to my grandfather for always believing in me and for teaching me to believe in myself; and to my friends in the Ubuntu, developer, sysadmin, cloud computing, and DevOps communities.

Acknowledgments

Matthew wishes to thank the many people who helped with past editions, with helpful comments and ideas, with technical edits, and with both formal and informal advice. I owe a huge debt of gratitude to the Ubuntu community, Canonical, and Mark Shuttleworth for inviting me to participate in in the community, including my role in the forums, a turn on the EMEA membership board, and two Ubuntu Developer Summits, back when we had to travel to be a part of them. Thanks to the Ubuntu All Stars for the chance to jam with you on guitar. Thank you to the entire Ubuntu community for your labor of love to create this wonderful operating system. Finally, thanks to my colleagues at Pearson, especially Debra Williams Cauley, for the trust placed in me and the opportunity to collaborate on projects like this one.

We Want to Hear from You!

As the reader of this book, *you* are our most important critic and commentator. We value your opinion and want to know what we're doing right, what we could do better, what areas you'd like to see us publish in, and any other words of wisdom you're willing to pass our way.

We welcome your comments. You can email or write to let us know what you did or didn't like about this book—as well as what we can do to make our books better.

Please note that we cannot help you with technical problems related to the topic of this book.

When you write, please be sure to include this book's title and author as well as your name and email address. We will carefully review your comments and share them with the author and editors who worked on the book.

Email: consumer@samspublishing.com

Mail: Sams Publishing
ATTN: Reader Feedback
800 East 96th Street
Indianapolis, IN 46240 USA

Reader Services

Visit our website and register this book at informit.com/register for convenient access to any updates, downloads, or errata that might be available for this book.

Introduction

We are pleased to present the 2017 edition of *Ubuntu Unleashed*. Ubuntu is a Linux-based computer operating system that has taken the world by storm. From its humble beginning in 2004, Ubuntu has risen to be the vanguard of desktop Linux, as well as a popular choice for servers.

Ubuntu descends from one of the oldest and most revered Linux distributions, Debian. Debian is assembled by a team of talented volunteers, is one of the most stable and customizable distributions of Linux, and is well respected for its quality and technological prowess. It is, however, an operating system for geeks; the bar for entry into the Debian realm is set high, and its userbase tends to be highly proficient and expects new users to learn the ropes before joining in. That is both appropriate and okay.

What Ubuntu has done is leverage the quality of Debian to create an operating system that ordinary people can use. That doesn't mean that Ubuntu users are not technologically proficient, just that they do not have to be. In fact, many talented and respected software developers love Ubuntu because it enables them to concentrate on their specific interests instead of the details of the operating system. This book is for these people and for those who aspire to join their ranks.

If you are new to Linux, you have made a great decision by choosing this book. Sams Publishing's *Unleashed* books offer an in-depth look at their subjects, taking in both beginner and advanced users and moving them to a new level of knowledge and expertise. Ubuntu is a fast-changing distribution that has an updated release twice a year. We have tracked the development of Ubuntu from early on to make sure that the information in this book mirrors closely the development of the distribution. A full copy of Ubuntu is included on the enclosed disc, and it is possible for you to install Ubuntu from that disc in less than an hour!

A QUICK WORD ABOUT MARKETING

Almost all of the content in this book applies regardless of what Ubuntu release version you are using, so long as it is reasonably current. The book has been written to try to focus on information that is useful for the longest amount of time possible. Some chapters, like those covering installation or the basics of the default Ubuntu graphical user interface, will have their information change frequently. Those chapters are the exception. The blurb on the cover of the book about which editions this book covers was added to account for these chapters and to denote clearly when the book was most recently revised.

Do not let the highly technical reputation of Linux discourage you, however. Many people who have heard of Linux think that it is found only on servers, looking after websites and email. Nothing could be further from the truth. Distributions like Ubuntu are making huge inroads in to the desktop market. Corporations are realizing the benefits of running a stable and powerful operating system that is easy to maintain and easy to secure. The best part is that as Linux distributions make improvements, the majority of those improvements are shared freely, allowing you to benefit from the additions and refinements made by one distribution, such as Red Hat, while continuing to use a different distribution, such as Ubuntu, which in turn shares its improvements. You can put Ubuntu to work today and be assured of a great user experience. Feel free to make as many copies of the software as you want; Ubuntu is freely and legally distributable all over the world—no copyright lawyers are going to pound on your door.

Licensing

Software licensing is an important issue for all computer users and can entail moral, legal, and financial considerations. Many consumers think that purchasing a copy of a commercial or proprietary operating system, productivity application, utility, or game conveys ownership, but this is not true. In the majority of cases, the *end user license agreement (EULA)* included with a commercial software package states that you have paid only for the right to use the software according to specific terms. This generally means you may not examine, make copies, share, resell, or transfer ownership of the software package. More onerous software licenses enforce terms that preclude you from distributing or publishing comparative performance reviews of the software. Even more insidious licensing schemes (and supporting legislation, especially in the United States) contain provisions allowing onsite auditing of the software's use!

This is not the case with the software included with this book. You are entirely free to make copies, share copies, and install the software on as many computers as you want—we encourage you to purchase additional copies of this book to give as gifts, however. Be sure to read the README file on the disc included with this book for important information regarding the included software and disk contents. After you install Ubuntu, go to www.gnu.org/licenses/gpl.html to find a copy of the GNU GPL. You will see that the GPL provides unrestricted freedom to use, duplicate, share, study, modify, improve, and even sell the software.

You can put your copy of Ubuntu to work right away in your home or at your place of business without worrying about software licensing, per-seat workstation or client licenses, software auditing, royalty payments, or any other type of payments to third parties. However, be aware that although much of the software included with Ubuntu is licensed under the GPL, some packages on this book's disc are licensed under other terms. There is a variety of related software licenses, and many software packages fall under a broad definition known as *open source*. Some of these include the Artistic License, the BSD License, the Mozilla Public License, and the Q Public License.

For additional information about the various GNU software licenses, browse to www.gnu.org/. For a definition of open source and licensing guidelines, along with links to the terms of nearly three dozen open-source licenses, browse to www.opensource.org/.

Who This Book Is For

This book varies its coverage from deep to shallow over its wide range of topics. This is intentional. There are some topics that are Ubuntu-specific and are not covered by any other book, and so deserve deep coverage here. There are some topics that every power user really must master. There are other topics that power users should know about, so that they understand some history, know some other options, or simply have what they need to be able to listen and participate in further discussions with other technical people without being completely confused.

Some topics, like using the Linux command line, receive deep and extensive coverage because I believe that information to be vital to anyone who wants to be a power user or become a skilled DevOps guru. That topic gets two full chapters.

Other topics, like the chapter that mentions ADA and Fortran, along with more than 15 other programming languages, only get brief coverage so that people who are interested get a few guideposts to help them continue if they are interested. In this case, around 20 programming languages are covered in about a dozen pages. These are useful topics to some, but not topics I would consider vital.

Additionally, some topics are just too broad to be covered in great depth in this book, but are topics that deserve a mention because, again, an intermediate to advanced user should have at least a foundational knowledge of them. These are covered and then information is provided to help you find more resources and expand your understanding, as needed.

Those Wanting to Become Intermediate or Advanced Users

Ubuntu Unleashed is intended for intermediate and advanced users or those who want to become one. Our goal is to give you a nudge in the right direction, to help you enter the higher stages by exposing you to as many different tools and ideas as possible; we want to give you some thoughts and methods to consider and spur you on to seek out more.

Although the contents are aimed at intermediate to advanced users, new users who pay attention will benefit from the advice, tips, tricks, traps, and techniques presented in each chapter. Pointers to more detailed or related information are also provided at the end of each chapter.

If you are new to Linux, you might need to learn some new computer skills, such as how to research your computer's hardware, how to partition a hard drive, and (occasionally) how to use a command line. This book helps you learn these skills and shows you how to learn more about your computer, Linux, and the software included with Ubuntu. Most important, it helps you overcome your fear of the system by telling you more about what it is and how it works.

We would like to take a moment to introduce a concept called "The Three Levels of Listening" from Alistair Cockburn's *Agile Software Development*, published by Addison Wesley. These describe how a person learns and masters a technique. We all start at the first stage and progress from there. Few reach the last stage, but those who do are incredibly effective and efficient. People aiming for this stage are the very ones for whom we intend this book.

▶ **Following**—The stage where the learner looks for one very detailed process that works and sticks to it to accomplish a task.

▶ **Detaching**—The stage where the learner feels comfortable with one method and begins to learn other ways to accomplish the same task.

▶ **Fluent**—The stage where the learner has experience with or understanding of many methods and doesn't think of any of them in particular while doing a task.

Myriad books focus on the first set of users. This is not one of them. It is our goal in *Ubuntu Unleashed* to write just enough to be sufficient to get you from where you are to where you want or need to be. This is not a book for newcomers who want or need every step outlined in detail, although we do that occasionally. This is a book for people who want help learning about what can be done and a way to get started doing it. The Internet is an amazing reference tool, so this is not a comprehensive reference book. This book is a tool to help you see the landscape; to learn enough about what you seek to get you started in the right direction with a quality foundational understanding.

Sysadmins, Programmers, and DevOps

Systems administrators, or Sysadmins, are the people who keep servers and networks up and running. Their role is sometimes called *operations*. They deal with software installation and configuration, security, and do all the amazing things behind the scenes that let others use these systems for their work. They are often given less respect than they deserve, but the pay is good and it is a ton of fun to wield the ultimate power over a computer system. It is also a great responsibility, and these amazing guys and gals work hard to make sure they do their jobs well, striving for incredible system uptime and availability. Ubuntu is an excellent operating system for servers and networks, and in this book you can find much of the knowledge needed to get started in this role.

Programmers are the people who write software. They are sometimes called *developers*. Programmers work with others to create the applications that run on top of those systems. Ubuntu is a great platform for writing and testing software. This is true whether you are doing web application development or writing software for desktop or server systems. It also makes a great platform for learning new programming languages and trying out new ideas. This book can help you get started.

DevOps is a portmanteau of *developer* and *operations*. It signifies a blending of the two roles already described. The information technology (IT) world is changing, and roles are becoming less clear cut and isolated from one another. In the past, it was common to witness battles between programmers excited about new technology and sysadmins in love with stability. DevOps realizes that neither goal is healthy in isolation, but that seeking a balance between the two can yield great results by removing the barriers to communication and understanding that sometimes cause conflict within a team. Because of the rise of cloud computing and virtualization, which are also covered in this book, and more agile forms of development, DevOps is a useful perspective that enables people working in IT to do an even better job of serving their ultimate clients: end users. This book is a great foundation for those wanting to learn knowledge that will help with both roles, hopefully presented in a way that balances them nicely.

What This Book Contains

Ubuntu Unleashed is organized into six parts, described here. A disc containing the entire distribution is included so that you have everything you need to get started.

Part I, "Installation and Configuration" takes you through installing Ubuntu on your computer in the place of any other operating system you might be running, such as Windows.

Part II, "Desktop Ubuntu," is aimed at users who want to use Ubuntu on desktop systems.

Part III, "System Administration," covers both elementary and sophisticated details of setting up a system for specific tasks and maintaining that system.

Part IV, "Ubuntu as a Server," gives you the information you need to start building your own file, web, and other servers for use in your home or office.

Part V, "Programming Linux," provides a great introduction to how you can extend Ubuntu capabilities even further using the development tools supplied with it.

In addition to what has already been mentioned, after the spring release of Ubuntu, bonus chapters will be available online at www.informit.com/title/9780134511184 .

In addition, this book is part of InformIT's exciting Content Update Program, which provides content updates for major technology improvements! As significant updates are made to Ubuntu, sections of this book will be updated or new sections will be added to match the updates to the technologies. As updates become available, they will be delivered to you via a free Web Edition of this book, which can be accessed with any Internet connection. To learn more, visit informit.com/cup.

How to access the Web Edition: Follow the instructions inside to learn how to register your book to access the FREE Web Edition.

Conventions Used in This Book

It is impossible to cover every option of every command included in Ubuntu. Besides, with the rise of the Internet and high-speed connections, reference materials are far less valuable than they used to be because most of these details are only a quick Google search away. Instead, we focus on teaching you how to find information you need while giving a quality overview worthy of the intermediate or advanced user. Sometimes this book offers tables of various options, commands, and keystrokes to help condense, organize, and present information about a variety of subjects.

To help you better understand code listing examples and sample command lines, several formatting techniques are used to show input and ownership. For example, if the command or code listing example shows typed input, the input is formatted in boldface after the sample command prompt, as follows:

```
matthew@seymour:~$ ls
```

If typed input is required, as in response to a prompt, the sample typed input also is in boldface, like so:

```
Delete files? [Y/n] y
```

All statements, variables, and text that should appear on your display use the same boldface formatting. In addition, command lines that require root or super-user access are prefaced with the sudo command, as follows:

```
matthew@seymour:~$ sudo printtool &
```

Other formatting techniques include the use of italic for placeholders in computer command syntax. Computer terms or concepts are also italicized upon first introduction in text.

Finally, you should know that all text, sample code, and screenshots in *Ubuntu Unleashed* were developed using Ubuntu and open-source tools.

Read on to start learning about and using the latest version of Ubuntu.

# CHAPTER 1

Installing Ubuntu and Post-Installation Configuration

Not that long ago, the mere mention of installing Linux struck fear into the hearts of mortal men. Thanks to a campaign of fear, uncertainty, and doubt (commonly referred to as FUD), Linux garnered a reputation as something of an elitist operating system that could be installed, configured, and used only by extreme computer geeks and professionals. Nowadays, it is a different story entirely, and Ubuntu is one of the easiest Linux distributions (distros) to install. This chapter covers how to get started with the install disc, including booting from an Ubuntu Live DVD or USB drive to test your system. The chapter then covers the actual installation of Ubuntu, looking at the various options available. The whole process is pain free with Ubuntu, as you are about to learn.

This chapter covers installation on a typical desktop or laptop computer system. It is not intended to provide information about installing Ubuntu on a tablet device or smart phone or anything else…yet.

Before You Begin the Installation

Installing a new operating system is a major event, and you should make sure that you have properly thought through what is going to take place. The first thing to consider is how the hardware will be affected by the software that you propose to install. Although Ubuntu runs well on a variety of hardware, it is worthwhile to check your hardware components because some bits of hardware do not work well with Ubuntu. This section provides some areas for you to investigate and think about; it might even save you hours of frustration when something goes wrong. Problems are becoming much less frequent, but they still crop up occasionally.

You start by researching and documenting your hardware. This information will prove helpful later on during the installation.

Researching Your Hardware Specifications

At the absolute minimum, you should know the basics of your system, such as how much RAM you have installed and what type of mouse, keyboard, and monitor you have. Knowing the storage capacity and type of hard drive you have is important because it helps you plan how you will divide it for Ubuntu and troubleshoot if problems occur. A small detail, such as whether your mouse uses the USB or PS/2 interface, ensures proper pointer configuration—something that should happen without any problem, but you will be glad you know it in case something does go wrong. The more information you have, the better prepared you are for any problems.

You can make an inventory or at least a quick list of some basic features of your system. Again, the items you most want to know include the amount of installed memory, the size of your hard drive, the type of mouse, the capabilities of the display monitor (such as maximum resolution), and the number of installed network interfaces (if any).

DVD INSTALLATION JUMP START

To install Ubuntu Desktop from the disc included with this book, you should first test whether your system is compatible by running Ubuntu from the DVD live. In general, a system must have at least a 1GHz processor, 5GB of hard drive space, and 512MB RAM. A monitor with a display resolution of at least 1024×768 is strongly recommended. Internet access is not required but is very helpful and also recommended. See https://help.ubuntu.com/community/Installation/SystemRequirements for a more detailed list of requirements.

Installation Options

Ubuntu is made available in two main forms: the Desktop DVD and the Server install DVD. (This list does not include derivative distributions like Kubuntu or Lubuntu or less commonly used methods such as the network install disk.) For most people, the Desktop DVD is what you want. The Server install DVD can get a LAMP (Linux, Apache, MySQL, and PHP) server up and running in about 20 minutes, but, as you learn in this book, all these components are available to the Ubuntu default distribution. An ISO image contains the entire contents of a CD or DVD in a single file that can be used as if it were a CD or DVD and that can be burned to a physical CD or DVD if desired. You can find a list of the currently available ISO images in a couple of places. The place that is best for most people to download from is www.ubuntu.com/download, which includes a nice graphical menu system and links to easy-to-read information and detailed instructions. Those with more specific requirements, such as a desire to use one of the official alternative Ubuntu versions like Kubuntu or Lubuntu, can find what they need by navigating the menus at cdimage.ubuntu.com.

OFFICIAL UBUNTU FLAVORS

Ubuntu has several official variants, called *flavors*, as follows:

- ▶ Ubuntu
- ▶ Ubuntu Server
- ▶ Ubuntu GNOME
- ▶ Kubuntu
- ▶ Xubuntu
- ▶ Edubuntu
- ▶ Mythbuntu
- ▶ Ubuntu Studio
- ▶ Lubuntu
- ▶ Ubuntu Kylin

Almost everything in this book applies to any of these flavors. The exceptions include GUI-specific content, such as Unity-specific descriptions, and content that refers to programs not installed by default, such as many of the server and programming options.

To install using the DVD included with in this book, ignore the next couple of paragraphs and then keep reading this chapter.

To install using a DVD that you create, download the ISO image you need from www.ubuntu.com/download or cdimage.ubuntu.com. You need to download a program to enable you to burn this image to physical media. For Windows, try either InfraRecorder (http://infrarecorder.org) or ISO Recorder (http://isorecorder.alexfeinman.com/isorecorder .htm) and follow the instructions given by the authors. For Mac OS X, you can use Apple's Disk Utility, which is installed by default. For Ubuntu, right-click the icon for an ISO image and select Write to Disc. After the DVD is created, use it as you follow the installation instructions in this section.

UBUNTU ON MAC HARDWARE

There are often problems installing Ubuntu on Mac hardware. Apple designs and configures their devices with the intent that only their software should be run on their hardware. Be warned if you want to try to install Ubuntu or anything else on Mac hardware: Here be dragons. It can work, but be prepared to search the web and maybe ask questions in some of the places listed in Chapter 2, "Background Information and Resources." The disc attached to this book will only boot on 64-bit Intel-processor machines. Macs require use of the 32-bit install disc, available from the download location above.

You can also install using a USB thumb drive (use one that holds at least 2GB). Download the ISO image you need. You need to download a program that enables you to use this image to create a bootable USB drive. For Windows, try Universal USB Installer (www.pendrivelinux.com/universal-usb-installer-easy-as-1-2-3/) or ISO Recorder (http://isorecorder.alexfeinman.com/isorecorder.htm) and follow the instructions given by the authors. For Ubuntu, use the installed Startup Disk Creator program available by searching in the Dash. After the ISO is written to the USB drive, use it as you follow the installation instructions in this section.

32-Bit vs 64-Bit Ubuntu

All users who can use it are better off using the 64-bit version of Ubuntu. The main difference has to do with how a computer processor is able to register and use memory, but speed is also a factor. Here is why.

A computer with a 32-bit processor will be able to use a maximum of 4GB of memory (actually a bit less, but this is a more practical-focused book and not a computer science text, so the approximation is close enough for our uses; and yes, there are exceptions, but this is a reasonable rule of thumb for those just getting started). A computer with a 64-bit processor will be able to use up to a theoretical limit of 17 billion GB. More memory addresses means that you can store more data in RAM, which is much faster than processing it while reading from and writing to disks or other storage media.

If you are dealing with large amounts of data, this is a huge benefit. Processing audio or video, manipulating large databases of weather data, or playing 3D video games will be much smoother. It will also happen faster.

Speed is increased for another reason. When you have more memory addresses, it is kind of like when the supermarket has more checkout lines open. You can process more operations simultaneously. As a result of the extra capacity, variables and arrays in programs are processed more efficiently, function arguments are passed more easily, and even new data models are available for programmers and languages to use.

This requires some adaptation. Programs written for 32-bit operating systems must generally be adapted to take advantage of the capabilities of 64-bit processors. Although it is (usually, or at least often) possible to run 32-bit programs on a 64-bit processor, it is not always advantageous to do so. However, in the Linux world, including Ubuntu, most software has been refactored and recompiled to take advantage of 64-bit processors and their capabilities. Software written for 64-bit processors is not backward compatible with 32-bit processors.

Early on, driver support and adaptation of software took time and was not complete enough to recommend using 64-bit Ubuntu by default. For about a decade, nearly all Intel- and AMD-based computer systems sold have been 64-bit, and the software has caught up. There is no reason to use anything else on this equipment. The disc attached to this book only boots on 64-bit machines

If you browse to ubuntu.com/releases, you will find downloadable .iso files that will allow you to create a DVD from which you can boot/install Ubuntu. Each is intended for a different sort of processor and setting, such as server and desktop:

▶ **i386:** This supports all Intel or compatible processors except those that require AMD64. This includes current Apple hardware. If you are not certain which you need, use this one. It works on either 32-bit or 64-bit systems, so it is the default choice.

▶ **AMD64:** If you know you are using a processor based on the AMD64 or EM64T architecture (for example, Athlon64, Opteron, EM64T Xeon, Core2), you should choose this version because it will be a bit more efficient on your hardware. This is the one on the attached DVD.

Planning Partition Strategies

Partitioning is a topic that can make novice Linux users nervous. Coming from a Microsoft world, where you might be used to having just one hard drive, it can seem a bit strange to use an operating system that makes partitioning a hard drive possible or even preferable and common.

Depending on your needs, you can opt to have a single large partition to contain everything, which is the official recommendation of the Ubuntu community and developers. You might prefer to segment your installation across several partitions if you have advanced knowledge and specific needs.

If you are installing Ubuntu in a corporate or business environment, the needs of the business should be a primary concern. Be careful to ensure that you build in an adequate upgrade path that allows you to extend the life of the system and add any additional storage or memory.

Knowing how software is placed on your hard drive for Linux involves knowing how Ubuntu organizes its file system. This knowledge helps you make the most out of hard drive space. In some instances, such as when you're planning to have user directories mounted via NFS or other means, this information can help head off data loss, increase security, and accommodate future needs. Create a great system, and you'll be the hero of information services. The Linux file system is covered along with commands to manipulate files and directories in Chapter 10, "Command-Line Beginner's Class."

To plan the best partitioning scheme, research and know the answers to these questions:

▶ How much disk space does your system require?

▶ Do you expect your disk space needs to grow significantly in the future?

▶ Will the system boot only Ubuntu, or do you need a dual-boot system?

▶ How much data requires backup, and what backup system will work best? (See Chapter 17, "Backing Up," for more information about backing up your system.)

The Boot Loader

During installation, Ubuntu automatically installs *GRUB2 (Grand Unified Boot Loader)* to the *Master Boot Record (MBR)* of your hard drive. Handily enough, it also detects any other operating systems, such as Windows, and adds entries in GRUB2 as appropriate. If you have a specific requirement not to install GRUB2 to the MBR, you need to install using the Alternate disc, which enables you to specify the install location for GRUB2.

DUAL BOOT NOT RECOMMENDED, BUT YOU CAN TRY IT IF YOU WANT

If you are attempting to create a dual-boot system using both Windows and Ubuntu, a system in which multiple operating systems exist on the hard drive and the user selects which one to use at boot time, you should install Windows first because it will overwrite the MBR and ignore any other operating systems on the disk. Ubuntu also overwrites the MBR, but does so in a way that creates a boot menu that includes all operating systems it detects on the disk. Dual-booting works, but in the past few years options have arisen that are better for most people.

If you decide you must dual boot, make sure you have your Windows recovery media available and that you either already have enough free space on your hard drive or know how to shrink the existing Windows partition and create a new partition on the hard drive for Ubuntu. No support or instructions for doing this are given in this book. If you need to use more than one operating system on the same hardware, this book recommends virtualization.

See Chapter 34, "Virtualization on Ubuntu," for more information.

Installing from DVD or USB Drive

The BIOS of most PCs support booting directly from a CD, DVD, or USB drive and enable you to set a specific order of devices (such as floppy, hard drive, CD-ROM, or USB) to search for bootable software. Turn on your PC and set its BIOS if required (usually accessed by pressing a function key or the Del key after powering on) and then insert your Ubuntu install media and boot to install Ubuntu.

UEFI

If you have hardware that is from 2010 or newer, it probably includes a firmware interface called UEFI. The Unified Extensible Firmware Interface is a specification that defines how an operating system and the hardware interact. It replaces the BIOS mentioned above. It has also been known to cause problems when you try to install a different operating system than the default one it came with on one of these machines. The 64-bit version of Ubuntu has become more reliable in supporting installation on these machines with each Ubuntu release. However, if you encounter difficulties, see https://help.ubuntu.com/community/UEFI for assistance.

Step-by-Step Installation

This section provides a basic step-by-step installation of Ubuntu from the install DVD included with this book, but these instructions also work with media you create yourself using an ISO image you downloaded and wrote to a disk or USB drive using the instructions provided earlier; just replace mentions of DVD with your install medium. The install process itself is fairly straightforward, and you should not encounter any real problems.

CAUTION

If you have anything at all on your computer that you want to save, back it up first. Installing an operating system has become easier to do, but it is still a major change. Your entire hard drive will be erased and new information written to it. This is expected when installing Ubuntu to the entire hard drive, but it can even happen due to user error or gremlins (unexplained problems) when attempting a dual-boot installation. Back up anything you want to preserve. Save data and files to an external hard drive or other medium. You may even want to back up your entire operating system and current installation using something like Clonezilla (http://clonezilla.org). Whatever you do, go in with the perspective that everything currently on the computer will disappear. If this is okay, continue.

It is useful and recommended to have your computer connected to the Internet as you proceed so that you can download updates while installing.

Installing

To get started, insert the DVD into your drive and reboot your computer.

NOTICE

The installation process occasionally changes when new releases occur, but the overall idea is consistent. The screenshots you see here are probably accurate, but it is possible you may see a change or two. If you understand what you need to do, any changes should be trivial to you.

The initial screen offers a variety of languages for you to use during installation (see Figure 1.1) and two options. The Try Ubuntu option boots and runs Ubuntu from the DVD without making any changes to your system so that when you remove the DVD and reboot, everything will be as it was before. Install Ubuntu installs Ubuntu instead of your current operating system or alongside it (for dual booting). Select Install Ubuntu to begin.

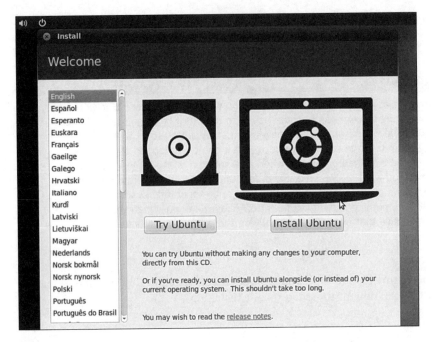

FIGURE 1.1   Choose a language for the installation in this opening screen.

Figure 1.2 shows the Preparing to Install Ubuntu screen. If you select the two check boxes at the bottom, Ubuntu downloads extra software, such as multimedia codecs and any software updates that have been released since the disk was created, and includes them in the installation. Doing so is recommended.

If other operating systems are found on your system, you are given the option to install Ubuntu alongside them or to erase them and use the whole disk for Ubuntu. See the dual-boot note and backup warning earlier in this chapter before continuing.

Next, you have the option either to erase and use the entire hard disk for your installation (recommended for people who are new to Linux and are nervous about partitioning a hard drive) or to specify partitions manually, which is not as difficult as it sounds, as shown in Figure 1.3.

Because this is a book for people who want a deeper understanding of their systems, we show a simple partitioning scheme here and give some reasons for our choices.

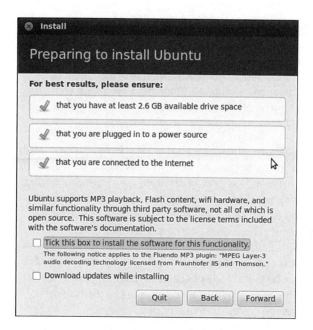

FIGURE 1.2   Before proceeding, double-check that your system meets the requirements shown.

FIGURE 1.3   What do you want to do with your hard drive?

Your needs may vary, so we give some principles to consider so that you may adjust our recommendations to your situation.

ENCRYPTED /HOME?

You are given the opportunity during installation to encrypt your /home partition, which is where your personal files will be stored. Doing so ensures that a password or passphrase must be entered for anyone to access the contents. The downside is that the contents won't be accessible even to you if you forget your password. Consider your needs and choose accordingly.

Many users benefit from three simple partitions, shown in Figure 1.4. Here we have a swap partition, a root partition (denoted by /), and a home partition in which data for each user on the system is stored. The swap partition was previously used for those times when there was not enough memory for running processes, so the Linux kernel, when moving stored information from RAM to the hard drive, could use that swap space as extra RAM. This is slow, but sometimes it is quite useful. These days, desktop systems come with more memory, and the swap space is used mainly for storing information during suspend and hibernate, which is an alternative you can use instead of turning your computer off. Having /home on a separate partition can be a good idea because it enables you to install a different Linux distribution or a different release of Ubuntu on your / partition while retaining your user data (neither of which are covered in this book).

FIGURE 1.4   A simple but useful partitioning scheme.

> **NOTE**
>
> *Suspend* saves your current system state to RAM and then turns off power to most of the system, but it maintains just enough power use to keep that state saved in RAM. When you restart your system, it comes back quickly to the same state it was in. Hibernate saves your current system state to the hard disk. These days, it is just as fast to boot from scratch as it is to hibernate and restore, so there isn't much point in using it.

If you choose to manually partition instead of using the entire disk, we recommend you have a / partition of at least 3GB and a swap partition that is about 1.5 to 2 times the size of your installed RAM; you can use the rest of the disk for /home. More complex partitioning schemes might be useful for more complex systems, such as servers, especially when multiple hard drives are available. Read Chapter 10, "Command-Line Beginner's Class," for a quick discussion of the parts of the Linux file system to get an idea of parts of the file system that could benefit from residing on their own (or even multiple!) partitions or disks.

> **NOTE**
>
> Adding, formatting, and partitioning a hard drive can be done at any time, not only during installation. You should not try to modify a drive you are currently using, such as the one on which you have installed Ubuntu, because doing so could make the computer unusable, and you would have to start over. However, if you are adding a second drive or if you want to reformat a flash drive, partitioning the drive you're using is a useful skill to know. In any case, this is an instance where the standard warning applies: Pay attention to what you are doing and know why you are doing it, because this powerful tool both is useful and has the potential to cause you serious problems and data loss if used incorrectly.
>
> The easiest and simplest method is to use GParted, which is a graphical partition manager. GParted is not installed by default, but it is available in the Ubuntu software repositories; see Chapter 9, "Managing Software" if you need help installing it.
>
> In addition to being useful for adding drives, GParted can also assist you in recovering from problems. You can run it after booting Ubuntu in a live session, running from a live cd or a USB drive. In this case, the system's hard drives are not mounted and you can manage them from the live session.

After you have made your partitioning selections, installation continues by asking about your current location; it helps you select the most appropriate keyboard layout for your system based on that location and the most common language used there, and it asks you to enter your name, a username that you will use to login to the system, and a password. You can even choose to encrypt your /home folder during the process.

A QUICK ASIDE ON PASSWORDS

When you create your password, be sure to remember what you entered. If you forget it, you cannot use your new system because you will not be able to log on to it.

When setting a password, the common advice is to make sure that it has a mixture of letters and numbers to make it more secure. For instance, a good example of a historically recommended style of password is `T1a5c0p`. Although this might seem like garbage at first glance, the easy way to remember it is by remembering the phrase This Is A Good Choice Of Password, shortened to Tiagcop, and finally substituting some of the letters with similar-looking numbers.

There are some reasons why this might not be the best recommendation anymore because computer systems are much faster than they used to be. It is a true statement that the longer a password is, the harder it is to break. For this reason, the newest recommendation is to use a passphrase consisting of at least four words, perhaps something like *green monkeys chortle often*. There is no doubt that a password the length of four common words combined together would be harder to break than the `T1a5c0p` example. From that perspective, it seems like a no-brainer. On the other hand, a longer password that does not use any words found in a dictionary would be even better, but the problem here is that these passwords, and even the `T1a5c0p` example, can be hard to remember and may end up being written down on a sticky note next to the computer, perhaps even stuck to the monitor. That is worse, especially if you use good security and create a different password for every website and computer system that requires one.

One solution is to choose a really good password for your system, one that you will remember, like the four words example or a long passphrase like PeanutButterandJelly $andwiches, and then create one more good password to use with a password manager program like KeyPassX (available in the Ubuntu software repositories; see Chapter 9, "Managing Software," for details on how to find and install it), which can generate long, completely random passwords for you and keep them in a list that can only be viewed by accessing your system and then accessing the program, both of which will use good passwords. Let's get back to the installation.

While you are answering the questions asked by the installer, the Ubuntu install has already begun to copy files to your hard drive. Performing these tasks in parallel makes the process even faster than it used to be. Now that you have input all necessary information, you see a series of information screens while the installation is completed. These are filled with interesting content about Ubuntu and are worth reading while you wait.

When the process is complete, you are prompted to restart the computer. Do so and remove the install media when it is ejected. Then log in when the reboot is complete. That's it.

In previous editions of this book, this chapter was longer and described a process that was sometimes confusing and fraught with peril. The Ubuntu developers deserve high praise for making this so incredibly easy and fast. The Linux kernel supports more hardware than ever, and the Ubuntu kernel gurus (who make the decisions about what hardware modules to enable, among other things) do a great job so that most hardware works out of the box.

First Update

It used to be that the first thing that you needed to do with your new system was update it to the latest package versions. You do this mainly to ensure that you have the latest security updates available. Remember that first installation step where we recommended checking the box to have software updates downloaded during the installation process? That means these updates were acquired during the installation and that your system should be up-to-the-minute current.

If you want to double-check that you have all the current versions of software and security updates installed, read Chapter 9, "Managing Software," and Chapter 10, "Command-Line Beginner's Class," for more information.

Shutting Down

At some point, you are going to want to shut down your computer. As with most things in Linux, there are different ways to do it. You can use the power icon located in the upper-right corner of your screen and its drop-down menu, as in Figure 1.5. From there, select Switch Off.

FIGURE 1.5   You have several options in the power icon menu.

If you are working at the command line, you can immediately shut down your system by using the shutdown command like this:

```
matthew@seymour:~$ sudo shutdown -h now
```

You can also use the shutdown command to restart your computer, as follows:

```
matthew@seymour:~$ sudo shutdown -r now
```

For new users, installing Ubuntu is the beginning of a new and highly rewarding journey on the path to learning Linux. For Ubuntu system administrators, the task ahead is to fine-tune the installation and to customize the server or user environment.

NOTE

Now that you have completed the primary task of installing Ubuntu, you can begin to customize your new operating system. This chapter looks at getting up and running with Ubuntu. Chapter 3, "Working with Unity," gives you a tour around the desktop. You should read these two chapters. Right now, you find out how to do some basic administration tasks. By the end of this chapter, you should feel comfortable enough to move on through the rest of the book.

Finding Programs and Files

In the past, Ubuntu used a system of menus to guide users in searching for programs, but now there is an easier, faster way. Use the Dash to find programs. You access the Dash by clicking the Ubuntu logo at the upper left of the screen. This brings up the menu shown in Figure 1.6. Start typing in the Search box to find specific programs or documents on your system. The icons in the row along the bottom of the Dash provide categories you can use to narrow searches. When you click the house icon, you go to the main Dash screen as shown in the figure. Click the second icon to see installed applications and a list of other applications that are available for installation. Click the arrow next to See More Results to view all installed software. Click the third icon to see documents or the fourth icon to see media. The Dash is covered in more detail in Chapter 3, "Working with Unity."

FIGURE 1.6 The Dash is the place to find programs and files.

Software Updater

This topic is covered in greater detail in Chapter 9, "Managing Software," but it is worthy of a quick mention now so that from the start you can benefit from any available security and bug fixes. The easiest way to check for updates is Software Updater. Open Software Updater from the Dash by typing **software updater** to search for it. When the window opens, Update Manager checks the Ubuntu software repositories to determine whether any updates are available. When it detects that new versions of installed software are available, they display in the window. Uncheck the check box next to any item if you don't want to install that particular software update. Click Install Updates to complete the process (see Figure 1.7). Software repositories are discussed later in this chapter.

FIGURE 1.7   Software Updater showing available software updates.

Another way of updating your system is to use the command line. This is vital on servers that do not have a GUI installed, and it is sometimes quicker than using Software Updater on a desktop computer. I like to use the command line to manage all the computers on my home network because I can use Secure Shell (SSH) to connect to each from a terminal and perform updates from another room in the house; anyone using that computer is left undisturbed while I'm making updates. You find out how to connect using the command line in Chapter 19, "Remote Access with SSH, Telnet, and VNC."

> **NOTE**
>
> In the second half of the "Software Updater" section and in "The `sudo` Command" section that follows, we introduce some commands that must be entered from the *command line*, also known as the *terminal*.
>
> Rather than a graphics-based user interface, this is a more traditional text-based user interface. Chapter 10, "Command-Line Beginner's Class," Chapter 11, "Command-Line Master Class Part 1" and Chapter 12, "Command-Line Master Class Part 2" cover this topic in much greater detail.
>
> For now, the goal is to introduce you to the idea and let you know what can be done. You are not yet expected to know what a lot of this means.
>
> To use the command line, open the Dash and type **terminal**.

When you open the terminal, you are greeted with a prompt similar to the one here:

```
matthew@seymour:~$
```

A blinking cursor also displays. Ubuntu is awaiting your first command. Issue the following command:

```
matthew@seymour:~$ sudo apt-get update
```

This command tells the package management utility `apt-get` to check the Ubuntu repositories and look for any updates to your installed software. In a matter of seconds, Ubuntu completes all of this, and your screen should look something like this:

```
matthew@seymour:~$ sudo apt-get update
[sudo] password for matthew:
Hit http://security.ubuntu.com xenial-security Release.gpg
Ign http://security.ubuntu.com/ubuntu/ xenial-security/main Translation-en
Hit http://us.archive.ubuntu.com xenial Release.gpg
Ign http://us.archive.ubuntu.com/ubuntu/ xenial/main Translation-en
Ign http://us.archive.ubuntu.com/ubuntu/ xenial/main Translation-en_US
Ign http://security.ubuntu.com/ubuntu/ xenial-security/main Translation-en_US
Ign http://security.ubuntu.com/ubuntu/ xenial-security/multiverse Translation-en
Ign http://security.ubuntu.com/ubuntu/ xenial-security/multiverse Translation-en_US
Ign http://security.ubuntu.com/ubuntu/ xenial-security/restricted Translation-en
Ign http://security.ubuntu.com/ubuntu/ xenial-security/restricted Translation-en_US
Ign http://security.ubuntu.com/ubuntu/ xenial-security/universe Translation-en
Ign http://security.ubuntu.com/ubuntu/ xenial-security/universe Translation-en_US
Ign http://us.archive.ubuntu.com/ubuntu/ xenial/multiverse Translation-en
Ign http://us.archive.ubuntu.com/ubuntu/ xenial/multiverse Translation-en_US
Ign http://us.archive.ubuntu.com/ubuntu/ xenial/restricted Translation-en
Ign http://us.archive.ubuntu.com/ubuntu/ xenial/restricted Translation-en_US
Ign http://us.archive.ubuntu.com/ubuntu/ xenial/universe Translation-en
Ign http://us.archive.ubuntu.com/ubuntu/ xenial/universe Translation-en_US
Hit http://us.archive.ubuntu.com xenial-updates Release.gpg
```

```
Hit http://security.ubuntu.com xenial-security Release
Ign http://us.archive.ubuntu.com/ubuntu/ xenial-updates/main Translation-en
Ign http://us.archive.ubuntu.com/ubuntu/ xenial-updates/main Translation-en_US
Ign http://us.archive.ubuntu.com/ubuntu/ xenial-updates/multiverse Translation-en
Ign http://us.archive.ubuntu.com/ubuntu/ xenial-updates/multiverse Translation-en_US
Ign http://us.archive.ubuntu.com/ubuntu/ xenial-updates/restricted Translation-en
Ign http://us.archive.ubuntu.com/ubuntu/ xenial-updates/restricted Translation-en_US
Ign http://us.archive.ubuntu.com/ubuntu/ xenial-updates/universe Translation-en
Ign http://us.archive.ubuntu.com/ubuntu/ xenial-updates/universe Translation-en_US
Hit http://security.ubuntu.com xenial-security/main Sources
Hit http://us.archive.ubuntu.com xenial Release
Hit http://us.archive.ubuntu.com xenial-updates Release
Hit http://security.ubuntu.com xenial-security/restricted Sources
Hit http://security.ubuntu.com xenial-security/universe Sources
Hit http://security.ubuntu.com xenial-security/multiverse Sources
Hit http://security.ubuntu.com xenial-security/main i386 Packages
Hit http://security.ubuntu.com xenial-security/restricted i386 Packages
Hit http://us.archive.ubuntu.com xenial/main Sources
Hit http://security.ubuntu.com xenial-security/universe i386 Packages
Hit http://security.ubuntu.com xenial-security/multiverse i386 Packages
Hit http://us.archive.ubuntu.com xenial/restricted Sources
Hit http://us.archive.ubuntu.com xenial/universe Sources
Hit http://us.archive.ubuntu.com xenial/multiverse Sources
Hit http://us.archive.ubuntu.com xenial/main i386 Packages
Hit http://us.archive.ubuntu.com xenial/restricted i386 Packages
Hit http://us.archive.ubuntu.com xenial/universe i386 Packages
Hit http://us.archive.ubuntu.com xenial/multiverse i386 Packages
Hit http://us.archive.ubuntu.com xenial-updates/main Sources
Hit http://us.archive.ubuntu.com xenial-updates/restricted Sources
Hit http://us.archive.ubuntu.com xenial-updates/universe Sources
Hit http://us.archive.ubuntu.com xenial-updates/multiverse Sources
Hit http://us.archive.ubuntu.com xenial-updates/main i386 Packages
Hit http://us.archive.ubuntu.com xenial-updates/restricted i386 Packages
Hit http://us.archive.ubuntu.com xenial-updates/universe i386 Packages
Hit http://us.archive.ubuntu.com xenial-updates/multiverse i386 Packages
Reading package lists... Done
matthew@seymour:~$
```

Upgrade your software by entering the following:

```
matthew@seymour:~$ apt-get dist-upgrade
```

Because you have already checked for updates, Ubuntu automatically knows to download and install only the packages it needs. The dist-upgrade option works intelligently to ensure that any dependencies that are needed can be satisfied and will be installed, even if major changes are needed. You can also use the option upgrade, which isn't as smart as dist-upgrade, but it might be a better choice on a production server because upgrade does not make major changes to software installations. It only makes those changes necessary for security and simple package updates. This allows the systems administrator more flexibility to keep up to date with security while keeping running setups otherwise unchanged.

The sudo Command

You will find as you work through this book that Ubuntu relies on the sudo command while you work at the command line. This command is used in front of other commands to tell Ubuntu that you want to run the specified command with super user powers. This sounds really special, and it actually is. When you work using the sudo command, you can make wide-ranging changes to your system that affect the way it runs. Be extra careful when running any command prefixed with sudo; however, a wrong option or incorrect command can have devastating consequences.

The use of sudo is straightforward. All you have to do is enter it like this:

```
matthew@seymour:~$ sudo command commandoptions
```

Just replace the word command with the command that you want to run, along with any options. For example, the following command opens your xorg.conf file in vi and enables you to make any changes as the super user before being able to save it:

```
matthew@seymour:~$ sudo vi /etc/X11/xorg.conf
```

Whenever you execute a command using sudo, you are prompted for your password. This is the same password that you use to log in to Ubuntu, so it is important that you remember it.

Sometimes, however, you might want to work with a classic root prompt instead of having to type sudo in front of every command (perhaps if you have to work with lots of commands at the command line that require super user access, for example). sudo enables you to do this by using the sudo -i command. Again, you are prompted for your password, which you should enter, after which Ubuntu gives you the standard root prompt, as follows:

```
matthew@seymour:~#
```

From here, you can execute any command without having to keep entering sudo.

WARNING

Working from the root prompt can be really dangerous unless you know what you are doing. Until you are experienced, we recommend you stick to using sudo, which is covered in more detail in Chapter 10, "Command-Line Beginner's Class."

Configuring Software Repositories

Ubuntu uses software repositories to get information about available software that can be installed on your system. Ubuntu is based on a much older Linux distribution called Debian. Debian has access to tens of thousands of different packages, which means that Ubuntu has access to these packages, too. The Debian packages are made available in Ubuntu's Universe repository. A set of volunteers called *Masters of the Universe (MOTUs)* are well trained and follow strict guidelines to package software and make even more packages available to Ubuntu users in the Universe repository. (See Chapter 40, "Helping with Ubuntu Development," for more about the MOTUs and how you can become one of them.) The Universe repository is filled with optional and often useful or fun software; it is enabled by default, along with other official repositories containing software necessary for Ubuntu to be installed and run in all its various official forms, security updates, and software updates.

You can adjust which repositories are enabled using the Software Sources GUI tool, available in Software Updater by clicking Settings. On the first tab (Ubuntu Software), you have five options to choose from. The default settings are shown in Figure 1.8. It is entirely up to you which options you check, but make sure that at least the first check box is selected to allow you access to Canonical-supported open source software, which includes all the packages necessary for a basic Ubuntu installation and a few more that are commonly used. The more boxes you check, the wider your selection of software. It's also a good idea to make sure that the Proprietary Drivers for Devices box is checked so that you can benefit from drivers that might enhance your system's performance.

FIGURE 1.8   You can find or add other options under the Other Software and Updates tabs.

OPEN SOURCE VERSUS PROPRIETARY

You might hear some arguments about using proprietary drivers or other software in Ubuntu. Some people feel that the use of such drivers goes against what *open source* stands for because the program code used for the drivers or software cannot be viewed and modified by the wider community but only by the original developers or company that owns it. There is also a strong argument that says users should have to undergo the least amount of work for a fully functional system.

Ubuntu takes a middle-of-the-road stance on this and leaves it up to the user to decide. Open source software is installed by default, but options are given to allow proprietary software to be installed easily.

After you are happy with your selections, switch to the Updates tab to configure Ubuntu's behavior when updates are available (see Figure 1.9). By default, both the important security updates and recommended updates are checked to ensure that you have the latest bug fixes and patches. You can also choose to receive proposed updates and *backports* (software that is released for a newer version of Ubuntu but reprogrammed to be compatible with the current release), but we recommend this only if you are happy to carry out testing for the community because any updated software from these repositories can adversely affect your system.

FIGURE 1.9   In the Updates tab of Software Sources, configure which updates you want and how you want them to be handled.

Ubuntu also enables you to configure how often it checks for updates and how they are installed. By default, Ubuntu checks daily for updates and, if any are available, notifies you. However, you can change the frequency and the actions Ubuntu carries out when it finds available updates. We recommend keeping the notification-only option because this enables you to see what updates are available prior to their installation. If you want to save time, choose Download All Updates in the Background to configure Ubuntu to silently download the updates before it gives you the option to install them.

Part of the magic of Ubuntu is the ease in which you can upgrade from major version to major version, such as moving from 16.04 to 16.10. Some Ubuntu releases are called LTS, for *long-term support*, and are intended for production use by most people. The interim releases are for those who feel they must have the most recent version of everything or those who help work on Ubuntu development. These releases are stable, but they are only supported for a short time, so if you choose to use them you should plan to upgrade to the new release every six months. By ensuring that the release upgrade option is set to long-term support releases only, you'll be prompted to upgrade your version of Ubuntu only every two years; the next LTS version, 18.04, is scheduled to be released in April 2018.

The Other Software tab enables you to add other repositories. It comes by default with everything you need to connect to and use Canonical's partner repository, with nonfree (usually in the licensing sense, but occasionally for payment) software from companies that have an agreement with Canonical to make it easily available to interested users. This repository is disabled by default, and if you want to use it, you must enable it by checking a box next to its entry in the Other Software tab.

System Settings

To configure system settings, search the Dash for System Settings. This brings up the menu in Figure 1.10, from which you can make adjustments as desired. A couple of the options are described in the following sections.

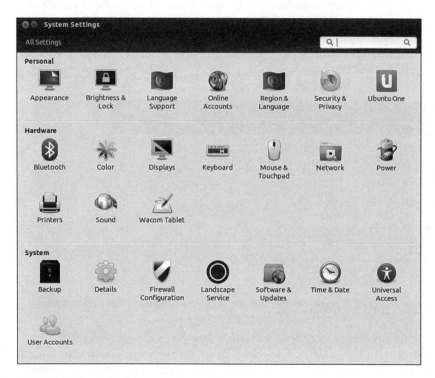

FIGURE 1.10   Adjust your system settings.

Detecting and Configuring a Printer

Setting up a printer in Linux used to be so difficult that previous editions of this book included an entire chapter filled with command-line magic and scary looking configuration files. The setup is no longer as difficult in most cases.

Ubuntu includes drivers for many printers, and it is usually easier to install and use a printer in Ubuntu than in other operating systems. (This is not an absolute rule, though.) Some printer manufacturers do not write and release drivers for Linux, and for some printers no open source driver exists. Before you buy a printer, it is a good idea to spend some time on the Internet searching for printers that are known to work with Linux. One great resource is the Open Printing database from The Linux Foundation, at www.openprinting.org/printers.

If you choose wisely, all you need to do is plug your printer into the computer and turn it on. In many cases, Ubuntu finds the printer and adds the driver automatically. Within a couple of minutes, you should be able to use it. You can find Printing in the System Settings menu and use it to see all installed and configured printers and change their settings. From here you can choose to enable printer sharing on a network, set options for default print quality, print a test page, and more.

Configuring Power Management in Ubuntu

Click the Power icon in the System Settings menu to control how Ubuntu handles power-saving features in specific situations (see Figure 1.11). You can have the display dim the backlight to use less power when on battery, put the display to sleep after a certain amount of inactivity, spin down your hard disks (kind of like turning them off, but not completely; this just makes them stop moving until a request is made from them, saving power in the interim), and set your computer to suspend, hibernate, or turn off when the battery reaches a certain level.

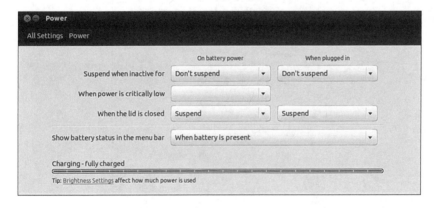

FIGURE 1.11   Configure specific power-related actions with Power Management Preferences.

Ubuntu provides good support for suspend. *Suspend* means that your computer writes its current state to memory and goes into a low-power mode. Your computer will start much faster the next time you use it because it does not need to perform a full boot, but rather brings the system up to its previous state out of memory instead of loading and starting every program again from scratch.

Setting the Time and Date

Linux provides a system time and date; your computer hardware provides a hardware clock-based time. In many cases, it is possible for the two times to drift apart. Linux system time is based on the number of seconds elapsed since January 1, 1970. Your computer's hardware time depends on the type of clock chips installed on your PC's motherboard, and many motherboard chipsets are notoriously subject to drift.

Keeping accurate time is important on a single workstation, but it is critically important in a network environment. Backups, scheduled downtimes, and other network-wide actions need to be accurately coordinated.

The Ubuntu installer sets the time and date during the installation process when it asks for your location. If you move or just want to change the settings (for example, to have your computer automatically synchronize its clock with official time servers on the Internet), you can do so.

Changing the Time and Date

Ubuntu's graphical tool is the simplest way to set your system date and time and the most obvious for a desktop user. The client is called Time & Date in the System Settings menu.

To make any changes to this tool, you need to unlock it by clicking the Unlock button. Only a user who has administrator privileges may use this tool, and you must enter your password to authenticate. After you've done this, you can change any of the options.

Manually set the date and time in the GUI (see Figure 1.12) or have your computer obtain updated date and time information via the Internet by selecting Automatically from the Internet. The Clock tab includes settings to adjust what is displayed at the upper right of your desktop.

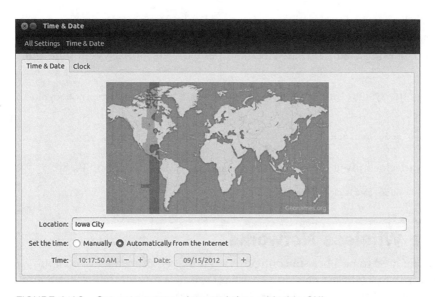

FIGURE 1.12   Set your system date and time with this GUI.

Using the date **Command**

Use the date command to display or set your Linux system time. This command requires you to use a specific sequence of numbers to represent the desired date and time. To see your Linux system's idea of the current date and time, use the date command like this:

```
matthew@seymour:~$ date
Fri Sep 28 18:03:14 CDT 2013
```

To adjust your system's time (for example, to September 28, 2012 at 10:33 a.m.), use a command line with the month, day, hour, minute, and year, like so:

```
matthew@seymour:~$ sudo date 092810332012
Fri Sep 28 18:03:14 CDT 2013
```

Using the hwclock **Command**

Use the hwclock command to display or set your Linux system time, display or set your PC's hardware clock, or to synchronize the system and hardware times. To see your hardware time and date, use hwclock with its --show option, like so:

```
matthew@seymour:~$ sudo hwclock --show
Fri 28 Sep 2013 06:04:43 PM CDT   -0.281699 seconds
```

Use hwclock with its --set and --date options to manually set the hardware clock, as follows:

```
matthew@seymour:~$ sudo hwclock --set --date "09/28/13 10:33:00"
matthew@seymour:~$ hwclock --show
Fri 28 Sep 2013 10:33:09 AM MST   -0.904668 seconds
```

In these examples, the hardware clock has been set using hwclock, which is then used again to verify the new hardware date and time. You can also use hwclock to set the Linux system time and date using your hardware clock's values with the Linux system time and date.

For example, to set the system time from your PC's hardware clock, use the --hctosys option, like so:

```
matthew@seymour:~$ sudo hwclock --hctosys
```

To set your hardware clock using the system time, use the --systohc option, like so:

```
matthew@seymour:~$ sudo hwclock --systohc
```

Configuring Wireless Networks

Wireless networking used to be a bear to configure for Linux, requiring a lot of complicated steps to connect to a wireless network. That has become a much easier task. Ubuntu includes a great utility called Network Manager that makes connecting to and managing wireless networks extremely easy.

When you log in to Ubuntu, the Network Manager applet appears in the top panel (see Figure 1.13). This applet handles and monitors network connections.

FIGURE 1.13   The Network Manager notification applet, shown here already connected to a wireless network.

Click the icon in the toolbar to connect to a wireless network. If your wireless access point broadcasts its *service set identifier (SSID)*, it should appear in the list under wireless networks. Click the desired network, and Network Manager detects what encryption (if any) is in use and asks you for the passkey. Enter this and Network Manager starts the wireless connection. The passkey is then stored in the default keyring, a secure area that is unique to your login. From now on, whenever you log in to Ubuntu and are in range of this network, Network Manager will start the connection automatically.

If for some reason your wireless network does not appear (you might have your SSID hidden), you must use the Connect to Other Wireless Network option, in which you enter the network name, wireless security type, and, when needed, the password for the connection.

Network Manager can handle WEP and WPA Personal encryption. You are advised to use WPA encryption because it is the stronger of the two. WEP encryption is easily broken.

Network Manager can also connect to Cisco VPN connections using the vpnc software. Install this from the Ubuntu repositories (see Chapter 9, "Managing Software"), and you can specify connection settings as appropriate, or if you have access to a predefined configuration file (PCF), you can import it directly into Network Manager.

Troubleshooting Post-Installation Configuration Problems

A lot of work has gone into Ubuntu to make it as versatile as possible, but sometimes you might come across a piece of hardware that Ubuntu is not sure about. Knowing what to do in these situations is important, especially when you are working with Ubuntu for the first time.

Because Ubuntu (and Linux in general) is built on a resilient UNIX foundation, it is much more stable than some operating systems. However, even though things might seem to be working fine, Ubuntu could have a problem that might not affect the appearance of the system. In this section, you learn how to examine some of Ubuntu's built-in error logs to help you discover or diagnose unseen problems.

Ubuntu has a command that responds with detailed messages that are output directly by the operating system: the `dmesg` command, which we introduce here and cover more completely in Chapter 12, "Command-Line Master Class Part 2." This command is commonly used with the `grep` command to filter output. The `dmesg` command takes its output directly from the `/var/log/messages` file, so you can choose to either run `dmesg` or to read the file directly by typing `less /var/log/messages`. The output is fairly detailed, so be prepared for an initial shock when you see how much information is generated. You might find it easier to generate a file with the `dmesg` output by using the following command:

```
matthew@seymour:~$ dmesg > dmesg.txt
```

This takes the output from the `dmesg` command and stores it in a new text file called `dmesg.txt`. You can then browse it at your leisure using your choice of text editor, such as `vi` or `emacs`. You can even use the `less` command, like so:

```
matthew@seymour:~$ less dmesg.txt
```

The messages are generated by the kernel, by other software run by `/etc/init.d`, and by Ubuntu's runlevel scripts. You might find what appear to be errors at first glance, but some errors are not really problems (for example, if a piece of hardware is configured but not present on your system).

Thanks to Google, troubleshooting is no longer the slow process it used to be. You can copy and paste error messages into Google's search bar to bring up a whole selection of results similar to the problem you face. Remember, Google is your friend, especially www.google.com/linux, which provides a specialized search engine for Linux. You can also try http://marc.info, which browses newsgroup and mailing list archives. Either way, you are likely to come across people who have had the same problem as you.

It is important to work on finding and testing only one solution to one problem at a time; otherwise, you might end up getting no work done whatsoever. You should also get into the habit of making backup copies of all files that you modify, just in case you make a bad situation worse. Use the copy (`cp`) command like this:

```
matthew@seymour:~$ cp file file.backup20160101
```

You should not use a .bak extension on your backup file because this could get overwritten by another automatic process and leave you frustrated when you try to restore the original file. I like to use `backupYYYYMMDD`, as in the preceding code where I used the date for New Year's Day 2016: 2016(year)01(month)01(day).

If something breaks as a result of your changing the original file, you can always copy the original back into place using the command like this:

```
matthew@seymour:~$ cp file.backup20160101 file
```

> **NOTE**
>
> Something as simple as this can really save you, especially when you are under pressure because you've changed something you shouldn't have changed on a production system. It is better not to make sweeping changes on a production system.

If you are having trouble with booting your system, you may find it helpful to read Chapter 15, "The Boot Process," as it details aspects like the bootloader and start up process. Understanding what happens during this process will give you an idea of what to look for and how to solve problems.

Ubuntu includes a comprehensive system testing application called Checkbox. Use it if you have problems and need some assistance tracking down the source, or if you simply want to put your system to the test. Search for Checkbox from the Dash to find and run the application.

References

▶ **www.ubuntu.com:** The place to start when looking for news, information, and documentation about installing, configuring, and using Ubuntu.

▶ **www.ubuntu.com/desktop/get-ubuntu/download:** This page has specific information and links for downloading, burning, and installing the current release of the Ubuntu Desktop edition. Replace *desktop* in the URL with *server* to download Ubuntu Server.

▶ **www.ubuntu.com/project/about-ubuntu/derivatives:** This page has information about Ubuntu derivatives, or flavors. These are based on Ubuntu but are modified to include different software or interfaces.

▶ **www.gnu.org/software/grub/:** Home page for the GRUB boot loader.

# CHAPTER 2

Background Information and Resources

As with any new thing, it's worthwhile finding out a bit about its history. Ubuntu is no different, and in this chapter you learn a little more about where Linux (and Ubuntu) came from. Additionally, this chapter gives you resources to help you learn more on your own.

What Is Linux?

Linux is the core, or kernel, of a free operating system first developed and released to the world by Linus Benedict Torvalds in 1991. Torvalds, then a graduate student at the University of Helsinki, Finland, is now a Fellow at the Linux Foundation (www.linuxfoundation.org/). He is an engineer and previously worked for the CPU design and fabrication company Transmeta, Inc. before leaving in 2003 to work for *Open Source Development Labs (ODSL)*, a consortium created by many high-tech companies to support Linux development and which has enabled him to focus on the Linux kernel full time. Fortunately for all Linux users, Torvalds chose to distribute Linux under a free software license named the GNU General Public License (GPL).

> **NOTE**
>
> The free online resource Wikipedia has a great biography of Linus Torvalds that examines his life and notable achievements. You can find it at http://en.wikipedia.org/wiki/Linus_Torvalds.

The GNU GPL is the brainchild of Richard M. Stallman, the founder of the Free Software Foundation. Stallman, the famous author of the Emacs editing environment and GCC compiler system, crafted the GPL to ensure that software that used the GPL for licensing would always be free and available in source-code form. The GPL is the guiding document for Linux and its ownership, distribution, and copyright. Torvalds holds the rights to the Linux trademark, but thanks to a combination of his generosity, the Internet, thousands of programmers around the world, GNU software, and the GNU GPL, Linux will remain forever free and unencumbered by licensing or royalty issues.

DISTRIBUTION VERSION AND KERNEL NUMBERING SCHEMA

There is a numbering system for Linux kernels, kernel development, and Ubuntu's kernel versions. Note that these numbers bear no relation to the version number of your Ubuntu Linux distribution. Ubuntu distribution version numbers are assigned by the Ubuntu developers, whereas most of the Linux kernel version numbers are assigned by Linus Torvalds and his legion of kernel developers.

To see the date your Linux kernel was compiled, use the `uname` command with its `-v` command-line option. To see the version of your Linux kernel, use the `-r` option. The numbers, such as 4.4.0-2s-generic, represent the major version (4), minor version (4), and patch level (0). The final number (22-generic) is the developer patch level and in our context is what is assigned by the Ubuntu developers.

Even minor numbers are considered "stable" and fit for use in production environments. You will find only stable versions of the Linux kernel included with this book. You can choose to download and install a beta (test) version of the kernel, but this is not recommended for a system destined for everyday use. When used, beta kernels are installed by developers to test support of new hardware or operating system features.

Linux, pronounced "lih-nucks," is free software. Combining the Linux kernel with GNU software tools—drivers, utilities, user interfaces, and other software such as the X.Org Foundation's X Window System—creates a Linux distribution. There are many different Linux distributions from different vendors, but many derive from or closely mimic the Debian Linux distribution, on which Ubuntu is founded.

NOTE

Debian lists several dozen other Linux distributions are based on Debian Linux, see: www .debian.org/misc/children-distros

While it is really the kernel itself that is most appropriately referred to as "Linux," colloquial language uses the term to refer to more than just the kernel. Most people who say they "use Linux" are referring to, at a minimum, a suite of software that includes several things. I have listed some of the more necessary ones here in the order in which they are loaded into your computer's memory during the boot cycle, after your computer's BIOS or UEFI firmware, which was included by the manufacturer of the motherboard and which runs from where it is stored on the motherboard, has run to get things started:

▶ A bootloader, like GRUB2, which is described in Chapter 1, "Installing Ubuntu and Post-Installation Configuration"

▶ The Linux kernel, which is described in Chapter 22, "Kernel and Module Management"

▶ Daemons, which are background processes that the system itself runs to perform tasks like logging or listening for attempted network connections and so on; daemons may be more easily understood as programs that are not run or invoked directly by a user, but which lie dormant until any of a specific set of conditions occurs

▶ The Shell, which is a command processor that most people know best because it is what they see when they login to the terminal; the shell is described in Chapter 14, "Automating Tasks and Shell Scripting"

▶ Shell utilities, such as most of the commands in Chapter 10, "Command-Line Beginner's Class," Chapter 11, "Command-Line Master Class Part 1," and Chapter 12, "Command-Line Master Class Part 2"

▶ A graphical server, such as the X Server, which is described in Chapter 3, "Working with Unity"

▶ A desktop environment, such as Unity, which is also described in Chapter 3, "Working with Unity," and others such as those discussed in Chapter 7, "Other Ubuntu Interfaces"

▶ Desktop software, such as web browsers, office suites, media players, games, and so on

A Linux distribution, like Ubuntu, collects all of these together, packages them, and makes them available to end users as a convenient set.

Why Use Linux?

Millions of clever computer users have been putting Linux to work for more than 20 years. Over the past year, many individuals, small office/home office (SOHO) users, businesses and corporations, colleges, nonprofits, and government agencies (local, state, and federal) in a number of countries have incorporated Linux with great success. And, today, Linux is being incorporated into many *information service/information technology (IS/IT)* environments as part of improvements in efficiency, security, and cost savings. Using Linux is a good idea for a number of reasons, including the following:

▶ **Linux provides an excellent return on investment (ROI)**—There is little or no cost on a per-seat basis. Unlike commercial operating systems, Linux has no royalty or licensing fees, and a single Linux distribution on CD-ROM or network shared folder can form the basis of an enterprise-wide software distribution, replete with applications and productivity software. Custom corporate CD-ROMs can be easily crafted or network shares can be created to provide specific installs on enterprise-wide hardware. This feature alone can save hundreds of thousands, if not millions, of dollars in IS/IT costs—all without the threat of a software audit from the commercial software monopoly or the need for licensing accounting and controls of base operating system installations.

▶ **Linux can be put to work on the desktop**—Linux, in conjunction with its supporting graphical networking protocol and interface (the X Window System), has worked well as a consumer UNIX-like desktop operating system since the mid-1990s.

The fact that UNIX is ready for the consumer desktop is now confirmed with the introduction, adoption, and rapid maturation of Apple Computer BSD UNIX—based on Mac OS X—supported, according to Apple, by more than 3,000 Mac OS X-specific programs that are known as native applications. This book's disc contains more than 800 software packages, including Internet connection utilities, games, a full office suite, many fonts, and hundreds of graphics applications.

▶ **Linux can be put to work as a server platform**—Linux is fast, secure, stable, scalable, and robust. The latest versions of the Linux kernel easily support multiple-processor computers, large amounts of system memory, individual file sizes in excess of hundreds of gigabytes, a choice of modern journaling file systems, hundreds of process monitoring and control utilities, and the (theoretical) capability to simultaneously support more than four billion users. IBM, Oracle, and other major database vendors all have versions of their enterprise software available for Linux.

▶ **Linux has a low entry-and-deployment cost barrier**—Maintenance costs can also be reduced because Linux works well on a variety of PCs. Although the best program performance will be realized with newer hardware, base installs can even be performed on lower-end computers or embedded devices . This feature provides for a much wider user base; extends the life of older working hardware; and can help save money for home, small business, and corporate users.

▶ **Linux appeals to a wide audience in the hardware and software industry**—Versions of Linux exist for nearly every CPU. Embedded-systems developers now turn to Linux when crafting custom solutions using ARM, MIPS, and other low-power processors on platforms like Raspberry Pi. Linux is also available for Intel's Itanium CPU, as well as the AMD64 group of CPUs.

▶ **Linux provides a royalty-free development platform for cross-platform development**—Because of the open-source development model and availability of free, high-quality development tools, Linux provides a low-cost entry point to budding developers and tech industry start-ups.

▶ **Big-player support in the computer hardware industry from such titans as IBM now lends credibility to Linux as a viable platform**—IBM has enabled Linux on the company's entire line of computers, from low-end laptops through "Big Iron" mainframes. New corporate customers are lining up and using Linux as part of enterprise-level computing solutions. It has been used on some of the world's fastest computers. Companies like HP and Dell also certify Linux across a large portion of their hardware offerings.

Look forward to even more support as usage spreads worldwide throughout all levels of business in search of lower costs, better performance, and stable and secure implementations.

What Is Ubuntu?

Ubuntu is an operating system based on the Linux kernel; created, improved, refined, and distributed by the Ubuntu Community at www.ubuntu.com/. Ubuntu, sponsored by Canonical Ltd. (www.canonical.com), is an open-source project supported by a worldwide community of software developers.

Ubuntu is one of the newer Linux distributions currently available today, having released its first version in October 2004. It quickly gained a reputation for ease of installation and use, combined with the slightly wacky code names given to each release. However, Ubuntu itself is based on Debian, which is a much older distribution steeped in respect from the wider Linux community. Ubuntu describes Debian as being the rock on which it is founded, and this is a good way to describe the relationship between the two.

Sponsored by Canonical Software and with the formidable resources of Mark Shuttleworth, Ubuntu got off to a great start with version 4.10, the Warty Warthog. From the start, Ubuntu specified clear goals: to provide a distribution that was easy to install and use, that did not overly confuse the user, and that came on a single CD (now one DVD image). Releasing every 6 months, Ubuntu made rapid progress into the Linux community and is now one of the most popular Linux distros across the world.

UBUNTU VERSION NUMBERS

As mentioned earlier, Ubuntu has chosen a unique numbering scheme and some peculiar code names for their releases since the first launch in October 2004. Doing away with the typical version numbering found elsewhere, Ubuntu decided to take the month and year of release and reverse them. Hence, the first release in October 2004 became 4.10, followed quickly by 5.04 (April 2005), 5.10, 6.06LTS, and so on up to the current 16.04.

The version covered in this book was released in April 2016, and therefore bears the version number 16.04. What's even more special about some releases is that they also carry the *LTS (long term support)* label, meaning that Canonical will support LTS versions for 3 years on the desktop and a total of 5 years for the server version after its release. LTS releases come out every 2 years, and the most recent LTS version is 16.04.

The code names during development are even better: 4.10 was christened the Warty Warthog in recognition that it was a first release, warts and all. The second release, 5.04, was dubbed the Hoary Hedgehog. Things got slightly better with 5.10, code-named the Breezy Badger. 6.06 was announced as the Dapper Drake and was the first Ubuntu distribution to carry the LTS badge. Beyond Dapper, there was the Edgy Eft (6.10) followed by the Feisty Fawn (7.04), and more. For a full list of development code names, see http://wiki.ubuntu.com/DevelopmentCodeNames

---

Ubuntu for Business

Linux has matured over the years. It includes all the essential features for use in enterprise-level environments, such as CPU architecture support, file systems, and memory handling.

Ubuntu includes a Linux kernel that can use multiple processors, which allows you to use Ubuntu in more advanced computing environments with greater demands on CPU power. This kernel can support at least 16 CPUs; in reality, however, small business servers typically use only dual- or quad-CPU workstations or servers. However, Ubuntu can run Linux on more powerful hardware.

Ubuntu automatically supports your multiple-CPU Intel-based motherboard, and you can take advantage of the benefits of *symmetric multiprocessors (SMPs)* for software development and other operations. The Linux kernels included with Ubuntu can use system RAM sizes up to 64GB, allow individual file sizes in excess of 2GB, and host the demands of—theoretically—billions of users.

Businesses that depend on high-availability, large-scale systems can also be served by Ubuntu, along with the specialist commercial support on offer from hundreds of support partners across the world.

However, Ubuntu can be used in many of these environments by customers with widely disparate computing needs. Some of the applications for Ubuntu include desktop support; small file, print, or mail servers; intranet web servers; and security firewalls deployed at strategic points inside and outside company LANs.

Debian itself is also available for multiple architectures, and is developed for and complied on about a dozen different architectures, from x86 to ARM and MIPS.

Small business owners can earn great rewards by stepping off the software licensing and upgrade treadmill and adopting a Linux-based solution. Using Ubuntu not only avoids the need for licensing accounting and the threat of software audits, but also provides viable alternatives to many types of commercial productivity software, often for free.

Using Ubuntu in a small business setting makes a lot of sense for other reasons, too, such as not having to invest in cutting-edge hardware to set up a productive shop. Ubuntu easily supports older, or *legacy*, hardware, and savings are compounded over time by avoiding unnecessary hardware upgrades. Additional savings will be realized because OS software and upgrades are free. New versions of applications can be downloaded and installed at little or no cost, and office suite software is free.

Ubuntu is easy to install on a network and plays well with others, meaning it works well in a mixed-computing situation with other operating systems such as Windows, Mac OS X, and of course, UNIX. A simple Ubuntu server can be put to work as an initial partial solution or made to mimic file, mail, or print servers of other operating systems. Clerical staff should quickly adapt to using familiar Internet and productivity tools, while your business gets the additional benefits of stability, security, and a virus-free computing platform.

By carefully allocating monies spent on server hardware, a productive and efficient multiuser system can be built for much less than the cost of comparable commercial software. Combine these benefits with support for laptops, PDAs, and remote access, and you will find that Ubuntu supports the creation and use of an inexpensive yet efficient work environment.

Ubuntu in Your Home

Ubuntu installs a special set of preselected software packages onto your hard drive; these are suitable for small office/home office (SOHO) users. This option provides a wealth of productivity tools for document management, printing, communication, and personal productivity.

The standard installation only requires about 2GB of hard drive space. Even with such a small footprint, the install also contains administrative tools, additional authoring and publishing clients, a variety of editors, a GNOME-based X11 desktop, support for sound, graphics editing programs, and graphical and text-based Internet tools.

Getting the Most from Ubuntu and Linux Documentation

Nearly all commercial Linux distributions include shrink-wrapped manuals and documentation covering installation and configuration. You will not find official documentation included on the DVD provided with this book. However, at www.ubuntu .com/ you find the links to various Ubuntu documentation projects.

Documentation for Ubuntu (and many Linux software packages) is distributed and available in a variety of formats. Some guides are available in PDF and can be read using Adobe's Acrobat Reader for Linux or the `evince` client. Guides are also available as bundled HTML files for reading with a web browser such as links, KDE's Konqueror, GNOME's Epiphany, or Firefox. Along with these guides, Ubuntu provides various tips, FAQs, and HOWTO documents.

You will find traditional Linux software package documentation, such as manual pages, under the `/usr/share/man` directory, with documentation for each installed software package under `/usr/share/doc`.

Linux manual pages are compressed text files containing succinct information about how to use a program. Each manual page generally provides a short summary of a command's use, a synopsis of command-line options, an explanation of the command's purpose, potential caveats or bugs, the name of the author, and a list of related configuration files and programs.

For example, you can learn how to read manual pages by using the `man` command to display its own manual page, as follows:

```
matthew@seymour:~$ man man
```

After you press Enter, a page of text appears on the screen or in your window on the desktop. You can then scroll through the information using your keyboard's cursor keys, read, and then press the Q key to quit reading.

Many of the software packages also include separate documents known as HOWTOs that contain information regarding specific subjects or software.

If the HOWTO documents are simple text files in compressed form (with filenames ending in .gz), you can easily read the document by using the zless command, which is a text pager that enables you to scroll back and forth through documents. (Use the less command to read plain-text files.) You can start the command by using less, followed by the complete directory specification and name of the file, or *pathname*, like this:

```
matthew@seymour:~$ less /usr/share/doc/httpd-2.0.50/README
```

To read a compressed version of this file, use the zless command in the same way:

```
matthew@seymour:~$ zless /usr/share/doc/attr-2.4.1/CHANGES.gz
```

After you press Enter, you can scroll through the document using your cursor keys. Press the Q key to quit.

If the HOWTO document is in HTML format, you can simply read the information using a web browser, such as Firefox. Or if you are reading from a console, you can use the links or lynx text-only web browsers, like this:

```
matthew@seymour:~$ links /usr/share/doc/stunnel-4.0.5/stunnel.html
```

The links browser offers drop-down menus, accessed by clicking at the top of the screen. You can also press the Q key to quit.

If the documentation is in PostScript format (with filenames ending in .ps), you can use the gv client to read or view the document like this:

```
matthew@seymour:~$ gv /usr/share/doc/iproute-2.4.7/ip-crefs.ps
```

Finally, if you want to read a document in Portable Document Format (with a filename ending in .pdf), use the evince client, as follows:

```
matthew@seymour:~$ evince /usr/share/doc/xfig/xfig-howto.pdf
```

NOTE

This book was developed and written using software from Ubuntu. You can use the disc included with this book for your install or download your own copy, available as ISO9660 images (with filenames ending in .iso), and burn it onto a DVD or create a bootable USB stick.

Along with the full distribution, you get access to the complete source code to the Linux kernel and source for all software in the distribution—more than 55 million lines of C and nearly 5 million lines of C++ code. Browse to www.ubuntu.com/download/ to get started.

Ubuntu Developers and Documentation

If you are interested in helping with Ubuntu, you can assist in the effort by testing beta releases (known as preview releases, and usually named after the animal chosen for the release name), writing documentation, and contributing software for the core or contributed software repositories. You should have some experience in installing Linux distributions, a desire to help with translation of documentation into different languages, or be able to use various software project management systems, such as Bazaar or Git. If you are interested in contributing, see Chapter 40, "Helping with Ubuntu Development."

Websites and Search Engines

Literally thousands of websites exist with information about Linux and Ubuntu. The key to getting the answers you need right away involves using the best search engines and techniques. Knowing how to search can mean the difference between frustration and success when troubleshooting problems. This section provides some Internet search tips and lists Ubuntu- and Linux-related sites sorted by various topics. The lists are not comprehensive, but they have been checked and were available at the time of this writing.

Web Search Tips

Troubleshooting problems with Linux by searching the Web can be an efficient and productive way to get answers to vexing problems. One of the most basic rules for conducting productive searches is to use specific search terms to find specific answers. For example, if you simply search for "Ubuntu," you end up with too many links and too much information. If you search for "Ubuntu sound," however, you are more likely to find the information you need. If you've received an error message, use it; otherwise, use the Linux kernel diagnostic message as your search criterion.

Other effective techniques include the following:

▶ Using symbols in the search string, such as the plus sign (+) to force matches of web pages containing both strings (if such features are supported by the search engine used by web search site)

▶ Searching within returned results

▶ Sorting results (usually by date to get the latest information)

▶ Searching for related information

▶ Stemming searches; for example, specifying returns for not only "link" but also "linking" and "linked"

Invest some time and experiment with your favorite search engine's features—the result will be more productive searches. In addition to sharpening your search skills, also take the time to choose the best search engine for your needs.

Google Is Your Friend

Some of the fastest and most comprehensive search engines on the Web are powered by Linux, so it makes sense to use the best available resources. Out of the myriad websites with search engines, http://google.com stands out from the crowd, with millions of users per month. The site uses advanced hardware and software to bring speed and efficiency to your searches.

Why is Google (named after a math number) so powerful? You can get a quick overview from the Google folks at www.google.com/corporate/tech. Part of its success is because of great algorithms, good programming, and simple interface design as well as lots of computing power and sophisticated networking of all that power; but most users really seem to appreciate Google's uncanny capability to provide links to what you are looking for in the first page of a search return. Google's early success was also assured because the site ran its search engine on clusters of thousands of PCs running a version of Red Hat Linux. It is also rumored that an Ubuntu-based distribution was seen in use on desktops at Google, with the informal moniker of Goobuntu.

Google has the largest database size of any search engine on the Web, with many billions of web pages searched and indexed. The database size is important because empty search results are useless to online users, and the capability to return hits on esoteric subjects can make the difference between success and failure or satisfaction and frustration.

To get a better idea of what Google can offer you, browse to www.google.com/options/. You will find links to many services and tools covering specialized searches, databases, information links, translators, and other helpful browsing tools.

Ubuntu Package Listings

You can quickly and easily view a list of the installed packages on your Ubuntu system, along with a short description of each package, by using the Ubuntu Software Center or Synaptic. Each also shows you descriptions of each package so you can decide whether you want it installed. For more information, see Chapter 9, "Managing Software."

Commercial Support

Commercial support for Ubuntu is an essential ingredient to the success of Linux in the corporate and business community. Although hundreds, if not thousands, of consultants well versed in Linux and UNIX are available on call for a fee, here is a short list of the best-known Linux support providers:

▶ **www.ubuntu.com/support**—Go straight to the source for a range of support options. You can get help on Ubuntu direct from Canonical software, or from a local support provider.

▶ **www.hp.com/linux**—HP offers a comprehensive package of Linux services and hardware that covers almost everything that you would want to do, including consultancy, business solutions, and hardware specification and implementation.

▶ **www.dell.com/linux**—Linux services are offered by Dell on a wide range of their hardware.

▶ **www.ibm.com/linux/**—Linux services offered by IBM include e-business solutions, open-source consulting, database migration, clustering, servers, and support.

In addition to service-oriented support companies, nearly every commercial distributor of Linux has some form of easily purchased commercial support. There are various ways in which to take advantage of support services (such as remote management, onsite consulting, device driver development, and so on), but needs vary according to customer circumstances and installations.

THE BENEFITS OF JOINING A LINUX USER GROUP

Join a local Linux Users Group (LUG). Joining and participating in a local LUG has many benefits. You will be able to get help, trade information, and learn many new and wonderful things about Linux. Most LUGs do not have membership dues, and many often sponsor regular lectures and discussions from leading Linux, GNU, and open-source experts. For one great place to start, browse to https://en.wikipedia.org/wiki/Linux_user_group. For Ubuntu-specific groups, check out Ubuntu Local Community, or LoCo Teams at http://loco.ubuntu.com/.

Documentation

Nearly all Linux distributions include thousands of pages of documentation in the form of manual pages, HOWTO documents (in various formats, such as text and HTML), mini-HOWTO documents, or software package documentation (usually found under the `/usr/share/doc/` directory). However, the definitive site for reading the latest versions of these documents is the Linux Documentation Project, found at www.tldp.org.

Linux Guides

If you are looking for more extensive and detailed information concerning a Linux subject, try reading one of the many Linux guides. These guides, available for a number of subjects, dwell on technical topics in more detail and at a more leisurely pace than a HOWTO. You can find copies of the following:

▶ "Advanced Bash-Scripting Guide," by Mendel Cooper; a guide to shell scripting using `bash`, available from http://tldp.org/LDP/abs/html/

▶ "LDP Author Guide," by Mark F. Komarinski; how to write Linux Documentation Project (LDP) documentation, available from www.tldp.org/LDP/LDP-Author-Guide/html/index.html

▶ "Linux Administration Made Easy," by Steve Frampton, available from www.tldp.org/LDP/lame/LAME/linux-admin-made-easy/index.html

▶ "Linux from Scratch," by Gerard Beekmans; creating a Linux distribution from software, available from www.linuxfromscratch.org/

▶ "Linux Kernel Module Programming Guide," by Peter J Salzman, Michael Burian, and Ori Pomerantz; is aging, but still a good guide to building modules, available from www.tldp.org/LDP/lkmpg/2.6/html/

▶ "Securing and Optimizing Linux," by Gerhard Mourani, available from www.tldp
.org/LDP/solrhe/Securing-Optimizing-Linux-RH-Edition-v1.3/index.html

▶ *A Practical Guide to Linux Commands, Editors, and Shell Programming*, Third Edition by
Mark G. Sobell, ISBN: 9780133085044

▶ *UNIX and Linux System Administration Handbook*, Fourth Edition by Evi Nemeth,
Garth Snyder, Trent R. Hein, and Ben Whaley, ISBN: 9780131480056

▶ *The Practice of System and Network Administration*, Second Edition by Thomas A.
Limoncelli, Christina J. Hogan, and Strata R. Chalup, ISBN: 9780321492661

Ubuntu

The best place to start for Ubuntu-specific information is at Ubuntu-focused websites.
Where better to start than the main website for the distribution and the official web
forums? Although these are not the only official Ubuntu resources, they are the most
likely to be immediately useful. You can easily find others under the Support tab on the
Ubuntu.com website:

▶ **www.ubuntu.com**—Home page for Ubuntu, Canonical's community-based free
Linux distribution. Ubuntu is the main release of this Linux distribution and
includes thousands of software packages that form the core of an up-to-date, cutting-
edge Linux-based desktop. You can also find links to the other *buntus, such as
Kubuntu, Xubuntu, and EdUbuntu.

▶ **https://help.ubuntu.com/**—The place to start for official Ubuntu documentation.

▶ **www.ubuntuforums.org**—A good place to go if you need specific community-
provided Ubuntu support.

▶ **http://askubuntu.com/**—Another good place to go if you need specific
community-provided Ubuntu support.

▶ **https://answers.launchpad.net/ubuntu**—The official bug reporting system and
tracker for Ubuntu.

Mailing Lists

Mailing lists are interactive or digest-form electronic discussions about nearly any
topic. To use a mailing list, you must generally send an email request to be subscribed
to the list, and then verify the subscription with a return message from the master list
mailer. After you subscribe to an interactive form of list, each message sent to the list will
appear in your email inbox. However, many lists provide a digest form of subscription in
which a single- or half-day's traffic is condensed in a single message. The digest form is
generally preferred unless you have set up email filtering.

The main Ubuntu mailing lists are detailed here, but there are quite a few Linux-related lists. You can search for nearly all online mailing lists by using a typical mailing list search web page, such as the one at www.lsoft.com/lists/list_q.html.

GNOME AND KDE MAILING LISTS

GNOME users and developers should know that more than two dozen mailing lists are available through http://mail.gnome.org/. KDE users will also benefit by perusing the KDE-related mailing lists at www.kde.org/mailinglists.html. Many open source projects run mailing lists. If there is a project that really interests you, search online to see if they have a mailing list available, especially if you are interested in contributing time or helping develop the software.

Ubuntu Project Mailing Lists

Email mailing lists are also available as an outlet or forum for discussions about Ubuntu. The lists are categorized. For example, general users of Ubuntu discuss issues on the ubuntu-users mailing list—beta testers and developers via the ubuntu-devel mailing list, and documentation contributors via the ubuntu-doc mailing list. You can subscribe to mailing lists by selecting the ones you are interested in at http://lists.ubuntu.com/mailman/listinfo/. Be warned, some of the mailing lists have in excess of 200 to 300 emails per day, so you may want to subscribe in batch format when available.

KEEP UP-TO-DATE

Keeping up to date with bug fixes and security updates is critical to the success and health of an Ubuntu system. You can simply install updates when you read your Ubuntu-provided notifications in your system (see Chapter 9, "Managing Software"). To keep abreast of the most important developments when using Ubuntu, you can register with the Ubuntu Announcements mailing list. From there, you will learn which updates have been issued and what has been fixed as a result. Go to https://lists.ubuntu.com/mailman/listinfo/ubuntu-security-announce to register for this mailing list. To keep up with bug fixes, new software packages, and security updates, also keep an eye out for Update Manager notifications.

You will find many other knowledgeable users with answers to your questions by participating in one of Ubuntu's mailing lists. The best etiquette is to read a list consistently for a while, until you get the feel for how people already using the list interact, before you post the first time. The lists are focused on using, testing, and developing and participating in Ubuntu's development:

▶ **http://lists.ubuntu.com/mailman/listinfo/ubuntu-security-announce**—Security announcements from the Ubuntu developers

▶ **http://lists.ubuntu.com/mailman/listinfo/ubuntu-announce**—Announcements concerning Ubuntu

▶ **http://lists.ubuntu.com/mailman/listinfo/ubuntu-users**—Discussions among users of Ubuntu releases

▶ **http://lists.ubuntu.com/mailman/listinfo/ubuntu-devel**—Queries and reports from developers and testers of Ubuntu test releases

Internet Relay Chat

Internet Relay Chat (IRC) is a popular form and forum of communication for many Linux developers and users because it allows an interactive, real-time exchange of information and ideas. To use IRC, you must have an IRC client and the address of a network and server hosting the desired chat channel for your discussions.

You can use the `irc.freenode.net` IRC server, or one listed at www.freenode.net/ to chat with other Ubuntu users. Some current channels are as follows:

▶ `#Ubuntu`—General chat about Ubuntu

▶ `#edubuntu`—General chat about Edubuntu

▶ `#xubuntu`—General chat about Xubuntu

▶ `#kubuntu`—General chat about Kubuntu

For more channels to look at, head over to https://help.ubuntu.com/community/InternetRelayChat for an exhaustive list of "official" channels.

However, Google can help you find other channels to explore. Enter the distro name and IRC into the search options to retrieve information on any IRC channels relevant to your requirements. To get help with getting started with IRC, browse to www.irchelp.org/. Among channels you might find interesting are the following:

▶ `#linux`—General discussions about Linux.

▶ `#linuxhelp`—A help chat discussion for new users.

Most IRC networks provide one or more Linux channels, although some providers require signup and registration before you can access any chat channel.

# CHAPTER 3

Working with Unity

Imagine a world of black screens with white text, or, for those of you who remember, dark green screens with light green text. That used to be the primary interface for users to access computers. Computing has moved on significantly and has adopted the *graphical user interface (GUI)* as standard on most desktop and workstation platforms. Not only that, but GUIs have gradually changed and evolved over time. This chapter starts with low-level information about what lies underneath the GUI and builds up to a description of the Unity desktop and how to use it.

Foundations and the X Server

Ubuntu uses the X Window System, the graphical networking interface found on many Linux distributions that provides the foundation for a wide range of graphical tools and window managers. More commonly known as just X, it can also be referred to as X11R7 and X11 (as found on Mac OS X). Coming from the world-renowned Massachusetts Institute of Technology, X has gone through several versions, each of which has extended and enhanced the technology. The open-source implementation is managed by the X.Org foundation, whose board includes several key figures from the open-source world. On September 15, 2012, X11 turned 25 years old, which is a very long time for any software to remain usable and be in active development.

The best way to think about how X works is to see it as a client/server system. The X server provides services to programs that have been developed to make the most of the graphical and networking capabilities that are available under the server and in the supported libraries. X.Org provides versions for many platforms, including Linux and Mac OS X. Originally implemented as XFree86, X.Org was forked when a fight broke out over certain restrictions that were going to be included in the XFree86 license. Taking a snapshot of code that was licensed under the previous version of the license, X.Org drove forward with its own implementation based on the code. Almost in unison, most Linux distributions turned away from XFree86 and switched their development and efforts to X.Org.

A desktop environment for X provides one or more window managers and a suite of clients that conform to a standard graphical interface based on a common set of software libraries. When used to develop associated clients, these libraries provide graphical consistency for the client windows, menus, buttons, and other onscreen components, along with some common keyboard controls and client dialogs. In this chapter, you find out how to work with Ubuntu's Unity interface and learn something about the version of X that is included with Ubuntu. If you want to discover more about some of the other desktop environments that are available to use with Ubuntu, including KDE and Xfce, take a look at Chapter 7, "Other Ubuntu Interfaces."

> **NOTE**
>
> Ubuntu is in the process of developing Mir, a replacement for X. This is being done because of Ubuntu's strong desire and commitment to creating a unified interface and user experience across multiple types of platforms and devices. Interaction with a touch screen, such as is found on a smart phone or tablet, is different than on a desktop or laptop system. This requires different backend processes, too. Mir is not yet in use by default, but is considered ready for use by testers. See https://wiki.ubuntu.com/Mir/ for more information.

Basic X Concepts

The underlying engine of X11 is the X protocol, which provides a system of managing displays on local and remote desktops. The protocol uses a client/server model that allows an abstraction of the drawing of client windows and other decorations locally and over a network. An X server draws client windows, dialog boxes, and buttons that are specific to the local hardware and in response to client requests. The client, however, does not have to be specific to the local hardware. This means that system administrators can set up a network with a large server and clients and enable users to view and use those clients on workstations with totally different CPUs and graphics displays.

Because X offers users a form of distributed processing, Ubuntu can be used as a very cheap desktop platform for clients that connect to a powerful X server. The more powerful the X server, the larger the number of X-based clients that can be accommodated. This functionality can breathe new life into older hardware, pushing most of the graphical processing on to the server. A fast network is a must if you intend to run many X clients because X can become bandwidth hungry.

> **NOTE**
>
> A great way to demonstrate the capability of X to handle remote clients is Edubuntu's use of LTSP, covered in Chapter 33, "Linux Terminal Server Project (LTSP)." It is designed to set up a main server and a set of dumb terminals that display programs that are being run on the server.

X is hugely popular in the UNIX and Linux world for a variety of reasons. That it supports nearly every hardware graphics system is a strong point. This and strong multiplatform programming standards give it a solid foundation of developers committed to X. Another key benefit of X is its networking capability, which plays a central point in administration of many desktops and can also assist in the deployment of a thin-client computing environment. Being able to launch applications on remote desktops and also standardize installations are examples of the versatility of this powerful application.

More recent versions of X have also included support for shaped windows (that is, nonrectangular), graphical login managers (also known as *display managers*), and compressed fonts. Each release of X brings more features designed to enhance the user experience, including being able to customize how X client applications appear, right down to buttons and windows. Most office and home environments run Linux and X on their local machines. The more-enlightened companies and users harness the power of the networking features of X, enabling thin-client environments and allowing the use of customized desktops designed specifically for that company. Having applications launch from a single location makes the lives of system administrators a lot easier because they have to work on only one machine, rather than several.

Using X

X.Org (www.x.org) is the X server that is used with Ubuntu. The base distribution consists of many packages including the server, support and development libraries, fonts, various clients, and documentation. An additional 1,000 or more X clients, fonts, and documentation are also available in the Ubuntu repositories.

The /usr directory and its subdirectories contain the majority of the xorg software (along with a lot of other stuff; the location is not exclusive to X). Some important subdirectories are as follows:

▶ **/usr/bin**—This is the location of the X server and various X clients. (Note that not all X clients require active X sessions.)

▶ **/usr/include**—This is the path to the files necessary for developing X clients and graphics such as icons.

▶ **/usr/lib**—This directory contains required software libraries to support the X server and clients.

▶ **/usr/lib/X11**—This directory contains fonts, default client resources, system resources, documentation, and other files that are used during X sessions and for various X clients. You will also find a symbolic link to this directory, named x11, under the /usr/lib directory.

▶ **/usr/lib/modules**—This path to drivers and the X server modules used by the X server enables use of various graphics cards.

The main components required for an active local X session are installed on your system if you choose to use a graphical desktop. These components are the X server, miscellaneous fonts, a *terminal client* (that is, a program that provides access to a shell prompt), and a client known as a *window manager*. Window managers administer onscreen displays, including overlapping and tiling windows, command buttons, title bars, and other onscreen decorations and features.

Elements of the `xorg.conf` File

Traditionally, the most important file for `Xorg` has been the `xorg.conf` configuration file. This file contained configuration information that was vital for X to function correctly and was usually created during the installation of Ubuntu.

BULLET PROOF X

Ubuntu is designed to work no matter what might happen. So in the event of some cataclysmic event that destroys your main X system, you still have some graphical way of getting yourself back into a fully functional X-based system. An additional upside is that much of the complexity of the information in this chapter is unnecessary for most users, in fact, the files are not even created or used by default and are only used if you create them. The downside to this is that much of the configurability of the X-server is now overwritten when an upgrade happens.

Modern versions of `Xorg` do not create an `xorg.conf` file by default. Instead, various files ending in `*.conf` reside in the `/usr/share/X11/xorg.conf.d` directory and are automatically loaded by X at boot, prior to reading any `xorg.conf`. These files can each contain one or more sections in the same format used by `xorg.conf`. Users can create the file and continue making custom configurations in `/etc/xorg.conf` as has been traditionally done, but the file is not created by default. What is included in the previously mentioned individual files should not be changed, but you may override those settings by creating your own `xorg.conf` file.

NOTE

We refer to using an `xorg.conf` file from here on, but keep the preceding information in mind to prevent confusion.

Let's take a look at the potential contents of `xorg.conf` so that you can get an idea of what X is looking for. The components, or sections, of the `xorg.conf` file specify the X session or *server layout*, along with pathnames for files that are used by the server, any options relating directly to the server, any optional support modules needed, information relating to the mouse and keyboard attached to the system, the graphics card installed, the monitor in use, and the resolution and color depth that Ubuntu uses. These are the essential components:

▶ `ServerLayout`—Defines the display, defines one or more screen layouts, and names input devices.

▶ `Files`—Defines the location of colors, fonts, or port number of the font server.

▶ `Module`—Tells the X server what graphics display support code modules to load.

▶ **InputDevice**—Defines the input devices, such as the keyboard and mouse; **multiple** devices can be used.

▶ **Monitor**—Defines the capabilities of any attached display; multiple monitors can be used.

▶ **Device**—Defines one or more graphics cards and specifies what optional features (if any) to enable or disable.

▶ **Screen**—Defines one or more resolutions, color depths, perhaps a default color depth, and other settings.

The following sections provide short descriptions of these elements; the `xorg.conf` man page contains full documentation of all the options and other keywords you can use to customize your desktop settings.

The ServerLayout Section

As noted previously, the `ServerLayout` section of the `xorg.conf` file defines the display and screen layouts, and it names the input devices. A typical `ServerLayout` section from an automatically configured `xorg.conf` file might look like this:

```
Section "ServerLayout"
        Identifier      "single head configuration"
        Screen        0 "Screen0" 0 0
        InputDevice     "Mouse0" "CorePointer"
        InputDevice     "Keyboard0" "CoreKeyboard"
        InputDevice     "DevInputMice" "AlwaysCore"
EndSection
```

In this example, a single display is used (the numbers designate the position of a screen), and two default input devices, Mouse0 and Keyboard0, are used for the session.

The `Files` Section

The `Files` section of the `xorg.conf` file might look like this:

```
Section "Files"
    RgbPath     "/usr/lib/X11/rgb"
    FontPath    "unix/:7100"
EndSection
```

This section lists available session colors (by name, in the text file `rgb.txt`) and the port number to the X font server. The font server, xfs, is started at boot and does not require an active X session. If a font server is not used, the `FontPath` entry could instead list each font directory under the `/usr/lib/X11/fonts` directory, as in this example:

```
FontPath "/usr/lib/X11/fonts/100dpi"
FontPath "/usr/lib/X11/fonts/misc"
FontPath "/usr/lib/X11/fonts/75dpi"
FontPath "/usr/lib/X11/fonts/type1"
FontPath "/usr/lib/X11/fonts/Speedo"
...
```

These directories contain the default compressed fonts that are available for use during the X session. The font server is configured by using the file named `config` under the `/etc/X11/fs` directory. This file contains a listing, or catalog, of fonts for use by the font server. By adding an alternate-server entry in this file and restarting the font server, you can specify remote font servers for use during X sessions. This can help centralize font support and reduce local storage requirements (even though only 25MB is required for the almost 5,000 fonts installed with Ubuntu and X).

The `Module` Section

The `Module` section of the `xorg.conf` file specifies loadable modules or drivers to load for the X session. This section might look like this:

```
Section "Module"
        Load   "dbe"
        Load   "extmod"
        Load   "fbdevhw"
        Load   "glx"
        Load   "record"
        Load   "freetype"
        Load   "type1"
        Load   "dri"


EndSection
```

These modules can range from special video card support to font rasterizers. The modules are located in subdirectories under the `/usr/lib/modules` directory.

The `InputDevice` Section

The `InputDevice` section configures a specific device, such as a keyboard or mouse, as in this example:

```
Section "InputDevice"
        Identifier   "Keyboard0"
        Driver       "kbd"


        Option   "XkbModel"     "pc105"
        Option   "XkbLayout"    "us"
EndSection
Section "InputDevice"
        Identifier   "Mouse0"
        Driver       "mouse"
        Option       "Protocol" "IMPS/2"
        Option       "Device" "/dev/input/mice"
        Option       "ZAxisMapping" "4 5"
        Option       "Emulate3Buttons" "yes"
EndSection
```

You can configure multiple devices, and multiple `InputDevice` sections might exist. The preceding example specifies a basic keyboard and a two-button PS/2 mouse (actually, a Dell touchpad pointer). An `InputDevice` section that specifies use of a USB device could be used at the same time (to enable mousing with PS/2 and USB pointers) and might look like this:

```
Section "InputDevice"
        Identifier   "Mouse0"
        Driver       "mouse"
        Option       "Device" "/dev/input/mice"
        Option       "Protocol" "IMPS/2"
        Option       "Emulate3Buttons" "off"
        Option       "ZAxisMapping" "4 5"
EndSection
```

The `Monitor` Section

The `Monitor` section configures the designated display device as declared in the `Server-Layout` section, as shown in this example:

```
Section "Monitor"
        Identifier   "Monitor0"
        VendorName   "Monitor Vendor"
        ModelName    "Monitor Model"
        DisplaySize  300      220
        HorizSync    31.5-48.5
        VertRefresh  50-70
        Option "dpms"
EndSection
```

Note that the X server automatically determines the best video timings according to the horizontal and vertical sync and refresh values in this section. If required, old-style mode-line entries (used by distributions and servers prior to XFree86 4.0) might still be used. If the monitor is automatically detected when you configure X (see the "Configuring X" section, later in this chapter), its definition and capabilities are inserted in your `xorg.conf` file from the MonitorsDB database. This database contains more than 600 monitors and is located in the `/usr/share/hwdata` directory.

The `Device` Section

The `Device` section provides details about the video graphics chipset used by the computer, as in this example:

```
Section "Device"
        Identifier       "Intel Corporation Mobile 945GM/GMS,\943/940GML Express
Integrated Graphics Controller"
        Driver           "intel"
        BusID            "PCI:0:2:0"
EndSection
```

This example identifies an installed video card as using an integrated Intel 945 graphics chipset. The `Driver` entry tells the `Xorg` server to load the intel kernel module. Different chipsets have different options. For example, here's the entry for a NeoMagic video chipset:

```
Section "Device"
        Identifier    "NeoMagic (laptop/notebook)"
        Driver        "neomagic"
        VendorName    "NeoMagic (laptop/notebook)"
        BoardName      "NeoMagic (laptop/notebook)"
    Option      "externDisp"
    Option      "internDisp"
EndSection
```

In this example, the `Device` section specifies the driver for the graphics card (`neomagic_drv.o`) and enables two chipset options (`externDisp` and `internDisp`) to allow display on the laptop's LCD screen and an attached monitor.

The `Xorg` server supports hundreds of different video chipsets. If you configure X11 but subsequently change the installed video card, you need to edit the existing `Device` section or generate a new `xorg.conf` file, using one of the X configuration tools discussed in this chapter, to reflect the new card's capabilities. You can find details about options for some chipsets in a companion man page. You should look at these sources for hints about optimizations and troubleshooting.

The `Screen` Section

The `Screen` section ties together the information from the previous sections (using the `Screen0`, `Device`, and `Monitor Identifier` entries). It can also specify one or more color depths and resolutions for the session. Here's an example:

```
Section "Screen"
        Identifier "Screen0"
        Device      "Videocard0"
        Monitor     "Monitor0"
        DefaultDepth    24
        SubSection "Display"
            Viewport    0 0
            Depth      16
            Modes       "1024x768"  "800x600"  "640x480"
        EndSubSection

EndSection
```

In this example, a color depth of thousands of colors and a resolution of 1024 × 768 is the default, with optional resolutions of 800 × 600 and 64 × 480. Multiple `Display` subsection entries with different color depths and resolutions (with settings such as Depth 24 for millions of colors) can be used if supported by the graphics card and monitor combination. You can also use a `DefaultDepth` entry (which is 24, or thousands of colors, in the example), along with a specific color depth to standardize display depths in installations.

You can also specify a desktop resolution larger than that supported by the hardware in your monitor or notebook display. This setting is known as a *virtual* resolution in the `Display` subsection. This allows, for example, an 800 × 600 display to pan (that is, slide around inside) a virtual window of 1024 × 768.

NOTE

If your monitor and graphics card support multiple resolutions and the settings are properly configured, you can use the key combination of Ctrl+Alt+(Keypad) + or Ctrl+Alt+(Keypad) − to change resolutions on-the-fly during your X session.

Starting X

You can start X sessions in a variety of ways. The Ubuntu installer sets up the system to have Linux boot directly to an X session using a display manager called *LightDM*, for Light(weight) Display Manager. This is an X client that provides a graphical login. After you log in, you use a local session (running on your computer) or, if the system is configured to do so, an X session running on a remote computer on the network.

Logging in via a display manager requires you to enter a username and password. You can also start X sessions from the command line. The following sections describe these two methods.

NOTE

If you have used the Server install, your system boots to a text login. See Chapter 10, "Command-Line Beginner's Class," for more information about what to do here.

Using a Display Manager

An X display manager presents a graphical login that requires a username and password to be entered before access is granted to the X desktop. It also enables you to choose a different desktop for your X session. Whether an X display manager is presented after you boot Linux is controlled by a *runlevel*—a system state entry in `/etc/event.d/`. The following runlevels as handled by Ubuntu are as follows:

▶ 0—Halt (Do *not* set `initdefault` to this.)

▶ 1—Multiuser text mode

▶ 2—X graphical multiuser mode

▶ 6—Reboot (Do *not* set `initdefault` to this.)

You may see mention of runlevels 3 through 5; you can ignore these because they are treated the same as runlevel 2 in Ubuntu. Historically, Ubuntu used the `/etc/inittab` file to handle runlevels, but this file no longer exists. (See Chapter 15, "The Boot Process," for information about runlevels.) Instead, there are several files under the `/etc/events.d/` directory, including an individual file for each of the virtual consoles (accessible by pressing Ctrl+Alt+F1 to F7). However, you can still create an `inittab` file if you want to override any defaults held by Ubuntu. Make sure you create the `inittab` file as root and include at least one line similar to the following:

```
id:1:initdefault:
```

This forces your system to start up in text mode.

Changing Window Managers

Ubuntu makes it fairly painless to switch to another window manager or desktop environment. *Desktop environment* refers to not only the window manager but also the suite of related applications, such as productivity or configuration tools.

First, you need to ensure that you have the relevant desktop environment installed on your system; the easiest way to do this is by installing the relevant `*-desktop` package. You can do this by installing the package `kubuntu-desktop`, for example (in the case of a KDE desktop); just search for "desktop" and look for Xubuntu or Kubuntu, and so on. After the download and installation is complete (you might want to grab a coffee while you wait because these packages include a ton of dependencies and take some time to download, install, and configure), you are all set to change environments.

Next, you need to log out of Ubuntu. When you return to the log-in page, select your name as usual and then select the session named for the desktop you want to use. Chapter 7, "Other Ubuntu Interfaces," provides a brief introduction to some of the desktop environments other than Unity that are available from the Ubuntu repositories.

Using Unity, a Primer

Unity is a fresh take on the GUI. It has been created with the assistance of user interface professionals and graphic designers and aims toward elegance, beauty, and efficiency while providing obvious ways to perform tasks. This section gives a tour of the basic features and use and then moves in to more specific details that are likely to thrill power users.

MARK SHUTTLEWORTH ON UNITY

"Our goal with Unity is unprecedented ease of use, visual style and performance on the Linux desktop."

From a blog post on August 16, 2011; www.markshuttleworth.com/archives/717

This chapter describes the current release version of Unity (7). Unity 8 is a multi-year project that is not yet ready for prime time, but nonetheless exciting and worth mentioning. With Unity 8, the goal is *convergence*, the ability to use the same operating system and have it adapt to the user. For example, what if you had a tablet device or a mobile phone that would use a typical mobile touch-screen interface until you connected a keyboard, an external display, or a mouse, in which case it would automatically switch to a standard desktop interface ready for you to get real work done? That is part of the goal with Unity 8, and it is worth watching.

The Desktop

When you boot your computer and log in to a Unity session, you are greeted by the desktop you see in Figure 3.1. This screen is made up of many parts, each of which is described in this chapter.

FIGURE 3.1   The default look of Ubuntu Unity.

The Launcher

To the left of the screen is a vertical bar. This is the Launcher (see Figure 3.2). Icons in the Launcher represent programs that are either running or which have been set to be included in the Launcher at all times. Click an icon to open a program. Right-click an icon for additional options, including an option to keep an item in the Launcher at all times.

FIGURE 3.2   You can customize the Launcher to include your most-used programs.

The Dash

Click the Ubuntu logo icon at the top of the Launcher to open the Dash (see Figure 3.3). The Dash is the primary way to find programs and files in Unity. At the bottom of the Dash is a row of icons. These represent *lenses*, which are different ways to focus your searching with the Dash.

The default Dash lens is represented by a house icon. This lens gives a set of shortcuts to often-used features. At the top is a Search box that searches your computer for programs, files, and directories that match any search terms you enter and then categorizes the results according to type (see Figure 3.4).

The applications Dash lens is represented by a ruler-pencil-pen icon. This lens lists and searches installed applications and also applications that are available from the Ubuntu Software Center (see Chapter 9, "Managing Software"), as in Figure 3.5. You can click to view more results and perform a visual search if you do not know the name of a program.

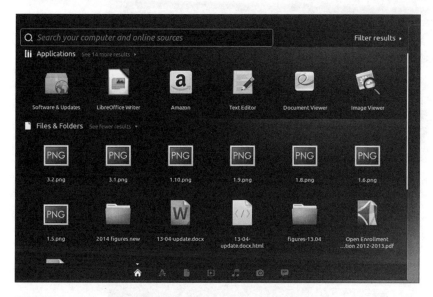

FIGURE 3.3   The Dash helps you find programs and files.

FIGURE 3.4   Sorted results in the main Dash lens.

FIGURE 3.5   Exploring applications in the Dash.

The files and folders Dash lens is represented by a sheet of paper icon. You can search by entering a term in the Search box or visually by clicking through what is shown here, as in Figure 3.6.

FIGURE 3.6   Exploring applications in the Dash.

Other Dash lenses may appear depending on your configuration. Possibilities include, but are not limited to, a Music lens for audio files and a Gwibber lens for interactive media such as Twitter and Facebook updates. More are likely to arrive as Unity matures.

In any Dash lens in which it appears, you can click Filter Results to view predefined ways to filter what is shown. Figure 3.7 shows a list of available filters for the Applications lens. The list you see may be different as new filters are created.

FIGURE 3.7   Filtering applications in the Dash.

The Panel

The panel is the bar across the top of the screen. When a program is being used, the panel houses various menus and buttons. (Some of these appear only when you hover your mouse over the panel; so if you can't find the File menu or close button, point at the panel with your mouse, and it is likely to appear.) The right side of the panel has a series of useful indicators. The Networking indicator was discussed in Chapter 1, "Installing Ubuntu and Post-Installation Configuration," because it is often needed right away to connect a computer to the Internet. Other indicators do the following:

▶ Help manage your mail and social applications such as chat (envelope icon)

▶ Show your battery status and provide quick access to power settings

▶ Provide volume and playback controls for the Rhythmbox media player

▶ Give quick access to the clock and calendar

▶ Show active users and sessions

▶ Give convenient access to commonly used system administration options and the logout menu

Customizing and Configuring Unity

Everyone likes to customize. Unity is quite new, and, as a result, not everything is customizable (yet). All existing options for customization and system settings are available in the System Settings menu.

System Settings

Search for "system settings" in the Dash. Click the System Settings icon to open the menu. The menu includes entries that enable you to change your desktop appearance, set up online accounts, configure additional languages for the system to use for displays, colors, keyboards, displays, and much more (see Figure 3.8).

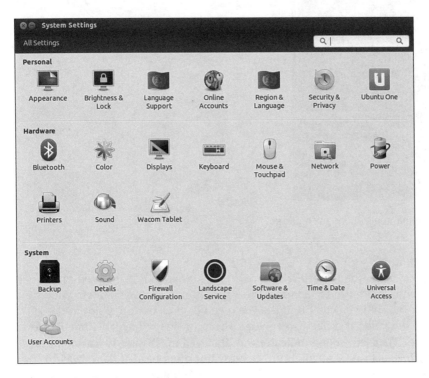

FIGURE 3.8   The System Settings menu.

Smart Scopes

Smart Scopes tries to provide a better Dash searching experience. It does so by using the search terms entered to change the set of locations being searched, that is, it changes the scope of the search. By default, Ubuntu includes a number of internal and external search locations when you use the Dash. Search terms entered may return results from a user's /home directory, the list of applications installed, recently used files, the Ubuntu software repositories, and even sites like Amazon.com. From the specification: "The Dash now gets and contributes information from a central server on which scopes are best able to answer Dash queries, in order to make the Dash home scope maximally useful through community-contributed scopes and usage data. As before, the Dash can be restricted from including any online content or contribution in the Privacy system settings" (from: https://wiki.ubuntu.com/SmartScopes1304Spec).

When you search for something, the Dash will attempt to show you results from appropriate categories and specific sources within those categories. For example, searching for the name of a famous musician or band may return results from your Music directory or maybe Wikipedia. The categories and locations that the Dash selects from can be changed; you can manually select or unselect categories. If you want to limit the scope of your search to include only local files, you may. If you only want to include specific websites and not others, you may. The scope of your search is limited or expanded by which Scopes (now with a capital "S") you select or deselect. A Scope is a single location in which the Dash may search.

Many Scopes include previews that display in the Dash. For example, a Wikipedia article will include the summary of the article from the site, to help you decide whether to click and read further or not.

To enable or disable specific Scopes:

1. Open the Applications Lens.

2. Select Search plugins.

3. Open the preview of the Scope.

4. Click Enable or Disable to toggle whether it is used or not.

If you want to search a specific source, you can. Just like on Google, power users can learn prefixes like wiki: to force the Dash to only return results from Wikipedia. Many are available, but a definitive list has not been released, so you may want to experiment.

Other Settings

You can configure or adjust many other GUI-related settings by installing a package from the Ubuntu repositories called the CompizConfig Settings Manager (CCSM) (see Chapter 9, "Managing Software," for information on how to install this and other packages). The documentation for these settings is not always clear, so go slowly.

A new community-developed tool called Unity Tweak Tool is available in the Ubuntu software repositories as `unity-tweak-tool`. It is a GUI tool for adjusting how Unity operates. It, like CCSM above, it is not an official software product and may change things that

Ubuntu developers never planned to be adjusted, so use with caution and make sure you know how to undo any changes you make before you make them.

Power Shortcuts

Often, power users want to avoid using the mouse. They don't want to take their hands off the keyboard unless absolutely necessary because doing so slows them down. Here are some of the more useful keyboard shortcuts that readers of this book are likely to appreciate. You can configure or adjust many of these by installing a package from the Ubuntu repositories called the CompizConfig Settings Manager:

▶ Use the Special key (that is, the Windows key) to open the Dash. Click Esc to close the Dash without selecting anything in it.

▶ Use the middle mouse button to click an icon in the Launcher to open more than one instance of the same program. On a laptop, you can do this by clicking both right and left buttons simultaneously.

▶ Holding Alt+Tab brings up a menu of icons showing open programs so that you may switch between them quickly. Hold Alt and press Tab repeatedly to move from one program to the next until you reach the one you desire. Shift+Alt+Tab scrolls through them in reverse order. This and the next shortcut work together as a powerful combination when the application you want has multiple windows or instances.

▶ Switching from Alt+Tab to Alt+` (on an English keyboard; for other keyboards, read on) modifies the Alt+Tab menu so that it shows miniature images of open program windows when there are multiple instances of the same program. Hold Alt and press ` repeatedly to scroll through and select a specific instance. If you begin this while the desktop focus is on an instance of a program that has multiple instances open, you automatically begin with this set of open instances to select from among them. (On an English keyboard, ` is the key just above the Tab key. For other language keyboards, it is whatever key is in this same location, regardless of the character represented on the key itself.)

▶ Icons in the Launcher indicate when multiple instances of a program are open or when a program has multiple windows. Click twice on an icon in the Launcher that shows multiple arrows next to it and all of its windows will be displayed for you to select the one you desire.

▶ Click PrtSc (Print Screen) to take a screenshot of the current workspace.

▶ Use Special+T to open the trash can.

▶ Click Ctrl+Alt+*arrow-key* to move up, down, right, and left from workspace to workspace.

References

▶ **www.gnome.org/**—The launch point for more information about GNOME, links to new clients, and GNOME development projects.

▶ **www.x.org/**—Curators of the X Window System.

▶ **www.x.org/Downloads_mirror.html**—Want to download the source to the latest revision of X? Start at this list of mirror sites.

▶ **www.xfree86.org/**—Home of The XFree86 Project, Inc., which provided a graphical interface for Linux for nearly 10 years.

▶ **https://wiki.ubuntu.com/X**—The place to get started when learning about X and Ubuntu.

▶ **https://wiki.ubuntu.com/X/Config**—Great information about configuring X on Ubuntu.

▶ **http://www.freedesktop.org/wiki/Software/LightDM**—LightDM, a new window manager.

# CHAPTER 4

On the Internet

The Internet is everywhere. From cell phones to offices, from game consoles to tablets, we are surrounded by multiple access routes to online information and communication. Ubuntu is no outsider when it comes to accessing information through the Internet; it comes equipped with all the tools you need to connect to other people across the globe.

In this chapter, we look at some of the popular Internet applications that are available with Ubuntu. You find out about Firefox and Google Chrome. The chapter also investigates some of the email clients available. Other topics include RSS feed readers, instant messaging (through IRC and other networks), and reading newsgroups.

A BRIEF INTRODUCTION TO THE INTERNET

The Internet itself was first brought to life by the U.S. Department of Defense in 1969. It was called ARPANET after the Department of Defense's Advanced Research Projects Agency. Designed to build a network that would withstand major catastrophe (this was the peak of the Cold War), it soon grew to encompass more and more networks to build the Internet. Then, in 1991, Tim Berners-Lee of CERN developed the idea of the World Wide Web, including *Hypertext Transfer Protocol (HTTP)* and *Hypertext Markup Language (HTML)*. This gave us what we now know to be the Internet.

Getting Started with Firefox

One of the most popular web browsers, and in fact the default web browser in Ubuntu, is Mozilla Firefox (see Figure 4.1). Built on a solid code base that is derived from the Mozilla suite, Firefox offers an open-source and more secure alternative to Internet Explorer for surfing the Internet, regardless of your operating system.

FIGURE 4.1   Mozilla Firefox—rediscover the Web. Firefox enables you to add on numerous extensions, further enhancing your experience.

In Ubuntu, you can find Firefox by searching the Dash for *firefox*.

Beyond the basic program are a wealth of plug-ins and extensions that can increase the capabilities of Firefox beyond simple web browsing. Plug-ins such as Shockwave, Flash, and Java are available for installation instantly, offered to you when first needed, as are multimedia codecs for viewing video content. Extensions provide useful additions to the browsing experience. For example, ForecastFox is an extension that gives you your local weather conditions, and Bandwidth Meter and Diagnostics is a tool that calculates your current bandwidth. There are many more extensions and plug-ins that you can use to enhance your browsing experience (Shift-Ctrl-A).

You can find and obtain these plug-ins and extensions easily because Mozilla developers have created a site dedicated to helping you get more from Firefox. You don't have to search to find the site as there is a link in the Firefox menu at Tools, Add-ons, Get Add-ons that takes you directly to it. Particular favorites are the Adblock Plus and the StumbleUpon plug-ins. Adblock Plus enables you to nuke all those annoying banners and animations that take up so much bandwidth while you are browsing. StumbleUpon is a neat plug-in that takes you to web pages based on your preferences. Be warned, though, that StumbleUpon can be quite addictive, and you will end up wasting away many hours clicking the [Stumble!] button.

FLASH

You can easily enable Flash in your browser by installing the `flashplugin-installer` package, or better yet, you can deal with the whole issue of codecs and functionality for your entire operating system right off by installing `ubuntu-restricted-extras`. Either way, Ubuntu downloads the official package from Adobe and installs it on your system. A browser restart is required before you try to access any Flash-enabled content. Note: Adobe recently stated it will cease to support Flash on Linux. However, Google Chrome includes Flash support and is doing so with Adobe's blessing. If you need Flash, you will probably need to use Google Chrome as your browser.

▶ To make things even easier, if you have not yet installed this package and visit a web page that requires Flash, a pop-up window appears with information and a link to help you install it easily.

Another plug-in that gets a lot of use of is Xmarks Sync. If, like us, you work across multiple computers and operating systems, you will no doubt have had to re-create bookmarks at every different computer and try to keep them the same. Xmarks makes this whole process much easier by allowing you to synchronize your bookmarks to multiple browsers (for example, Firefox and Google Chrome) running on different operating systems (Windows, Mac OS X, Linux).

Checking Out Google Chrome and Chromium

Anyone who has been paying attention to tech news has heard about the explosive appearance of Google Chrome (Figure 4.2), which has gone from being the new kid on the block to a firm contender for most popular browser in just a few years. This browser is fast, secure, expandable with extensions, and the hottest new toy on geek desktops. It is based on WebKit and other technologies, and it downloads and renders quickly while being standards compliant. You can learn more about the easy installation of Google Chrome at www.google.com/chrome.

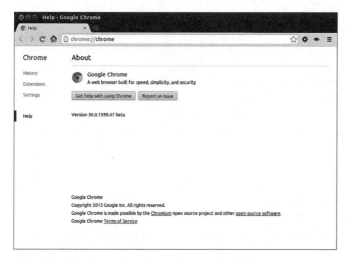

FIGURE 4.2   Google Chrome running in Ubuntu.

Chrome is not completely open-source, but the main foundational parts are open-source and are made available as Google Chromium, shown in Figure 4.3, which has most of the functionality of Chrome, but it is missing the Google branding, automatic updates, and is used as the test and development foundation for Chrome releases. As a point of interest, chromium is the metal from which chrome is made, hence the names.

You can learn more about Chromium at www.chromium.org. It used to be necessary to install Chromium from the Google website or from the Personal Package Archive of the Google Chromium developers. Now, you may simply install `chromium-browser` from the Ubuntu repositories.

FIGURE 4.3   Chromium is the source from which Chrome is made, and it works very well.

Choosing an Email Client

Back in the earlier days of UNIX there were various text-based email clients such as elm and pine (Pine Is Not Elm). Although they looked basic, they allowed the average user to interact with email, both for composing and reading correspondence, and had some sophisticated and useful features that might not have been expected, such as filtering and searching tools. Still, when computing became mainstream, there was a realization that people wanted friendly *graphical user interfaces (GUIs)*. Soon there came a flood of email clients, some of them even cross-platform and compatible among Linux, Windows, Mac OS X, and even traditional UNIX.

Mozilla Thunderbird

Mozilla Thunderbird (see Figure 4.4) is the sister program to Firefox and the default email application in Ubuntu. Whereas Firefox is designed to browse the Web, Thunderbird's specialty is communication. It can handle email, network news (see later in this chapter), and RSS feeds.

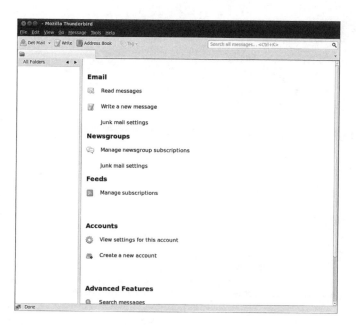

FIGURE 4.4   The natural companion to Firefox, Mozilla's lightweight email client, Thunderbird, can be found in use all over the world.

As with Firefox, there are many plug-ins and extensions to enhance your email. You can also use Thunderbird for Usenet news reading.

Evolution

Up until Ubuntu 11.10, Evolution was the default email client in Ubuntu, although to call it simply an email client is to sincerely underrate its usefulness as an application. Not only does it handle email, but it can also look after contacts and calendars and help you manage your tasks (see Figure 4.5).

You need to have the following information to successfully configure Evolution (or any email client):

▶ Your email address

▶ Your incoming email server name and type (that is, pop.email.com, POP, and IMAP)

▶ Your username and password for the incoming mail server

▶ Your outgoing mail server name (that is, smtp.email.com)

FIGURE 4.5   With Evolution you can handle all your email and contacts, as well as make appointments and track tasks.

As many people are moving to web-based mail options such as Google's Gmail or Yahoo! Mail, client-side email programs have started to decline in popularity. One thing that sets Evolution apart is that you can still use it for the other features and disable the email portion of the program by selecting "none" as your mail transfer agent instead of POP, IMAP, and so on. In addition, Evolution can interact with an existing web calendar program if it uses one of the common formats, such as CalDAV. This enables you to use your calendar remotely as you are used to, but also permits the Ubuntu desktop to have access to your events and embed them into your desktop panel (which it does by default using Evolution).

Other Mail Clients

The mail clients that we've covered are only a few of those available. Claws is very popular because it offers spell check while typing and is well suited for use in large network environments in which network overhead and RAM usage are important considerations. Mutt is an older text-based email program that is still beloved by sysadmins for its configurability and feature set, including the easy use of GPG keys for signing email. Alpine is another text-based program based on the classic Pine, with a few upgrades. Kmail is commonly used by lovers of the KDE desktop that is commonly run as a part of many Linux-based operating systems. All of these and more are available for installation from the Ubuntu software repositories. In addition, all of the web-based email applications work just fine with Ubuntu, such as Gmail, Hotmail, and Yahoo! Mail.

RSS Readers

RSS is one of the protocols of Web 2.0, the current generation of Internet content. RSS has really taken off, thanks to adoption by a large number of websites and portals.

The key advantage of RSS is that you can quickly read news from your choice of websites at a time that suits you and from one location, meaning you don't have to go to each site to view their content. Some services offer just the articles' headlines, whereas others offer full articles for you to view. RSS feeds can be accessed in various ways, even through your web browser!

Firefox

Firefox implements RSS feeds as what it calls Live Bookmarks (shown in Figure 4.6), which are essentially bookmarks with sub-bookmarks, each linking to a new page from your chosen website. Some people like to have several news sites grouped together in a folder called News in the Firefox toolbar because this allows them to quickly browse through a collection of sites and pick out articles of interest.

FIGURE 4.6   Live Bookmarks for Firefox, making all your news fixes just a mouse click away.

Liferea

Of course, not everyone wants to read RSS feeds with the browser. The main problem with reading RSS feeds with Firefox is that you get to see only the headline, rather than any actual text. This is where a dedicated RSS reader comes in handy, and in many peoples opinion, Liferea is one of the best readers out there (see Figure 4.7).

Read your daily news feeds with Liferea, a fantastic and easy-to-use RSS feed reader. Liferea is not installed by default, but it is available from the repositories under the name `liferea`. After you install it, you can find it by searching the Dash for Liferea.

By default, Liferea offers a number of RSS feeds, including Planet Debian, Groklaw, and Slashdot. Adding a new feed is straightforward. You select New Subscription under the Feeds menu and paste the URL of the RSS feed into the box. Liferea then retrieves all the current items available through that field and displays the feed name on the left side for you to select and start reading.

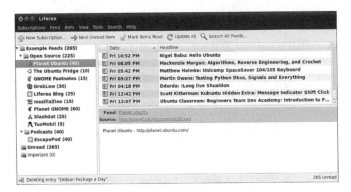

FIGURE 4.7   Read your daily news feeds with Liferea, a fantastic and easy-to-use RSS feed reader.

Internet Relay Chat

As documented in RFC 2812 and RFC 2813, the *Internet Relay Chat (IRC)* protocol is used for text conferencing. Like mail and news, IRC uses a client/server model. Although it is rare for an individual to set up and run an IRC server, it can be done. Most people use public IRC servers and access them with IRC clients. IRC is also the favorite and most common form of quick communication among developers in the Ubuntu community, so if that interests you, you will certainly want to learn to use this tool.

Ubuntu provides a number of graphical IRC clients in the repositories, including XChat, Pidgin, and Quassel. Ubuntu also makes the console clients epic and irssi available in the repositories for those who eschew X and a graphical interface. Don't laugh, there are actually many who do this, and not just server admins, especially because they can be run on a remote server and accessed over *Secure Shell (SSH)* using Byobu or Screen allowing them to be left running 24/7 on that remote server. For more about Byobu and Screen, see Chapter 12, "Command-Line Master Class Part 2." If you don't already have a favorite IRC client, you should try them all.

XChat is a very popular IRC client, and the most common recommendation for IRC newcomers using Ubuntu, so we use it as an example. After you install the program, the documentation for XChat is available in /usr/share/doc/xchat. It is a good idea to read that before you begin because it includes an introduction and covers some of the basics of IRC.

The XChat application enables you to assign yourself up to three nicknames. You can also specify your real name and your username. Because many people choose not to use their real names in IRC chat, you are free to enter any names you desire in any of the spaces provided. You can select multiple nicknames; you might be banned from an IRC channel under one name, and you could then rejoin using another. If this seems slightly juvenile to you, you are beginning to get an idea of the type of behavior on many IRC channels (but not the ones where serious developer and Ubuntu community interactions take place).

When you open the main XChat screen, a list of IRC servers appears, as shown in Figure 4.8. After you choose a server by double-clicking it, you can view a list of channels available on that server by choosing Window, Channel List. The XChat Channel List window appears. In that window, you can choose to join channels featuring topics that interest you. To join a channel, you double-click it. Ubuntu uses irc.freenode.net for the server, and the primary support channel is #ubuntu.

FIGURE 4.8   The main XChat screen presents a list of available public servers from which to select.

THE WILD SIDE OF IRC

Do not be surprised at the number of lewd topics and the use of crude language on public IRC servers. For a humorous look at the topic of IRC cursing, see www.irc.org/fun_docs/nocuss.html. This site also offers some tips for maintaining IRC etiquette, which is essential if you do not want to be the object of any of that profanity. Here are some of the most important IRC etiquette rules:

▶ Do not use colored text, all-capitalized text, blinking text, or "bells" (beeps caused by sending ^G to a terminal).

▶ Show respect for others.

▶ Ignore people who act inappropriately.

After you select a channel, you can join in the conversation, which appears as onscreen text. The messages scroll down the screen as new messages appear. For an example, see Figure 4.9. You can continue learning about IRC at https://help.ubuntu.com/community/InternetRelayChat.

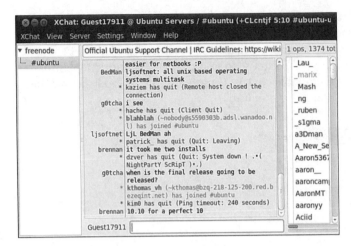

FIGURE 4.9   Join in an online chatroom about your favorite distro, with XChat.

TIP

You can establish your own IRC server even though Ubuntu does not provide one. Setting up a server is not a task for anyone who is not well versed in Linux or IRC.

A popular server is IRCd, which you can obtain from http://www.irc.org/ftp/irc/server/. Before you download IRCd, look at the README file to determine what files you need to download and read the information at www.irchelp.org/irchelp/ircd/.

Usenet Newsgroups

The concept of newsgroups revolutionized the way information was exchanged between people across a network. The Usenet network news system created a method for people to electronically communicate with large groups of people with similar interests. Many of the concepts of Usenet news are embodied in other forms of collaborative communication.

Usenet newsgroups act as a form of public bulletin board system. Any user can subscribe to individual newsgroups and send (or post) messages (called articles) to the newsgroup so that all the other subscribers of the newsgroup can read them. Some newsgroups include an administrator, who must approve each message before it is posted. These are called *moderated newsgroups*. Other newsgroups are open, allowing any subscribed member to post a message. When an article is posted to the newsgroup, it is transferred to all the other hosts in the news network.

Usenet newsgroups are divided into a hierarchy to make it easier to find individual newsgroups. The hierarchy levels are based on topics, such as computers, science, recreation, and social issues. Each newsgroup is named as a subset of the higher-level topic. For example, the newsgroup comp relates to all computer topics. The newsgroup `comp.laptops` relates to laptop computer issues. Often the hierarchy goes several layers deep. For example, the newsgroup `comp.databases.oracle.server` relates to Oracle server database issues.

NOTE

The format of newsgroup articles follows the strict guidelines defined in the Internet standards document *Request for Comments (RFC)* 1036. Each article must contain two distinct parts: header lines and a message body.

The header lines identify information about when and by whom the article was posted. The body of the message should contain only standard ASCII text characters. No binary characters or files should be posted within news articles. To get around this restriction, binary files are converted to text data through use of either the standard UNIX uuencode program or the newer *Multipurpose Internet Mail Extensions (MIME)* protocol. The resulting text file is then posted to the newsgroup. Newsgroup readers can then decode the posted text file back into its original binary form.

A collection of articles posted in response to a common topic is called a *thread*. A thread can contain many articles as users post messages in response to other posted messages. Some newsreader programs allow users to track articles based on the threads to which they belong. This helps simplify the organization of articles in the newsgroup.

TIP

The free news server `news.gmane.org` makes the Red Hat and Ubuntu mail lists available via newsgroups. The beta list is available as `gmane.linux.redhat.rhl.beta`. It is a handy way to read threaded discussions, and some prefer it to using the Ubuntu mail list archives.

The protocol used to transfer newsgroup articles from one host to another is *Network News Transfer Protocol (NNTP)*, defined in RFC 975. (You can search RFCs at ftp://metalab.unc.edu/pub/docs/rfc/; look at the file `rfc-index.txt`.) NNTP was designed as a simple client/server protocol that enables two hosts to exchange newsgroup articles in an efficient manner.

Whether or not your Ubuntu machine is set up as a news server, you can use a newsreader program to read newsgroup articles. The newsreader programs require just a connection to a news server. It does not matter whether the news server is on the same machine or is a remote news server on the other side of the world.

Several programs are available to connect to news servers to read and post articles in newsgroups. If you are interested in Usenet, you might want to check out a program from the Ubuntu repositories called Pan. Pan is a graphical newsreader client that can download and display all the newsgroups available on a server and display posted news articles. However, Usenet is an old system that predates the creation of the World Wide Web. It was the place to be in the early days and the source of many great memories, but today is little better than a ghost town with wind-blown tumbleweeds, spam, and illegal exchanges of pirated content. Most Internet service providers used to run free Usenet servers, and connecting was easy and common, but most of the free ones are gone now, and traffic has dwindled. Feel free to experiment or try to relive the glory days, but Usenet is, alas, well past its prime.

References

▶ www.mozilla.com/—The home page for Mozilla Firefox, Thunderbird, and the Mozilla Suite.

▶ http://en.wikipedia.org/wiki/Usenet—A history of Usenet.

CHAPTER 5

Productivity Applications

Many businesses have already found a way to benefit from free and open-source software, such as office productivity suites like LibreOffice. These have the cost benefits of not having to pay license fees or support costs. However, more applications beyond these are available in Ubuntu. In this chapter, we explore some of them.

> **NOTE**
>
> It's important to understand that even though free and open-source software does very well most of the time, especially with less-complex documents, it is not 100 percent compatible with Microsoft Office. Why is this? Microsoft is notoriously secretive about its proprietary file formats, and the only way that free and open-source alternatives could ensure compatibility would be to reverse-engineer each file format, an exercise akin to taking apart a telephone to see how it works. This reverse-engineering is difficult to do in a legal way and is rarely perfect. However, many manage to maintain a very high standard of importing and exporting, so you should not experience too many problems except with documents of great complexity. As an example, this book was written using LibreOffice, whereas the post-production at the publisher uses Microsoft tools.
>
> The biggest compatibility issue between Microsoft Office and others like LibreOffice is that Microsoft's *Visual Basic for Applications (VBA)* and scripts produced using it do not transfer. If you use VBA scripts, you need to find another way to perform the functions for which they were written.

A *productivity suite* is defined as two or more applications bundled together and used for creating documents, presentations, spreadsheets, and databases. Other applications that might be included in the bundle are email clients, calculators/formula editors, illustration or drawing software, and more. Commonly, they are all tied together by a default look and feel, which makes sticking to one particular suite much easier. Because Ubuntu uses LibreOffice as its standard office suite, we introduce you to that first. We also take a brief look at some of the other Linux-based productivity applications.

PRODUCTIVITY FOR THE TYPICAL USER

For the majority of users of productivity suites, LibreOffice should fulfill most, if not all, of your requirements. However, the first hurdle is not whether it can do what you require of it, but rather whether it can successfully import and export to proprietary Microsoft formats at a standard that is acceptable to your needs. Most of the time, LibreOffice should import and export with minimal hassle, perhaps getting a bit stuck with some of the more esoteric Microsoft Office formatting. Given that most users do not go much beyond tabs, columns, and tables, this level of compatibility should suffice.

However, you are strongly advised to round up a selection of documents and spreadsheets that seem the most likely to be difficult for the import/export filter and test them thoroughly (of course, keeping a backup of the originals). There is nothing worse for a system administrator who has deployed a new productivity suite than to suddenly get users complaining that they cannot read their files. This would quickly destroy any benefits gained from the other useful functions within LibreOffice, and could even mark the return of proprietary formats and expensive office suites.

On the positive side, LibreOffice supports a huge array of file formats and can export to nearly 70 types of documents. Such a variety of file formats means that you should be able to successfully use LibreOffice in nearly any environment, including formats no longer used by currently produced and maintained software, so it may be able to open some old files and documents you had once given up for lost.

Introducing LibreOffice

LibreOffice contains a number of productivity applications for use in creating text documents, preparing spreadsheets, organizing presentations, managing projects, and so on. The following components of the LibreOffice package are included with Ubuntu:

▶ **Writer**—This word processing program enables you to compose, format, and organize text documents. If you are accustomed to using Microsoft Word, the functionality of LibreOffice Writer will be familiar to you.

▶ **Calc**—This spreadsheet program enables you to manipulate numbers in a spreadsheet format. Support for all but the most esoteric Microsoft Excel functions means that trading spreadsheets with Excel users should be successful. Calc offers some limited compatibility with Excel macros, but those macros generally have to be rewritten.

▶ **Impress**—This presentation program is similar to Microsoft PowerPoint and enables you to create slideshow presentations that include graphs, diagrams, and other graphics. Impress also works well with most PowerPoint files.

NOTE

The following five applications are not included by default with Ubuntu but are quite useful. All but Dia are a part of the LibreOffice project and add features to the suite that are not used as often as those Ubuntu installs by default. You must install them from the Ubuntu repositories if you want or require their functionality.

▶ **Math**—This math formula editor enables you to write mathematical formulas with a number of math fonts and symbols for inclusion in a word processing document. Such symbols are highly specialized and not easily included in the basic functionality of a word processor. This is of interest primarily to math and science writers, but Math can be useful to anyone who needs to include a complex formula in text.

▶ **Base**—This is a fully functional database application.

▶ **Draw**—This graphics application allows you to create images for inclusion in the documents produced with LibreOffice. It saves files only in LibreOffice format, but it can import most common image formats.

▶ **Dia**—This technical drawing editor from the GNOME Office suite enables you to create measured drawings, such as those used by architects and engineers. Its functionality is similar to that of Microsoft Visio.

▶ **Planner**—You can use this project management application for project planning, scheduling, and tracking; this application is similar to, but not compatible with, Microsoft Project. After you install it, you will find it under the name Project Management.

A BRIEF HISTORY OF LIBREOFFICE

LibreOffice started as a fork of the OpenOffice.org office suite. The OpenOffice.org office suite is based on a commercial suite called StarOffice. Originally developed by a German company, StarOffice was purchased by Sun Microsystems in the United States. One of the biggest complaints about the old StarOffice was that all the component applications were integrated under a StarOffice "desktop" that looked very much like a Microsoft Windows desktop, including a Start button and menus. This meant that to edit a simple document, unneeded applications had to be loaded, making the office suite slow to load, slow to run, and quite demanding on system resources.

After the purchase of StarOffice, Sun Microsystems released a large part of the StarOffice code under the GNU Public License, and development began on what has become OpenOffice.org, which was freely available under the GPL. Sun also continued development on StarOffice. The significant differences between the free and commercial versions of the software were that StarOffice provided more fonts and even more import/export file filters than OpenOffice.org (these filters were not provided in the GPL version because of licensing restrictions), and StarOffice provided its own relational database, Software AGs Adabas D database.

Sun was bought by Oracle. Oracle suffered from a major disagreement with the developer community surrounding OpenOffice.org and the developers left to form The Document

Foundation, hoping that Oracle would eventually join. Because the code for OpenOffice.org was licensed using a free software license, The Document Foundation created a fork, or a new version of the same software, using what they intended as a temporary name, LibreOffice. The hope was merely to change how the project was governed, from being led by one company to being led by a community with many companies and individuals participating. Oracle chose not to join The Document Foundation and instead relicensed the OpenOffice.org code for all future versions, which they may do as the owners of that code, and gave the code to the Apache Software Foundation, who is licensing it under the less-restrictive Apache license that allows open-source code to be used in proprietary products. To make things more interesting, IBM is using this Apache-licensed version of OpenOffice.org as the foundation for its own free-as-in-cost office suite based on it called Lotus Symphony, which also has some proprietary additions.

As the saga continues, the ultimate winner may be the end user as this effectively creates three competing office suites. For now, LibreOffice has the most developers, the strongest community, and the most mature software with the most rapid addition of new or improved features.

Other Office Suites for Ubuntu

As mentioned earlier, LibreOffice is the default application suite for Ubuntu. However, as is common in the open-source world, there are plenty of alternatives should you find that LibreOffice does not meet your specific requirements. These include the popular GNOME Office and also KOffice, the default KDE productivity suite. You are likely to hear more about LibreOffice, especially as more and more people realize that it is generally compatible with Microsoft Office file formats. Interestingly, the state of Massachusetts not long ago elected to standardize on two file formats for use in government: the Adobe Acrobat PDF format and the OASIS OpenDocument format, both of which are supported natively in LibreOffice.

> **NOTE**
>
> The decision by the state of Massachusetts to standardize on PDF and OpenDocument has huge ramifications for the open-source world. It is the first time that OpenDocument, an open standard, has been specified in this way. It means that anyone who wants to do business with the state government must use OpenDocument-based file formats, and not the proprietary formats in use by Microsoft. Unfortunately for Microsoft, it does not have support for OpenDocument in any of its applications, making them useless to anyone wanting to work with the state government. This is despite Microsoft being a founding member of OASIS, who developed and ratified the OpenDocument standard.

Working with GNOME Office

The other office suite available for Ubuntu is GNOME Office, which is a collection of individual applications. Unlike LibreOffice, GNOME Office does not have a coherent suite of applications, meaning that you have to get used to using a word processor that offers no integration with a spreadsheet and cannot work directly with a presentation package. However, if you need only one or two components, it is worthwhile investigating GNOME Office.

THE GTK WIDGET SET

Open-source developers are always trying to make it easier for people to build applications and help in development. To this end, there are a number of widgets or toolkits that other developers can use to rapidly create and deploy GUI applications. These widgets control things such as drop-down lists, Save As dialogs, window buttons, and general look and feel. Unfortunately, whereas Windows and Apple developers have to worry about only one set of widgets each, Linux has a plethora of different widgets, including GTK+, QT, and Motif. What is worse is that these widgets are incompatible with one another, making it difficult to easily move a finished application from one widget set to another.

GTK is an acronym for *GIMP Tool Kit*. GIMP, the *GNU Image Manipulation Program*, is a graphics application very similar to Adobe Photoshop. By using the GTK-based jargon, we save ourselves several hundred words of typing and help move along our discussion of GNOME Office. You might also see similar references to QT and Motif, as well as other widget sets, in these chapters.

Here are some of the primary components of the GNOME Office suite that are available in Ubuntu:

► **AbiWord**—This word processing program enables you to compose, format, and organize text documents and has some compatibility with the Microsoft Word file format. It uses plug-ins (programs that add functionality such as language translation) to enhance its functionality.

► **Gnumeric**—This spreadsheet program enables you to manipulate numbers in a spreadsheet format. Support for all but the most esoteric Microsoft Excel functions means that users should have little trouble trading spreadsheets with Excel users.

► **GIMP**—This graphics application allows you to create images for general use. It can import and export all common graphic file formats. GIMP is similar to Adobe's Photoshop application and is described in Chapter 6, "Multimedia Applications."

► **Evolution**—Evolution is a mail client with an interface similar to Microsoft Outlook, providing email, scheduling, and calendaring. It is described in Chapter 4, "On the Internet."

The loose association of applications known as GNOME Office includes several additional applications that duplicate the functionality of applications already provided by Ubuntu. Those extra GNOME applications are not included in a default installation of Ubuntu to eliminate redundancy. They are all available from the GNOME Office website, at `www.gnome.org/gnome-office/`, and in the Ubuntu software repositories.

Working with KOffice

The KDE office suite KOffice was developed to provide tight integration with the KDE desktop. Integration enables objects in one application to be inserted in other applications via drag and drop, and all the applications can communicate with each other, so a change in an object is instantly communicated to other applications. The application integration provided by KDE is a significant enhancement to productivity. (Some GNOME desktop applications share a similar communication facility with each other.) If you use the KDE desktop instead of the default GNOME desktop, you can enjoy the benefits of this integration, along with the Konqueror web and file browser.

The word processor for KOffice is KWord. KWord is a frames-based word processor, meaning that document pages can be formatted in framesets that hold text, graphics, and objects in enclosed areas. You can use framesets to format text on a page that includes text and images within columns that the text needs to flow around, making KWord an excellent choice for creating documents other than standard business letters, such as newsletters and brochures.

KWord and other components of KOffice are stable, but are still under development and lack all the polished features of LibreOffice and AbiWord. However, it does have the capability to work with the OpenDocument format found in LibreOffice, as well as limited compatibility with Microsoft file formats.

The KOffice KSpread client is a functional spreadsheet program that offers graphing capabilities along with all the other standard spreadsheet functionality.

KDE includes other productivity options in KOffice. These include an address book, time tracker, calculator, notepad, and scheduler. One popular application is Kontact, which provides daily, weekly, workweek, and monthly views of tasks, to-do lists, and scheduled appointments with background alarms.

Other Useful Productivity Software

The office suites already discussed in this chapter are ideal for typical office-focused file interactions: creating basic documents, spreadsheets, and so on. However, some of us have more complex or precise needs. This section covers some of the options available to help you be productive in those instances.

Working with PDF

Reading a PDF in Ubuntu is simple. The functionality is available by default thanks to an installed program called Evince. Open a PDF, and Evince opens and so you read the document. Sometimes filling out forms is less straightforward as the form might have been created using functionality only available from Adobe. You can install Adobe Reader from the Ubuntu Software Center from the Canonical Partners section. Adobe Reader should work with any PDF form created using Adobe software, whether it was created on Windows, Mac OS X, or Linux.

On occasion, you find that you have a PDF file that you want to edit. That is a little more complex, but not as difficult as it used to be. There is a program created just for editing PDF files.

Install PDF Editor (`pdfedit`) from the Ubuntu Software Center. On the surface, this program seems simple enough, but it has great power that is not immediately obvious. Advanced users can learn to use `pdfedit` in scripts to make sweeping changes quickly. Of course, as with most powerful tools, it comes with the cost of complexity and learning how to use it.

Working with XML and DocBook

Like its ancestor SGML and cousin HTML, XML is a markup language. It is designed for use in a plain-text document. Tags surround specific sections of the text to denote how that section is to be displayed. Listing 5.1 contains a short example.

LISTING 5.1   Sample XML Excerpt

```
<?xml version="1.0"?>
<xml-stylesheet type="text/css" href="book.css"?>
<book>
<title>Ubuntu Unleashed 2013</title>
<edition>8</edition>
<chapter>
        <number>1</number>
        <title>Installing Ubuntu</title>
        <text>
                <paragraph><dropcap>N</dropcap>ot that long ago,the mere mention...
                </paragraph>
        ...
        </text>
</chapter>
...
</book>
```

This could easily be written using a simple text editor like the one installed by default, Gedit (called Text Editor in the Dash and the listings in the Ubuntu Software Center). However, doing it that way would be tedious for most people. A better option is to use an editor expressly designed and intended for dealing with XML files. Because DocBook is an open-source standard form of XML that has been designed explicitly for use with documentation, many editors that can work with one will work with both. If you only need to do something quick, one of these should be suitable. Start with Gedit, which is installed by default. If it is not suitable, look in the Ubuntu Software Center for other options like the ones discussed next.

If you intend to write a lot of complicated documentation in only the DocBook format, the most common recommendation for Ubuntu is a program called Publican. Publican is not just an editor; it is also a publication system for DocBook. It tests your XML to ensure it is in a valid DocBook form so that your output conforms to publication standards. It automates output into multiple formats such as HTML and PDF, and it allows complete control for custom skinning and formatting. You can install Publican from the Ubuntu Software Center.

A more powerful option is XML Copy Editor. It is designed for editing most markup languages including XML, DocBook, DITA, and more. It also features schema validation, syntax highlighting, tag completion, and spell checking. This is the most useful option for the professional documentation specialist. You can install XML Copy Editor from the Ubuntu Software Repositories, and their website has a version available for use on Windows. See `http://xml-copy-editor.sourceforge.net` for more.

Working with LaTeX

LaTeX was created for and is widely used in academia. It is a WYGIWYW (What You Get Is What You Want) document markup language created for the TeX typesetting system. Multiple editors are available for use with LaTeX, and they are likely to be found for just about every operating system in existence.

> **NOTE**
>
> WYSIWYG is an acronym for "what you see is what you get" that has often been used to describe word processors and document creation systems that use a graphical interface. Unfortunately, anyone who has created documents with these programs, including the ones mentioned earlier in this chapter, such as LibreOffice, knows that what you see on the screen is not always what appears in the printed version on paper. There are no promises about how things will or will not look on the screen while using a LaTeX editor for your TeX document, but the format promises that the ultimate output will be exactly what you ask for.

A couple of the more popular LaTeX editors available from the Ubuntu Software Center are discussed in this section. You can also create and edit using any text editor, including Gedit.

Texmaker not only has a version in the Ubuntu Software Center, but also offers versions for Windows and Mac OS X from `www.xmlmath.net/texmaker/`. It is free, easy to use, and mature. The program has been around for a while, it is stable, has many useful features, and is rather popular in the TeX world.

LyX follows suit with both a version in the Ubuntu Software Center and versions available for Windows and Mac OS X from its website at `www.lyx.org`. The main appeal for LyX users is its graphical interface, which makes it an interesting bridge from WYSIWYG to LaTeX. It also has many plug-ins available to expand functionality.

Kile was written and designed for use with KDE. As such, it blends in well to Kubuntu but will run well on a standard Ubuntu installation. It also has a Windows version available; see `http://kile.sourceforge.net` for details.

Productivity Applications Written for Microsoft Windows

Microsoft Windows is fundamentally different from Linux, yet you can install and run some Microsoft Windows applications in Linux by using an application named Wine. Wine enables you to use Microsoft Windows and DOS programs on UNIX-based systems. Wine includes a program loader that you can use to execute a Windows binary, along with a DLL library that implements Windows command calls, translating them to the equivalent UNIX and X11 command calls. Because of frequent updates to the Wine code base, Wine is not included with Ubuntu. Download a current version of Wine from `www.winehq.org/`. To see whether your favorite application is supported by Wine, you can look at the Wine application database at `https://appdb.winehq.org/`.

Other solutions, primarily CrossOver Office from CodeWeavers, enable use of Microsoft productivity applications. If you are after a closer-to-painless way of running not only Microsoft Office, but also Apple iTunes and other software, you should investigate CodeWeavers. CrossOver Office is one of the simplest programs you can use to get Windows-based programs to work. Check out `www.codeweavers.com` to download a trial version of the latest software.

References

▶ www.libreoffice.org—The home page for the LibreOffice suite.

▶ www.documentfoundation.org—The home page for The Document Foundation.

▶ www.openoffice.org—The home page for the OpenOffice.org office suite.

▶ https://wiki.gnome.org/Projects/GnomeOffice—The GNOME Office site.

▶ www.koffice.org/—The home page for the KOffice suite.

▶ http://www.pdfedit.cz/en/index.html—The home page for PDF Edit.

▶ www.codeweavers.com/—The home page for CrossOver Office from CodeWeavers that enables you to run some Windows programs under Linux.

Multimedia Applications

The twenty-first century has become the century of the digital lifestyle, with millions of computer users around the world embracing new technologies, such as digital cameras, MP3 players, and other assorted multimedia gadgets. Whereas 10 years ago you might have had a small collection of WAV files scattered about your Windows installation, today you are more likely to have hundreds, if not thousands, of MP3 files scattered across various computers. Along with video clips, animations, and other graphics, the demand for organizing and maintaining these vast libraries is driving development of applications. Popular proprietary applications such as iTunes and Google's Picasa were once coveted by Linux users, but open-source applications now exist that provide real alternatives, and for some people these are the final reasons they need to move to Linux full time.

This chapter provides an overview of some of the basic multimedia tools included with Ubuntu. In this chapter, you discover how to create your own CDs, watch TV, rip audio CDs into the open-source Ogg audio format for playback, as well as manage your media library. You also find out about how Ubuntu handles graphics and pictures and more.

Sound and Music

Linux had a reputation of lacking good support for sound and multimedia applications in general. However, great strides have been made in recent years to correct this, and support is now a lot better than it used to be. (It might make you smile to know that Microsoft no longer supports the Microsoft Sound Card, but Linux users still enjoy support for it, no doubt just to annoy the folks in Redmond.) UNIX, however, has always had good multimedia support, as David Taylor, UNIX author and guru, points out:

> The original graphics work for computers was done by Evans and Sutherland on UNIX systems. The innovations at MIT's Media Lab were done on UNIX workstations. In 1985, we at HP Labs were creating sophisticated multimedia immersive work environments on UNIX workstations, so maybe UNIX is more multimedia than suggested. Limitations in Linux support doesn't mean UNIX had the same limitations. I think it was more a matter of logistics, with hundreds of sound cards and thousands of different possible PC configurations.

That last sentence sums it up quite well. UNIX had a limited range of hardware to support; Linux has hundreds of sound cards. Sound card device driver support has been long lacking from manufacturers, and there is still no single standard for the sound subsystem in Linux.

In this section, you learn about sound cards, sound file formats, and the sound applications provided with Ubuntu.

Sound Cards

Ubuntu supports a wide variety of sound hardware and software. Two models of sound card drivers compete for prominence in today's market:

▶ ALSA, the *Advanced Linux Sound Architecture*, which is entirely open source

▶ OSS, the *Open Sound System*, which offers free and commercial drivers

Ubuntu uses ALSA because ALSA is the sound architecture for the linux kernel, starting with the 2.6 series, all the way to the current the 4.x series. OSS might still be found here and there, but it is no longer in widespread use and should be considered deprecated.

ALSA supports a long list of sound cards. You can review the list at www.alsa-project.org/main/index.php/Main_Page if you are interested, but Ubuntu detects most sound cards during the original installation and should detect any new additions to the system during boot. To configure the sound card at any other time, use the sound preferences graphical tool by searching the Dash for sound.

In addition, Ubuntu uses an additional layer of software called *PulseAudio*. PulseAudio is a sound server and acts as a mediator between the various multimedia programs that have sound output and the ALSA kernel drivers. Over the years, there have been many different sound servers used in Linux, each with different strengths, usability issues, and levels of documentation. These various sound servers have often been forced to run side by side on the same computer, causing all sorts of confusion and issues. PulseAudio aims to replace all of them and work as a single handler to accept output from applications that use the APIs for any of the major sound servers already in use, such as ESD, OSS, GStreamer, and aRts, and route the various output streams together through one handler. This gives several advantages, including the ability to control the output volume of various programs individually.

PulseAudio is still quite young, and its full potential has not yet been realized; however, it has matured over the last several releases and is better and more powerful than ever. Although there were stability issues and complaints in the first release that included PulseAudio, those don't seem to be a problem anymore except in unusual hardware combinations and special cases, and more and more features have been implemented. For more information about PulseAudio, see www.pulseaudio.org/.

Adjusting Volume

Ubuntu offers a handy utility that you can use to control the volumes for various outputs from your computer. For a simple master volume control, just click the speaker icon in the top-right corner of the screen and move the slider left or right, as shown in Figure 6.1.

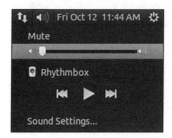

FIGURE 6.1   Control the master volume level with the volume slider.

Alternatively, you can control all the output volumes for the system to make sure that you have set everything to your taste, as shown in Figure 6.2. To access the volume control, left-click the speaker icon and select Sound Preferences.

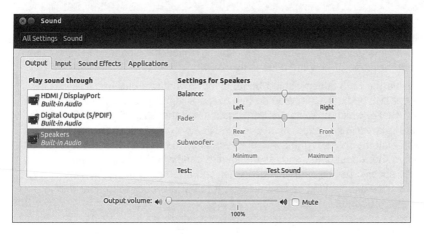

FIGURE 6.2   Use the volume control to manage volume settings for all your sound output devices.

Sound Formats

A number of formats exist for storing sound recordings. Some of these formats are associated with specific technologies, and others are used strictly for proprietary reasons. Ubuntu supports several of the most popular sound formats, including the following:

▶ **RAW (.raw)**—More properly known as *headerless format,* audio files using this format contain an amorphous variety of specific settings and encodings. All other sound files contain a short section of code at the beginning—a header—that identifies the format type.

▶ **MP3 (.mp3)**—A popular, but commercially licensed, format for the digital encoding used by many Linux and Windows applications. MP3 is not supported by any software included with Ubuntu by default, but you can easily install software that supports MP3 later. In fact, the first time you try to play an MP3 file, Ubuntu asks whether you want to install the codec needed and walks you through the whole, simple process.

▶ **WAV (.wav)**—The popular uncompressed Windows audio-visual sound format. It is often used as an intermediate file format when encoding audio.

▶ **Ogg-Vorbis (.ogg)**—Ubuntu's preferred audio encoding format. You enjoy better compression and audio playback and freedom from lawsuits when you use this open-source encoding format for your audio files.

▶ **FLAC (.flac)**—This is a lossless format popular with audiophiles. The name stands for *Free Lossless Audio Format* and it is a compressed format, like MP3, but does not suffer from any loss of quality.

NOTE

Because of patent and licensing issues, Ubuntu does not by default support the MPEG, MPEG2, and MPEG3 (MP3) file formats. Although we cannot offer any legal advice, it appears that individuals using MP3 software are okay; it is just that Ubuntu cannot distribute the code because of how the code is licensed.

You can also enable the MP3 codec within Ubuntu by downloading a plug-in for GStreamer, the GNOME audio system. You do this by installing the gstreamer0.10-plugins-ugly package, which enables the MP3 codec in all the GNOME applications. Even better, there is a package called ubuntu-restricted-extras that you can install that enables all the major formats you are ever likely to encounter. You can find the package in the repositories, and, as mentioned earlier in the chapter, Ubuntu also recommends specific packages as needed when you attempt to use a file type that does not currently have an installed codec package. It really is that easy to deal with multimedia formats in Ubuntu.

Ubuntu even includes software in the repositories (such as the `sox` command used to convert between sound formats) so that you can more easily listen to audio files provided in a wide variety of formats, such as AU (from NeXT and Sun), AIFF (from Apple and SGI), IFF (originally from Commodore's Amiga), RA (from Real Audio), and VOC (from Creative Labs).

TIP

For an introduction to audio formats, check out the list of audio file formats at www.fileinfo .com/filetypes/audio, with links to detailed information for each.

Ubuntu also offers several utilities for converting sound files from one format to another. Conversion utilities come in handy when you want to use a sound in a format not accepted by your current application of choice. The easiest one to use is also the easiest to install. Install the `soundconverter` package and then look for the application in the menu at Applications, Sound & Video, and Sound Converter. It has a clear graphical interface and easy-to-understand configuration options.

Listening to Music

If you're anything like us, you might be a huge music fan. One of the downsides of having a fairly large music collection is the physical problem of having to store so many CDs. Wouldn't it be great if you could pack them all away somewhere, yet still have access to all the music when you want it? Some manufacturers experimented with rather bulky jukeboxes that stored 250 CDs at once. The main downside with that was that finding a particular piece of music could take hours, having to cycle through each CD in the hope that it would match your mood.

Fortunately for us, Ubuntu is fantastic at working with CDs, even enabling you to rip your entire CD collection into a vast searchable music library, letting you quickly create playlists, and enabling you to create your own customized CDs. Getting started couldn't be easier, mainly because Ubuntu comes preconfigured with everything you need.

Rhythmbox

Rhythmbox is a useful application that plays CDs if you insert an audio CD into your computer. It also attempts to obtain information about the CD from the Internet. If it's successful, you see the name of the CD appear in Rhythmbox.

When you're ready to play your CD, click the name of the CD under the Devices section and then click the Play button. You can also define whether the CD should repeat itself until stopped or whether you want to shuffle the music (randomize the playlist).

Of course, just listening to your CDs doesn't really change anything; Rhythmbox acts like a regular CD player, enabling you to listen to specific tracks and define how you want to listen to your music by using playlists or sorting it by artists. The real fun starts when you click the Copy to Library button on your toolbar. Rhythmbox starts to extract, or rip, the audio from your CD and store it within the `Music` directory under your `/home` directory.

Depending on the speed of your optical drive and the power of your computer, the ripping process can take up to 15 minutes to complete a full CD. As it goes along, Rhythmbox automatically adds the files to your media library, which you can access by clicking the Music button on the left side of the Rhythmbox screen, as you can see in Figure 6.3.

FIGURE 6.3   Rhythmbox displays a list of the music you have available.

Within the Rhythmbox interface, you can easily browse through the list of artist names or album titles, which affects the track listing that appears at the bottom of the screen. The numbers after each artist and album tell you how many tracks are assigned to that specific entry, giving you a heads up before you click them. Double-clicking any entry automatically starts the music playing. So, for example, double-clicking an artist's name causes the music tracks associated with that artist to start playing. When a track starts to play, Rhythmbox automatically attempts to retrieve the CD artwork, which it then displays in the lower-left corner of the screen.

There's a lot more that you can do with Rhythmbox, including download and listen to podcasts. A good place to start is the Ubuntu UK podcast at http://podcast.ubuntu-uk.org/. All you have to do is click an RSS link for the feed on that page, copy the link URL, and go to Rhythmbox. There, press Ctrl+P, or go to Music, New Podcast Feed, paste the link into the field, and click the Add button. Rhythmbox then contacts the server and attempts to download the most recent episodes of your chosen podcast.

Banshee

Banshee (Figure 6.4) is another music application that can handle ripping and playing back music, download cover art, sync with portable players, and can even play video.

FIGURE 6.4   Banshee gives you a neat interface to browse through your music collection.

GETTING MUSIC INTO UBUNTU WITH SOUND JUICER

A handy utility that is included with Ubuntu is Sound Juicer, found under Applications, Sound & Video as the Audio CD Extractor. Sound Juicer automatically detects when you install a CD and attempts to retrieve the track details from the Internet. From there, it rips the CD tracks into Ogg files for storage on your file system. You can see Sound Juicer in action in Figure 6.5.

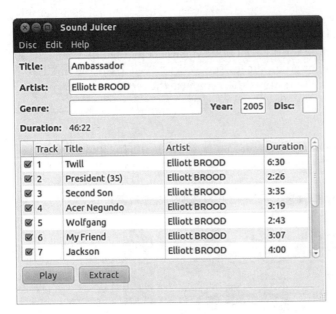

FIGURE 6.5   Create your own digital music collection with Sound Juicer.

Graphics Manipulation

Over a short period of time, digital cameras and digital imagery have become extremely popular—so popular that some traditional film camera manufacturers are switching solely to digital. This meteoric rise has led to an increase in the number of applications that can handle digital imagery. Linux, thanks to its rapid pace of development, is now highly regarded as a multimedia platform for editing digital images.

By default, Ubuntu installs the useful Shotwell Photo Manager in Applications, Graphics, and Shotwell Photo Manager (see Figure 6.6). This application is similar to other photo managers, such as iPhoto, and includes simple tools that are adequate for many users, such as red-eye reduction, cropping, color adjustment, and the ability to interact with online photo hosts such as Facebook, Flickr, and Picasa.

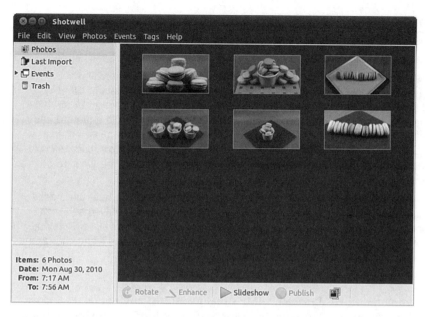

FIGURE 6.6   For most people, the simple tools in Shotwell Photo Manager are sufficient.

The rest of this section discusses GIMP, a powerful graphics manipulation tool that intermediate and advanced users are likely to enjoy. You also learn about graphic file formats supported by Ubuntu and some tools you can use to convert them if the application you want to use requires a different format.

The GNU Image Manipulation Program

One of the best graphics clients available is GIMP. GIMP is a free, GPL-licensed image editor with sophisticated capabilities that can import and export more than 30 different graphics formats, including files created with Adobe Photoshop. It is often compared with Photoshop, and GIMP represents one of the first significant successes of GNU Projects. Many images in Linux were prepared with GIMP.

GIMP is not installed by default, but after you install it from the repositories you can find it by searching the Dash for Gimp in the menu at Applications, Graphics, and GIMP Image Editor.

You see an installation dialog box when GIMP is started for the first time, and then a series of dialog boxes that display information regarding the creation and contents of a local GIMP directory. This directory can contain personal settings, preferences, external application resource files, temporary files, and symbolic links to external software tools used by the editor.

WHAT DOES PHOTOSHOP HAVE THAT GIMP DOES NOT?

Although GIMP is powerful, it does lack two features Adobe Photoshop offers that are important to some graphics professionals.

The first of these is the capability to generate color separations for commercial press printers (CMYK, for the colors cyan, magenta, yellow, and key [or black]). GIMP uses RGB (red, green, and blue), which is great for video display, but not so great for printing presses. The second feature GIMP lacks is the use of Pantone colors (a patented color specification) to ensure accurate color matching. These deficiencies might not last long. A CMYK plug-in is in the works (an early version is available from http://cue.yellow magic.info/softwares/separate-plus/index.html), and the Pantone issues are likely to be addressed in the near future, as well.

If these features are unimportant to you, GIMP is an excellent tool. If you must use Adobe Photoshop, you might want to explore using Wine or Codeweavers; there have been consistent reports of success running Photoshop on Linux with these tools. Bear in mind, though, that both Ubuntu and Photoshop release regularly, so check www.winehq.org/ and www.codeweavers.com/ for the current info before assuming it will work.

After the initial configuration has finished, GIMP's main windows and toolboxes appear (see Figure 6.7). GIMP's main window contains tools used for selecting, drawing, moving, view enlarging or reducing, airbrushing, painting, smudging, copying, filling, and selecting color.

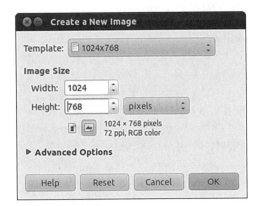

FIGURE 6.7   Right-click an image window to access GIMP's cascading menus.

Using Scanners in Ubuntu

With the rise of digital photography, there has been an equal decline in the need for image scanners. However, there are still times that you want to use a scanner, and Ubuntu makes it easy with a program installed by default called Simple Scan. Simple Scan is designed to do one thing, scan photos or documents easily (see Figure 6.8). It has few settings or options but does all the things most people would want or need.

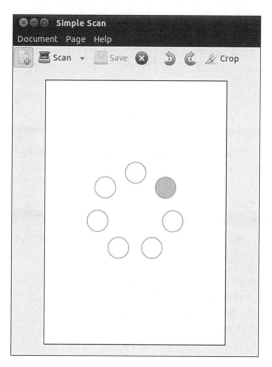

FIGURE 6.8   Simple Scan makes scanning easy.

You can also use many types of image scanners with GIMP, which is likely to be the choice of people who like to tinker with settings and options or who need greater flexibility than is offered by Simple Scan. If it wasn't installed when you installed GIMP, install the xsane package. Then, when you scan from GIMP, you will have an abundance of settings and options that you can use. You can also use XSane by itself; search the Dash for XSane.

Working with Graphics Formats

Image file formats are developed to serve a specific technical purpose (lossless compression, for example, where the file size is reduced without sacrificing image quality) or to meet a need for a proprietary format for competitive reasons. Many file formats are covered by one or more patents. For example, the GIF format had fallen into disfavor with the open-source crowd because the patent holder waited a while before deciding to enforce his patent rights rather than being upfront with requests for patent royalties.

If you want to view or manipulate an image, you need to identify the file format to choose the proper tool for working with the image. The file's extension is your first indicator of the file's format. The graphics image formats supported by the applications included with Ubuntu include the following:

▶ **BMP** (.bmp)—Bitmapped graphics, commonly used in Microsoft Windows

▶ **GIF** (.gif)—CompuServe Graphics Interchange Format

▶ **JPG** (`.jpg`)—Joint Photographic Experts Group

▶ **PCX** (`.pcx`)—IBM Paintbrush

▶ **PNG** (`.png`)—Portable Network Graphics

▶ **SVG** (`.svg`)—Scalable Vector Graphics

▶ **TIF** (`.tif`)—Tagged Image File format

You can find an extensive list of image file extensions in the man page for ImageMagick, an excellent application included with Ubuntu, which you read more about in upcoming sections of this chapter.

> **TIP**
>
> Ubuntu includes dozens of graphics conversion programs in its software repositories that are accessible through the command line and from a *graphical user interface (GUI)*, and there are few, if any, graphics file formats that cannot be manipulated when using Linux. These programs can be called in Perl scripts, shell scripts, or command-line pipes to support many types of complex format-conversion and image-manipulation tasks. See the man pages for the ppm, pbm, pnm, and pgm families of commands. Also see the man page for the `convert` command, which is part of a suite of extremely capable programs included with the ImageMagick suite.

Sometimes, a file you want to manipulate in some way is in a format that cannot be used by either your graphics application or the final application. The solution is to convert the image file—sometimes through several formats. The convert utility from ImageMagick is useful, as is the `netpbm` family of utilities. If it is not already installed, you can easily install ImageMagick from the Ubuntu repositories; the `netpbm` tools are always installed by default. convert is super simple to use from the command line. Here is an example:

```
matthew@seymour~:$ convert image.gif image.png
```

The convert utility converts between image formats recognized by ImageMagick. You can also manipulate color depth and size during the conversion process. You can use ImageMagick to append images, surround them with borders, add labels, rotate and shade them, and perform other manipulations well suited to scripting. Other commands associated with ImageMagick include display, animate, identify, and import. The application supports more than 130 different image formats (all listed in the man page for ImageMagick).

The `netpbm` tools are installed by default because they compose the underpinnings of graphics format manipulation. The man page for each image format lists related conversion utilities; the number of those utilities gives you some indication of the way that format is used and shows how one is built on another:

▶ The man page for ppm, the *portable pixmap* file format, lists 47 conversion utilities related to ppm. This makes sense because ppm, or *portable pixmap*, is considered the lowest common denominator for color image files. It is therefore often used as an intermediate format.

▶ The man page for pgm, the *portable graymap* file format, lists 22 conversion utilities. This makes sense because pgm is the lowest common denominator for grayscale image files.

▶ The man page for pnm, the *portable anymap* file format, lists 31 conversion utilities related to it. However, there is no format associated with PNM because it operates in concert with ppm, pgm, and pbm.

▶ An examination of the man page for pbm, the *portable bitmap* file format, reveals no conversion utilities. It's a monochrome format and serves as the foundation of the other related formats.

▶ The easiest way to resize or rotate image files is to install the nautilus-image-converter package from the repositories. This enables you to right-click an image when you are viewing files in the File Browser (for example, from Places, Pictures) and choose menu options to resize or rotate one or multiple images without opening another program.

Capturing Screen Images

You can use graphics-manipulation tools to capture images that are displayed on your computer screen. Although this technique was used for the production of this book, it has broader uses; there is truth to the cliché that a picture is worth a thousand words. Sometimes it is easier to show an example than it is to describe it.

You can use a captured screen image (also called a screen grab or a screenshot) to illustrate an error in the display of an application (a font problem, for example) or an error dialog that is too complex to copy down by hand. You might just want to share an image of your beautifully crafted custom desktop configuration with your friends or illustrate your written documents.

When using the default desktop, you can take advantage of the built-in screenshot mechanism (gnome-screenshot). You can use this tool by pressing the Print Screen key. (Alt+Print Screen takes a screenshot of only the window that has focus on a desktop.) Captured images are saved in PNG format. You can also find the tool in the Dash by searching for screenshot.

Other Graphics Manipulation Options

If you have very specific requirements for working with graphics, you may find one of the following better suits your needs than the general options and comments above. Some of these are in the Ubuntu repositories, but not all of them.

▶ **Blender** is a 3-D image and animation editor that you can find at http://www.blender.org/.

▶ **CinePaint** is a powerful and complex tool used by many Hollywood studios that you can find at http://www.cinepaint.org/.

▶ **darktable** is a RAW editor and can be found at http://www.darktable.org/.

▶ **digiKam** is photo management software and can be found at http://www.digikam .org/.

▶ **Hugin** is a panoramic photo stitcher and can be found at http://hugin.sourceforge .net/.

▶ **Inkscape** is a vector graphics creation and editing tool that you can find at http://inkscape.org/.

▶ **POV-Ray** is a powerful and complex 3-D graphics program that uses ray tracing and can be found at http://www.povray.org/.

▶ **Radiance** is intended for the analysis and visualization of lighting in design and can be found at http://www.radiance-online.org/.

▶ **Xara Xtreme** is a general purpose graphics editor that you can find at http://www .xaraxtreme.org/.

Using Digital Cameras with Ubuntu

Most digital cameras used with Ubuntu fall into one of two categories: webcams (small, low-resolution cameras connected to the computer's interface) or handheld digital cameras that record image data on disks or memory cards for downloading and viewing on a PC. Ubuntu supports both types. Other types of cameras, such as surveillance cameras that connect directly to a network via wired or wireless connections, need no special support (other than a network connection and viewing software) to be used with a Linux computer.

Ubuntu supports hundreds of different digital cameras, from early parallel-port (CPiA chipset-based) cameras to today's USB-based cameras. You can even use Intel's QX3 USB microscope with Ubuntu. The following sections describe some of the more commonly used types of still camera hardware and software supported by Ubuntu.

Handheld Digital Cameras

Because of the good development carried out in the Linux world, you can plug almost any digital camera in to your computer through a USB interface, and Ubuntu automatically recognizes the camera as a USB mass storage device. You can even set Ubuntu to recognize when a camera is plugged in so that it automatically imports your photographs for you.

Using Shotwell Photo Manager

Ubuntu comes by default with a pretty good photo manager called Shotwell Photo Manager that includes simple adjustment tools (see Figure 6.9). You can import your photos into Shotwell, assign tags to them, sort and arrange them, and even upload them to your favorite Internet photo-hosting sites such as Facebook, Flickr, and Picasa.

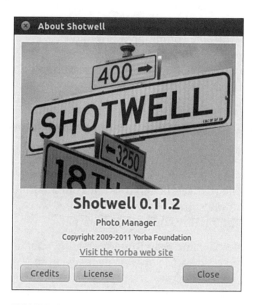

FIGURE 6.9   Browse your photo collection and correct minor problems with Shotwell Photo Manager.

Burning CDs and DVDs in Ubuntu

Linux is generally distributed via the Internet as disc images called ISOs that are ready to be written to CDs or DVDs. Therefore, learning how to burn discs is essential if you have to download and install a Linux distribution. You can use CDs and DVDs to do the following:

▶ Record and store multimedia data, such as backup files, graphics images, and music.

▶ Rip audio tracks from music CDs (*ripping* refers to extracting music tracks from a music CD) and compile your own music CDs for your personal use.

Although USB storage devices such as thumb drives are making CDs and DVDs almost as rare as floppy disks, they aren't quite gone, and many people still find them useful. As long as that remains true, we want to make sure this information is available.

Creating CDs and DVDs with Brasero

Although adequate for quick burns and use in shell scripting, the command-line technique for burning CDs and DVDs is an awkward choice for many people (but we still cover doing so later in this chapter because others find it useful and desirable). Fortunately, Ubuntu provides several graphical clients; the most useful is Brasero.

Brasero is an easy-to-use graphical CD and DVD burning application that is installed by default.

Brasero takes a project-based approach to disc burning, opening up with a wizard from which you can select from four different tasks that people commonly want to do. Figure 6.10 shows the opening screen. Brasero also remembers previous "projects," enabling you to quickly create several copies of a disc, which is ideal if you're planning to pass on copies of Ubuntu to your friends and family.

Burning a data CD or DVD is as easy as selecting the option in the opening screen and dragging and dropping the files you want to include from the directory tree on the left to the drop area on the right. If you insert a blank CD or DVD in your writer, Brasero keeps an eye on the disc size and tells you when you reach or exceed the limits. It also creates ISO files, which are disc images that contain everything that would exist on the medium if you burned a real CD or DVD in one file that can be mounted by computer file systems, which is useful if you want to create multiple copies of the same disc or if you want to share a disc image, perhaps using a USB thumb drive or over the Internet.

Finally, click the Burn button, input a label for the disc, and Brasero starts creating your new CD or DVD or image file. How long it takes to create a CD or DVD depends on the amount of data you are writing and the speed of your drive.

Creating CDs from the Command Line

In Linux, creating a CD at the command line is a two-step process. You first create the ISO9660-formatted image, and you then burn or write the image onto the CD. The ISO9660 is the default file system for CD-ROMs.

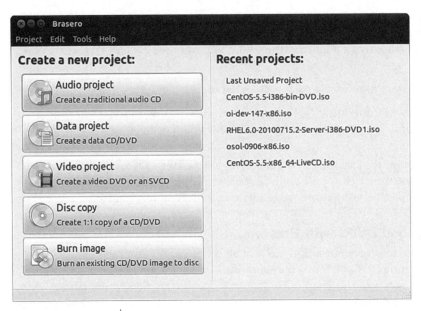

FIGURE 6.10   Brasero gives you an intuitive way to create data and audio CDs and DVDs.

Use the `mkisofs` command to create the ISO image. The `mkisofs` command has many options (see the man page for a full listing), but use the following for quick burns:

```
matthew@seymour~:$ mkisofs -r -v -J -1 -o /tmp/our_special_cd.iso /source_directory
```

The options used in this example are as follows:

▶ `-r`—Sets the permission of the files to more useful values. `UID` and `GID` (individual and group user ID requirements) are set to `0`, all files are globally readable and searchable, and all files are set as executable (for Windows systems).

▶ `-v`—Displays verbose messages (rather than terse messages) so that you can see what is occurring during the process; these messages can help you resolve problems if they occur.

▶ `-J`—Uses the Joliet extensions to ISO9660 so that your Windows-using buddies can more easily read the CD. The Joliet (for Windows), Rock Ridge (for UNIX), and HSF (for Mac) extensions to the ISO9660 standard are used to accommodate long filenames rather than the eight-character DOS filenames that the ISO9660 standard supports.

▶ `-1`—Allows 31-character filenames; DOS does not like it, but everyone else does.

▶ `-o`—Defines the directory where the image will be written (that is, the output) and its name. The `/tmp` directory is convenient for this purpose, but the image could go anywhere you have write permissions.

▶ `/source_directory`—Indicates the path to the source directory; that is, the directory containing the files you want to include. There are ways to append additional paths and exclude directories (and files) under the specified path; it is all explained in the man page, if you need that level of complexity. The simple solution is to construct a new directory tree and populate it with the files you want to copy and then make the image using that directory as the source.

Many more options are available, including options to make the CD bootable.

After you have created the ISO image, you can write it to the CD with the `cdrecord` command:

```
matthew@seymour~:$ cdrecord -eject -v speed=12 dev=0,0,0 /tmp/our_special_cd.iso
```

The options used in this example are as follows:

▶ `-eject`—Ejects the CD when the write operation is finished.

▶ `-v`—Displays verbose messages.

▶ `speed=`—Sets the speed; the rate depends on the individual drive's capabilities. If the drive or the recordable medium is poor, you can use lower speeds to get a good burn.

▶ `dev=`—Specifies the device number of the CD writer.

NOTE

You can also use the `blank = option` with the `cdrecord` command to erase CD-RW discs. The cdrecord command has fewer options than `mkisofs` does, but it offers the `-multi option`, which enables you to make multisession CDs. A multisession CD enables you to write a data track, quit, and then add more data to the CD later. A single-session CD can be written to only once; any leftover CD capacity is wasted. Read about other options in the `cdrecord` man page.

Current capacity for CD media is 700MB of data or 80 minutes of music. (There are 800MB/90-minute CDs, but they are rare.) Some CDs can be overburned; that is, recorded to a capacity in excess of the standard. The `cdrecord` command and some graphical programs are capable of overburning if your CD-RW drive supports it. You can learn more about overburning CDs at www.cdmediaworld.com/hardware/cdrom/cd_oversize.shtml/.

Creating DVDs from the Command Line

There are several competing formats for DVD, as follows:

▶ DVD+R

▶ DVD-R

▶ DVD+RW

▶ DVD-RW

Differences in the + and - formats have mostly to do with how the data is modulated onto the DVD itself, with the + format having an edge in buffer underrun recovery. How this is achieved affects the playability of the newly created DVD on any DVD player. The DVD+ format also has some advantages in recording on scratched or dirty media. Most drives support the DVD+ format. As with any technology, your mileage may vary.

We focus on the DVD+RW drives because most drives support that standard. The software supplied with Ubuntu has support for writing to DVD-R/W (rewritable) media, as well. It will be useful for you to review the DVD+RW/+R/-R[W] for Linux HOWTO at http://fy.chalmers.se/~appro/linux/DVD+RW/ before you attempt to use dvd+rw-tools, which you need to install to enable DVD creation (also known as *mastering*) and the cdrtools package. You can ignore the discussion in the HOWTO about kernel patches and compiling the tools.

TIP

The 4.7GB size of DVD media is measured as 1000 megabytes per gigabyte, instead of the more traditionally used, but not entirely accurate, 1024 megabytes per gigabyte (more appropriately written GiB), so do not be surprised when the actual formatted capacity, about 4.4GB, is less than you anticipated. A good explanation of the difference and the need for the correction is available at http://en.wikipedia.org/wiki/Gibibyte. Most hard drive manufacturers have also made the switch. dvd+rw-tools does not allow you to exceed the capacity of the disc.

You need to have the `dvd+rw-tools` package installed (as well as the `cdrtools` package). The `dvd+rw-tools` package contains the `growisofs` application (which acts as a front end to `mkisofs`) and the DVD formatting utility.

You can use DVD media to record data in two ways. The first way is much the same as that used to record CDs in a session, and the second way is to record the data as a true file system using packet writing.

Session Writing

To record data in a session, you use a two-phase process:

1. Format the disc with `dvd+rw-format /dev/scd0` (only necessary the first time you use a disc, where `/dev/scd0` is the device name for your drive).

2. Write your data to the disc with `growisofs -Z /dev/scd0 -R -J /your_files`.

The `growisofs` command simply streams the data to the disc. For subsequent sessions, use the `-M` argument rather than `-z`. The `-z` argument is used only for the initial session recording; if you use the `-z` argument on an already used disc, it erases the existing files.

> **CAUTION**
>
> Some DVDs come preformatted; formatting them again when you use them for the first time can make the DVD useless. Always be sure to carefully read the packaging your DVD comes in to ensure that you are not about to create another coaster.

> **TIP**
>
> Writing a first session of at least 1GB helps maintain compatibility of your recorded data with other optical drives. DVD players calibrate themselves by attempting to read from specific locations on the disc; you need data there for the drive to read it and calibrate itself.
>
> Also, because of limitations to the ISO9660 file system in Linux, do not start new sessions of a multisession DVD that would create a directory past the 4GB boundary. If you do so, it causes the offsets used to point to the files to "wrap around" and point to the wrong files.

Packet Writing

Packet writing treats the CD or DVD like a hard drive in which you create a file system (like ext3) and format the disc and then write to it randomly as you would to a conventional hard drive. This method, although commonly available on Windows-based computers, was long considered experimental for Linux and was never used much anyway because USB thumb drives became common before the use of CD or DVD-RWs had the opportunity. We do not cover this in detail here, but a quick overview is appropriate.

> **TIP**
>
> DVD+RW media are capable of only about 1,000 writes, so it is useful to mount them with the `noatime` option to eliminate any writing to update their inodes or simply mount them read-only when it's not necessary to write to them.

It is possible to pipe data to the `growisofs` command:

```
matthew@seymour~:$ sudo your_application | growisofs -Z /dev/scd0=/dev/fd/0
```

It is also possible to burn from an existing image (or file, named pipe, or device):

```
matthew@seymour~:$ sudo growisofs -Z /dev/scd0=image
```

The `dvd+rw-tools` documentation, found at `/usr/share/doc/dvd+rw-tools/index.html`, is required reading before your first use of the program. We also suggest that you experiment with DVD-RW (rewritable) media first because if you make mistakes you can still reuse the disc instead of creating several new coasters for your coffee mug.

Viewing Video

You can use Ubuntu tools and applications to view movies and other video presentations on your PC. This section presents some TV and motion picture video software tools included with the Ubuntu distribution you received with this book.

TV and Video Hardware

To watch TV and video content on your PC, you must install a supported TV card or have a video/TV combo card installed. You can find a current list of TV and video cards supported in Linux at http://linuxtv.org/wiki/index.php/Main_Page.

Freely available Linux support for TV display from video cards that have a TV-out jack is improved over a couple of years ago, but still rather poor. That support must come from the X driver, not from a video device that Video4Linux supports with a device driver. Some of the combo TV-tuner/video display cards have support, including the Matrox Marvel, the Matrox Rainbow Runner G-Series, and the RivaTV cards. Many other combo cards lack support, although an independent developer might have hacked something together to support his own card. Your best course of action is to perform a thorough Internet search with Google.

Many of the TV-only PCI cards are supported. In Linux, however, they are supported by the video chipset they use, and not by the name some manufacturer has slapped on a generic board. (The same board is typically sold by different manufacturers under different names.) The most common chipset is the Brooktree `Bt***` series of chips; they are supported by the `bttv` device driver.

If you have a supported card in your computer, it should be detected during installation. If you add it later, the hardware-detection utility should detect it and configure it. It is possible to try to configure it by hand, but because the Ubuntu kernel czars try to compile every hardware option available as a module and make it available, doing so isn't likely to be of much use. Even so, this is what you would do.

First, to determine what chipset your card has, use the lspci command to list the PCI device information, find the TV card listing, and look for the chipset that the card uses. For example, the lspci output for one computer shows the following.

```
matthew@seymour~:$ lspci
00:00.0 Host bridge: Advanced Micro Devices [AMD] AMD-760 [IGD4-1P] System ↙
Controller (rev 13)
00:01.0 PCI bridge: Advanced Micro Devices [AMD] AMD-760 [IGD4-1P] AGP Bridge
00:07.0 ISA bridge: VIA Technologies, Inc. VT82C686 [Apollo Super South] (rev 40)
00:07.1 IDE interface: VIA Technologies, Inc. VT82C586B PIPC Bus Master IDE (rev 06)
00:07.2 USB Controller: VIA Technologies, Inc. USB (rev 1a)
00:07.3 USB Controller: VIA Technologies, Inc. USB (rev 1a)
00:07.4 SMBus: VIA Technologies, Inc. VT82C686 [Apollo Super ACPI] (rev 40)
00:09.0 Multimedia audio controller: Ensoniq 5880 AudioPCI (rev 02)
00:0b.0 Multimedia video controller: Brooktree Corporation Bt878 Video Capture ↙
(rev 02)
00:0b.1 Multimedia controller: Brooktree Corporation Bt878 Audio Capture (rev 02)
00:0d.0 Ethernet controller: Realtek Semiconductor Co., Ltd. RTL-8029(AS)
00:0f.0 FireWire (IEEE 1394): Texas Instruments TSB12LV23 IEEE-1394 Controller
00:11.0 Network controller: Standard Microsystems Corp [SMC] SMC2602W EZConnect
01:05.0 VGA compatible controller: nVidia Corporation NV15 [GeForce2 Ti] (rev a4)
```

Here, the lines listing the multimedia video controller and multimedia controller say that this TV board uses a Brooktree Bt878 Video Capture chip and a Brooktree Bt878 Audio Capture chip. This card uses the Bt878 chipset. Your results will be different, depending on what card and chipset your computer has. This card happened to be an ATI All-in-Wonder VE (also known as ATI TV-Wonder). (The VE means *Value Edition*; hence, there is no TV-out connector and no radio chip on the card; what a value!)

Then you figure out what module is needed, probably using Google to search for "Bt878 linux" or "Bt878 Ubuntu," and start reading documentation. You want to look for official pages first rather than blog posts. Finally, you need to enter some information into /etc/modules.conf. This file does not exist anymore in a default Ubuntu installation but may be created as needed and will be read at boot time. Then, you calculate the module and kernel dependencies with sudo depmod -a and sudo modprobe *module name* to load the module. Again, this is not necessary in Ubuntu because the people doing kernel configuration create a module for everything that exists, so if it is available to them, they will make it available to you with no extra work on your part, and the system scans to see what should be loaded at boot and pulls in what is needed then.

Video Formats

Ubuntu recognizes a variety of video formats. The formats created by the MPEG group, Apple, and Microsoft dominate, however. At the heart of video formats are the *codecs*—the encoders and decoders of the video and audio information. These codecs are typically proprietary, but free codecs do exist. Here is a list of the most common video formats and their associated file extensions, although many more exist:

▶ **AVI** (`.avi`)—The Windows audio visual format

▶ **FLV** (`.flv`)—Used in Adobe Flash, supports H.264 and others

▶ **MPEG** (`.mpeg`)—The MPEG video format; also known as. `mpg`

▶ **MOV** (`.mov`)—Another QuickTime video format

▶ **OGV/OGG** (`.ogv/.ogg`)—The Ogg Theora freely licensed video format

▶ **QT** (`.qt`)—The QuickTime video format from Apple

▶ **WEBM** (`.webm`)—Google's royalty-free container for audio and video (such as in VP8 format) designed for HTML5

Viewing Video in Linux

Out of the box, Ubuntu does not support any of the proprietary video codecs due to licensing restrictions. However, this functionality can be acquired if you install the `ubuntu-restricted-extras` package from the Ubuntu software repositories. You can learn more about this at https://help.ubuntu.com/community/RestrictedFormats.

You can watch video files and video DVDs with Totem Movie Player (Figure 6.11), which is installed by default. This may also be used with several other file formats and for both video and audio and is especially well suited for almost anything you are likely to want to use after you install the `ubuntu-restricted-extras` package.

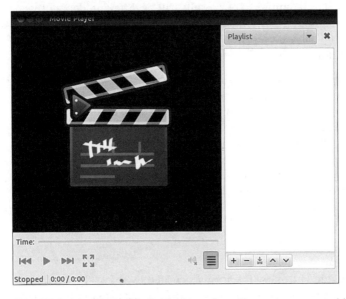

FIGURE 6.11   Totem Movie Player works with most common video and audio formats.

ADOBE FLASH

The Adobe Flash plug-in for the Firefox browser is a commercial multimedia application that isn't provided with Ubuntu out of the box, but many people find it useful. Adobe Flash enables you to view Flash content at websites that support it. The easiest way of getting a hold of the official version of Flash is to install the `ubuntu-restricted-extras` package. After you've done this, any Flash animations play quite happily within any Firefox-based browsers. Note that Adobe recently announced they are discontinuing support for Flash on Linux. However, the Google Chrome browser supports Flash and Google has committed to making sure it continues to work on Linux, so if Flash is vital to you, using Google Chrome might be your best option.

Another interesting video viewer application is VLC, which is available in the software repositories and also for other operating systems like Windows and Mac OS X (see Figure 6.12). VLC uses its own set of audio and video codecs and supports a wider range of video formats than any other media player we have encountered. If VLC can't play it, it probably can't be played.

FIGURE 6.12   VLC is a powerful and capable media player.

Personal Video Recorders

The best reason to attach a television antenna to your computer, however, is to use the video card and the computer as a personal video recorder.

The commercial personal video recorder, TiVo, started a new trend by using Linux running on a PowerPC processor to record television programming with a variety of customizations. You can turn your computer into a personal digital video recorder with Myth TV from www.mythtv.org/, a Linux-based digital video recorder software project, made even easier for Ubuntu users by the Mythbuntu project at www.mythbuntu.org/. Everything you need is available in the Ubuntu repositories and may be installed and configured easily thanks to the people involved in these projects.

Video Editing

You can now create and edit video in Ubuntu using PiTiVi (see Figure 6.13). It is not installed by default, but a quick search for "PiTiVi Video Editor" in the Ubuntu Software Center gets you started. You may import any video clip in any format that is supported by GStreamer, the main multimedia framework used in Ubuntu. This should include the files created by your digital camera, which should mount in Ubuntu as a storage device, making the transfer of the files from the camera to your computer quick and easy. PiTiVi lets you move scenes around, cut things, add your own soundtrack, and more.

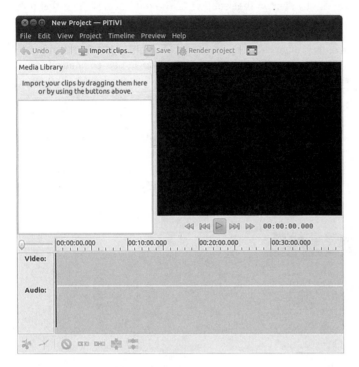

FIGURE 6.13   PiTiVi Video Editor.

Several other video editing options exist. If you have very specific requirements for working with video, you may find one of the following better suits your needs:

▶ **Avidemux** is designed for people with simple needs and can be found at http://fixounet.free.fr/avidemux/.

▶ **Blender** is a 3-D image and animation editor that you can find at http://www .blender.org/.

▶ **Cinelerra** has been around for years, but recently made some big changes and is rebuilding its community. You can find it at http://cinelerra.org/.

▶ **CinePaint** is a powerful and complex tool used by many Hollywood studios that you can find at http://www.cinepaint.org/.

▶ **Kdenlive** comes from the KDE folks and can be found at http://kdenlive.org/.

▶ **OpenShot Video Editor** can be found at http://www.openshot.org/.

Some of the above options are in the Ubuntu repositories, so check there first, but some you will have to download directly from their website.

References

▶ **www.videolan.org/**—A multimedia player project with good documentation that will play almost anything.

▶ **http://fy.chalmers.se/~appro/linux/DVD+RW/**—The DVD+RW/+R/-R[W] for Linux, a HOWTO for creating DVDs under Linux.

▶ **www.gimp.org**—Home page of The GIMP (*GNU Image Manipulation Program*).

▶ **http://f-spot.org**—Home page of the F-Spot project.

▶ **www.sane-project.org**—Home page of the SANE (*Scanner Access Now Easy*) project.

▶ **www.imagemagick.org**—Home page for ImageMagick.

▶ **http://gimp.net/tutorials/**—Official tutorials for The GIMP.

Other Ubuntu Interfaces

When you install Ubuntu, by default you use the Unity graphical user interface (GUI). This is sometimes called a desktop, but this term is gradually becoming obsolete as the interface is being used on more and more types of devices. Unity is discussed in Chapter 3, "Working with Unity," and has specific strengths that appeal to many users. However, some of us have unique requirements or just like to tinker. This chapter discusses some of the alternatives to Unity, their strengths and weaknesses, and how to install them. This is not a complete listing of all the options available, but rather a brief survey of some of the more popular options to consider as you get your feet wet in the realm of Linux desktop software.

UNITY IS NOT THE ONLY OPTION

When you install Ubuntu, you also install the Unity interface. However, this is neither your only option nor are you limited to only one interface or desktop environment installed at a time. Each of the options we discuss in this chapter may be installed alongside Unity in standard Ubuntu, and you are allowed to choose which one to use each time you log in and which one to use by default. This makes testing a new option less risky because switching back to what you already know is simple.

Because Unity is one of the first GUIs to strive to be usable across devices, most of the others that are available still use the term "desktop." This makes it worthwhile to include a brief introduction to why, especially as many of the details cross over and apply to Unity.

Desktop Environment

Traditionally, a *GUI* for computers has used a desktop metaphor; specifically, the interface uses the idea of a physical office desk as a metaphor to make interacting with the computer simple to comprehend. As in a real-world office, a computer desktop environment uses files to store documents that contain information that is necessary for office tasks to be done. Computer systems take the metaphor further by adding applications, programs that enable users to create, manipulate, and delete those documents as needed, much as might be done in the real world, but with greater efficiency and often with greater power.

A computer desktop includes a windowing system, another metaphoric way to deal with information that makes conceptualizing the complexity occurring behind the scenes in the digital realm easier. Files, folders (or directories), and applications open in a graphic display that may be moved around the user's desktop just as paper documents and file folders may be moved to different locations on a physical desktop for convenience and efficiency. This windowing system includes the graphical bits (called *widgets*) needed to draw the windows on the screen and all the program code needed to perform the actions desired behind the scenes while displaying those actions using the pretty metaphor. For example, moving a document from one folder to another on a desktop involves little more than a mouse click followed by a drag and drop. Behind the scenes, the desktop environment is listening to the window manager's instructions to move a file from one directory to another and then telling the window manager to draw the event on the screen as it is accomplished.

The Ubuntu software repositories include all the popular desktop environments available for Linux and make installing and trying them out easy to do. It is also possible for an adventurous person to find other desktop environments that will work on Ubuntu and download and install them. We don't cover that process here.

It is also possible to use one desktop environment while substituting a different window manager into that environment instead of using the one that comes with the desktop environment by default. For example, the standard GNOME window manager is called Metacity. It is stable and works quite well. However, Ubuntu uses a different window manager called Compiz. To make matters more interesting, you can replace either of those with other window managers such as Enlightenment (Figure 7.1), which does things in a unique and interesting manner.

This chapter focuses on complete desktop environments using the default window manager. In addition, because this is an Ubuntu-focused book, it focuses on Ubuntu-refined versions of environments such as KDE and Xfce rather than their default versions, although the default versions are also available in the Ubuntu repositories if you want to seek them out.

FIGURE 7.1   Enlightenment is a unique and interesting desktop environment option.

KDE and Kubuntu

The KDE project began back in 1996 with the goal of creating a quality desktop environment for the Linux desktop that was free, worked well, and which was well integrated, meaning that programs and interfaces would have a consistent look and feel where all the parts fit together seamlessly, rather than looking like a jumbled compilation of a bunch of assorted bits.

The project has always been focused on end users rather than creating a simple GUI for the systems administrator. This is an important point because since the beginning, the intent has been to make any computer user comfortable and able to do what they want to do without necessarily requiring a full grasp of what is happening behind the scenes. This focus continues today and is shared by other desktop environments, notably GNOME, which was started in 1997 by people once involved in the KDE project who left after a dispute over software licensing.

The cause of that dispute no longer exists as the licenses today are equivalently free, but the projects diverged a bit in their focus: GNOME offers a desktop of zenlike simplicity with simple and elegant defaults and use whereas KDE presents more flash and configuration options. Honestly, they are each great desktop environments that are well integrated with a high degree of professionalism and quality and are easily the top two in the Linux world—if you have never used either, try them both and see which you prefer.

Kubuntu is a project that started in the Ubuntu community very early on with the simple goal of enabling users to install and use KDE in Ubuntu. To make this even easier for people who already know they prefer KDE over GNOME, you can download an install disk for Kubuntu, which is Ubuntu minus GNOME plus KDE plus a few Kubuntu-specific enhancements. You may also install Kubuntu in standard Ubuntu and alongside GNOME by installing the `kubuntu-desktop` package from the Ubuntu software repositories.

Kubuntu (Figure 7.2) uses a different set of default programs for most tasks: web browsing, email, and so on. Most were written specifically for the KDE desktop environment, making KDE one of the most closely integrated and consistent Linux desktops available.

FIGURE 7.2   The Kubuntu desktop.

Xfce and Xubuntu

Xfce is a lighter desktop environment that requires less memory and processing power than either GNOME or KDE and is therefore often suggested for use on older machines. It does not deserve to be relegated to that role because it also works great on current hardware and is often a quality choice for a different reason. Xfce has been developed using the traditional UNIX philosophy of software: Do one thing, do it well, and play well with others.

Each part of the Xfce desktop environment is modular; you may add or remove bits at will, substitute other programs that perform the same function, and everything created by or included in Xfce is expected to work according to simple standards that allow other programs to interact with it easily.

On one hand, this sometimes means that people look at Xfce and think it isn't as seamlessly integrated and smooth as the two main desktop environments. On the other hand, it means that if you prefer the GNOME file manager (Nautilus) over the one included with Xfce (Thunar), then just install Nautilus and use it, either side by side with Thunar or remove Thunar completely. This is a huge part of what makes Xfce so lightweight that it has very few dependency requirements and is highly flexible.

Originally, Xubuntu (Figure 7.3) was designed to create a lighter weight version of Ubuntu that would run well on older hardware because of the lighter code dependencies of Xfce. Over time, some people discovered they liked the desktop environment for other reasons, and the older hardware use case became less of a focus. It was the modularity of Xfce combined with a smoothness of operation that won people over, and the distribution began to take some of the favored bits from Ubuntu's customized version of GNOME and added them to Xfce to replace some of its defaults. What we have today is a nice amalgamation of Ubuntu GNOME bits, Xfce bits, and a few other things not included by default in either.

FIGURE 7.3   The Xubuntu desktop.

Xubuntu still uses less memory and fewer CPU cycles than a standard Ubuntu or Kubuntu install; however, thinking of it only in those terms doesn't do it justice. To install Xubuntu with the Xfce desktop environment, install the `xubuntu-desktop` package.

LXDE and Lubuntu

Lubuntu is based on LXDE, an extremely fast desktop environment that uses less memory and fewer CPU cycles than any of the others discussed. It is being developed specifically with lower-powered computers such as netbooks in mind, but that isn't the sole use case. For example, Knoppix, which is a Linux distribution that runs from a live, bootable CD or DVD, now uses LXDE. Knoppix is a long-time favorite of sysadmins for emergency repairs of unbootable systems and for its portability. It recently switched from KDE to LXDE to benefit from this lightness because running an operating system from a CD or DVD is generally much slower than when it is installed on a hard drive.

As the focus in Xubuntu turned from speed and lightness to enjoying the flexibility of Xfce, a gap was created. Users and developers interested in less-expensive hardware, such as mobile Internet devices and ARM or MIPS processor-based computers, wanted to find a way to run a distribution of Linux that shared the community of Ubuntu, a beautiful and useful desktop, and that did not get bogged down on slower machines. LXDE is quite new, and its development philosophy fits quite well with the hopes and dreams of these users, so it seems a perfect fit.

The Lubuntu (see Figure 7.4) distribution is still very new. The developers are working within the Ubuntu community and making consistent progress, and if you are inclined, they are also appealing for interested people to join the development team and help out. Install `lubuntu-desktop` from the Ubuntu repositories to check it out.

FIGURE 7.4   The Lubuntu desktop is quite attractive.

GNOME3 and Ubuntu GNOME

Starting with Ubuntu 4.10, the default desktop for Ubuntu has been based on GNOME. Until a couple years ago, it was close to a standard GNOME desktop with only a few customizations. After development began on GNOME 3, the desktop took a turn that did not suit the needs or desires of Ubuntu quite as well. This was when development began on Unity, as described in Chapter 3, "Working with Unity."

GNOME 3 is available in Ubuntu for those who prefer it over Unity. As development and support are ending for the classic GNOME 2 environment, it is no longer recommended.

GNOME 3 is somewhat similar to Unity in that both are trying to push the Linux desktop into new territory. They both discard older metaphors and require a bit of adjusting for the user. The goal of GNOME 3 is to create an elegant desktop that is easy to use, uncluttered, and consistent (Figure 7.5). If you just want to try GNOME 3, install `gnome-shell` from the Ubuntu software repositories. Most of the programs are the same as are used in Unity, which is based on GNOME 3, but with a different user interface.

FIGURE 7.5   The GNOME 3 desktop.

A project called Ubuntu GNOME has been approved, and Ubuntu community members have already begun development. It provides a way to use GNOME similar to how Kubuntu provides a way to use KDE. You can download an install disk for Ubuntu GNOME, which is Ubuntu minus Unity plus GNOME. You may also install Ubuntu GNOME alongside standard Ubuntu by installing the `ubuntu-gnome-desktop` package from the Ubuntu software repositories.

MATE and Ubuntu MATE

Remember in the last section where we said that GNOME 2 was no longer supported and therefore not recommended? That is true, however, the code was forked into MATE. Basically, MATE is a continuation of GNOME 2. MATE has the features, look, and feel of the older version of GNOME, the same code foundation, but with continued development (Figure 7.6).

GNOME 3 is somewhat similar to Unity in that both are trying to push the Linux desktop into new territory. They both discard older metaphors and require a bit of adjusting for the user. The goal of GNOME 3 is to create an elegant desktop that is easy to use, uncluttered, and consistent (Figure 7.5). If you just want to try GNOME 3, install `gnome-shell` from the Ubuntu software repositories. Most of the programs are the same as are used in Unity, which is based on GNOME 3, but with a different user interface.

FIGURE 7.6   The MATE desktop.

Ubuntu Kylin

Ubuntu Kylin is Ubuntu, localized for China. It starts out the same as standard Ubuntu and is modified with Chinese-language, calendar, and cultural customizations for the world's largest market. As it is in a different language than this book, we are only giving it a cursory mention. However, if you are a Chinese speaker, you will probably find this interesting and worth a look.

References

▶ http://blogs.gnome.org/metacity/2007/12/23/start-reading-here/—Metacity does not have an official home page, as this post on the official Metacity blog explains.

▶ www.compiz.org/—The official site of Compiz.

▶ www.enlightenment.org/—The official site of Enlightenment.

▶ www.kde.org/—The official site for the KDE desktop.

▶ www.kubuntu.org/—The official Kubuntu site.

▶ www.xfce.org/—The official site for the Xfce desktop.

▶ www.xubuntu.org/—The official Xubuntu site.

▶ www.lxde.org/—The official site for the LXDE desktop.

▶ http://lubuntu.net/—The official Lubuntu site.

▶ www.gnome.org/—The official site for the GNOME desktop.

▶ **http://ubuntugnome.org/**—The official Ubuntu GNOME site.

▶ **https://ubuntu-mate.org**—The official Ubuntu MATE site.

▶ **https://wiki.ubuntu.com/UbuntuKylin**—The English language resource for Ubuntu Kylin.

▶ **http://www.ubuntu.com/project/about-ubuntu/derivatives**—The official Ubuntu list of recognized derivatives.

▶ **www.knoppix.net/**—The site for the live CD/DVD Linux distribution, Knoppix.

▶ **http://xwinman.org/**—A nice discussion of many of the different window managers and desktop environments available for Linux and UNIX systems. Much of the discussion on this site is dated, but the links are generally valid and useful, and the site gives a good overview of the many options available.

▶ **http://en.wikipedia.org/wiki/Desktop_environment**—A detailed definition of a desktop environment, how they work, why they exist, and so on.

▶ **http://en.wikipedia.org/wiki/Comparison_of_X_Window_System_desktop_environments**—An amazing list of available desktop environments complete with a comparison of features.

7

CHAPTER 8

Games

Playing games is a fun part of computing. For some of us, games are a big part of the appeal of any operating system, at least for uses beyond the business or corporate environment. From the humble card games that entertain millions during their coffee breaks, to the heavily involved first-person shooters that involve players dotted around the globe, Linux offers a quality gaming platform that might surprise you.

In this chapter, we explore some of the common games available for you to download and install easily in Ubuntu.

Ubuntu Gaming

A small number of games come installed by default with standard desktop Ubuntu, mostly simple things to divert your attention for a few minutes between tasks, games such as solitaire or sudoku. These are easy to try out and learn, and you might find them enjoyable.

Most of us who enjoy games will want to find something more. Thankfully, games for Linux do not stop there—several popular games have native Linux support. We discuss a small number of our favorites here.

Emulators enable you to play classic games, such as the LucasArts ScummVM games like Secret of Monkey Island, natively under Linux. There are emulators for DOS, NES, SNES, and many more. If you are interested in them, do a search online for Dgen/SDL, DosBox, xtrs, FCEUltra, GnGeo, SDLMama, ScummVM, and Stella. The documentation for emulators is hit or miss, but if you are lucky you might be able to play your favorite old games for consoles or operating systems that no longer exist or that current OS versions do not support.

Installing Proprietary Video Drivers

A major gripe of Linux users has been the difficulty involved in getting modern 3D graphics cards to work. Thankfully, both AMD (owner of the now-defunct ATI brand) and Nvidia support Linux, albeit by using closed-source drivers. This means that Ubuntu does not ship with native 3D drivers activated for either graphics card, but they are easily installed, often during or just after the operating system is installed. These drivers are needed for most of the more visually spectacular games.

> **NOTE**
>
> As of the time this chapter was last edited, because of issues with the way the drivers function, Ubuntu has ceased to provide the AMD proprietary video drivers; instead, it provides an open source option that is easier to work with and that works more consistently. However, the open source option does not currently work as well as the AMD proprietary driver for high-end graphics work. Accordingly, the author's current suggestion is to avoid AMD video cards until this is sorted out.

Both Nvidia and AMD produce proprietary drivers, meaning that the source code is not open or available for outside developers to read or modify. Because of this it is hard for some Linux distros to include them as part of their standard installation. The Ubuntu community has taken a pragmatic approach of including both Nvidia and AMD drivers within the main Ubuntu distro, but they're disabled by default. That way, anyone who has Nvidia or AMD hardware can activate those drivers to take advantage of their features.

> **NOTE**
>
> If you think that proprietary drivers are the only way on Linux, we should mention that there is a lot of development going into providing totally free and open-source drivers for slightly older graphics cards. Ubuntu automatically selects the best "free" driver for your system and allows you to switch the proprietary driver should you want to. Although the open-source drivers provide 3D acceleration, this support doesn't always extend to a full feature set or to the more recent graphics cards.

It's easy to activate the proprietary driver if you need to; from the Dash search for "additional drivers."

Installing a different hardware driver requires super user privileges, so a confirmation check is run to determine whether you are permitted, and then you are asked for your password. After the Hardware Drivers dialog window has opened, read the descriptions and look for the recommended entry for your hardware, highlight it, and click Activate at the lower right. Ubuntu confirms that you want to use the proprietary driver and, if you agree, automatically downloads and configures the relevant driver. If you want to revert to the open driver then do the same thing but select the activated driver and click Remove at the lower right, as shown in Figure 8.1, in the same place where the previously mentioned Activate button was.

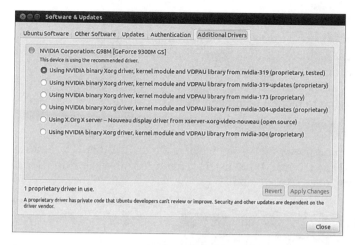

FIGURE 8.1   Use the Additional Drivers manager to activate or deactivate the appropriate proprietary graphics driver for your graphics card.

Steam

Steam is a cross-platform entertainment platform. When you install it on Ubuntu, you get access to a ton of games and other fun things. Some of these are free, but most require you to pay. Steam has become the primary method that most current Linux-based gamers use these days to find, install, and play.

Steam has grown into the premier source for quality professional games on Linux and for a lot of indie content as well. Steam is created by Valve Software, usually referred to as just "Valve," a well-established gaming company with a great reputation because of games like *Half-Life*.

On September 16, 2013, Gabe Newell, the cofounder and managing director of Valve, said that Linux is the future of gaming despite its current minuscule share of the market, and the Steam website proclaims Ubuntu as Steam's favorite version of Linux. Steam is Newell's company's means of pursuing that future.

To learn more about Valve and about Steam, see www.valvesoftware.com/ and http://store.steampowered.com/.

Installing Games in Ubuntu

In this section, you learn how to install some of the more popular games for Ubuntu, all of which can be easily installed using Ubuntu Software Center, along with hundreds more listed under Games. Alongside the usual shoot-'em-up games, you'll also find one or two strategy-focused titles.

Warsow

Warsow is a free and fast-paced *first-person shooter (FPS)* game that is available on Windows, Mac OS X, and Linux. Members of the Ubuntu community have packaged the game and make it available directly and easily for Ubuntu users from the software repositories. The game involves quick movements, grabbing power-ups and weapons before your enemies do, and trying to plant a bomb and steal your enemy's flag without anyone seeing you. You can jump, dash, dodge, and even wall jump your way throughout the colorful 3D environment. Figure 8.2 shows a game just getting started, with lots of weapons, platforms and ramps, and power-ups in sight. There are many other FPS games available, such as Alien Arena, Urban Terror, Wolfenstein: Enemy Territory, Smokin' Guns, Nexuiz, World of Padman, and Cube 2: Sauerbraten.

FIGURE 8.2   Warsow is one of the newest and fastest FPS games available.

Scorched 3D

Scorched 3D is based on an old DOS game called Scorched Earth. The object and game play are similar: There are multiple players, and you enter targeting details to try to destroy the other players using a variety of missile-like weapons. You earn points for each win and can buy new weapons at the end of each round. This time around, there is an amazing array of weapons available, and the game play is completely in stunning 3D, as shown in Figure 8.3.

FIGURE 8.3   Scorched 3D in action.

Scorched 3D is based on turns. Each player shoots once, and then all other players take a shot before the first player shoots again. The game allows you to have more than 20 players at the same time, including both human and computer-controlled players. You may play a local game, over a LAN, or even over the Internet. Scorched 3D runs on Windows, Mac OS X, and Linux, so you may play with your friends regardless of what platforms their computers use.

Frozen Bubble

Frozen Bubble is an amusing little game with sharp graphics, nice music, and easy game play. You may play alone or against another player. The goal is to use your colored marbles to knock down the ones above you within a certain amount of time. You have to hit at least two at a time that are the same color as the one you shoot for anything to fall; otherwise, your shot joins the menagerie above and brings your demise somewhat more quickly, as illustrated in Figure 8.4. There is a lot more to Frozen Bubble, but even with the details it is easy enough for a child to play and interesting enough to hold the interest of most adults.

8

FIGURE 8.4   Move left or right to aim, press up to fire.

SuperTux

Many of us grew up in the era when game play was more important than graphics. Even so, we still liked flashy and pretty-looking games. SuperTux is a throwback to the Mario era. It is a 2D side scroller in which you jump, run, and occasionally shoot something if you have the appropriate power-up. This time, your hero is Tux, the Linux penguin. More than 25 levels are available, as is a level editor for you to create your own. If you enjoy running, jumping, hitting your head to get money, and jumping on your enemies, this game is for you. Figure 8.5 gives you the basic look and feel.

Battle for Wesnoth

One of the most popular games currently available for Linux is Battle for Wesnoth (see Figure 8.6), a strategy game featuring both single and multiplayer options. Based in a fantasy land, you are responsible for building armies to wage war against your foes who are attacking you. Game play may be based on scenarios, such as in single-player mode where some scenarios are preinstalled and others may be easily downloaded, or based on trying to better your friends at a LAN party or online.

Battle for Wesnoth also comes with a map editor that lets you create your own scenarios. An active community shares their work and welcomes new contributions. You can find more information about Battle for Wesnoth at http://wesnoth.org/.

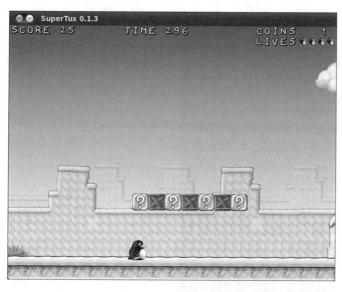

FIGURE 8.5   Although the look and feel of this game takes me back to my childhood, it is far from dull or boring.

FIGURE 8.6   Flex your strategic brain by playing Battle for Wesnoth, a rich and full land of fantasy of adventure.

Frets on Fire

Frets on Fire is similar to games like Guitar Hero, as seen in Figure 8.7. Players try to keep up with a song and "play" it correctly. It supports songs from Guitar Hero I and II and, unlike these proprietary games, is expandable by the community, as well, with more songs available for download from the Internet. The game is completely open source and has content-compatible versions for Linux, Windows, and Mac OS X.

FIGURE 8.7   Frets on Fire offers flashy graphics and familiar game play.

FlightGear

If you like flight simulators, you should try out FlightGear (see Figure 8.8). It is cross platform, sophisticated, and fun. It is completely open source and developed by volunteers, but it's also very professional looking and smooth. If you like this, you can also try others, such as Thunder and Lightning, GL-117, and Search and Rescue II.

FIGURE 8.8   FlightGear features stunning landscapes and technically accurate control panels.

Speed Dreams

There are many racing games available. One of the newer ones is Speed Dreams (Figure 8.9), which started as a fork of an older racing game, TORCS. It features a variety of tracks, vehicles, and options. Speed Dreams is open source, free, and multiplatform. Similar games include TORCS, Rigs of Rods, vDrift, Tile Racer, Trigger, and Mania Drive.

Games for Kids

Kids, both young and old, are not left out. Check out game packages such as gCompris, Childsplay, and TuxPaint to get started. Some of these are educational, some teach computer skills such as using a mouse or a keyboard, and others are just for amusement. Many developers are also parents who have placed a high priority on making quality software for their children to enjoy on their favorite platform. You can search for children's games in the Ubuntu Software Center and find lots of great things to try.

FIGURE 8.9   Many views of the race are available, including one from your car's hood.

Commercial Games

Something new in the past few years is that Ubuntu and Canonical have made a way for commercial software companies to make their products available for installation in Ubuntu via the Ubuntu Software Center. This includes games. A special section of the Ubuntu Software Center labeled For Purchase has been created. Look here for some new and flashy options from commercial vendors. Payment is required, and the details are taken care of within the Ubuntu Software Center.

One interesting and cool option is the Humble Indie Bundle from www.humblebundle. com/, which is a collection of cross-platform software made by independent developers with a "pay what you can" price tag. These bundles are made available intermittently, and sometimes you can find them available directly from the Ubuntu Software Center. This is a great way to find some fun games with a low cost while feeling good about supporting people who write software for fun.

Playing Windows Games

Ubuntu is primarily aimed at desktop computer users who want a system that is stable, powerful, and easy to use. It is not primarily a gaming platform. In fact, compared to Windows, there are not nearly as many games available or being developed (although the number is growing and has improved). This doesn't mean hard-core gamers need to feel left out, though. There are two projects that exist to help game lovers play most Windows-based games on Linux.

A project called Wine uses application interfaces to make Windows programs believe they are running on a Windows platform and not a Linux platform. Bear in mind that Wine, which is a compatibility layer, stands for *Wine is not an emulator*, so do not start thinking of it as such—the community can get quite touchy about it! Although the open-source, free software project won't run everything, it does run a very large number of Windows programs, including many games.

Crossover Games is another commercial option available in the Ubuntu Software Center under For Purchase.

> **TIP**
>
> The keys to successful gaming in Linux are to always read the documentation thoroughly, always investigate the Internet resources thoroughly, and always understand your system. Installing games is a great way to learn about your system because the reward of success is so much fun.

References

- ▶ www.linuxgames.com/—A good source of up-to-date information about the state of Linux gaming.
- ▶ www.warsow.net/—The official site of Warsow.
- ▶ www.scorched3d.co.uk/—The official site of Scorched 3D.
- ▶ www.frozen-bubble.org/—The official site of Frozen Bubble.
- ▶ http://supertux.lethargik.org/—The official site of SuperTux.
- ▶ http://wesnoth.org/—The official site of Battle for Wesnoth.
- ▶ http://gcompris.net/—The official site of gCompris.
- ▶ http://fretsonfire.sourceforge.net—The official site of Frets on Fire.
- ▶ http://childsplay.sourceforge.net/index.php—The official site of Childsplay.
- ▶ www.tuxpaint.org/—The official site of TuxPaint.
- ▶ www.flightgear.org/—The official site of FlightGear.
- ▶ www.speed-dreams.org/—The official site of Speed Dreams.

▶ **https://help.ubuntu.com/community/Games**—Ubuntu community documentation for playing Games on Ubuntu.

▶ **www.nvnews.net/vbulletin/forumdisplay.php?f=14**—The Official Nvidia Linux driver support forum.

▶ **www.nvidia.com/object/unix.html**—The home page for the Nvidia Unix/Linux drivers.

▶ **http://support.amd.com/us/gpudownload/Pages/index.aspx**—The home page for the ATI Linux drivers, including drivers for Linux.

▶ **https://help.ubuntu.com/community/Wine**—Ubuntu community documentation for Wine.

▶ **www.winehq.org/**—The official site of Wine, which includes good information about software that is known to work with the current version in an application database subsite at http://appdb.winehq.org/.

CHAPTER 9

Managing Software

In this chapter, we look at the options you have to manage your software in Ubuntu. If you are used to an environment where you are reliant on visiting different vendor websites to download updates, you are in for a pleasant surprise. Updating a full Ubuntu installation, including all the application software, is as simple as running the Update Manager program. You will discover just how easy it is to install and even remove various software packages.

Ubuntu provides a variety of tools for system resource management. The following sections introduce the graphical software management tools that you will use for most of your software management. This chapter also covers monitoring and managing memory and disk storage on your system.

Ubuntu Software

Ubuntu Software is a graphical utility for package management in Ubuntu. You can find it in the Applications menu as Ubuntu Software; the package and executable program is named `ubuntu-software`. Ubuntu Software enables you to easily select and install a large array of applications by using the intuitive built-in search and easy one-click installation. When you open the program, you see the main screen, as shown in Figure 9.1.

Along the top side of the screen, you have three menu options: All, Installed, and Updates. Just below that is a search bar you can use to search for packages. Scroll down to find software listed by categories.

FIGURE 9.1   The initial Ubuntu Software screen enables you to browse through packages sorted by groups.

Installing new software via Ubuntu Software is as simple as finding it in the package list, double-clicking, and clicking the Install button. When you do so, you may be asked for your password; then the application is downloaded and installed. You can remove an application by finding it in Ubuntu Software and clicking the Remove button.

Using Synaptic for Software Management

Ubuntu Software works just fine for adding and removing applications, but if you need to install something specific—such as a library—you need to use Synaptic (Figure 9.2). You can install Synaptic using Ubuntu Software described earlier; it is not installed by default.

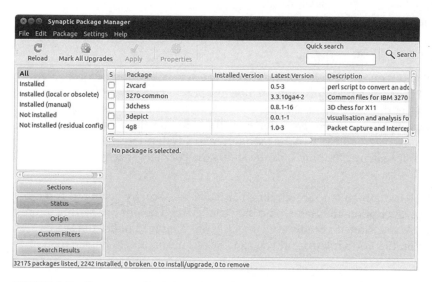

FIGURE 9.2   For more advanced software management in a GUI, Synaptic is the preferred tool.

Along the left are software categories (although this time there are more of them), along the top right are the package selections for that category, and on the bottom right is the Package Information window that shows information about the currently selected package. To install or remove software, click the check box to the left of its name, and you'll see a menu that offers the following options:

▶ **Unmark**—If you have marked this package for installation, upgrade, or one of the other options, this option removes that mark.

▶ **Mark for Installation**—Add this package to the list that will be installed.

▶ **Mark for Re-installation**—If you have some software already installed, but for some reason it's not working, this option reinstalls it from scratch. Existing configuration files are retained, so any edits you have made are safe.

▶ **Mark for Upgrade**—If the software has updates available, this option downloads and installs them.

▶ **Mark for Removal**—This option deletes the selected package from your system but leaves its configuration files intact so that if you ever reinstall it you do not have to reconfigure it.

▶ **Mark for Complete Removal**—This option deletes the selected package from your system but also removes any configuration files, purging everything from the system.

After you have made your changes, click the Apply button to have Synaptic download, install, upgrade, and uninstall as necessary. If you close the program without clicking Apply, your changes are lost.

Beneath the categories on the left side of the screen, you see six buttons: Sections, Status, Origin, Custom Filters, Search Results, and Architecture. These customize the left list: Sections is the Categories view; Status enables you to view packages that are installed or upgradable; Origin lists the different repositories available to download packages; Custom Filters has some esoteric groupings that are useful only to advanced users, Search Results stores results of your searches; and Architecture shows the packages specific to each architecture of Ubuntu.

You can press Ctrl+F at any time to search for a particular package. By default, it is set to search by package description and name. You may change the Look In box setting to only search for Name. As mentioned already, your search terms are saved under the Search view (the button on the bottom left), and you can click from that list to re-search on that term.

As well as providing the method of installing and removing software, Synaptic provides the means to configure the servers you want to use for finding packages. In fact, this is where you can make one of the most important changes to your Ubuntu system: You can open it up to the Ubuntu Universe and Multiverse.

Ubuntu is based on the Debian distribution, which has thousands software packages available for installation. Ubuntu uses only a subset of that number but makes it easy for you to install the others, along with many packages that are not available in Debian. When you use Synaptic, you see small orange Ubuntu logos next to many packages; this identifies them as being officially supported by the Canonical-supported Ubuntu developers. The packages that do not have this logo are supported by the wider Ubuntu community of developers.

To enable the Universe and Multiverse repositories, go to Settings, Repositories. This list shows all the servers you have configured for software installation and updates and includes the Universe and Multiverse repositories. When you find them, check them, and then click Close.

Synaptic shows a message box warning you that the repository listings have changed and that you need to click the Reload button (near the top left of the Synaptic window) to have it refresh the package lists. Go ahead and do that, and you should see a lot more software appear for your selection. However, notice that only a small number have the official Ubuntu "seal" attached, which means you may want to be a bit more careful when installing software.

NOTE

Much of the software discussed in this book is available only through the Universe repository. Therefore, we highly recommend enabling it to get full use out of this book and your Ubuntu installation.

Staying Up-to-Date

Although you can manage your software updates through Synaptic, Ubuntu provides a dedicated tool called Software Updater (shown in Figure 9.3). This tool is designed to be simple to use: When you run it, Software Updater automatically downloads the list of updates available and checks them all in the list it shows. If the update list was downloaded automatically not too long ago, you can force Ubuntu to refresh the list of available updates by clicking the Check button. Otherwise, all you need to do is click Install Updates to bring your system up to date. If you want a little more information about the updates, click Show Details at the bottom to see what has changed in the update.

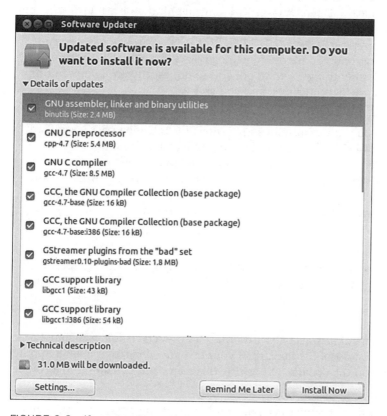

FIGURE 9.3   If you need to update your software to apply bug fixes and security upgrades, use Software Updater.

Ubuntu automatically checks for updates periodically and notifies you when critical updates are available. However, there's no harm running Software Updater yourself every so often, just to make sure; it's better to be safe than sorry.

Working on the Command Line

With so much software available for installation, it is no surprise that Debian-based distros have many ways to manage software installation. At their root, however, they all use Debian's world-renowned *Advanced Package Tool (APT)*. A person posting on Slashdot.com once said, "Welcome to Slashdot. If you can't think of anything original, just say how much APT rocks and you'll fit right in." You see, even though many other distros have tried to equal the power of APT, nothing else even comes close.

Why is APT so cool? Well, it was the first system to properly handle dependencies in software. Other distros, such as Red Hat, used RPM files that had dependencies. For example, an RPM for Gimp would have a dependency on Gtk, the graphical toolkit on which Gimp is based. As a result, if you tried to install your Gimp RPM without having the Gtk RPM, your install would fail. So, you grab the Gtk RPM and try again. Aha: Gtk has a dependency on three other things that you need to download. And those three other things have dependencies on 20 other things. And so on, and so on, usually until you can't find a working RPM for one of the dependencies, and you give up.

APT, on the other hand, was designed to automatically find and download dependencies for your packages. So, if you want to install Gimp, it downloads Gimp's package and any other software it needs to work. No more hunting around by hand, no more worrying about finding the right version, and certainly no more need to compile things by hand. APT also handles installation resuming, which means that if you lose your Internet connection part-way through an upgrade (or your battery runs out, or you have to quit, or whatever), APT picks up where it left off the next time you rerun it.

Day-to-Day Usage

To enable you to search for packages both quickly and thoroughly, APT uses a local cache of the available packages. Try running this command:

```
matthew@seymour:~$ sudo apt-get update
```

The `apt-get` update command instructs APT to contact all the servers it is configured to use and download the latest list of file updates. If your lists are outdated, it takes a minute or two for APT to download the updates. Otherwise, this command executes it in a couple of seconds.

After the latest package information has been downloaded, you are returned to the command line. You can now ask APT to automatically download any software that has been updated, using this command:

```
matthew@seymour:~$ sudo apt-get upgrade
```

If you have a lot of software installed on your machine, there is a greater chance of things being updated. APT scans your software and compares it to the latest package information from the servers and produces a report something like this:

```
mmatthew@seymour:~$ sudo apt-get upgrade
Reading package lists... Done
```

```
Building dependency tree
Reading state information... Done
The following packages will be upgraded:
  cabextract google-chrome-beta icedtea6-plugin language-pack-en
  language-pack-en-base language-pack-gnome-en language-pack-gnome-en-base
  libfreetype6 libfreetype6-dev libsmbclient libwbclient0 openjdk-6-jre
  openjdk-6-jre-headless openjdk-6-jre-lib samba-common samba-common-bin
  smbclient upstart winbind xserver-common xserver-xorg-core
21 upgraded, 0 newly installed, 0 to remove and 0 not upgraded.
Need to get 84.8MB of archives.
After this operation, 623kB of additional disk space will be used.
Do you want to continue [Y/n]?
```

Each part of that report tells you something important. Starting at the top, the line "the following packages will be upgraded" gives you the exact list of packages for which updates are available. If you're installing new software or removing software, you see lists titled "The following packages will be installed" and "The following packages will be removed." A summary at the end shows a total of 21 packages that APT will upgrade, with 0 new packages, 0 to remove, and 0 not upgraded. Because this is an upgrade rather than an installation of new software, all those new packages take up only 623KB of additional space. Although you have an 84.8MB download, the packages are overwriting existing files.

It's important to understand that a basic `apt-get` upgrade never removes software or adds new software. As a result, it is safe to use to keep your system fully patched because it should never break things. However, occasionally you will see the "0 not upgraded" status change, which means some things cannot be upgraded. This happens when some software must be installed or removed to satisfy the dependencies of the updated package, which, as previously mentioned, `apt-get` upgrade will never do.

In this situation, you need to use `apt-get dist-upgrade`, so named because it's designed to allow users to upgrade from one version of Debian/Ubuntu to a newer version—an upgrade that inevitably involves changing just about everything on the system, removing obsolete software, and installing the latest features. This is one of the most-loved features of Debian because it enables you to move from version to version without having to download and install new CDs. Keeping regular upgrades and distro upgrades separate is very useful for making sure that security updates and simple bug fixes don't change software configurations that you may be counting on, especially on a machine that needs to be consistently available and working, such as a server.

Whereas `apt-get upgrade` and `apt-get dist-upgrade` are there for upgrading packages, `apt-get install` is responsible for adding new software. For example, if you want to install the MySQL database server, you run this:

```
matthew@seymour:~$ sudo apt-get install mysql-server
```

6

Internally, APT queries "mysql-server" against its list of software and find that it matches the mysql-server-5.5 package. It then finds which dependencies it needs that you don't already have installed and gives you a report like this one:

```
matthew@seymour:~$ sudo apt-get install mysql-server
[sudo] password for matt:

Reading package lists... Done
Building dependency tree
Reading state information... Done
The following extra packages will be installed:
  libaio1 libdbd-mysql-perl libdbi-perl libhtml-template-perl libmysqlclient18
  libnet-daemon-perl libplrpc-perl libterm-readkey-perl mysql-client-5.5
  mysql-client-core-5.5 mysql-server-5.5 mysql-server-core-5.5
Suggested packages:
  libipc-sharedcache-perl tinyca mailx
The following NEW packages will be installed:
  libaio1 libdbd-mysql-perl libdbi-perl libhtml-template-perl libmysqlclient18
  libnet-daemon-perl libplrpc-perl libterm-readkey-perl mysql-client-5.5
  mysql-client-core-5.5 mysql-server mysql-server-5.5 mysql-server-core-5.5
0 upgraded, 13 newly installed, 0 to remove and 0 not upgraded.
Need to get 26.8 MB of archives.
After this operation, 96.2 MB of additional disk space will be used.
Do you want to continue [Y/n]?
```

This time, you can see that APT has picked up and selected all the dependencies required to install MySQL Server 5.5, but it has also listed one recommended package and two suggested packages that it has not selected for installation. The "recommended" package is just that: The person who made the MySQL package (or its dependencies) thinks it would be a smart idea for you to also have the mailx package. If you want to add it, press N to terminate apt-get and rerun it like this:

```
matthew@seymour:~$ sudo apt-get install mysql-server mailx
```

The "suggested" packages are merely a lower form of recommendation. They don't add any crucial features to the software you selected for install, but it's possible that you might need them for certain non-crucial (to the main piece of software being installed) features or tasks.

> **NOTE**
>
> APT maintains a package cache where it stores DEB files it has downloaded and installed. This usually lives in /var/cache/apt/archives and can sometimes take up many hundreds of megabytes on your computer. You can have APT clean out the package cache by running apt-get clean, which deletes all the cached DEB files. Alternatively, you can run apt-get autoclean, which deletes cached DEB files that are beyond a certain age, thereby keeping newer packages.

If you try running `apt-get` install with packages you already have installed, APT considers your command to be `apt-get update` and looks to see whether new versions are available for download.

The last day-to-day package operation is removing things you no longer want, which you do through the `apt-get remove` command, as follows:

matthew@seymour:~$ **sudo apt-get remove firefox**

Removing packages can be dangerous because APT also removes any software that relies on the packages you selected. For example, if you were to run `apt-get remove libgtk2.0-0` (the main graphical toolkit for Ubuntu), you would probably find that APT insists on removing more than a hundred other things. The moral of the story is this: When you remove software, read the APT report carefully before pressing `Y` to continue with the uninstall.

A straight `apt-get remove` leaves behind the configuration files of your program so that if you ever reinstall it you do not also need to reconfigure it. If you want to remove the configuration files as well as the program files, run this command instead:

matthew@seymour:~$ **sudo apt-get remove —purge firefox**

Or:

matthew@seymour:~$ **sudo apt-get purge firefox**

Either will perform a full uninstall.

> **NOTE**
>
> You can see a more extensive list of `apt-get` parameters by running `apt-get` without any parameters. The cryptic line at the bottom, "This APT has Super Cow Powers," is made even more cryptic if you run the command `apt-get moo`.

Finding Software

With so many packages available, it can be hard to find the exact thing you need using command-line APT. The general search tool is called `apt-cache` and is used like this:

matthew@seymour:~$ **apt-cache search kde**

Depending on which repositories you have enabled, that tool returns about a thousand packages. Many of those results will not even have KDE in the package name but will be matched because the description contains the word *KDE*.

You can filter through this information in several ways. First, you can instruct `apt-cache` to search only in the package names, not in their descriptions. You do this with the –n parameter, like this:

matthew@seymour:~$ **apt-cache –n search kde**

Now the search has gone down from more than 1,000 packages to a few hundred.

Another way to limit search results is to use some basic regular expressions, such as ^, meaning "start," and $, meaning "end." For example, you might want to search for programs that are part of the main KDE suite and not libraries (usually named something like libkde), additional bits (such as xmms-kde), and things that are actually nothing to do with KDE yet still match our search (like tkdesk). Do this by searching for packages that have a name starting with kde, as follows:

matthew@seymour:~$ **apt-cache -n search ^kde**

Perhaps the easiest way to find packages is to combine apt-cache with grep, to search within search results. For example, if you want to find all games-related packages for KDE, you could run this search:

matthew@seymour:~$ **apt-cache search games | grep kde**

When you've found the package you want to install, run it through apt-get install as usual. If you first want a little more information about that package, you can use apt-cache showpkg, like this:

matthew@seymour:~$ **apt-cache showpkg mysql-server-5.0**

This shows information on "reverse depends" (which packages require, recommend, or suggest mysql-server-5.0), "dependencies" (which packages are required, recommended, or suggested to install mysql-server-5.0), and "provides" (which functions this package gives you). The "provides" list is quite powerful because it allows different packages to provide a given resource. For example, a MySQL database-based program requires MySQL to be installed, but isn't fussy whether you install MySQL 4.1 or MySQL 5.5. In this situation, the Debian packages for MySQL 4.1 and MySQL 5.0 both have "mysql-server-4.1" in the provides list, meaning that they offer the functionality provided by MySQL 4.1. Therefore, you can install either version to satisfy the MySQL-based application.

Using apt Instead of apt-get

There is a new, simplified interface to APT that removes the hyphen and the second part of the command. It also includes lovely updates like a progress bar. Although this is new, in testing for this edition of the book, it was stable and pleasant to use. Table 9.1 lists some of the new commands and what they replace. Both versions work, so no relearning is necessary if you do not want to switch.

TABLE 9.1   apt-get versus apt

apt-get Command	apt Command
apt-get install	apt install
apt-get remove	apt remove
apt-get update	apt update
apt-get upgrade	apt upgrade

apt-get dist-upgrade	apt full-upgrade
apt-get remove –purge	apt purge
apt-get autoremove	apt autoremove
apt-get purge	apt purge

Compiling Software from Source

Compiling applications from source is not that difficult. There are two ways to do this: You can use the source code available in the Ubuntu repositories, or you can use source code provided by upstream developers (most useful for those projects that are not available in the Ubuntu repositories). For either method, you need to install the `build-essential` package to ensure that you have the tools you need for compilation. You may also need to install `automake` and `checkinstall`, which are build tools.

Compiling from a Tarball

Most source code that is not in the Ubuntu repositories is available from the original writer or from a company's website as compressed source *tarballs*—that is, `tar` files that have been compressed using `gzip` or `bzip`. The compressed files typically uncompress into a directory containing several files. It is always a good idea to compile source code as a regular user to limit any damage that broken or malicious code might inflict, so create a directory named `source` in your home directory.

From wherever you downloaded the source tarball, uncompress it into the `~/source` directory using the `-C` option to `tar`:

```
matthew@seymour:~$ tar zxvf packagename.tgz -C ~/source
matthew@seymour:~$ tar zxvf packagename.tar.gz -C ~/source
matthew@seymour:~$ tar jxvf packagename.bz -C ~/source
matthew@seymour:~$ tar jxvf packagename.tar.bz2 -C ~/source
```

If you are not certain what file compression method was used, use the `file` command to figure it out:

```
matthew@seymour:~$ file packagename
```

Now, change directories to `~/source/packagename` and look for a file named README, INSTALL, or a similar name. Print out the file if necessary because it contains specific instructions on how to compile and install the software. Typically, the procedure to compile source code is as follows:

```
matthew@seymour:~/source/packagename$ ./configure
```

This runs a script to check whether all dependencies are met and the build environment is correct. If you are missing dependencies, the configure script normally tells you exactly which ones it needs. If you have the Universe and Multiverse repositories enabled in Synaptic, chances are you will find the missing software (usually libraries) in there.

When your configure script succeeds, run the following to compile the software:

```
matthew@seymour:~/source/packagename$ make
```

And finally, run the following:

```
matthew@seymour:~/source/packagename$ sudo make install
```

If the compile fails, check the error messages for the reason and run the following before you start again:

```
matthew@seymour:~/source/packagename$ make clean
```

You can also run the following to remove the software if you do not like it:

```
matthew@seymour:~/source/packagename$ sudo make uninstall
```

Compiling from Source from the Ubuntu Repositories

You might sometimes want to recompile a package, even though a binary package is available in the Ubuntu repositories. For example, a program might have been compiled into a binary with a specific feature disabled that you would like to use. Here is how you can do this. We will call the software package we want to compile *foo*.

First, get the source from the Ubuntu repositories:

```
matthew@seymour:~$ apt-get source foo
```

Install the build dependencies for the package:

```
matthew@seymour:~$ sudo apt-get build-dep foo
```

Change to the directory for the source code (may include the version number):

```
matthew@seymour:~$ cd foo-4.5.2
```

Make whatever changes you want to make to the package or to the compilation flags. You can do this using ./configure and make, or sometimes by making manual changes to a configuration file. Each package has the potential to do this differently, so you need to see that program's documentation. Try looking for a README file in the source code to get started.

Next, create a new debian/changelog entry. After you enter this command, you need to enter a message that tells why a new version was made, perhaps something like *Matthew's flight of fancy with extra sauce.*

NOTE

Ubuntu package numbering follows a specific pattern. To help yourself later, you should stick to this pattern. Using the foo numbers shown here, a typical Ubuntu package that was inherited from Debian with no changes would then be 4.5.2-1. A package inherited from Debian, but changed for Ubuntu would be 4.5.2-1ubuntu1 (and then ubuntu2 for a second version, and so on). A package that did not have a version in Debian but which was created for Ubuntu would be 4.5.2-0ubuntu1 (and ubuntu2 and so on).

```
matthew@seymour:~$ dch -i
```

Build the source package. This creates all the files necessary for uploading a package:

```
matthew@seymour:~$ debuild -S
```

Finally, you are left with a `foo-4.5.2-1ubuntu1custom.deb` package (using whatever version number or suffix you created earlier) that you can install, and later uninstall as well, using your package manager. In some instances, multiple DEB files might be created, in which case you would replace the individual package name in the example here with `*.deb`.

```
matthew@seymour:~$ sudo dpkg -Oi foo-4.5.2-1ubuntu1custom.deb
```

Configuration Management

This section provides a quick introduction to a couple tools that might be useful for those who want more control over system configuration management. For larger needs, see Chapter 36, "Managing Sets of Servers."

dotdee

If you run Linux-based systems, you will find a series of directories that end with a `.d` and that store configuration files. These are sometimes called .d or "dot dee" directories. If you look in `/etc/`, you find many (such as `apparmor.d` and `pam.d`). Opening these directories reveals a large number of configuration files and perhaps other directories containing even more. In Ubuntu or other Debian-based systems, it is a violation of etiquette (and Debian policy) for any software package to be allowed to directly change the configuration files of another package. This can be problematic if you want to use system configuration management software.

dotdee solves this problem by allowing you to take any flat file in your filesystem and replace it with a symlink pointing to a file that is generated from a .d-style directory. It saves the original file and then updates the generated file automatically and dynamically any time any file in the original .d directory is added, deleted, or modified. This way, the Debian policy and general etiquette standards are met, but configurations can be modified as needed by an external program.

dotdee works its magic using `inotify` to dynamically and instantly update the master file. The master file can be built three different ways: using flat files, which are concatenated; using diff/patch files, which are applied in a quiltlike manner; and using executables, which process `stdin` and dump to `stdout`. This flexibility should make any system administrator or developer guru happy.

Snappy Ubuntu Core

Snappy Ubuntu Core takes the absolute minimum of files and code necessary for a usable Ubuntu server image and adds to it a new means of managing software packages. The idea is similar to how smart phones like Android-based phones provide software. In this method, the software packages include everything they need to run on the operating system, effectively making it so that a package is isolated from the operating system more completely. This is designed to protect from the possibility of a package breaking other packages or an entire operating system installation. It is also intended to make updates easier and cleaner. With the idea of convergence, where Ubuntu is aiming to use the same set of software for traditional desktops, laptops, tablets, and phones, all these devices will share the core operating system and Unity interface, and packages that work on any one should also work on the others. This feature first appeared in Ubuntu 16.04 LTS.

Using Snaps

Software bundles packaged this way are called *snaps*. Snaps can be installed using Ubuntu Software or from the command line. On the command line, snaps have a new command. Use the following to interact with snaps.

To show a list of snap packages that are available to be installed:

```
matthew@seymour:~$ snap find
```

Because snaps are new, few packages are available today. However, this list is growing and is likely to become unwieldy at some point. Sure, you can use grep to search through the output to try to find a specific package in the list, but you can also use:

```
matthew@seymour:~$ snap find searchterm
```

To install a snap package:

```
matthew@seymour:~$ sudo snap install packagename
```

To show a list of snap packages that are currently installed:

```
matthew@seymour:~$ snap list
```

To update a snap package:

```
matthew@seymour:~$ sudo snap refresh packagename
```

To remove a snap package:

```
matthew@seymour:~$ sudo snap remove packagename
```

To display a list of changes, such as when snaps were installed, updated, or removed:

```
matthew@seymour:~$ snap changes
```

It is possible for you to create a snap package. See Chapter 39, "Opportunistic Development," to learn how. Learn more and keep up to date as Ubuntu Snappy Core continues develop by checking out https://developer.ubuntu.com/en/snappy/.

References

▶ **www.debian.org/doc/manuals/project-history/ch-detailed.en.html**—History of the Debian Linux package system.

▶ **www.nongnu.org/synaptic/**—Home of the Synaptic package manager.

▶ **www.ubuntu.com/usn**—The official list of Ubuntu security notices.

CHAPTER **10**

Command-Line Beginner's Class

The Linux command line is one of the most powerful tools available for computer system administration and maintenance. The command line is also known as the terminal, shell, the console, the command prompt, and the *command-line interface (CLI)*. For the purposes of this chapter and the next, these terms are interchangeable, although fine-grained differences do exist between them.

The command line is an efficient way to perform complex tasks accurately and much more easily than it would seem at a first glance. Knowledge of the commands available to you and also how to string them together makes using Ubuntu easier for many tasks. Many of the commands were created by the GNU Project as free software analogs to previously existing proprietary UNIX commands. If you are interested, you can learn more about the GNU Project at www.gnu.org/gnu/thegnuproject.html.

This chapter covers some of the basic commands that you need to know to be productive at the command line. You find out how to get to the command line and discover some of the commands used to navigate the file system and perform basic operations with files, directories, and users. This chapter does not give comprehensive coverage of all the commands discussed, but it does give you enough to get started. Chapter 11, "Command-Line Master Class Part 1," advances the subject further while expanding on some of the commands from this chapter. The skills you discover in this chapter help you get started using the command line with confidence.

What Is the Command Line?

If you spend any amount of time with experienced Linux users, you have heard them mention the command line. Some, especially those who have begun their journey in the Linux world using distributions that make it easy to complete many tasks using a *graphical user interface (GUI),* such as Ubuntu, might speak with trepidation about the mysteries of the text interface. Others either praise its power or comment about doing something via the command line as if it is the most natural and obvious way to complete a task.

It is not necessary for you to embrace either extreme. You might develop an affinity for the command line when performing some tasks and prefer the GUI for others. This is where most users end up today. Some might say that you will never need to access the command line because Ubuntu offers a slew of graphical tools that enable you to config-ure most things on your system. Although the premise might be true most of the time, there are some good reasons to acquire a fundamental level of comfort with the command line that you should consider before embracing that view.

Sometimes things go wrong, and you might not have the luxury of a graphical interface to work with. In these situations, a fundamental understanding of the command line and its uses can be a real lifesaver. Also, some tasks end up being far easier and faster to accom-plish from the command line. More important, though, you will be able to make your way around a command-line-based system, which you will encounter if you ever work with a Linux server because most Linux servers have no GUI, and all administration is done using a command-line interface.

> **NOTE**
>
> Don't be tempted to skip over this chapter as irrelevant. You should take the time to work through the chapter and ensure that you are comfortable with the command line before moving on. Doing so will benefit you greatly for years to come.

Initially, you might be tempted to think of the command line as the product of some sort of black and arcane art, and in some ways it can appear to be extremely difficult and complicated to use. However, with a little perseverance, by the end of this chapter you will start to feel comfortable using the command line, and you'll be ready to move on to Chapter 11, "Command-Line Master Class Part 1," and Chapter 12, "Command-Line Master Class Part 2."

This chapter introduces you to commands that enable you to perform the following:

▶ **Routine tasks**—Logging in and out, changing passwords, listing and navigating file directories

▶ **Basic file management**—Creating files and folders, copying or moving them around the file system, renaming and deleting them

▶ **Basic system management**—Shutting down or rebooting, changing file permissions, and reading man pages, which are entries for commands included as files already on your computer in a standardized manual format

The information in this chapter is valuable for individual users or system administrators who are new to Linux and are learning to use the command line for the first time.

> **TIP**
>
> Those of you who have used a computer for many years will probably have come into contact with MS-DOS, in which case being presented with a black screen will fill you with a sense of nostalgia. Don't get too comfy; the command line in Linux is different from (and actually more powerful than) its distant MS-DOS cousin. Even cooler is that whereas MS-DOS skills are transferable only to other MS-DOS environments, the skills that you learn at the Linux command line can be transferred easily to other UNIX and UNIX-like operating systems, such as Solaris, OpenBSD, FreeBSD, and even Mac OS X, which provides access to the terminal.

Accessing the Command Line

You can quickly access the terminal using the desktop menu option Terminal. This opens `gnome-terminal`, from which you can access the terminal while remaining in a GUI environment. This time, the terminal appears as white text on an aubergine (dark purple) background. This is the most common method for accessing the terminal for most desktop users.

> **NOTE**
>
> Finding and running programs, such as Terminal, from a GUI is covered in Chapter 3, "Working with Unity," as is logging it to a Linux system using a graphical interface. This chapter focuses on text-based logins and the use of Linux.

The second most common way for graphical desktop users to access the command line is to press the key combination Ctrl+Alt+F1, after which Ubuntu switches to a black screen and a login prompt like this:

```
Ubuntu 16.04 seymour tty1
seymour login:
```

> **TIP**
>
> This is tty1, one of six virtual consoles that Ubuntu provides. After you have accessed a virtual console, you can use Ctrl+Alt + any of F1 through F6 to switch to a different console, tty1 through tty6. If you want to get back to the graphical interface, press Ctrl+Alt+F7. You can also switch between consoles by holding the Alt key and pressing either the left or the right cursor key to move down or up a console, such as tty1 to tty2.

Regardless of which way you access the terminal, using the virtual tty consoles accessible at Ctrl+Alt+F1-6 or via the windowed version atop your GUI desktop, you will find the rest of the usage details that we cover work the same. As you continue to learn and

10

experiment beyond the contents of this book, you might start to discover some subtle differences between the two and develop a preference. For our purposes, either method works quite well.

There are many other ways to access and use the command line. You could use a traditional console with a monitor, keyboard, and mouse attached to the PC, but which boots into a command-line interface instead of a GUI. You can also connect to your system through a wired or wireless network using the `telnet` or `ssh` commands, as covered in Chapter 19, "Remote Access with SSH, Telnet, and VNC."

With that, let's begin.

Text-Based Console Login

However you connect to a command-line interface, you start with a prompt similar to this one:

```
Ubuntu 16.04 seymour tty1
seymour login:
```

Your prompt might vary, depending on the version of Ubuntu you are using and the method you are using to connect. In any event, at this prompt, type in your username and press Enter. When you are prompted for your password, type it in and press Enter.

> **NOTE**
>
> Your password is not echoed back to you, which is a good idea. Why is it a good idea? Well, people are prevented from looking over your shoulder and seeing your screen input. It is not difficult to guess that a five-letter password might correspond to the user's spouse's first name. After typing your username and pressing the Enter key, you are asked for your password, which you type. Note that Ubuntu does not show any characters while you are typing your password in. This is a good thing because it prevents any shoulder surfers from seeing what you've typed or the length of the password.

Pressing the Enter key drops you to a shell prompt, signified by the dollar sign:

```
matthew@seymour:~$
```

This particular prompt tells me that I am logged in as the user `matthew` on the system `seymour` and I am currently in my home directory; Linux uses the tilde (~) as shorthand for the home directory, which would usually be something like `/home/matthew`.

> **TIP**
>
> Navigating through the system at the command line can get confusing at times, especially when a directory name occurs in several places. Fortunately, Linux includes a simple command that tells you exactly where you are in the file system. It's easy to remember because the command is just an abbreviation of the present working directory, so type `pwd` at any point to get the full path of your location. For example, typing `pwd` after

following these instructions shows /home/*yourusername*, meaning that you are currently in your home directory.

Using the pwd command can save you a lot of frustration when you have changed directory half a dozen times and have lost track.

Logging Out

Use the exit or logout command or Ctrl+D to exit your session. You are then returned to the login prompt. If you use virtual consoles, remember to exit each console before leaving your PC. (Otherwise, someone could easily sit down and use your account.)

Logging In and Out from a Remote Computer

Although you can happily log in on your computer, an act known as a *local* login, you can also log in to your computer via a network connection from a remote computer. Linux-based operating systems provide a number of remote access commands you can use to log in to other computers on your *local area network (LAN)*, *wide area network (WAN)*, or the Internet. Note that you must have an account on the remote computer, *and* the remote computer must be configured to support remote logins; otherwise, you won't be able to log in.

> **NOTE**
>
> See Chapter 18, "Networking," to see how to set up network interfaces with Linux to support remote network logins and Chapter 19, "Remote Access with SSH, Telnet, and VNC," to see how to start remote access services (such as sshd).

The best and most secure way to log in to a remote Linux computer is to use ssh, the Secure Shell client. Your login and session are encrypted while you work on the remote computer. The ssh client features many command-line options but can be simply used with the name or IP address of the remote computer, as follows:

```
matthew@seymour:~$ ssh 192.168.0.41
The authenticity of host '192.168.0.41 (192.168.0.41)' can't be established.
RSA key fingerprint is e1:db:6c:da:3f:fc:56:1b:52:f9:94:e0:d1:1d:31:50.
Are you sure you want to continue connecting (yes/no)?
```

```
yes
```

The first time you connect with a remote computer using ssh, Linux displays the remote computer's encrypted identity key and asks you to verify the connection. After you type yes and press Enter, you are warned that the remote computer's identity (key) has been entered in a file named known_hosts under the .ssh directory in your home directory. You are also prompted to enter your password:

```
Warning: Permanently added '192.168.0.41' (RSA) \
to the list of known hosts.
```

```
matthew@192.168.0.41's password:
matthew@babbage~$
```

After entering your password, you can work on the remote computer, which you can confirm by noticing the changed prompt that now uses the name of the remote computer on which you are working. Again, because you are using ssh, everything you enter on the keyboard in communication with the remote computer is encrypted. When you log out, you return to the shell on your computer:

```
matthew@babbage~$ logout
matthew@seymour:~$
```

User Accounts

A good place to start is with the concept of user-based security. For the most part, only two types of people access the system as users. (Although there are other accounts that run programs and processes, here we are talking about accounts that represent human beings rather than something like an account created for a web server process.) Most people have a regular user account. These users can change anything that is specific to their accounts, such as the wallpaper on the desktop, their personal preferences, and the configuration for a program when it is run by them using their account. Note that the emphasis is on anything that is *specific to their accounts*. This type of user cannot make systemwide changes that could affect other users.

To make systemwide changes, you need to use super user privileges, such as can be done using the account you created when you started Ubuntu for the first time (see Chapter 1, "Installing Ubuntu and Post-Installation Configuration"). With super user privileges you have access to the entire system and can carry out any task, even destructive ones. To help prevent this from happening, this user does not run with these powers enabled at all times, but instead spends most of the time as a regular user.

To use super user privileges from the command line, you need to preface the command you want to execute with another command, sudo, followed by a space and the command you want to run. As a mnemonic device, some think of this as "super user do." When you press Enter (after typing the remaining command), you are prompted for your password, which you should type and then press the Enter key. As usual on any UNIX-based system, the password does not appear on the screen while you are typing it as a security measure, in case someone is watching over your shoulder. Ubuntu then carries out the command, but with super user privileges.

An example of the destructive nature of working as the super user is the age-old example sudo rm -rf /, which erases everything on your hard drive. If you enter a command using sudo as a regular user who does not have an account with super user privileges, an error message appears and nothing happens because the command will not run. We recommend that you don't try this particular command as a test, though. If you enter this command using an account with super user privileges, you will soon find yourself starting over with a fresh installation and hoping you have a current backup of all your data.

You need to be especially careful when using your super user privileges; otherwise, you might do irreparable damage to your system.

However, the ability to work as the super user is fundamental to a healthy Linux system and should not be feared, but rather respected, even while used only with focused attention. Without this ability, you could not install new software, edit system configuration files, or do a large number of important administration tasks. By the way, you have already been performing operations with super user privileges from the GUI if you have ever been asked to enter your password to complete a specific task, such as installing software updates. The difference is that most graphical interfaces limit the options that users have and make it a little more difficult to do some of the big, disruptive tasks, even the ones that are incredibly useful.

Ubuntu works slightly differently from many other Linux distributions. If you study some other Linux distros, especially older or more traditional ones, you will hear about a specific user account called root, which is a super user account. In those distros, instead of typing in `sudo` before a command while using a regular user account with super user privileges, you log in to the root account and simply issue the command without entering a password (at least by default; in almost all cases, `sudo` can be installed and configured in these distros). In those cases, you can tell when you are using the root account at the command line because you will see a pound sign (#) in the command line prompt in the place of the dollar sign ($).

For example: `matthew@seymour:~#` versus the usual `matthew@seymour:~$`

In Ubuntu, the root account is disabled by default because forcing regular users with super user privileges to type a specific command every time they want to execute a command as a super user should have the benefit of making them carefully consider what they are doing when they use that power. It is easy to forget to log out of a root account, and entering a powerful command while logged in to root can be catastrophic. However, if you are more experienced and comfortable with the more traditional method of using super user privileges and want to enable the root account, you can use the command `sudo passwd`. When prompted, enter your user password to confirm that your user account has super user privileges. You are then asked for a new UNIX password, which will be the password for the root account, so make sure to remember it. You are also prompted to repeat the password, in case you've made any mistakes. After you've typed it in and pressed Enter, the root account is active. You find out how to switch to root later on.

An alternative way of getting a root prompt, without having to enable the root account, is to issue the command `sudo -i`. After entering your password, you find yourself at a root prompt (#). Do what you need to do, and when you are finished, type `exit`, and press Enter to return to your usual prompt. You can learn more about `sudo` and root from an Ubuntu perspective at https://help.ubuntu.com/community/RootSudo.

Reading Documentation

Although you learn the basics of using Ubuntu in this book, you need time and practice to master and troubleshoot more complex aspects of the Linux operating system and your distribution. As with any operating system, you can expect to encounter some problems or perplexing questions as you continue to work with Linux. The first place to turn for help with these issues is the documentation included with your system; if you cannot find the information you need there, check Ubuntu's website.

Using Man Pages

To learn more about a command or program, use the man command followed by the name of the command. Man pages are stored in places like /usr/share/man and /usr/local/share/man, but you don't need to know that. To read a man page, such as the one for the rm command, use the man command like this:

```
matthew@seymour:~$ man rm
```

After you press Enter, the less command (a Linux command known as a *pager*) displays the man page. The less command is a text browser you can use to scroll forward and backward (even sideways) through the document to learn more about the command. Type the letter h to get help, use the forward slash (/) to enter a search string, or press q to quit.

No one can remember everything. Even the best and most experienced systems administrators use man pages regularly. Looking up complicated information is easy because this frees you from having to recall it all, enabling you to focus on your task rather than punishing you for not remembering syntax.

> **NOTE**
>
> Nearly all the hundreds of commands included with Linux each have a man page; however, some do not or may only have simple pages. You may also use the info command to read more detailed information about some commands or as a replacement for others. For example, to learn even more about info (which has a rather extensive manual page), use the info command like this:
>
> ```
> matthew@seymour:~$ info info
> ```
>
> Use the arrow keys to navigate through the document and press q to quit reading.

Using apropros

Linux, like UNIX, is a self-documenting system, with man pages accessible through the man command. Linux offers many other helpful commands for accessing its documentation. You can use the apropos command (for example, with a keyword such as partition) to find commands related to partitioning, like this:

```
matthew@seymour:~$ apropos partition
addpart        (8)    - Simple wrapper around the "add partition" ioctl
all-swaps      (7)    - Event signaling that all swap partitions have been ac...
cfdisk         (8)    - Curses/slang based disk partition table manipulator fo...
delpart        (8)    - Simple wrapper around the "del partition" ioctl
fdisk          (8)    - Partition table manipulator for Linux
```

```
gparted       (8)    - Gnome partition editor for manipulating disk partitions.
Mpartition    (1)    - Partition an MSDOS hard disk
Partprobe     (8)    - Inform the OS of partition table changes
Partx         (8)    - Telling the kernel about presence and numbering of on-...
Pvcreate      (8)    - Initialize a disk or partition for use by LVM
Pvresize      (8)    - Resize a disk or partition in use by LVM2
Sfdisk        (8)    - Partition table manipulator for Linux
```

Using whereis

To find a command and its documentation, you can use the whereis command. For example, if you are looking for the fdisk command, you can do this:

```
matthew@seymour:~$ whereis fdisk
fdisk: /sbin/fdisk /usr/share/man/man8/fdisk.8.gz
```

Understanding the Linux File System Hierarchy

Linux has inherited from UNIX a well-planned hierarchy for organizing things. It isn't perfect, but it is generally logical and mostly consistent, although distributions do tend to make some modifications that force some thinking and adaptation when moving between, say, Fedora, Slackware, and Ubuntu. Table 10.1 shows some of the top-level directories that are part of a standard Linux distro.

TABLE 10.1   Basic Linux Directories

Name	Description
/	The root directory
/bin	Essential commands
/boot	Boot loader files, Linux kernel
/dev	Device files
/etc	System configuration files
/home	User home directories
/lib	Shared libraries, kernel modules
/lost+found	Directory for recovered files (if found after a file system check)
/media	Mount point for removable media, such as DVDs and floppy disks
/mnt	Usual mount point for local, remote file systems
/opt	Add-on software packages
/proc	Kernel information, process control
/root	Super user (root) home
/sbin	System commands (mostly root only)
/srv	Holds information relating to services that run on your system
/sys	Real-time information on devices used by the kernel
/tmp	Temporary files

10

| /usr | Software not essential for system operation, such as applications |
| /var | Variable data (such as logs); spooled files |

Knowing these directories can help you find files when you need them. This knowledge can even help you partition hard drives when you install new systems by letting you choose to put certain directories on their own distinct partition, which can be useful for things like isolating directories from one another, such as a server security case like putting a directory like /boot that doesn't change often on its own partition and making it read-only and unchangeable without specific operations being done by a super user during a maintenance cycle. Desktop users probably won't need to think about that, but the directory tree is still quite useful to know when you want to find the configuration file for a specific program and set some program options systemwide to affect all users.

> **NOTE**
>
> This is a lot to remember, especially at first. For reference, there is a man page for the Linux filesystem hierarchy:
>
> matthew@seymour:~$ **man hier**
>
> This returns a detailed listing, with descriptions of each part.

Some of the important directories in Table 10.1, such as those containing user and root commands or system configuration files, are discussed in the following sections. You may use and edit files under these directories when you use Ubuntu.

Essential Commands in /bin and /sbin

The /bin directory contains essential commands used by the system for running and booting the system. In general, only the root operator uses the commands in the /sbin directory. The software in both locations is essential to the system; they make the system what it is, and if they are changed or removed, it could cause instability or a complete system failure. Often, the commands in these two directories are *statically* linked, which means that the commands do not depend on software libraries residing under the /lib or /usr/lib directories. Nearly all the other applications on your system are *dynamically* linked, meaning that they require the use of external software libraries (also known as *shared* libraries) to run. This is a feature for both sets of software.

The commands in /bin and /sbin are kept stable to maintain foundational system integrity and do not need to be updated often, if at all. For the security of the system, these commands are kept in a separate location and isolated where changes are more difficult and where it will be more obvious to the system administrator if unauthorized changes are attempted or made.

Application software changes more frequently, and applications often use the same functions that other pieces of application software use. This was the genesis of shared libraries. When a security update is needed for something that is used by more than one program, it has to be updated in only one location, a specific software library. This enables easy and quick security updates that will affect several pieces of non-system-essential software at the same time by updating one shared library, contained in one file on the computer.

Configuration Files in /etc

System configuration files and directories reside under the /etc directory. Some major software packages, such as Apache, OpenSSH, and xinetd, have their own subdirectories in /etc filled with configuration files. Others like crontab or fstab use one file. Examples of system-related configuration files in /etc include the following:

- ▶ **fstab**—The file system table is a text file listing each hard drive, CD-ROM, floppy, or other storage device attached to your PC. The table indexes each device's partition information with a place in your Linux file system (directory layout) and lists other options for each device when used with Linux (see Chapter 22, "Kernel and Module Management"). Nearly all entries in fstab can be manipulated by root using the mount command.

- ▶ **modprobe.d/**—This folder holds all the instructions to load kernel modules that are required as part of the system startup.

- ▶ **passwd**—The list of users for the system, including special-purpose nonhuman users like syslog and CouchDB, along with user account information.

- ▶ **sudoers**—A list of users or user groups with super user access.

User Directories: /home

The most important data on a non-server Linux system often resides in the user's directories, found under the /home directory. User directories are named by default according to account usernames, so on a computer where I have an account named matthew, my home directory would generally be found in /home/matthew. This can be changed, and if you're curious you can read more about it in Chapter 11, "Command-Line Master Class Part 1."

Segregating the system and user data can be helpful in preventing data loss and making the process of backing up easier. For example, having user data reside on a separate file system or mounted from a remote computer on the network might help shield users from data loss in the event of a system hardware failure. For a laptop or desktop computer at home, you might place /home on a separate partition from the rest of the file system, so that if the operating system is upgraded, damaged, or reinstalled, /home would be more likely to survive the event intact.

10

Using the Contents of the /proc Directory to Interact with the Kernel

The content of the /proc directory is created from memory and exists only while Linux is running. This directory contains special files that either extract information from or send information to the kernel. Many Linux utilities extract information from dynamically created directories and files under this directory, also known as a *virtual file system*. For example, the free command obtains its information from a file named meminfo:

```
matthew@seymour:~$ free
```

```
            total      used       free     shared   buffers    cached
Mem:      4055680    2725684    1329996    0        188996     1551464
-/+ buffers/cache:    985224    3070456
Swap:     8787512    0          8787512
```

This information constantly changes as the system is used. You can get the same information by using the cat command to see the contents of the meminfo file:

```
matthew@seymour:~$ cat /proc/meminfo
MemTotal:          4055680 KB
MemFree:           1329692 KB
Buffers:            189208 KB
Cached:            1551488 KB
SwapCached:              0 KB
Active:            1222172 KB
Inactive:          1192244 KB
Active(anon):       684092 KB
Inactive(anon):         16 KB
Active(file):       538080 KB
Inactive(file):    1192228 KB
Unevictable:            48 KB
Mlocked:                48 KB
SwapTotal:         8787512 KB
SwapFree:          8787512 KB
Dirty:                 136 KB
Writeback:               0 KB
AnonPages:          673760 KB
Mapped:             202308 KB
Shmem:               10396 KB
Slab:               129248 KB
SReclaimable:       107356 KB
SUnreclaim:          21892 KB
KernelStack:          2592 KB
PageTables:          30108 KB
NFS_Unstable:            0 KB
Bounce:                  0 KB
WritebackTmp:            0 KB
```

```
CommitLimit:                  10815352 KB
Committed_AS:                  1553172 KB
VmallocTotal:              34359738367 KB
VmallocUsed:                    342300 KB
VmallocChunk:              34359387644 KB
HardwareCorrupted:                   0 KB
HugePages_Total:                     0
HugePages_Free:                      0
HugePages_Rsvd:                      0
HugePages_Surp:                      0
Hugepagesize:                     2048 KB
DirectMap4k:                     38912 KB
DirectMap2M:                   4153344 KB
```

The /proc directory can also be used to dynamically alter the behavior of a running Linux kernel by "echoing" numerical values to specific files under the /proc/sys directory. For example, to "turn on" kernel protection against one type of denial-of-service (DoS) attack known as *SYN flooding*, use the echo command to send the number 1 to the following /proc path:

matthew@seymour:~$ **sudo echo 1 >/proc/sys/net/ipv4/tcp_syncookies**

Other ways to use the /proc directory include the following:

▶ Getting CPU information, such as the family, type, and speed from /proc/cpuinfo.

▶ Viewing important networking information under /proc/net, such as active interfaces information under /proc/net/dev, routing information in /proc/net/route, and network statistics in /proc/net/netstat.

▶ Retrieving file system information.

▶ Reporting media mount point information via USB; for example, the Linux kernel reports what device to use to access files (such as /dev/sda) if a USB camera or hard drive is detected on the system. You can use the dmesg command to see this information.

▶ Getting the kernel version in /proc/version, performance information such as uptime in /proc/uptime, or other statistics such as CPU load, swap file usage, and processes in /proc/stat.

Working with Shared Data in the /usr Directory

The /usr directory contains software applications, libraries, and other types of shared data for use by anyone on the system. Many Linux system administrators give /usr its own partition. A number of subdirectories under /usr contain manual pages (/usr/share/man), software package shared files (/usr/share/name_of_package, such as /usr/share/emacs), additional application or software package documentation (/usr/share/doc), and an entire subdirectory tree of locally built and installed software, /usr/local.

Temporary File Storage in the `/tmp` Directory

As its name implies, the `/tmp` directory is used for temporary file storage; as you use Linux, various programs create files in this directory. Files in this directory are cleared daily by a cron job and every time the system is booted.

Accessing Variable Data Files in the `/var` Directory

The `/var` directory contains subdirectories used by various system services for spooling and logging. Many of these variable data files, such as print spooler queues, are temporary, whereas others, such as system and kernel logs, are renamed and rotated in use. Incoming email is usually directed to files under `/var/spool/mail`.

Linux also uses `/var` for other important system services, such as the topmost *File Transfer Protocol (FTP)* directory under `/var/ftp` (see Chapter 27, "Remote File Serving with FTP"), and the Apache web server's initial home page directory for the system, `/var/www/html`. (See Chapter 24, "Apache Web Server Management," for more information about using Apache.)

> **NOTE**
>
> There is a recent trend to move data that is served from `/var/www` and `/var/ftp` to `/srv`, but this is not universal.

Navigating the Linux File System

In the Linux file system, as with its predecessor UNIX, everything is a file: data files, binary files, executable programs, even input and output devices. These files are placed in a series of directories that act like file folders. A directory is nothing more than a special type of file that contains a list of other files/directories. These files and directories are used to create a hierarchical structure that enables logical placement of specific types of files. Later this chapter discusses the standard hierarchy of the Linux file system. First, you learn how to navigate and interact with the file system.

> **NOTE**
>
> A directory with contents is called a *parent*, and its contents are called *children*, as in "`/home/matthew/Documents` is a child directory of `/home/matthew`, its parent."

Listing the Contents of a Directory with `ls`

The `ls` command lists the contents of the current directory. It is commonly used by itself, but a number of options (also known as switches) are available for `ls` and give you more information. If you have just logged in as described earlier, this command lists the files and directories in your user's home directory:

```
matthew@seymour:~$ ls
Documents    Music      file.txt  Pictures  Music
```

By itself, the `ls` command shows just a list of names. Some are files and some are directories. This is useful if I know what I am looking for but cannot remember the exact name. However, using `ls` in this matter has some limitations. First, it does not show hidden files. Hidden files use filenames that start with a period (.) as the first character. They are often used for configuration of specific programs and are not accessed frequently. For this reason, they are not included in a basic directory listing. You can see all the hidden files by adding a switch to the command like this:

```
matthew@seymour:~$ ls -a
.                   .bash_logout     Documents     Music
..                  .bashrc          file.txt      Pictures
.bash_history  .config          .local        .profile
```

There is still more information available about each item in a directory. To include details such as the file/directory permissions, owner and group (all of which are discussed later in this chapter), as well as the size, and the date and time it was last modified, enter the following:

```
matthew@seymour:~$ ls -al
total 608
drwxr-xr-x 38 matthew matthew   4096 2015-06-04 08:20 .
drwxr-xr-x  3 root    root      4096 2015-05-16 16:48 ..
-rw-------  1 matthew matthew    421 2015-06-04 10:27 .bash_history
-rw-r--r--  1 matthew matthew    220 2015-05-16 16:48 .bash_logout
-rw-r--r--  1 matthew matthew   3353 2015-05-16 16:48 .bashrc
drwxr-xr-x 13 matthew matthew   4096 2015-05-21 10:42 .config
drwxr-xr-x  2 matthew matthew   4096 2015-05-16 17:07 Documents
-rw-r--r--  1 matthew matthew    335 2015-05-16 16:48 file.txt
drwxr-xr-x  3 matthew matthew   4096 2015-05-16 17:07 .local
drwxr-xr-x  2 matthew matthew   4096 2015-05-16 17:07 Music
drwxr-xr-x  3 matthew matthew   4096 2015-05-16 18:07 Pictures
-rw-r--r--  1 matthew matthew    675 2015-05-16 16:48 .profile
```

The listing (abbreviated here) is now given with one item per line, but with multiple columns. The listing starts with the number of items in the directory. (Both files and subdirectories are included; remember that the listing here is abbreviated.) Then, the details are as shown in Figure 10.1.

10

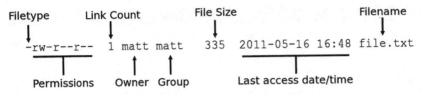

FIGURE 10.1   Decoding the output of a detailed directory listing.

These details are discussed more completely later in the chapter in the "Working with Permissions" section.

Another useful switch is this:

```
matthew@seymour:~$ ls -R
```

This command scans and lists all the contents of the subdirectories of the current directory. This is likely to be a lot of information, so you might want to redirect the output to a text file so that you can browse through it at your leisure by using the following:

```
matthew@seymour:~$ ls -laR > listing.txt
```

TIP

The previous command sends the output of ls -laR to a file called listing.txt and demonstrates part of the power of the Linux command line. At the command line, you can use files as inputs to commands, or you can generate files as outputs as shown. For more information about redirects and combining commands, see Chapter 14, "Automating Tasks and Shell Scripting." In the meantime, note that you can read the contents of that text file using the command less listing.txt, which lets you read the file bit by bit using the arrow keys to navigate in the file (or Enter to move to the next line), the spacebar to move to the next page, and q to exit when done.

Changing Directories with cd

Use the cd command to move within the file system from one directory to another. It might help you remember this command to think of it meaning "change directory." The most basic usage of cd is this:

```
matthew@seymour:~$ cd somedir
```

That looks in the current directory for the somedir subdirectory, and then moves you into it. You can also specify an exact location for a directory, like this:

```
matthew@seymour:~$ cd /home/matthew/stuff/somedir
```

You can also use the cd command with several shortcuts. For example, to quickly move up to the *parent* directory, the one above the one you are currently in, use the cd command like this:

```
matthew@seymour:~$ cd ..
```

To return to your home directory from anywhere in the Linux file system, use the `cd` command like this:

`matthew@seymour:~$` **`cd`**

You can also use the $HOME shell environment variable to accomplish the same thing. Environment variables are discussed in greater detail in Chapter 12, "Command-Line Master Class Part 2." Type this command and press Enter to return to your home directory:

`matthew@seymour:~$` **`cd $HOME`**

You can accomplish the same thing by using the tilde (~) like this:

`matthew@seymour:~$` **`cd ~`**

Finding Your Current Directory with pwd

Use `pwd` to remind you where you are within the file system:

`matthew@seymour:~$` **`pwd`**

Working with Permissions

Under Linux (and UNIX), everything in the file system, including directories and devices, is a file. And every file on your system has an accompanying set of permissions based on ownership. These permissions provide data security by giving specific permission settings to every single item denoting who may read, write, or execute the file. These permissions are set individually for the file's owner, for members of the group the file belongs to, and for all others on the system.

You can examine the default permissions for a file you create by using the `umask` command, which lists default permissions using the number system explained next, or by using the `touch` command and then the `ls` command's long-format listing like this:

```
matthew@seymour:~$ touch file
matthew@seymour:~$ ls -l file
-rw-r--r-- 1 matthew matthew 0 2015-06-30 13:06 file
```

In this example, the `touch` command is used to quickly create a file. The `ls` command then reports on the file, displaying the following (from left to right):

▶ **The type of file created**—Common indicators of the type of file are in the leading letter in the output. A blank (which is represented by a dash, as in the preceding example) designates a plain file, `d` designates a directory, `c` designates a character device (such as `/dev/ttyS0`), and `b` is used for a block device (such as `/dev/sda`).

▶ **Permissions**—Read, write, and execute permissions for the owner, group, and all others on the system. (You learn more about these permissions later in this section.)

10

▶ **Number of links to the file**—The number 1 designates that there is only one file, whereas any other number indicates that there might be one or more hard-linked files. Links are created with the ln command. A hard-linked file is an exact copy of the file, but it might be located elsewhere on the system. Symbolic links of directories can also be created, but only the root operator can create a hard link of a directory.

▶ **The owner**—The account that owns the file; this is originally the file creator, but you can change this designation using the chown command.

▶ **The group**—The group of users allowed to access the file; this is originally the file creator's main group, but you can change this designation using the chgrp command.

▶ **File size and creation/modification date**—The last two elements indicate the size of the file in bytes and the date the file was created or last modified.

Assigning Permissions

Under Linux, permissions are grouped by owner, group, and others, with read, write, and execute permission assigned to each, as follows:

```
Owner    Group    Others
rwx      rwx      rxw
```

Permissions can be indicated by mnemonic or octal characters. Mnemonic characters are listed here:

▶ r indicates permission for an owner, member of the owner's group, or others to open and read the file.

▶ w indicates permission for an owner, member of the owner's group, or others to open and write to the file.

▶ x indicates permission for an owner, member of the owner's group, or others to execute the file (or read a directory).

In the previous example for the file named file, the owner, matthew, has read and write permission. Any member of the group named matthew may only read the file. All other users may only read the file. Also note that default permissions for files created by the root operator (while using sudo or a root account) will differ because of umask settings assigned by the shell.

Many users prefer to use numeric codes, based on octal (base 8) values, to represent permissions. Here's what these values mean:

▶ 4 indicates read permission.

▶ 2 indicates write permission.

▶ 1 indicates execute permission.

In octal notation, the previous example file has a permission setting of 644 (read + write or 4 + 2, read-only or 4, read-only or 4). Although you can use either form of permissions notation, octal is easy to use quickly after you visualize and understand how permissions are numbered.

> **NOTE**
>
> In Linux, you can create groups to assign a number of users access to common directories and files, based on permissions. You might assign everyone in accounting to a group named `accounting` and allow that group access to accounts payable files while disallowing access by other departments. Defined groups are maintained by the root operator, but you can use the `newgrp` command to temporarily join other groups to access files (as long as the root operator has added you to the other groups). You can also allow or deny other groups' access to your files by modifying the group permissions of your files.

Directory Permissions

Directories are also files under Linux. For example, again use the `ls` command to show permissions like this:

```
matthew@seymour:~$ mkdir directory
matthew@seymour:~$ ls -ld directory
drwxr-xr-x  2 matthew  matthew  4096 2015-06-30 13:23 directory
```

In this example, the `mkdir` command is used to create a directory. The `ls` command, and its `-ld` option, is used to show the permissions and other information about the directory (not its contents). Here you can see that the directory has permission values of 755 (read + write + execute or 4 + 2 + 1, read + execute or 4 + 1, and read + execute or 4 + 1).

This shows that the owner can read and write to the directory and, because of execute permission, also list the directory's contents. Group members and all other users can list only the directory contents. Note that directories require execute permission for anyone to be able to view their contents.

You should also notice that the `ls` command's output shows a leading d in the permissions field. This letter specifies that this file is a directory; normal files have a blank field in its place. Other files, such as those specifying a block or character device, have a different letter.

For example, if you examine the device file for a Linux serial port, you will see the following:

```
matthew@seymour:~$ ls -l /dev/ttyS0
crw-rw---- 1 root dialout 4, 64 2015-06-30 08:13 /dev/ttyS0
```

Here, /dev/ttyS0 is a character device (such as a serial communications port and designated by a c) owned by root and available to anyone in the dialout group. The device has permissions of 660 (read + write, read + write, no permission).

On the other hand, if you examine the device file for an IDE hard drive, you see this:

```
matthew@seymour:~$ ls -l /dev/sda
brw-rw-- -- 1 root disk 8, 0 2015-06-30 08:13 /dev/sda
```

In this example, `b` designates a block device (a device that transfers and caches data in blocks) with similar permissions. Other device entries you will run across on your Linux system include symbolic links, designated by `s`.

Altering File Permissions with `chmod`

You can use the `chmod` command to alter a file's permissions. This command uses various forms of command syntax, including octal or a mnemonic form (such as `u`, `g`, `o`, or `a` and `rwx`, and so on) to specify a desired change. You can use the `chmod` command to add, remove, or modify file or directory permissions to protect, hide, or open up access to a file by other users (except for the root account or a user with super user permission and using sudo, either of which can access any file or directory on a Linux system).

The mnemonic forms of `chmod`'s options are (when used with a plus character, +, to add, or a minus sign, -, to remove):

▶ `u`—Adds or removes user (owner) read, write, or execute permission

▶ `g`—Adds or removes group read, write, or execute permission

▶ `o`—Adds or removes read, write, or execute permission for others not in a file's group

▶ `a`—Adds or removes read, write, or execute permission for all users

▶ `r`—Adds or removes read permission

▶ `w`—Adds or removes write permission

▶ `x`—Adds or removes execution permission

For example, if you create a file, such as a `readme.txt`, the file has the following default permissions (set by the `umask` setting in `/etc/bashrc`, covered in the next section):

```
-rw-r--r-- 1 matthew matthew 0 2015-06-30 13:33 readme.txt
```

As you can see, you can read and write the file. Anyone else can only read the file (and only if it is outside your home directory, which will have read, write, and execute permission set only for you, the owner). You can remove all write permission for anyone by using `chmod`, the minus sign (-), and `aw`, as follows:

```
matthew@seymour:~$ chmod a-w readme.txt
matthew@seymour:~$ ls -l readme.txt
-r--r--r-- 1 matthew matthew 0 2015-06-30 13:33 readme.txt
```

Now, no one can write to the file (except you, if the file is in your /home or /tmp directory because of directory permissions). To restore read and write permission for only you as the owner, use the plus sign (+) and the u and rw options like so:

```
matthew@seymour:~$ chmod u+rw readme.txt
matthew@seymour:~$ ls -l readme.txt
-rw-r--r-- 1 matthew matthew 0 2015-06-30 13:33 readme.txt
```

You can also use the octal form óf the chmod command (for example, to modify a file's permissions so that only you, the owner, can read and write a file). Use the chmod command and a file permission of 600, like this:

```
matthew@seymour:~$ chmod 600 readme.txt
matthew@seymour:~$ ls -l readme.txt
-rw------- 1 matthew matthew 0 2015-06-30 13:33 readme.txt
```

If you take away execution permission for a directory, files might be hidden inside and may not be listed or accessed by anyone else (except the root operator, of course, who has access to any file on your system). By using various combinations of permission settings, you can quickly and easily set up a more secure environment, even as a normal user in your /home directory.

File Permissions with umask

When you create a file, it is created with a default set of permissions. You can view and modify the default permissions for files with umask, which works like a filter. When a file is created by a user account, whether that account is owned by a human like matthew or a process like init, the file will be created using specific permissions.

The numbers we used above when discussing file permissions are also used with umask, but with an interesting change. Now, the numbers defined in umask are subtracted from the ultimate file permissions. So, if we wanted all new files to be created with a default permission of 777, we would type:

```
matthew@seymour:~$ umask 000
```

Of course, we would never want to have all our files accessible by default because this would be incredibly insecure and unsafe. The default umask is 022, which means that files are created by default with 755 permissions, except in your /home directory where the umask is 002 and files are created with 775.

To find the current umask setting, use:

```
matthew@seymour:~$ umask
```

This may list four digits instead of three. If so, don't be confused. The additional digit is the first one; it is explained later in this chapter in the sections covering setuid, setgid, and the sticky bit.

10

To change the `umask` setting—for example, if you wanted the default to be 740—use:

```
matthew@seymour:~$ umask 037
```

File Permissions with `chgrp`

You can use the `chgrp` command to change the group to which a file belongs:

```
matthew@seymour:~$ chgrp wheel filename
```

Changing File Permissions with `chown`

You can use the `chown` command to change the owner of a file:

```
matthew@seymour:~$ chown matthew filename
```

You can also use the `chown` command to change the group of a file at the same time:

```
matthew@seymour:~$ chown matthew:wheel filename
```

Understanding Set User ID, Set Group ID, and Sticky Bit Permissions

The first two of the three listed types of permission are "set user ID," known as *suid*, and "set group ID," or *sgid*. These settings, when used in a program, enable any user running that program to have program owner or group owner permissions for that program. These settings enable the program to be run effectively by anyone, without requiring that each user's permissions be altered to include specific permissions for that program.

One commonly used program with suid permissions is the `passwd` command:

```
matthew@seymour:~$ ls -l /usr/bin/passwd
-rwsr-xr-x 1 root root 42856 2015-01-26 10:09 /usr/bin/passwd
```

This setting allows normal users to execute the command (as root) to make changes to a root-only-accessible file `/etc/passwd`.

By default, these are turned off on files. To set them, add an extra digit to the beginning of a number in a `chmod` command. Suid uses 4. Sgid uses 2. You can set both at the same time using a 6 (4+2). For example, for a file owned by root with current 711 permissions allowing anyone to run it, you can make it run as root with:

```
matthew@seymour:~$ chmod 4711 filename
```

> **NOTE**
>
> Other files that might have suid or guid permissions include `at`, `rcp`, `rlogin`, `rsh`, `chage`, `chsh`, `ssh`, `crontab`, `sudo`, `sendmail`, `ping`, `mount`, and several UNIX-to-UNIX Copy (UUCP) utilities. Many programs (such as games) might also have this type of permission to access a sound device.

Files or programs that have suid or guid permissions can sometimes present security holes because they bypass normal permissions. This problem is compounded if the permission extends to an executable binary (a command) with an inherent security flaw because it could lead to any system user or intruder gaining root access. In past exploits, this typically happened when a user fed a vulnerable command with unexpected input (such as a long pathname or option); the command would fail, and the user would be presented a root prompt. Although Linux developers are constantly on the lookout for poor programming practices, new exploits are found all the time, and can crop up unexpectedly, especially in newer software packages that haven't had the benefit of peer developer review.

Savvy Linux system administrators keep the number of suid or guid files present on a system to a minimum. The `find` command can be used to display all such files on your system:

```
matthew@seymour:~$ sudo find / -type f -perm /6000 -exec ls -l {} \;
```

> **NOTE**
>
> The `find` command is quite helpful and can be used for many purposes, such as before or during backup operations.

Note that the programs do not necessarily have to be removed from your system. If your users really do not need to use the program, you can remove the programs execute permission for anyone. You have to decide, as the root operator, whether your users are allowed, for example, to mount and unmount CD-ROMs or other media on your system. Although Linux-based operating systems can be set up to accommodate ease of use and convenience, allowing programs such as `mount` to be suid might not be the best security policy. Other candidates for suid permission change could include the `chsh`, `at`, or `chage` commands.

An additional setting called the *sticky bit* is available using this same additional first digit. A sticky bit limits who may rename or delete files within a directory. When set, files in that directory may be unlinked or renamed only by a super user, the directory owner, or the file owner. Set the sticky bit to on using a 1, like this for a directory with 755 permissions:

```
matthew@seymour:~$ chmod 1755 directoryname
```

You can set the sticky bit concurrently with suid and sgid, like this (4+2+1):

```
matthew@seymour:~$ chmod 7755 directoryname
```

Setting Permissions with Access Control Lists

POSIX is a family of standards created to maintain stability and consistency across operating systems for UNIX and UNIX-like systems, such as Linux. One important feature of POSIX is the access control list or ACL (often pronounced *ak-el*). ACLs permit even more fine-grained control over access permissions.

By default, all files have an ACL. To view the ACL for a file, use:

matthew@seymour:~$ **getfacl** *filename*

A typical getfacl output includes multiple lines, like this for filename.txt:

```
# file: filename.txt
# owner: matthew
# group: matthew
user::rw-
group::rw-
other::r--
```

The information listed here is standard and clear, based on what we already know. The real power of ACLs is that you can add to them. You are not restricted to the standard set of user, group, or other. You can add multiple users and groups with permissions specific to each.

To add the user sandra with read, write, and execute permissions to the ACL for a file named secrets.txt, use:

matthew@seymour:~$ **setfacl -m u:sandra:rwx secrets.txt**

To remove and reset sandra's permissions on the file to the file's defaults, use:

matthew@seymour:~$ **setfacl -r u:sandra: secrets.txt**

From these two examples, you can see that -m is for modify, -r is for remove.

ACLs permit similar actions with groups and others, just as we did with a user. Instead of the u: before the name, use a g: for groups and an o: for others, like this:

matthew@seymour:~$ **setfacl -m g:*groupname*:rwx secrets.txt**
matthew@seymour:~$ **setfacl -m o:r secrets.txt**

Notice that with others there is no user name or group name to include in the commands.

A useful feature is masking, by which you only list those permissions that are available. For example:

matthew@seymour:~$ **setfacl -m m:rx secrets.txt**

This limits everyone, regardless of any other settings. So, in this case, a group may have rwx settings on the file, but the mask here says to only permit rx, so rx will be the only settings that are available.

As an exercise to the reader, see if you can figure out the meaning of this output from getfacl for a file named coffeecup.conf.

```
# file: coffeecup.conf
# owner: matthew
```

```
# group: yirgacheffe
user::rw-
group::rw-
other::r--
group:qa:rwx
group:uat:rwx
mask::rwx
```

Working with Files

Managing files in your home directory involves using one or more easily remembered commands.

Creating a File with touch

To create an empty file called filename within your current directory, use the following command:

```
matthew@seymour:~$ touch filename
```

To edit this file, you must use a text editor. Several are discussed in Chapter 14, "Automating Tasks and Shell Scripting." However, it is sometimes useful to create an empty file as this creates an access record because of the time and date information that is connected to the file. You can also use touch to update this information, called a timestamp, without otherwise accessing or modifying a file.

You can create a file in a different location by changing what is after touch. To create a new file in /home/matthew/randomdirectory, if I am already in my home directory, I can use the following:

```
matthew@seymour:~$ touch randomdirectory/newfile
```

Or from anywhere using an absolute path, I use this:

```
matthew@seymour:~$ touch /home/matthew/randomdirectory/newfile
```

Or from anywhere using a path shortcut, I use the following command:

```
matthew@seymour:~$ touch ~/randomdirectory/newfile
```

Creating a Directory with mkdir

To create an empty directory called newdirectory within your current directory, use this command:

```
matthew@seymour:~$ mkdir newdirectory
```

10

You can create a directory in a different location by changing what is after `mkdir`. To create a new directory in `/home/matthew/music`, if I am already in my `/home` directory, I can use the following:

```
matthew@seymour:~$ mkdir music/newdirectory
```

Or from anywhere using an absolute path, I can use this:

```
matthew@seymour:~$ mkdir /home/matthew/music/newdirectory
```

Or from anywhere using a path shortcut, I can use the following command:

```
matthew@seymour:~$ mkdir ~/music/newdirectory
```

The `-p` option is valuable. It enables you to create a directory and its parent directories at the same time, if they do not already exist. This can be a real-time saver. If the parent directories exist, the command works normally. For example, suppose I want to make a new directory with two layers of subdirectories. In this example, `music` and `newdirectory` already exist, but `subdir1` and `subdir2` are to be created:

```
matthew@seymour:~$ mkdir -p ~/music/newdirectory/subdir1/subdir2
```

Deleting a Directory with `rmdir`

To delete an empty directory named `directoryname`, use the following command:

```
matthew@seymour:~$ rmdir directoryname
```

You can remove a directory in a different location by changing what is after `rmdir`. To remove a directory in `/home/matthew/music`, if I am already in my `/home` directory, I can use the following:

```
matthew@seymour:~$ rmdir music/directoryname
```

Or from anywhere using an absolute path, I can use this:

```
matthew@seymour:~$ rmdir /home/matthew/music/directoryname
```

Or from anywhere using a path shortcut, I can use the following command:

```
matthew@seymour:~$ rmdir ~/music/directoryname
```

The directory must be empty to be removed using `rmdir`. However, there is a way to remove a directory with its contents using `rm`.

CAUTION

You cannot easily recover anything that has been deleted using `rmdir` or `rm`, so proceed carefully. Be absolutely certain you will never need what you are about to delete before you do so. Only a professional data recovery service is likely to be able to recover the files, and even then at great expense.

Deleting a File or Directory with `rm`

To delete a file named filename, use this command:

```
matthew@seymour:~$ rm filename
```

You can remove a file in a different location by changing what is after `rm`. To remove a directory in /home/matthew/randomdirectory, if I am already in my /home directory, I can use the following:

```
matthew@seymour:~$ rm randomdirectory/filename
```

Or from anywhere using an absolute path, I can use this:

```
matthew@seymour:~$ rm /home/matthew/randomdirectory/filename
```

Or from anywhere using a path shortcut, I can use the following command:

```
matthew@seymour:~$ rm ~/randomdirectory/filename
```

If you try to use `rm` to remove an empty directory, you will receive an error message: `rm: cannot remove 'random/': Is a directory`. In this case, you must use `rmdir`. However, you can remove a directory and its contents using `rm`.

CAUTION

Be sure that all the contents of a directory are known and unwanted if you choose to delete them. There is no way to recover them later. Also, be careful that you don't have extra spaces, mistype the name of the directory, or use `sudo` to delete something that you shouldn't be deleting. Linux gives you great power, and it will let you use that power without questioning you about it; that's the human's job.

To delete a directory and all its contents, use the `-r` recursive switch. This switch works with many commands, not only `rm`:

```
matthew@seymour:~$ rm -r /home/matthew/randomdirectory/
```

Everything in randomdirectory as well as in the directory itself will be deleted, including other subdirectories, without considering whether they are empty or have contents.

Moving or Renaming a File with `mv`

In Linux land, moving and renaming a file are the same thing. It doesn't matter whether you are moving the directory to another or from one filename to another filename in the same directory, there is only one command to remember. To move a file named filename from ~/documents to ~/archive, use this command:

```
matthew@seymour:~$ mv documents/filename archive
```

Notice that the filename is not included in the destination. The destination here must be an existing directory. If it is not, the file is renamed to the term used. Some examples will make this clear.

To rename a file that is in my current directory, I could use the following:

```
matthew@seymour:~$ mv oldfilename newfilename
```

To rename a file as I move it from ~/documents to ~/archive, I could use this:

```
matthew@seymour:~$ mv documents/oldfilename archive/newfilename
```

Or from anywhere using an absolute path, I could use the following command:

```
matthew@seymour:~$ mv /home/matthew/documents/oldfilename
➥/home/matthew/archive/newfilename
```

Or from anywhere using a path shortcut, I could use this:

```
matthew@seymour:~$ mv ~/documents/oldfilename ~/archive/newfilename
```

Copying a File with cp

Copying works similarly to moving, but retains the original in the original location. To copy a file named filename from ~/documents to ~/archive, use this command:

```
matthew@seymour:~$ cp documents/filename archive
```

Notice that the filename is not included in the destination. The destination here must be an existing directory. If it is not, the file is renamed to the term used. Some examples will make this clear.

To copy a file that is in my current directory I could use the following, and it will work exactly the same as mv, except that both files will exist afterward:

```
matthew@seymour:~$ cp oldfilename newfilename
```

To rename a file as I copy it from ~/documents to ~/archive, I could use this:

```
matthew@seymour:~$ cp documents/oldfilename archive/newfilename
```

Or from anywhere using an absolute path, I could use the following command:

```
matthew@seymour:~$ cp /home/matthew/documents/oldfilename
➥/home/matthew/archive/newfilename
```

Or from anywhere using a path shortcut, I can use this:

```
matthew@seymour:~$ cp ~/documents/oldfilename ~/archive/newfilename
```

Displaying the Contents of a File with `cat`

To view the contents of a text file named `filename` on your screen, use this command:

matthew@seymour:~$ **cat filename**

Notice that the text is displayed on your screen but that you cannot edit or work with the text in any way. This command is convenient when you want to know the contents of a file but don't need to make any changes. Text editors for the terminal are covered in Chapter 12, "Command-Line Master Class Part 2." This command works best with short files because the contents of longer files will scroll off of the screen too quickly to be read.

Displaying the Contents of a File with `less`

When you need to view the contents of a longer text file from the command line, you can use `less`. This produces a paged output, meaning that output stops each time your screen is full. You can then use your up- and down-arrow keys and page-up and page-down keys to scroll through the contents of the file. Then, use `q` to quit and return to the command line:

matthew@seymour:~$ **less filename**

There was a program that did give paged output in the early days of UNIX called `more`. It was the first paged output program but did not include the ability to scroll up and down. `less` was written to add that capability and was named as a bit of hacker humor because "`less` is more." You can also use `more`, but today it is merely an alias for `less`.

Using Wildcards and Regular Expressions

Each of these commands can be used with pattern-matching strings known as *wildcards* or *regular expressions*. For example, to delete all files in the current directory beginning with the letters `abc`, you can use an expression beginning with the first three letters of the desired filenames. An asterisk (*) is then appended to match all these files. Use a command line with the `rm` command like this:

matthew@seymour:~$ **rm abc***

Linux shells recognize many types of file naming wildcards, but this is different from the capabilities of Linux commands supporting the use of more complex expressions. You learn more about using wildcards in Chapter 11, "Command-Line Master Class Part 1," and in Chapter 14, "Automating Tasks and Shell Scripting."

10

> **NOTE**
>
> You can also learn more about using expressions by reading the `grep` manual pages (man grep), but because both `man` and `grep` are covered in Chapter 11, "Command-Line Master Class Part 1," consider this mention as included only to whet your appetite.

Working as Root

The root, or super user account, is a special account and user on UNIX and Linux systems. Super user permissions are required in part because of the restrictive file permissions assigned to important system configuration files. You must have root permission to edit these files or to access or modify certain devices (such as hard drives). When logged in as root, you have total control over your system, which can be dangerous.

When you work in root, you can destroy a running system with a simple invocation of the `rm` command like this:

```
matthew@seymour:~$ sudo rm -rf /
```

This command line not only deletes files and directories but also could wipe out file systems on other partitions and even remote computers. This alone is reason enough to take precautions when using root access.

The only time you should run Linux as the super user is when you are configuring the file system, for example, or to repair or maintain the system. Logging in and using Linux as the root operator isn't a good idea because it defeats the entire concept of file permissions.

Knowing how to run commands as the super user (root) without logging in as root can help avoid serious missteps when configuring your system. In Ubuntu, you can use `sudo` to allow you to execute single commands as root and then quickly return to normal user status. For example, if you would like to edit your system's file system table (a text file that describes local or remote storage devices, their type, and location), you can use `sudo` like this:

```
matthew@seymour:~$ sudo nano -w /etc/fstab
[sudo] password for matthew:
```

After you press Enter, you are prompted for a password that gives you access to root. This extra step can also help you "think before you leap" into the command. Enter the root password, and you are then editing `/etc/fstab`, using the `nano` editor with line wrapping disabled (thanks to the `-w`).

CAUTION

Before editing any important system or software service configuration file, make a backup copy. Then make sure to launch your text editor with line wrapping disabled. If you edit a configuration file without disabling line wrapping, you could insert spurious carriage returns and line feeds into its contents, causing the configured service to fail when restarting. By convention, nearly all configuration files are formatted for 80-character text width, but this is not always the case. By default, the `vi` and `emacs` editors don't use line wrap.

Understanding and Fixing `sudo`

Most Ubuntu users never have a problem here, but sometimes, people who like to experiment break things, especially while learning. This section exists to help you first understand more completely how sudo works and also how to restore sudo access to a specific user when, for some reason, it has ceased to function for that user.

NOTE

You will usually know a problem has occurred because an error message like this will appear when a user tries to issue a command using sudo:

```
matthew@seymour:~$ sudo shutdown -h now
[sudo] password for matthew:
matthew is not in the sudoers file. This incident will be reported.
```

Sometimes, you might not even receive an error message, but the command issued simply does nothing. Either way, you can fix the problem using the following knowledge and procedure.

In order for a user to use sudo, the user account must belong to the *sudo* group and also be listed in the */etc/sudoers* file. If both conditions are met, the user will be permitted to temporarily use root powers for specific commands that are issued at the command line by that user account by prefacing the command with the word sudo.

A PROBLEM CAN OCCUR FOR A SPECIFIC USER WITH sudo WHEN

A user is taken out of the *sudo* group but should not have been. The permissions for the */etc/sudoers* file has been changed to anything other than 440. The */etc/sudoers* file has been changed in a way that does not allow members of the *sudo* group to use root powers.

TIP

Generally, these things are the result of a user doing something they should not have done, such as changing the permissions on all files rather than taking the time to figure out a specific file that is causing problems due to permissions issues. Take heed, it is better to spend a bit more time learning than it is to take a shortcut that causes bigger problems.

Fixing any of these problems requires the use of root powers. This is an obvious problem because if sudo is not working, then the account does not have access to root. To fix it, we must gain root access. You can do this by booting into *recovery mode* using the following steps:

1. Hold down the Shift key while the computer is booting.

2. When the GRUB menu page appears, use the arrow keys on your keyboard to scroll to the entry that ends with (recovery mode) and press Enter to select it.

3. When the boot process finishes, you have several options. Select the menu entry for root, which is described as Drop to Root Shell Prompt. You are now at the command line with full root access to the computer.

10

4. Ubuntu mounts filesystems as read-only by default in recovery mode, so you need to remount the root filesystem, /, as read-write so that you can fix the problem. Enter the following:

```
root@seymour:~# mount -o rw,remount /
```

NOTE

You now have complete root access and read-write privileges on the machine. This is an example of why security of a physical machine is important. If someone has physical access to your computer, he can easily and quickly gain full control over the machine and all it contains if he knows what he is doing.

If the problem exists because the user account was removed from the admin group, enter

```
root@seymour:~# adduser username admin
```

If the problem exists because the permissions for /etc/sudoers are wrong, enter

```
root@seymour:~# chmod 440 /etc/sudoers
```

If the problem exists because of an internal problem in /etc/sudoers, make a backup of the existing file and use visudo to edit it (this is a special use of the vi editor, covered in Chapter 12, "Command-Line Master Class Part 2," that runs a check on the file after editing to be certain that it is correct—this particular problem usually occurs when someone edits the file using another editor that does not make this check). The contents of the file should be the following:

```
#
# This file MUST be edited with the 'visudo' command as root.
#
# Please consider adding local content in /etc/sudoers.d/ instead of
# directly modifying this file.
#
# See the man page for details on how to write a sudoers file.
#
Defaults env_reset
Defaults secure_path="/usr/local/sbin:/usr/local/bin:/usr/sbin:/usr/bin:/sbin:/bin"

# Host alias specification

# User alias specification

# Cmnd alias specification

# User privilege specification
root ALL=(ALL:ALL) ALL
```

```
# Members of the admin group may gain root privileges
%admin ALL=(ALL) ALL

# Allow members of group sudo to execute any command
%sudo ALL=(ALL:ALL) ALL

# See sudoers(5) for more information on "#include" directives:

#includedir /etc/sudoers.d
```

After your fix is complete, exit the root command line:

```
root@seymour:~# exit
```

You return to the recovery mode menu. Select resume, described as Resume Normal Boot, to finish and return to a normal boot. When the boot completes, you should be able to use sudo correctly again.

Creating Users

When a Linux system administrator creates a user, an entry in /etc/passwd for the user is created. The system also creates a directory, labeled with the user's username, in the /home directory. For example, if you create a user named sandra, the user's home directory is /home/sandra.

> **NOTE**
>
> In this chapter, you learn how to manage users from the command line. See Chapter 13, "Managing Users," for more information on user administration including doing so using graphical administration utilities.

Use the adduser command, along with a user's name, to quickly create a user:

```
matthew@seymour:~$ sudo adduser sandra
```

After creating the user, you must also create the user's initial password with the passwd command:

```
matthew@seymour:~$ sudo passwd sandra

Changing password for user sandra.
New password:
Retype new password:
passwd: all authentication tokens updated successfully.
```

Enter the new password twice. If you do not create an initial password for a new user, the user cannot log in.

The `adduser` command has many command-line options. The command can be used to set policies and dates for the new user's password, assign a login shell, assign group membership, and other aspects of a user's account. See `man adduser` as well as Chapter 13, "Managing Users," for more info.

Deleting Users

Use the `deluser` command to delete users from your system. This command removes a user's entry in the system's `/etc/passwd` file. You should also use the command's `--remove-all-files` and `--remove-home` option to remove all the user's files and directories (such as the user's mail spool file under `/var/spool/mail`):

```
matthew@seymour:~$ sudo deluser --remove-all-files --remove-home andrew
```

If you do not use the `-remove-home` option, you have to manually delete the user's directory under `/home`, along with the user's `/var/spool/mail` queue.

Shutting Down the System

Use the `shutdown` command to shut down your system. The `shutdown` command has a number of different command-line options (such as shutting down at a predetermined time), but the fastest way to cleanly shut down Linux is to use the `-h` or halt option, followed by the word `now` or the numeral zero (0), like this:

```
matthew@seymour:~$ sudo shutdown -h now
```

or

```
matthew@seymour:~$ sudo shutdown -h 0
```

To incorporate a timed shutdown and a pertinent message to all active users, use `shutdown`'s time and message options, as follows:

```
matthew@seymour:~$ sudo shutdown -h 18:30 "System is going down for maintenance this
evening at 6:30 p.m. Please make sure you have saved your work and logged out by
then or you may lose data."
```

This example shuts down your system and provides a warning to all active users 15 minutes before the shutdown (or reboot). Shutting down a running server can be considered drastic, especially if there are active users or exchanges of important data occurring (such as a backup in progress). One good approach is to warn users ahead of time. This can be done by editing the system *Message of the Day (MOTD)* `motd` file, which displays a message to users when they log in using the command-line interface, as is common on multi-user systems.

It used to be that to create a custom MOTD you only had to use a text editor and change the contents of `/etc/motd`. However, this has changed in Ubuntu as the developers have added a way to automatically and regularly update some useful information contained in MOTD using `cron`. To modify how the MOTD is updated, you should install `update-motd` and read the man page.

You can also make downtimes part of a regular schedule, perhaps to coincide with security audits, software updates, or hardware maintenance.

You should shut down Ubuntu for only a few very specific reasons:

▶ You are not using the computer, no other users are logged in or expected to need or use the system, such as your personal desktop or laptop computer, and you want to conserve electrical power.

▶ You need to perform system maintenance that requires any or all system services to be stopped.

▶ You want to replace integral hardware.

TIP

Do not shut down your computer if you suspect that intruders have infiltrated your system; instead, disconnect the machine from any or all networks and make a backup copy of your hard drives. You might want to also keep the machine running to examine the contents of memory and to examine system logs. Exceptions to this are when the system contains only trivial data files and nonessential services, such as a personal computer that is only used to run a web browser, and when you have no intention of trying to track down what an intruder might have changed, either to repair the damage or to try to catch them using computer forensics, but rather plan to merely wipe everything clean and rebuild or reinstall the system from scratch.

Rebooting the System

You should also use the `shutdown` command to reboot your system. The fastest way to cleanly reboot Linux is to use the `-r` option, and the word `now` or the numeral zero (`0`):

```
matthew@seymour:~$ sudo shutdown -r now
```

or

```
matthew@seymour:~$ sudo shutdown -r 0
```

Both rebooting and shutting down can have dire consequences if performed at the wrong time (such as during backups or critical file transfers, which arouses the ire of your system's users). However, Linux-based operating systems are designed to properly stop active system services in an orderly fashion. Other commands you can use to shut down and reboot Linux are the `halt` and `reboot` commands, but the `shutdown` command is more flexible.

Commonly Used Commands and Programs

The following programs and built-in shell commands are commonly used when working at the command line. These commands are organized by category to help you understand the command's purpose. If you need to find full information for using the command, you can find that information under the command's man page.

▶ **Managing users and groups**—chage, chfn, chsh, edquota, gpasswd, groupadd, groupdel, groupmod, groups, mkpasswd, newgrp, newusers, passwd, umask, useradd, userdel, usermod

▶ **Managing files and file systems**—cat, cd, chattr, chmod, chown, compress, cp, dd, fdisk, find, gzip, ln, mkdir, mksfs, mount, mv, rm, rmdir, rpm, sort, swapon, swapoff, tar, touch, umount, uncompress, uniq, unzip, zip

▶ **Managing running programs**—bg, fg, kill, killall, nice, ps, pstree, renice, top, watch

▶ **Getting information**—apropos, cal, cat, cmp, date, diff, df, dir, dmesg, du, env, file, free, grep, head, info, last, less, locate, ls, lsattr, man, more, pinfo, ps, pwd, stat, strings, tac, tail, top, uname, uptime, vdir, vmstat, w, wc, whatis, whereis, which, who, whoami

▶ **Console text editors**—ed, jed, joe, mcedit, nano, red, sed, vim

▶ **Console Internet and network commands**—bing, elm, ftp, host, hostname, ifconfig, links, lynx, mail, mutt, ncftp, netconfig, netstat, pine, ping, pump, rdate, route, scp, sftp, ssh, tcpdump, traceroute, whois, wire-test

References

▶ https://help.ubuntu.com/community/UsingTheTerminal—The Ubuntu community help page for using the terminal.

▶ https://help.ubuntu.com/community/LinuxFilesystemTreeOverview— The Ubuntu community help page for and overview of the Linux file system tree.

▶ https://help.ubuntu.com/community/RootSudo—An Ubuntu community page explaining sudo, the philosophy behind using it by default, and how to use it.

CHAPTER 11

Command-Line Master Class Part 1

Some Linux users like to focus on the graphical environments that are available—they rush to tell new users that the command line isn't vital when using Linux. Although there are some amazing *graphical user interface (GUI)* desktops and this statement is mostly true, avoiding the command line limits your options and makes some tasks more difficult. The command-line interface is where the greatest power and flexibility are found, and those who actively avoid learning how to use it are also actively limiting their abilities and options. You learned the basics earlier in Chapter 10, "Command-Line Beginner's Class." In this chapter, we dig in deeper.

It is with some trepidation that this two-chapter set retains its classic title "Command-Line Master Class." Entire books have been published covering the depth and breadth of the command line. To believe that two short chapters make any reader a true master is foolish. Our greatest hope is to give enough information to enable any reader to perform all basic and vital tasks from the command line while inspiring readers to go on a quest to discover all the beauty and grandeur that we do not have space to cover here. Please keep this in mind as we continue.

In his book *The Art of Unix Programming*, Eric Raymond wrote a short story that perfectly illustrates the power of the command line versus the GUI. It's reprinted here with permission, for your reading pleasure:

> One evening, Master Foo and Nubi attended a gathering of programmers who had met to learn from each other. One of the programmers asked Nubi to what school he and his master

belonged. Upon being told they were followers of the Great Way of Unix, the programmer grew scornful.

"The command-line tools of Unix are crude and backward," he scoffed.

"Modern, properly designed operating systems do everything through a graphical user interface."

Master Foo said nothing, but pointed at the moon. A nearby dog began to bark at the master's hand.

"I don't understand you!" said the programmer.

Master Foo remained silent, and pointed at an image of the Buddha. Then he pointed at a window. "What are you trying to tell me?" asked the programmer.

Master Foo pointed at the programmer's head. Then he pointed at a rock.

"Why can't you make yourself clear?" demanded the programmer.

Master Foo frowned thoughtfully, tapped the programmer twice on the nose, and dropped him in a nearby trash can.

As the programmer was attempting to extricate himself from the garbage, the dog wandered over and piddled on him.

At that moment, the programmer achieved enlightenment.

Whimsical as the story is, it does illustrate that there are some things that the GUI just does not do well. Enter the command line: It is a powerful and flexible operating environment and—if you practice—can actually be quite fun, too!

In this chapter, you learn more commands to help you master the command line so that you can perform common tasks through it.

Why Use the Command Line?

Moving from the GUI to the command line is a conscious choice for most people, although it is increasingly rare that it is an absolute choice accompanied by a complete abandoning of GUIs.

Reasons for using the command line include the following:

▶ You want to chain two or more commands together.

▶ You want to use a command or parameter available only on the shell.

▶ You are working on a text-only system.

▶ You have used it for a long time and feel comfortable there.

▶ You want to automate a task.

Chaining two or more commands together, or *piping*, is what gives the shell its real power. Hundreds of commands are available, and by combining them in different ways you get tons of new options. Some of the shell commands are available through the GUI, but these commands usually have only a small subset of their parameters available, which limits what you can do with them.

Working from a text-only system is useful both for working locally with a broken GUI and for connecting to a remote, text-only system. If your Linux server is experiencing problems, the last thing you want to do is load it down with a GUI connection; working in text mode is faster and more efficient.

Many people use the shell simply because it is familiar to them. Some people even use the shell to start GUI applications just because it saves them taking their hands off the keyboard for a moment. This is not a bad thing; it provides fluency and ease with the system and is a perfectly valid way of working. Working from the command line is faster. The mouse is slow, and taking your fingers away from the keyboard makes your work even slower. Anyone looking to achieve the Zen-like power user state hinted at by Eric Raymond will understand this after making the effort to learn.

Knowing how to work in the shell is also essential if you wish to automate tasks on your system without use of the GUI. Whether you want to add a periodic task to cron or update a configuration management system, you will need to know what text commands to give in order to run programs from the command line.

Using Basic Commands

It is impossible to know how many commands the average command-line citizen uses, but if we had to guess, we would place it at about 25. Some of these were introduced in Chapter 10, "Command-Line Beginner's Class," but are covered here with greater depth. Others will be new to the reader. Still others are only mentioned in this list to give the reader ideas for further study. Here are some commands that every command-line user will want to learn:

- ▶ `cat`—Prints the contents of a file
- ▶ `cd`—Changes directories
- ▶ `chmod`—Changes file access permissions
- ▶ `cp`—Copies files
- ▶ `du`—Prints disk usage
- ▶ `emacs`—Edits text files
- ▶ `find`—Finds files by searching
- ▶ `grep`—Searches for a string in input
- ▶ `less`—Filters for paging through output
- ▶ `ln`—Creates links between files

▶ `locate`—Finds files from an index

▶ `ls`—Lists files in the current directory

▶ `make`—Compiles and installs programs

▶ `man`—Displays manual pages for reading

▶ `mkdir`—Makes directories

▶ `mv`—Moves files

▶ `nano`—Edits text files

▶ `rm`—Deletes files and directories

▶ `sort`—Takes a text file as input and outputs the contents of the file in the order you specify

▶ `ssh`—Connects to other machines using a secure shell connection

▶ `tail`—Prints the last lines of a file

▶ `vim`—Edits text files

▶ `which`—Prints the location of a command

Many other commands also are available to you that get used fairly often—`cut`, `diff`, `gzip`, `history`, `ping`, `su`, `tar`, `uptime`, `who`, and so on—but if you can understand the ones listed here, you have sufficient skill to concoct your own command combinations.

Note that we say *understand* the commands, not know all their possible parameters and usages. This is because several of the commands, although commonly used, are used only in any complex manner by people with specific needs. `make` is a good example of this: Unless you plan to become a programmer, you need not worry about this beyond just typing `make` and `make install` now and then. If you want to learn more, see Chapter 38, "Using Programming Tools for Ubuntu."

Similarly, `emacs`, `nano` and `vim` are text editors that have a text-based interface all their own and are covered later in this chapter, and SSH is covered in detail in Chapter 19, "Remote Access with SSH, Telnet, and VNC."

What remains is a set of commands, each of which has many parameters you can use to customize what it actually does. Again, we can eliminate much of this because many of the parameters are esoteric and rarely used, and the few times in your Linux life that you need them, you can just read the manual page.

We go over these commands one by one, explaining the most common ways to use them.

Printing the Contents of a File with `cat`

Many of Ubuntu's shell commands manipulate text strings, so if you want to be able to feed them the contents of files, you need to be able to output those files as text. Enter the `cat` command, which prints the contents of any files you pass to it.

Its most basic use is like this:

```
matthew@seymour:~$ cat myfile.txt
```

That prints the contents of myfile.txt. For this usage there are two extra parameters that are often used: -n numbers the lines in the output, and -s ("squeeze") prints a maximum of one blank line at a time. That is, if your file has 1 line of text, 10 blank lines, 1 line of text, 10 blank lines, and so on, -s shows the first line of text, a single blank line, the next line of text, a single blank line, and so forth. When you combine -s and -n, cat numbers only the lines that are printed—the 10 blank lines shown as one will count as 1 line for numbering.

This command prints information about your CPU, stripping out multiple blank lines and numbering the output:

```
matthew@seymour:~$ cat -sn /proc/cpuinfo
```

You can also use cat to print the contents of several files at once, like this:

```
matthew@seymour:~$ cat -s myfile.txt myotherfile.txt
```

In that command, cat merges myfile.txt and myotherfile.txt on the output, stripping out multiple blank lines. The important thing is that cat does not distinguish between the files in the output; there are no filenames printed and no extra breaks between the two. This allows you to treat the 2 as 1 or, by adding more files to the command line, to treat 20 files as 1.

Changing Directories with cd

Changing directories is surely something that has no options, right? Not so. cd is actually more flexible than most people realize. Unlike most of the other commands here, cd is not a command in itself—it is built in to bash (or whichever shell interpreter you are using), but it is still used like a command.

The most basic usage of cd is this:

```
matthew@seymour:~$ cd somedir
```

That looks in the current directory for the somedir subdirectory and then moves you into it. You can also specify an exact location for a directory, like this:

```
matthew@seymour:~$ cd /home/matthew/stuff/somedir
```

The first part of cd's magic lies in the characters (– and ~, a dash and a tilde). The first means "switch to my previous directory," and the second means "switch to my home directory." This conversation with cd shows this in action:

```
matthew@seymour:~$ cd /usr/local
matthew@seymour/usr/local$ cd bin
matthew@seymour/usr/local/bin$ cd -
```

```
/usr/local
matthew@seymour/usr/local$ cd ~
matthew@seymour:~$
```

In the first line, we change to `/usr/local` and get no output from the command. In the second line, we change to bin, which is a subdirectory of `/usr/local`. Next, `cd -` is used to change back to the previous directory. This time `bash` prints the name of the previous directory so we know where we are. Finally, `cd ~` is used to change back to our `/home` directory, although if you want to save an extra few keystrokes, just typing `cd` by itself is equivalent to `cd ~`.

The second part of `cd`'s magic is its capability to look for directories in predefined locations. When you specify an absolute path to a directory (that is, one starting with a /), `cd` always switches to that exact location. However, if you specify a relative subdirectory— for example, `cd subdir`—you can tell `cd` where you would like that to be relative to. This is accomplished with the `CDPATH` environment variable. If this variable is not set, `cd` always uses the current directory as the base; however, you can set it to any number of other directories.

This next example shows a test of this. It starts in `/home/matthew/empty`, an empty directory, and the lines are numbered for later reference:

```
1  matthew@seymour:~/empty$ pwd
2  /home/matthew/empty
3  matthew@seymour:~/empty$ ls
4  matthew@seymour:~/empty$ mkdir local
5  matthew@seymour:~/empty$ ls
6  local
7  matthew@seymour:~/empty$ cd local
8  matthew@seymour:~/empty/local$ cd ..
9  matthew@seymour:~/empty$ export CDPATH=/usr
10 matthew@seymour:~/empty$ cd local
11 /usr/local
12 matthew@seymour:/usr/local$ cd -
13 /home/matthew/empty
14 matthew@seymour:~/empty$ export CDPATH=.:/usr
15 matthew@seymour:~/empty$ cd local
16 /home/matthew/empty/local
17 matthew@seymour:~/empty/local$
```

Lines 1–3 show that we are in `/home/matthew/empty` and that it is indeed empty; `ls` had no output. Lines 4–6 show the `local` subdirectory being made, so that `/home/matthew/empty/local` exists. Lines 7 and 8 show you can `cd` into `/home/matthew/empty/local` and back out again.

In line 9, `CDPATH` is set to `/usr`. This was chosen because Ubuntu has the directory `/usr/local`, which means our current directory (`/home/matthew/empty`) and our `CDPATH` directory (`/usr`) both have a local subdirectory. In line 10, while in the `/home/matthew/empty` directory, we use `cd local`. This time, `bash` switches us to `/usr/local` and even prints the new directory to ensure we know what it has done.

Lines 12 and 13 move us back to the previous directory, `/home/matthew/empty`. In line 14, CDPATH is set to be `.:/usr`. The `:` is the directory separator, so this means `bash` should look first in the current directory, `.`, and then in the `/usr` directory. In line 15 `cd local` is issued again, this time moving to `/home/matthew/empty/local`. Note that `bash` has still printed the new directory; it does that whenever it looks up a directory in CDPATH.

Changing File Access Permissions with chmod

Your use of `chmod` can be greatly extended through one simple parameter: `-c`. This instructs `chmod` to print a list of all the changes it made as part of its operation, which means we can capture the output and use it for other purposes. For example:

```
matthew@seymour:~$ chmod -c 600 *
mode of '1.txt' changed to 0600 (rw------)
mode of '2.txt' changed to 0600 (rw------)
mode of '3.txt' changed to 0600 (rw------)
matthew@seymour:~$ chmod -c 600 *
matthew@seymour:~$
```

There the `chmod` command is issued with `-c`, and you can see it has output the result of the operation: Three files were changed to `rw------` (read and write by user only). However, when the command is issued again, no output is returned. This is because `-c` prints only the changes that it made. Files that already match the permissions you are setting are left unchanged and therefore are not printed.

There are two other parameters of interest: `--reference` and `-R`. The first allows you to specify a file to use as a template for permissions rather than specifying permissions yourself. For example, if you want all files in the current directory to have the same permissions as the file `/home/matthew/myfile.txt`, you use this:

```
chmod --reference /home/matthew/myfile.txt *
```

You can use `-R` to enable recursive operation, which means you can use it to `chmod` a directory and it will change the permissions of that directory as well as all files and subdirectories under that directory. You could use `chmod -R 600 /home` to change every file and directory under `/home` to become read/write to their owner(s).

Copying Files with cp

Like `mv`, which is covered later, `cp` is a command that is easily used and mastered. However, two marvelous parameters rarely see much use (which is a shame) despite their power. These are `--parents` and `-u`. The first copies the full path of the file into the new directory; the second copies only if the source file is newer than the destination.

Using `--parents` requires a little explanation, so here is an example. You have a file,`/home/matthew/desktop/documents/work/notes.txt`, and want to copy it to your `/home/`

`matthew/backup folder`. You could do a normal `cp`, but that would give you `/home/matthew/backup/notes.txt`, so how would you know where that came from later? If you use `--parents`, the file is copied to `/home/matthew/backup/desktop/ documents/work/notes.txt`.

The `-u` parameter is perfect for synchronizing two directories because it allows you to run a command like `cp -Ru myfiles myotherfiles` and have `cp` recopy only files that have changed. The `-R` parameter means recursive and enables you to copy directory contents.

Printing Disk Usage with `du`

The `du` command prints the size of each file and directory that is inside the current directory. Its most basic usage is as easy as it gets:

`matthew@seymour:~$ du`

That outputs a long list of directories and how much space their files take up. You can modify that with the `-a` parameter, which instructs `du` to print the size of individual files as well as directories. Another useful parameter is `-h`, which makes `du` use human-readable sizes like 18M (18MB) rather than 17532 (the same number in bytes, unrounded). The final useful basic option is `-c`, which prints the total size of files.

So, using `du` we can get a printout of the size of each file in our `/home` directory, in human-readable format, and with a summary at the end, like this:

`matthew@seymour:~$ du -ahc /home/matthew`

Two advanced parameters deal with filenames you want excluded from your count. The first is `--exclude`, which enables you to specify a pattern that should be used to exclude files. This pattern is a standard shell file matching pattern as opposed to a regular expression, which means you can use `?` to match a single character or `*` to match zero or many characters. You can specify multiple `--exclude` parameters to exclude several patterns. For example:

`matthew@seymour:~$ du --exclude="*.xml" --exclude="*.xsl"`

However, typing numerous `--exclude` parameters repeatedly is a waste of time, so you can use `-x` to specify a file that has the list of patterns you want excluded. The file should look like this:

`*.xml`
`*.xsl`

That is, each pattern you want excluded should be on a line by itself. If that file were called `xml_exclude.txt`, we could use it in place of the previous example, like this:

`matthew@seymour:~$ du -X xml_exclude.txt`

You can make your exclusion file as long as you need, or you can just specify multiple `-x` parameters.

> **TIP**
>
> Running du in a directory where several files are hard-linked to the same inode counts the size of the file only once. If you want to count each hard link separately for some reason, use the -1 parameter (lowercase *L*).

Using echo

You can do many things with echo, especially with redirection (see Chapter 12, "Command-Line Master Class Part 2," for more about redirecting output). In its simplest use, echo sends whatever you tell it to send to standard output. If you want to repeat text on the screen (useful in a shell script, for example), just enter the text string in single quotation marks ('), and the output appears below it, like this:

```
matthew@seymour:~$ echo 'I have the power!'
I have the power!
```

If you want to know the value of a system variable, such as, say, TERM, enter the variable name to ouput the value, like this:

```
matthew@seymour:~$ echo $TERM
xterm
```

You can redirect the output of echo into a text file, as when I want to add a new directory to my PATH, like this:

```
matthew@seymour:~$ echo 'export PATH=$PATH:/usr/local/bin' >> ~/.bashrc
```

You can change or set a kernel setting (1=on, 0=off) in /proc, like this:

```
matthew@seymour:~$ sudo sh -c 'echo "1"
>/proc/sys/location/of/setting'
```

Note that you can read the setting of a kernel value in /proc using cat.

Finding Files by Searching with find

The find command is one of the darkest and least understood areas of Linux, but it is also one of the most powerful. Admittedly, the find command does not help itself by using X-style parameters. The UNIX standard is -c, -s, and so on, whereas the GNU standard is --dosomething, --mooby, and so forth. X-style parameters merge the two by having words preceded by only one dash.

However, the biggest problem with find is that it has more options than most people can remember; it truly is capable of doing most things you could want. The most basic usage is this:

```
matthew@seymour:~$ find -name "*.txt"
```

That option searches the current directory and all subdirectories for files that end in .txt. The previous search finds files ending in .txt but not .TXT, .Txt, or other case variations.

To search without case sensitivity, use -iname rather than -name. You can optionally specify where the search should start before the -name parameter, like this:

```
matthew@seymour:~$ find /home -name "*.txt"
```

Another useful test is -size, which you use to specify how big the files should be to match. You can specify your size in kilobytes and optionally use + or - to specify greater than or less than. For example:

```
matthew@seymour:~$ find /home -name "*.txt" -size 100k
matthew@seymour:~$ find /home -name "*.txt" -size +100k
matthew@seymour:~$ find /home -name "*.txt" -size -100k
```

The first example brings up files of exactly 100KB, the second only files larger than 100KB, and the last only files under 100KB.

Moving on, the -user option enables you to specify the user who owns the files you are looking for. So, to search for all files in /home that end with .txt, that are under 100KB, and that are owned by user matthew, you use this:

```
matthew@seymour:~$ find /home -name "*.txt" -size -100k -user matthew
```

You can flip any of the conditions by specifying -not before them. For example, you can add a -not before -user matthew to find matching files owned by everyone but matthew:

```
matthew@seymour:~$ find /home -name "*.txt" -size -100k -not -user matthew
```

You can add as many -not parameters as you need, even using -not -not to cancel each other out. (Yes, that is pointless.) Keep in mind, though, that -not -size -100k is essentially equivalent to -size +100k, with the exception that the former will match files of exactly 100KB whereas the latter will not.

You can use -perm to specify which permissions a file should have for it to be matched. This is tricky, so read carefully. The permissions are specified in the same way as with the chmod command: u for user, g for group, o for others, r for read, w for write, and x for execute. However, before you give the permissions, you need to specify a plus, a minus, or a blank space. If you specify neither a plus nor a minus, the files must exactly match the mode you give. If you specify -, the files must match all the modes you specify. If you specify +, the files must match any the modes you specify. Confused yet?

The confusion can be cleared up with some examples. This next command finds all files that have permission o=r (readable for other users). Notice that if you remove the -name parameter, it is equivalent to * because all filenames are matched:

```
matthew@seymour:~$ find /home -perm -o=r
```

Any files that have o=r set are returned from that query. Those files also might have u=rw and other permissions, but as long as they have o=r, they will match. This next query matches all files that have o=rw set:

```
matthew@seymour:~$ find /home -perm -o=rw
```

However, that query does not match files that are `o=r` or `o=w`. To be matched, a file must be readable and writeable by other users. If you want to match readable or writeable (or both), you need to use `+`, like this:

```
matthew@seymour:~$ find /home -perm +o=rw
```

Similarly, this next query matches only files that are readable by user, group, and others:

```
matthew@seymour:~$ find /home -perm -ugo=r
```

Whereas this query matches files as long as they are readable by the user, or by the group, or by others, or by any combination of the three:

```
matthew@seymour:~$ find /home -perm +ugo=r
```

If you use neither `+` or `-`, you are specifying the exact permissions to search for. For example, the next query searches for files that are readable by user, group, and others but not writeable or executable by anyone:

```
matthew@seymour:~$ find /home -perm ugo=r
```

You can be as specific as you need to be with the permissions. For example, this query finds all files that are readable for the user, group, and others and writeable by the user:

```
matthew@seymour:~$ find /home -perm ugo=r,u=w
```

To find files that are not readable by others, use the `-not` condition, like this:

```
matthew@seymour:~$ find /home -not -perm +o=r
```

Now, on to the most advanced aspect of the find command: the `-exec` parameter. This enables you to execute an external program each time a match is made, passing in the name of the matched file wherever you want it. This has very specific syntax: Your command and its parameters should follow immediately after `-exec`, terminated by `\;`. You can insert the filename match at any point using `{}` (an opening and a closing brace side by side).

So, you can match all text files on the entire system (that is, searching recursively from `/` rather than from `/home` as in our previous examples) over 10KB, owned by `matthew`, that are not readable by other users, and then use `chmod` to enable reading, like this:

```
matthew@seymour:~$ find / -name "*.txt" -size +10k -user matthew -not -perm +o=r
➥-exec chmod o+r {} \;
```

When you type your own `-exec` parameters, be sure to include a space before `\;`. Otherwise, you might see an error such as `missing argument to '-exec'`.

Do you see now why some people think the `find` command is scary? Many people learn just enough about `find` to be able to use it in a very basic way, but hopefully you will see how much it can do if you give it a chance.

Searches for a String in Input with grep

The grep command, like find, is an incredibly powerful search tool in the right hands. Unlike find, though, grep processes any text, whether in files, or just in standard input.

The basic usage of grep is this:

```
matthew@seymour:~$ grep "some text" *
```

That searches all files in the current directory (but not subdirectories) for the string some text and prints matching lines along with the name of the file. To enable recursive searching in subdirectories, use the -r parameter, as follows:

```
matthew@seymour:~$ grep -r "some text" *
```

Each time a string is matched within a file, the filename and the match are printed. If a file contains multiple matches, each of the matches is printed. You can alter this behavior with the -1 parameter (lowercase *L*), which forces grep to print the name of each file that contains at least one match, without printing the matching text. If a file contains more than one match, it is still printed only once. Alternatively, the -c parameter prints each filename that was searched and includes the number of matches at the end, even if there were no matches.

You have a lot of control when specifying the pattern to search for. You can, as we did previously, specify a simple string like some text, or you can invert that search by specifying the -v parameter. For example, the following returns all the lines of the file myfile.txt that do not contain the word *hello*:

```
matthew@seymour:~$ grep -v "hello" myfile.txt
```

You can also use regular expressions for your search term. For example, you can search myfile.txt for all references to *cat*, *sat*, or *mat* with this command:

```
matthew@seymour:~$ grep "[cms]at" myfile.txt
```

Adding the -i parameter to that removes case sensitivity, matching *Cat*, *CAT*, *MaT*, and so on:

```
matthew@seymour:~$ grep -i [cms]at myfile.txt
```

You can also control the output to some extent with the -n and —color parameters. The first tells grep to print the line number for each match, which is where it appears in the source file. The —color parameter tells grep to color the search terms in the output, which helps them stand out when among all the other text on the line. You choose which color you want using the GREP_COLOR environment variable: export GREP_COLOR=36 gives you cyan, and export GREP_COLOR=32 gives you lime green.

This next example uses these two parameters to number and color all matches to the previous command:

```
matthew@seymour:~$ grep -in —color [cms]at myfile.txt
```

Later you learn how important grep is for piping with other commands.

Paging Through Output with `less`

The `less` command enables you to view large amounts of text in a more convenient way than the `cat` command. For example, your `/etc/passwd` file is probably more than a screen long, so if you run `cat /etc/passwd`, you are not able to see what the lines at the top were. Using `less /etc/passwd` enables you to use the cursor keys to scroll up and down the output freely. Type `q` to quit and return to the shell.

On the surface, `less` sounds like an easy command; however, it has the infamy of being one of the few Linux commands that have a parameter for every letter of the alphabet. That is, `-a` does something, `-b` does something else, `-c`, `-d`, `-e` ... `-x`, `-y`, `-z`; they all do things, with some letters even differentiating between upper- and lowercase. Furthermore, these parameters are only used when invoking `less`. After you are viewing your text, even more commands are available. Make no mistake, `less` is a complex beast to master.

Input to `less` can be divided into two categories: what you type before running `less` and what you type while running it. The former category is easy, so we start there.

We have already discussed how many parameters `less` can take, but they can be distilled down to three that are very useful: `-M`, `-N`, and `+`. Adding `-M` (this is different from `-m`) enables verbose prompting in `less`. Instead of just printing a colon and a flashing cursor, `less` prints the filename, the line numbers being shown, the total number of lines, and the percentage of how far you are through the file. Adding `-N` (again, this is different from `-n`) enables line numbering.

The last option, `+`, enables you to pass a command to `less` for it to execute as it starts. To use this, you first need to know the commands available to you in `less`, which means it's time to move to the second category of `less` input: what you type while `less` is running.

The basic navigation keys are the up, down, left, and right cursors; Home and End (for navigating to the start and end of a file); and Page Up and Page Down. Beyond that, the most common command is /, which initiates a text search. You type what you want to search for and press Enter to have `less` find the `first` match and highlight all subsequent matches. Type / again and press Enter to have `less` jump to the next match. The inverse of that is ?, which searches backward for text. Type ?, enter a search string, and press Enter to go to the first previous match of that string, or just use ? and press Enter to go to the next match preceding the current position. You can use / and ? interchangeably by searching for something with / and then using ? to go backward in the same search.

Searching with / and ? is commonly used with the + command-line parameter from earlier, which passes `less` a command for execution after the file has loaded. For example, you can tell `less` to load a file and place the cursor at the first match for the search *hello*, like this:

```
matthew@seymour:~$ less +/hello myfile.txt
```

Or, to place the cursor at the last match for the search *hello*:

```
matthew@seymour:~$ less +?hello myfile.txt
```

Beyond the cursor keys, the controls primarily involve typing a number and then pressing a key. For example, to go to line 50 you type 50g, or to go to the 75 percent point of the file you type 75p. You can also place invisible mark points through the file by pressing m and then typing a single letter. Later, while in the same less session, you can press ' (a single quote) and then type the letter, and it moves you back to the same position. You can set up to 52 marks, named a–z and A–Z.

One clever feature of less is that you can, at any time, press v to have your file open inside your text editor. This defaults to vim, but you can change that by setting the EDITOR environment variable to something else.

If you have made it this far, you can already use less better than most users. You can, at this point, justifiably skip to the next section and consider yourself proficient with less. However, if you want to be a less guru, there are two more things to learn: how to view multiple files simultaneously and how to run shell commands.

Like most other file-based commands in Linux, less can take several files as its parameters. For example:

```
matthew@seymour:~$ less -MN 1.txt 2.txt 3.txt
```

That loads all three files into less, starting at 1.txt. When viewing several files, less usually tells you which file you are in, as well as numbering them: 1.txt (file 1 of 3) should be at the bottom of the screen. However, certain things make that go away, so you should use -M anyway.

You can navigate between files by typing a colon and then pressing n to go to the next file or press p to go to the previous file; these are referred to from now on as :n and :p. You can open another file for viewing by typing :e and providing a filename. This can be any file you have permission to read, including files outside the local directory. Use Tab to complete filenames. Files you open in this way are inserted one place after your current position, so if you are viewing file 1 of 4 and open a new file, the new file is numbered 2 of 5 and is opened for viewing right away. To close a file and remove it from the list, use :d.

Viewing multiple files simultaneously has implications for searching. By default, less searches within only one file, but it is easy to search within all files. When you type / or ? to search, follow it with a *. You should see EOF-ignore followed by a search prompt. You can now type a search and it searches in the current file; if nothing is found, it looks in subsequent files until it finds a match. You can repeat searches by pressing Esc and then either n or N. The lowercase option repeats the search forward across files, and the uppercase repeats it backward.

The last thing you need to know is that you can get to a shell from less and execute commands. The simplest way to do this is just to type ! and press Enter. This launches a shell and leaves you free to type all the commands you want, as per normal. Type exit to return to less. You can also type specific commands by entering them after the exclamation mark, using the special character % for the current filename. For example, du -h % prints the size of the current file. Finally, you can use !! to repeat the previous command.

Creating Links Between Files with `ln`

Linux allows you to create links between files that look and work like normal files for the most part. Moreover, it allows you to make two types of links, known as hard links and *symbolic links (symlinks)*. The difference between the two is crucial, although it might not be obvious at first.

Each filename on your system points to what is known as an inode, which is the absolute location of a file. Linux allows you to point more than one filename to a given inode, and the result is a hard link—two filenames pointing to the same file. Each of these files shares the same contents and attributes. So, if you edit one, the other changes because they are both the same file.

On the other hand, a symlink—sometimes called a soft link—is a redirect to the real file. When a program tries to read from a symlink, it automatically is redirected to what the symlink is pointing at. The fact that symlinks are really just dumb pointers has two advantages: You can link to something that does not exist (and create it later if you want), and you can link to directories.

Both types of links have their uses. Creating a hard link is a great way to back up a file on the same disk. For example, if you delete the file in one location, it still exists untouched in the other location. Symlinks are popular because they allow a file to appear to be in a different location; you could store your website in `/var/www/live` and an under-construction holding page in `/var/www/construction`. Then you could have Apache point to a symlink `/var/www/html` that is redirected to either the live or construction directory, depending on what you need.

> **TIP**
>
> The `shred` command overwrites a file's contents with random data, allowing for safe deletion. Because this directly affects a file's contents, rather than just a filename, this means that all filenames hard linked to an inode are affected.

Both types of link are created using the `ln` command. By default, it creates hard links, but you can create symlinks by passing it the `-s` parameter. The syntax is `ln [-s] something somewhere`, for example:

```
matthew@seymour:~$ ln -s myfile.txt mylink
```

That creates the symlink `mylink` that points to `myfile.txt`. You don't see it here, but the file I created is 341 bytes. This is important later. Remove the `-s` to create a hard link. You can verify that your link has been created by running `ls -l`. Your symlink should look something like this:

```
lrwxrwxrwx  1 matthew matthew    5 Feb 19 12:39 mylink -> myfile.txt
```

Note how the file properties start with l (lowercase *L*) for link and how ls -l also prints where the link is going. Symlinks are always very small in size; the previous link is 5 bytes. If you created a hard link, it should look like this:

```
-rw-rw-r    2 matthew matthew    341 Feb 19 12:39 mylink
```

This time the file has normal attributes, but the second number is 2 rather than 1. That number is how many hard links point to this file, which is why it is 2 now. The file size is also the same as that of the previous filename because it is the file, as opposed to just being a pointer.

Symlinks are used extensively in Linux. Programs that have been superseded, such as sh, now point to their replacements (in this case bash), and library versioning is accomplished through symlinks. For example, applications that link against zlib load /usr/lib/libz. so. Internally, however, that is just a symlink that points to the actual zlib library: /usr/lib/libz.so.1.2.1.2. This enables multiple versions of libraries to be installed without application developers needing to worry about these specific details.

Finding Files from an Index with locate

When you use the find command, it searches recursively through each directory each time you request a file. This is slow, as you can imagine. Fortunately, Ubuntu ships with a cron job that creates an index of all the files on your system every night. Searching this index is extremely fast, which means that if the file you are looking for has been around since the last index, this is the preferable way of searching.

To look for a file in your index, use the command locate followed by the names of the files you want to find, like this:

```
matthew@seymour:~$ locate myfile.txt
```

On a relatively modern computer (say, with at least one processor that runs at 1.5GHz or higher), locate should be able to return all the matching files in less than one second. The trade-off for this speed is lack of flexibility. You can search for matching filenames, but, unlike find, you cannot search for sizes, owners, access permissions, or other attributes. The one thing you can change is case sensitivity; use the -i parameter to do a search that is not case sensitive.

Although Ubuntu rebuilds the filename index nightly, you can force a rebuild whenever you want by running the command updatedb with sudo. This usually takes a few minutes, but when it's done the new database is immediately available.

Listing Files in the Current Directory with ls

The ls command, like ln, is one of those you expect to be very straightforward. It lists files, but how many options can it possibly have? In true Linux style, the answer is many, although again you need only know a few to wield great power!

The basic usage is simply ls, which lists the files and directories in the current location. You can filter that using normal wildcards, so all these are valid:

```
matthew@seymour:~$ ls *
matthew@seymour:~$ ls *.txt
matthew@seymour:~$ ls my*ls *.txt *.xml
```

11

Any directories that match these filters are recursed into one level. That is, if you run `ls my*` and you have the files `myfile1.txt` and `myfile2.txt` and a directory `mystuff`, the matching files are printed first. Then `ls` prints the contents of the `mystuff` directory.

The most popular parameters for customizing the output of `ls` are as follows:

- ▶ `-a`—Includes hidden files
- ▶ `-h`—Uses human-readable sizes
- ▶ `-l` **(lowercase *L*)**—Enables long listing
- ▶ `-r`—Reverse order
- ▶ `-R`—Recursively lists directories
- ▶ `-s`—Shows sizes
- ▶ `--sort`—Sorts the listing

All files that start with a period are hidden in Linux, so that includes the `.gnome` directory in your `/home` directory, as well as `.bash_history` and the `.` and `..` implicit directories that signify the current directory and the parent. By default, `ls` does not show these files, but if you run `ls -a`, they are shown. You can also use `ls -A` to show all the hidden files except `.` and `...`.

The `-h` parameter needs to be combined with the `-s` parameter, like this:

```
matthew@seymour:~$ ls -sh *.txt
```

That outputs the size of each matching file in a human-readable format, such as 108KB or 4.5MB.

Using the `-l` parameter enables you to get much more information about your files. Instead of just providing the names of the files, you get output like this:

```
drwxrwxr-x 24 matthew matthew  4096 Dec 24 21:33 arch
-rw-r--r--  1 matthew matthew 18691 Dec 24 21:34 COPYING
-rw-r--r--  1 matthew matthew 88167 Dec 24 21:35 CREDITS
drwxrwxr-x  2 matthew matthew  4096 Dec 24 21:35 crypto
```

That shows four matches and prints a lot of information about each of them. The first row shows the arch directory; you can tell it is a directory because its file attributes starts with a `d`. The `rwxrwxr-x` following that shows the access permissions, and this has special meanings because it is a directory. Read access for a directory enables users to see the directory contents, write access enables you to create files and subdirectories, and execute access enables you to `cd` into the directory. If a user has execute access but not read access, the user can `cd` into the directory but not list files.

Moving on, the next number on the line is 24, which also has a special meaning for directories: It is the number of subdirectories (including . and . .). After that is matthew matthew, which is the name of the user owner and the group owner for the directory. Next is the size and modification time, and finally the directory name itself.

The next line shows the file COPYING, and most of the numbers have the same meaning, with the exception of the 1 immediately after the access permissions. For directories, this is the number of subdirectories, but for files this is the number of hard links to this file. A 1 in this column means this is the only filename pointing to this inode, so if you delete it, it is gone.

Ubuntu comes configured with a shortcut command for ls -l: ll.

The --sort parameter enables you to reorder the output from the default alphabetic sorting. You can sort by various things, although the most popular are extension (alphabetically), size (largest first), and time (newest first). To flip the sorting (making size sort by smallest first), use the -r parameter also. So, the following command lists all .ogg files, sorted smallest to largest:

```
matthew@seymour:~$ ls --sort size -r *.ogg
```

Finally, the -R parameter recurses through subdirectories. For example, typing ls /etc lists all the files and subdirectories in /etc, but ls -R /etc lists all the files in and subdirectories in /etc, all the files and subdirectories in /etc/acpi, all the files and subdirectories in /etc/acpi/actions, and so on until every subdirectory has been listed.

Listing System Information with lsblk, lshw, lsmod, and lspci

These commands are not really related to ls, but they work in a similar way. Here, the focus is on listing information about your system rather than the contents of a directory.

To list the storage, or *block*, devices that are attached to your system, use:

```
matthew@seymour:~$ lsblk
NAME    MAJ:MIN RM    SIZE RO TYPE MOUNTPOINT
sda       8:0    0 465.8G  0 disk
├─sda1    8:1    0     1K  0 part
├─sda2    8:2    0 453.7G  0 part /
└─sda5    8:5    0  12.1G  0 part [SWAP]
sdb       8:16   0   1.4T  0 disk
└─sdb1    8:17   0   1.4T  0 part
sr0      11:0    1  1024M  0 rom
```

The next command must be run as root for a full listing. Note that the output may be quite long, so this command may be most useful if you pipe it into grep and search for a specific bit of text, as described in Chapter 12, "Command-Line Master Class Part 2." To list the hardware detected in your system, use:

```
matthew@seymour:~$ sudo lshw
```

To list the status of modules in the Linux kernel, use this, which takes the contents of /proc/modules and formats it nicely:

```
matthew@seymour:~$ lsmod
```

To list the PCI devices attached to your system, use:

```
matthew@seymour:~$ lspci
```

Reading Manual Pages with man

Time for a much-needed mental break: The man command is easy to use. Most people use only the topic argument, like this: man gcc. However, two other commands work closely with man that are very useful: whatis and apropos.

The whatis command returns a one-line description of another command, which is the same text you get at the top of that command's man page. For example:

```
matthew@seymour:~$ whatis ls
ls    (1) - list directory contents
```

The output explains what ls does but also provides the man page section number for the command so you can query it further.

The apropos command takes a search string as its parameter and returns all man pages that match the search. For example, apropos mixer returns this list:

```
alsamixer (1) - soundcard mixer for ALSA soundcard driver
mixer (1) - command-line mixer for ALSA soundcard driver
aumix (1) - adjust audio mixer
```

So, use apropos to help you find commands and use whatis to tell you what a command does.

One neat trick is that many of the tips and tricks we learned for less also work when viewing man pages (for example, using / and ? to search). This is one of the beautiful things about UNIX systems: Gaining knowledge in one area often benefits you in other areas.

You can use a number of other commands to search the file system, including the following:

▶ **whereis command**—Returns the location of the command (for example, /bin, /sbin, or /usr/bin/*command*) and its man page, which is an entry for the command included as a file already on your computer in a standardized manual format.

▶ **whatis command**—Returns a one-line synopsis from the command's man page.

▶ **type name**—Returns how a name would be interpreted if used as a command. This generally shows options or the location of the binary that will be used. For example, type ls returns ls is aliased to 'ls –color=auto'.

Making Directories with `mkdir`

Making directories is as easy as it sounds, although there is one parameter you should be aware of: `-p`. If you are in `/home/matthew` and you want to create the directory `/home/matthew/audio/sound`, you get an error like this:

```
mkdir: cannot create directory 'audio/sound': No such file or directory
```

At first glance, this seems wrong; `mkdir` cannot create the directory because it does not exist. What it actually means is that it cannot create the directory sound because the directory audio does not exist. This is where the `-p` parameter comes in: If you try to make a directory within another directory that does not exist, like the previous, `-p` creates the parent directories, too. So:

```
matthew@seymour:~$ mkdir -p audio/sound
```

That first creates the audio directory and then creates the sound directory inside it.

Moving Files with `mv`

This command is one of the easiest around. There are two helpful parameters to `mv`: `-f`, which overwrites files without asking; and `-u`, which moves the source file only if it is newer than the destination file. That's it. You can use absolute paths to indicate the destination directory (starting from /) or relative paths from the current directory (starting without a slash). This is generally entered in the source directory, but it doesn't have to be; you can use an absolute path to indicate the source directory, too.

```
matthew@seymour:~$ mv filename /newdirectory/newfilename
```

Renaming Files with `rename`

We often use `mv` to rename a single file. This would be tedious, however, for renaming multiple files. For this, we use `rename`. The basic syntax is simple:

```
matthew@seymour:~$ rename 's/filename/newfilename/'
```

The part in the single quotes is a Perl expression, meaning the command is far more powerful than this example suggests. Let's say we have a directory filled with files that end with a .htm extension, and we want to rename them all to .html:

```
matthew@seymour:~$ rename 's/\.htm/\.html/' *.htm
```

Notice here that the . characters must be preceded with a \ to let the command know they are part of the text being searched out and replaced rather than part of the command. This is called "escaping" the characters. Next, notice the replace part of the command is followed by a wildcard character (*) and the remainder of the filename to search for in the directory. Anything matching the combination of *filename*.htm will be renamed to *filename*.html.

`rename` is incredibly powerful. See the man page for more.

Deleting Files and Directories with rm

The rm command has only one parameter of interest: –preserve-root. By now, you should know that issuing rm -rf / with sudo destroys your Linux installation because -r means recursive and -f means force (do not prompt for confirmation before deleting). It is possible for a clumsy person to issue this command by accident—not by typing the command on purpose, but by putting a space in the wrong place. For example:

```
matthew@seymour:~$ rm -rf /home/matthew
```

That command deletes the /home directory of the user matthew. This is not an uncommon command; after you have removed a user and backed up the user's data, you will probably want to issue something similar. However, if you add an accidental space between the / and the *h* in *home*, you get this:

```
matthew@seymour:~$ rm -rf / home/matthew
```

This time the command means "delete everything recursively from / and then delete home/matthew"—quite a different result! You can stop this from happening by using the --preserve-root parameter, which stops you from catastrophe with this message:

```
rm: it is dangerous to operate recursively on '/'
rm: use --no-preserve-root to override this failsafe.
```

However, no one wants to keep typing --preserve-root each time when running rm, so you could add this line to the .bashrc file in your /home directory:

```
alias rm='rm --preserve-root'
```

That alias automatically adds --preserve-root to all calls to rm in future bash sessions. Ubuntu (and Debian and perhaps other distributions now) have done this by default, not by adding an alias in bashrc, but by making --preserve-root the default for the command.

Sorting the Contents of a File with sort

You have a text file. You want to sort its contents alphabetically. That is easy. Let's assume our test file is filled with one letter on each line, upper or lower case.

```
matthew@seymour:~$ sort testfile.txt
a
A
b
B
```

That is useful. You can also sort in reverse order:

```
matthew@seymour:~$ sort -r testfile.txt
```

This will output the same contents, but this time from Z to a.

You can use sort with files of numbers, but you don't want a normal sort. That will give you output like this.

```
matthew@seymour:~$ sort numberfile.txt
1
14
5
58
6
```

The command performs a rather useless alphabetic style sorting. Fortunately, there is a switch we can use.

```
matthew@seymour:~$ sort -n numberfile.txt
1
5
6
14
58
```

There are tons of neat tricks you can do with sort and many more parameters explained in the man file. For files with a number of columns, such as a directory listing maybe, you can pick which column you use to sort by using the -k switch and the number of the column, such as with this example of a directory of old Conky files. We will start with an ls command for comparison.

```
matthew@seymour:~/conky$ ls -la
total 60
drwxr-xr-x  2 matt matt 4096 Dec 25  2012 .
drwxr-xr-x 91 matt matt 4096 Jul 28 18:42 ..
-rwxr-xr-x  1 matt matt 5526 Dec 25  2012 conkyrc_main
-rwxr-xr-x  1 matt matt 5502 Dec 25  2012 conkyrc_main~
-rwxr-xr-x  1 matt matt 5387 Apr 16  2008 conkyrc_main (old)
-rwxr-xr-x  1 matt matt 1326 Mar 15  2008 conkyrc_weather
-rwxr-xr-x  1 matt matt 2549 Oct 23  2009 sample_conky.conf
-rwxr-xr-x  1 matt matt  128 Apr  8  2008 start_conky (copy).sh
-rwxr-xr-x  1 matt matt  139 Dec 25  2012 start_conky.sh
-rwxr-xr-x  1 matt matt  140 Dec 25  2012 start_conky.sh~
-rwxr-xr-x  1 matt matt 1503 Sep 30  2007 weather.sh
-rwxr-xr-x  1 matt matt 2379 Sep 30  2007 weather.xslt
And here is the same listing, this time sorted by file size.

matthew@seymour:~$ ls -la | sort -n -k5
total 60
-rwxr-xr-x  1 matt matt  128 Apr  8  2008 start_conky (copy).sh
-rwxr-xr-x  1 matt matt  139 Dec 25  2012 start_conky.sh
-rwxr-xr-x  1 matt matt  140 Dec 25  2012 start_conky.sh~
-rwxr-xr-x  1 matt matt 1326 Mar 15  2008 conkyrc_weather
```

```
-rwxr-xr-x  1 matt matt 1503 Sep 30  2007 weather.sh
-rwxr-xr-x  1 matt matt 2379 Sep 30  2007 weather.xslt
-rwxr-xr-x  1 matt matt 2549 Oct 23  2009 sample_conky.conf
drwxr-xr-x  2 matt matt 4096 Dec 25  2012 .
drwxr-xr-x 91 matt matt 4096 Jul 28 18:42 ..
-rwxr-xr-x  1 matt matt 5387 Apr 16  2008 conkyrc_main (old)
-rwxr-xr-x  1 matt matt 5502 Dec 25  2012 conkyrc_main~
-rwxr-xr-x  1 matt matt 5526 Dec 25  2012 conkyrc_main
```

Printing the Last Lines of a File with `tail`

If you want to watch a log file as it is written to, or want to monitor a user's actions as they are occurring, you need to be able to track log files as they change. In these situations, you need the `tail` command, which prints the last few lines of a file and updates as new lines are added. This command tells tail to print the last few lines of `/var/log/apache2/access.log`, the Apache hit log:

```
matthew@seymour:~$ tail /var/log/apache2/access.log
```

To get tail to remain running and update as the file changes, add the `-f` parameter (follow):

```
matthew@seymour:~$ tail -f /var/log/apache2/access.log
```

You can tie the lifespan of a tail follow to the existence of a process by specifying the `--pid` parameter. When you do this, `tail` continues to follow the file you asked for until it sees that the process identified by *process ID (PID)* is no longer running, at which point it stops tailing.

If you specify multiple files on the command line, `tail` follows both, printing file headers whenever the input source changes. Press Ctrl+C to terminate `tail` when in follow mode.

Printing the Location of a Command with `which`

The purpose of `which` is to tell you the exact command that would be executed if you typed it. For example, `which mkdir` returns `/bin/mkdir`, telling you that running the command `mkdir` runs `/bin/mkdir`.

Download Files with `wget`

Let's say you see a website with useful content that you need to download to your server, say http://releases.ubuntu.com/, because you want to make a copy of the ISO of the current release of Ubuntu available to students that work in your computer lab. This is called *mirroring* and is a commonly accepted practice. Or, maybe you want to download the latest Minecraft server file to your server and don't want to download it from the website to your local machine first, before you upload it to your server. You can do this with wget, which exists to download files using HTTP, HTTPS, and FTP, like this:

```
matthew@seymour:~$ wget http://releases.ubuntu.com/16.04/ubuntu-16.04-desktop-
➥amd64.iso
```

This downloads the linked file directly to the directory in which you issue the command.

What if you wanted to copy all of the content files from your existing web server onto a new server? You can use the `-m` or the `--mirror` flag to do this. This example downloads all of the contents of the directory you specify, assuming you have access, to your current directory:

```
matthew@seymour:~$ wget http://youroldserver.com/website/files
```

> **TIP**
>
> You can use `wget` with any standard URL syntax, including specifying ports and usernames and passwords, but you should realize that the username and password information will be transmitted in plain text; therefore, this is not considered a secure method of data transfer. For that, use `scp.`, which is covered in Chapter 19, "Remote Access with SSH, Telnet, and VNC."

References

▶ www.gnu.org/—The website of the GNU project, it contains manuals and downloads for lots of command-line software.

▶ http://shop.oreilly.com/product/9780596154493.do—A wide selection of Linux commands and explanations of what they do taken from O'Reilly's excellent book *Linux in a Nutshell*, which is a dictionary of Linux commands.

▶ www.linuxcommand.org/—Describes itself as "your one-stop command-line shop!" It contains a wealth of useful information about the console.

▶ Understanding the way UNIX works at the nuts and bolts level can be both challenging and rewarding, and there are several good books that will help guide you on your way. Perhaps the best is *The Art of UNIX Programming* by Eric Raymond (Addison-Wesley, ISBN: 0-13-142901-9), which focuses on the philosophy behind UNIX and manages to mix in much about the command line.

CHAPTER 12

Command-Line Master Class Part 2

In Chapter 11, you learned a number of useful commands. In this chapter, we follow that up with information about how to link commands together to create new command groups. We also look at the three most popular Linux text editors: vim, emacs, and nano, as well as the sed and awk tools. We then add more commands and command-line interface (CLI) based tools to help you become successful and efficient. Let's jump right in.

Redirecting Output and Input

Sometimes, the output of a command is too long to view on one screen. At other times, there might be an advantage to preserving the output as a file, perhaps to be edited later. You can't do that using cat or less, at least not using them as we have described so far. Good news: It is possible using redirection.

Commands take their input and give their output in a standard place. This is called standard input and standard output. By default, this is configured as the output of a keyboard for standard input because it comes in to the computer from the keyboard, and the screen for standard output because the computer displays the results of a command to the user using that screen. Standard input and standard output can be redirected.

To redirect output, the command line uses >. Sometimes people read this as "in to." Here is an example:

```
matthew@seymour:~$ cat /proc/cpuinfo > file.txt
```

We know the first part of this line reads the information about the CPU from the file /proc/cpuinfo. Usually this would print it to the screen, but here the output is redirected into a file called `file.txt`, created in my `/home` directory, because that is the directory in which I issued the command. I can now read, edit, or use this file in any way I like.

CAUTION

Be aware that you can overwrite the contents of a file using a redirect in this manner, so be certain that the destination file you name either does not exist or that its current contents do not need to be preserved.

What if we want to take the contents of an existing file and use that data as an input to a command? It is as simple as reversing the symbol from `>` to `<`:

```
matthew@seymour:~$ cat < file.txt
```

This takes the contents of `file.txt` and displays them on the screen. At first glance, that does not seem useful because the command is doing the same thing it usually does, it is printing the contents of a file to the screen. Perhaps a different example would be helpful.

Ubuntu uses a software packaging system called `apt`, which is discussed in Chapter 9, "Managing Software." Using a command from the `apt` stable, `dpkg`, you can quickly list all software that has been installed using `apt` on a system and record that info into a file using a redirect:

```
matthew@seymour:~$ sudo dpkg --get-selections > pkg.list
```

This creates a text file named `pkg.list` that contains the list we want. You can open it with a text editor to confirm this. Now, we can use this file as input to `dpkg`, perhaps on another system on which we want the exact same software to be installed:

```
matthew@seymour:~$ sudo dpkg --set-selections < pkg.list
```

This tells `dpkg` to mark for installation any of the items in the list that are not already installed on the second system. One more quick command and these will be installed (included here for completeness of the example, even though it has nothing to do with redirection...): `sudo apt-get -u dselect-upgrade`.

Earlier in the chapter we gave an example of using `cat` to display several files simultaneously. This example can be modified slightly to redirect the output into a file, thereby making a new file that includes the contents of the previous two using the order in which they are listed:

```
matthew@seymour:~$ cat myfile.txt myotherfile.txt > combinedfile.txt
```

If you want to append information to the end of a text file, rather than replace its contents, use two greater than signs, like this:

```
matthew@seymour:~$ echo "This is a new line being added." >> file.txt
```

If you want to suppress the output that you do not want to keep from a process, so that it does not get sent to standard output or saved, send it instead to a special location called the Null Device, like this, where `verboseprocess` is an example process that produces lots of output:

```
matthew@seymour:~$ verboseprocess > /dev/null
```

Add the power of redirection to the information in this next section and you will finally begin to understand the potential and the power that a command-line-savvy user has and why so many who learn the command line absolutely love it.

stdin, stdout, stderr, **and Redirection**

When a program runs, it automatically has three input/output streams opened for it; one for input, one for output, and one for error messages. Typically, these are attached to the user's terminal (so they take input from or give output to the command line), but they can be directed elsewhere, such as to or from a file. These three streams are referred to and abbreviated as shown here:

Stream	Abbreviation	Number
Standard input	stdin	0
Standard output	stdout	1
Standard error, or error stream	Stderr	2

Each of these is assigned a number, shown in the third column.

In the "Redirecting Output and Input" section, you learned how to redirect input and output without needing to know about `stdin` or `stdout`. You can also redirect where the `stderr` messages are sent as well as do some more powerful things.

If you are running a program and want any error messages that appear to be directed into a text file instead of having them printed on a screen that might not be monitored, you can use the following command when starting the program or running a command (substitute *program* with the name of the program or command you are running):

```
matthew@seymour:~$ program 2> error.log
```

Here, any error messages from *program* are added to the end of a file named *error.log* in the current working directory.

If you want to redirect both `stderr` and `stdout` to a file, use the following:

```
matthew@seymour:~$ program &> filename
```

You can do the same thing using

```
matthew@seymour:~$ program >> filename 2>&1
```

Here, any output from *program* is added to the end of a file named *filename*.

To redirect `stderr` to `stdout`, so that error messages are printed to the screen instead of another location (such as when a program or command is written in a way that already redirects those error messages to a file), use:

matthew@seymour:~$ **program 2>&1**

Comparing Files

The two most common things a user wants to know when comparing two files is what in the files is the same and what is different. This is especially useful when comparing current versions of configuration files with backup versions of the same files. These commands make that task easy. Because looking for differences is more common, we start there.

Finding Differences in Files with `diff`

The `diff` command compares files line by line and outputs any lines that are not identical. For example:

matthew@seymour:~$ **diff file1 file2**

This command outputs every line that is different between the two. If `file1` and `file2` are different versions of a configuration file, say the current and a backup, the output quickly tells you what, if anything, has changed. This can help when a config file is automatically updated during an operating system upgrade or when you make a change that doesn't work as well as you had planned and then go back a couple of weeks later to change the configuration back.

There are several options you may use when running `diff` (the original UNIX-style versions like `-i` and the newer style versions like `--ignore-case` are identical in what they do; it might simply be easier for you to remember one than the other). Here are a few of the more useful ones to get you started:

▶ `-i` or `-ignore-case` ignores case differences in file contents.

▶ `-b` or `-ignore-space-change` ignores changes in the amount of white space.

▶ `-w` or `-ignore-all-space` ignores all white space.

▶ `-q` or `--brief` outputs only whether the files differ.

▶ `-l` or `--paginate` passes the output through `pr` to paginate it.

Finding Similarities in Files with `comm`

The `comm` command compares files line by line and outputs any lines that are identical. For example:

matthew@seymour:~$ **comm file1 file2**

This command output displays in three columns: column 1 shows lines only in `file1`, column2 shows every line only in `file2`, and column 3 shows every line that is the same between the two files. This is a much more detailed comparison than with `diff`, and the output can be overwhelming when all you want is to find or check for one or two simple changes. However, it can be incredibly useful when you aren't terribly familiar with either file and want to see how they compare.

There are fewer options available when running `comm`. These three are the ones you are most likely to be interested in:

▶ `-1` **(the number one)** suppresses the output of column 1.

▶ `-2` **(the number two)** suppresses the output of column 2.

▶ `-3` **(the number three)** suppresses the output of column 3.

Limiting Resource Use and Job Control

Computer systems run many processes at the same time. This is a good thing and allows users or multiple users to multitask. Some processes require more system resources than others. Occasionally, a resource-intensive process may take up or require so many resources that it slows down the system for other processes. There are ways to deal with this. This section describes a few of the basics. You must have admin privileges to perform any of the actions in this section.

Listing Processes with `ps`

The `ps` command lists processes and gives you an extraordinary amount of control over its operation. A process is any running program or instance of a running program. There can be many copies of the same program running at the same time, and when that happens, each will have its own process. Every process has its own address space, or designated part of the computer's memory that is reserved just for this process and its needs. A process group is created when any process begins and will include that process and any processes started by it.

In the Unix/Linux world, a process (parent) has the ability to create another process (child) that executes some given code independently. This can be really useful for programs that need a lot of time to finish. For example, if you have a program that needs to calculate some complex equation, search large databases, or delete and cleanup a lot of files, you can write it so that it will "spawn" a child process that performs the task, while the parent returns control to the user. In such a case, the user does not have to wait for the task to finish, because the child process is running in the background.

The first thing to know is that `ps` is typically used with what are known as BSD-style parameters. In the section of the previous chapter, "Finding Files by Searching with `find`," we discussed UNIX-style, GNU-style, and X-style parameters (`-c`, `--dosomething`, and `-dosomething`, respectively), but BSD-style parameters are different because they use single letters without a dash.

So, the default use of `ps` lists all processes that you are running that are attached to the terminal. However, you can ask it to list all your processes attached to any terminal (or indeed no terminal) by adding the x parameter: ps x. You can ask it to list all processes for all users with the a parameter or combine that with x to list all processes for all users, attached to a terminal or otherwise: ps ax.

However, both of these are timid compared with the almighty u option, which enables user-oriented output. In practice, that makes a huge difference because you get important fields such as the username of the owner, how much CPU time and RAM are being used, when the process was started, and more. This outputs a lot of information, so you might want to try adding the f parameter, which creates a process forest by using ASCII art to connect parent commands with their children. You can combine all the options so far with this command: ps faux. (Yes, with a little imagination, you spell words with the parameters.)

You can control the order in which the data is returned by using the --sort parameter. This takes either a + or a - (although the + is default) followed by the field you want to sort by: command, %cpu, pid, and user are all popular options. If you use the minus sign, the results are reversed. This next command lists all processes, ordered by CPU usage descending:

```
matthew@seymour:~$ ps aux --sort=-%cpu
```

There are many other parameters for ps, including a large number of options for compatibility with other UNIXes. If you have the time to read the man page, give it a try.

Listing Jobs with jobs

A job is any program you interactively start that doesn't then detach from the user and run on its own (like a daemon does). If you're running an interactive program, you can press Ctrl+Z to suspend it. Then you can start it back in the foreground (using fg, covered next) or in the background (using bg, covered with fg).

While the program is suspended or running in the background, you can start another program. Then you have two jobs running. You can also start a program running in the background by appending an "&" like this:

```
matthew@seymour:~$ programname &
```

When started this way, a program runs as a background job. To list all the jobs you are running, you can use jobs.

```
matthew@seymour:~$ jobs
```

There are several useful parameters that you can use with jobs. The most generally useful are:

- ▶ -l, which then lists the process IDs along with the normal output
- ▶ -n, which displays information only about jobs that have changed status since the user was last notified of their status
- ▶ -r, which restricts output to running jobs
- ▶ -s, which restricts output to stopped jobs

Running One or More Tasks in the Background

Put the & (ampersand) symbol at the end of any command to make it run in the background. A background process runs without any user input. The shell is not forced to wait until the process is complete before it is freed up to allow more commands to be input and run. When you tell a command to run in the background, you are given its job number in brackets followed by its PID, or process ID number. You can use this to manage the process later, if necessary.

```
matthew@seymour:~$ command &
[1] 11423
```

You can input a list of several commands to run in the background. Each will run separately and have its own PID. In this sample, a, b, and c represent commands.

```
matthew@seymour:~$ a & b & c &
[1] 11427
[2] 11428
[3] 11429
```

You can even use pipes within background processes, and combine multiples of each. The letters here represent individual commands.

```
matthew@seymour:~$ d & | e & f & g & | h &
[1] 11432
[2] 11433
[3] 11434
```

Notice that the line above becomes three separate background processes, even though five commands were issued. That is because commands piped together are treated as one process.

Moving Jobs to the Background or Foreground with bg and fg

The shell has the concept of "foreground" jobs and "background" jobs. Foreground jobs are process groups with control of the terminal, and background jobs are process groups without control of the terminal.

Let's say you started a job by running a program at the command line. Maybe something like this, which could take a while to run.

```
matthew@seymour:~$ find . -type f -printf "%s\t%p\n" | sort -n
```

When you run this, it starts in the foreground, meaning the terminal will be interactive with you only for this job until the job is complete. This particular job will find all files in the current directory and its subdirectories and then list them according to their size. You wouldn't likely want to tie up your terminal session the whole time the job is running. You meant to run it with a & at the end so that it would run in the background, but you forgot. No worries. You can hit Ctrl+Z to suspend the job, then you type this:

```
matthew@seymour:~$ bg
```

That's it. This will resume the process, but this time with it running in the background.

Both `bg` and `fg`, if entered with no further arguments, will operate on the most recent job you interacted with.

Remember that the `jobs` command will list all current jobs and their status (running, stopped, etc.). If you want to move a job running in the background to the foreground, first list the running jobs. They will each have a number next to them in the listing. Use the job number to move a job to the foreground, like this:

```
matthew@seymour:~$ fg %2
```

If you want to move a specific job to the background, just add the job number the same way.

```
matthew@seymour:~$ bg %2
```

Remember, jobs running in this manner will terminate when the shell is closed. If you want a job to continue after you exit, you should consider using a tool like byobu, covered later in this chapter, or learn to run the process as a daemon, which is beyond the scope of this chapter and will require you to do some further research.

Printing Resource Usage with `top`

The `top` command is unusual in this list because the few parameters it takes are rarely, if ever, used. Instead, it has a number of commands you can use while it is running to customize the information it shows you. To get the most from these instructions, open two terminal windows. In the first, run the program `yes` and leave it running; in the second run `top`.

When you run `top`, you see a display as shown in Figure 12.1.

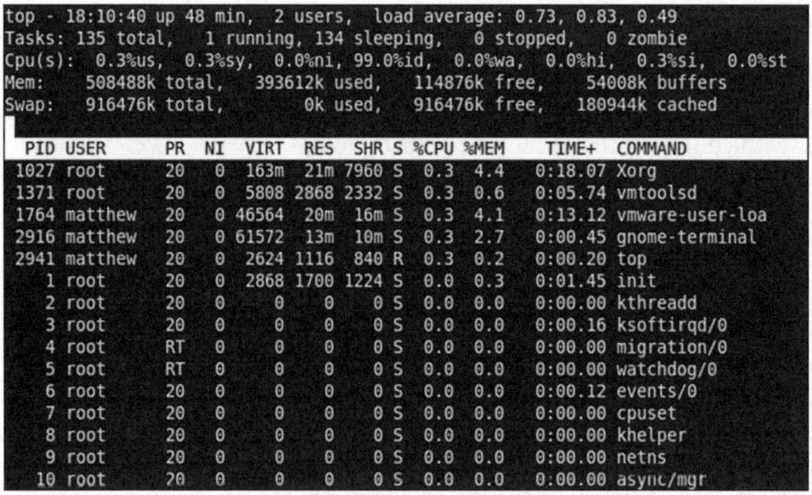

```
top - 18:10:40 up 48 min,  2 users,  load average: 0.73, 0.83, 0.49
Tasks: 135 total,   1 running, 134 sleeping,   0 stopped,   0 zombie
Cpu(s):  0.3%us,  0.3%sy,  0.0%ni, 99.0%id,  0.0%wa,  0.0%hi,  0.3%si,  0.0%st
Mem:    508488k total,   393612k used,   114876k free,    54008k buffers
Swap:   916476k total,        0k used,   916476k free,   180944k cached

  PID USER      PR  NI  VIRT  RES  SHR S %CPU %MEM    TIME+  COMMAND
 1027 root      20   0  163m  21m 7960 S  0.3  4.4  0:18.07 Xorg
 1371 root      20   0  5808 2868 2332 S  0.3  0.6  0:05.74 vmtoolsd
 1764 matthew   20   0 46564  20m  16m S  0.3  4.1  0:13.12 vmware-user-loa
 2916 matthew   20   0 61572  13m  10m S  0.3  2.7  0:00.45 gnome-terminal
 2941 matthew   20   0  2624 1116  840 R  0.3  0.2  0:00.20 top
    1 root      20   0  2868 1700 1224 S  0.0  0.3  0:01.45 init
    2 root      20   0     0    0    0 S  0.0  0.0  0:00.00 kthreadd
    3 root      20   0     0    0    0 S  0.0  0.0  0:00.16 ksoftirqd/0
    4 root      RT   0     0    0    0 S  0.0  0.0  0:00.00 migration/0
    5 root      RT   0     0    0    0 S  0.0  0.0  0:00.00 watchdog/0
    6 root      20   0     0    0    0 S  0.0  0.0  0:00.12 events/0
    7 root      20   0     0    0    0 S  0.0  0.0  0:00.00 cpuset
    8 root      20   0     0    0    0 S  0.0  0.0  0:00.00 khelper
    9 root      20   0     0    0    0 S  0.0  0.0  0:00.00 netns
   10 root      20   0     0    0    0 S  0.0  0.0  0:00.00 async/mgr
```

FIGURE 12.1   Use the `top` command to monitor and control processes.

The default sort order in `top` shows the most CPU-intensive tasks first. The first command there should be the `yes` process you just launched from the other terminal, but there should be many others also. First, we want to filter out all the other users and focus on the user running `yes`. To do this, press `u` and enter the username you used when you ran `yes`. When you press Enter, `top` filters out processes not being run by that user.

The next step is to kill the PID of the `yes` command, so you need to understand what each of the important fields means:

▶ `PID`—The process ID

▶ `User`—The owner of the process

▶ `PR`—Priority

▶ `NI`—Niceness

▶ `virt`—Virtual image size in kilobytes

▶ `Res`—Resident size in kilobytes

▶ `shr`—Shared memory size in kilobytes

▶ `S`—Status

▶ `%CPU`—CPU usage

▶ `%Mem`—Memory usage

▶ `Time+`—CPU time

▶ `Command`—The command being run

Several of them are unimportant unless you have a specific problem. The ones we are interested in are `PID`, `User`, `Niceness`, `%CPU`, `%MEM`, `Time+`, and `Command`. The `Niceness` of a process is how much time the CPU allocates to it compared to everything else on the system: 19 is the lowest, and –19 is the highest.

With the columns explained, you should be able to find the PID of the errant `yes` command launched earlier; it is usually the first number below `PID`. Now type `k`, enter that PID, and press Enter. You are prompted for a signal number (the manner in which you want the process killed), with 15 provided as the default. Signal 15 (also known as `SIGTERM`, for terminate) is a polite way of asking a process to shut down, and all processes that are not wildly out of control should respond to it. Give `top` a few seconds to update itself, and hopefully the `yes` command should be gone. If not, you need to be more forceful: Type `k` again, enter the PID, and press Enter. When prompted for a signal to send, enter `9` and press Enter to send `SIGKILL`, or "terminate whether you like it or not."

You can choose the fields to display by pressing `f`. A new screen appears that lists all possible fields, along with the letter you need to press to toggle their visibility. Selected fields are marked with an asterisk and have their letter, as follows:

```
* A: PID        = Process Id
```

If you press the a key, the screen changes to this:

```
a: PID        = Process Id
```

When you have made your selections, press Enter to return to the normal top view with your normal column selection.

You can also press F to select the field you want to use for sorting. This works in the same way as the field selection screen, except that you can select only one field at a time. Again, press Enter to get back to top after you have made your selection, and it will be updated with the new sorting.

If you press B, text bolding is enabled. By default, this bolds some of the header bar as well as any programs that are currently running (as opposed to sleeping), but if you press x you can also enable bolding of the sorted column. You can use y to toggle bolding of running processes.

The last command to try is r, which enables you to renice—or adjust the nice value of—a process. You need to enter the PID of the process, press Enter, and enter a new nice value. Keep in mind that 19 is the lowest and –19 is the highest; anything less than 0 is considered "high" and should be used sparingly.

You can combine the information you learn here with the information in Chapter 16, "System-Monitoring Tools" for even more power over your system.

Setting Processes Priority with nice

You can set the priority for individual processes, to tell the kernel to either limit or give extra priority to a specific process. This is most useful when multiple concurrent processes are demanding more resources than are actually available, since this is the condition that generally causes slowdowns and bottlenecks. Processes set with a higher priority get a larger portion of the CPU time than lower priority processes.

You can set this priority when you first run a program by putting the command nice before whatever you are going to run, and assigning the process a value that designates its priority. By default, all processes start with a priority of 0 (zero). nice can set that to a maximum of –20, which is the highest priority, to a minimum of 19, the lowest priority.

Here is an example that takes the tar command we used earlier in this chapter and sets its priority very low, because tar can demand significant system resources, but is often not something whose output we require immediately. We could run the same command as above, but with nice set to 19 to allow us to do something else with the system at the same time.

```
matthew@seymour:~$ sudo nice -n 19 tar czf compressedfilename.tgz directoryname
```

If a process is already running, you can reset the priority (some say "renice it") using renice. To adjust a specific process, first use top to learn the PID for the process. Then, use -p PID, as follows in this example where we renice PID 20136 to priority 19:

```
matthew@seymour:~$ sudo renice 19 -p 20136
```

This command is a little more flexible, as it also allows priority adjustments to be made on all processes owned by a specific user or group in the system. Notice that `renice` is most commonly used to lower the priority of a system-slowing task, but it can also be used to bump up the priority for an urgent task, as shown in these examples. Here we first give all tasks by the user `mysql` (using `-u` *username*) a priority of –20 (top priority, remember?) and then give all tasks belonging to system users in the `website` group (using `-g` *groupname*) a priority of –20:

```
matthew@seymour:~$ sudo renice -20 -u mysql
matthew@seymour:~$ sudo renice -20 -g website
```

With the `ionice` command, you can adjust priority for disk access, similar to how `nice` and `renice` set priority for CPU access. The difference here is that there are only three class settings for priority. The lowest priority is Idle (3), which permits the process to access the disk only when other processes are not using the disk. In the middle is Best Effort (2), which is the default and allows the kernel to schedule access as its algorithms deem appropriate. The highest priority is Real Time (1), which gives this process the first access to the disk whenever it demands it, regardless of what other processes are running. The Real Time setting can be dangerous as it can cause other processes to lose their data— this isn't guaranteed to happen, but you should consider yourself warned and you probably want to spend some time studying the man page for `ionice` before you set anything to Real Time.

To use `ionice`, find the PID for a process and use it to set the priority. Notice that there are no spaces between the flag and the value using this command. Here is an example where we set the priority (using the `-c` flag, for class) to 3 for PID 24351 (using the `-p` flag).

```
matthew@seymour:~$ sudo ionice -c3 -p24351
```

You will find other useful tips for managing your system in Chapter 16, "System-Monitoring Tools."

Combining Commands

So far, we have been using commands only individually, and for the most part that is what you do in practice. However, some of the real power of these commands lies in the capability to join them together to get exactly what you want. There are some extra little commands that we have not looked at that are often used as glue because they do one very simple thing that enables a more complex process to work.

Pipes

All the commands we have looked at have printed their information to the screen, but this is often flexible.

A pipe is a connector between one command's output and another's input. Instead of sending its output to your terminal, using a pipe sends that output directly to another command as input.

Two of the commands we have looked at so far are `ps` and `grep`: the process lister and the string matcher. We can combine the two to find out which users are playing Nethack right now:

```
matthew@seymour:~$ ps aux | grep nethack
```

That creates a list of all the processes running right now and sends that list to the `grep` command, which filters out all lines that do not contain the word `nethack`. Ubuntu allows you to pipe as many commands as you can sanely string together. For example, we could add in the `wc` command, which counts the numbers of lines, words, and characters in its input, to count precisely how many times Nethack is being run:

```
matthew@seymour:~$ ps aux | grep nethack | wc -l
```

The `-l` (lowercase *L*) parameter to `wc` prints only the line count.

Using pipes in this way is often preferable to using the `-exec` parameter to find simply because many people consider `find` to be a black art and using it less frequently is better. This is where the `xargs` command comes in: It converts output from one command into arguments for another.

For a good example, consider this mammoth `find` command from earlier:

```
matthew@seymour:~$ find / -name "*.txt" -size +10k -user matthew -not -perm +o=r
➥-exec chmod o+r {} \;
```

That searches every directory from / onward for files matching `*.txt` that are greater than 10KB, are owned by user `matthew`, and do not have read permission for others. Then it executes `chmod` on each of the files. It is a complex command, and people who are not familiar with the workings of `find` might have problems understanding it. So, what you can do is break it into two—a call to `find` and a call to `xargs`. The most simple conversion would look like this:

```
matthew@seymour:~$ find / -name "*.txt" -size +10k -user matthew -not -perm +o=r |
➥xargs chmod o+r
```

That has eliminated the confusing `{} \;` from the end of the command, but it does the same thing, and faster, too. The speed difference between the two is because using `-exec` with `find` causes it to execute `chmod` once for each file. However, `chmod` accepts many files at a time and, because we are using the same parameter each time, we should take advantage of that. The second command, using `xargs`, is called once with all the output from find, and so saves many command calls. The `xargs` command automatically places the input at the end of the line, so the previous command might look something like this:

```
matthew@seymour:~$ xargs chmod o+r file1.txt file2.txt file3.txt
```

Not every command accepts multiple files, though, and if you specify the `-l` parameter, `xargs` executes its command once for each line in its input. If you want to check what it is doing, use the `-p` parameter to have `xargs` prompt you before executing each command.

For even more control, the -i parameter allows you to specify exactly where the matching lines should be placed in your command. This is important if you need the lines to appear before the end of the command or need it to appear more than once. Either way, using the -i parameter also enables the -1 parameter so each line is sent to the command individually. This next command finds all files in /home/matthew that are larger than 10,000KB in size (10MB) and copies them to /home/matthew/archive:

```
matthew@seymour:~$ find /home/matthew -size +10000k | xargs -i cp {} ./home/matthew/
➥archive
```

Using find with xargs is a unique case. All too often, people use pipes when parameters would do the job just as well. For example, the following two commands are identical:

```
matthew@seymour:~$ ps aux --sort=-%cpu | grep -v 'whoami'
matthew@seymour:~$ ps -N ux --sort=-%cpu
```

The former prints all users and processes and then pipes that to grep, which in turn filters out all lines that contain the output from the program whoami (our username). So, line one prints all processes being run by other users, sorted by CPU use. Line two does not specify the a parameter to ps, which makes it list only our parameters. It then uses the -N parameter to flip that, which means it is everyone but us, without the need for grep.

The reason people use the former is often just simplicity: Many people know only a handful of parameters to each command, so they can string together two commands simply rather than write one command properly. Unless the command is to be run regularly, this is not a problem. Indeed, the first line would be better because it does not drive people to the manual to find out what ps -N does.

You can string together any commands that use standard input and output formats. Another useful example is this series, which will verify the installation of a named software package, in this example we are showing a search for FTP-related software:

```
matthew@seymour:~$ dpkg --get-selections | grep ftp | sort
ftp                          install
lftp                         install
```

Here, dpkg is being told to list all installed packages, grep is searching that list for any line containing "ftp", and sort is sorting alphabetically (not so vital in our two-line example, but really useful if you have a large number of results).

Combining Commands with Boolean Operators

If you want to run a second command only if the first command is successfully completed, you can. Every command you issue to the system outputs an exit status, 0 for true (successful) and 1 for false (failed). The system receives these, even if they are not displayed to the user. The && operator, when added to the end of a command, reads that exit status and confirms its value as 0 for true before allowing the next command to be run. Again, the letters represent commands.

```
matthew@seymour:~$ i && k
```

You can do the exact opposite with ||, which only runs the following command if the first one returns an exit status of 1 for false.

```
matthew@seymour:~$ m || n
```

Running Separate Commands in Sequence

If you want to have a set of commands run in order, but not use the output from one as the input to the next one, you can. Separating commands with a ; (semicolon) will cause the system to treat each item as if it was entered on a new line after the previous item finished running. Let's say you have three commands called doctor, rose, and tardis. You could run each in order using this command:

```
matthew@seymour:~$ doctor ; rose ; tardis
```

Note that the spaces before and after the semicolon are optional, but they do make the line easier to read.

Process Substitution

Sometimes the output of one or more commands is precisely what you want to use as the input to another command. You can use output redirection for this as well, using what we call *process substitution*. In process substitution, you surround one or more commands with ()s and precede each list with a <. When you do this, do NOT insert a space between the < and the opening (. The resulting command looks like this:

```
matthew@seymour:~$ cat <(ls -al)
```

This first example is really the same as `ls -al | cat`. With only the output of one process being involved, it doesn't seem worth learning an additional command.

But, here we take the output of two `ls` commands as input to a `diff` command to compare the contents of two directories:

```
matthew@seymour:~$ diff <(ls firstdirectory) <(ls seconddirectory)
```

This is faster because you don't have to wait for temporary files to be written and then read; it saves both disk space and the time needed to clean up temporary files. One especially neat advantage of doing this is that Bash automatically runs the multiple tasks being used as input in parallel, which is faster than doing them sequentially with redirects like this:

```
matthew@seymour:~$ ls firstdirectory > file1.txt
matthew@seymour:~$ ls seconddirectory > file2.txt
matthew@seymour:~$ diff file1.txt file2.txt
```

Using Environment Variables

A number of in-memory variables are assigned and loaded by default when you log in. These variables are known as *environment variables* and can be used by various commands to get information about your environment, such as the type of system you are running, your /home directory, and the shell in use. Environment variables are used to help tailor the computing environment of your system and include helpful specifications and setup, such as default locations of executable files and software libraries. If you begin writing shell scripts, you might use environment variables in your scripts. Until then, you need to be aware only of what environment variables are and do.

The following list includes a number of environment variables, along with descriptions of how the shell uses them:

▶ **PWD**—Provides the full path to your current working directory, used by the pwd command, such as /home/matthew/Documents

▶ **USER**—Declares the user's name, such as matthew

▶ **LANG**—Sets the default language, such as English

▶ **SHELL**—Declares the name and location of the current shell, such as /bin/bash

▶ **PATH**—Sets the default locations of executable files, such as /bin, /usr/bin, and so on

▶ **TERM**—Sets the type of terminal in use, such as vt100, which can be important when using screen-oriented programs, such as text editors

You can print the current value of any environment variable using echo $VARIABLENAME, like this:

```
matthew@seymour:~$ echo $USER
matthew
matthew@seymour:~$
```

> **NOTE**
>
> Each shell can have its own feature set and language syntax, as well as a unique set of default environment variables.

You can use the env or printenv command to display all environment variables, as follows:

```
matthew@seymour:~$ env
ORBIT_SOCKETDIR=/tmp/orbit-matthew
SSH_AGENT_PID=1729
TERM=xterm
SHELL=/bin/bash
WINDOWID=71303173
GNOME_KEYRING_CONTROL=/tmp/keyring-qTEFTw
GTK_MODULES=canberra-gtk-module
USER=matt
hew
SSH_AUTH_SOCK=/tmp/keyring-qTEFTw/ssh
DEFAULTS_PATH=/usr/share/gconf/gnome.default.path
SESSION_MANAGER=local/seymour:/tmp/.ICE-unix/1695
```

```
USERNAME=matthew
XDG_CONFIG_DIRS=/etc/xdg/xdg-gnome:/etc/xdg
DESKTOP_SESSION=gnome
PATH=/usr/local/sbin:/usr/local/bin:/usr/sbin:/usr/bin:/sbin:/bin:/usr/games
PWD=/home/matthew
hew
GDM_KEYBOARD_LAYOUT=us
LANG=en_US.utf8
GNOME_KEYRING_PID=1677
MANDATORY_PATH=/usr/share/gconf/gnome.mandatory.path
GDM_LANG=en_US.utf8
GDMSESSION=gnome
HISTCONTROL=ignoreboth
SPEECHD_PORT=7560
SHLVL=1
HOME=/home/matt
hew
LOGNAME=matt
hew
LESSOPEN=| /usr/bin/lesspipe %s
DISPLAY=:0.0
LESSCLOSE=/usr/bin/lesspipe %s %s
XAUTHORITY=/var/run/gdm/auth-for-matthew-PzcGqF/database
COLORTERM=gnome-terminal
OLDPWD=/var/lib/mlocate
_=/usr/bin/env
```

This abbreviated list shows some of the common variables. These variables are set by configuration or *resource* files contained in the /etc, /etc/skel, or in the user's /home directory. You can find default settings for bash, for example, in /etc/profile and /etc/bashrc as well as .bashrc or .bash_profile files in your /home directory. Read the man page for bash for details about using these configuration files.

One of the most important environment variables is $PATH, which defines the location of executable files. For example, if, as a regular user, you try to use a command that is not located in your $PATH (such as the imaginary command command), you see something like this:

```
matthew@seymour:~$ command
-bash: command: command not found
```

If the command that you're trying to execute exists in the Ubuntu software repositories but is not yet installed on your system, Ubuntu responds with the correct command to install the command:

```
matthew@seymour:~$ command
```

```
The program 'command' is currently not installed. You can install it by typing:
```

```
sudo apt-get install command
```

However, you might know that command is definitely installed on your system, and you can verify this by using the whereis command, like this:

```
matthew@seymour:~$ whereis command
command: /sbin/command
```

You can also run the command by typing its full pathname or complete directory specification, as follows:

```
matthew@seymour:~$ /sbin/command
```

As you can see in this example, the command command is indeed installed. What happened is that by default, the /sbin directory is not in your $PATH. One of the reasons for this is that commands under the /sbin directory are normally intended to be run only by root. You can add /sbin to your $PATH by editing the file .bash_profile in your /home directory (if you use the bash shell by default, like most Linux users). Look for the following line:

```
PATH=$PATH:$HOME/bin
```

You can then edit this file, perhaps using one of the text editors discussed later in this chapter, to add the /sbin directory, like so:

```
PATH=$PATH:/sbin:$HOME/bin
```

Save the file. The next time you log in, the /sbin directory is in your $PATH. One way to use this change right away is to read in the new settings in .bash_profile by using the bash shell's source command, as follows:

```
matthew@seymour:~$ source .bash_profile
```

You can now run commands located in the /sbin directory without the need to explicitly type the full pathname.

Some Linux commands also use environment variables to acquire configuration information (such as a communications program looking for a variable such as BAUD_RATE, which might denote a default modem speed).

To experiment with the environment variables, you can modify the PS1 variable to manipulate the appearance of your shell prompt. If you are working with bash, you can use its built-in export command to change the shell prompt. For example, if your default shell prompt looks like this:

```
matthew@seymour:~$
```

You can change its appearance by using the PS1 variable like this:

```
matthew@seymour:~$ export PS1='$OSTYPE r00lz ->'
```

After you press Enter, you see the following:

```
linux-gnu r00lz ->
```

NOTE

See the `bash` man page for other variables you can use for prompt settings.

Using Common Text Editors

Linux distributions include a number of applications known as *text editors* that you can use to create text files or edit system configuration files. Text editors are similar to word processing programs but generally have fewer features, work only with text files, and might or might not support spell checking or formatting. Text editors range in features and ease of use and are found on nearly every Linux distribution. The number of editors installed on your system depends on what software packages you've installed on the system.

The more popular console-based text editors include the following:

▶ `emacs`—The comprehensive GNU `emacs` editing environment, which is much more than an editor; see the section "Working with `emacs`," later in this chapter.

▶ `nano`—A simple text editor similar to the classic `pico` text editor that was included with the once-common `pine` email program.

▶ `vim`—An improved, compatible version of the `vi` text editor (which we call `vi` in the rest of this chapter because it has a symbolic link named `vi` and a symbolically linked manual page).

Note that not all text editors are *screen oriented*, meaning designed for use from a terminal. Some of the text editors are designed to run from a graphical desktop and that provide a graphical interface with menu bars, buttons, scrollbars, and so on, are the following:

▶ `gedit`—A GUI text editor for GNOME, which is installed by default with Ubuntu

▶ `kate`—A simple KDE text editor

▶ `kedit`—Another simple KDE text editor

A good reason to learn how to use a text-based editor, such as `vi` or `nano`, is that system maintenance and recovery operations almost never take place during GUI sessions, negating the use of a GUI editor. Many larger, more complex, and capable editors do not work when Linux is booted to its single-user or maintenance mode. If anything does go wrong with your system and you can't log into the GUI, knowledge and experience of using both the command line and text editors will turn out to be very important. Make a point of opening some of the editors and playing around with them. You never know; you might just thank us someday.

Another reason to learn how to use a text-based editor under the Linux console mode is so that you can edit text files through remote shell sessions because many servers will not host graphical desktops.

> **NOTE**
>
> Before you take the time to get familiar with a nonstandard text editor, consider this: All three of the editors included here are readily available and common. Two of them, nano and vi, are almost universally installed. If you spend your time learning a nonstandard editor, you will find yourself having to install it on every system or fighting against the software that is already there instead of using your time productively. Feel free to use any text editor you prefer, but we strongly recommend that you make sure you have at least a basic working knowledge of these standard editors so that you can walk up to any system and start working when necessary.

Working with nano

This one is listed first as it has the easiest learning curve. It is neither the most powerful nor the most "guru approved," but nano is a respectable text editor that you can run from the command line, and it's often perfect for quick tasks such as editing configuration files.

Learning how to use nano is quick and easy. You might need to edit files on a Linux system with a minimal install, or a remote server without a more extensive offering of installed text editors. Chances are nearly 100 percent that nano will be available.

You can start an editing session by using the nano command like this:

```
matthew@seymour:~$ nano file.txt
```

When you first start editing, you see the text on the screen with a title bar across the top and a list of simple commands across the bottom. The editor is simple enough that you can use it without any instruction. Here are the basic commands, just so you can compare them with other listed editors (^ is the Control key):

▶ **Cursor movement**—Arrow keys (left, down, up, and right), Page Up and Page Down keys, or ^y and ^v page up and down

▶ **Add characters**—Type at the cursor location

▶ **Delete character**—Backspace or Delete

▶ **Exit**—^x (prompts to ask whether to save changes)

▶ **Get Help**—^g

> **NOTE**
>
> nano really is that easy to use, but that does not mean that it cannot be used by power users. Take a little time and read the contents of Help to discover some of the more interesting and powerful capabilities of this editor.

Working with vi

The one editor found on nearly every UNIX and Linux system is the vi editor, originally written by Bill Joy. This simple-to-use but incredibly capable editor features a somewhat cryptic command set, but you can put it to use with only a few commands. Although many experienced UNIX and Linux users use vi extensively during computing sessions, many users who do only quick and simple editing might not need all its power and might prefer an easier-to-use text editor such as nano. Diehard GNU fans and programmers often use emacs for pretty much everything.

However, learning how to use vi is a good idea. You might need to edit files on a Linux system with a minimal install or on a remote server without a more extensive offering of installed text editors. Chances are nearly 100 percent that vi will be available.

You can start an editing session by using the vi command like this:

```
matthew@seymour:~$ vi file.txt
```

The vi command works by using an insert (or editing) mode and a viewing (or command) mode.

When you first start editing, you are in the viewing mode. You can use your arrow or other navigation keys (as shown later) to scroll through the text. To start editing, press the i key to insert text or the a key to append text. When you're finished, use the Esc key to toggle out of the insert or append modes and into the viewing (or command) mode. To enter a command, type a colon (:), followed by the command, such as w to write the file, and press Enter.

Although vi supports many complex editing operations and numerous commands, you can accomplish work by using a few basic commands. These basic vi commands are as follows:

▶ **Cursor movement**—h, j, k, l (left, down, up, and right)

▶ **Delete character**—x

▶ **Delete line**—dd

▶ **Mode toggle**—Esc, Insert (or i)

▶ **Quit**—:q

▶ **Quit without saving**—:q!

▶ **Run a shell command**—:sh (use `exit` to return)

▶ **Save file**—:w

▶ **Text search**—/

NOTE

Use the vimtutor command to quickly learn how to use vi's keyboard commands. The tutorial takes less than 30 minutes, and it teaches new users how to start or stop the editor, navigate files, insert and delete text, and perform search, replace, and insert operations.

Working with emacs

Richard M. Stallman's GNU emacs editor, like vi, is available with Ubuntu and nearly every other Linux distribution. Unlike other UNIX and Linux text editors, emacs is much more than a simple text editor. It's an editing environment, and you can use it to compile and build programs and act as an electronic diary, appointment book, and calendar. Use it to compose and send email, read Usenet news, and even play games. The reason for this capability is that emacs contains a built-in language interpreter that uses the Elisp (emacs LISP) programming language. emacs is not installed in Ubuntu by default. To use emacs, the package you need to install is called emacs. See Chapter 9, "Managing Software."

You can start an emacs editing session like this:

```
matthew@seymour:~$ emacs file.txt
```

> **TIP**
>
> If you start emacs when using X11, the editor launches in its own floating window. To force emacs to display inside a terminal window instead of its own window (which can be useful if the window is a login at a remote computer), use the -nw command-line option like this: emacs -nw file.txt.

The emacs editor uses an extensive set of keystroke and named commands, but you can work with it by using a basic command subset. Many of these basic commands require you to hold down the Ctrl key, or to first press a *meta* key (generally mapped to the Alt key). Table 12.1 lists the basic commands.

TABLE 12.1   emacs Editing Commands

Action	Command
Cursor left	Ctrl+B
Cursor down	Ctrl+N
Cursor right	Ctrl+F
Cursor up	Ctrl+P
Delete character	Ctrl+D
Delete line	Ctrl+K
Go to start of line	Ctrl+A
Go to end of line	Ctrl+E
Help	Ctrl+H
Quit	Ctrl+X, Ctrl+C
Save as	Ctrl+X, Ctrl+W
Save file	Ctrl+X, Ctrl+S
Search backward	Ctrl+R
Search forward	Ctrl+S
Start tutorial	Ctrl+H, T
Undo	Ctrl+X, U

One of the best reasons to learn how to use emacs is that you can use nearly all the same keystrokes to edit commands on the bash shell command line, although it is possible to change the default to use vi keybindings. Another reason is that like vi, emacs is universally available for installation on nearly every UNIX and Linux system, including Apple's Mac OS X.

Working with sed **and** awk

sed, from Stream EDitor, is a command that is used to perform transformations on text. It works from the command line and processes text via standard in and standard out. It does not modify the original input and does not save the output unless you redirect that output to a file. It is most useful this way or when piped between other commands.

awk is a small programming language for processing strings. It takes in text, transforms it in whatever way you tell it to, and then outputs the transformed text. It doesn't do as much as other languages, but what it does do it does with elegance and speed.

Both sed and awk run from the command line. There is a lot to them, more than can be covered in a short section of one chapter of a long book, but you can learn enough of each in just a few minutes to find them useful. If you want to continue, there are great resources available online and in the aptly named book by Dale Dougherty and Arnold Robbins, Sed & Awk.

sed and awk aren't used much anymore, at least not by people who have entered the profession in the 21st century, but they are beloved by those who take the time to learn them. For this edition of the book, we are only including a brief mention and a couple quick examples, certainly not enough to really learn to use either in a large capacity. If there is significant interest, we may break this out and expand it into a separate chapter in a future edition.

You use sed with sed commands, like this:

```
matthew@seymour:~$ sed sedcommand inputfile
matthew@seymour:~$ sed -e sedcommand inputfile
matthew@seymour:~$ sed -e sedcommand -e anothersedcommand inputfile
```

The second example does the same thing as the first example, except that it specifically denotes the command to run. This is optional when there is only one command, but useful when you want to run other commands, as in the third example.

Let's say I want to change every instance of *camel* in the text file transportation.txt to *dune buggy*. Here is how to do that:

```
matthew@seymour:~$ sed -e 's/camel/dune buggy/g' transportation.txt
```

The s command stands for *substitution*. It is surrounded by ' marks to prevent confusion by spaces or other characters in the strings it contains. The s is followed by / (slash), which is a delimiter separating the parts of the command from one another. Then we have the pattern to match. Next, what it will be changed to. Finally, the letter g, which means to replace it globally, or everywhere in the text file that *camel* occurs.

You can process text based on line numbers in the file. If I wanted to delete lines 4 through 17 in the file longtext.txt, I would do this:

```
matthew@seymour:~$ sed -e '4,17d' longtext.txt
```

The characters used for `sed` commands are generally obvious, like the `d` above standing for delete. You can use a regular expression in the place of the line numbers. You can use other commands besides substitute and delete. You can use `sed` in scripts and chain commands together.

The most common use of `awk` is to manipulate files that consist of fields separated by delimiters, such as a comma separated values (CSV) file output from a spreadsheet program or a configuration file that assigns default values to program variables.

You define the delimiter that awk will look for, and it will then assign an internal awk variable to each item on a line. For example, if you have a set of parameters and values in a file where each parameter is listed, followed by an equal sign as the delimiter, then a value, you define this for `awk` in your command and the parameter will be assigned as $1 and the value as $2.

Most files contain more than lists of parameters and values, though. What if we had a comma-delimited file containing names of things on my desk, a category for each, a color for each, and a date corresponding to the last time I picked that item up. That is 4 columns: name, category, color, and date. If I only really cared about the names and dates, then I could use awk to process the file quickly and list just these for me, like this:

```
matthew@seymour:~$ awk -F',' '{print $1, "was last picked up on", $4}' deskstuff.txt
```

The output would be displayed on the screen (but could be redirected to a file) and would contain a list of only the information I wanted. In the command above, `-F` defines the delimiter, which is placed in ' marks, and the {}s within a set of ' marks defines what to output, first variable 1, then the text "was last picked up on", followed by variable 4. At the end, the text file to process is named.

You can define multiple delimiters using []s (brackets), like this: `-F'[;,-]'`. You can adjust how to format the text that is output. You can output placeholders when there are blank variables. You can place several `awk` statements in a file and then run it as if it was a shell script.

To close this introduction, consider this idea. What if you have a large text file containing delimited lists of data, and that file contains far more information than you need, and once you extract the data you need from the file, you want to replace a subset of that data with a different value? Give yourself a minute to think at a high level of how you might be able to process the file through awk, then pipe it into sed, and then redirect the output to a file. Think about how long that would take you to perform by hand or even with most programming languages like Python or Perl. Consider how long those programs would be and, in the case of Perl, how difficult it might be to read it later. Now you know why people who know them love `sed` and `awk`.

If you are reading this and think it would be useful to expand this introduction into a full treatment of `sed` and `awk`, drop me a line at matthew@matthewhelmke.com and I'll consider it for a future edition.

Working with Compressed Files

Another file management operation is compression and decompression of files, or the creation, listing, and expansion of file and directory archives. Linux distributions usually include several compression utilities you can use to create, compress, expand, or list the contents of compressed files and archives. These commands include the following:

▶ `bunzip2`—Expands a compressed file

▶ `bzip2`—Compresses or expands files and directories

▶ `gunzip`—Expands a compressed file

▶ `gzip`—Compresses or expands files and directories

▶ `tar`—Creates, expands, or lists the contents of compressed or uncompressed file or directory archives known as *tape archives* or *tarballs*

Most of these commands are easy to use. However, the `tar` command, which is the most commonly used of the bunch, has a somewhat complex set of command-line options and syntax. This flexibility and power are part of its popularity; you can quickly learn to use `tar` by remembering a few of the simple command-line options. For example, to create a compressed archive of a directory, use `tar`'s `czf` options, like this:

```
matthew@seymour:~$ tar czf compressedfilename.tgz directoryname
```

The result is a compressed archive (a file ending in .tgz) of the specified directory (and all files and directories under it). Add the letter `v` to the preceding options to view the list of files added during compression and archiving while the archive is being created. To list the contents of the compressed archive, substitute the `c` option with the letter `t`, like this:

```
matthew@seymour:~$ tar tzf archive
```

However, if many files are in the archive, a better invocation (to easily read or scroll through the output) is this:

```
matthew@seymour:~$ tar tzf archive | less
```

To expand the contents of a compressed archive, use `tar`'s `zxf` options, as follows:

```
matthew@seymour:~$ tar zxf archive
```

The `tar` utility decompresses the specified archive and extracts the contents in the current directory.

Using Multiple Terminals with byobu

Many Linux veterans have enjoyed and use the screen command, which was designed to enable you to use one terminal to control several terminal sessions easily. Although screen has been a welcome and useful tool, a better one has appeared called byobu; it is an enhanced version of screen. *Byobu* is a Japanese term for decorative, multipanel, vertically folding screens that are often used as room dividers.

Picture this scene: You connect to a server via *Secure Shell (SSH)* and are working at the remote shell. You need to open another shell window so you can have the two running side by side; perhaps you want the output from top in one window while typing in another. What do you do? Most people would open another SSH connection, but that is both wasteful and unnecessary. Like screen, byobu is a terminal multiplexer, which is a fancy term for a program that enables you to run multiple terminals inside one terminal.

The best way to learn byobu is to try it yourself. So, open a console, type byobu and then press Enter. Your display blinks momentarily and is then replaced with a new console with new information in a panel at the bottom. Now, do something with that terminal. Run top and leave it running for the time being. Press F2. Your prompt clears again, leaving you able to type. Run the uptime command.

Pop quiz: What happened to the old terminal running top? It is still running, of course. You can press F3 to return to it. Press F4 to go back to your uptime terminal. While you are viewing other terminals, the commands in the other terminals carry on running as normal so you can multitask. Here are some of the basic commands in byobu:

▶ F2—Create a new window

▶ F3—Go to the previous window

▶ F4—Go to the next window

▶ F9—Open the Byobu menu for help and configuration

To close a terminal within byobu, simply log out of it normally using exit or Ctrl+D. When you exit the last terminal session that is open in byobu, the program closes as well and drops you to the regular terminal session you used to start byobu.

However, there are two alternatives to quitting a byobu session: locking and disconnecting. The first, activated with F12, locks access to your screen data until you enter your system password.

The second is the most powerful feature of screen and also works beautifully in byobu: You can exit it and do other things for a while and then reconnect later; both screen and byobu pick up where you left off. For example, you could be typing at your desk, detach from a session and go home, reconnect, and carry on as if nothing had changed. What's more, all the programs you ran from screen or byobu carry on running even while screen or byobu is disconnected. It even automatically disconnects for you if someone closes your terminal window while it is in a locked state (with Ctrl+A+X).

To disconnect, press F6. You are returned to the prompt from which you launched `screen` or `byobu` and can carry on working, close the terminal you had opened, or even log out completely. When you want to reconnect, run the command `screen -r` or `byobu -r`. You can, in the meantime, just run `screen` or `byobu` and start a new session without resuming the previous one, but that is not wise if you value your sanity. You can disconnect and reconnect the same session as many times you want, which potentially means you need never lose your session again.

Although this has been a mere taste of what `byobu` and `screen` can do, hopefully you can see how useful they can be. Check the man pages for each to learn more. You can also find Byobu documentation at http://byobu.co and https://help.ubuntu.com/community/Byobu.

Polite System Reset Using REISUB

Sometimes computer systems freeze. I'm not talking about the times when one program starts acting weird and the program freezes, but everything else works fine. In those cases, you can use `kill` to terminate the program and move on, as described in the section earlier in this chapter on using `top` or by using the `kill` command described in Chapter 16, "System Monitoring Tools." I'm talking about those times when nothing will work. Nothing responds to any keyboard or other input, not even a Ctrl+Alt+Del key combination. What then? The absolute worst case scenario is to perform a power cycle, which is a fancy way of saying, "Turn it off and back on again." The problem is that power cycling can cause you to lose data because it can corrupt the filesystem. This doesn't always happen, but it is a large enough risk that you want to avoid performing a power cycle unless absolutely necessary. Instead, here is something to try first.

The Linux kernel has a set of key combination commands that are built in, at the kernel level. These are referred to using the name of one of the keys, the SysRq key, often labeled PrtScr. The *Magic SysRq Key* combinations send commands directly to the kernel, bypassing any programs running on top of the kernel, including your window manager and probably anything that is frozen. To use these commands, press SysRq+Alt+ one other key. Here we will focus on the six most useful to most of us; there is a full list of available commands available at https://en.wikipedia.org/wiki/Reisub.

REISUB is an acronym used as a mnemonic device to help users remember the Magic SysRq Key sequence that is best to use when trying to restart a frozen system without risking damage to the filesystem. You hold down SysRq+Alt and press the R, E, I, S, U, B keys one at a time, in order. This performs the following series of actions, listed in order with the letter corresponding to the command capitalized:

▶ **unRaw**—takes control of the keyboard back from the X server

▶ **tErminate**—sends a SIGTERM command to all processes, which allows time for the processes to terminate gracefully

▶ **kIll**—sends a SIGKILL to all processes, forcing any still running to terminate immediately

▶ **Sync**—flush data from memory to disk

▶ **Unmount**—unmount and remount all filesystems as read only

▶ **reBoot**—turn off and back on again, restarting the computer

If you have to use REISUB, allow several seconds for each step. Be patient. Doing it this way can save you from the heartache of lost data.

Fixing an Ubuntu System That Will Not Boot

Although it's uncommon, it happens. There are many reasons a system won't boot. The goal here is to help you discover one that may help you recover your system. The ideas in this section are for computers that have had a working Ubuntu installation; however, they may also be useful if you attempted an install but it did not work. They are not going to help with troubleshooting computers running Windows or other operating systems.

Checking BIOS

If your computer is unable to boot at all, not even from a known-good bootable USB drive or live DVD, there are two options. It is possible you accidentally reset the boot devices and/or order in your system BIOS. If making sure those settings are correct does not help, you may have a hardware problem.

Checking GRUB

If you are able to turn the computer on and get past the initial BIOS startup, then you should consider whether you can access GRUB. As discussed in greater detail in Chapter 15, "The Boot Process," the GRUB boot loader takes over after the BIOS has completed its initial work. Hold down the Shift key after the BIOS part is done to bring up the GRUB menu. If GRUB does not appear, then perhaps it has been overwritten, in which case the next section will help. If GRUB is working fine, skip to the "Use Recovery Mode" section.

Reinstalling GRUB

Note: If you have a dual-boot system, you must be extremely careful with the steps in this section because the details in Step 2 may differ depending on the other operating system residing on your system. Troubleshooting dual-boot systems is outside the scope of this book.

To restore GRUB, follow these steps:

1. Boot Ubuntu from a live DVD or bootable USB drive that has the same Ubuntu release as your system, such as 16.04.

2. Determine the boot drive on your system:

   a. Open a terminal and use `sudo fdisk -l` to list the drives attached to this system.

   b. Look for an entry in the output with an * in the Boot column. This is your boot device. It will look something like `/dev/sda1`.

3. Mount the Ubuntu partition at `/mnt` using this command, replacing `/dev/sda1` with the information you just found: `sudo mount /dev/sda1 /mnt`.

4. Reinstall GRUB with this, again replacing `/dev/sda1` with what you found earlier: `sudo grub-install --boot-directory=/mnt/boot /dev/sda1`.

5. Restart the computer, and Ubuntu should boot properly.

Using Recovery Mode

If GRUB is already working but you are unable to access Ubuntu, you may be able to use recovery mode. Press Shift after the BIOS is done to access the GRUB menu. Select Advanced Options for Ubuntu. From the new menu, select an entry with the words *recovery mode*. This boots into a recovery menu with options to automatically fix several possible problems, or at least it lets you boot into a minimal recovery-mode version of Ubuntu with only the most necessary processes loaded. From here, you may be able to fix disks, check filesystems, drop to a root prompt to fix file permissions, and so on. If you don't understand the entries in this menu, they aren't likely to help you much, and you should consider the next option.

Reinstalling Ubuntu

If you are able to boot using a live DVD or bootable USB drive using the same Ubuntu release or one just newer than the one on the hard drive, and if there are no hardware problems with your system, you can usually recover all your files by reinstalling Ubuntu. Boot from the install medium and select Install Ubuntu. Make sure you are paying attention. The installer will detect an existing Ubuntu installation and give you the option to reinstall Ubuntu. When you do this, it should not overwrite existing files in your /home directory. Note, we said *should*, not *will*, so consider this an option of last resort.

Tips and Tricks

This last section is a motley collection of useful command line tidbits that don't really fit well in the other categories, but which are worth sharing. Enjoy.

Running the Previous Command

You can rerun the previous command with the up arrow and Enter. You can also rerun it with !! (referred to as "bang bang"). This is especially useful for those moments when you typed the command correctly, but forgot to preface it with sudo.

```
matthew@seymour:~$ apt-get update
E: Could not open lock file /var/lib/apt/lists/lock - open (13: Permission denied)
E: Unable to lock directory /var/lib/apt/lists/
E: Could not open lock file /var/lib/dpkg/lock - open (13: Permission denied)
E: Unable to lock the administration directory (/var/lib/dpkg/), are you root?
matthew@seymour:~$ sudo !!
```

This will run `sudo apt-get update`.

Running Any Previous Command

You found this neat trick and ran it, but you can't remember it. That is frustrating. You know you can use the up and down arrows to search through your command history and try to find it, but you last ran it earlier in the week and you aren't sure how long that will take. No worries. You can search your command history.

Type Ctrl+R at the command line to start what is called a "reverse-i search" and begin typing. Whatever you type will be matched to previously run commands, so if you know it was a cool combination of commands piped together that had `sort` in the middle, start typing "sort" and watch as the displayed commands from your history appear. When you find it, hit Enter and run it again.

Running a Previous Command that Started with Specific Letters

You are listing the contents of a directory that is several layers deep and you last ran it about 9 commands ago, but you don't feel like scrolling. No sweat. Use ! (bang) and the letters that make up that command or its beginning.

```
matthew@seymour:~$ !ls
```

This will run the most recently run command that started with "ls".

Running the Same Thing You Just Ran with a Different First Word

You just used `ls` to list a file and you have confirmed it is present. Now you want to use `nano` to edit the file. Use !* (bang star).

```
matthew@seymour:~$ ls stuff/article.txt
article.txt
matthew@seymour:~$ nano !*
```

Viewing Your History and More

By default, the previous 1000 commands you have run are saved in your /home directory in a file called .bash_history. You can edit this file. You can delete this file.

You can change the number of commands saved in your history by editing this line in the .bashrc file in your /home directory to whatever number you want.

```
HISTSIZE=1000
```

Doing Two or More Things

There are a few ways you can do this.

Separating commands with a ; (semicolon) will execute the second command after the first command is complete, regardless of the result of the first command.

```
matthew@seymour:~$ command1 ; command2
```

If you want the second command to be run only if the first command exited with no errors, use && (two ampersands).

```
matthew@seymour:~$ command1 && command2
```

If you want the second command to be run only if the first command fails, use || (two pipes).

```
matthew@seymour:~$ command1 || command2
```

Using Shortcuts

We all make typing errors while entering commands. When you notice an error in a long line of text, just before you hit Enter, it is frustrating to use the backspace key to erase the entire line one character at a time. There are faster ways.

Use Ctrl+U to erase the entire line.

Use Ctrl+W to erase word by word.

Use the left and right arrow key to move along the line to where the error is.

Use Ctrl+A to move your cursor to the beginning of the line.

Use Ctrl+E to move your cursor to the end of the line.

Use Ctrl+K to erase everything to the right of your cursor's position.

Use Ctrl+Y to restore something you just deleted, but shouldn't have.

Confining a Script to a Directory

Sometimes you want to isolate a process from the rest of the system, such as when you want to test a script you have written, but you also want to make sure the script is only able to affect what you want it to and not anything else. To do this, you can set up what is called a *chroot jail*. Really, all you are doing is creating a new directory, copying the files you need for the process to run into that directory, and then using the `chroot` command to change the root directory to the base of this new file system tree. Explained differently, you are making the system act temporarily as if the directory you just named is root, when in reality nothing in the filesystem has changed.

For example, let's say you have a simple filesystem like this:

```
/
├─etc
├─home
|  └testing
|     └fakeetc
|        └www
└var
└www
```

If you enter:

```
matthew@seymour:~$ chroot testing
```

And follow it with:

```
matthew@seymour:~$ ls /
```

You will receive this output:

```
/
├─fakeetc
└─www
```

> **TIP**
>
> It is possible for processes that run as root to "break out" of a chroot environment, so maybe *chroot jail* is not the most accurate term, but it is commonly used. Better to think of this as a means to do some isolated testing, but not truly secure testing.

Using Coreutils

You have already learned about some of the contents of a package of useful command line tools called GNU Coreutils. It includes some of the most used commands like `ls`, `mv`, `cp`, `rm`, and `cat`. It also contains a ton of lesser known, but incredibly useful tools. This package is installed by default. Few people ever make use of its richness. You will want to explore it more deeply. Coreutils contains so much, it is worthy of a chapter and maybe a book of its own. What we can do here is point you to the GNU website entry for Coreutils as https://www.gnu.org/software/coreutils/ and also the info page at `info coreutils` (there is no man page for Coreutils).

Reading the Contents of the Kernel Ring Buffer with `dmesg`

Although it sounds fancy and ominous, the *kernel ring buffer* is actually quite simple, at least conceptually. It records a limited set of messages related to the operation of the Linux kernel. When it reaches a certain number of messages, then it deletes the oldest message every time a new message is written to the list. Looking at the contents of the kernel ring buffer with `dmesg` can be helpful in determining what is happening with your system. If you enter:

```
matthew@seymour:~$ dmesg
```

You will receive an incredibly long and scary-looking list of data. Alone, this is too much information to be really helpful. The best use of `dmesg`, then, is to combine it with a filter and look for specific entries in the output. You might search for a part of the system, like "memory" or a specific vendor, like "nvidia," to read messages containing that text as in:

```
matthew@seymour:~$ dmesg | grep nvidia
```

References

▶ **www.vim.org/**—Home page for the `vim` (`vi` clone) editor included with Linux distributions. Check here for updates, bug fixes, and news about this editor.

▶ **www.gnu.org/software/emacs/emacs.html**—Home page for the FSF's GNU `emacs` editing environment; you can find additional documentation and links to the source code for the latest version here.

▶ **www.nano-editor.org/**—Home page for the GNU `nano` editor environment.

▶ *Sed & Awk* by Dale Dougherty and Arnold Robbins is the standard book for learning Sed and Awk.

▶ O'Reilly's *The UNIX CD Bookshelf* (ISBN: 0-596-00392-7) contains seven highly respected books in one, although it retails for more than $120 as a result. However, it is incomparable in its depth and breadth of coverage.

# CHAPTER 13

Managing Users

System administrators would have a boring, but much easier life without users. In reality, it's impossible to have a system with absolutely no users, so it is important that you learn how to effectively manage and administer your users as they work with your system. Whether you are creating a single user account or modifying a group that holds hundreds of user accounts, the fundamentals of user administration are the same.

User management and administration includes allocating and managing /home directories, putting in place good password policies, and applying an effective security policy that includes things such as disk quotas and file and directory access permissions. This chapter covers all these areas as well as some of the different types of users that you are likely to find on a typical Linux system.

User Accounts

You normally find three types of users on Linux systems: the super user, the day-to-day user, and the system user. Each type is essential to the smooth running of your system. Learning the differences between the three is essential if you are to work efficiently and safely within your Linux environment.

All users who access your system must have accounts on the system. Ubuntu uses the /etc/passwd file to store information on the user accounts that are present on the system. All users, regardless of their type, have a one-line entry in this file that contains their username (typically used for logging in to the system), an encrypted field for the password (which contains an X to denote that a password is present), a user ID (commonly referred to as the UID), and a group ID (commonly referred to as the GID). The last two fields show the location of the /home directory (usually /home/username) and the default shell for the user (/bin/bash is the default for new users). There is also a field called GECOS that uses a comma-delimited list to record information about the account or the user; most often when this field is used it records the user's full name and contact information.

> **NOTE**
>
> Although the Password field contains an **X**, this doesn't mean that what you read here is the actual password. All passwords are stored in /etc/shadow in an encrypted format for safekeeping. Ubuntu automatically refers to this file whenever a password is required. You can read more about this later in the chapter in the "Shadow Passwords" section.

In keeping with long-standing tradition in UNIX-style operating systems, Ubuntu makes use of the well-established UNIX file ownership and permission system. To start with, everything in these systems is treated as a file, and all files (which can include directories and devices) can be assigned to one or more of read, write, and execute permissions. These three "flags" can also be assigned as desired to each of three categories: the owner of the file, a member of a group, or anyone else on the system. The security for a file is drawn from these permissions and from file ownership. As the system administrator (also commonly referred to as the *super user*), it is your responsibility to manage these settings effectively and ensure that the users have proper UIDs and GIDs. Perhaps most important, the system administrator can lock away sensitive files from users who should not have access to them through these file permissions.

The Super User/Root User

No matter how many system administrators there are for a system, there can only be one super user account. The super user account, more commonly referred to as the *root user*, has total and complete control over all aspects of the system. That account can access any part of the file system; read, change, or delete any file; grant and revoke access to files and directories; and can carry out any operation on the system, including destroying it if the root user so wishes. The root user is unique in that it has a UID of 0 and GID of 0.

In other words, the root user has supreme power over your system. With this in mind, it's important that you do not work as root all the time because you might inadvertently cause serious damage to your system, perhaps even making it totally unusable. Instead, rely on root only when you need to make specific changes to your system that require root privileges. As soon as you've finished your work, you can switch back to your normal user account to carry on working.

In Ubuntu, you execute a command with root, or super user, privileges using the sudo command, like this:

```
matthew@seymour:~$ sudo apt-get update
```

You are then prompted for your password, which will not show on the screen as you enter it. After typing in your password, press Enter. Ubuntu then carries out the command (in this case updating information about available software) as if you were running it as root.

THE ROOT USER

If you've used other Linux distros, you might be a little puzzled by the use of the `sudo` command because not all distros use it. In short, Ubuntu allows the first user on the system access to full root privileges using the `sudo` command. It also disables the root account so that no one can actually log in with the username *root*.

In other Linux distros, you change to the root user by issuing the command `su -nd` and then entering the root password when prompted. This lands you at the root prompt, which is shown as a pound sign (#). From here, you can execute any command you want. To get to a root prompt in Ubuntu you need to execute the command `sudo -i` which, after you enter your password, gives you the prompt so familiar to other Linux distros. When you've finished working as root, type `exit` and press Enter to get back to a normal user prompt ($).

13

A regular user is someone who logs on to the system to use it for nonadministrative tasks such as word processing or email. These users do not need to make system-wide changes or manage other users. However, they might want to be able to change settings specific to their accounts (for instance, a desktop background). Depending on how much control the system administrator (the root or super user) likes to wield, regular users might not even be able to do that.

The super user grants privileges to regular users using file and directory permissions (as covered in Chapter 10, "Command-Line Beginner's Class"). For example, if the super user does not want you to change your settings in `~/.profile` (the ~ is a shell shortcut representing your `/home` directory), then as root she can alter the permissions so that you may read from, but not write to, that file.

CAUTION

Because of the potential for making a catastrophic error as the super user, always use your system as a regular user and only use your super user powers temporarily to do specific administration tasks. This is easier to remember in Ubuntu where the use of `sudo` is default and the root account is initially disabled. If you work on a multiuser system, consider this advice an absolute rule; if root were to delete the wrong file or kill the wrong process, the results could be disastrous for the system (and likely the business that owns and operates it). On your home system, you can do as you please. Running as root makes many things easier, but much less safe, and we still do not recommend doing so. In any setting, however, the risks of running as root are significant, and we cannot stress how important it is to be careful when working as root.

The third type of user is the system user. The system user is not a person, but rather an administrative account that the system uses during day-to-day running of various services. For example, the system user named `www-data` owns the Apache web server and all the associated files. Only that user and root can have access to these files; no one else can access or make changes to these files. System users do not have a home directory or password, nor do they permit access to the system through a login prompt.

You can find a list of all the users on a system in the `/etc/passwd` file.

User IDs and Group IDs

A computer is, by its very nature, a number-oriented machine. It identifies users and groups by numbers known as the *user ID (UID)* and *group ID (GID)*. The alphabetic names display on your screen just for ease of use.

As previously mentioned, the root user is UID 0. Numbers from 1 through 499 and number 65,534 are the system, sometimes called logical or pseudo-users. Regular users have UIDs beginning with 1,000; Ubuntu assigns them sequentially beginning with this number.

With only a few exceptions, the GID is the same as the UID.

Ubuntu creates a private GID for every UID of 1,000 and greater. The system administrator can add other users to a GID or create a totally new group and add users to it. Unlike Windows NT and some UNIX variants, a group cannot be a member of another group in Ubuntu (or any Linux distribution).

File Permissions

There are three types of permissions: read, write, and execute (`r`, `w`, `x`). For any file or directory, permissions are assigned to three categories: user, group, and other. This section focuses on group permissions. First, though, we want to highlight three commands used to change the group, user, or access permissions of a file or directory:

- ▶ `chgrp`—Changes the group ownership of a file or directory
- ▶ `chown`—Changes the owner of a file or directory
- ▶ `chmod`—Changes the access permissions of a file or directory

You can use these commands to reproduce organizational structures and permissions in the real world in your Ubuntu system (see the next section, "Managing Groups"). For example, a human resources department can share health-benefit memos to all company employees by making the files readable (but not writable) by anyone in an accessible directory. Programmers in the company's research and development section, although able to access each other's source code files, would not have read or write access to HR pay scale or personnel files (and certainly would not want HR or marketing poking around R&D).

These commands are used to easily manage group and file ownerships and permissions from the command line. It is essential that you know these commands because there are times when you are likely to have only a command-line interface to work with, such as when a well-meaning but fat-fingered system administrator set incorrect permissions on X11, rendering the system incapable of working with a graphical interface. (No, we won't tell that story, but if you press them, most systems administrators have similar tales of woe.)

USER STEREOTYPES

As is the case in many professions, exaggerated stereotypes have emerged for users and system administrators. Many stereotypes contain elements of truth mixed with generous amounts of hyperbole and humor and serve to assist us in understanding the characteristics of and differences in the stereotyped subjects. The stereotypes of the *luser* and the *BOFH* (not-so-nice terms for users and administrators, respectively) serve as cautionary tales describing what behavior is acceptable and unacceptable in the computing community.

Understanding these stereotypes enables you to better define the appropriate and inappropriate roles of system administrators, users, and others. You can find a description of each on Wikipedia at http://en.wikipedia.org/wiki/BOFH and http://en.wikipedia.org/wiki/Luser.

Managing Groups

Groups can make managing users a lot easier. Instead of having to assign individual permissions to every user, you can use groups to grant or revoke permissions to a large number of users quickly and easily. Setting group permissions enables you to set up workspaces for collaborative working and to control what devices can be used, such as external drives or DVD writers. This approach also represents a secure method of limiting access to system resources to only those users who need them. As an example, the system administrator could put the users matthew, ryan, sandra, holly, debra, and mark in a new group named unleashed. Those users could each create files intended for their group work and chgrp those files to unleashed.

Now, everyone in the unleashed group—but no one else except root—can work with those files. The system administrator would probably create a directory owned by that group so that its members could have an easily accessible place to store those files. The system administrator could also add other users such as chris and shannon to the group and remove existing users when their part of the work is done. The system administrator could make the user matthew the group administrator so that matthew could decide how group membership should be changed. You could also put restrictions on the DVD writer so that only matthew could burn DVDs, thus protecting sensitive material from falling into the wrong hands.

Group Listing

Different UNIX operating systems implement the group concept in various ways. Ubuntu uses a scheme called *UPG (user private group)* in which the default is that all users are assigned to a group with their own name. (The user's username and group name are identical.) All the groups on a system are listed in /etc/group file.

Here is an example of a portion of the /etc/group file:

```
matthew@seymour:~$ cat /etc/group
root:x:0:
daemon:x:1:
```

```
bin:x:2:
sys:x:3:
adm:x:4:matthew
tty:x:5:
disk:x:6:
mail:x:8:
news:x:9:
fax:x:21:matthew
voice:x:22:
cdrom:x:24:matthew
floppy:x:25:matthew
tape:x:26:matthew
www-data:x:33:
crontab:x:107:
ssh:x:109:
admin:x:115:matthew
saned:x:116:
gdm:x:119:
matthew:x:1000:
ntp:x:122:
```

In this example, you see a number of groups, mostly for services (mail, news, and so on) and devices (floppy, disk, and so on). As previously mentioned, the system services groups allow those services to have ownership and control of their files. For example, adding postfix to the mail group, as shown previously, enables the postfix application to access mail's files in the manner that mail would decide for group access to its file. Adding a regular user to a device's group permits the regular user to use the device with permissions granted by the group owner. Adding user matthew to the group cdrom, for example, allows matthew to use the optical drive device. You learn how to add and remove users from groups in the next section.

AN ALTERNATE WAY TO FIND YOUR GROUPS

You can also find which groups your user account belongs to with the group command, like this:

```
matthew@seymour:~$ groups

matthew adm cdrom sudo audio dip plugdev lpadmin sambashare
```

Add a username after the command to list the groups for that user.

Group Management Tools

Ubuntu provides several command-line tools for managing groups, but it also provides graphical tools for doing so. Most experienced system administrators prefer the command-line tools because they are quick and easy to use, are always available even when there is no graphic user interface, and because they can be included in scripts she may write if the system administrator wants to write a quick program to perform a repetitive task.

Here are the most commonly used group management command-line tools:

▶ **groupadd**—This command creates and adds a new group.

▶ **groupdel**—This command removes an existing group.

▶ **groupmod**—This command creates a group name or GIDs but doesn't add or delete members from a group.

▶ **gpasswd**—This command creates a group password. Every group can have a group password and an administrator. Use the -A argument to assign a user as group administrator.

▶ **useradd -G**—The -G argument adds a user to a group during the initial user creation. (More arguments are used to create a user.)

▶ **usermod -G**—This command allows you to add a user to a group so long as the user is not logged in at the time.

▶ **grpck**—This command checks the /etc/group file for typos.

Let's say there is a DVD-RW device (/dev/scd0) on our computer that the system administrator wants a regular user named ryan to have permission to access. This is the process to grant ryan that access:

1. Add a new group with the groupadd command:

matthew@seymour:~$ **sudo groupadd dvdrw**

2. Change the group ownership of the device to the new group with the chgrp command:

matthew@seymour:~$ **sudo chgrp dvdrw /dev/scd0**

3. Add the approved user to the group with the usermod command:

matthew@seymour:~$ **sudo usermod -G dvdrw ryan**

4. Make user ryan the group administrator with the gpasswd command so that he can add new users to the group:

matthew@seymour:~$ **sudo gpasswd -A ryan**

Now ryan has permission to use the DVD-RW drive, as would anyone else added to the group by either the super user or ryan because he is now also a group administrator and can add users to the group.

The system administrator can also use the graphical interface that Ubuntu provides, as shown in Figure 13.1. It is accessed from the menu at System, Administration, Users, and Groups.

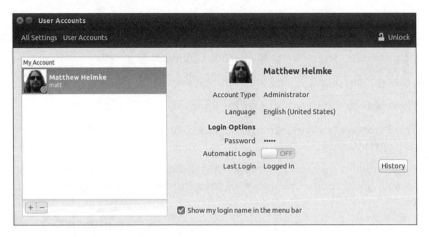

FIGURE 13.1   Use Manage Groups to assign users to groups.

Note that the full set of group commands and options are not available from the graphical interface. This limits the usefulness of the GUI to a subset of the most frequently used commands. You learn more about using the Ubuntu User Manager GUI in the next section of this chapter.

Managing Users

Users must be created, assigned a UID, provided a /home directory, provided an initial set of files for their home directory, and assigned to groups so that they can use the system resources securely and efficiently. The system administrator in some situations might want or need to not only restrict a user's access to specific files and folders, but also the amount of disk space an account may use.

User Management Tools

As with groups, Ubuntu provides several command-line tools for managing users, but also provides graphical tools for doing so. Most experienced system administrators prefer the command-line tools because they are quick and easy to use, are always available even when there is no GUI, and because they can be included in scripts she may write if the system administrator wants to write a quick program to perform a repetitive task. Here are the most common commands to manage users:

▶ **useradd**—This command adds a new user account to the system. Its options permit the system administrator to specify the user's /home directory and initial group or to create the user with the default /home directory and group assignments (based on the new account's username).

▶ **useradd -D**—This command sets the system defaults for creating the user's /home directory, account expiration date, default group, and command shell. See the specific options in the useradd man page. Used without any arguments, it displays the defaults for the system. The default set of files for a user are in /etc/skel.

13

NOTE

The set of files initially used to populate a new user's home directory are kept in `/etc/skel`. This is convenient for the system administrator because any special files, links, or directories that need to be universally applied can be placed in `/etc/skel` and will be duplicated automatically with appropriate permissions for each new user:

```
matthew@seymour:~$ ls -la /etc/skel
total 32
drwxr-xr-x     2 root root    4096 2010-04-25 12:14 .
drwxr-xr-x 154 root root   12288 2010-07-01 16:30 ..
-rw-r--r--     1 root root     220 2009-09-13 22:08 .bash_logout
-rw-r--r--     1 root root    3103 2010-04-18 19:15 .bashrc
-rw-r--r--     1 root root     179 2010-03-26 05:31 examples.desktop
-rw-r--r--     1 root root     675 2009-09-13 22:08 .profile
```

Each line provides the file permissions, the number of files housed under that file or directory name, the file owner, the file group, the file size, the creation date, and the filename.

As you can see, root owns every file here. The `useradd` command copies everything in `/etc/skel` to the new home directory and resets file ownership and permissions to the new user.

▶ Certain user files might exist that the system administrator doesn't want the user to change; the permissions for those files in `/home/username` can be reset so that the user can read them but can't write to them. `deluser`—This command removes a user's account (thereby eliminating that user's home directory and all files it contains). There is an older version of this command, `userdel`, that previous versions of this book discussed. `deluser` is preferred because it provides finer control over what is deleted. Whereas `userdel` automatically removes both the user account and also all the user's files, such as the associated `/home` directory, `deluser` only deletes the user account, unless you use a command-line option to tell it to do more. With `deluser`, using these options you can still `--remove-home`, you can `--remove-all-files`, you can `--backup` that user's files first, and more. See the `man page` for more information.

▶ `passwd`—This command updates the "authentication tokens" used by the password management system.

TIP

To lock a user out of his account, use the following command:

```
matthew@seymour:~$ sudo passwd -l username
```

This prepends an `!` (exclamation point, also called a bang) to the user's encrypted password; the command to reverse the process uses the `-u` option.

▶ `usermod`—This command changes several user attributes. The most commonly used arguments are `-s` to change the shell and `-u` to change the UID. No changes can be made while the user is logged in or running a process.

▶ **chsh**—This command changes the user's default shell. For Ubuntu, the default shell is /bin/bash, known as the Bash, or Bourne Again Shell.

Adding New Users

The command-line approach to adding a user is quite simple and can be accomplished on a single line. In the following example, the system administrator uses the useradd command to add the new user sandra. The command adduser (a variant found on some UNIX systems) is a symbolic link to useradd, so both commands work the same. This example uses the -p option to set the password the user requested and the -u option to specify her UID. (If you create a user with the default settings, you do not need to use these options.) All you want to do can be accomplished on one line:

```
matthew@seymour:~$ sudo useradd sandra -p c00kieZ4ME -u 1042
```

The system administrator can also use the graphical interface that Ubuntu provides to add the same account as shown in the preceding command, but with fewer setting options available:

1. Launch the Ubuntu User Manager graphical interface by searching the Dash for User Accounts.

2. Click Unlock at the upper right and enter your password to authorize making changes to user accounts (refer to Figure 13.1).

3. Click + at the lower left to open the Add Account window (refer to Figure 13.1).

4. Fill in the form with the new user's name and desired username and click Add (Figure 13.2).

FIGURE 13.2   Adding a new user is simple. The GUI provides a set of options for user management spread over several screens as shown here.

5. Select the user from the list. On the right, click Account disabled (Figure 13.3) to bring up the Change Password window (Figure 13.4).

6. Under Action, select Enable this account and click Change.

7. Repeat step 5 to reopen the Change Password window. This time, under Action, select Set a password now. Assign a good password and click Change.

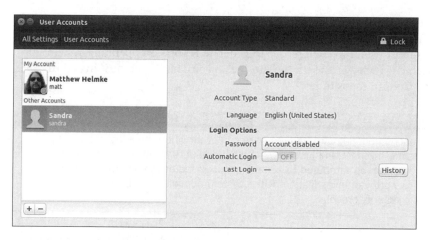

FIGURE 13.3   Select the new user from the list.

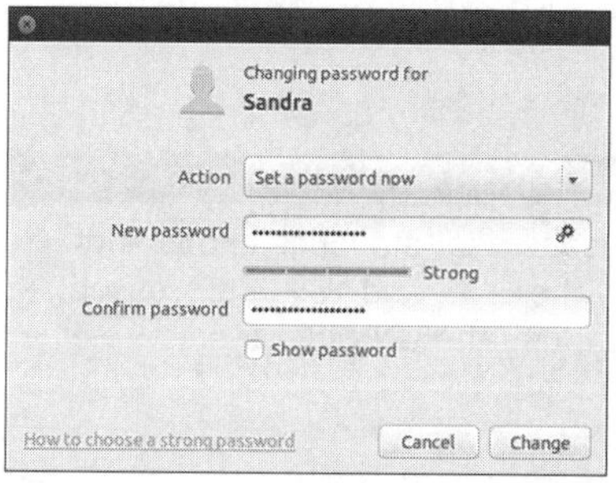

FIGURE 13.4   Change user password.

NOTE

A Linux username can be any alphanumeric combination that does not begin with a special character reserved for shell script use. (See Chapter 14, "Automating Tasks and Shell Scripting," for disallowed characters, mostly <space> and punctuation characters.) Usernames are often the user's first name plus the first initial of her last name or the first initial of the user's first name and his entire last name. These are common practices on larger systems with many users because it makes life simpler for the system administrator, but neither is a rule nor a requirement.

Monitoring User Activity on the System

Monitoring user activity is part of the system administrator's duties and an essential task in tracking how system resources are being used. The w command tells the system administrator who is logged in, where he is logged in, and what he is doing. No one can hide from the super user. The w command can be followed by a specific user's name to show only that user.

The `ac` command provides information about the total connect time of a user measured in hours. It accesses the `/var/log/wtmp` file for the source of its information. The `ac` command proves most useful in shell scripts to generate reports on operating system usage for management review. Note that to use the `ac` command you must install the `acct` package from the Ubuntu repositories.

TIP

Interestingly, a phenomenon known as *time warp* can occur where an entry in the `wtmp` files jumps back into the past and `ac` shows unusual amounts of time accounted for users. Although this can be attributed to some innocuous factors having to do with the system clock, it is worthy of investigation by the system administrator because it can also be the result of a security breach.

The last command searches through the `/var/log/wtmp` file and lists all the users logged in and out since that file was first created. The user reboot exists so that you might know who has logged in since the last reboot. A companion to `last` is the command `lastb`, which shows all failed, or bad, logins. It is useful for determining whether a legitimate user is having trouble or a hacker is attempting access.

NOTE

The accounting system on your computer keeps track of usage user statistics and is kept in the current `/var/log/wtmp` file. That file is managed by the `init` and `login` processes. If you want to explore the depths of the accounting system, use the GNU info system: `info accounting`.

Managing Passwords

Passwords are an integral part of Linux security, and they are the most visible part to the user. In this section, you learn how to establish a minimal password policy for your system, where the passwords are stored, and how to manage passwords for your users.

System Password Policy

An effective password policy is a fundamental part of a good system administration plan. The policy should cover the following:

▶ Allowed and forbidden passwords

▶ Frequency of mandated password changes

▶ Retrieval or replacement of lost or forgotten passwords

▶ Password handling by users

The Password File

The password file is `/etc/passwd`, and it is the database file for all users on the system. The format of each line is as follows:

```
username:password:uid:gid:gecos:homedir:shell
```

The fields are self-explanatory except for the `gecos` field. This field is for miscellaneous information about the user, such as the user's full name, office location, office and home phone numbers, and possibly a brief text message. For security and privacy reasons, this field is little used today, but the system administrator should be aware of its existence because the `gecos` field is used by traditional UNIX programs such as `finger` and `mail`. For that reason, it is commonly referred to as the *finger information field*. The data in this field is comma delimited; you can change the `gecos` field with the `chfn` (change `finger`) command.

Note that a colon separates all fields in the `/etc/passwd` file. If no information is available for a field, that field is empty, but all the colons remain.

If an asterisk appears in the password field, that user is not permitted to log on. Why does this feature exist? The feature exists so that a user can be easily disabled and (possibly) reinstated later without having to be created all over again. The traditional UNIX way of accomplishing this task is for the system administrator to manually edit this field. Ubuntu provides a more elegant method with the `passwd -l` command mentioned earlier in this chapter.

Several services run as pseudo-users, usually with root permissions. These are the system, or logical, users mentioned previously. You would not want these accounts available for general login for security reasons, so they are assigned `/sbin/nologin` or `/bin/false` as their shell, which prohibits any logins from these accounts.

A list of `/etc/passwd` reveals the following (abridged for brevity):

```
matthew@seymour:~$ cat /etc/passwd
root:x:0:0:root:/root:/bin/bash
bin:x:2:2:bin:/bin:/bin/sh
sys:x:3:3:sys:/dev:/bin/sh
games:x:5:60:games:/usr/games:/bin/sh
man:x:6:12:man:/var/cache/man:/bin/sh
mail:x:8:8:mail:/var/mail:/bin/sh
news:x:9:9:news:/var/spool/news:/bin/sh
uucp:x:10:10:uucp:/var/spool/uucp:/bin/sh
www-data:x:33:33:www-data:/var/www:/bin/sh
gnats:x:41:41:Gnats Bug-Reporting System (admin):/var/lib/gnats:/bin/sh
nobody:x:65534:65534:nobody:/nonexistent:/bin/sh
messagebus:x:102:106::/var/run/dbus:/bin/false
avahi:x:105:111:Avahi mDNS daemon,,,:/var/run/avahi-daemon:/bin/false
couchdb:x:106:113:CouchDB Administrator,,,:/var/lib/couchdb:/bin/bash
haldaemon:x:107:114:Hardware abstraction layer,,,:/var/run/hald:/bin/false
kernoops:x:109:65534:Kernel Oops Tracking Daemon,,,:/:/bin/false
gdm:x:112:119:Gnome Display Manager:/var/lib/gdm:/bin/false
```

```
matthew:x:1000:1000:Matthew Helmke,,,,:/home/matthew:/bin/bash
sshd:x:114:65534::/var/run/sshd:/usr/sbin/nologin
ntp:x:115:122::/home/ntp:/bin/false
pulse:x:111:117:PulseAudio daemon,,,:/var/run/pulse:/bin/false
```

Note that none of the password fields show a password, but rather contain an *X*. This is because they are shadow passwords, a useful security enhancement to Linux.

Shadow Passwords

It is considered a security risk to keep passwords in /etc/passwd because anyone with read access could run a cracking program on the file and obtain the passwords with little trouble. To avoid this risk, *shadow passwords* are used so that only an *X* appears in the password field of /etc/passwd; the real passwords are kept in /etc/shadow, a file that can only be read by the system administrator (and *PAM*, the *Pluggable Authentication Modules* authentication manager; see the "PAM Explained" sidebar for an explanation of PAM).

Special versions of the traditional password and login programs must be used to enable shadow passwords. Shadow passwords are automatically enabled during installation of Ubuntu. Examine the following abbreviated listing of the shadow companion to /etc/passwd, the /etc/shadow file:

```
matthew@seymour:~$ sudo cat /etc/shadow
root:!:14547:0:99999:7:::
daemon:*:14544:0:99999:7:::
bin:*:14544:0:99999:7:::
sys:*:14544:0:99999:7:::
games:*:14544:0:99999:7:::
man:*:14544:0:99999:7:::
mail:*:14544:0:99999:7:::
www-data:*:14544:0:99999:7:::
irc:*:14544:0:99999:7:::
nobody:*:14544:0:99999:7:::
libuuid:!:14544:0:99999:7:::
syslog:*:14544:0:99999:7:::
messagebus:*:14544:0:99999:7:::
kernoops:*:14544:0:99999:7:::
gdm:*:14544:0:99999:7:::
matthew:$6$wtML.mV4$.I5WeTp9tgGkIjJM4uLR5p6TVUqPrSvJ0N2W/t//0jVBrWQrOySEEDvXsA/sKSEl
QsfmNmfPJYxVrjZ21/Ir70:14564:0:99999:7:::
sshd:*:14547:0:99999:7:::
ntp:*:14548:0:99999:7:::
usbmux:*:14724:0:99999:7:::
pulse:*:14725:0:99999:7:::
```

The fields are separated by colons and are, in order:

▶ The user's login name.

▶ The encrypted password for the user.

▶ The day on which the last password change occurred, measured in the number of days since January 1, 1970. This date is known in UNIX circles as the *epoch*. Just so you know, the billionth second since the epoch occurred was in September 2001; that was the UNIX version of Y2K—as with the real Y2K, nothing much happened.

▶ The number of days before the password can be changed (prevents changing a password and then changing it back to the old password right away—a dangerous security practice).

▶ The number of days after which the password must be changed. This can be set to force the change of a newly issued password known to the system administrator.

▶ The number of days before the password expiration that the user is warned it will expire.

▶ The number of days after the password expires that the account is disabled (for security).

▶ Similar to the password change date, although this is the number of days since January 1, 1970, that the account has been disabled.

▶ The final field is a "reserved" field and is not currently allocated for any use.

Note that password expiration dates and warnings are disabled by default in Ubuntu. These features are not often used on home systems and usually not even used for small offices. It is the system administrator's responsibility to establish and enforce password expiration policies if they are to exist.

The permissions on the `/etc/shadow` file should be set so that it is not writable or readable by regular users: The permissions should be `600`.

PAM EXPLAINED

Pluggable Authentication Modules (PAM) is a system of libraries that handle the tasks of authentication on your computer. It uses four management groups: account management, authentication management, password management, and session management. This allows the system administrator to choose how individual applications will authenticate users. Ubuntu has preinstalled and preconfigured all the necessary PAM files for you.

The configuration files in Ubuntu are in `/etc/pam.d`. These files are named for the service they control, and the format is as follows:

```
type control module-path module-arguments
```

The `type` field is the management group that the rule corresponds to. The `control` field tells PAM what to do if authentication fails. The final two items deal with the PAM module used and any arguments it needs. Programs that use PAM typically come packaged with appropriate entries for the `/etc/pam.d` directory. To achieve greater security, the system administrator can modify the default entries. Misconfiguration can have unpredictable results, so back up the configuration files before you modify them. The defaults provided by Ubuntu are adequate for home and small office users.

An example of a PAM configuration file with the formatted entries as described previously is shown next. Here are the contents of `/etc/pam.d/gdm`:

```
#%PAM-1.0
auth      requisite        pam_nologin.so
auth      required         pam_env.so readenv=1
auth      required         pam_env.so readenv=1 envfile=/etc/default/locale
auth      sufficient        pam_succeed_if.so user ingroup nopasswdlogin
@include common-auth
auth      optional         pam_gnome_keyring.so
@include common-account
session [success=ok ignore=ignore module_unknown=ignore default=bad]
➥pam_selinux.so open
session required         pam_limits.so
@include common-session
session [success=ok ignore=ignore module_unknown=ignore default=bad]
➥pam_selinux.so close
session optional         pam_gnome_keyring.so auto_start
@include common-password
```

Amusingly, even the PAM documents state that you do not really need (or want) to know a lot about PAM to use it effectively.

You will likely need only the PAM system administrator's guide. You can find it at www.kernel.org/pub/linux/libs/pam/Linux-PAM-html/Linux-PAM_SAG.html.

Managing Password Security for Users

Selecting appropriate user passwords is always an exercise in trade-offs. A password such as *password* (do not laugh, it has been used often in the real world and with devastating consequences) is just too easy to guess by an intruder. So are simple words or number combinations (the numbers from a street address or date of birth, for example). You would be surprised how many people use easily guessed passwords such as 123456, iloveyou, Qwerty, or abc123.

In contrast, a password such as 2a56u'"F($84u&#^Hiu44Ik%$([#EJD is sure to present great difficulty to an intruder (or an auditor). However, that password is so difficult to remember that it would be likely that the password owner would write that password down on a sticky note attached to his monitor.

The system administrator has control, with settings in the `/etc/shadow` file, over how often the password must be changed. The settings can be changed by the super user using a text editor, or the `chage` command. (See the `shadow` and `chage` man pages for details.)

Changing Passwords in a Batch

On a large system, there might be times when a large number of users and their passwords need some attention. The super user can change passwords in a batch by using the `chpasswd` command, which accepts input as a name/password pair per line in the following form:

```
matthew@seymour:~$ sudo chpasswd username:password
```

Passwords can be changed *en masse* by redirecting a list of name and password pairs to the command. An appropriate shell script can be constructed with the information gleaned from Chapters 11 and 12, "Command-Line Master Class Parts 1 and 2," combined with information on writing scripts from Chapter 14, "Automating Tasks and Shell Scripting."

However, Ubuntu also provides the `newusers` command to add users in a batch from a text file. This command also allows a user to be added to a group, and a new directory can be added for the user, too.

Granting System Administrator Privileges to Regular Users

On occasion, it might be necessary for regular users to run a command as if they were the root user. They usually do not need these powers, but a user might on a special occasion—for example, to temporarily access certain devices or run a command for testing purposes.

There are two ways to run commands with root privileges. The first way is useful if you are the owner of both the super user account (an enabled root account) and a regular user; the second way is useful if you are not a regular user but are not privileged to access all super user functions. (This might happen on a large, multiuser network with senior and junior administrators as well as regular users.) Let's look at each.

Temporarily Changing User Identity with the `su` Command

This first scenario requires the existence of a root account, which is not enabled by default on Ubuntu systems and is not generally recommended in the Ubuntu community. However, there are times when it makes sense. Discussing that is beyond the scope of this chapter, but for the sake of argument, for the scenario and details in this section assume we are operating in one of those special cases and that a root account has been enabled.

What if you have access to an enabled root account as a super user but are logged on as a regular user because you are performing nonadministrative tasks, and you find you need to do something that only the super user can do? The `su` command is available for this purpose.

> **NOTE**
>
> A popular misconception is that the `su` command is short for *super user*; it really just means *substitute user*. An important but often overlooked distinction is that between `su` and `su -`. In the former instance, you become that user but keep your own environmental variables (such as paths). In the latter, you inherit the environment of that user. This is most noticeable when you use `su` to become the super user, `root`. Without appending the `-`, you do not inherit the path variable that includes `/bin` or `/sbin`, so you must always enter the full path to those commands when you just `su` to `root`.

Don't forget that on a standard Ubuntu system, the first created user is classed as root, whereas the true root account is disabled. To enable the root account, you enter the command `sudo passwd` at the command line and enter your password and a new root password. After this has been completed, you can `su` to root. We suggest you read the information the following website before doing so to ensure you understand the reason the root account is not enabled by default: https://help.ubuntu.com/community/RootSudo.

Because almost all Linux file system security revolves around file permissions, it can be useful to occasionally become a different user with permission to access files belonging to other users or groups or to access special files (such as the communications port `/dev/ttyS0` when using a modem or the sound device `/dev/audio` when playing a game). You can use the `su` command to temporarily switch to another user identity, and then switch back.

The `su` command spawns a new shell, changing both the UID and GID of the existing user and automatically changes the environmental variables associated with that user, known as *inheriting the environment*. For more information about environment variables, see Chapter 5, "Productivity Applications."

The syntax for the `su` command is as follows:

```
matthew@seymour:~$ su option username arguments
```

The man page for `su` gives more details, but some highlights of the `su` command are here:

```
-c, --command COMMAND
        pass a single COMMAND to the shell with -c


-m, --preserve-environment
        do not reset environment variables


-l     a full login simulation for the substituted user,
        the same as specifying the dash alone
```

You can invoke the `su` command in different ways that yield diverse results. By using `su` alone, you can become root, but you keep your regular user environment. This can be verified by using the `printenv` command before and after the change. Note that the working directory (you can execute `pwd` at the command line to print the current working directory) has not changed. By executing the following, you become root and inherit root's environment:

```
matthew@seymour:~$ su -
```

By executing the following, you become that user and inherit the super user's environment—a pretty handy tool. (Remember: Inheriting the environment comes from using the dash in the command; omit that, and you keep your "old" environment.) To become another user, specify a different user's name on the command line:

```
matthew@seymour:~$ su - other_user
```

When leaving an identity to return to your usual user identity, use the `exit` command. For example, while logged on as a regular user

```
matthew@seymour:~$ su - root
```

the system prompts for a password:

```
Password:
```

When the password is entered correctly, the root user's prompt appears:

```
root~#
```

To return to the regular user's identity, just type the following:

```
root~# exit
```

This takes you to the regular user's prompt:

```
matthew@seymour:~$
```

If you need to allow other users access to certain commands with root privileges, you must give them the password for the root account (often referred to as the root password) so that they can use `su`; that definitely is not a secure solution. The next section describes a more flexible and secure method of allowing normal users to perform selected root tasks and the preferred method for sharing and using super user privileges in Ubuntu.

Granting Root Privileges on Occasion: The `sudo` Command

It is often necessary to delegate some of the authority that root wields on a system. For a large system, this makes sense because no single individual will always be available to perform super user functions. The problem is that UNIX permissions come with an all-or-nothing authority. Enter `sudo`, an application that permits the assignment of one, several, or all the root-only system commands.

> **NOTE**
>
> As mentioned earlier, the `sudo` command is pervasive in Ubuntu because it is used by default. If you want to get to a root shell, thereby removing the need to type `sudo` for every command, just enter `sudo -i` to get the root prompt. To return to a normal user prompt, enter `exit` and press Enter. Again, this is a bit dangerous because if you are not paying attention and forget to exit root, you could cause severe damage to the system. It is usually better to choose one method or the other and use it consistently, and the Ubuntu community consistently uses and recommends using `sudo` for each command, even if it gets tedious, because it is a good reminder to think about what you are doing.

After it is configured, using `sudo` is simple. An authorized user merely precedes a super user authority-needed command with `sudo`, like this:

```
matthew@seymour:~$ sudo command
```

When the command is entered, sudo checks the /etc/sudoers file to see whether the user is authorized to wield super user privileges; if so, sudo use is authorized for a specific length of time. The user is then prompted for her password (to preserve accountability and provide some measure of security), and then the command is run as if root had issued it. During the time allotted, which is 15 minutes by default in Ubuntu, sudo can be used again once or multiple times without a password. If an unauthorized user attempts to execute a sudo command, a record of the unauthorized attempt is kept in the system log, and a mail message is sent to the super user.

Three man pages are associated with sudo: sudo, sudoers, and visudo. The first covers the command itself, the second the format of the /etc/sudoers file, and the third the use of the special editor for /etc/sudoers. You should use the special editing command because it checks the file for parse errors and locks the file to prevent others from editing it at the same time. The visudo command uses the vi editor, so you might need a quick review of the vi editing commands found in Chapter 12, "Command-Line Master Class Part 2," in the section "Working with vi." You begin the editing by executing the visudo command with this:

matthew@seymour:~$ **sudo visudo**

The default /etc/sudoers file looks like this:

```
# /etc/sudoers
#
# This file MUST be edited with the 'sudo' command as root.
#
# See the man page for details on how to write a sudoers file.
#
Defaults        env_reset

# Host alias specification

# User alias specification

# Cmnd alias specification

# User privilege specification
root     ALL=(ALL) ALL

# Uncomment to allow members of group sudo to not need a password
# (Note that later entries override this, so you might need to move
# it further down)
# %sudo ALL=NOPASSWD: ALL

# Members of the admin group may gain root privileges
%admin ALL=(ALL) ALL
```

The basic format of a `sudoers` line in the file is as follows:

```
user host_computer=command
```

The user can be an individual user or a group. (A `%` in front identifies a name as a group.) The `host_computer` is normally `ALL` for all hosts on the network and `localhost` for the local machine, but the host computer can be referenced as a subnet or any specific host. The command in the `sudoers` line can be `ALL`, a list of specific commands, or a restriction on specific commands (formed by prepending a `!` to the command). A number of options are available for use with the `sudoers` line, and aliases can be used to simplify the assignment of privileges. Again, the `sudoers` man page gives the details, but here are a few examples:

If we add the line

```
%wheel        ALL=(ALL)        NOPASSWD: ALL
```

any user we add to the wheel group can execute any command without a password.

Suppose that we want to give a user `john` permission across the network to be able to add users with the graphical interface. We would add the following line:

```
john ALL=/users-admin
```

Or perhaps we would grant permission only on her local computer:

```
john 192.168.1.87=/usr/bin/users-admin
```

If we want to give the editor group system-wide permission with no password required to delete files, we use the following:

```
%editors ALL=NOPASSWD: /bin/rm
```

If we want to give every user permission with no password required to mount the CD drive on the `localhost`, we do so as follows:

```
ALL localhost=NOPASSWD:/sbin/mount /dev/scd0 /mnt/cdrom /sbin/umount /mnt/cdrom
```

It is also possible to use wildcards in the construction of the `sudoers` file. Aliases can be used, as well, to make it easier to define users and groups. The man page for `sudoers` contains some examples, and www.komar.org/pres/sudo/toc.html provides illustrative notes and comments about `sudo` use at a large company. The `sudo` home page at www.sudo.ws/ is also a useful resource for additional explanations and examples.

The following command presents users with a list of the commands they are entitled to use:

```
matthew@seymour:~$ sudo -l
```

ADDING EXTRA sudo **USERS**

As mentioned earlier, by default Ubuntu grants the first created user full root access through the sudo command. If you need to add this capability for other users, you can do this easily by adding each user to the admin group (in Ubuntu 11.10 or older) or the sudo group (any release after 12.04) or by using the User Manager tool to allow them to administer the System, which can be found in the User Privileges tab when you edit the properties for a user. The group change is described in this comment from the official release notes for Ubuntu 12.04: "Up until Ubuntu 11.10, administrator access using the sudo tool was granted via the admin Unix group. In Ubuntu 12.04, administrator access will be granted via the sudo group. This makes Ubuntu more consistent with the upstream implementation and Debian. For compatibility purposes, the admin group will continue to provide sudo/administrator access in 12.04."

Disk Quotas

On large systems with many users, you often need to control the amount of disk space a user can use. Disk quotas are designed specifically for this purpose. Quotas, managed per partition, can be set for both individual users and for groups; quotas for the group need not be as large as the aggregate quotas for the individuals in the groups.

When files are created, both a user and a group own them; ownership of the files is always part of the metadata about the files. This makes quotas based on both users and groups easy to manage.

NOTE

Disk quota management is not really useful or needed on a home system and rarely, if ever, on a small office system. It is unlikely you will see or implement this in either circumstance.

To manage disk quotas, you must have the quota and quotatool packages installed on your system. Quota management with Ubuntu is not enabled by default and has traditionally been enabled and configured manually by system administrators. System administrators use the family of quota commands, such as quotacheck to initialize the quota database files, edquota to set and edit user quotas, setquota to configure disk quotas, and quotaon or quotaoff to control the service. (Other utilities include warnquota for automatically sending mail to users over their disk space usage limit.)

Implementing Quotas

Quotas are not enabled by default, even if the quota software package is installed on your Ubuntu system. When quotas are installed and enabled, you can see which partitions have either user quotas, group quotas, or both by looking at the fourth field in the /etc/fstab file. For example, one line in /etc/fstab shows that quotas are enabled for the /home partition:

```
/dev/hda5     /home     ext3          defaults,usrquota,grpquota 1 1
```

The root of the partition with quotas enabled will have the files `quota.user` or `quota.group` in them (or both files, if both types of quotas are enabled), and the files will contain the actual quotas. The permissions of these files should be `600` so that users cannot read or write to them. (Otherwise, users would change them to allow ample space for their music files and Internet art collections.) To initialize disk quotas, the partitions must be remounted. This is easily accomplished with the following:

```
matthew@seymour:~$ sudo mount -o ro,remount partition_to_be_remounted mount_point
```

The underlying console tools (complete with man pages) are as follows:

- ▶ `quotaon, quotaoff`—Toggles quotas on a partition

- ▶ `repquota`—A summary status report on users and groups

- ▶ `quotacheck`—Updates the status of quotas (compares new and old tables of disk usage); run after `fsck`

- ▶ `edquota`—A basic quota management command

Manually Configuring Quotas

Manual configuration of quotas involves changing entries in your system's file system table, `/etc/fstab`, to add the `usrquota` mount option to the desired portion of your file system. As an example in a simple file system, you can enable quota management like this:

```
LABEL=/          /               ext3    defaults,usrquota    1 1
```

You can also enable group-level quotas by using the `grpquota` option. As the root operator, you must then create a file (using our example of creating user quotas) named `quota.user` in the designated portion of the file system, like so:

```
matthew@seymour:~$ sudo touch /quota.user
```

You should then turn on the use of quotas using the `quotaon` command:

```
matthew@seymour:~$ sudo quotaon -av
```

You can then edit user quotas with the `edquota` command to set hard and soft limits on file system use. The default system editor (`vi` unless you change your `EDITOR` environment variable) is launched when editing a user's quota.

Any user can find out what their quotas are with the following:

```
matthew@seymour:~$ quota -v
```

> **NOTE**
>
> Ubuntu does not support any graphical tools that enable you to configure disk quotas. A Quota mini-HOWTO is maintained at www.tldp.org/HOWTO/Quota.html.

Related Ubuntu Commands

You use these commands to manage user accounts in Ubuntu:

- ▶ `ac`—A user account-statistics command
- ▶ `change`—Sets or modifies user password expiration policies
- ▶ `chfn`—Creates or modifies user finger information in `/etc/passwd`
- ▶ `chgrp`—Modifies group memberships
- ▶ `chmod`—Changes file permissions
- ▶ `chown`—Changes file ownerships
- ▶ `chpasswd`—Batch command to modify user passwords
- ▶ `chsh`—Modifies a user's shell
- ▶ `groups`—Displays existing group memberships
- ▶ `logname`—Displays a user's login name
- ▶ `newusers`—Batches user management command
- ▶ `passwd`—Creates or modifies user passwords
- ▶ `su`—Executes shell or command as another user
- ▶ `sudo`—Manages selected user execution permissions
- ▶ `useradd`—Creates, modifies, or manages users
- ▶ `usermod`—Edits a user's login profile

References

- ▶ **http://tldp.org/HOWTO/User-Authentication-HOWTO/**—The User-Authentication HOWTO describes how user and group information is stored and used for authentication.

- ▶ **http://tldp.org/HOWTO/Shadow-Password-HOWTO.html**—The Shadow-Password HOWTO delves into the murky depths of shadow passwords and even discusses why you might not want to use them.

- ▶ **http://tldp.org/HOWTO/Security-HOWTO/**—A must-read HOWTO, the Security HOWTO is a good overview of security issues. Especially applicable to this chapter are sections on creating accounts, file permissions, and password security.

- ▶ **http://tldp.org/LDP/sag/html/index.html**—A general guide, the Linux System Administrator's Security Guide has interesting sections on limiting and monitoring users.

- ▶ **www.kernel.org/pub/linux/libs/pam**—The Pluggable Authentication Modules suite contains complex and highly useful applications that provide additional security and logging for passwords. PAM is installed by default in Ubuntu. It isn't necessary to understand the intricacies of PAM to use it effectively.

# CHAPTER 14

Automating Tasks and Shell Scripting

In this chapter, we cover ways to automate tasks on your system using task schedulers. This chapter is also an introduction to the basics of creating *shell scripts*, or executable text files written to conform to shell syntax. Shell scripts run like any other command under Linux and can contain complex logic or a simple series of Linux command-line instructions. You can also run other shell scripts from within a shell program. The features and functions for several Linux shells are discussed in this chapter after a short introduction to working from the shell command line. You find out how to write and execute a simple shell program using `bash`, one of the most popular Linux shells and the default shell in Ubuntu and most other distributions.

Scheduling Tasks

There are three ways to schedule commands in Ubuntu, all of which work in different ways. The first is the `at` command, which specifies a command to run at a specific time and date relative to today. The second is the `batch` command, which is actually a script that redirects you to the `at` command with some extra options set so your command runs when the system is quiet. The last option is the `cron` daemon, which is the Linux way of executing tasks at a given time.

Using `at` and `batch` to Schedule Tasks for Later

If there is a time-intensive task you want to run, but you do not want to do it while you are still logged in, you can tell Ubuntu to run it later with the `at` command, which you must install. The package name is the same as the tool: at.. To use at, you need to tell it the time at which you want to run and then press Enter. You will then see a new prompt that starts with at>, and everything you type there until you press Ctrl+D will be the commands you want at to run.

When the designated time arrives, at performs each action individually and in order, which means later commands can rely on the results of earlier commands. In this next example, run at just after 8:00 p.m., at is used to download and extract the latest Linux kernel at a time when the network should be quiet:

```
matthew@seymour:~$ at now + 7 hours
at> wget http://www.kernel.org/pub/linux/kernel/v3.0/linux-3.0.tar.bz2
at> tar xvfjp linux-3.0.tar.bz2
at> <EOT>
job 2 at 2011-07-08 20:01
```

Specifying now + 7 hours as the time does what you would expect: at was run at 8:00 p.m., so the command will run just after 3:00 a.m.

If you have a more complex job, you can use the -f parameter to have at read its commands from a file, like this:

```
echo wget http://www.kernel.org/pub/linux/kernel/v3.0/linux-3.00.tar.bz2\;
tar xvfjp linux-3.0.tar.bz2 > myjob.job
at -f myjob.job tomorrow
```

As you can see, at is flexible about the time format it takes; you can specify it in three ways:

▶ Using the now parameter, you can specify how many minutes, hours, days, or weeks relative to the current time. For example, now + 4 weeks runs the command 1 month from today.

▶ You can also specify several special times, including tomorrow, midnight, noon, or teatime (4:00 p.m.). If you do not specify a time with tomorrow, your job is set for precisely 24 hours from the current time.

▶ You can specify an exact date and time using HH:MM MM/DD/YY format (for example, 16:40 22/12/12 for 4:40 p.m. on the 22nd of December 2012).

When your job is submitted, at reports the job number, date, and time that the job will be executed; the queue identifier; plus the job owner (you). It also captures all your environment variables and stores them along with the job so that when your job runs, it can restore the variables, preserving your execution environment.

The job number and job queue identifier are both important. When you schedule a job using at, it is placed into queue "a" by default, which means it runs at your specified time and takes up a normal amount of resources.

There is an alternative command, `batch`, which is really just a shell script that calls `at` with a few extra options. These options (`-q b -m now`, if you were interested) set `at` to run on queue b (`-q b`), mailing the user on completion (`-m`), and running immediately (`now`). The queue part is what is important: Jobs scheduled on queue b will only be executed when system load falls below 0.8—that is, when the system is not running at full load. Furthermore, it runs with a lower niceness, meaning a queue jobs usually have a niceness of 2, whereas b queue jobs have a niceness of 4.

Because `batch` always specifies `now` as its time, you need not specify your own time; it will simply run as soon as the system is quiet. Having a default niceness of 4 means that batched commands get fewer system resources than a queue job's (`at`'s default) and fewer system resources than most other programs. You can optionally specify other queues using `at`. Queue c runs at niceness 6, queue d runs at niceness 8, and so on. However, it is important to note that the system load is only checked before the command is run. If the load is lower than 0.8, your batch job runs. If the system load subsequently rises beyond 0.8, your batch job continues to run, albeit in the background, thanks to its niceness value.

When you submit a job for execution, you are also returned a job number. If you forget this or just want to see a list of other jobs you have scheduled to run later, use the `atq` command with no parameters. If you run this as a normal user, it prints only your jobs; running it as a super user prints everyone's jobs. The output is in the same format as when you submit a job, so you get the ID number, execution time, queue ID, and owner of each job.

If you want to delete a job, use the `atrm` command followed by the ID number of the job you want to delete. This next example shows `atq` and `atrm` being used to list jobs and delete one:

```
matthew@seymour:~$ atq
14        2012-01-20 23:33 a matthew
16        2012-02-03 22:34 a matthew
17        2012-01-25 22:34 a matthew
15        2012-01-22 04:34 a matthew
18        2012-01-22 01:35 b matthew
matthew@seymour:~$ atrm 16
matthew@seymour:~$ atq
14        2012-01-20 23:33 a matthew
17        2012-01-25 22:34 a matthew
15        2012-01-22 04:34 a matthew
18        2012-01-22 01:35 b matthew
```

In the preceding example, job 16 is deleted using `atrm`, and so it does not show up in the second call to `atq`.

The default configuration for `at` and `batch` is to allow everyone to use it, which is not always the desired behavior. Access is controlled through two files: `/etc/at.allow` and `/etc/at.deny`. By default, `at.deny` exists but is empty, which allows everyone to use at and batch. You can enter usernames into at.deny, one per line, to stop those users scheduling jobs.

Alternatively, you can use the at.allow file; this does not exist by default. If you have a blank at.allow file, no one except root is allowed to schedule jobs. As with at.deny, you can add usernames to at.allow one per line, and those users are able to schedule jobs. You should use either at.deny or at.allow: When someone tries to run at or batch, Ubuntu checks for her username in at.allow. If it is in there, or if at.allow does not exist, Ubuntu checks for her username in at.deny. If her username is in at.deny or at.deny does not exist, she is not allowed to schedule jobs.

Using cron to Run Jobs Repeatedly

The at and batch commands work well if you just want to execute a single task at a later date, but they are less useful if you want to run a task frequently. Instead, the cron daemon exists for running tasks repeatedly based on system (and user) requests. The cron daemon has a similar permissions system to at: Users listed in the cron.deny file are not allowed to use cron, and users listed in the cron.allow file are. An empty cron.deny file—the default—means everyone can set jobs. An empty cron.allow file means that no one (except root) can set jobs.

There are two types of jobs: system jobs and user jobs. Only root can edit *system* jobs, whereas any user whose name appears in cron.allow or does not appear in cron.deny can run *user* jobs. System jobs are controlled through the /etc/crontab file, which by default looks like this:

```
SHELL=/bin/sh
PATH=/usr/local/sbin:/usr/local/bin:/sbin:/bin:/usr/sbin:/usr/bin

# m h dom mon dow user    command
17 *   * * *      root    cd / && run-parts —report /etc/cron.hourly
25 6   * * *      root    test -x /usr/sbin/anacron || ( cd / && run-parts -report
➥/etc/cron.daily )
47 6   * * 7      root    test -x /usr/sbin/anacron || ( cd / && run-parts -report
➥/etc/cron.weekly )
52 6   1 * *      root    test -x /usr/sbin/anacron || ( cd / && run-parts -report
➥/etc/cron.monthly )
```

The first two lines specify which shell should be used to execute the job (defaults to the shell of the user who owns the crontab file, usually /bin/bash) and the search path for executables that will be used. It's important that you avoid using environment variables in this path statement because they might not be set when the job runs.

The next line starts with a pound sign (#) and so is treated as a comment and ignored. The next four lines are the important parts: They are the jobs themselves.

Each job is specified in seven fields that define the time to run, owner, and command. The first five commands specify the execution time in quite a quirky order: minute (0–59), hour (0–23), day of the month (1–31), month of the year (1–12), and day of the week

(0–7). For day of the week, both 0 and 7 are Sunday, which means that 1 is Monday, 3 is Wednesday, and so on. If you want to specify "all values" (that is, every minute, every hour, every day, and so on), use an asterisk, `*`.

The next field specifies the username of the owner of the job. When a job is executed, it uses the username specified here. The last field is the command to execute.

So, the first job runs at minute 17, every hour of every day of every month, and executes the command `run-parts /etc/cron.hourly`. The `run-parts` command is a simple script that runs all programs inside a given directory (in this case, `/etc/cron.hourly`). So, in this case, the job executes at 00:17 (17 minutes past midnight), 01:17, 02:17, 03:17, and so on, and uses all the programs listed in the `cron.hourly` directory.

The next job runs at minute 25 and hour 6 of every day of every month, running `run-parts /etc/cron.daily`. Because of the hour limitation, this script runs only once per day, at 6:25 a.m. Note that it uses minute 25 rather than minute 17 so that daily jobs do not clash with hourly jobs. You should be able to guess what the next two jobs do, simply by looking at the commands they run.

Inside each of those four directories (`cron.hourly`, `cron.daily`, `cron.weekly`, and `cron.monthly`) are a collection of shell scripts that are run by `run-parts`. For example, in `cron.daily` you have scripts like `logrotate`, which handles backing up of log files, and `makewhatis`, which updates the `whatis` database. You can add other system tasks to these directories if you want to, but be careful to ensure your scripts are correct.

> **CAUTION**
>
> The `cron` daemon reads all the system `crontab` files and all user `crontab` files once a minute (on the minute; that is, at 6:00:00, 6:01:00, and so on) to check for changes. However, any new jobs it finds will not be executed until at least 1 minute has passed.
>
> For example, if it is 6:01:49 (that is, 49 seconds past 1 minute past 6:00 a.m.) and you set a `cron` job to run at 6:02, it does not execute. At 6:02, the `cron` daemon rereads its configuration files and sees the new job, but it is not able to execute it. If you set the job to run at 6:02 a.m. every day, it is executed the following morning and every subsequent morning.
>
> This same situation exists when deleting jobs. If it is 6:01:49 and you have a job scheduled to run at 6:02, deleting it makes no difference: `cron` runs it before it rereads the `crontab` files for changes. However, after it has reread the `crontab` file and noticed the job is no longer there, it will not be executed in subsequent days.

There are alternative ways of specifying dates. For example, you can use sets of dates and times by using hyphens of commas, for example hours 9–15 would execute at 9, 10, 11, 12, 13, 14, and 15 (from 9:00 a.m. to 3:00 p.m.), whereas 9, 11, 13, and 15 would miss out at the even hours. Note that it is important you do not put spaces into these sets because the `cron` daemon interprets them as the next field. You can define a step value with a slash (/) to show time division: `*/4` for hours means "every 4 hours all day," and `0-12/3` means "every 3 hours from midnight to noon." You can also specify day and month names rather than numbers, using three-character abbreviations: Sun, Mon, Tue, Fri, Sat for days, or Jan, Feb, Mar, Oct, Nov, Dec for months.

As well as system jobs, there are user jobs for those users who have the correct permissions. User jobs are stored in the `/var/spool/cron` directory, with each user having his own file named after his username (for instance, `/var/spool/cron/philip` or `/var/spool/cron/root`). The contents of these files contain the jobs the user wants to run and take roughly the same format as the `/etc/crontab file`, with the exception that the owner of the job should not be specified because it is always the same as the filename.

To edit your own `crontab` file, type `crontab -e`. This brings up a text editor (`vim`, also known by its older name `vi`, by default, but you can set the `EDITOR` environment variable to change that) where you can enter your entries. The format of this file is a little different from the format for the main `crontab` because this time there is no need to specify the owner of the job—it is always you.

So, this time each line is made up of six fields: minute (0–59), hour (0–23), day of the month (1–31), month of the year (1–12), day of the week (0–7), and then the command to run. If you are using `vim` and are new to it, press `i` to enter insert mode to edit your text; then press Esc to exit insert mode. To save and quit, type a colon followed by `wq` and press Enter.

When programming, we tend to use a `sandbox` subdirectory in our home directory where we keep all sorts of temporary files that we were just playing around with. We can use a personal job to empty that directory every morning at 6:00 a.m. so that we get a fresh start each morning. Here is how that would look in our `crontab` file:

```
0 6 * * * rm -rf /home/matthew/sandbox/*
```

If you are not allowed to schedule jobs, you will be stopped from editing your `crontab` file.

After your jobs are placed, you can use the command `crontab -l` to list your jobs. This just prints the contents of your `crontab` file, so its output is the same as the line you just entered.

If you want to remove just one job, the easiest thing to do is type `crontab -e` to edit your `crontab` file in `vim`; then, after having moved the cursor to the job you want to delete, type `dd` (two *d*'s) to delete that line. If you want to delete all your jobs, you can use `crontab -r` to delete your `crontab` file.

Read the man page for more about cron.

Using `rtcwake` to Wake Your Computer from Sleep Automatically

Some of us keep our computers running 24/7. Perhaps you don't want to do so, but you need to have your system up and running at a certain time every day, and you can't guarantee that you will be able to be present to turn it on. It is possible to use `rtcwake` to place the computer in sleep or suspend mode instead of turning it off and then wake up the computer later. To do this, you must have sudo permissions. Here is an example:

```
matthew@seymour:~$ sudo rtcwake -m mem -s -3600
```

The command above tells the computer to suspend to RAM, or sleep, which means to save the current state of the computer in memory and shut everything else down, and then to wake the computer after 3600 seconds, which is one hour.

Here is the basic syntax of the command:

```
sudo rtcwake -m [type of suspend] -s [number of seconds]
```

There are five types of suspend available to use with -m:

- ▶ disk—(hibernate) The current state of the computer is written to disk and the computer is powered off.

- ▶ mem—(sleep) The current state of the computer is written to RAM and the computer is put into a low-power state, using just enough power to keep the memory preserved.

- ▶ no—The computer is not suspended immediately. Only the wakeup time is set. This allows you to continue working; you have to remember to put the computer to sleep manually.

- ▶ off—The computer is turned off completely. Wake will not work with this setting for everyone and is not officially supported, but it does work with some computers. It is included here for those who like to live dangerously.

- ▶ standby—The computer is put into standby mode, which saves some power over running normally, but not nearly as much as the other options. This is the default setting and will be used if you omit -m.

Setting the wake time can be done more than one way:

- ▶ Above, we use -s, which specifies the number of seconds before waking.

- ▶ You can also use -t, which allows you to set a specific time to wake, but formatted in the number of seconds since the beginning of Unix time (00:00:00 UTC on 1/1/1970). The date command can help you find this number, which is a commonly used method of performing time-related tasks in the Unix/Linux world. You can do so like this: sudo rtcwake -m no -t $(date +%s -d 'tomorrow 06:30').

See the man files for rtcwake and date for help and more options.

Here are a few tips to help you get started:

- ▶ The letters RTC stand for "real time clock," which refers to the hardware clock that is set in your BIOS and which is kept running by the battery on your motherboard. If your computer needs a new battery, as evidenced by the time needing to be reset every time you turn the computer back on, or if you have other clock-related problems, this command will not work for you.

▶ If you have problems using sleep, hibernate, or suspend on your system, this command will not work for you.

▶ You probably want to avoid using this command on a notebook computer. Overheating and/or dead batteries are a real possibility if a system wakes itself while the computer is in a laptop bag.

▶ If you want to run a specific command when the computer wakes up, you can do this the same way you chain other commands to run in a series, put && after rtcwake and before the command you want to run when rtcwake has completed, as discussed in Chapter 12, "Command-Line Master Class Part 2."

Basic Shell Control

Ubuntu includes a rich assortment of capable, flexible, and powerful shells. Each shell is different but has numerous built-in commands and configurable command-line prompts and might include features such as command-line history, the ability to recall and use a previous command line, and command-line editing. As an example, the bash shell is so powerful that it is possible to write a minimal web server entirely in bash's language using 114 lines of script. (See the link at the end of this chapter.)

Although there are many shells to choose from, most people stick with the default, bash. This is because bash does everything most people need to do, and more. Only change your shell if you really need to.

Table 14.1 lists each shell, along with its description and location, in your Ubuntu file system. Most of these are not installed by default, so if you want or need a shell other than bash, you can install it from the Ubuntu repositories.

TABLE 14.1   Shells with Ubuntu

Name	Description	Location
bash	The Bourne Again SHell	/bin/bash
ksh	The Korn shell	/bin/ksh, /usr/bin/ksh
pdksh	A symbolic link to ksh	/usr/bin/pdksh
rsh	The restricted shell (for network operation)	/usr/bin/rsh
sh	A symbolic link to bash	/bin/sh
tcsh	A csh-compatible shell	/bin/tcsh
zsh	A compatible csh, ksh, and sh shell	/bin/zsh

LEARNING MORE ABOUT YOUR SHELL

All the shells listed in Table 14.1 have accompanying man pages, along with other documentation under the `/usr/share/doc` directory. Some of the documentation can be quite lengthy, but it is generally much better to have too much documentation than too little. The `bash` shell includes more than 100 pages in its manual, and the `zsh` shell documentation is so extensive that it includes the `zshall` meta man page (use `man zshall` to read this overview).

The Shell Command Line

Having a basic understanding of the capabilities of the shell command line can help you write better shell scripts. If, after you have finished reading this short introduction, you want to learn more about the command line, check out Chapter 11, "Command-Line Master Class Part 1." You can use the shell command line to perform a number of different tasks, including the following:

▶ Searching files or directories with programs using pattern matching or expressions. These commands include the GNU `gawk` (linked as `awk`) and the `grep` family of commands, including `egrep` and `fgrep`.

▶ Getting data from and sending data to a file or command, known as *input* and *output redirection*.

▶ Feeding or filtering a program's output to another command (called using *pipes*).

A shell can also have built-in *job-control* commands to launch the command line as a background process, suspend a running program, selectively retrieve or kill running or suspended programs, and perform other types of process control.

You can run multiple commands on a single command line using a semicolon to separate commands:

```
matthew@seymour:~$ w ; free ; df
 18:14:13 up  4:35,  2 users,  load average: 0.97, 0.99, 1.04
USER     TTY       FROM            LOGIN@   IDLE   JCPU   PCPU WHAT
matthew   tty7      :0              13:39   4:35m 24:34   0.32s gnome-session
matthew   pts/0     :0.0            17:24   0.00s  1.19s  4.98s gnome-terminal
             total      used       free     shared    buffers     cached
Mem:       4055692    1801104    2254588         0     134096     757532
-/+ buffers/cache:     909476    3146216
Swap:      8787512          0    8787512
Filesystem          1K-blocks     Used Available Use% Mounted on
/dev/sda1           14421344   6509276   7179508  48% /
none                 2020136       336   2019800   1% /dev
none                 2027844      3004   2024840   1% /dev/shm
none                 2027844       224   2027620   1% /var/run
```

14

```
none                   2027844        0   2027844   0% /var/lock
none                   2027844        0   2027844   0% /lib/init/rw
/dev/sda6            284593052 144336704 125799860  54% /home
```

This example displays the output of the w, free, and df commands. You can extend long shell command lines inside shell scripts or at the command line by using the backslash character (\), as follows:

```
matthew@seymour:~$ echo "this is a long \
> command line and" ; echo "shows that multiple commands \
> may be strung out."
this is a long command line and
shows that multiple commands may be strung out.
```

The first three lines of this example are a single command line. In that single line are two instances of the echo command. Note that when you use the backslash as a line-continuation character, it must be the last character on the command line (or in your shell script, as you see later in the "Writing and Executing a Shell Script" section).

Using the basic features of the shell command line is easy, but mastering use of all features can be difficult. Entire books have been devoted to using shells, writing shell scripts, and using pattern-matching expressions. The following sections provide an overview of some features of the shell command line relating to writing scripts.

UNDERSTANDING GREP

If you plan to develop shell scripts to expand the capabilities of pattern-matching commands such as grep, you will benefit from learning more about using expressions. One of the definitive guides to using the pattern-matching capabilities of UNIX and Linux commands is *Mastering Regular Expressions* by Jeffrey E. F. Freidl (O'Reilly).

Shell Pattern-Matching Support

The shell command line enables you to use strings of specially constructed character patterns for wildcard matches. This is a different simpler capability than that supported by GNU utilities such as grep, which can use more complex patterns, known as *expressions*, to search through files or directories or to filter data input to or out of commands.

The shell's pattern strings can be simple or complex, but even using a small subset of the available characters in simple wildcards can yield constructive results at the command line. Common characters used for shell pattern matching include the following:

▶ *—Matches any character. For example, to find all files in the current directory ending in .txt, you could use this:

```
matthew@seymour:~$ ls *.txt
```

▶ ?—Matches a single character. For example, to find all files in the current directory ending in the extension .d?c (where ? could be 0–9, a–z, or A–Z), you could use the following:

```
matthew@seymour:~$ ls *.d?c
```

▶ [xxx] or [x-x]—Matches a range of characters. For example, to list all files in a directory with names containing numbers, you could use this:

```
matthew@seymour:~$ ls *[0-9]*
```

▶ \x—Matches or escapes a character such as ? or a tab character. For example, to create a file with a name containing a question mark, you could use the following:

```
matthew~$ touch foo\?
```

Note that the shell might not interpret some characters or regular expressions in the same manner as a Linux command, and mixing wildcards and regular expressions in shell scripts can lead to problems unless you're careful. For example, finding patterns in text is best left to regular expressions used with commands such as grep; simple wildcards should be used for filtering or matching filenames on the command line. And although both Linux command expressions and shell scripts can recognize the backslash as an escape character in patterns, the dollar sign ($) will have two wildly different meanings (single-character pattern matching in expressions and variable assignment in scripts).

CAUTION

Make sure you read your command carefully when using wildcards; an all-too-common error is to type something like rm -rf * .txt with a space between the * and the .txt. By the time you wonder why the command is taking so long, Bash will already have deleted most of your files. The problem is that it will treat the * and the .txt separately. * will match everything, so Bash will delete all your files.

Redirecting Input and Output

You can create, overwrite, and append data to files at the command line, using a process called *input* and *output redirection*. The shell recognizes several special characters for this process, such as >, <, or >>.

In this example, the output of the ls command is redirected to create a file named textfiles.listing:

```
matthew@seymour:~$ ls *.txt >textfiles.listing
```

Use output redirection with care because it is possible to overwrite existing files. For example, specifying a different directory but using the same output filename overwrites the existing textfiles.listing:

```
matthew@seymour:~$ ls /usr/share/doc/mutt-1.4/*.txt >textfiles.listing
```

14

Fortunately, most shells are smart enough to recognize when you might do something foolish. Here, the bash shell warns that the command is attempting to redirect output to a directory:

```
matthew@seymour:~$ mkdir foo
matthew@seymour:~$ ls >foo
bash: foo: Is a directory
```

Output can be appended to a file without overwriting existing content by using the append operator, >>. In this example, the directory listing is appended to the end of textfiles.listing instead of overwriting its contents:

```
matthew@seymour:~$ ls /usr/share/doc/mutt-1.4/*.txt >>textfiles.listing
```

You can use *input redirection* to feed data into a command by using the < like this:

```
matthew@seymour:~$ cat < textfiles.listing
```

You can use the shell *here* operator, <<, to specify the end of input on the shell command line:

```
matthew@seymour:~$ cat >simple_script <<DONE
> echo ""this is a simple script""
> DONE
matthew@seymour:~$ cat simple_script
echo ""this is a simple script""
```

In this example, the shell feeds the cat command you are typing (input) until the pattern DONE is recognized. The output file simple_script is then saved and its contents verified. You can use this same technique in scripts to create content based on the output of various commands and define an end-of-input or delimiter.

Piping Data

Many Linux commands can be used in concert in a single, connected command line to transform data from one form to another. Stringing Linux commands together in this fashion is known as using or creating *pipes*. Pipes are created on the command line with the bar operator (|). For example, you can use a pipe to perform a complex task from a single command line like this:

```
matthew@seymour:~$ find /d2 -name '*.txt' -print | xargs cat | \
tr ' ' '\n' | sort | uniq >output.txt
```

This example takes the output of the find command to feed the cat command (via xargs) the name of all text files in the /d2 directory. The content of all matching files is then fed through the tr command to change each space in the data stream into a carriage return. The stream of words is then sorted, and identical adjacent lines are removed using the uniq command. The output, a raw list of words, is then saved in the file named output.txt.

Background Processing

The shell allows you to start a command and then launch it into the background as a process by using an ampersand (&) at the end of a command line. This technique is often used at the command line of an X terminal window to start a client and return to the command line. For example, to launch another terminal window using the `xterm` client, you can use the following:

```
matthew@seymour:~$ xterm &
[3] 1437
```

The numbers echoed back show a number (3 in this example), which is a *job* number, or reference number for a shell process, and a *process ID* number, or PID (1437 in this example). You can kill the `xterm` window session by using the shell's built-in `kill` command, along with the job number like this:

```
matthew@seymour:~$ kill %3
```

Or you can kill the process by using the `kill` command, along with the PID, as follows:

```
matthew@seymour:~$ kill 1437
```

You can use background processing in shell scripts to start commands that take a long time, such as backups:

```
matthew@seymour:~$ tar -czf /backup/home.tgz /home &
```

Writing and Executing a Shell Script

Why should you write and use shell scripts? Shell scripts can save you time and typing, especially if you routinely use the same command lines multiple times every day. Although you could also use the history function (press the Up or Down keys while using `bash` or use the `history` command), a shell script can add flexibility with command-line argument substitution and built-in help.

Although a shell script doesn't execute faster than a program written in a computer language such as C, a shell program can be smaller in size than a compiled program. The shell program does not require any additional library support other than the shell or, if used, existing commands installed on your system. The process of creating and testing shell scripts is also generally simpler and faster than the development process for equivalent C language commands.

> **NOTE**
>
> Hundreds of commands included with Ubuntu are actually shell scripts, and many other good shell script examples are available over the Internet—a quick search yields numerous links to online tutorials and scripting guides from fellow Linux users and developers. For example, the `startx` command, used to start an X Window session from the text

console, is a shell script used every day by most users. To learn more about shell scripting with `bash`, see the "Advanced Bash-Scripting Guide," listed in the "Reference" section
at the end of this chapter. You'll also find *Sams Teach Yourself Shell Programming in 24
Hours* a helpful guide to learning more about using the shell to build your own commands.

When you are learning to write and execute your first shell scripts, start with scripts for
simple but useful tasks. Begin with short examples, and then expand the scripts as you
build on your experience and knowledge. Make liberal use of comments (lines preceded
with a pound sign, #) to document each section of your script. Include an author statement and overview of the script as additional help, along with a creation date or version
number. Write shell scripts using a text editor such as `vi` because it does not automatically
wrap lines of text. Line wrapping can break script syntax and cause problems. If you use
the `nano` editor, include its `-w` flag to disable line wrap.

In this section, you learn how to write a simple shell script to set up a number of *aliases*
(command synonyms) whenever you log on. Instead of typing all the aliases every time
you log on, you can put them in a file by using a text editor, such as `vi`, and then execute
the file. Normally these changes are saved in system-wide shell configuration files under
the `/etc` directory to make the changes active for all users or in your `.bashrc`, `.cshrc`
(if you use `tcsh`), or `.bash_profile` files in your home directory.

Here is what is contained in `myenv`, a sample shell script created for this purpose (for `bash`):

```
#!/bin/sh
alias ll='ls –L'
alias ldir='ls –aF'
alias copy='cp'
```

This simple script creates command *aliases*, or convenient shorthand forms of commands,
for the `ls` and `cp` commands. The `ll` alias provides a long directory listing: The `ldir` alias
is the `ls` command, but prints indicators (for directories or executable files) in listings.
The `copy` alias is the same as the `cp` command. You can experiment and add your own
options or create aliases of other commands with options you frequently use.

You can execute `myenv` in a variety of ways under Linux. As shown in this example, you
can make `myenv` executable by using the `chmod` command and then execute it as you
would any other native Linux command:

```
matthew@seymour:~$ chmod +x myenv
```

This line turns on the executable permission of `myenv`, which can be checked with the `ls`
command and its `-1` option like this:

```
matthew@seymour:~$ ls -l myenv
-rwxr-xr-x    1 matthew matthew   0 2010-07-08 18:19 myenv
```

Running the New Shell Program

You can run your new shell program in several ways. Each method produces the same results, which is a testament to the flexibility of using the shell with Linux. One way to run your shell program is to execute the file myenv from the command line as if it were a Linux command:

```
matthew@seymour:~$ ./myenv
```

A second way to execute myenv under a particular shell, such as pdksh, is as follows:

```
matthew@seymour:~$ pdksh myenv
```

This invokes a new pdksh shell and passes the filename myenv as a parameter to execute the file. A third way requires you to create a directory named bin in your home directory and to then copy the new shell program into this directory. You can then run the program without the need to specify a specific location or to use a shell. You do so like this:

```
matthew@seymour:~$ mkdir bin
matthew@seymour:~$ mv myenv bin
matthew@seymour:~$ myenv
```

This works because Ubuntu is set up by default to include the executable path $HOME/bin in your shell's environment. You can view this environment variable, named PATH, by piping the output of the env command through fgrep like so:

```
matthew@seymour:~$ env | fgrep PATH
/usr/kerberos/bin:/usr/local/bin:/bin:/usr/bin: \
/usr/X11R6/bin:/sbin:/home/matthew/bin
```

As you can see, the user (matthew in this example) can use the new bin directory to hold executable files. Another way to bring up an environment variable is to use the echo command along with the variable name (in this case, $PATH):

```
matthew@seymour:~$ echo $PATH
/usr/kerberos/bin:/usr/local/bin:/usr/bin:/bin:/usr/X11R6/bin:/home/bball/bin
```

> **CAUTION**
>
> Never put . in your $PATH to execute files or a command in the current directory—this presents a serious security risk, especially for the root operator, and even more so if . is first in your $PATH search order. Trojan scripts placed by crackers in directories such as /tmp can be used for malicious purposes, and will be executed immediately if the current working directory is part of your $PATH.

Storing Shell Scripts for System-Wide Access

After you execute the command myenv, you should be able to use ldir from the command line to get a list of files under the current directory and ll to get a list of files with attributes displayed. However, the best way to use the new commands in myenv is to put them into your shell's login or profile file. For Ubuntu, and nearly all Linux users, the default shell is `bash`, so you can make these commands available for everyone on your system by putting them in the `/etc/bashrc` file. System-wide aliases for `tcsh` are contained in files with the extension `.csh` under the `/etc/profile.d` directory. The `pdksh` shell can use these command aliases, as well.

> **NOTE**
>
> To use a shell other than `bash` after logging in, use the `chsh` command from the command line or the `system-config-users` client during an X session. You'll be asked for your password (or the root password if using `system-config-users`) and the location and name of the new shell. The new shell will become your default shell, but only if its name is in the list of acceptable system shells in `/etc/shells`.

Interpreting Shell Scripts Through Specific Shells

The majority of shell scripts use a *shebang line* (`#!`) at the beginning to control the type of shell used to run the script; this bang line calls for an `sh`-incantation of `bash`:

```
#!/bin/sh
```

A shebang line (it is short for "sharp" and "bang," two names for # and !) tells the Linux kernel that a specific command (a shell, or in the case of other scripts, perhaps `awk` or Perl) is to be used to interpret the contents of the file. Using a shebang line is common practice for all shell scripting. For example, if you write a shell script using `bash` but want the script to execute as if run by the Bourne shell, `sh`, the first line of your script contains `#!/bin/sh`, which is a link to the `bash` shell. Running bash as `sh` causes `bash` to act as a Bourne shell. This is the reason for the symbolic link `sh`, which points to `bash`.

> **THE SHEBANG LINE**
>
> The shebang line is a magic number, as defined in `/usr/share/misc/magic`—a text database of magic numbers for the Linux `file` command. Magic numbers are used by many different Linux commands to quickly identify a type of file, and the database format is documented in the section five manual page named `magic` (read by using `man 5 magic`). For example, magic numbers can be used by the Linux `file` command to display the identity of a script (no matter what filename is used) as a shell script using a specific shell or other interpreter such as `awk` or Perl.

You might also find different or new environmental variables available to your scripts by using different shells. For example, if you launch `csh` from the `bash` command line, you find several new variables or variables with slightly different definitions, such as the following:

```
matthew@seymour:~$ env
...
VENDOR=intel
MACHTYPE=i386
HOSTTYPE=i386-linux
HOST=thinkpad.home.org
```

On the other hand, bash might provide these variables or variables of the same name with a slightly different definition, such as

```
$ env
...
HOSTTYPE=i386
HOSTNAME=thinkpad.home.org
```

Although the behavior of a shebang line is not defined by POSIX, variations of its use can prove helpful when you are writing shell scripts. For example, as described in the wish man page, you can use a shell to help execute programs called within a shell script without needing to hard code pathnames of programs. The wish command is a windowing *Tool Control Language* (tcl) interpreter that can be used to write graphical clients. Avoiding the use of specific pathnames to programs increases shell script portability because not every UNIX or Linux system has programs in the same location.

For example, if you want to use the wish command, your first inclination might be to write this:

```
#!/usr/local/bin/wish
```

Although this works on many other operating systems, the script fails under Linux because wish is located under the /usr/bin directory. However, if you write the command line this way

```
#!/bin/sh
exec wish "$@"
```

you can use the wish command (as a binary or a shell script itself).

Using Variables in Shell Scripts

When writing shell scripts for Linux, you work with three types of variables:

▶ **Environment variables**—Part of the system environment, you can use them in your shell program. You can define new variables, and you can also modify some of them, such as PATH, within a shell program.

▶ **Built-in variables**—Variables such as options used on the command (interpreted by the shell as a *positional argument*) are provided by Linux. Unlike environment variables, you cannot modify them.

▶ **User variables**—Variables defined within a script when you write a shell script. You can use and modify them at will within the shell script, but they are not available to be used outside of the script.

A major difference between shell programming and other programming languages is that in shell programming, variables are not *typed*—that is, you do not have to specify whether a variable is a number or a string, and so on.

Assigning a Value to a Variable

Suppose that you want to use a variable called `lcount` to count the number of iterations in a loop within a shell program. You can declare and initialize this variable as follows:

Command	Environment
`lcount=0`	`pdksh` and `bash`
`set lcount=0`	`tcsh`

> **NOTE**
>
> Under `pdksh` and `bash`, you must ensure that the equal sign (=) does not have spaces before and after it.

To store a string in a variable, you can use the following:

Command	Environment
`myname=Sedona`	`pdksh` and `bash`
`set myname=Sedona`	`tcsh`

Use the preceding variable form if the string doesn't have embedded spaces. If a string has embedded spaces, you can do the assignment as follows:

Command	Environment
`myname="Saralyn"`	`pdksh` and `bash`
`set myname="Saralyn"`	`tcsh`

Accessing Variable Values

You can access the value of a variable by prefixing the variable name with a dollar sign ($). That is, if the variable name is `var`, you can access the variable by using `$var`.

If you want to assign the value of `var` to the variable `lcount`, you can do so as follows:

Command	Environment
`lcount=$var`	`pdksh` and `bash`
`set lcount=$var`	`tcsh`

Positional Parameters

It is possible to pass options from the command line or from another shell script to your shell program.

These options are supplied to the shell program by Linux as *positional parameters*, which have special names provided by the system. The first parameter is stored in a variable called 1 (number 1) and can be accessed by using $1 within the program. The second parameter is stored in a variable called 2 and can be accessed by using $2 within the program, and so on. One or more of the higher numbered positional parameters can be omitted while you're invoking a shell program.

Understanding how to use these positional parameters and how to access and use variables retrieved from the command line is necessary when developing more advanced shell programs.

A Simple Example of a Positional Parameter

For example, if a shell program mypgm expects two parameters—such as a first name and a last name—you can invoke the shell program with only one parameter, the first name. However, you cannot invoke it with only the second parameter, the last name.

Here is a shell program called mypgm1, which takes only one parameter (a name) and displays it on the screen:

```
#!/bin/sh
#Name display program
if [ $# -eq 0 ]
then
    echo "Name not provided"
else
    echo "Your name is "$1
fi
```

If you execute mypgm1, as follows:

```
matthew@seymour:~$ bash mypgm1
```

you get the following output:

```
Name not provided
```

However, if you execute mypgm1, as follows:

```
matthew@seymour:~$ bash   mypgm1 Heather
```

you get the this output:

```
Your name is Heather
```

The shell program mypgm1 also illustrates another aspect of shell programming: the built-in variables provided to the shell by the Linux kernel. In mypgm1, the built-in variable $# provides the number of positional parameters passed to the shell program. You learn more about working with built-in variables in the next major section of this chapter.

Using Positional Parameters to Access and Retrieve Variables from the Command Line

Using positional parameters in scripts can be helpful if you need to use command lines with piped commands requiring complex arguments. Shell programs containing positional parameters can be even more convenient if the commands are infrequently used. For example, if you use your Ubuntu system with an attached voice modem as an answering machine, you can write a script to issue a command that retrieves and plays the voice messages. The following lines convert a saved sound file (in .rmd or voice-phone format) and pipe the result to your system's audio device:

```
#!/bin/sh
# play voice message in /var/spool/voice/incoming
rmdtopvf /var/spool/voice/incoming/$1 | pvfspeed -s 8000 | \
pvftobasic >/dev/audio
```

You can then easily play back a voice message using this script (perhaps named pmm):

```
matthew@seymour:~$ pmm name_of_message
```

Shell scripts that contain positional parameters are often used for automating routine and mundane jobs, such as system log report generation, file system checks, user resource accounting, printer use accounting, and other system, network, or security administration tasks.

Using a Simple Script to Automate Tasks

You could use a simple script, for example, to examine your system log for certain keywords. If the script is run via your system's scheduling table, /etc/crontab, it can help automate security monitoring. By combining the output capabilities of existing Linux commands with the language facilities of the shell, you can quickly build a useful script to perform a task normally requiring a number of command lines. For example, you can create a short script, named greplog, like this:

```
#!/bin/sh
#     name:  greplog
#      use:  mail grep of designated log using keyword
# version:  v.01 08aug02
#
#   author: bb
#
# usage: greplog [keyword] [logpathname]
#
#   bugs: does not check for correct number of arguments

# build report name using keyword search and date
log_report=/tmp/$1.logreport.`date '+%m%d%y'`
```

```
# build report header with system type, hostname, date and time
echo "================================================================" \
       >$log_report
echo "              S Y S T E M    M O N I T O R    L O G" >>$log_report
echo uname -a >>$log_report
echo "Log report for" `hostname -f` "on" `date '+%c'`        >>$log_report
echo "================================================================" \
       >>$log_report ; echo "" >>$log_report

# record log search start
echo "Search for->" $1 "starting" `date '+%r'` >>$log_report
echo "" >>$log_report

# get and save grep results of keyword ($1) from logfile ($2)
grep -i $1 $2 >>$log_report

# build report footer with time
echo "" >>$log_report
echo "End of" $log_report at `date '+%r'` >>$log_report

# mail report to root
mail -s "Log Analysis for $1" root <$log_report

# clean up and remove report
rm $log_report
exit 0
```

In this example, the script creates the variable $log_report, which will be the filename of the temporary report. The keyword ($1) and first argument on the command line is used as part of the filename, along with the current date (with perhaps a better approach to use $$ instead of the date, which will append the script's PID as a file extension). Next, the report header containing some formatted text, the output of the uname command, and the hostname and date is added to the report. The start of the search is then recorded, and any matches of the keyword in the log are added to the report. A footer containing the name of the report and the time is then added. The report is mailed to root with the search term as the subject of the message, and the temporary file is deleted.

You can test the script by running it manually and feeding it a keyword and a pathname to the system log, /var/log/messages, like this:

matthew@seymour:~# **greplog FAILED /var/log/messages**

Note that your system should be running the syslogd daemon. If any login failures have occurred on your system, the root operator might get an email message that looks like this:

```
Date: Sun, 23 Oct 2016 16:23:24 -0400
From: root <root@righthere.home.org>
```

```
To: root@righthere.home.org
Subject: FAILED


=============================================================
            S Y S T E M   M O N I T O R   L O G
Linux system 4.4.0-22-generic #1 Sun Oct 9 20:21:24 EDT 2016
+GNU/Linux
Log report for righthere.home.org on Sun 23 Oct 2016 04:23:24 PM EDT
=============================================================


Search for-> FAILED starting 04:23:24 PM


Oct 23 16:23:04 righthere login[1769]: FAILED LOGIN 3 FROM (null) FOR bball,
+Authentication failure


End of /tmp/FAILED.logreport.102303 at 04:23:24 PM
```

To further automate the process, you can include command lines using the script in another script to generate a series of searches and reports.

Built-In Variables

Built-in variables are special variables provided to shell by Linux that you can use to make decisions within a shell program. You cannot modify the values of these variables within the shell program.

Some of these variables are:

- ▶ $#—Number of positional parameters passed to the shell program
- ▶ $?—Completion code of the last command or shell program executed within the shell program (returned value)
- ▶ $0—The name of the shell program
- ▶ $*—A single string of all arguments passed at the time of invocation of the shell program

To show these built-in variables in use, here is a sample program called mypgm2:

```
#!/bin/sh
#my test program
echo "Number of parameters is $#"
echo "Program name is $0"
echo "Parameters as a single string is $*"
```

If you execute mypgm2 from the command line in pdksh and bash as follows:

```
matthew@seymour:~$ bash mypgm2 Sanjiv Guha
```

you get the following result:

```
Number of parameters is 2
Program name is mypgm2
Parameters as a single string is Sanjiv Guha
```

Special Characters

Some characters have special meaning to Linux shells; these characters represent commands, denote specific use for surrounding text, or provide search parameters. Special characters provide a sort of shorthand by incorporating these rather complex meanings into a simple character. Some special characters are shown in Table 14.2.

TABLE 14.2   Special Shell Characters

Character	Explanation
$	Indicates the beginning of a shell variable name
|	Pipes standard output to next command
#	Starts a comment
&	Executes a process in the background
?	Matches one character
*	Matches one or more characters
>	Output redirection operator
<	Input redirection operator
`	Command substitution (the backquote or backtick—the key above the Tab key on most keyboards)
>>	Output redirection operator (to append to a file)
<<	Wait until following end-of-input string (HERE operator)
[ ]	Range of characters
[a-z]	All characters a through z
[a,z] or [az]	Characters a or z
Space	Delimiter between two words

Special characters are very useful to you when you're creating shell scripts, but if you inadvertently use a special character as part of variable names or strings, your program behaves incorrectly. As you learn in later parts of this section, you can use one of the special characters in a string if you precede it with an *escape character* (\, or backslash) to indicate that it isn't being used as a special character and shouldn't be treated as such by the program.

A few special characters deserve special note. They are the double quotes ("), the single quotes ('), the backslash (\), and the backtick (`)—all discussed in the following sections.

Using Double Quotes to Resolve Variables in Strings with Embedded Spaces

If a string contains embedded spaces, you can enclose the string in double quotes (") so that the shell interprets the whole string as one entity instead of more than one.

For example, if you assigned the value of `abc def` (abc followed by one space, followed by `def`) to a variable called x in a shell program as follows, you would get an error because the shell would try to execute `def` as a separate command:

Command	Environment
x=abc def	pdksh and bash
set x = adb def	tcsh

The shell executes the string as a single command if you surround the string in double quotes as follows:

Command	Environment
x="abc def"	pdksh and bash
set x="abc def"	tcsh

The double quotes resolve all variables within the string. Here is an example for pdksh and bash:

```
var="test string"
newvar="Value of var is $var"
echo $newvar
```

Here is the same example for tcsh:

```
set var="test string"
set newvar="Value of var is $var"
echo $newvar
```

If you execute a shell program containing the preceding three lines, you get the following result:

```
Value of var is test string
```

Using Single Quotes to Maintain Unexpanded Variables

You can surround a string with single quotes (') to stop the shell from expanding variables and interpreting special characters. When used for the latter purpose, the single quote is an *escape character*, similar to the backslash, which you learn about in the next section. Here, you learn how to use the single quote to avoid expanding a variable in a shell script. An unexpanded variable maintains its original form in the output.

In the following examples, the double quotes in the preceding examples have been changed to single quotes:

```
pdksh and bash:
var='test string'
newvar='Value of var is $var'
echo $newvar
tcsh:
set var = 'test string'
set newvar = 'Value of var is $var'
echo $newvar
```

If you execute a shell program containing these three lines, you get the following result:

```
Value of var is $var
```

As you can see, the variable var maintains its original format in the results, rather than having been expanded.

Using the Backslash as an Escape Character

As you learned earlier, the backslash (\) serves as an escape character that stops the shell from interpreting the succeeding character as a special character. Say that you want to assign a value of $test to a variable called var. If you use the following command, the shell reads the special character $ and interprets $test as the value of the variable test. No value has been assigned to test; a null value is stored in var as follows:

Command	Environment
var=$test	pdksh and bash
set var=$test	tcsh

Unfortunately, this assignment might work for bash and pdksh, but it returns an error of "undefined variable" if you use it with tcsh. Use the following commands to correctly store $test in var:

Command	Environment
var=\$test	pdksh and bash
set var = \$test	tcsh

The backslash before the dollar sign (\$) signals the shell to interpret the $ as any other ordinary character and *not to associate any sp*ecial meaning to it. You could also use single quotes (') around the $test variable to get the same result.

Using the Backtick to Replace a String with Output

You can use the backtick (`) character to signal the shell to replace a string with its output when executed. This is called *command substitution*. You can use this special character in shell programs when you want the result of the execution of a command to be stored in a variable. For example, if you want to count the number of lines in a file called `test.txt` in the current directory and store the result in a variable called `var`, you can use the following command:

Command	Environment
`var=`wc -l test.txt` `	`pdksh` and `bash`
`set var = `wc -l test.txt` `	`tcsh`

Comparison of Expressions in pdksh **and** bash

Comparing values or evaluating the differences between similar bits of data—such as file information, character strings, or numbers—is a task known as *comparison of expressions*. Comparison of expressions is an integral part of using logic in shell programs to accomplish tasks. The way the logical comparison of two operators (numeric or string) is done varies slightly in different shells. In `pdksh` and `bash`, a command called `test` can be used to achieve comparisons of expressions. In `tcsh`, you can write an expression to accomplish the same thing.

This section covers comparison operations using the `pdksh` or `bash` shells. Later in the chapter, you learn how to compare expressions in the `tcsh` shell.

The `pdksh` and `bash` shell syntax provide a command named `test` to compare strings, numbers, and files. The syntax of the `test` command is as follows:

```
test expression
or
[ expression ]
```

Both forms of the `test` commands are processed the same way by `pdksh` and `bash`. The `test` commands support the following types of comparisons:

▶ String comparison

▶ Numeric comparison

▶ File operators

▶ Logical operators

String Comparison

You can use the following operators to compare two string expressions:

▶ `=`—To compare whether two strings are equal

▶ `!=`—To compare whether two strings are not equal

▶ `-n`—To evaluate whether the string length is greater than zero

▶ `-z`—To evaluate whether the string length is equal to zero

Next are some examples using these operators when comparing two strings, string1 and string2, in a shell program called compare1:

```
#!/bin/sh
string1="abc"
string2="abd"
if [ $string1 = $string2 ]; then
    echo "string1 equal to string2"
else
    echo "string1 not equal to string2"
fi

if [ $string2 != string1 ]; then
    echo "string2 not equal to string1"
else
    echo "string2 equal to string2"
fi

if [ $string1 ]; then
    echo "string1 is not empty"
else
    echo "string1 is empty"
fi

if [ -n $string2 ]; then
    echo "string2 has a length greater than zero"
else
    echo "string2 has length equal to zero"
fi

if [ -z $string1 ]; then
    echo "string1 has a length equal to zero"
else
  echo "string1 has a length greater than zero"
fi
```

If you execute compare1, you get the following result:

```
string1 not equal to string2
string2 not equal to string1
string1 is not empty
string2 has a length greater than zero
string1 has a length greater than zero
```

If two strings are not equal in size, the system pads out the shorter string with trailing spaces for comparison. That is, if the value of string1 is "abc" and that of string2 is "ab", string2 is padded with a trailing space for comparison purposes; it has a value of "ab " (with a space after the letters).

Number Comparison

The following operators can be used to compare two numbers:

▶ -eq—To compare whether two numbers are equal

▶ -ge—To compare whether one number is greater than or equal to the other number

▶ -le—To compare whether one number is less than or equal to the other number

▶ -ne—To compare whether two numbers are not equal

▶ -gt—To compare whether one number is greater than the other number

▶ -lt—To compare whether one number is less than the other number

The following shell program compares three numbers, number1, number2, and number3:

```
#!/bin/sh
number1=5
number2=10
number3=5

if [ $number1 -eq $number3 ]; then
    echo "number1 is equal to number3"
else
    echo "number1 is not equal to number3"
fi

if [ $number1 -ne $number2 ]; then
    echo "number1 is not equal to number2"
else
    echo "number1 is equal to number2"
fi

if [ $number1 -gt $number2 ]; then
    echo "number1 is greater than number2"
else
    echo "number1 is not greater than number2"
fi

if [ $number1 -ge $number3 ]; then
    echo "number1 is greater than or equal to number3"
else
    echo "number1 is not greater than or equal to number3"
fi
```

```
if [ $number1 -lt $number2 ]; then
    echo "number1 is less than number2"
else
    echo "number1 is not less than number2"
fi


if [ $number1 -le $number3 ]; then
    echo "number1 is less than or equal to number3"
else
    echo ""number1 is not less than or equal to number3"
fi
```

When you execute the shell program, you get the following results:

```
number1 is equal to number3
number1 is not equal to number2
number1 is not greater than number2
number1 is greater than or equal to number3
number1 is less than number2
number1 is less than or equal to number3
```

File Operators

You can use the following operators as file comparison operators:

- ▶ -d—To ascertain whether a file is a directory

- ▶ -f—To ascertain whether a file is a regular file

- ▶ -r—To ascertain whether read permission is set for a file

- ▶ -s—To ascertain whether a file exists and has a length greater than zero

- ▶ -w—To ascertain whether write permission is set for a file

- ▶ -x—To ascertain whether execute permission is set for a file

Assume that a shell program called compare3 is in a directory with a file called file1 and a subdirectory dir1 under the current directory. Assume that file1 has a permission of r-x (read and execute permission) and dir1 has a permission of rwx (read, write, and execute permission). The code for the shell program would look like this:

```
#!/bin/sh
if [ -d $dir1 ]; then
    echo ""dir1 is a directory"
else
    echo ""dir1 is not a directory"
fi
```

```
if [ -f $dir1 ]; then
   echo ""dir1 is a regular file"
else
   echo ""dir1 is not a regular file"
fi

if [ -r $file1 ]; then
   echo ""file1 has read permission"
else
   echo ""file1 does not have read permission"
fi

if [ -w $file1 ]; then
   echo ""file1 has write permission"
else
   echo ""file1 does not have write permission"
fi

if [ -x $dir1 ]; then
   echo ""dir1 has execute permission"
else
   echo ""dir1 does not have execute permission"
fi
```

If you execute the shell program, you get the following results:

```
dir1 is a directory
file1 is a regular file
file1 has read permission
file1 does not have write permission
dir1 has execute permission
```

Logical Operators

You use logical operators to compare expressions using Boolean logic, which compares values using characters representing NOT, AND, and OR:

▶ !—To negate a logical expression

▶ -a—To logically AND two logical expressions

▶ -o—To logically OR two logical expressions

This example named logic uses the file and directory mentioned in the previous compare3 example:

```
#!/bin/sh
if [ -x file1 -a -x dir1 ]; then
   echo file1 and dir1 are executable
```

```
else
   echo at least one of file1 or dir1 are not executable
fi

if [ -w file1 -o -w dir1 ]; then
   echo file1 or dir1 are writable
else
   echo neither file1 or dir1 are executable
fi

if [ ! -w file1 ]; then
   echo file1 is not writable
else
   echo file1 is writable
fi
```

If you execute logic, it will yield the following result:

```
file1 and dir1 are executable
file1 or dir1 are writable
file1 is not writable
```

Comparing Expressions with `tcsh`

As stated earlier, the method for comparing expressions in `tcsh` is different from the method used under `pdksh` and `bash`. The comparison of expression demonstrated in this section uses the syntax necessary for the `tcsh` shell environment.

String Comparison

You can use the following operators to compare two string expressions:

▶ `==`—To compare whether two strings are equal

▶ `!=`—To compare whether two strings are not equal

The following examples compare two strings, `string1` and `string2`, in the shell program `compare1`:

```
#!/bin/tcsh
set string1 = "abc"
set string2 = ""abd"

if  (string1 == string2)  then
   echo "string1 equal to string2"
else
   echo ""string1 not equal to string2"
endif
```

```
if   (string2 != string1)   then
   echo ""string2 not equal to string1"
else
   echo ""string2 equal to string1"
endif
```

If you execute `compare1`, you get the following results:

```
string1 not equal to string2
string2 not equal to string1
```

Number Comparison

You can use the following operators to compare two numbers:

▶ `>=`—To compare whether one number is greater than or equal to the other number

▶ `<=`—To compare whether one number is less than or equal to the other number

▶ `>`—To compare whether one number is greater than the other number

▶ `<`—To compare whether one number is less than the other number

The next examples compare three numbers, `number1`, `number2`, and `number3`, in a shell program called `compare2`:

```
#!/bin/tcsh
set number1=5
set number2=10
set number3=5

if   (number1 > number2)   then
   echo "number1 is greater than number2"
else
   echo "number1 is not greater than number2"
endif

if   (number1 >= number3) then
   echo "number1 is greater than or equal to number3"
else
   echo ""number1 is not greater than or equal to number3"
endif

if   (number1 < number2)   then
   echo ""number1 is less than number2"
else
   echo ""number1 is not less than number2"
endif
```

```
if  (number1 <= number3) then
    echo ""number1 is less than or equal to number3"
else
    echo ""number1 is not less than or equal to number3"
endif
```

When executing the shell program `compare2`, you get the following results:

```
number1 is not greater than number2
number1 is greater than or equal to number3
number1 is less than number2
number1 is less than or equal to number3
```

File Operators

You can use the following operators as file comparison operators:

▶ -d—To ascertain whether a file is a directory

▶ -e—To ascertain whether a file exists

▶ -f—To ascertain whether a file is a regular file

▶ -o—To ascertain whether a user is the owner of a file

▶ -r—To ascertain whether read permission is set for a file

▶ -w—To ascertain whether write permission is set for a file

▶ -x—To ascertain whether execute permission is set for a file

▶ -z—To ascertain whether the file size is zero

The following examples are based on a shell program called `compare3`, which is in a directory with a file called `file1` and a subdirectory `dir1` under the current directory. Assume that `file1` has a permission of `r-x` (read and execute permission) and `dir1` has a permission of `rwx` (read, write, and execute permission).

The following is the code for the `compare3` shell program:

```
#!/bin/tcsh
if  (-d dir1) then
    echo "dir1 is a directory"
else
    echo "dir1 is not a directory"
endif

if (-f dir1) then
    echo "file1 is a regular file"
else
    echo "file1 is not a regular file"
endif
```

```
if (-r file1) then
    echo "file1 has read permission"
else
    echo "file1 does not have read permission"
endif

if (-w file1) then
    echo "file1 has write permission"
else
    echo "file1 does not have write permission"
endif

if (-x dir1) then
    echo "dir1 has execute permission"
else
    echo "dir1 does not have execute permission"
endif

if (-z file1) then
    echo "file1 has zero length"
else
    echo "file1 has greater than zero length"
endif
```

If you execute the file compare3, you get the following results:

```
dir1 is a directory
file1 is a regular file
file1 has read permission
file1 does not have write permission
dir1 has execute permission
file1 has greater than zero length
```

Logical Operators

You use logical operators with conditional statements. You use the following operators to negate a logical expression or to perform logical ANDS and ORS:

▶ !—To negate a logical expression

▶ &&—To logically AND two logical expressions

▶ ||—To logically OR two logical expressions

This example named logic uses the file and directory mentioned in the previous compare3 example:

```
#!/bin/tcsh
if ( -x file1 && -x dir1 ) then
```

```
      echo file1 and dir1 are executable
   else
      echo at least one of file1 or dir1 are not executable
   endif

   if ( -w file1 || -w dir1 ) then
      echo file1 or dir1 are writable
   else
      echo neither file1 or dir1 are executable
   endif

   if ( ! -w file1 ) then
      echo file1 is not writable
   else
      echo file1 is writable
   endif
```

If you execute `logic`, it yields the following result:

```
file1 and dir1 are executable
file1 or dir1 are writable
file1 is not writable
```

The `for` Statement

You use the `for` statement to execute a set of commands once each time a specified condition is true. The `for` statement has a number of formats. The first format used by `pdksh` and `bash` is as follows:

```
for curvar in list
do
     statements
done
```

You should use this form if you want to execute `statements` once for each value in `list`. For each iteration, the current value of the list is assigned to `vcurvar`. `list` can be a variable containing a number of items or a list of values separated by spaces. The second format is as follows:

```
for curvar
do
     statements
done
```

In this form, the `statements` are executed once for each of the positional parameters passed to the shell program. For each iteration, the current value of the positional parameter is assigned to the variable `curvar`.

You can also write this form as follows:

```
for curvar in $
do
    statements
done
```

Remember that $@ gives you a list of positional parameters passed to the shell program, quoted in a manner consistent with the way the user originally invoked the command.

Under tcsh, the for statement is called foreach. The format is as follows:

```
foreach curvar (list)
    statements
end
```

In this form, statements are executed once for each value in list, and, for each iteration, the current value of list is assigned to curvar.

Suppose that you want to create a backup version of each file in a directory to a subdirectory called backup. You can do the following in pdksh and bash:

```
#!/bin/sh
for filename in *
do
    cp $filename backup/$filename
    if [ $? -ne 0 ]; then
        echo "copy for $filename failed"
    fi
done
```

In the preceding example, a backup copy of each file is created. If the copy fails, a message is generated.

The same example in tcsh is as follows:

```
#!/bin/tcsh
foreach filename (`/bin/ls`)
    cp $filename backup/$filename
    if ($? != 0) then
        echo "copy for $filename failed"
    endif
end
```

The while Statement

You can use the while statement to execute a series of commands while a specified condition is true. The loop terminates as soon as the specified condition evaluates to false. It is possible that the loop will not execute at all if the specified condition initially evaluates to false. You should be careful with the while command because the loop never terminates if the specified condition never evaluates to false.

ENDLESS LOOPS HAVE THEIR PLACE IN SHELL PROGRAMS

Endless loops can sometimes be useful. For example, you can easily construct a simple command that constantly monitors the 802.11 link quality of a network interface by using a few lines of script:

```
#!/bin/sh
while :
 do
    /sbin/iwconfig eth0 |  grep Link | tr '\n' '\r'
 Done
```

The script outputs the search, and then the `tr` command formats the output. The result is a simple animation of a constantly updated single line of information:

```
Link Quality:92/92 Signal level:-11 dBm Noise level:-102 dBm
```

You can also use this technique to create a graphical monitoring client for X that outputs traffic information and activity about a network interface:

```
#!/bin/sh
xterm -geometry 75x2 -e \
bash -c \
  "while :; do \
     /sbin/ifconfig eth0 | \
     grep 'TX bytes' |
      tr '\n' '\r' ; \
 done"
```

The simple example uses a bash command-line script (enabled by `-c`) to execute a command line repeatedly. The command line pipes the output of the `ifconfig` command through `grep`, which searches the output of `ifconfig` and then pipes a line containing the string `"TX bytes"` to the `tr` command. The `tr` command then removes the carriage return at the end of the line to display the information inside an `/xterm X11` terminal window, automatically sized by the `-geometry` option:

```
RX bytes:4117594780 (3926.8 Mb)  TX bytes:452230967 (431.2 Mb)
```

Endless loops can be so useful that Linux includes a command that repeatedly executes a given command line. For example, you can get a quick report about a system's hardware health by using the sensors command. Instead of using a shell script to loop the output endlessly, you can use the `watch` command to repeat the information and provide simple animation:

```
$ watch "sensors -f | cut -c 1-20"
```

In pdksh and bash, use the following format for the while flow control construct:

```
while expression
do
    statements
done
```

In tcsh, use the following format:

```
while (expression)
    Statements
End
```

If you want to add the first five even numbers, you can use the following shell program in pdksh and bash:

```
#!/bin/bash
loopcount=0
result=0
while [ $loopcount -lt 5 ]
do
    loopcount=`expr $loopcount + 1`
    increment=`expr $loopcount \* 2`
    result=`expr $result + $increment`
doneecho "result is $result"
```

In tcsh, you can write this program as follows:

```
#!/bin/tcsh
set loopcount = 0
set result = 0
while ($loopcount < 5)
    set loopcount = `expr $loopcount + 1`
    set increment = `expr $loopcount \* 2`
    set result = `expr $result + $increment`

end

echo "result is $result"
```

The until **Statement**

You can use the until statement to execute a series of commands until a specified condition is true.

The loop terminates as soon as the specified condition evaluates to true.

In pdksh and bash, the following format is used:

```
until expression
do
    statements
done
```

As you can see, the format of the until statement is similar to that of the while statement, but the logic is different: In a while loop, you execute until an expression is false, but in an until loop, you loop until the expression is true. An important part of this difference is that while is executed zero or more times (potentially not executed at all), but until is repeated one or more times, meaning it is executed at least once.

If you want to add the first five even numbers, you can use the following shell program in pdksh and bash:

```
#!/bin/bash
loopcount=0
result=0
until [ $loopcount -ge 5 ]
do
    loopcount=`expr $loopcount + 1`
    increment=`expr $loopcount \* 2`
    result=`expr $result + $increment`
done

echo "result is $result"
```

The example here is identical to the example for the while statement except that the condition being tested is just the opposite of the condition specified in the while statement.

The tcsh shell does not support the until statement.

The repeat **Statement** (tcsh)

You use the repeat statement to execute only one command a fixed number of times.

If you want to print a hyphen (-) 80 times with one hyphen per line on the screen, you can use the following command:

```
repeat  80 echo '-'
```

The select **Statement** (pdksh)

You use the select statement to generate a menu list if you are writing a shell program that expects input from the user online. The format of the select statement is as follows:

```
select  item in itemlist
do
    Statements
Done
```

itemlist is optional. If it isn't provided, the system iterates through the item entries one at a time. If itemlist is provided, however, the system iterates for each entry in itemlist and the current value of itemlist is assigned to item for each iteration, which then can be used as part of the statements being executed.

If you want to write a menu that gives the user a choice of picking a Continue or a Finish, you can write the following shell program:

```
#!/bin/ksh
select  item in Continue Finish
```

```
do
   if [ $item = "Finish" ]; then
      break
   fi
done
```

When the select command is executed, the system displays a menu with numeric choices to the user—in this case, 1 for Continue and 2 for Finish. If the user chooses 1, the variable item contains a value of Continue; if the user chooses 2, the variable item contains a value of Finish. When the user chooses 2, the if statement is executed and the loop terminates.

The shift **Statement**

You use the shift statement to process the positional parameters, one at a time, from left to right. Recall that the positional parameters are identified as $1, $2, $3, and so on. The effect of the shift command is that each positional parameter is moved one position to the left and the current $1 parameter is lost.

The shift statement is useful when you are writing shell programs in which a user can pass various options. Depending on the specified option, the parameters that follow can mean different things or might not be there at all.

The format of the shift command is as follows:

```
shift   number
```

The parameter number is the number of places to be shifted and is optional. If not specified, the default is 1; that is, the parameters are shifted one position to the left. If specified, the parameters are shifted number positions to the left.

The if **Statement**

The if statement evaluates a logical expression to make a decision. An if condition has the following format in pdksh and bash:

```
if [ expression ]; then
    Statements
elif [ expression ]; then
    Statements
else
    Statements
fi
```

The if conditions can be nested. That is, an if condition can contain another if condition within it. It isn't necessary for an if condition to have an elif or else part. The else part is executed if none of the expressions that are specified in the if statement and are optional if subsequent elif statements are true. The word fi is used to indicate the end of the if statements, which is very useful if you have nested if conditions. In such a case, you should be able to match fi to if to ensure that all if statements are properly coded.

In the following example for bash or pdksh, a variable var can have either of two values: Yes or No. Any other value is invalid. This can be coded as follows:

```
if [ $var = "Yes" ]; then
    echo "Value is Yes"
elif [ $var = "No" ]; then
    echo "Value is No"
else
    echo "Invalid value"
fi
```

In tcsh, the if statement has two forms. The first form, similar to the one for pdksh and bash, is as follows:

```
if (expression) then
    Statements
else if (expression) then
    Statements
Else
    Statements
endif
```

Using the example of the variable var having only two values, Yes and No, here is how it is coded with tcsh:

```
if ($var == "Yes") then
    echo "Value is Yes"
else if ($var == "No" ) then
    echo "Value is No"
else
    echo "Invalid value"
endif
```

The second form of the if condition for tcsh is as follows:

```
if (expression) command
```

In this format, only a single command can be executed if the expression evaluates to true.

The case Statement

You use the case statement to execute statements depending on a discrete value or a range of values matching the specified variable. In most cases, you can use a case statement instead of an if statement if you have a large number of conditions.

The format of a case statement for pdksh and bash is as follows:

```
case str in
    str1 | str2)
        Statements;;
```

```
   str3|str4)
      Statements;;
   *)
      Statements;;
esac
```

You can specify a number of discrete values—such as str1, str2, and so on—for each condition, or you can specify a value with a wildcard. The last condition should be an asterisk (*) and is executed if none of the other conditions are met. For each of the specified conditions, all the associated statements until the double semicolon (;;) are executed.

You can write a script that echoes the name of the month if you provide the month number as a parameter. If you provide a number that isn't between 1 and 12, you get an error message. The script is as follows:

```
#!/bin/sh

case $1 in
   01 | 1) echo "Month is January";;
   02 | 2) echo "Month is February";;
   03 | 3) echo "Month is March";;
   04 | 4) echo "Month is April";;
   05 | 5) echo "Month is May";;
   06 | 6) echo "Month is June";;
   07 | 7) echo "Month is July";;
   08 | 8) echo "Month is August";;
   09 | 9) echo "Month is September";;
   10) echo "Month is October";;
   11) echo "Month is November";;
   12) echo "Month is December";;
   *) echo "Invalid parameter";;
esac
```

You need to end the statements under each condition with a double semicolon (;;). If you do not, the statements under the next condition are also executed.

The format for a case statement for tcsh is as follows:

```
switch (str)
   case str1|str2:
      Statements
      breaksw
   case str3|str4:
      Statements
      breaksw
   default:
      Statements
      breaksw
endsw
```

You can specify a number of discrete values—such as str1, str2, and so on—for each condition, or you can specify a value with a wildcard. The last condition should be default and is executed if none of the other conditions are met. For each of the specified conditions, all the associated statements until breaksw are executed.

You can write the example that echoes the month when a number is given, shown earlier for pdksh and bash, in tcsh as follows:

```
#!/bin/tcsh

set month = 5
switch  ( $month )
   case 1: echo "Month is January" ;  breaksw
   case 2: echo "Month is February" ;  breaksw
   case 3: echo "Month is March" ;  breaksw
   case 4: echo "Month is April" ;  breaksw
   case 5: echo "Month is May" ;  breaksw
   case 6: echo "Month is June" ;  breaksw
   case 7: echo "Month is July" ;  breaksw
   case 8: echo "Month is August"  ;  breaksw
   case 9: echo "Month is September" ;  breaksw
   case 10: echo "Month is October" ;  breaksw
   case 11: echo "Month is November" ;  breaksw
   case 12: echo "Month is December" ;  breaksw
   default: echo "Oops! Month is Octember!" ;  breaksw
endsw
```

You need to end the statements under each condition with breaksw. If you do not, the statements under the next condition are also executed.

The break **and** exit **Statements**

You should be aware of two other statements: the break statement and the exit statement.

You can use the break statement used to terminate an iteration loop, such as a for, until, or repeat command.

You can use exit statements to exit a shell program. You can optionally use a number after exit. If the current shell program has been called by another shell program, the calling program can check for the code (the $? or $status variable, depending on shell) and make a decision accordingly.

Using Functions in Shell Scripts

As with other programming languages, shell programs also support functions. A function is a piece of a shell program that performs a particular process; you can reuse the same function multiple times within the shell program. Functions help eliminate the need for duplicating code as you write shell programs.

The following is the format of a function in `pdksh` and `bash`:

```
func(){
    Statements
}
```

You can call a function as follows:

```
func param1 param2 param3
```

The parameters `param1`, `param2`, and so on are optional. You can also pass the parameters as a single string—for example, `$@`. A function can parse the parameters as if they were positional parameters passed to a shell program from the command line as command-line arguments, but instead use values passed inside the script. For example, the following script uses a function named `Displaymonth()` that displays the name of the month or an error message if you pass a month number out of the range 1 to 12. This example works with `pdksh` and `bash`:

```
#!/bin/sh
Displaymonth() {
    case $1 in
        01 | 1) echo "Month is January";;
        02 | 2) echo "Month is February";;
        03 | 3) echo "Month is March";;
        04 | 4) echo "Month is April";;
        05 | 5) echo "Month is May";;
        06 | 6) echo "Month is June";;
        07 | 7) echo "Month is July";;
        08 | 8) echo "Month is August";;
        09 | 9) echo "Month is September";;
        10) echo "Month is October";;
        11) echo "Month is November";;
        12) echo "Month is December";;
        *) echo "Invalid parameter";;
    esac
}
Displaymonth 8
```

The preceding program displays the following output:

```
Month is August
```

References

▶ **www.gnu.org/software/bash/**—The `bash` home page at the GNU Software Project.

▶ **www.tldp.org/LDP/abs/html/**—Mendel Cooper's "Advanced Bash-Scripting Guide."

▶ **www.freeos.com/guides/lsst/**—Linux shell scripting tutorial.

▶ **http://kornshell.com/**—The Korn Shell website.

▶ **http://web.cs.mun.ca/~michael/pdksh/**—The `pdksh` home page.

▶ **www.tcsh.org/**—Find out more about `tcsh` here.

▶ **www.zsh.org/**—Examine `zsh` in more detail here.

14

CHAPTER 15

The Boot Process

In this chapter, you learn about making tasks into services that run as your system starts, and making them into services you can start and stop by hand. You also learn about the entire boot process.

After you turn on the power switch, the boot process begins with the computer executing code stored in a chip called the *BIOS*, or *basic input/output system*; this process occurs no matter what operating system you have installed. The Linux boot process begins when the code known as the *boot loader* starts loading the Linux kernel and ends only when the login prompt appears.

As a system administrator, you will use the skills you learn in this chapter to control your system's services and manage runlevels on your computer. Understanding the management of the system services and states is essential to understanding how Linux works (especially in a multi-user environment) and helps untangle the mysteries of a few of your Ubuntu system's configuration files. Furthermore, a good knowledge of the cron daemon that handles task scheduling is essential for administrators at all skill levels, so you will want to combine this knowledge with that in Chapter 14, "Automating Tasks and Shell Scripting."

Running Services at Boot

Although most people consider a computer to be either on or off, in Ubuntu and Linux in general, there are a number of states in between. Known as *runlevels*, they define what system services are started upon boot. These services are simply applications running in the background that provide some needed function to your system, such as getting information from your mouse and sending it to the display; or a service could monitor the partitions to see whether they have enough free space left on them. Services are typically loaded and run (also referred to as being started) during the boot process, in the same way as Microsoft Windows services are. For a while, Ubuntu used a system known as Upstart instead of the classic and venerable SysVinit; Upstart had a special backward-compatibility layer that can use runlevels in the way that Linux veterans are accustomed to doing for services not otherwise handled by Upstart. Starting in 2015, Ubuntu has switched to another system called systemd. There is more on runlevels, Upstart and systemd later in this chapter.

INIT SYSTEMS

There are many ways to describe init systems, but this quote from a thread at Reddit. com, is hard to beat (capitalization and spelling errors are from the original):

"To understand the fuss, there are 3 init systems that you should be aware of: sysvinit, upstart and systemd. SyvVinit is really old, outdated and only allows for a sequential startup of services, that is, all services started by init must wait for the previous service to have completed their startup process before the next can startup. Both upstart and systemd are designed to tackle the limitations of init, and allows for concurrent service initialization, that is, multiple services can startup at the same time, as long as they are not dependent on each other, and allows taking advantage of multi core processing. They also allow for services to startup and shutdown for specific events, such as a network connection going up or another service has started. Upstart was developed by Canonical was initially released in 2006 and was used in Ubuntu, Debian, Fedora, RHEL, CentOS, and many others. Systemd is a much younger system that was initally released in 2011, however, most major distros has already migrated to using systemd by default.

"Both Upstart and Systemd are event based, however their architecture and configuration setup are very different and this is where the worrying comes from. If the configurations aren't ported correctly then systems are going to behave differently to what's expected and this can lead to issues for may users." - hitsujiTMO in https://www.reddit.com/r/ Ubuntu/comments/2yeyyi/grab_your_pitchforks_ubuntu_to_switch_to_systemd/cp92iro

You can manage nearly every aspect of your computer and how it behaves after booting via configuring and ordering boot scripts and by using various system administration utilities included with Ubuntu. In this chapter, you learn how to work with these boot scripts and system administration utilities. This chapter also offers advice for troubleshooting and fixing problems that might arise with software configuration or the introduction or removal of various types of hardware from your system.

Beginning the Boot Loading Process

Although the actual boot loading mechanism for Linux varies on different hardware platforms (such as the SPARC, Alpha, or PowerPC systems), Intel-based PCs running Ubuntu most often use the same mechanism throughout product lines. This process is traditionally accomplished through a basic input/output system, or BIOS. The BIOS is an application stored in a chip on the motherboard that initializes the hardware on the motherboard (and often the hardware that's attached to the motherboard). The BIOS gets the system ready to load and run the software that we recognize as the operating system.

As a last step, the BIOS code looks for a special program known as the boot loader or boot code. The instructions in this little bit of code tell the BIOS where the Linux kernel is located, how it should be loaded into memory, and how it should be started.

If all goes well, the BIOS looks for a bootable volume such as a floppy disk, CD-ROM, hard drive, RAM disk, USB drive, or other media. The bootable volume contains a special hexadecimal value written to the volume by the boot loader application (such as Ubuntu's default, GRUB2) when the boot loader code was first installed in the system's drives. The BIOS searches volumes in the order established by the BIOS settings (for example, USB first, followed by a DVD-ROM, and then a hard drive) and then boots from the first bootable volume it finds. Modern BIOSs allow considerable flexibility in choosing the device used for booting the system.

> **NOTE**
>
> If the BIOS detects a hardware problem, the boot process fails, and the BIOS generates a few beeps from the system speaker. These "beep codes" indicate the nature of the problem the BIOS has encountered. The codes vary among manufacturers, and the diagnosis of problems occurring during this phase of the boot process is beyond the scope of this book and does not involve Linux. If you encounter a problem, consult the motherboard manual or contact the manufacturer of the motherboard. Another good source for learning about beep codes is www.computerhope.com/beep.htm.

Next, the BIOS looks on the bootable volume for boot code in the partition boot sector also known as the *Master Boot Record (MBR)* of the first hard disk. The MBR contains the boot loader code and the partition table—think of it like an index for a book, plus a few comments on how to start reading the book. If the BIOS finds a boot loader, it loads the boot loader code into memory. At that point, the BIOS's job is completed, and it passes control of the system to the boot loader.

As computing has evolved, the BIOS began to be a limiting factor because some of its limitations were not easy to overcome. Intel was the first company to notice this as they developed their Itanium systems back in the late 1990s. That work eventually became the foundation for the Unified Extensible Firmware Interface (UEFI).

> **NOTE**
>
> Wikipedia has a nice article that includes the history of UEFI at https://en.wikipedia.org/wiki/Unified_Extensible_Firmware_Interface.

UEFI serves a similar role to BIOS and has replaced BIOS in most modern systems. For most end users, the difference is negligible, except that if you have a UEFI computer, you may need to do some research to install Ubuntu. UEFI firmware often has a BIOS-mode that allows the firmware to work like a traditional BIOS and that is more easily compatible, especially if you are installing Ubuntu as the sole operating system on the computer, rather than as a dual-boot. There were some significant problems early on, but those seem to have lessened as the Linux community learned more about UEFI and made things more easily compatible. To learn more, especially if you are having trouble, see https://help.ubuntu.com/community/UEFI.

One interesting aspect of using UEFI involves hard disk partitioning. When UEFI is used with Windows 8.x or 10, often the partitioning is set up using GPT (GUID Partition Table) rather than the existing MBR (master boot record) standard. You can use GPT with Ubuntu, but if only Ubuntu is to be installed on the drive, it is often easier to reformat the hard disk to use MBR. As with BIOS and UEFI, most people do not need to know or care whether they are using MBR or GPT. To learn more, see http://www.howtogeek .com/193669/whats-the-difference-between-gpt-and-mbr-when-partitioning-a-drive/.

The boot loader locates the Linux kernel on the disk and loads it into memory. After that task is completed, the boot loader passes control of the system to the Linux kernel. You can see how one process builds on another in an approach that enables many different operating systems to work with the same hardware.

> **NOTE**
>
> Linux is very flexible and can be booted from multiple images on a CD-ROM, over a network using PXE (pronounced "pixie") or NetBoot, or on a headless server with the console display sent over a serial or network connection. Work is even underway to create a special Linux BIOS at www.coreboot.org/ that will expedite the boot process because Linux does not need many of the services offered by the typical BIOS.
>
> This kind of flexibility enables Linux to be used in a variety of ways, such as remote servers or diskless workstations, which are not generally seen in personal home use.

Loading the Linux Kernel

In a general sense, the kernel manages the system resources. As the user, you do not often interact with the kernel, but instead you interact with the applications that you are using. Linux refers to each application as a process, and the kernel assigns each process a number called a *process ID (PID)*. Traditionally, the Linux kernel loads and runs a process named init, which is also known as the "ancestor of all processes" because it starts every subsequent process. The traditional init system was SysVinit. It has been replaced by newer options. Until recently, Ubuntu replaced init with Upstart, which was written by Ubuntu developers and made available for any distribution to use. Upstart has now been replaced by systemd as of Ubuntu 15.04. This chapter walks through the traditional SysVinit method first and then provides details on Upstart and systemd.

This next step of the boot process traditionally begins with a message that the Linux kernel is loading, and a series of messages that are printed to the screen, giving you the status of each command. A failure should display an error message. The quiet option may be passed to the kernel at boot time to suppress many of these messages. Ubuntu does not display these messages by default, but instead uses a boot process created by the Fedora/Red Hat developers called Plymouth that is fast and incorporates a beautiful boot screen.

If the boot process were halted at this point, the system would just sit idle and the screen would be blank. To make the system useful for users, you need to start the system services. Those services are some of the applications that enable you to interact with the system.

System Services and Runlevels

The `init` command traditionally boots a Linux system to a specific system state, commonly referred to as its *runlevel*.

Runlevels determine which of the many available system services are started, as well as in which order they start. A special runlevel is used to stop the system, and a special runlevel is used for system maintenance. As you will see, there are other runlevels for special purposes.

You traditionally use runlevels to manage the system services running on a Linux computer. All these special files and scripts are set up during installation, but you can change and control them manually.

With the integration of systemd, much of the interest and concern about runlevels is unnecessary. This is because systemd replaces much of the functionality previously performed by runlevels. For example, you don't even see the runlevel concept used anymore, but instead you hear generic terms like booting into the default.target, multi-user.target, graphical.target, or reboot.target. This information remains in the book for historic context, but most users can simply skim the runlevel sections.

Runlevel Definitions

The runlevels are defined in a traditional Linux system in `/etc/init.d`. Some distributions use the traditional `/etc/inittab` file to manage boot services. Ubuntu has not used this for several years. Because it is not standard in Ubuntu, this book does not cover `/etc/inittab`.

Each runlevel tells the `init` command what services to start or stop. Although runlevels might all have custom definitions, Ubuntu has adopted some standards:

▶ **Runlevel 0**—Known as "halt," this runlevel shuts down the system.

▶ **Runlevel 1**—This is a special runlevel, defined as "single," which boots Ubuntu to a root access shell prompt where only the root user may log in. It has networking, X, and multi-user access turned off. This is the maintenance or rescue mode. It enables the system administrator to perform work on the system, make backups, or repair configuration or other files.

▶ **Runlevels 2–5**—These runlevels aren't used in Ubuntu in any way that distinguishes them from each other, but are often used in other Linux distributions.

▶ **Runlevel 6**—This runlevel reboots the system.

Runlevel 1 (also known as single-user mode or maintenance mode) is most commonly used to repair file systems and change the root password on a system when the password has been forgotten. Trespassers with physical access to the machine can also use runlevel 1 to access your system.

> **CAUTION**
>
> Never forget that uncontrolled physical access is a virtual guarantee of access to your data by an intruder.

Booting into the Default Runlevel

Traditionally, Ubuntu boots into runlevel 5 by default, which means it starts the system as normal and leaves you inside the X Window System looking at the graphical login prompt. It knows what runlevel 5 needs to load by looking in the `rc*.d` directories in `/etc`. Ubuntu contains directories for rc0.d through to rc5.d and rcS.d.

Assuming that the value is `1`, the `rc` script executes all the scripts under the `/etc/rc.1` directory and then launches the graphical login.

If Ubuntu is booted to runlevel 1, for example, scripts beginning with the letter *K* followed by scripts beginning with the letter *S* under the `/etc/rc1.d` directory are then executed:

```
matthew@seymour:~$ ls /etc/rc1.d/
K10jackd         K20rsync            K20vboxdrv    K80cups      S70pppd-dns
K15pulseaudio    K20saned            K20winbind    README       S90single
K20acpi-support  K20saslauthd        K74bluetooth  S30killprocs
K20kerneloops    K20speech-dispatcher K77ntp       S70dns-clean
```

These scripts, as with all scripts in the `rc*.d` directories, are actually symbolic links to system service scripts that reside in the `/etc/init.d` directory.

The `rc1.d` links are prefaced with a letter and number, such as K15 or S10. The *K* or *S* in these prefixes indicate whether a particular service should be killed (K) or started (S) and pass a value of stop or start to the appropriate `/etc/init.d` script. The number in the prefix executes the specific `/etc/init.d` script in a particular order. The symlinks have numbers to delineate the order in which they are started. Nothing is sacred about a specific number, but some services need to be running before others are started. You would not want your Ubuntu system to attempt, for example, to mount a remote *Network File System (NFS)* volume without first starting networking and NFS services.

Understanding `init` Scripts and the Final Stage of Initialization

Each `/etc/init.d` script, or `init` script, contains logic that determines what to do when receiving a start or stop value. The logic might be a simple switch statement for execution, as in this example:

```
case "$1" in
  start)
        start
        ;;
  stop)
        stop
        ;;
```

```
restart)
      restart
      ;;
reload)
      reload
      ;;
status)
      rhstatus
      ;;
condrestart)
      [ -f /var/lock/subsys/smb ] && restart || :
      ;;
*)
      echo $"Usage: $0 {start|stop|restart|status|condrestart}"
      exit 1
esac
```

Although you can use the scripts to customize the way that the system runs from power-on, absent the replacement of the kernel, this script approach also means that you do not have to halt the system in total to start, stop, upgrade, or install new services.

Note that not all scripts use this approach and that other messages might be passed to the service script, such as restart, reload, or status. Also, not all scripts respond to the same set of messages (with the exception of start and stop, which they all have to accept by convention) because each service might require special commands.

After all the system scripts have been run, your system is configured and all the necessary system services have been started. If you are using a runlevel other than 5, the final act of the `init` process is to launch the user shell—`bash`, `tcsh`, `zsh`, or any of the many command shells available. The shell launches and you see a login prompt on the screen.

Controlling Services at Boot with Administrative Tools

You can configure what services run at startup from the Dash with a search for Startup Applications (shown in Figure 15.1). Here Ubuntu lists all the services that you can have automatically start at boot time. They are usually all enabled by default, but you can uncheck the ones you don't want and click OK. It is not recommended that you disable services randomly "to make things go faster." Some services might be vital for the continuing operation of your computer, such as the graphical login manager and the system communication bus.

FIGURE 15.1   You can enable and disable Ubuntu's boot services by toggling the check boxes in the Services dialog.

Changing Runlevels

After making changes to system services and runlevels, you can use the `telinit` command to change runlevels on-the-fly on a running Ubuntu system. Changing runlevels this way enables system administrators to alter selected parts of a running system to make changes to the services or to put changes into effect that have already been made (such as reassignment of network addresses for a networking interface).

For example, in the past a system administrator could quickly change the system to maintenance or single-user mode by using the `telinit` command with its s option like this:

```
matthew@seymour:~$ sudo telinit S
```

Today, the same thing would be done using this `systemd` command:

```
matthew@seymour:~$ sudo systemctl rescue
```

The `telinit` command uses the `init` command to change runlevels and shut down currently running services. However, under `systemd`, `telinit` is deprecated.

After booting to single-user mode, you used to then return to multi-user mode, like this:

```
matthew@seymour:~$ sudo telinit 2
```

Today, the same thing would be done using this `systemd` command:

```
matthew@seymour:~$ systemctl default
```

> **TIP**
>
> Linux is full of shortcuts:
>
> If you don't want to use the `systemctl default` command, you can just click Ctrl+D.
>
> If you exit the single-user shell by typing `exit` at the prompt, you go back to the default runlevel without worrying about using `telinit` or `systemctl`.

Troubleshooting Runlevel Problems

Reordering or changing system services during a particular runlevel is rarely necessary when using Ubuntu unless some disaster occurs. But system administrators should have a basic understanding of how Linux boots and how services are controlled in order to perform troubleshooting or to diagnose problems. By using additional utilities such as the `dmesg | less` command to read kernel output after booting or by examining system logging with `cat /var/log/messages | less`, it is possible to gain a bit more detail about what is going on when faced with troublesome drivers or service failure.

Starting and Stopping Services Manually

If you change a configuration file for a system service, it is usually necessary to stop and restart the service to make it read the new configuration. If you are reconfiguring the X server, it is often convenient to change from runlevel 5 to runlevel 1 to make testing easier and then switch back to runlevel 5 to reenable the graphical login. If a service is improperly configured, it is easier to stop and restart it until you have it configured correctly than it is to reboot the entire machine.

The traditional way to manage a service (as root) is to call the service's `/etc/init.d` name on the command line with an appropriate keyword, such as `start`, `status`, `restart`, or `stop`. For example, to start the Apache web server, call the `/etc/init.d/apache2` script like this:

```
matthew@seymour:~$ sudo /etc/init.d/apache2 start
Starting apache 2.2 web server                              [  OK  ]
```

The script executes the proper programs and reports the status of it/them. Stopping services is equally easy, using the `stop` keyword.

Using Upstart

Starting in 2015, Ubuntu has switched to systemd instead of Upstart. This content is being retained in the book for users of LTS versions like 14.04 LTS that are still supported, but for anyone doing a new installation, you should skip this section and move immediately to the next section, systemd. If you are upgrading from an earlier release of Ubuntu, you may benefit from reading https://wiki.ubuntu.com/SystemdForUpstartUsers.

Upstart was originally developed for Ubuntu. It is an event-based replacement for the `/sbin/init` daemon and System-V init system. It handles starting of tasks and services during boot and stops them during shutdown. It also supervises them while the system is running and is intended to become a way to have tasks and services start or stop automatically based on specific events that happen rather than having to call a script manually to start or stop them. This is a big change and a big deal because it will make the overall system much more flexible, configurable, and responsive to conditions.

Basically, in Upstart, tasks and services are started and stopped by events. Events are generated as other tasks and services are started and stopped and may be received from any other process on the system. Services may be respawned if they die unexpectedly and communication with the `init` daemon occurs over D-Bus. Planned features that have not yet been implemented include the ability for events to be created at timed intervals or at scheduled times or as files or directories are changed and the creation of user services that users can start and stop themselves. This means that eventually Upstart jobs could even replace the venerable `cron` and do things previously impossible on any UNIX or Linux version.

For now, Upstart is being used for many jobs including boot and shutdown, but not all services have Upstart jobs written. Those that exist reside as expected in /etc/init and are easily accessible in the same basic manner as `init` jobs. If an Upstart job exists and you try to manage it using the traditional method, you get a message like this:

```
matthew@seymour:~$ sudo /etc/init.d/ufw stop
[sudo] password for matthew:

Rather than invoking init scripts through /etc/init.d, use the service(8)

utility, e.g. service ufw stop



Since the script you are attempting to invoke has been converted to an

Upstart job, you may also use the stop(8) utility, e.g. stop ufw

ufw stop/waiting
```

In this case, to start or stop Ubuntu's *Uncomplicated Firewall (UFW)*, you just enter `sudo start ufw` or `sudo stop ufw`. Simple. If you want to learn more about Upstart, start with http://upstart.ubuntu.com/. There is also an excellent cookbook filled with Upstart recipes at http://upstart.ubuntu.com/cookbook/.

Read the systemd section that follows this one before you dig too deeply into Upstart.

systemd

Starting 2015, Upstart has been replaced with systemd. systemd was developed at the same time as Upstart and the two have been competing for the title of "init replacement of the future." systemd won. There isn't much point in learning a ton about Upstart, other than what you need for the moment. The future lies with systemd.

To interact with systemd, you typically use the `systemctl` command. The main interactions you are likely to have with systemd involve starting and stopping services. Table 15.1 shows commands related to services.

TABLE 15.1   systemd Service-related Commands

Command	Description
`systemctl start servicename service`	Start a service
`systemctl stop servicename service`	Stop a service
`systemctl restart servicename service`	Restart a service
`systemctl reload servicename service`	Reload a service (this only tells the service to reload its configuration files, rather than restart the entire service—typically, restarting is a safer option)
`systemctl status servicename service`	Show the status of a service
`systemctl condrestart servicename service`	Restart a service if it is already running
`systemctl enable servicename service`	Enable a service at startup
`systemctl disable servicename service`	Disable a service at startup (typically done to remove a service from the list of those starting automatically at boot)
`systemctl is-enabled servicename service`	List all services currently enabled at startup

There are a few standard commands that are replaced, like the ones in Table 15.2.

TABLE 15.2   Other systemd Commands

Command	Description
`systemctl halt`	Halt the system
`systemctl reboot`	Reboot the system
`journalctl -f`	Follow the system log file, replaces `tail -f /var/log/message`

Services are defined in systemd Unit files, which end with `.service`. Many examples of these are found in `/lib/systemd/system`.

There is much more to learn about systemd than is appropriate for a book with such a wide range of topics to cover, especially as few people need to know it. See the official documentation listed in References to learn more, if you find yourself in need.

Boot Repair

Sometimes, such as when you install both Windows and Ubuntu on the same hard
drive, boot problems can develop. Boot Repair is a simple GUI tool to fix those problems.
Typically, it just reinstalls GRUB2, but using the program is a much easier solution
for many users. The program is not yet in the Ubuntu repositories, although plans for
including it have been discussed. In the meanwhile, should you need it, take a look at
https://help.ubuntu.com/community/Boot-Repair or the official documentation at
http://sourceforge.net/projects/boot-repair/.

References

- ▶ **/usr/src/linux/init/main.c**—This file is found on your computer after you
  install the kernel source code; it's the best place to learn about how Linux boots.
  Fascinating reading, really. Get it from the source.

- ▶ **https://help.ubuntu.com/community/Grub2**—Ubuntu community documentation
  for GRUB2.

- ▶ **https://wiki.freedesktop.org/www/Software/systemd/**—The official systemd
  documentation.

# CHAPTER 16

System-Monitoring Tools

To keep your system in optimum shape, you need to be able to monitor it closely. This is imperative in a corporate environment where uptime is vital and any system failures and downtime can be quite expensive. Whether it is checking processes for errant daemons or keeping a close eye on CPU and memory usage, Ubuntu provides a wealth of utilities designed to give you as little or as much feedback as you want. This chapter looks at some of the basic monitoring tools, along with some tactics designed to keep your system up longer. Some of the monitoring tools cover network connectivity, memory, and hard drive usage, and in this chapter you learn how to manipulate active system processes using a mixture of graphical and command-line tools.

Console-Based Monitoring

Those familiar with UNIX system administration already know the ps, or process display, command commonly found on most flavors of UNIX. Because of the close relationship between Linux and UNIX, it also includes this command, which enables you to see the current processes running on the system and who owns them and how resource-hungry they are.

Although the Linux kernel has its own distinct architecture and memory management, it also benefits from enhanced use of the /proc file system, the virtual file system found on many UNIX flavors. Through the /proc file system, you can communicate directly with the kernel to get a deep view of what is currently happening. Developers tend to use the /proc file system as a way of extracting information from the kernel and for their programs to manipulate that information into human-readable formats. A full discussion of the /proc file system is beyond the scope of this book. To get a better idea of what it contains you can take a look at http://en.tldp.org/LDP/Linux-Filesystem-Hierarchy/html/ proc.html for an excellent and in-depth guide.

Processes can also be controlled at the command line, which is important because you might sometimes have only a command-line interface. Whenever an application or command is launched, either from the command line or a clicked icon, the process that comes from the kernel is assigned an identification number called a *process ID (PID)*. This number is shown in the shell if the program is launched via the command line:

```
matthew@seymour:~$ gedit &
[1] 9649
```

In this example, gedit has been launched in the background, and the (bash) shell reported a shell job number ([1] in this case). A job number or job control is a shell-specific feature that allows a different form of process control, such as sending or suspending programs to the background and retrieving background jobs to the foreground. (See your shell's man pages for more information if you are not using bash.)

The second number displayed (9649 in this example) represents the PID. You can get a quick list of your processes by using the ps command like this:

```
matthew@seymour:~$ ps
  PID TTY          TIME CMD

 9595 pts/0     00:00:00 bash

 9656 pts/0     00:00:00 gedit

 9657 pts/0     00:00:00 ps
```

As you can see, the output includes the PID along with other information, such as the name of the running program. As with any UNIX command, many options are available; the proc man page has a full list. One useful option is -e, which lists all processes running on the system. Another is aux, which provides a more detailed list of all the processes. You should also know that ps works not by polling memory, but through the interrogation of the Linux /proc or process file system.

The /proc directory contains many files, some of which include constantly updated hardware information (such as battery power levels and so on). Linux administrators often pipe the output of ps through grep to display information about a specific program, like this:

```
matthew@seymour:~$ ps aux | grep bash
matthew      9656  0.0  0.1  21660  4460 pts/0     Ss   11:39   0:00 bash
```

This example returns the owner (the user who launched the program) and the PID, along with other information such as the percentage of CPU and memory usage, size of the command (code, data, and stack), time (or date) the command was launched, and name of the command for any process that includes the match "bash". Processes can also be queried by PID as follows:

```
matthew@seymour:~$ ps 9656
  PID TTY      STAT    TIME COMMAND
 9656 pts/0    S       0:00 gedit
```

You can use the PID to stop a running process by using the shell's built-in `kill` command. This command asks the kernel to stop a running process and reclaim system memory. For example, to stop gedit in the example, use the `kill` command like this:

```
matthew@seymour:~$ kill 9656
```

After you press Enter and then press Enter again, the shell reports the following:

```
[1]+  Terminated              gedit
```

Note that users can kill only their own processes, but root can kill them all. Controlling any other running process requires root permission, which you should use judiciously (especially when forcing a kill by using the `-9` option); by inadvertently killing the wrong process through a typo in the command, you could bring down an active system.

Using the `kill` Command to Control Processes

The `kill` command is a basic UNIX system command. You can communicate with a running process by entering a command into its interface, such as when you type into a text editor. But some processes (usually system processes rather than application processes) run without such an interface, and you need a way to communicate with them as well, so you use a system of signals. The `kill` system accomplishes that by sending a signal to a process, and you can use it to communicate with any process. The general format of the `kill` command is as follows:

```
matthew@seymour:~$ kill option PID
```

Note that if you are using `kill` on a process you do not own, you need to have super user privileges and preface the `kill` command with `sudo`.

A number of signal options can be sent as words or numbers, but most are of interest only to programmers. One of the most common is the one used previously to kill `gedit`:

```
matthew@seymour:~$ kill PID
```

This tells the process with PID to stop; you supply the actual PID. However, without a signal option, there is no guarantee that a process will be killed because programs can catch, block, or ignore some terminate signals (and this is a good thing, done by design).

```
matthew@seymour:~$ kill -9 PID
```

This includes a signal for `kill` that cannot be caught (9 is the number of the SIGKILL signal); you can use this combination when the plain `kill` shown previously does not work. Be careful, though. Using this does not allow a process to shut down gracefully, and shutting down gracefully is usually preferred because it closes things out that the process might have been using and ensures that things such as logs are written before the process disappears. Instead, try this first.

```
matthew@seymour:~$ kill -1 PID
```

This is the signal to "hang up"—stop—and then clean up all associated processes as well (1 is the number of the SIGHUP signal).

In fact, some system administrators and programmers prefer something like this progression of signals:

▶ `kill -15` sends a SIGTERM, which is a clean shutdown that flushes data that needs to be written to disk, cleans up memory registers, and closes the PID.

▶ `kill -1`, mentioned above, sends a SIGHUP, which cleans up and usually also causes the program to restart.

▶ `kill -2` sends a SIGINT, which is an interrupt from the keyboard, the equivalent to sending a CTRL+C. Say you want to stop a program that is running in the background as a daemon instead of in the terminal foreground, this is a good way to do it.

▶ `kill -11` sends a SIGSEGV, which causes the problem to experience a segmentation fault and close. It does not flush data to disk, but it may create a core dump file that could be useful for debugging and learning why the program was misbehaving (or behaving exactly as you told it to behave, but not as you intended it to behave).

▶ `kill -9` sends a SIGKILL, which should be used as a last resort because it does not sync any data. Nothing is written to disk, no logging, no debugging, nothing. You stop the PID (usually, but not always), but you get nothing that helps you either save data that needed to be written to disk or assists you in figuring out what happened.

As you become proficient at process control and job control, you will learn the utility of a number of `kill` options. You can find a full list of signal options in the `kill` man page.

Using Priority Scheduling and Control

Two useful applications included with Ubuntu are the `nice` and `renice` commands. They are covered in Chapter 12, "Command-Line Master class Part 2." Along with `nice`, system administrators can also use the `time` command to get an idea of how much time and what proportion of a system's resources are required for a task, such as a shell script. (Here, `time` is used to measure the duration of elapsed time; the command that deals with civil and sidereal time is the `date` command.) This command is used with the name of another command (or script) as an argument, like this:

```
matthew@seymour:~$ sudo time -p find / -name conky
/home/matthew/conky
/etc/conky
/usr/lib/conky
```

```
/usr/bin/conky
real 30.19
user 1.09
sys 2.77
```

Output of the command displays the time from start to finish, along with the user and system time required. Other factors you can query include memory, CPU usage, and file system *input/output (I/O)* statistics. See the `time` command's man page for more details.

The `top` command is covered in Chapter 12, "Command-Line Master class Part 2." It has some even-more-powerful cousins worth mentioning here.

One option for monitoring resource usage called `htop`. It is not installed by default, but is available from the Ubuntu software repositories and is worth a minute or two of your consideration after you're familiar with `top`. Here are some key differences:

In `htop`, you can scroll the list vertically and horizontally to see all processes and complete command lines.

In `top` you are subject to a delay for each unassigned key you press (especially annoying when multikey escape sequences are triggered by accident).

`htop` starts faster (top seems to collect data for a while before displaying anything).

In `htop` you don't need to type the process number to kill a process; in `top` you do.

In `htop` you don't need to type the process number or the priority value to renice a process; in `top` you do.

`htop` supports mouse operation; `top` doesn't.

`top` is older, hence, more used and tested.

See http://hisham.hm/htop/ for more details, if you are interested.

Displaying Free and Used Memory with `free`

Although `top` includes some memory information, the free utility displays the amount of free and used memory in the system in kilobytes. (The `-m` switch displays in megabytes.) On one system, the output looks like this:

```
matthew@seymour:~$ free
                total        used        free      shared     buffers      cached
Mem:          4055680     3327764      727916           0      280944     2097568
-/+ buffers/cache:         949252     3106428
Swap:         8787512           0     8787512
```

This output describes a machine with 4GB of RAM memory and a swap partition of 8GB. Note that none of the swap is being used and that the machine is not heavily loaded. Linux is very good at memory management and "grabs" all the memory it can in anticipation of future work.

> **TIP**
>
> A useful trick is to employ the watch command; it repeatedly reruns a command every two seconds by default. If you use
>
> ```
> matthew@seymour:~$ watch free
> ```
>
> you can see the output of the free command updated every two seconds. Use Ctrl+C to quit.

Another useful system-monitoring tool is vmstat *(virtual memory statistics)*. This command reports on processes, memory, I/O, and CPU, typically providing an average since the last reboot; or you can make it report usage for a current period by telling it the time interval in seconds and the number of iterations you desire, like this:

```
matthew@seymour:~$ vmstat 5 10
```

This runs vmstat every five seconds for 10 iterations.

Use the uptime command to see how long it has been since the last reboot and to get an idea of what the load average has been; higher numbers mean higher loads.

Disk Space

Along with system load, it is important to keep an eye on the amount of free hard drive space that your computer has remaining.

It is easy to do this, mainly by using the df command, as follows:

```
matthew@seymour:~$ df
```

Just using the command alone returns this output:

```
Filesystem          1K-blocks       Used Available Use% Mounted on
/dev/sda1           14421344     6584528   7104256  49% /
none                 2020124         348   2019776   1% /dev
none                 2027840        2456   2025384   1% /dev/shm
none                 2027840         220   2027620   1% /var/run
none                 2027840           0   2027840   0% /var/lock
none                 2027840           0   2027840   0% /lib/init/rw
/dev/sda6          284593052   147323812 122812752  55% /home
```

Here you can see each drive as mounted on your system, as well as the used space, the available space, the percentage of the total usage of the disk, and finally where it is mounted on your system.

Unless you are good at doing math in your head, you might find it difficult to work out exactly what the figures mean in megabytes and gigabytes, so it is recommended that you use the -h switch to make the output human readable, like this:

```
matthew@seymour:~$ df -h
Filesystem          Size  Used Avail Use% Mounted on
```

```
/dev/sda1          14G   6.3G   6.8G   49%  /
none              2.0G   348K   2.0G    1%  /dev
none              2.0G   2.4M   2.0G    1%  /dev/shm
none              2.0G   220K   2.0G    1%  /var/run
none              2.0G      0   2.0G    0%  /var/lock
none              2.0G      0   2.0G    0%  /lib/init/rw
/dev/sda6         272G   141G   118G   55%  /home
```

Disk Quotas

Disk quotas are a way to restrict the usage of disk space either by user or by groups. Although rarely—if ever—used on a local or standalone workstation, quotas are definitely a way of life at the enterprise level of computing. Usage limits on disk space not only conserve resources, but also provide a measure of operational safety by limiting the amount of disk space any user can consume.

Disk quotas are more fully covered in Chapter 13, "Managing Users."

Checking Log Files

Many of the services and programs that run on your computer save data in log files. Typical data include success and error messages for processes that are attempted and lists of actions. Some of these log files are extremely technical while others are easily read and parsed by regular users, if you know what you are looking for. Most log files can be found in /var/log/ or its subdirectories.

Typically, these logs are used to learn about something that happened recently, so most admins are interested in the most recent entries. In this case, using tail is common to read just the most recent 10 lines:

```
matthew@seymour:~$ tail /var/log/boot.log
 * Starting                                                          [ OK ] *
Starting save kernel messages                                  [ OK ] * Starting
                                         [ OK ] * Starting   [ OK ] *
Starting deferred execution scheduler                      [ OK ] *
Starting regular background program processing daemon      [ OK ] * Stopping
save kernel messages                                    [ OK ] * Stopping
anac(h)ronistic cron                                    [ OK ] * Starting CUPS
printing spooler/server                        [ OK ] * Starting CPU interrupts
balancing daemon                   [ OK ]
```

There isn't anything terribly interesting in this quote of today's boot.log on my machine, but it is sufficient to show how reading the last few lines of a log file works.

More often, I want to find out whether something specific is mentioned in a log. Let's use cat and grep to see if we can find mentions of "pnp" in dmesg, the display message buffer log for the Linux kernel, to see if there is any mention of a Plug-and-Play device:

matthew@seymour:~$ **cat /var/log/dmesg | grep pnp**

```
[     0.426212] pnp: PnP ACPI init[     0.426223] ACPI: bus type pnp registered[
0.426303] pnp 00:01: [dma 4][     0.426315] pnp 00:01: Plug and Play ACPI device, IDs
PNP0200 (active)[     0.426338] pnp 00:02: Plug and Play ACPI device, IDs PNP0b00
(active)[     0.426351] pnp 00:03: Plug and Play ACPI device, IDs PNP0800 (active)[
0.426369] pnp 00:04: Plug and Play ACPI device, IDs PNP0c04 (active)[     0.426531] pnp
00:05: [dma 0 disabled][     0.426568] pnp 00:05: Plug and Play ACPI device, IDs PNP0501
(active)[     0.426872] pnp 00:08: Plug and Play ACPI device, IDs PNP0103 (active)[
0.427298] pnp: PnP ACPI: found 12 devices[     0.427299] ACPI: ACPI bus type pnp
unregistered
```

Here are a few of the most commonly used log files. Your system will have many others, in addition to these:

▶ /var/log/apport.log saves information about system crashes and reports.

▶ /var/log/auth.log saves information about system access and authentication, including when a user does something using sudo.

▶ /var/log/boot.log saves information about what happens when the computer starts up.

▶ /var/log/kern.log saves information from kernel messages, such as warnings and errors.

▶ /var/log/syslog saves information from system events.

▶ /var/log/ufw.log saves information from the Ubuntu Firewall.

▶ /var/log/apt/history.log saves information about package installation and removal.

Notice that the last one is in its own subdirectory. Many applications create their own directory and may even create multiple log files within that directory.

There are a couple of special cases that deserve a separate mention. These two are not read using standard methods, but each has its own program for reading them from the command line. The commands are the same as the log names. faillog reads from /var/log/faillog and lists recent login failures. lastlog reads from /var/log/lastlog and lists the most recent login for each account.

For those who love GUI applications, there is a log-reader installed by default in Ubuntu. Find System Log in the Dash to run it. It does not include every log in /var/log, but it does include the most important ones that serve the widest audience.

Rotating Log Files

Log files are great, but sometimes they can get unwieldy as time passes and more information is logged. Rotating log files prevents that problem. Rotating a log file means to archive the current log file, start a fresh log, and delete older log files. This means you always have a current log file to peruse, the previous log file, and that the log files never grow too large.

Typically, log rotation is set up by an administrator to happen nightly, at a time when the system is not being heavily used. This is done with a utility called `logrotate`, running as a `cron` job (`cron` is described in Chapter 14, "Automating Tasks and Shell Scripting").

Ubuntu comes with `logrotate` installed. There is a `cron` job already set as well. You can find the script at /etc/cron.daily/logrotate. This file is a `bash` script and looks like this:

```
#!/bin/sh


# Clean nonexistent log file entries from status filecd /var/lib/logrotatetest -e
status || touch statushead -1 status > status.cleansed 's/"//g' status | while read
logfile datedo     [ -e "$logfile" ] && echo "\"$logfile\" $date"done >> status.
cleanmv
status.clean status
test -x /usr/sbin/logrotate || exit 0/usr/sbin/logrotate /etc/logrotate.conf
```

Don't worry if you don't yet understand everything in that script. You don't need to understand it to configure `logrotate` to do what you want. You can learn more about `bash` and shell scripting in Chapter 14, "Automating Tasks and Shell Scripting."

The important line right now is that last one, which lists the location of the configuration file for `logrotate`. Here are the default contents of /etc/logrotate.conf.

```
# see "man logrotate" for details


# rotate log files weeklyweekly
# use the syslog group by default, since this is the owning group# of /var/log/
syslog.su root syslog
# keep 4 weeks' worth of backlogsrotate 4
# create new (empty) log files after rotating old onescreate


# uncomment this if you want your log files compressed#compress
# packages drop log rotation information into this directoryinclude /etc/logrotate.d
# no packages own wtmp, or btmp -- we'll rotate them here/var/log/wtmp {    missingok
monthly    create 0664 root utmp    rotate 1}
/var/log/btmp {    missingok    monthly    create 0660 root utmp    rotate 1}
# system-specific logs may be configured here
```

16

This file includes useful comments and what it can configure is straightforward. If you can read the file, you probably already have a pretty accurate guess as to what the various settings do. As the first comment in the file says, the man page for `logrotate` has an explanation of everything if it is not already clear.

One interesting entry says that packages drop log rotation information into /etc/logrotate.d. This is worth a closer look.

The directory contains a config file for applications that are installed using the package manager and that log information. These files are named after the applications whose log files they control. Let's look at two examples. This first one is for `apt`, the package manager.

```
/var/log/apt/term.log { rotate 12 monthly compress missingok notifempty}
/var/log/apt/history.log { rotate 12 monthly compress missingok notifempty}
```

There are two entries here, each for a different log file that is created and used by apt. The entries define how many old versions of the log files to keep, how frequently `logrotate` will rotate the logs, whether to compress the log files, whether it is okay for the log file to be missing, and whether to bother rotating if the file is empty. Pretty straightforward again. Here is a more complex example, for `rsyslog`, the system logging program.

```
/var/log/syslog
{
    rotate 7
    daily
    missingok
    notifempty
    delaycompress
    compress
    postrotate
       reload rsyslog >/dev/null 2>&1 || true
    endscript
}

/var/log/mail.info
/var/log/mail.warn
/var/log/mail.err
/var/log/mail.log
/var/log/daemon.log
/var/log/kern.log
/var/log/auth.log
/var/log/user.log
/var/log/lpr.log
```

```
/var/log/cron.log
/var/log/debug
/var/log/messages
{
     rotate 4
     weekly
     missingok
     notifempty
     compress
     delaycompress
     sharedscripts
     postrotate
        reload rsyslog >/dev/null 2>&1 || true
     endscript
}
```

The man page for logrotate defines all the commands used in these configuration files, but many are probably clear to you already. Here are some of the more important ones:

▶ rotate—defines how many archived logs are kept at any one time

▶ *interval*—defines how often to rotate the log; the actual setting will be daily, weekly, monthly, or yearly

▶ size—defines how large a log file can become before it is rotated; this setting supercedes the time interval setting above and the format will be a number and a unit, such as size 512k or size 128M or size 100G.

▶ compress—configures the log file to be compressed

▶ nocompress—configures the log file to not be compressed

What is more important to cover here than all of the individual options, which you can look up in the man entry, is that these individual configuration files for specific applications will override the default settings in /etc/logrotate.conf. If a setting is assigned a value in that file, it will be used by all applications that logrotate affects unless an application-specific file in /etc/logrotate.d includes the same setting.

Graphical Process and System Management Tools

The GNOME and KDE desktop environments offer a rich set of network and system-monitoring tools. Graphical interface elements, such as menus and buttons, and graphical output, including metering and real-time load charts, make these tools easy to use. These clients, which require an active X session and (in some cases) root permission, are included with Ubuntu.

If you view the graphical tools locally while they are being run on a server, you must have X properly installed and configured on your local machine. Although some tools can be used to remotely monitor systems or locally mounted remote file systems, you have to properly configure pertinent X11 environment variables, such as $DISPLAY, to use the software or use the ssh client's -x option when connecting to the remote host.

System Monitor

You can find a graphical monitoring tool called System Monitor by searching the Dash. This tool is informative, easy to use and understand, and very useful. It has tabs for information about running processes, available resources, and local file systems.

Conky

Conky is a highly configurable, rather complex system monitor that is light on system resources and can give you information about nearly anything. The downside is that you need to learn how to configure it. Simply installing Conky from the software repositories only gets you started. However, for those who want specific information displayed on our desktop at all times, it is invaluable and well worth the time it takes to figure it out. We give an example here, but to truly appreciate the power, flexibility, and possibilities of Conky, visit http://conkyhardcore.com/ and this long-running thread on the Ubuntu Forums http://ubuntuforums.org/showthread.php?t=281865.

Conky uses text files for configuration and is often started using a short script. The example shown in Figure 16.1 is from Matthew's personal configuration on his desktop and is intended as a simple example to get you started.

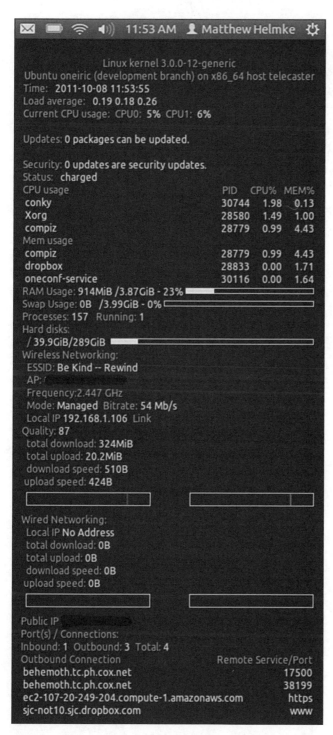

FIGURE 16.1 You can configure Conky to give up-to-the-moment information about anything.

In this example, Conky gives information about the kernel, the operating system, the hostname of the system, and the current time and date. It continually updates with information on load averages, CPU usage and temperature, battery status, and RAM and disk usage. In addition, it shows networking details, including the internal network IP address and the IP address assigned to the outside-facing router the network uses to connect to the wider world and current inbound and outbound network connections. (The IP address is assigned by the ISP, and it changes, so if you try to attack Matthew's home network using it, you will find that the IP address is being used by someone else now.) That is a lot of information in a small space. This setup is not as pretty as some you will see at the previous links, nearly all of which have their setup details made freely available by the person who wrote the configurations.

In this example, Matthew is using two files to run Conky. The first is called `conkyrc` and is a text file that includes the configuration details for what you see in Figure 16.1:

```
# Use Xft?
use_xft yes
# Xft font when Xft is enabled
xftfont Ubuntu:size=9
# gap is the number of pixels from the starting point under alignment
#minimum_size 10 10
gap_x 13
gap_y 45
# Text alignment, other possible values are commented#alignment top_left
alignment top_right
#alignment bottom_left
#alignment bottom_right
# Add spaces to keep things from moving about?  This only affects certain objects.
use_spacer right
# Subtract file system buffers from used memory?
no_buffers yes
# Use double buffering (reduces flicker, may not work for everyone)
double_buffer yes
# Allows icons to appear, window to be moved, and transparency
own_window yes
own_window_type override
own_window_transparent yes
#own_window_hints undecorated,below,skip_taskbar
# set to yes if you want Conky to be forked in the background
background yes
# Update interval in seconds
update_interval 1
cpu_avg_samples 1
net_avg_samples 1
# -- start display config -
TEXT
${alignc}${color #EA6B36}$sysname kernel $kernel
```

```
${alignc}${color #EA6B36}${exec cat /etc/issue.net} on $machine host $nodename
${color #EA6B36}Time:${color #E7E7E7}    $time
${color #EA6B36}Load average:${color #E7E7E7}    $loadavg
${color #EA6B36}Current CPU usage:${color #E7E7E7}  ${color #EA6B36}CPU0:${color
➥#E7E7E7}  ${cpu cpu0}%  ${color #EA6B36}CPU1:${color #E7E7E7}  ${cpu cpu1}%
➥${color #EA6B36}CPU2:${color #E7E7E7}  ${cpu cpu2}%  ${color #EA6B36}CPU3:${color
➥#E7E7E7}  ${cpu cpu3}%

  ${color #EA6B36}CPU4:${color #E7E7E7}  ${cpu cpu4}%  ${color #EA6B36}CPU5:${color
➥#E7E7E7}  ${cpu cpu5}%  ${color #EA6B36}CPU6:${color #E7E7E7}  ${cpu cpu6}%
➥${color #EA6B36}CPU7:${color #E7E7E7}  ${cpu cpu7}%${color #EA6B36}Updates:
➥${color #E7E7E7}${execi 3600 /usr/lib/update-notifier/apt_check.py
➥--human-readable | grep updated}

${color #EA6B36}Security: ${color #E7E7E7}${execi 3600 /usr/lib/update-
➥notifier/apt_check.py --human-readable | grep security}
${color #EA6B36}Status:${color #E7E7E7}    ${battery BAT0}
${color #EA6B36}CPU usage            ${alignr}PID    CPU%   MEM%
${color #E7E7E7} ${top name 1}${alignr}${top pid 1}    ${top cpu 1}    ${top mem 1}
${color #E7E7E7} ${top name 2}${alignr}${top pid 2}    ${top cpu 2}    ${top mem 2}
${color #E7E7E7} ${top name 3}${alignr}${top pid 3}    ${top cpu 3}    ${top mem 3}
${color #EA6B36}Mem usage
${color #E7E7E7} ${top_mem name 1}${alignr}${top_mem pid 1}    ${top_mem cpu 1}
➥${top_mem mem 1}
${color #E7E7E7} ${top_mem name 2}${alignr}${top_mem pid 2}    ${top_mem cpu 2}
➥${top_mem mem 2}
${color #E7E7E7} ${top_mem name 3}${alignr}${top_mem pid 3}    ${top_mem cpu 3}
➥${top_mem mem 3}
${color #EA6B36}RAM Usage:${color #E7E7E7} $mem/$memmax - $memperc% $membar
${color #EA6B36}Swap Usage:${color #E7E7E7} $swap/$swapmax - $swapperc% ${swapbar}
${color #EA6B36}Processes:${color #E7E7E7} $processes  ${color
➥#EA6B36}Running:${color #E7E7E7} $running_processes ${color #EA6B36}
${color #EA6B36}Hard disks:
  / ${color #E7E7E7}${fs_used /}/${fs_size /} ${fs_bar /}
  ${color #EA6B36}/TheLair ${color #E7E7E7}${fs_used /media/TheLair}/${fs_size
➥/media/TheLair} ${fs_bar /media/TheLair}
${color #EA6B36}Wireless Networking:
  ${color #EA6B36}ESSID: ${color #E7E7E7}${wireless_essid wlan0}  ${color
➥#EA6B36}AP: ${color #E7E7E7}${wireless_ap wlan0}
  ${color #EA6B36}${exec iwconfig wlan0 | grep "Frequency" | cut -c 24-44}
  ${color #EA6B36}Mode: ${color #E7E7E7}${wireless_mode wlan0}  ${color
➥#EA6B36}Bitrate: ${color #E7E7E7}${wireless_bitrate wlan0}
  ${color #EA6B36}Local IP ${color #E7E7E7}${addr wlan0}  ${color #EA6B36}Link
Quality: ${color #E7E7E7}${wireless_link_qual_perc wlan0}
  ${color #EA6B36}total download: ${color #E7E7E7}${totaldown wlan0}
  ${color #EA6B36}total upload: ${color #E7E7E7}${totalup wlan0}
```

```
${color #EA6B36}download speed: ${color #E7E7E7}${downspeed wlan0}${color #E7E7E7}
${color #EA6B36} upload speed: ${color #E7E7E7}${upspeed wlan0}
  ${color #E7E7E7}${downspeedgraph wlan0 15,150 ff0000 0000ff} $alignr${color
➥#E7E7E7}${upspeedgraph wlan0 15,150 0000ff ff0000}
${color #EA6B36}Wired Networking:
  ${color #EA6B36}Local IP ${color #E7E7E7}${addr eth0} ${color #EA6B36}
  ${color #EA6B36}total download: ${color #E7E7E7}${totaldown eth0}
  ${color #EA6B36}total upload: ${color #E7E7E7}${totalup eth0}

  ${color #EA6B36}download speed: ${color #E7E7E7}${downspeed eth0}${color #E7E7E7}
${color #EA6B36} upload speed: ${color #E7E7E7}${upspeed eth0}
  ${color #E7E7E7}${downspeedgraph eth0 15,150 ff0000 0000ff} $alignr${color
➥#E7E7E7}${upspeedgraph eth0 15,150 0000ff ff0000}
${color #EA6B36}Public IP ${color #E7E7E7}${execi 5 curl 'http://***a-website-that-
➥returns-your-ip-address—see below***'}
${color #EA6B36}Port(s) / Connections:
${color #EA6B36}Inbound: ${color #E7E7E7}${tcp_portmon 1 32767 count}  ${color
➥#EA6B36}Outbound: ${color #E7E7E7}${tcp_portmon 32768 61000 count}  ${color
➥#EA6B36}Total: ${color #E7E7E7}${tcp_portmon 1 65535 count}
${color #EA6B36}Outbound Connection ${alignr} Remote Service/Port${color #E7E7E7}
 ${tcp_portmon 1 65535 rhost 0} ${alignr} ${tcp_portmon 1 65535 rservice 0}
 ${tcp_portmon 1 65535 rhost 1} ${alignr} ${tcp_portmon 1 65535 rservice 1}
 ${tcp_portmon 1 65535 rhost 2} ${alignr} ${tcp_portmon 1 65535 rservice 2}
 ${tcp_portmon 1 65535 rhost 3} ${alignr} ${tcp_portmon 1 65535 rservice 3}
 ${tcp_portmon 1 65535 rhost 4} ${alignr} ${tcp_portmon 1 65535 rservice 4}
 ${tcp_portmon 1 65535 rhost 5} ${alignr} ${tcp_portmon 1 65535 rservice 5}
```

Most of these details are clear, but one is particularly interesting. There are commercial and other sites that, if you visit them, will return your IP address. This is easily accomplished several ways. Matthew chose to put the following PHP in a file named myip.php on a server he owns, and he calls it directly. Doing so can help you not to feel guilty about constantly hitting someone else's server for this information.

```
<?
$remote = $_SERVER["REMOTE_ADDR"];
  echo $remote;
?>
```

Finally, although you can run Conky from the command line at any time after it is set up, to make it more convenient many people choose to keep their config files in their /home directory somewhere and then write a script with the custom location. If you add a pause to the beginning of the script, you can add the script to Startup Applications (search in the Dash to find it) and have it come up after all your other desktop processes are up and running. Here is a simple example:

```
#!/bin/bash
sleep 45 &&
```

```
exec conky -d -c ~/conky/conkyrc &
# sleep 50 &&
# exec conky -d -c ~/conky/conkyrc_weather &
exit
```

Save it in /home/username/conky along with all your Conky config files, make it executable, and then have the startup applications process call it at boot. Notice that this way you can also run more than one instance of Conky at a time, perhaps having your regular instance in the upper right of the screen and a weather instance or something else in a different location. The possibilities are vast.

A lovely GUI program for creating and managing Conky configurations exists, but it is not in the Ubuntu software repositories. If you are interested in exploring it further, there is a PPA from which you can install Conky Manager at https://launchpad.net/conky-manager. Installation directions and other documentation are available from the maintainer's website at http://www.teejeetech.in/p/conky-manager.html.

Other

Graphical system- and process-monitoring tools that are available for Ubuntu include the following:

- ▶ **vncviewer**—AT&T's open-source remote session manager (part of the Xvnc package), which you can use to view and run a remote desktop session locally. This software (discussed in more detail in Chapter 19, "Remote Access with SSH, Telnet, and VNC") requires an active, background, X session on the remote computer.

- ▶ **gnome-nettool**—A GNOME-developed tool that enables system administrators to carry out a wide range of diagnostics on network interfaces, including port scanning and route tracing.

- ▶ **wireshark**—A graphical network protocol analyzer that can be used to save or display packet data in real time and has intelligent filtering to recognize data signatures or patterns from a variety of hardware and data captures from third-party data-capture programs, including compressed files. Some protocols include AppleTalk, Andrew File System (AFS), AOL's Instant Messenger, various Cisco protocols, and many more.

KDE Process- and System-Monitoring Tools

KDE provides several process- and system-monitoring clients. Integrate the KDE graphical clients into the desktop taskbar by right-clicking the taskbar and following the menus.

These KDE monitoring clients include the following:

- ▶ **kdf**—A graphical interface to your system's file system table that displays free disk space and enables you to mount and unmount file systems with a pointing device.

- ▶ **ksysguard**—Another panel applet that provides CPU load and memory use information in animated graphs.

Enterprise Server Monitoring

Servers used in enterprise situations require extreme uptime. It is beyond the scope of this book to discuss topics such as redundancy, failsafe and failover safeguards, and so on. However, there are a couple of tools we wanted to mention to help an enterprise sysadmin get started.

Landscape

Canonical, the company that finances much of the Ubuntu development, has a monitoring service incorporated into its proprietary, fee-based systems administration tool, Landscape. Landscape has a special dashboard that gives monitoring information and creates an interface for managing multiple Ubuntu systems easily including Ubuntu Enterprise Cloud and Amazon EC2 installations. For more information, see https://landscape.canonical.com/.

Other

A number of top-quality monitoring tools are available. We have touched on only one of the more basic options. For more information about other enterprise server monitoring options, such as Zenoss and Nagios, take a look at https://help.ubuntu.com/community/Servers#Monitoring.

References

▶ **http://and.sourceforge.net/**—Home page of the *auto nice daemon (AND)*, which can be used to prioritize and reschedule processes automatically.

▶ **http://sourceforge.net/projects/schedutils/**—Home page for various projects offering scheduling utilities for real-time scheduling.

CHAPTER 17

Backing Up

This chapter examines the practice of safeguarding data by creating backup copies, restoring that same data if necessary, and recovering data in case of a catastrophic hardware or software failure. The chapter gives you a full understanding of the reasons for sound backup practices. You can use the information here to make intelligent choices about which strategies are best for you. The chapter also shows you how to perform some types of data recovery and system restoration on your own and provides advice about when to seek professional assistance.

Choosing a Backup Strategy

Backups are always trade-offs. Any backup consumes time, money, and effort on an ongoing basis; backups must be monitored, validated, indexed, and stored, and you must continuously purchase new media. Sound expensive? The cost of not having backups is the loss of your critical data. Re-creating the data from scratch costs time and money, and if the cost of doing it all again is greater than the cost associated with backing up, you should be performing backups. At their most basic, backups are nothing more than insurance against financial loss for you or your business.

Your first step in formulating and learning to use an effective backup strategy is to choose the strategy that is right for you. First, you must understand some of the most common (and not so common) causes of data loss so that you are better able to understand the threats your system faces. Then, you need to assess your own system, how it is used and by whom, your available hardware and software resources, and your budget constraints. The following sections look at each of these issues in detail and provide some backup system examples and discuss their use.

Why Data Loss Occurs

Files disappear for any number of reasons: They can be lost because the hardware fails and causes data loss; your attention might wander and you accidentally delete or overwrite a file. Some data loss occurs as a result of natural disasters, and other circumstances beyond your control. A tornado, flood, or earthquake could strike, the water pipes could burst, or the building could catch on fire. Your data, as well as the hardware, would likely be destroyed in such a disaster. A disgruntled employee might destroy files or hardware in an attempt at retribution. Equipment can be stolen. And any equipment might fail; all equipment fails at some time—most likely when it is extremely important for it not to fail.

A CASE IN POINT

A recent Harris poll of Fortune 500 executives found that roughly two-thirds of them had problems with their backups and disaster recovery plans. How about you?

Data can also be lost because of malfunctions that corrupt the data as it attempts to write to the disk. Other applications, utilities, and drivers might be poorly written, buggy (the phrase most often heard today is "still beta quality"), or might suffer some corruption and fail to correctly write that all-important data you have just created. If that happened, the contents of your data file would be indecipherable garbage of no use to anyone.

All these accidents and disasters offer important reasons for having a good backup strategy; however, the most frequent cause of data loss is human error. Who among us has not overwritten a new file with an older version or unintentionally deleted a needed file? This applies not only to data files, but also to configuration files and binaries. While perusing the mail lists, Usenet newsgroup postings, or online forums, stories about deleting entire directories such as /home, /usr, or /lib seem all too common. On a stable server that is not frequently modified or updated, you can choose to mount /usr read-only to prevent writing over or deleting anything in it. Incorrectly changing a configuration file and not saving the original in case it has to be restored (which happens more often than not because the person reconfigured it incorrectly) is another common error.

TIP

To make a backup of a configuration file you are about to edit, use the cp command:

matthew@seymour:~$ **cp filename filename.original**

To restore it, use the following:

matthew@seymour:~$ **cp *filename*.original *filename***

Never edit or move the *.original file, or the original copy will be lost. You can change the file's mode to be unwriteable; then if you try to delete it, you are prevented from doing so and receive a warning.

Proper backups can help you recover from these problems with a minimum of hassle, but you have to put in the effort to keep backups current, verify they are intact, and practice restoring the data in different disaster scenarios.

Assessing Your Backup Needs and Resources

By now you have realized that some kind of plan is needed to safeguard your data, and, like most people, you are overwhelmed by the prospect. Entire books, as well as countless articles and white papers, have been written on the subject of backing up and restoring data. What makes the topic so complex is that each solution is truly individual.

Yet, the proper approach to making the decision is very straightforward. You start the process by asking the following:

▶ What data must be safeguarded?

▶ How often does the data change?

The answers to these two questions determine how important the data is, determine the volume of the data, and determine the frequency of the backups. This in turn determines the backup medium. Only then can the software be selected to accommodate all these considerations. (You learn about choosing backup software, hardware, and media later in this chapter.)

Available resources are another important consideration when selecting a backup strategy. Backups require time, money, and personnel. Begin your planning activities by determining what limitations you face for all these resources. Then, construct your plan to fit those limitations, or be prepared to justify the need for more resources with a careful assessment of both backup needs and costs.

17

> **TIP**
>
> If you are not willing or capable of assessing your backup needs and choosing a backup solution, legions of consultants, hardware vendors, and software vendors would love to assist you. The best way to choose one in your area is to ask other UNIX and Linux system administrators (located through user groups, discussion groups, or mail lists) who are willing to share their experiences and make recommendations. If you cannot get a referral, ask the consultant for references and check them out.

Many people also fail to consider the element of time when formulating their plan. Some backup devices are faster than others, and some recovery methods are faster than others. You need to consider that when making choices.

To formulate your backup plan, you need to determine the frequency of backups. The necessary frequency of backups should be determined by how quickly the important data on your system changes. On a home system, most files never change, a few change daily, and some change weekly. No elaborate strategy needs to be created to deal with that. A good strategy for home use is to back up (to any kind of removable media) critical data frequently and back up configuration and other files weekly.

At the enterprise level on a larger system with multiple users, a different approach is called for. Some critical data is changing constantly, and it could be expensive to re-create; this typically involves elaborate and expensive solutions. Most of us exist somewhere in between these extremes. Assess your system and its use to determine where you fall in this spectrum.

Backup schemes and hardware can be elaborate or simple, but they all require a workable plan and faithful follow-through. Even the best backup plan is useless if the process is not carried out, data is not verified, and data restoration is not practiced on a regular basis. Whatever backup scheme you choose, be sure to incorporate in it these three principles:

- ▶ **Have a plan**—Design a plan that is right for your needs and have equipment appropriate to the task. This involves assessing all the factors that affect the data you are backing up. We delve into more detail later in the chapter.

- ▶ **Follow the plan**—Faithfully complete each part of your backup strategy and then verify the data stored in the backups. Backups with corrupt data are of no use to anyone. Even backup operations can go wrong.

- ▶ **Practice your skills**—Practice restoring data from your backup systems from time to time, so when disaster strikes, you are ready (and able) to benefit from the strength of your backup plan. (For restoring data, see the section "Using Backup Software.") Keep in mind that it is entirely possible that the flaws in your backup plan will become apparent only when you try restoring.

SOUND PRACTICES

You have to create your own best backup plan, but here are some building blocks that go into the foundation of any sound backup program:

- ▶ Maintain more than one copy of critical data.
- ▶ Label the backups.
- ▶ Store the backups in a climate-controlled and secure area.
- ▶ Use secure, offsite storage of critical data. Many companies choose bank vaults for their offsite storage, and this is highly recommended.
- ▶ Establish a backup policy that makes sense and can be followed religiously. Try to back up your data when the system is consistent (that is, no data is being written), which is usually overnight.
- ▶ Keep track of who has access to your backup media and keep the total number of people as low as possible. If you can, allow only trusted personnel near your backups.
- ▶ Routinely verify backups and practice restoring data from them.
- ▶ Routinely inspect backup media for defects and regularly replace them (after destroying the data on them if it is sensitive).

Evaluating Backup Strategies

Now that you are convinced you need backups, you need a strategy. It is difficult to be specific about an ideal strategy because each user or administrator's strategy will be highly individualized, but here are a few general examples:

▶ **Home user**—At home, the user has the Ubuntu installation DVD that takes less than an hour to reinstall, so the time issue is not a major concern. The home user will want to back up any configuration files that have altered, keep an archive of any files that have been downloaded, and keep an archive of any data files created while using any applications. Unless the home user has a special project in which constant backups are useful, a weekly backup is probably adequate. The home user will likely use a consumer-focused online cloud service like Dropbox, an external hard drive, or other removable media for backups.

▶ **Small office**—Many small offices tend to use the same strategy as the home user but are more likely to back up critical data daily and use manually changed tape drives. If they have a tape drive with adequate storage, they will likely have a full system backup as well because restoring from the tape is quicker than reinstalling from the CDs. They also might be using a CD-RW or DVD writers for backups. Although they will use scripts to automate backups, most of it is probably done by hand. This category is also moving to online cloud services for backup as technology is becoming more mature and less expensive.

▶ **Small enterprise**—Here is where backups begin to require higher-end equipment such as auto-loading tape drives with fully automated backups. Commercial backup software usually makes an introduction at this level, but a skillful system administrator on a budget can use one of the basic applications discussed in this chapter. Backups are highly structured and supervised by a dedicated system administrator. You might have guessed that small enterprises are also moving their backups to online cloud services.

▶ **Large enterprise**—These are the most likely setting for the use of expensive, proprietary, and highly automated backup solutions. At this level, data means money, lost data means lost money, and delays in restoring data means money lost as well. These system administrators know that backups are necessary insurance and plan accordingly. Often, these own their own online, distributed cloud systems, with multiple redundant data centers in geographically diverse locations.

Does all this mean that enterprise-level backups are better than those done by a home user? Not at all. The "little guy", with Ubuntu, can do just as well as the enterprise operation at the expense of investing more time in the process. By examining the higher-end strategies, we can apply useful concepts across the board.

This chapter focuses on the local-level activities, not the cloud-services activities that are based on techniques like those listed here, but combined with networking and cloud-service specific additional details. It also discusses some technologies that are a bit outdated for the enterprise but might be useful to the hobbyist with cheap and easy access to older equipment. If you want to use an online cloud service, take what you learn here, read everything made available by your cloud service provider, and then do your homework to design a suitable backup solution for your unique needs. This could be as simple as putting all your important files in a Dropbox–style cloud folder that automatically updates to another computer you own—if you are a casual consumer-grade user backing up simple documents and a few legally owned media files, remembering that services like these generally do not guarantee your data to be permanently backed up, especially the free versions, so although we've not had problems, we warn that they are not enterprise backup solutions. Or it could be as detailed as studying up on Amazon Web Services, OpenStack, or other cloud providers and learning the fine details of their services to suit your needs.

> **NOTE**
>
> If you are a new system administrator, you might inherit an existing backup strategy. Take some time to examine it and see if it meets the current needs of the organization. Think about what backup protection your organization really needs and determine if the current strategy meets that need. If it does not, change the strategy. Consider whether the current policy is being practiced by the users, and, if not, why it is not.

> **BACKUP LEVELS**
>
> UNIX uses the concept of backup levels as a shorthand way of referring to how much data is backed up in relation to a previous backup. It works this way:
>
> A level 0 backup is a full backup. The next backup level is 1.
>
> Backups at the other numbered levels will back up everything that has changed since the last backup at that level or a numerically higher level. (The `dump` command, for example, offers 10 different backup levels.) For example, a level 3 followed by a level 4 generates an incremental backup from the full backup, and a level 4 followed by a level 3 generates a differential backup between the two.

The following sections examine a few of the many strategies in use today. Many strategies are based on these sample schemes; one of them can serve as a foundation for the strategy you construct for your own system.

Simple Strategy

If you need to back up just a few configuration files and some small data files, copy them to a USB stick, label it, and keep it someplace safe. You can copy the important files to a CD-RW disk (up to 700MB in size), or a DVD-RW disk (up to 8GB for data) if you still have that hardware. Most users have switched to using an external hard drive for backups because they are becoming less and less expensive and hold a great amount of data, or they have moved backups online.

In addition to configuration and data files, you should archive each user's /home directory and their entire /etc directory. Between the two, that backup would contain most of the important files for a small system. Then you can easily restore this data from the backup media device you have chosen after a complete reinstall of Ubuntu, if necessary.

Experts used to say that if you have more data than can fit on a floppy disk, you really need a formal backup strategy. Because a floppy disk only held a little over 1MB (and is now incredibly obsolete), perhaps we should change that to "if you have more data than can fit on a cheap USB stick." In any case, some formal backup strategies are discussed in the following sections. We use a tape media backup as an example for convenience because they have been incredibly popular and standard in the past and are still quite common, even as people move to new options such as portable hard drives and cloud storage.

Full Backup on a Periodic Basis

This backup strategy involves a backup of the complete file system on a weekly, bi-weekly, or other periodic basis. The frequency of the backup depends on the amount of data being backed up, the frequency of changes to the data, and the cost of losing those changes.

This backup strategy is not complicated to perform, and it can be accomplished with the swappable disk drives discussed later in the chapter. If you are connected to a network, it is possible to mirror the data on another machine (preferably offsite); the `rsync` tool is particularly well suited to this task. Recognize that this does not address the need for archives of the recent state of files; it only presents a snapshot of the system at the time the update is done.

Full Backups with Incremental Backups

This scheme involves performing a full backup of the entire system once a week, along with a daily incremental backup of only those files that have changed in the previous day, and it begins to resemble what a system administrator of a medium-to-large system traditionally uses.

This backup scheme can be advanced in two ways. In one way, each incremental backup can be made with reference to the original full backup. In other words, a level 0 backup is followed by a series of level 1 backups. The benefit of this backup scheme is that a restoration requires only two tapes (the full backup and the most recent incremental backup). But because it references the full backup, each incremental backup might be large (and grow ever larger) on a heavily used system.

Alternatively, each incremental backup could reference the previous incremental backup. This is a level 0 backup followed by a level 1, followed by a level 2, and so on. Incremental backups are quicker (less data each time) but require every tape to restore a full system. Again, it is a classic trade-off decision.

Modern commercial backup applications such as Amanda or BRU assist in organizing the process of managing complex backup schedules and tracking backup media. Doing it yourself using the classic `dump` or employing shell scripts to run `tar` requires that system administrators handle all the organization themselves. For this reason, complex backup situations are typically handled with commercial software and specialized hardware that are packaged, sold, and supported by vendors.

17

Mirroring Data or RAID Arrays

Given adequate (and often expensive) hardware resources, you can always mirror the data somewhere else, essentially maintaining a real-time copy of your data on hand. This is often a cheap, workable solution if no large amounts of data are involved. The use of *redundant array of independent disks (RAID)* arrays (in some of their incarnations) provides for a recovery if a disk fails.

Note that RAID arrays and mirroring systems just as happily write corrupt data as valid data. Moreover, if a file is deleted, a RAID array will not save it. RAID arrays are best suited for protecting the current state of a running system, not for backup needs.

Making the Choice

Only you can decide what is best for your situation. After reading about the backup options in this book, put together some sample backup plans; run through a few likely scenarios and assess the effectiveness of your choice.

In addition to all the other information you have learned about backup strategies, here are a couple good rules of thumb to remember when making your choice:

▶ If the backup strategy and policy is too complicated (and this holds true for most security issues), it will eventually be disregarded and fall into disuse.

▶ The best scheme is often a combination of strategies; use what works.

Choosing Backup Hardware and Media

Any device that can store data can be used to back it up, but that is like saying that anything with wheels can take you on a cross-country trip. Trying to fit 10GB worth of data on a big stack of CD-RWs is an exercise in frustration, and using an expensive automated tape device to save a single copy of an email is a waste of resources.

Many people use what hardware they already have for their backup operations. Many consumer-grade workstations have a DVD-RW drive, but they usually do not have the abundant free disk space necessary for performing and storing multiple full backups.

In this section, you find out about some of the most common backup hardware available and how to evaluate its appropriateness for your backup needs. With large storage devices becoming increasingly affordable (you can now get 2TB hard drives for around $100), decisions about backup hardware for the small business and home users have become more interesting.

Removable Storage Media

Choosing the right media isn't as easy as it used to be when floppy drives were the only choice. Today, most machines have DVD-ROM drives that can read but not write DVDs, which rules them out for backup purposes. Instead, USB hard drives and solid-state "pen" drives have taken over the niche previously held by floppy drives. Both USB hard drives and solid-state drives are highly portable. Support for these drives under Ubuntu is very good, and the storage space is rising while prices are continuing to fall. A 1TB USB external hard drive is also within the budgets of most and are preferred for anything more than could be held on one pen drive. The biggest benefits of USB drives are data transfer speed and portability.

CD-RW and DVD+RW/-RW Drives

Compared to floppy drives and some removable drives, CD-RW drives and their cousins, DVD+RW/-RW drives, can store large amounts of data and are useful for a home or small business. CD writers and media that were once very common are cheap if you can find them but are gradually disappearing, and automated CD changing machines, necessary for automatically backing up large amounts of data, are still quite costly, if you can find them at all. A benefit of CD and DVD storage over tape devices is that the archived uncompressed file system can be mounted and its files accessed randomly just like a hard drive (you do this when you create a data CD, see Chapter 6, "Multimedia Applications"), making the recovery of individual files easier.

Each CD-RW disk can hold 650MB to 700MB of data (the media comes in both capacities at roughly the same cost); larger chunks of data can be split to fit on multiple disks. Some backup programs support this method of storage. After they are burned and verified, the shelf life for the media is at least a decade or longer.

DVD+RW/-RW is similar to CD-RW, but it is more expensive and can store up to 8GB of uncompressed data per disk.

Honestly, though, these are an old technology, and although they haven't completely died off, the use of either CDs or DVDs for backup has dropped off considerably. It won't be long before they become almost as rare as floppy disks and drives.

Network Storage

For network backup storage, remote arrays of hard drives provide one solution to data storage. With the declining cost of mass storage devices and the increasing need for larger storage space, network storage (*NAS* or *network-attached storage*) is available and supported in Linux. These are cabinets full of hard drives and their associated controlling circuitry, as well as special software to manage all of it. These NAS systems are connected to the network and act as a huge (and expensive) mass storage device.

More modest and simple network storage can be done on a remote desktop-style machine that has adequate storage space (up to eight 1TB drives is a lot of storage space, easily accomplished with off-the-shelf parts), but then that machine (and the local system administrator) has to deal with all the problems of backing up, preserving, and restoring its own data, doesn't it? Several hardware vendors offer such products in varying sizes.

Tape Drive Backup

Tape drives have been used in the computer industry from the beginning. Tape drive storage has been so prevalent in the industry that the `tar` command (the most commonly used command for archiving) is derived from the words *tape archive*. Capacities and durability of tapes vary from type to type and range from a few gigabytes to hundreds of gigabytes with commensurate increases in cost for the equipment and media. Autoloading tape-drive systems can accommodate archives that exceed the capacity of the file systems.

> **TIP**
>
> Older tape equipment is often available in the used equipment market and might be useful for smaller operations that have outgrown more limited backup device options.

Tape equipment is well supported in Linux and, when properly maintained, is extremely reliable. The tapes themselves are inexpensive, given their storage capacity and the ability to reuse them. Be aware, however, that tapes do deteriorate over time and, being mechanical, tape drives can and will fail.

> **CAUTION**
>
> Neglecting to clean, align, and maintain tape drives puts your data at risk. The tapes themselves are also susceptible to mechanical wear and degradation. Hardware maintenance is part of a good backup policy. Do not ever forget that it is a question of when—not if—hardware will fail.

Cloud Storage

Services such as Amazon's AWS and S3 or Dropbox offer a way to create and store backups offsite. Larger companies may create their own offsite, online storage options as well. In each of these and similar cases, data is copied and stored remotely on a file server set aside specifically for that purpose. The data backups may be scheduled with great flexibility and according to the plans and desires of the customer.

Cloud storage is a backup solution that is recent and growing in popularity, but it is also a technology that is changing rapidly. To learn more about the options mentioned here, take a look at www.dropbox.com/ and http://aws.amazon.com/s3/. Although these are not the only services of the kind available, they offer a good introduction to the concept. If you like to roll your own, you definitely want to take a look at Ubuntu Enterprise Cloud at www.ubuntu.com/cloud.

Using Backup Software

Because there are thousands of unique situations requiring as many unique backup solutions, it comes as no surprise that Linux offers many backup tools. Along with command-line tools such as `tar` and `dd`, Ubuntu also provides a graphical archiving tool for desktop installations called *Déjà Dup* that is quite powerful. Another excellent, but complicated alternative is the Amanda backup application—a sophisticated backup application that works well over network connections and can be configured to automatically back up all the computers on your network. Amanda works with drives as well as tapes.

> **NOTE**
>
> The software in a backup system must support the hardware, and this relationship can determine which hardware or software choices you make. Many system administrators choose particular backup software not because they prefer it to other options, but because it supports the hardware they own.
>
> The price seems right for free backup tools, but consider the software's ease of use and automation when assessing costs. If you must spend several hours implementing, debugging, documenting, and otherwise dealing with overly elaborate automation scripts, the real costs go up.

`tar`: **The Most Basic Backup Tool**

The `tar` tool, the bewhiskered old man of archiving utilities, is installed by default. It is an excellent tool for saving entire directories full of files. For example, here is the command used to back up the `/etc` directory:

```
matthew@seymour:~$ sudo tar cvf etc.tar /etc
```

Here, the options use `tar` to create an archive, be verbose in the message output, and use the filename `etc.tar` as the archive name for the contents of the directory `/etc`.

Alternatively, if the output of `tar` is sent to the standard output and redirected to a file, the command appears as follows:

```
matthew@seymour:~$ sudo tar cv /etc > etc.tar
```

The result is the same.

All files in the `/etc` directory will be saved to a file named `etc.tar`. With an impressive array of options (see the man page), `tar` is quite flexible and powerful in combination with shell scripts. With the `-z` option, it can even create and restore `gzip` compressed archives, and the `-j` option works with `bzipped` files.

Creating Full and Incremental Backups with `tar`

If you want to create a full backup, the following creates a `bzip2` compressed tarball (the `j` option) of the entire system:

```
matthew@seymour:~$ sudo tar cjvf fullbackup.tar.bz2 /
```

To perform an incremental backup, you must locate all the files that have been changed since the last backup. For simplicity, assume that you do incremental backups on a daily basis. To locate the files, use the `find` command:

```
matthew@seymour:~$ sudo find / -newer name_of_last_backup_file ! -a -type f -print
```

When run alone, `find` generates a list of files system-wide and prints it to the screen. The `! -a -type` eliminates everything but regular files from the list; otherwise, the entire directory is sent to `tar` even if the contents were not all changed.

Pipe the output of our `find` command to `tar` as follows:

```
matthew@seymour:~$ sudo find / -newer name_of_last_backup_file ! -type d -print |\
  tar czT - backup_file_name_or_device_name
```

Here, the `T -` option gets the filenames from a buffer (where the `-` is the shorthand name for the buffer).

NOTE

The `tar` command can back up to a raw device (one with no file system) and to a formatted partition. For example

```
matthew@seymour:~$ sudo tar cvzf /dev/hdd  /boot  /etc /home
```

backs up those directories to device `/dev/hdd` (not `/dev/hda1`, but to the unformatted device itself).

The `tar` command can also back up over multiple floppy disks:

```
matthew@seymour:~$ sudo tar czvMf /dev/fd0 /home
```

This backs up the contents of `/home` and spreads the file out over multiple floppies, prompting you with this message:

```
Prepare volume #2 for '/dev/fd0' and hit return:
```

Restoring Files from an Archive with `tar`

The `xp` option in `tar` restores the files from a backup and preserves the file attributes, as well, and `tar` creates any subdirectories it needs. Be careful when using this option because the backups might have been created with either relative or absolute paths. You should use the `tvf` option with `tar` to list the files in the archive before extracting them so that you know where they will be placed.

For example, to restore a `tar` archive compressed with `bzip2`, use the following:

```
matthew@seymour:~$ sudo tar xjvf ubuntutest.tar.bz2
```

To list the contents of a tar archive compressed with `bzip2`, use this:

```
matthew@seymour:~$ sudo tar tjvf ubuntutest.tar.bz2
tar: Record size = 8 blocks

drwxr-xr-x matthew/matthew        0 2013-07-08 14:58 other/

-rwxr-xr-x matthew/matthew     1856 2013-04-29 14:37 other/matthew helmke public.
➥asc

-rwxr-xr-x matthew/matthew      170 2013-05-28 18:11 backup.sh

-rwxr-xr-x matthew/matthew     1593 2013-10-11 10:38 backup method
```

Note that because the pathnames do not start with a backslash, they are relative pathnames and will install in your current working directory. If they were absolute pathnames, they would install exactly where the paths state.

The GNOME File Roller

The GNOME desktop file archiving graphical application File Roller (`file-roller`) views, extracts, and creates archive files using `tar`, `gzip`, `bzip`, `compress`, `zip`, `rar`, `lha`, and several other compression formats. Note that File Roller is only a front end to the command-line utilities that actually provide these compression formats; if a format is not installed, File Roller cannot use that format.

CAUTION

File Roller does not complain if you select a compression format that is not supported by installed software until after you attempt to create the archive. So, install any needed compression utilities first.

File Roller is well-integrated with the GNOME desktop environment to provide convenient drag-and-drop functionality with the Nautilus file manager. To create a new archive, select Archive, New to open the New Archive dialog box and navigate to the directory where you want the archive to be kept. Type your archive's name in the Selection: /root text box at the bottom of the New Archive dialog box. Use the Archive type drop-down menu to select a compression method. Now, drag the files that you want to be included from Nautilus into the empty space of the File Roller window, and the animated icons will show that files are being included in the new archive. When you have finished, a list of files appears in the previously blank File Roller window. To save the archive, select Archive, Close. Opening an archive is as easy as using the Archive, Open dialog to select the appropriate archive file. You can learn more at https://help.ubuntu.com/community/File%20Roller.

Ubuntu also offers the KDE `ark` and `kdat` GUI tools for backups; they are installed only if you select the KDE desktop during installation, but you can search through Synaptic to find them. Archiving has traditionally been a function of the system administrator and not seen as a task for the individual user, so no elaborate GUI was believed necessary. Backing up has also been seen as a script-driven, automated task in which a GUI is not as useful. Although that's true for system administrators, home users usually want something a little more attractive and easier to use, and that's the gap `ark` was created to fill.

The KDE `ark` Archiving Tool

You launch `ark` by launching it from the command line. It is integrated with the KDE desktop (such as File Roller is with GNOME), so it might be a better choice if you use KDE. This application provides a graphical interface for viewing, creating, adding to, and extracting from archived files. Several configuration options are available with `ark` to ensure its compatibility with Microsoft Windows. You can drag and drop from the KDE desktop or Konqueror file browser to add or extract files, or you can use the `ark` menus.

As long as the associated command-line programs are installed, `ark` can work with `tar`, `gzip`, `bzip2`, `zip`, and `lha` files (the last four being compression methods used to save space by compaction of the archived files).

Existing archives are opened after launching the application itself. You can add files and directories to the archive or delete them from the archive. After opening the archive, you can extract all of its contents or individual files. You can also perform searches using patterns (all `*.jpg` files, for example) to select files.

Choosing New from the File menu creates new archives. You then type the name of the archive, providing the appropriate extension (.`tar`, .`gz`, and so on), and then proceed to add files and directories as you desire.

Déjà Dup

Déjà Dup is a simple backup tool with a useful GUI. It supports local, remote, or cloud backups. It can encrypt and compress your data for secure and fast transfers and more. Search the Dash to find Déjà Dup (Figure 17.1).

FIGURE 17.1   The Déjà Dup icon is easy to find in the Dash.

Start with Déjà Dup Backup Preferences. This menu item brings up a configuration wizard that lets you set where the backup will be stored, what will be backed up, a schedule for automatic backups, and more. The following screenshots tell the story (see Figures 17.2–17.4).

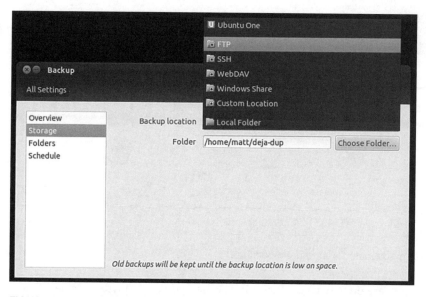

FIGURE 17.2   Storage options include cloud storage, local, via FTP or SSH and more.

FIGURE 17.3   Set the files and folders you want to back up or exclude.

17

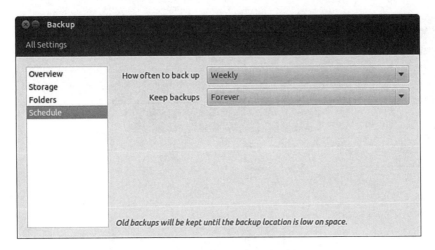

FIGURE 17.4   Set a schedule for automatic backups.

Click Close when you are done with configuration. When you are ready to run Déjà Dup at a later time, click the same icon in the Dash. This brings up the same interface showing the Overview tab. Click Restore to restore from a previous backup. Click Back Up Now to back up using the settings enabled earlier (see Figure 17.5).

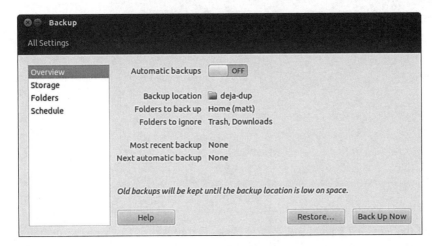

FIGURE 17.5   Backing up and restoring is easy from the Déjà Dup Overview.

Back In Time

Back In Time is a viable alternative to Déjà Dup for many users. It is easily available from the Ubuntu Software Center, stable, has a clear and easy-to-understand interface, and is actually little more than a GUI front end for well-established tools.

Back In Time uses `rsync`, `diff`, and `cp` to monitor, create, and manipulate files, and it uses `cron` to schedule when it will run. Using these command-line tools is described later in this chapter. Back In Time is little more than a well-designed GUI front end designed for GNOME that also works well with Ubuntu's Unity interface. Back In Time also offers a separate package in the Ubuntu Software Center with a front end for KDE, if that is your preference. If you use the standard Ubuntu interface, install a package from the Ubuntu Software Center called `nautilus-actions` to get context menu access to some of the backup features.

The first time you run Back In Time, it takes a snapshot of your drive. This takes a long time, depending on the amount of data you have. You designate which files and directories to back up and where to back them up. Then set when to schedule the backup. The program takes care of the rest.

To restore, select the most recent snapshot from the list at the left of the screen (see Figure 17.6). Then browse through the list of directories and files at the right until you find the file that interests you. You may right-click the file to view a pop-up menu, from which you may open a file, copy a file to a desired location, or view the various snapshots of a file and compare them to determine which you might want to restore.

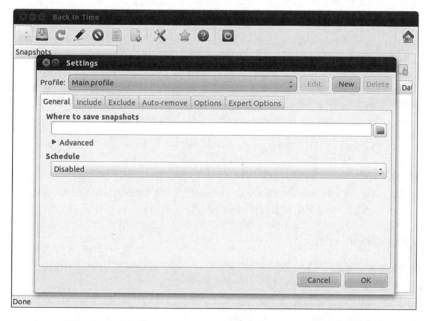

FIGURE 17.6   Back In Time makes finding and restoring files easy.

Back In Time keeps multiple logs of actions and activities, file changes and versions, and is a useful tool. It does have one main weakness: For the moment, it remains unable to schedule backups to be made over a network. If you are backing up to a second hard drive or if you always have a network drive mounted on your system, this is not an issue. However, if you want to back up to cloud storage or via ssh, this tool might not suit your needs.

You can find the official documentation for Back In Time at http://backintime.le-web.org.

Unison

Unison is a file-synchronization tool that works on multiple platforms, including Linux, other flavors of UNIX such as Solaris and Mac OS X, and Windows. After Unison is set up, it synchronizes files in both directions and across platforms. If changes are made on both ends, files are updated in both directions. When file conflicts arise, such as when the same file was modified on each system, the user is prompted to decide what to do. Unison can connect across a network using many protocols, including ssh. It can connect with and synchronize many systems at the same time and even to the cloud.

Unison was a project developed at the University of Pennsylvania as a research project among several academics. It is no longer under active development as a research project, but it does appear to continue to be maintained with bug fixes and very occasional feature additions. The original developers claim to still be using it daily, so it is not completely abandoned.

Unison is powerful and configurable. The foundation is based on rsync, but with some additions that enable functionality that is generally only available from a version control system. See Chapter 39, "Opportunistic Development," for an introduction to these, as well as a brief mention later in this chapter in the context of backing up configuration files.

Even though the project is no longer the primary focus of any of the developers, many people still use Unison, and it still gets press, as in a recent *Linux Journal* article. For that reason, it gets a mention in this chapter and might be worthy of your time and effort if you are interested. Unison is released under the free GPL license, so you might decide you want to dig in to the code. The developers do not have time to maintain it regularly but welcome patches and contributions. If this sounds like a project that interests you, see www.cis.upenn.edu/~bcpierce/unison/.

Using the Amanda Backup Application

Amanda is a powerful network backup application created by the University of Maryland at College Park. Amanda is a robust backup and restore application best suited to unattended backups with an autoloading tape drive of adequate capacity. It benefits from good user support and documentation.

Amanda's features include compression and encryption. It is intended for use with high-capacity tape drives, floptical, CD-R, and CD-RW devices.

Amanda uses GNU tar and dump; it is intended for unattended, automated tape backups and is not well suited for interactive or ad hoc backups. The support for tape devices in Amanda is robust, and file restoration is relatively simple. Although Amanda does not support older Macintosh clients, it uses Samba to back up Microsoft Windows clients, as well as any UNIX client that can use GNU tools (which includes Mac OS X). Because Amanda runs on top of standard GNU tools, file restoration can be made using those tools on a recovery disk even if the Amanda server is not available. File compression can be done on either the client or server, thus lightening the computational load on less-powerful machines that need to be backed up.

CAUTION

Amanda does not support `dump` images larger than a single tape and requires a new tape for each run. If you forget to change a tape, Amanda continues to attempt backups until you insert a new tape, but those backups will not capture the data as you intended them to. Do not use too small a tape or forget to change a tape; otherwise, you will not be happy with the results.

There is no GUI for Amanda. Configuration is done in the time-honored UNIX tradition of editing text configuration files located in `/etc/amanda`. The default installation in Ubuntu includes a sample `cron` file because it is expected that you will be using `cron` to run Amanda regularly. The client utilities are installed with the package `amanda-client`; the Amanda server is called `amanda-server`. Install both. As far as backup schemes are concerned, Amanda calculates an optimal scheme on-the-fly and schedules it accordingly. It can be forced to adhere to a traditional scheme, but other tools are possibly better suited for that job.

The man page for Amanda (the client is `amdump`) is well written and useful, explaining both the configuration of Amanda and detailing the several programs that actually make up Amanda. The configuration files found in `/etc/amanda` are well commented; they provide a number of examples to assist you in configuration.

The program's home page is www.amanda.org. There you can find information about subscribing to the mail list and links to Amanda-related projects and a FAQ.

Alternative Backup Software

Commercial and other freeware backup products do exist; BRU and Veritas are good examples of effective commercial backup products. Here are some useful free software backup tools that are not installed with Ubuntu:

▶ **flexbackup**—This backup tool is a large file of Perl scripts that makes `dump` and `restore` easier to use. `flexbackup`'s command syntax can be found by using the command with the `-help` argument. It also can use `afio`, `cpio`, and `tar` to create and restore archives locally or over a network using `rsh` or `ssh` if security is a concern. Its home page is www.edwinh.org/flexbackup/. Note that it has not received any updates or changes in a very long time.

▶ **afio**—This tool creates `cpio` formatted archives but handles input data corruption better than `cpio` (which does not handle data input corruption very well at all). It supports multi-volume archives during interactive operation and can make compressed archives. If you feel the need to use `cpio`, you might want to check out `afio` at http://freshmeat.net/projects/afio/.

Many other alternative backup tools exist, but covering all of them is beyond the scope of this book. Two good places to look for free backup software are Freshmeat (www.freshmeat.net) and Google (www.google.com/linux).

17

Copying Files

Often, when you have only a few files that you need to protect from loss or corruption, it might make better sense to simply copy the individual files to another storage medium rather than to create an archive of them. You can use the tar, cp, rsync, or even the cpio commands to do this; you can also use a handy file management tool known as mc. Using tar is the traditional choice because older versions of cp did not handle symbolic links and permissions well at times, causing those attributes (characteristics of the file) to be lost; tar handled those file attributes in a better manner. cp has been improved to fix those problems, but tar is still more widely used. rsync has recently been added to Ubuntu and is an excellent choice for mirroring sets of files, especially when done over a network.

To illustrate how to use file copying as a backup technique, the examples here show how to copy (not archive) a directory tree. This tree includes symbolic links and files that have special file permissions we need to keep intact.

Copying Files Using tar

One choice for copying files into another location is to use the tar command; you just create a tar file that is piped to tar to be uncompressed in the new location. To accomplish this, first change to the source directory. Then the entire command resembles this:

```
matthew@seymour:~$ tar -cvf files | (cd target_directory ; tar -xpf)
```

In this command, *files* are the filenames you want to include; use * to include the entire current directory.

Here is how this command works: You have already changed to the source directory and executed tar with the cvf arguments that tell tar to

- ▶ c—Create an archive.
- ▶ v—Verbose; lists the files processed so you can see that it is working.
- ▶ f—The filename of the archive will be what follows. (In this case, it is -.)

The following tar commands can be useful for creating file copies for backup purposes:

- ▶ l—Stay in the local file system (so that you do not include remote volumes).
- ▶ atime-preserve—Do not change access times on files, even though you are accessing them now (to preserve the old access information for archival purposes).

The contents of the tar file (held for us temporarily in the buffer, which is named -) are then piped to the second expression, which extracts the files to the target directory. In shell programming (refer to Chapter 14, "Automating Tasks and Shell Scripting"), enclosing an expression in parentheses causes it to operate in a subshell and be executed first.

First you change to the target directory, and then

- ▶ x—Extract files from a `tar` archive.

- ▶ p—Preserve permissions.

- ▶ f—The filename will be -, the temporary buffer that holds the files archived with `tar`.

Compressing, Encrypting, and Sending `tar` Streams

The file copy techniques using the `tar` command in the previous section can also be used to quickly and securely copy a directory structure across a LAN or the Internet (using the `ssh` command). One way to make use of these techniques is to use the following command line to first compress the contents of a designated directory and then decompress the compressed and encrypted archive stream into a designated directory on a remote host:

```
matthew@seymour:~$ tar -cvzf data_folder | ssh remote_host '( cd ~/mybackup_dir;
➥tar -xvzf )'
```

The `tar` command is used to create, list, and compress the files in the directory named `data_folder`. The output is piped through the `ssh` (Secure Shell) command and sent to the remote computer named `remote_host`. On the remote computer, the stream is then extracted and saved in the directory named `/mybackup_dir`. You are prompted for a password to send the stream.

Copying Files Using `cp`

To copy files, we could use the `cp` command. The general format of the command when used for simple copying is as follows:

```
matthew@seymour:~$ cp -a source_directory target_directory
```

The -a argument is the same as giving -dpR, which would be

- ▶ -d—Preserves symbolic links (by not dereferencing them) and copies the files that they point to instead of copying the links.

- ▶ -p—Preserves all file attributes if possible. (File ownership might interfere.)

- ▶ -R—Copies directories recursively.

The `cp` command can also be used to quickly replicate directories and retain permissions by using the -avR command-line options. Using these options preserves file and directory permissions, gives verbose output, and recursively copies and re-creates subdirectories. You can also create a log of the backup during the backup by redirecting the standard output like this:

```
matthew@seymour:~$ sudo cp -avR directory_to_backup destination_vol_or_dir 1 >
➥/root/backup_log.txt
```

or

```
matthew@seymour:~$ sudo cp -avR ubuntu /test2 1 > /root/backup_log.txt
```

This example makes an exact copy of the directory named /ubuntu on the volume named /test2 and saves a backup report named backup_log.txt under /root.

Copying Files Using mc

The Midnight Commander (available in the Universe repository, under the package mc; see Chapter 9, "Managing Software," for how to enable the Universe and Multiverse repositories) is a command-line file manager that is useful for copying, moving, and archiving files and directories. The Midnight Commander has a look and feel similar to the Norton Commander of DOS fame. By executing mc at a shell prompt, a dual-pane view of the files is displayed. It contains drop-down menu choices and function keys to manipulate files. It also uses its own virtual file system, enabling it to mount FTP directories and display the contents of tar files, gzip tar files (.tar.gz or .tgz), bzip files, DEB files, and RPM files, as well as extract individual files from them. As if that is not enough, mc contains a File Undelete virtual file system for ext2/3 partitions. By using cd to "change directories" to an FTP server's URL, you can transfer files using FTP. The default font chosen for Ubuntu makes the display of mc ugly when used in a tty console (as opposed to an xterm), but does not affect its performance.

In the interface, pressing the F9 key drops down the menu, and pressing F1 displays the Help file. A "feature" in the default GNOME terminal intercepts the F10 key used to exit mc, so use F9 instead to access the menu item to quit, or just click the menu bar at the bottom with your mouse. The configuration files are well documented, and it would appear easy to extend the functionality of mc for your system if you understand shell scripting and regular expressions. It is an excellent choice for file management on servers not running X.

Using rsync

An old favorite for backing up is rsync. One big reason for this is because rsync enables you to copy only those files that have changed since the last backup. So although the initial backup might take a long time, subsequent backups are much faster. It is also highly configurable and can be used with removable media such as USB hard drives or over a network. Here is one way to use rsync.

First, create an empty file and call it backup.sh:

```
matthew@seymour:~$ sudo touch backup.sh
```

Then, using your favorite text editor, enter the following command into the file and save it:rsync --force --ignore-errors --delete --delete-excluded --exclude-

```
from=/home/matthew-exclude.txt --backup --backup-dir='date +%Y-%m-%d' -av /
/media/externaldrive/backup/Seymour
```

Make the file executable:

```
matthew@seymour:~$ sudo chmod +x backup.sh
```

This command uses several options with `rsync` and puts them in a script that is quick and easy to remember and run. You can run the script at the command line using `sudo sh ./backup.sh` or as an automated `cron` job.

Here is a rundown of what is going on in the command. Basically, `rsync` is told to copy all new and changed files (what to back up) and delete from any existing backup any files that have been deleted on the source (and back them up in a special directory, just to be safe). It is told where to place the backup copy and is given details on how to deal with specific issues in the process. Read the `rsync` man page for more options and to customize to your needs.

Following are the options used here:

▶ `--force`—Forces deletion of directories in the target location that are deleted in the source, even if the directories in the destination are not empty.

▶ `--ignore-errors`—Tells `--delete` to go ahead and delete files even when there are I/O errors.

▶ `--delete`—Deletes extraneous files from destination directories.

▶ `--delete-excluded`—Also deletes excluded files from destination directories.

▶ `--exclude-from=/home/matt-exclude.txt`—Prevents backing up files or directories listed in this file. (It is a simple list with each excluded directory on its own line.)

▶ `--backup`—Creates backups of files before deleting them from a currently existing backup.

▶ `--backup-dir='date +%Y-%m-%d'`—Creates a backup directory for the previously mentioned files that looks like this: 2013-07-08. Why this format for the date? Because it is standard, as outlined in ISO 8601 (see: http://www.iso.org/iso/home/standards/iso8601.htm). It is clear, works with scripts, and sorts beautifully, making your files easy to find.

▶ `-av`—Tells `rsync` to use archive mode and verbose mode.

▶ `/`—Denotes the directory to back up. In this case, it is the root directory of the source, so everything in the file system is being backed up. You could put `/home` here to back up all user directories or make a nice list of directories to exclude in the file system.

▶ `/media/externaldrive/backup/seymour`—Sets the destination for the backup as the `/backup/seymour` directory on an external hard drive mounted at `/mount/externaldrive`.

To restore from this backup to the same original location, you reverse some of the details and may omit others. Something like this works nicely:

```
matthew@seymour:~$ rsync --force --ignore-errors --delete --delete-excluded
/media/externaldrive/backup/seymour /
```

This becomes even more useful when you think of ways to script its use. You could create an entry in crontab, as described in Chapter 14, "Automating Tasks and Shell Scripting." Even better, you could set two computers to allow for remote SSH connections using private keys created with `ssh-keygen`, as described in Chapter 19, "Remote Access with SSH, Telnet, and VNC," so that one could back up the files from one computer to the other computer without needing to login manually. Then you could place that in an automated script.

Version Control for Configuration Files

For safety and ease of recovery when configuration files are corrupted or incorrectly edited, the use of a version control system is recommended. In fact, this is considered an industry best practice. Many top-quality version control systems are available, such as Git, Subversion, Mercurial, and Bazaar. If you already have a favorite, perhaps one that you use for code projects, you can do what we describe in this section using that version control system. The suggestions here are to get people thinking about the idea of using version control for configuration files and to introduce a few well-used and documented options for those who are unfamiliar with version control. First, some background.

Version control systems are designed to make it easy to revert changes made to a file, even after the file has been saved. This is done a little bit differently by each system, but the basic idea is that not only is the current version of the file saved, but each and every version that existed previously is also saved. Some version control systems do this by saving the entire file every time. Some use metadata to describe just the differences between each version. In any case, it is possible to roll back to a previous version of the file, to restore a file to a state before changes were made. Developers who write software are well aware of the power and benefit to being able to do this quickly and easily; it is no longer required that the file editor remember the technical details of where, what, or even how a file has been edited. When a problem occurs, the file is simply restored to its previous state. The version control system is also able to inform the user where and how each file has changed at each save.

Using a version control system for configuration files means that every time a configuration is changed, those changes are recorded and tracked. This enables easy discovery of intruders (if a configuration has been changed by an unauthorized person trying to reset, say, the settings for Apache so that the intruder can allow a rogue web service or site to run on your server), easy recovery from errors and glitches, and easy discovery of new features or settings that have been enabled or included in the configuration by software upgrades.

Many older and well-known tools do this task, such as `changetrack`, which is quite a good example. All of them seek to make the job of tracking changes to configuration files easier and faster, but with the advances in version control systems, most provide very little extra benefit. Instead of suggesting any of these tools, you are probably better off learning a modern and good version control system. One exception is worth a bit of discussion because of its ability to work with your software package manager, which saves you the task of remembering to commit changes to your version control system each time the package manager runs. This exception is `etckeeeper`.

`etckeeper` takes all of your `/etc` directory and stores the configuration files from it in a version control system repository. You can configure the program by editing the `etckeeper.conf` file to store data in a Git, Mercurial, Bazaar, or Subversion repository. In addition, `etckeeper` connects automatically to the APT package management tool used by Ubuntu and automatically commits changes made to `/etc` and the files in it during normal software package upgrades. Other package managers, such as Yum, can also be tracked when using other Linux distributions such as Fedora. It even tracks file metadata that is often not easily tracked by version control systems, like the permissions in `/etc/shadow`.

> **CAUTION**
>
> Using any version control system to track files that contain sensitive data such as passwords can be a security risk. Tracked files and the version control system itself should be treated with the same level of care as the sensitive data itself.

By default, `etckeeper` uses Git. On Ubuntu, this is changed to Bazaar (`bzr`) because it is the version control system used by Ubuntu developers. Because this is configurable, we mention just the steps here and leave it to you to adapt them for your particular favorite version control system.

First, edit `/etc/etckeeper/etckeeper.conf` to use your desired settings, such as the version control system to use, the system package manager being used, and whether to have changes automatically committed daily. After `etckeeper` is installed from the Ubuntu repositories, it must be initiated from the command line:

```
matthew@seymour:~$ etckeeper init
```

If you are only going to use `etckeeper` to track changes made to `/etc` when software updates are made using APT, you do not need to do anything else. If you edit files by hand, make sure you use your version control system's commands to commit those changes or use the following:

```
matthew@seymour:~$ etckeeper commit "Changed prompt style"
```

The message in quotes should reflect the change just made. This makes reading logs and finding exact changes much easier later.

Recovering or reverting file changes is then done using your version control system directly. Suppose, for example, that you have made a change in `/etc/bash.bashrc`, the file that sets the defaults for your `bash` shell. You read somewhere how to change the prompt and did not like the result. However, because the changes are being tracked, you can roll it back to the previous version. Because `bzr` is the default for `etckeeper` in Ubuntu, here is how you do that with `bzr`. First, check the log to find the commit number for the previous change:

```
matthew@seymour:~$ bzr log /etc/bash.bashrc
------------------------------------------------------------
revno: 2
committer: matthew <matthew@seymour>
branch nick: seymour etc repository
timestamp: Tue 2013-07-16 11:08:22 -0700
message:
  Changed /etc/bash.bashrc
------------------------------------------------------------
revno: 1
committer: matthew <matthew@seymour>
branch nick: seymour etc repository
timestamp: Tue 2013-07-16 11:00:16 -0700
message:
  Changed /etc/bash.bashrc
------------------------------------------------------------
```

I know the change was made in the most recent revision, denoted `revno 2` (for revision number two), so I now revert back to that version:

```
matthew@seymour:~$ bzr revert -revision 2 /etc/bash.bashrc
```

Today it is common for programmers, systems administrators, and developer types to back up their dotfiles using version control. Dotfiles are the configuration files and directories in a user's /home directory, all of which begin with a dot, like .bashrc. These are not necessarily backed up by all software, and because they are often customized by highly technical people to suit their desires, backing them up is a good idea. Version control systems are commonly used. A new program for Ubuntu called *dotdee* performs this task for a different type of configuration file or directory that ends with .d and is stored in /etc. You can find more information about dotdee in Chapter 9, "Managing Software."

System Rescue

There will come a time when you need to engage in system rescue efforts. This need arises when the system will not even start Linux so that you can recover any files. This problem is most frequently associated with the boot loader program or partition table, but it could be that critical system files have been inadvertently deleted or corrupted. If you have been making backups properly, these kinds of system failures are easily, though not quickly, recoverable through a full restore. Still, valuable current data might not have been backed up since the last scheduled backup, and the backup archives are found to be corrupt, incomplete, or missing. A full restore also takes time you might not have. If the problem causing the system failure is simply a damaged boot loader, a damaged partition table, a missing library, or misconfiguration, a quick fix can get the system up and running, and the data can then be easily retrieved.

In this section, you learn a couple of quick things to try to restore a broken boot loader or recover your data when your system fails to boot.

The Ubuntu Rescue Disc

The Ubuntu installation DVD works quite well as a live DVD. To use it, insert the disc and reboot the computer, booting from the DVD just as you did when you installed Ubuntu originally and ran it from the DVD.

Restoring the GRUB2 Boot Loader

The easiest way to restore a broken system's GRUB2 files is simply to replace them. This works with Ubuntu 9.10 or later only and only if the system uses GRUB2 (which it does if it was originally installed using 9.10 or later, but might not if Ubuntu was originally installed using an older Ubuntu release and upgraded as GRUB2 is not automatically installed during release upgrades). In any case, your best bet is to use a DVD from the same release as what you have installed on the hard drive.

To get started, boot using the live DVD and open a terminal from the Dash. Then determine which of the hard drive's partitions holds the Ubuntu installation, which you can discover using the following:

```
matthew@seymour:~$ sudo fdisk -l
```

You may find this block ID command useful, as it tends to return a bit more information:

```
matthew@seymour:~$ sudo blkid
```

Unless you customized your installation, in which case you probably already know your partitioning scheme and the location of your Ubuntu installation, the partition will probably be on a drive called sda on the first partition, which you can mount now using this:

```
matthew@seymour:~$ sudo mount /dev/sda1 /mnt
```

This mounts the drive in the current file system (running from the live DVD) at /mnt, where it will be accessible to you for reading and modifying as needed. Next, you reinstall GRUB2 on this device:

```
matthew@seymour:~$ sudo grub-install --boot-directory=/mnt/boot /dev/sda
```

At this point, reboot (using your hard drive and not the live DVD), and all should be well. After the reboot is complete, enter the following:

```
matthew@seymour:~$ sudo update-grub
```

This refreshes the GRUB2 menu and completes the restoration. You can find a lot of great information about GRUB2 at https://help.ubuntu.com/community/Grub2.

17

Saving Files from a Nonbooting Hard Drive

If restoring the GRUB2 boot loader fails and you still cannot boot from the hard drive, try to use the live DVD to recover your data. Boot and mount the hard drive as shown previously and then attach an external storage device such as a USB thumb drive or an external hard drive. Then copy the files you want to save from the mounted drive to the external drive.

If you cannot mount the drive at all, your options become more limited and possibly more expensive. It is likely that either the hardware has failed or the file system has become badly corrupted. In either case, recovery is either impossible or more difficult and best left to experts if the data is important to you. But, the good news is that you have been making regular backups, right? So, you probably only lost a day or maybe a week of work and can buy a new drive, install it, and start from scratch, putting the data from your backup on your new Ubuntu installation on the new hardware.

Every experienced system administrator has had this happen because no hardware is infallible. We expect occasional hardware failures, and that's why we have good backup and recovery schemes in place for data. There are two types of system administrators: those who lose data when this happens and those who have good schemes in place. Be forewarned and be wise.

If you did not have a backup, which happens to most system administrators only once in their lives (because they learn from the mistake), immediately stop messing with the hard drive. Your best bet to recover the data will be very expensive, but you should look for a company that specializes in the task and pay them to do it. If your data is not worth the expense for recovery and you want to try to recover it yourself, you can try, but this is not a task for the faint of heart, and more often than not, the data is simply lost. Again, the moral of the story is back up regularly, check your backups to be sure they are valid, and repeat. Practice restoring from backups before you need to do it, perhaps with a test system that is not vital and will not hurt anything if you make a mistake.

References

▶ **https://help.ubuntu.com/community/BackupYourSystem**—An excellent place to start for learning and examining backup methods in Ubuntu.

▶ **www.tldp.org/**—The Linux Documentation Project offers several useful HOWTO documents that discuss backups and disk recovery.

CHAPTER 18
Networking

One of the benefits of open-source technology in general and Linux in particular is that it can be used effortlessly across several networking environments and the Internet. With strong support for the standard Internet protocol TCP/IP, Linux can talk to all the UNIX flavors, including Mac OS X, Windows (with the help of Samba), NetWare (IPX), and even older protocols such as DECNET and Banyan Vines. Many organizations use Linux as an Internet gateway, allowing many different clients to access the Internet through Linux, as well as communicate via email and instant messaging. Most important is its built-in support for IPv6, which has begun to see a significant uptake in the commercial/enterprise world. It's safe to say that whatever networking protocol you'll come across, Linux will be able to work with it in some way.

This chapter covers network and Internet connectivity, as most networks invariably end up connected to the Internet in some shape or form. You learn about how to get the basics right, including configuration and management of network interface cards (*NICs*) and other network services with Ubuntu. You also find out how to manage network services from the command line—again an important lesson in case you are ever confined to a command prompt. We also look at connectivity options, both for inbound and outbound network traffic, and the importance of *Point-to-Point Protocol (PPP)*.

We focus on the use of text interfaces and manual configurations in this chapter. We also include an overview of basic graphical network management in Ubuntu, which is becoming more and more popular. The *graphical user interface (GUI)* option has become much more stable, useful, and easy to comprehend, to the point that this will be the way most desktop users now interact with networking.

However, this is a book for power users who want to learn about the guts of their system, roll up your sleeves and prepare to get your hands dirty.

Laying the Foundation: The `localhost` Interface

The first thing that needs to be in place before you can successfully connect to a network or even to the Internet is a `localhost` interface, sometimes called a *loopback interface*, but more commonly referenced as `lo`. The TCP/IP protocol (see the section "Networking with TCP/IP" later in this chapter) uses this interface to assign an IP address to your computer and is needed for Ubuntu to establish a PPP interface.

Checking for the Availability of the Loopback Interface

You should not normally have to manually create a loopback interface because Ubuntu creates one automatically for you during installation. To check that one is set up, you can use the `ifconfig` command, which lists all networking interfaces available, including the `lo` interface if it exists, like this:

```
matthew@seymour:~$ ifconfig

lo         Link encap:Local Loopback
           inet addr:127.0.0.1  Mask:255.0.0.0
           inet6 addr: ::1/128 Scope:Host
           UP LOOPBACK RUNNING  MTU:16436  Metric:1
           RX packets:270 errors:0 dropped:0 overruns:0 frame:0
           TX packets:270 errors:0 dropped:0 overruns:0 carrier:0
           collisions:0 txqueuelen:0
           RX bytes:20748 (20.7 KB)  TX bytes:20748 (20.7 KB)
```

What you see in this example is evidence that the loopback interface is present and active. The `inet addr` is the IP number assigned to the `localhost`, typically `127.0.0.1` along with the broadcast mask of `255.0.0.0` and that there has been little activity on this interface (`RX` = receive and `TX` = transmit). If your output does not look like the one shown previously, you must hand-configure the `localhost` interface after you finish the rest of this section. You can also see the IPv6 address that is assigned to `lo`, which is `::1/128`, referred to as the `inet6 addr`.

Configuring the Loopback Interface Manually

The `localhost` interface's IP address is specified in a text configuration file that is used by Ubuntu to keep record of various network-wide IP addresses. The file is called `/etc/hosts` and usually exists on a system, even if it is empty. The file is used by the Linux kernel and other networking tools to enable them to access local IP addresses and hostnames. If you have not configured any other networking interfaces, you might find that the file looks something like this:

```
127.0.0.1    localhost
127.0.1.1    seymour
```

```
# The following lines are desirable for IPv6 capable hosts
::1      localhost ip6-localhost ip6-loopback
fe00::0 ip6-localnet
ff00::0 ip6-mcastprefix
ff02::1 ip6-allnodes
ff02::2 ip6-allrouters
ff02::3 ip6-allhosts127.0.0.1      localhost
```

The first line defines the special `localhost` interface and assigns it an IP address of `127.0.0.1`. You might hear or read about terms such as `localhost`, *loopback*, and *dummy interface*; all these terms refer to the use of the IP address `127.0.0.1`. The term *loopback interface* is used to describe how to Linux networking drivers, it looks as though the machine is talking to a network that consists of only one machine; the kernel sends network traffic to and from itself on the same computer. This is sometimes referred to as a *dummy interface* because the interface doesn't really exist; it is not a real address as far as the outside world is concerned; it exists only for the local machine, to trick the kernel into thinking that it and any network-aware programs running that require a network interface to operate have one available without them actually being aware that the connection is a connection to the same machine. It is a dummy, not in the sense of stupid or silent, but in the sense that it is a mockup or substitute for something real.

Each networked Ubuntu machine on a LAN uses this same IP address for its `localhost`. If for some reason you discover that an Ubuntu computer does not have this interface, perhaps because some well-meaning person deleted it without understanding it was needed, you can use `sudo` and edit the `/etc/hosts` file to add the `localhost` entry as you saw previously and then use the `ifconfig` and `route` commands using your `sudo` permissions to create the interface like this:

```
matthew@seymour:~$ sudo /sbin/ifconfig lo 127.0.0.1
matthew@seymour:~$ sudo /sbin/route add 127.0.0.1 lo
```

These commands create the `localhost` interface in memory (all interfaces, such as `eth0` or `ppp0`, are created in memory when using Linux), and then add the IP address `127.0.0.1` to an internal (in-memory) table so that the Linux kernel's networking code can keep track of routes to different addresses.

Use the `ifconfig` command as shown previously to test the interface.

Checking Connections with `ping`, `traceroute`, and `mtr`

If all worked properly in the preceding section, you should now be able to use the `ping` command to check that the interface is responding properly like this (using either `localhost` or its IP address):

```
matthew@seymour:~$ ping -c 3 localhost
PING localhost (127.0.0.1) 56(84) bytes of data.
```

```
64 bytes from localhost (127.0.0.1): icmp_seq=1 ttl=64 time=0.154 ms
64 bytes from localhost (127.0.0.1): icmp_seq=2 ttl=64 time=0.159 ms
64 bytes from localhost (127.0.0.1): icmp_seq=3 ttl=64 time=0.153 ms

--- localhost ping statistics ---
3 packets transmitted, 3 received, 0% packet loss, time 1998ms
rtt min/avg/max/mdev = 0.153/0.155/0.159/0.010 ms
```

You use the -c option to set the number of pings, and the command, if successful (as it was here), returns information regarding the round-trip speed of sending a test packet to the specified host.

The second line in the /etc/hosts file uses the actual hostname of the computer and assigns it to a similar private IP address that is unique to that computer. In the earlier code example, you can see that 127.0.1.1 is assigned to seymour, which is the name of the computer on which that hosts file resides.

The remaining lines are used for IPv6 and can be ignored with the exception of the line that begins ::1. This is used to define the localhost connection for IPv6, which you can test with the ping6 command at the terminal, as follows:

```
matthew@seymour:~$ ping6 -c 3 ::1
PING ::1(::1) 56 data bytes
64 bytes from ::1: icmp_seq=1 ttl=64 time=0.102 ms
64 bytes from ::1: icmp_seq=2 ttl=64 time=0.140 ms
64 bytes from ::1: icmp_seq=3 ttl=64 time=0.140 ms
--- ::1 ping statistics ---
3 packets transmitted, 3 received, 0% packet loss, time 1998ms
rtt min/avg/max/mdev = 0.102/0.127/0.140/0.020 ms
```

This is a good place to pause and discuss three tools that are useful for checking a network: ping/ping6, traceroute, and mtr. A network timeout while you're using any of these indicates that there is a connectivity problem. If you get a response back, then your network is working. Depending on the command, you might also receive information that helps you find and troubleshoot slow network problems.

You just used the first one, ping, and its new ipv6 version, ping6. These send a request to the specified network host (another computer that you specify on the same network), and if that computer receives the message, it sends a response. It is recommended that you use the -c option followed by a number to limit the number of times the ping request is made. If not stated, ping continues to make requests until you use Ctrl+C to stop the process. Here is an example, which is useful to determine whether your local connection is working:

```
matthew@seymour:~$ ping -c 3 google.com
PING google.com (74.125.225.103) 56(84) bytes of data.
64 bytes from ord08s08-in-f7.1e100.net (74.125.225.103): icmp_req=1 ttl=53 time=22.0 ms
64 bytes from ord08s08-in-f7.1e100.net (74.125.225.103): icmp_req=2 ttl=53 time=20.1 ms
64 bytes from ord08s08-in-f7.1e100.net (74.125.225.103): icmp_req=3 ttl=53 time=21.0 ms
```

```
--- google.com ping statistics ---
3 packets transmitted, 3 received, 0% packet loss, time 2004ms
rtt min/avg/max/mdev = 20.111/21.097/22.085/0.814 ms
```

The second tool, `traceroute/traceroute6`, tracks the route that packets take on an IP
network from the local computer to the network host specified. The 6 version is intended
for use with IPv6, although it isn't necessary unless you want to force the command
to trace using only IPv6—otherwise `traceroute` tries to resolve the name given and
automatically uses whichever protocol is most appropriate. Here is an example:

```
matthew@seymour:~$ traceroute google.com
traceroute to google.com (74.125.225.99), 30 hops max, 60 byte packets
 1  Cisco02420 (192.168.1.1)  0.149 ms  0.181 ms  0.304 ms
 2  10.2.0.1 (10.2.0.1)  3.190 ms  3.227 ms  3.217 ms
 3  65.201.51.216.sta.southslope.net (216.51.201.65)  3.397 ms  3.611 ms  3.720 ms
 4  ss-dsl-sec1.nl.southslope.net (167.142.151.30)  3.622 ms  3.637 ms  3.649 ms
 5  167.142.50.13 (167.142.50.13)  6.660 ms  6.665 ms  6.678 ms
 6  ins-dc2-et-8-4.desm.netins.net (167.142.67.17)  6.599 ms  6.503 ms  7.482 ms
 7  ins-db3-te-0-7-0-0.desm.netins.net (167.142.67.182)  7.845 ms  5.145 ms  5.131 ms
 8  216.176.4.29 (216.176.4.29)  20.557 ms  20.981 ms  20.978 ms
 9  216.176.4.58 (216.176.4.58)  20.124 ms  20.085 ms  20.103 ms
10  209.85.254.120 (209.85.254.120)  21.424 ms  22.390 ms  22.382 ms
11  209.85.240.150 (209.85.240.150)  23.318 ms  22.823 ms  22.821 ms
12  ord08s08-in-f3.1e100.net (74.125.225.99)  22.306 ms  23.269 ms  23.252 ms
```

The third tool, `mtr`, combines the functionality of `ping` and `traceroute` and gives you a live
display of the data as it runs. It is not useful for creating a text file for analysis, but like the live
systems monitoring tool `top` (discussed in Chapter 16, "System-Monitoring Tools"), it gives
real-time data and is quite powerful. As with `top`, you press the Q key to exit `mtr`.

```
                     My traceroute  [v0.80]
          example.lan                        Sat Jul 14 14:07:50 2012

                            Packets               Pings
Hostname                 %Loss  Rcv  Snt   Last Best  Avg  Worst
 1. example.lan              0%   11   11      1    1    1      2
 2. ae-31-51.ebr1.Chicago1.Level3.n  19%    9   11      3    1    7     14
 3. ae-1.ebr2.Chicago1.Level3.net     0%   11   11      7    1    7     14
 4. ae-2.ebr2.Washington1.Level3.ne  19%    9   11     19   18   23     31
 5. ae-1.ebr1.Washington1.Level3.ne  28%    8   11     22   18   24     30
 6. ge-3-0-0-53.gar1.Washington1.Le   0%   11   11     18   18   20     36
 7. 63.210.29.230                     0%   10   10     19   19   19     19
 8. t-3-1.bas1.re2.yahoo.com          0%   10   10     19   18   32    106
 9. p25.www.re2.yahoo.com             0%   10   10     19   18   19     19
```

Networking with TCP/IP

The basic building block for any network based on UNIX hosts is the *Transport Control Protocol/Internet Protocol (TCP/IP)* suite, which includes three protocols even though only two get to be in the abbreviation. The suite consists of the *Internet Protocol (IP), Transport Control Protocol (TCP)*, and *Universal Datagram Protocol (UDP)*. IP is the base protocol. The TCP/IP suite is *packet* based, which means that data is broken into little chunks on the transmit end for transmission to the receiving end. Breaking data up into manageable packets allows for faster and more accurate transfers. In TCP/IP, all data travels via IP packets, which is why addresses are referred to as IP addresses. It is the lowest level of the suite.

TCP is also a connection-based protocol. Before data is transmitted between two machines, a connection is established between them. When a connection is made, a stream of data is sent to the IP to be broken into the packets that are then transmitted. At the receiving end, the packets are put back in order and sent to the proper application port. TCP/IP forms the basis of the Internet; without it the Internet would be a very different place indeed, if it even existed. In contrast, UDP is a connectionless protocol. Applications using this protocol just choose their destination and start sending. UDP is normally used for small amounts of data or on fast and reliable networks. If you are interested in the internals of TCP/IP, see the "References" section at the end of this chapter for places to look for more information.

UBUNTU AND NETWORKING

Chances are that your network card was configured during the installation of Ubuntu. You can use the `ifconfig` or `ip` commands or Ubuntu's graphical network configuration tools to edit your system's network device information or to add or remove network devices on your system. Hundreds of networking commands and utilities are included with Ubuntu—far too many to cover in this chapter and more than enough for coverage in two or three volumes.

Nearly all Ethernet cards can be used with Linux, along with many PCMCIA wired and wireless network cards. The great news is that many USB wireless networking devices also work just fine with Linux, and more are supported with each new version of the Linux kernel. You can check the Linux USB Project at www.linux-usb.org/ for the latest developments or to verify support for your device.

After reading this chapter, you might want to learn more about other graphical network clients for use with Linux. For example, you can use the GNOME `ethereal` client (more at www.ethereal.com/) to monitor all traffic on your LAN or specific types of traffic. You can use another client, Nmap, to scan a specific host for open ports and other running services (more at http://nmap.org/). You may also find utilities like netcat (more at http://nc110.sourceforge.net/), Wireshark (more at www.wireshark.org), and tcpdump (more at www.tcpdump.org/) useful.

TCP/IP Addressing

To understand networking with Linux, you need to know the basics of TCP/IP addressing. Internet IP addresses (also known as *public* IP addresses) are different from those used internally on a *local area network* (LAN). Internet IP addresses are assigned (for the United States and some other hosts) by the American Registry for Internet Numbers, available at www.arin.net/. Entities that need an Internet address apply to this agency to be assigned an address. The agency assigns *Internet service providers (ISPs)* one or more blocks of IP addresses, which the ISPs can then assign to their subscribers.

You will quickly recognize the current form of TCP/IP addressing, known as *IP version 4 (IPv4)*. In this method, a TCP/IP address is expressed of a series of four decimal numbers: a 32-bit value expressed in a format known as dotted-decimal format, such as `192.168.0.1`. Each set of numbers is known as an *octet* (eight 1s and 0s, such as `10000000` to represent `128`) and ranges from 0 to 255.

The first octet usually determines what *class* the network belongs to. There are three classes of networks:

▶ **Class A**—Consists of networks with the first octet ranging from 1 to 126. There are only 126 Class A networks, each composed of up to 16,777,214 hosts. (If you are doing the math, there are potentially 16,777,216 addresses, but no host portion of an address can be all 0s or 255s.) The 10. network is reserved for local network use, and the 127. network is reserved for the loopback address of 127.0.0.1. Loopback addressing is used by TCP/IP to enable Linux network-related client and server programs to communicate on the same host. This address does not appear and is not accessible on your LAN.

NOTE

Notice that 0 is not included in Class A. The 0 address is used for network-to-network broadcasts. Also, note that there are two other classes of networks, Classes D and E. Class D networks are reserved for multicast addresses and not for use by network hosts. Class E addresses are deemed experimental and thus are not open for public addressing.

▶ **Class B**—Consists of networks defined by the first two octets with the first ranging from 128 to 191. The 128. network is also reserved for local network use. There are 16,382 Class B networks, each with 65,534 possible hosts.

▶ **Class C**—Consists of a network defined by the first three octets with the first ranging from 192 to 223. The 192. network is another that is reserved for local network use. There are a possible 2,097,150 Class C networks of up to 254 hosts each.

No host portion of an IP address can be all 0s or 255s. These addresses are reserved for broadcast addresses. IP addresses with all 0s in the host portion are reserved for network-to-network broadcast addresses. IP addresses with all 255s in the host portion are reserved for local network broadcasts. Broadcast messages are not typically seen by users.

These classes are the standard, but a *netmask* also determines what class your network is in. The netmask determines what part of an IP address represents the network and what part represents the host. Common netmasks for the different classes are as follows:

▶ **Class A**—255.0.0.0

▶ **Class B**—255.255.0.0

▶ **Class C**—255.255.255.0

Because of the allocation of IP addresses for Internet hosts, it is now impossible to get a Class A network. It is also nearly impossible to get a Class B network (all the addresses have been given out, but some companies are said to be willing to sell theirs), and Class C network availability is dropping rapidly with the continued growth of Internet use worldwide.

LIMITS OF IPV4 ADDRESSING

The IPv4 address scheme is based on 32-bit numbering and limits the number of available IP addresses to about 4.1 billion. Many companies and organizations (particularly in the United States) were assigned very large blocks of IP addresses in the early stages of the growth of the Internet, which has left a shortage of "open" addresses. Even with careful allocation of Internet-connected host IP addresses and the use of *network address translation (NAT)* to provide communication to and from machines behind an Internet-connected computer, the Internet might run out of available addresses.

To solve this problem, a newer scheme named *IP version 6 (IPv6)* is being implemented. It uses a much larger addressing solution that is based on 128-bit addresses, with enough room to include much more information about a specific host or device, such as *global positioning server (GPS)* or serial numbering. Although the specific details about the entire contents of the an IPv6 address have yet to be finalized, all Internet-related organizations appear to agree that something must be done to provide more addresses.

You can get a good overview of the differences between IPv4 and IPv6 policies regarding IP address assignments, and the registration process of obtaining IP addresses at www.arin.net/knowledge/v4-v6.html and www.arin.net/resources/request.html.

Ubuntu supports the use of IPv6 and includes a number of networking tools conforming to IPv6 addressing.

Migration to IPv6 is slow in coming, however, because the majority of computer operating systems, software, hardware, firmware, and users are still in the IPv4 mindset. Supporting IPv6 requires rewriting many networking utilities, portions of operating systems currently in use, and firmware in routing and firewall hardware.

See the IPv6 Basics section later in this chapter for more on IPv6.

Using IP Masquerading in Ubuntu

Three blocks of IP addresses are reserved for use on internal networks and hosts not directly connected to the Internet. The address ranges are from 10.0.0.0 to 10.255.255.255, or 1 Class A network; from 172.16.0.0 to 172.31.255.255, or 16 Class B networks; and from 192.168.0.0 to 192.168.255.255, or 256 Class C networks. Use these IP addresses when building a LAN for your business or home. Which class you choose can depend on the number of hosts on your network.

Internet access for your internal network can be provided by another PC or a router. The host or device is connected to the Internet and is used as an Internet gate-way to forward information to and from your LAN. The host should also be used as a firewall to protect your network from malicious data and users while functioning as an Internet gateway.

A PC used in this fashion typically has at least two network interfaces. One is connected to the Internet and the other connected to the computers on the LAN (via a hub or switch). Some broadband devices also incorporate four or more switching network interfaces. Data is then passed between the LAN and the Internet using NAT, sometimes known in networking circles as *IP masquerading*.

NOTE

Do not rely on a single point of protection for your LAN, especially if you use wireless networking, provide dial-in services, or allow mobile (laptop or PDA) users internal or external access to your network. Companies, institutions, and individuals relying on a "moat mentality" have often discovered to their dismay that such an approach to security is easily breached. Make sure that your network operation is accompanied by a security policy that stresses multiple levels of secure access, with protection built into every server and workstation—something easily accomplished when using Linux.

Ports

Most servers on your network have perform more than one task. For example, web servers often have to serve both standard and secure pages. You might also be running an FTP server on the same host. For this reason, applications are provided *ports* to use to make "direct" connections for specific software services. These ports help TCP/IP distinguish services so that data can get to the correct application. If you check the file /etc/ services, you see the common ports and their usage. For example, for FTP, HTTP, and POP3 (email retrieval server), you see the following:

```
ftp        21/tcp
http       80/tcp       http      # WorldWideWeb HTTP
pop3       110/tcp      pop-3     # POP version 3
```

The ports defined in /etc/services in this example are 21 for FTP, 80 for HTTP, and 110 for POP3. Some other common port assignments are 25 for *Simple Mail Transport Protocol (SMTP)* and 22 for *Secure Shell (SSH)* remote login. Note that these ports are not set in stone, and you can set up your server to respond to different ports. For example, although port 22 is listed in /etc/services as a common default for SSH, the sshd server can be configured to listen on a different port by editing its configuration file /etc/ssh/sshd_config. The default setting (commented out with a pound sign, #) looks like this:

```
#Port 22
```

Edit the entry to use a different port, making sure to select an unused port number, as follows:

```
Port 2224
```

Save your changes, and then restart the sshd server with sudo service ssh restart. Remote users must now access the host through port 2224, which can be done using ssh's -p (port) option, like this:

```
matthew@seymour:~$ ssh -p 2224 remote_host_name_or_IP
```

18

IPv6 Basics

Much of what this chapter discusses is valid regardless of whether you are using IPv4 or IPv6. We start here with a short description of each to lay a foundation for further understanding. As IPv6 receives greater acceptance and use, this understanding should be adequate to help you transition between the two, even if specific issues are not addressed in the chapter. If you missed the "Limits of IPv4 Addressing" note in the earlier "TCP/IP Addressing" section, you should go back and read through it to get started.

IPv4 is based on 32-bit numbering and limits the number of available IP addresses to about 4.1 billion. This and how those addresses were assigned has led to the realization that there are not enough IPv4 addresses available for the number of devices that need IP addresses. This is only one of the problems with IPv4 that was noticed back in the 1990s. Others include large routing tables, which are lists of the routes to particular network destinations, and sometimes the network distances and topography associated with those routes. These tables are stored in routers and networked computers.

To deal with these issues, IPv6 uses 128-bit numbering that can theoretically allow well over 340,282,366,920,938,463,463,374,607,431,768,211,456 IP addresses, which is normally expressed in scientific notation as about $3.4*1038$ addresses. That's about 340 trillion, trillion, trillion addresses, meaning we are unlikely to run out again anytime soon. Gives each computer its own globally routable address. You don't need NAT in IPv6 to translate IP addresses as packets pass through a routing device, as there are an adequate number of addresses available. We can go back to the easier-to-configure peer-to-peer style of Internet networking originally conceived of and used in the 1980s. Creates routing tables that are much smaller because fewer subroutes need to be generated.

Some other useful features of IPv6 include the following:

▶ Address autoconfiguration (RFC2462)

▶ Anycast addresses ("one-out-of many")

▶ Mandatory multicast addresses

▶ IPsec (IP security)

▶ Simplified header structure

▶ Mobile IP

▶ IPv6-to-IPv4 transition mechanisms

There are different types of IPv6 addresses. Unicast addresses are the well-known addresses; packets sent to these addresses arrive directly at the interface that belongs to the address. Anycast addresses look the same as unicast addresses, but they actually address a group of interfaces; packets sent to an anycast address arrive at the nearest (in the router metric sense) interface. Anycast addresses may only be used by routers. Finally, multicast addresses identify a group of interfaces; packets sent to a multicast address arrive at all interfaces belonging to the multicast group.

IPv6 addresses are created using eight sets of numbers, like this:

`F734:0000:0000:0000:3458:79B2:D07B:4620`

Each of the eight sections is made of a four-digit number in hexadecimal, which means that each digit can from 0 to 9 or A to F (A=10, B=11, and so on). Hexadecimal is a denser format than binary. In binary, there are only two options, 0 or 1. This means that in hexadecimal, 4 digits can be used to represent 16 binary digits, like this:

- ▶ Bin 0000000000000000 = Hex 0000 (or just 0)

- ▶ Bin 1111111111111111 = Hex FFFF

- ▶ Bin 1101010011011011 = Hex D4DB

So, a 128-bit address written in binary would be very long indeed. This 128-bit address written in binary and separated by dots

`1111111111111111.1111111111111111.1111111111111111.1111111111111111.111111111111`
`1111.1111111111111111.1111111111111111.1111`

is the same as this 128-bit address, written in hexadecimal and separated by colons:

`FFFF:FFFF:FFFF:FFFF:FFFF:FFFF:FFFF:FFFF`

So, understandably, we use the latter hexidecimal format for IPv6 (and the binary format is not used, just in case you were wondering).

Often an address has long substrings of all zeros; the longest and first run of all zero sections is abbreviated as a double colon ("`::`"). Because :: is variable in length, it can only be used once per address. Leading 0s are also omitted, up to three per section. When this is done, the result is called the canonical form. For example, `fe80::1` is the canonical form of `fe80:0000:0000:0000:0000:0000:0000:0001` and `2001:db8:b:23c1:49:4592:efe:9982` is the canonical form of `2001:0db8:000b:23c1:0049:4592:0efe:9982`.

It is also possible to write the last 32 bits of an IPv6 address using the well-known IPv4 format. For example, `2002::10.0.0.1` corresponds to the long form `2002:0000:0000:0000:0000:0000:0a00:0001`, which then can be compressed to the canonical form `2002::a00:1`.

As in IPv4, an IPv6 address has sections for the network and for the device. However, an IPv6 address has a dedicated section for subnetting. The following examples use 1s to show the section of the address being described (in binary because that is easier for us humans) and 0s for the rest of the address.

In IPv6, the first 48 bits are for Internet routing (network addressing):

`1111111111111111.1111111111111111.1111111111111111.0000000000000000. 00000000000`
`00000.0000000000000000.0000000000000000.0000000000000000`

The 16 bits from the 49th to the 54th are for defining subnets:

0000000000000000.0000000000000000.0000000000000000.1111111111111111. 00000000000
00000.0000000000000000.0000000000000000.0000000000000000

The last 64 bits are for device (interface) IDs:

0000000000000000.0000000000000000.0000000000000000.0000000000000000. 11111111111
11111.1111111111111111.1111111111111111.1111111111111111

It is easier for humans to conceive of these using binary, but to actually use this information you have to convert numbers from binary to hexadecimal. Fortunately, this is easily accomplished on the Web using a quick Google search for "binary to hex" conversion.

Let's say you want to break your corporate network into 64 subnets. The binary mask just for the subnetting range would be 1111110000000000, which translates to a hex value of FC00. Some IPv6 masking tools work with just this one hex word; otherwise a full 128-bit hex mask would be FFFF:FFFF:FFFF:FC00:0:0:0:0.

Here are some special-use, reserved IPv6 addresses:

▶ ::1/128 is the loopback address.

▶ ::/128 is the unspecified address.

▶ ::*IPv4-address*/96 are the IPv4-compatible addresses.

▶ The 2001:db8::/32 are the documentation addresses. They are used for documentation purposes such as user manuals, RFCs, and so on.

▶ ::/0 is the default unicast route address.

▶ ff00::/8 are multicast addresses.

This section of the book is certain to grow as time passes and IPv6 becomes more commonly used. For now, this introduction is probably all you are likely to need, especially since IPv4 is not going away. This transition is a process of adding IPv6 into existing worldwide networking schemes and system abilities and is neither intended nor likely to completely replace IPv4.

Network Organization

Properly organizing your network addressing process grows more difficult as the size of your network grows. Setting up network addressing for a Class C network with fewer than 254 devices is simple. Setting up addressing for a large, worldwide company with a Class A network and many different users can be extremely complex. If your company has fewer than 254 *hosts* (meaning any device that requires an IP address, including computers, printers, routers, switches, and other devices) and all your workgroups can share information, a single Class C network is sufficient.

Subnetting

Within Class A and B networks, there can be separate networks called *subnets*. Subnets are considered part of the host portion of an address for network class definitions. For example, in the 128. Class B network, you can have one computer with an address of 128.10.10.10 and another with an address of 128.10.200.20; these computers are on the same network (128.10.), but they have different subnets (128.10.10. and 128.10.200.). Because of this, communication between the two computers requires either a router or a switch. Subnets can be helpful for separating workgroups within your company.

Often subnets can be used to separate workgroups that have no real need to interact with or to shield from other groups' information passing among members of a specific workgroup. For example, if your company is large enough to have its own HR department and payroll section, you could put those departments' hosts on their own subnet and use your router configuration to limit the hosts that can connect to this subnet. This configuration prevents networked workers who are not members of the designated departments from being able to view some of the confidential information the HR and payroll personnel work with.

Subnet use also enables your network to grow beyond 254 hosts and share IP addresses. With proper routing configuration, users might not even know they are on a different subnet from their co-workers. Another common use for subnetting is with networks that cover a wide geographic area. It is not practical for a company with offices in Chicago and London to have both offices on the same subnet, so using a separate subnet for each office is the best solution.

Subnet Masks

Subnet masks are used by TCP/IP to show which part of an IP address is the network portion and which part is the host. Subnet masks are usually referred to as *netmasks*. For a pure Class A network, the netmask is 255.0.0.0; for a Class B network, the netmask is 255.255.0.0; and for a Class C network, the netmask is 255.255.255.0. You can also use netmasks to deviate from the standard classes.

By using customized netmasks, you can subnet your network to fit your needs. For example, your network has a single Class C address. You have a need to subnet your network. Although this is not possible with a normal Class C subnet mask, you can change the mask to break your network into subnets. By changing the last octet to a number greater than zero, you can break the network into as many subnets as you need.

For more information on how to create customized subnet masks, see Day 6, "The Art of Subnet Masking," in *Sams Teach Yourself TCP/IP Network Administration in 21 Days*. That chapter goes into great detail on how to create custom netmasks and explains how to create an addressing cheat sheet for hosts on each subnet. The Linux Network Administrator's Guide also has good information about how to create subnets at www.tldp.org/LDP/nag2/index.html.

Broadcast, Unicast, and Multicast Addressing

Information can get to systems through three types of addresses: unicast, multicast, and broadcast. Each type of address is used according to the purpose of the information being sent, as explained here:

▶ **Unicast**—Sends information to one specific host. Unicast addresses are used for Telnet, FTP, SSH, or any other information that needs to be shared in a one-to-one exchange of information. Although it is possible that any host on the subnet/network can see the information being passed, only one host is the intended recipient and will take action on the information being received.

▶ **Multicasting**—Broadcasts information to groups of computers sharing an application, such as a video conferencing client or online gaming application. All the machines participating in the conference or game require the same information at precisely the same time to be effective.

▶ **Broadcasting**—Transmits information to all the hosts on a network or subnet. *Dynamic Host Configuration Protocol (DHCP)* uses broadcast messages when the DHCP client looks for a DHCP server to get its network settings, and *Reverse Address Resolution Protocol (RARP)* uses broadcast messages for hardware address to IP address resolution. Broadcast messages use .255 in all the host octets of the network IP address. (10.2.255.255 broadcasts to every host in your Class B network.)

Hardware Devices for Networking

As stated at the beginning of this chapter, networking is one of the strong points of the Linux operating system. This section covers the classes of devices used for basic networking. Note that this section talks about hardware devices, and not Linux networking devices, which are discussed in the section "Using Network Configuration Tools."

Network Interface Cards

A computer must have a *network interface card (NIC)* to connect to a network. Currently, there are several topologies (ways of connecting computers) for network connections. These topologies range from the old and mostly outdated 10BASE-2 to the much newer and popular wireless WiFi or 802.11 networking.

Each NIC has a unique address (the hardware address, known as *Media Access Control [MAC]*), which identifies that NIC. This address is six pairs of hexadecimal bits separated by colons (:). A MAC address looks similar to this: 00:60:08:8F:5A:D9. The hardware address is used by DHCP (see the section "Dynamic Host Configuration Protocol," later in this chapter) to identify a specific host. It is also used by the *Address Resolution Protocol (ARP)* and *Reverse Address Resolution Protocol (RARP)* to map hosts to IP addresses.

This section covers some of the different types of NIC used to connect to your network.

Token Ring

Token Ring networking was developed by IBM. As the name implies, the network is set up in a ring. A single "token" is passed from host to host, indicating the receiving host's permission to transmit data.

Token Ring has a maximum transfer rate of 16Mbps (16 million bits per second). Unlike 10BASE-2 and 10BASE-5, Token Ring uses what is called *unshielded twisted pair (UTP)* cable. This cable looks a lot like the cable that connects your phone to the wall. Almost all Token Ring NICs are recognized by Linux.

10BASE-T

10BASE-T was the standard for a long time. A large number of networks still use it. 10BASE-T also uses UTP cable. Instead of being configured in a ring, 10BASE-T mostly uses a star architecture. In this architecture, the hosts all connect to a central location (usually a hub, which you learn about later in the "Hubs and Switches" section). All the data is sent to all hosts, but only the destination host takes action on individual packets. 10BASE-T has a transfer rate of 10Mbps.

10BASE-T has a maximum segment length of 100 meters (about 325 feet). There are many manufacturers of 10BASE-T NICs, and most are recognized by Ubuntu.

100BASE-T

100BASE-T was popular around the turn of the millennium, keeping the same ease of administration as 10BASE-T while increasing the speed by a factor of 10. For most networks, the step from 10BASE-T to 100BASE-T is as simple as replacing NICs and hubs. Most 100BASE-T NICs and hubs can also handle 10BASE-T and can automatically detect which is in use. This allows for a gradual network upgrade and usually does not require rewiring your whole network. Nearly every known 100BASE-T NIC and most generic NICs are compatible with Linux. 100BASE-T requires Category 5 UTP cabling.

1000BASE-T

1000BASE-T—usually referred to as *Gigabit Ethernet*—is the accepted standard in enterprise networking, with most NICs being detected and configured correctly by Ubuntu. Like 100BASE-T NICs, gigabit NICs automatically downgrade if they are plugged in to a slower network. Also like 100BASE-T, gigabit NICs require Category 5 UTP cabling; however, many institutions are now deploying Category 6 cables because they have much longer range and so are often worth the extra cost. You will find that most newer computers are sold with gigabit NICs.

Fiber Optic and Gigabit Ethernet

Fiber optic is more commonly used in newer and high-end installations because the cost of upgrading can be prohibitive for older sites.

Fiber optics were originally used on *fiber distributed data interface (FDDI)* networks, similar to token ring in structure except that there are two rings (one primary, the other secondary). The primary ring is used exclusively, and the secondary sits idle until there is a break in the primary ring. That is when the secondary ring takes over, keeping the network alive. FDDI has a speed of 100Mbps and has a maximum ring length of 100 kilometers

(62 miles). FDDI uses several tokens at the same time that, along with the faster speed of fiber optics, account for the drastic increase in network speed.

As stated, switching to a fiber-optic network can be very costly. To make the upgrade, the whole network has to be rewired, and all NICs must be replaced at the same time. Most FDDI NICs are recognized by Linux.

Fiber-related gigabit that uses fiber-optics is termed *1000BASE-X*, whereas 1000BASE-T Gigabit Ethernet uses twisted-pair cabling (see the "Unshielded Twisted Pair" section, later in this chapter).

Wireless Network Interfaces

Wireless networking, as the name states, works without network cables and is an extremely popular option. Upgrading is as easy as replacing network cards and equipment, such as routers and switches. Wireless networking equipment can also work along with the traditional wired networking using existing equipment.

Wireless networking is still generally slower than a traditional wired network. However, this situation is changing with wider adoption of newer protocols.

Network Cable

Currently, three types of network cable are available: coaxial, UTP, and fiber. Coaxial cable looks a lot like the coaxial cable used to connect your television to the cable jack or antenna. UTP looks a lot like the cable that runs from your phone to the wall jack (the jacks are a bit wider). Fiber cable looks sort of like the RCA cables used on your stereo or like the cable used on your electrical appliances in your house (two separate segments connected together). The following sections discuss UTP and fiber network cable in more detail.

Unshielded Twisted Pair

UTP uses color-coded pairs of thin copper wire to transmit data. The six categories of UTP each serve a different purpose:

▶ **Category 1 (Cat1)**—Used for voice transmissions such as your phone. Only one pair is used per line (one wire to transmit and one to receive). An RJ-11 plug is used to connect the cable to your phone and the wall.

▶ **Category 2 (Cat2)**—Used in early Token Ring networks. Has a transmission rate of 4Mbps and has the slowest data transfer rate. An RJ-11 plug is also used for cable connections.

▶ **Category 3 (Cat3)**—Used for 10BASE-T networks. It has a transmission rate of 10Mbps. Three pairs of cables are used to send and receive signals. RJ-11 or RJ-45 plugs can be used for Cat3 cables, usually deferring to the smaller RJ-11. RJ-45 plugs are similar in design to RJ-11, but are larger to handle up to four pairs of wire and are used more commonly on Cat5 cables.

▶ **Category 4 (Cat4)**—Used in modern Token Ring networks. It has a transmission rate of 16Mbps and is less and less common because companies are switching to better alternatives. RJ-45 plugs are used for cable connections.

▶ **Category 5 (Cat5)**—The fastest of the UTP categories with a transmission rate of up to 1000Mbps. It is used in both 100BASE-T and 1000BASE-T networks and uses four pairs of wire. Cat5 cable came out just as 10BASE-T networks were becoming popular and isn't much more expensive than Cat3 cable. As a result, most 10BASE-T networks use Cat5 UTP rather than Cat3. Cat5 cable uses RJ-45 plugs. Cat 5e (which stands for Category 5, *enhanced*) cable is similar to basic Cat 5, except that it fulfills higher standards of data transmission. While Cat 5 is common in existing cabling systems, Category 5e has almost entirely replaced it in *new* installations. Cat 5e can handle data transfer at 1000 Mbps, is suitable for Gigabit Ethernet, and experiences much lower levels of near-end crosstalk (NEXT) than Cat 5.

▶ **Category 6 (Cat6)**—Also rated at 1000Mbps, this cable is available in two forms: stranded for short runs (25-meter runs, about 80 feet) and solid for up to 100-meter runs (about 325 feet), but which should not be flexed.

Fiber-Optic Cable

Fiber-optic cable (fiber) is usually orange or red in color. The transmission rate is 100Mbps and has a maximum length of 100 kilometers (62 miles). Fiber uses a two-pronged plug to connect to devices. Fiber provides a couple of advantages because it uses light rather than electricity to transmit its signal: It is free from the possibility of electromagnetic interference, and it is also more difficult to tap into and eavesdrop.

Hubs and Switches

Hubs and switches are used to connect several hosts together on a star architecture network. They can have any number of connections; the common sizes are 4, 8, 16, 24, and 48 connections (ports); each port has a light that comes on when a network connection is made (link light). Their use enables you to expand your network easily; you can just add new hubs or switches when you need to add new connections. Each unit can connect to the other hubs or switches on the network, typically, through a port on the hub or switch called an *uplink* port. This enables two hubs or switches, connected by their uplink ports, to act as one hub or switch. Having a central location where all the hosts on your network can connect allows for easier troubleshooting of problems. If one host goes down, none of the other hosts are affected (depending on the purpose of the downed host). Because hubs and switches are not directly involved with the Linux operating system, compatibility is not an issue.

If you are constructing a small to midsize network, it is important to consider whether you intend to use either hubs or switches. Hubs and switches are visually the same in that they have rows of network ports. However, under the hood, the difference is quite important. Data is sent as packets of information across the network; with a hub the data is transmitted simultaneously to all the network ports, irrespective of which port the destination computer is attached to.

Switches, however, are more intelligent because they can direct packets of information to the correct network port that leads to the destination computer. They do this by "learning" the MAC addresses of each computer that is attached to them. In short, using switches minimizes excess packets being sent across the network, thus increasing network bandwidth available. In a small network with a handful of computers, the use of hubs might be perfectly acceptable, and you will find that hubs are generally cheaper than switches. However, for larger networks of 15 computers or more, you should consider implementing a switched network.

TIP

Troubleshooting network connections can be a challenge, especially on large networks. If a user complains that he has lost his network connection, the hub or switch is a good place to start. If the link light for the user's port is lit, chances are the problem is with the user's network configuration. If the link light is not on, the host's NIC is bad, the cable is not inserted properly, or the cable has gone bad for some reason.

Routers and Bridges

Routers and bridges are used to connect different networks to your network and to connect different subnets within your network. Routers and bridges both serve the same purpose of connecting networks and subnets, but they do so with different techniques. The information in the following sections helps you choose the connection method that best suits your needs.

Bridges

Bridges are used within a network to connect different subnets. A bridge blindly relays all information from one subnet to another without any filtering and is often referred to as a *dumb gateway*. This can be helpful if one subnet in your network is becoming overburdened and you need to lighten the load. A bridge is not very good for connecting to the Internet, however, because it lacks filtering. You really do not want all traffic traveling the Internet to be able to get through to your network.

Routers

Routers can pass data from one network to another, and they allow for filtering of data. Routers are best suited to connect your network to an outside network, such as the Internet. If you have a web server for an internal intranet that you do not want people to access from the Internet, for example, you can use a router's filter to block port 80 from outside of your internal network. These filters can be used to block specific hosts from accessing the Internet, as well. For these reasons, routers are also called *smart gateways*.

Routers range in complexity and price from an enterprise-grade Cisco brand router that can cost thousands of dollars to consumer brands designed for home or small office use that can cost less than $50.

Initializing New Network Hardware

All the initial network configuration and hardware initialization for Ubuntu is normally done during installation. At times, however, you could have to reconfigure networking on your system, such as when a host needs to be moved to a different subnet or a different network, or if you replace any of your computer's networking hardware.

Linux creates network interfaces in memory when the kernel recognizes that a NIC or other network device is attached to the system. These interfaces are unlike other Linux interfaces, such as serial communications ports, and they do not have a corresponding device file in the /dev directory. Unless support for a particular NIC is built in to your kernel, Linux must be told to load a specific kernel module to support your NIC. More than 100 such modules are located in the /lib/modules/2.6.XX-XX/kernel/net directory (where XX-XX is your version of the kernel).

You can initialize a NIC in several ways when using Linux. When you first install Ubuntu, automatic hardware probing detects and configures your system to use any installed NICs. If you remove the original NIC and replace it with a different make and model, your system will not automatically detect and initialize the device unless you configure Ubuntu to use automatic hardware detection when booting. Ubuntu should detect the absence of the old NIC and the presence of the new NIC at boot time.

If you do not use automatic hardware detection and configuration, you can initialize network hardware by doing the following:

▶ Manually editing the /etc/modprobe.conf file to prompt the system to recognize and support the new hardware upon reboot

▶ Manually loading or unloading the new device's kernel module with the modprobe command

The following sections explain these methods in greater detail.

Editing the /etc/modprobe.conf File

This file might not be present when you first look for it, so you might need to create a blank file in a text editor. You can manually edit the /etc/modprobe.conf file to add a module dependency entry (also known as a *directive*) to support a new NIC or other network device. This entry includes the device's name and its corresponding kernel module. After you add this entry, the Linux kernel recognizes your new networking hardware upon reboot. Ubuntu runs a module dependency check upon booting.

For example, if your system uses a RealTek NIC, you could use an entry like this:

```
alias eth0 8139too
```

The example entry tells the Linux kernel to load the 8139too.o kernel module to support the eth0 network device. On the other hand, if you have an Intel Ethernet Pro NIC installed, you use an entry like this:

```
alias eth0 eepro100
```

You can pass other parameters to a kernel module using one or more option entries, if need be, to properly configure your NIC. See the `modprobe.conf` man page for more information about using entries. For more specifics regarding NIC kernel modules, examine the module's source code. (No man pages are yet available [a good opportunity for anyone willing to write the documentation].)

Using `modprobe` to Manually Load Kernel Modules

You do not have to use an `/etc/modprobe.conf` entry to initialize kernel support for your new network device. As root (using `sudo`), you can manually load or unload the device's kernel module using the `modprobe` command, along with the module's name. For example, use the following command line to enable the example RealTek NIC:

```
matthew@seymour:~$ sudo modprobe 8139too
```

After you press Enter, you see this device reported from the kernel's ring buffer messages, which you can display by using the `dmesg` command. Here's a portion of that command's output:

```
matthew@seymour:~$ dmesg
...
eth0: RealTek RTL8139 Fast Ethernet at 0xce8ee000, 00:30:1b:0b:07:0d, IRQ 11
eth0: Identified 8139 chip type ÔRTL-8139C'
eth0: Setting half-duplex based on auto-negotiated partner ability 0000.
...
```

Note that at this point an IP address or other settings have not been assigned to the device. Linux can use multiple Ethernet interfaces, and the first Ethernet device is numbered `eth0`, the second `eth1`, and so on. Each different Ethernet device recognized by the kernel might have additional or different information reported, depending on its kernel module. For example:

```
matthew@seymour:~$ dmesg
...
eepro100.c:v1.09j-t 9/29/99 Donald Becker http://cesdis.gsfc.nasa.gov/linux/drive
rs/eepro100.html
eepro100.c: $Revision: 1.36 $ 2000/11/17 Modified by Andrey V. Savochkin
&#x194;<saw@saw.sw.com.sg> and others
PCI: Found IRQ 10 for device 00:0d.0
eth0: Intel Corporation 82557 [Ethernet Pro 100], 00:90:27:91:92:B5, IRQ 10.
 Board assembly 721383-007, Physical connectors present: RJ45
 Primary interface chip i82555 PHY #1.
 General self-test: passed.
 Serial sub-system self-test: passed.
 Internal registers self-test: passed.
 ROM checksum self-test: passed (0x04f4518b).
...
```

In this example, an Intel Ethernet Pro 100 NIC has been recognized. To disable support for a NIC, the kernel module can be unloaded, but usually only after the device is no longer in use. Read the next section to learn how to configure a NIC after it has been recognized by the Linux kernel and how to control its behavior.

Using Network Configuration Tools

If you add or replace networking hardware after your initial installation, you must configure the new hardware. You can do so using either the command line or the graphical configuration tools. To configure a network client host using the command line, you can use a combination of commands or edit specific files under the /etc directory. To configure the hardware through a graphical interface, you can use Ubuntu's graphical tool for X called nm-connection-editor, found by clicking the Network indicator and then Edit Connections.. This section introduces command-line and graphical software tools you can use to configure a network interface and network settings on your Ubuntu system. You'll see how to control your NIC and manage how your system interacts with your network.

Using the command-line configuration tools can seem difficult if you are new to Linux. For anyone new to networking, the nm-connection-editor graphical tool is the way to go. Both manual and graphical methods require super user privileges to work. You should not edit any scripts or settings files used by graphical network administration tools on your system. Your changes will be lost the next time the tool is run. Either use a manual approach all the time and write your own network setup script or stick to using graphical configuration utilities. Don't switch back and forth between the two methods.

Command-Line Network Interface Configuration

You can configure a network interface from the command line using the basic Linux networking utilities. You configure your network client hosts either with commands to change your current settings or by editing a number of system files. Traditionally, two commands, ifconfig (which many have abandoned for ip) and route, are used for network configuration. The netstat command displays information about the network connections.

/sbin/ifconfig

ifconfig is used to configure your network interface. You can use it to do the following:

▶ Activate or deactivate your NIC or change your NIC's mode

▶ Change your machine's IP address, netmask, or broadcast address

▶ Create an IP alias to allow more than one IP address on your NIC

▶ Set a destination address for a point-to-point connection

You can change as many or as few of these options as you want with a single command. The basic structure for the command is as follows:

```
ifconfig [network device] options
```

18

Table 18.1 shows a subset of ifconfig options and examples of their uses.

TABLE 18.1 `ifconfig` Options

Use	Option	Example
Create alias	[network device]	ifconfig eth0:0_:[number] 10.10.10.10
Change IP address		ifconfig eth0 10.10.10.12
Change the netmask	netmask [netmask]	ifconfig eth0 netmask 255.255.255.0
Change the broadcast	broadcast [address]	ifconfig eth0 broadcast 10.10.10.255
Take interface down	down	ifconfig eth0 down
Bring interface up	up (add IP address)	ifconfig eth0 up (ifconfig eth0 10.10.10.10)
Set NIC promiscuous	[-]promisc [ifconfig eth0 -promisc]	ifconfig eth0 promisc mode on [off]
Set multicasting mode	[-]allmulti	ifconfig eth0_on [off] allmulti [ifconfig eth0 -allmulti]
Enable or disable	[-]pointo- point [address] eth0_pointopoint	ifconfig_point-to-point address 10.10.10.20 [ifconfig eth0 pointopoint_10.10.10.20]

The `ifconfig` man page shows other options that enable your machine to interface with a number of network types such as AppleTalk, Novell, IPv6, and others. Again, read the man page for details on these network types.

NOTE

Promiscuous mode causes the NIC to receive all packets on the network. It is often used to sniff a network. Multicasting mode enables the NIC to receive all multicast traffic on the network.

If no argument is given, `ifconfig` displays the status of active interfaces. For example, the output of `ifconfig`, without arguments and one active and configured NIC, looks similar to this:

```
matthew@seymour:~$ ifconfig
eth0      Link encap:Ethernet  HWaddr 00:90:f5:8e:52:b5
          UP BROADCAST MULTICAST  MTU:1500  Metric:1
          RX packets:0 errors:0 dropped:0 overruns:0 frame:0
          TX packets:0 errors:0 dropped:0 overruns:0 carrier:0
          collisions:0 txqueuelen:1000
          RX bytes:0 (0.0 B)  TX bytes:0 (0.0 B)
          Interrupt:30 Base address:0xc000
lo        Link encap:Local Loopback
          inet addr:127.0.0.1  Mask:255.0.0.0
```

```
              inet6 addr: ::1/128 Scope:Host
              UP LOOPBACK RUNNING  MTU:16436  Metric:1
              RX packets:314 errors:0 dropped:0 overruns:0 frame:0
              TX packets:314 errors:0 dropped:0 overruns:0 carrier:0
              collisions:0 txqueuelen:0
              RX bytes:25204 (25.2 KB)  TX bytes:25204 (25.2 KB)

wlan0         Link encap:Ethernet  HWaddr 00:16:ea:d4:58:88
              inet addr:192.168.1.106  Bcast:192.168.1.255  Mask:255.255.255.0
              inet6 addr: fe80::216:eaff:fed4:5888/64 Scope:Link
              UP BROADCAST RUNNING MULTICAST  MTU:1500  Metric:1
              RX packets:325832 errors:0 dropped:0 overruns:0 frame:0
              TX packets:302754 errors:0 dropped:0 overruns:0 carrier:0
              collisions:0 txqueuelen:1000
              RX bytes:207381807 (207.3 MB)  TX bytes:40442735 (40.4 MB)
```

The output is easily understood. The `inet` entry displays the IP address for the interface. UP signifies that the interface is ready for use; BROADCAST denotes that the interface is connected to a network that supports broadcast messaging (`ethernet`); RUNNING means that the interface is operating; and LOOPBACK shows which device (`lo`) is the loopback address. The *maximum transmission unit (MTU)* on `eth0` is 1500 bytes. This determines the size of the largest packet that can be transmitted over this interface (and is sometimes "tuned" to other values for performance enhancement). Metric is a number from 0 to 3 that relates to how much information from the interface is placed in the routing table. The lower the number, the smaller the amount of information.

The `ifconfig` command can be used to display information about or control a specific interface using commands that are listed in Table 18.1. For example, to deactivate the first Ethernet device on a host, use the `ifconfig` command, the interface name, and the command `down`:

```
matthew@seymour:~$ sudo ifconfig eth0 down
```

You can also configure and activate the device by specifying a hostname or IP address and network information. For example to configure and activate (bring up) the `eth0` interface with a specific IP address, use the `ifconfig` command:

```
matthew@seymour:~$ sudo ifconfig eth0 192.168.2.9 netmask 255.255.255.0 up
```

If you have a host defined in your system's `/etc/hosts` file (see the section "Network Configuration Files," later in this chapter), you can configure and activate the interface according to the defined hostname like this:

```
matthew@seymour:~$ sudo ifconfig eth0 catcat.fakeurl.com up
```

18

`/sbin/ip`

In preparing for this edition, `ifconfig` still worked well on our testing system. However, it is losing favor as `ip` sees more use. This command works with a series of subcommands to perform its tasks. Many of the common subcommands also have short aliases, which are also listed here. Note that the IP addresses listed below are examples; the addresses in your network will likely be different.

To get information about all your network interfaces:

`matthew@seymour:~$` **`sudo ip addr show`**

To assign an IP address to a specific interface, in this case "eth1":

`matthew@seymour:~$` **`sudo ip addr add 192.168.2.9 dev eth1`**

To remove an assigned IP address:

`matthew@seymour:~$` **`sudo ip addr del 192.168.2.9 dev eth1`**

To enable a network interface:

`matthew@seymour:~$` **`sudo ip link set eth1 up`**

To disable a network interface:

`matthew@seymour:~$` **`sudo ip link set eth1 down`**

To check the routing table:

`matthew@seymour:~$` **`sudo ip route show`**

To add a static route:

`matthew@seymour:~$` **`sudo ip route add 10.10.30.0/24 via 192.168.50.100 dev eth0`**

To remove a static route:

`matthew@seymour:~$` **`sudo ip route del 10.10.30.0/24`**

To add a default gateway:

`matthew@seymour:~$` **`sudo ip route add default via 192.168.36.100`**

The next section explains how to configure your system to work with your LAN.

`/sbin/route`

The second command used to configure your network is the `route` command. `route` is used to build the routing tables (in memory) implemented for routing packets and to display the routing information. It is used after `ifconfig` has initialized the interface. `route` is normally used to set up static routes to other networks via the gateway or to other hosts. The command configuration is as follows:

`route [options] [commands] [parameters]`

To display the routing table, use the route command with no options. The display will look similar to this:

```
matthew@seymour:~$ route
Kernel IP routing table
```

Destination	Gateway	Genmask	Flags	Metric	Ref	Use	Iface
192.168.1.0	*	255.255.255.0	U	2	0	0	wlan0
link-local	*	255.255.0.0	U	1000	0	0	wlan0
default	WirelessAccessPt	0.0.0.0	UG	0	0	0	wlan0

In the first column, Destination is the IP address (or, if the host is in /etc/hosts or /etc/networks, the hostname) of the receiving host. The default entry is the default gateway for this machine. The Gateway column lists the gateway that the packets must go through to reach their destination. An asterisk (*) means that packets go directly to the host. Genmask is the netmask. The Flags column can have several possible entries. In our example, U verifies that the route is enabled and G specifies that Destination requires the use of a gateway. The Metric column displays the distance to the Destination. Some daemons use this to figure the easiest route to the Destination. The Ref column is used by some UNIX flavors to convey the references to the route, but this isn't used by Linux. The Use column indicates the number of times this entry has been looked up. Finally, the Iface column is the name of the interface for the corresponding entry.

Using the -n option to the route command gives the same information, substituting IP addresses for names and asterisks (*), and looks like this:

```
matthew@seymour:~$ route -n
Kernel IP routing table
```

Destination	Gateway	Genmask	Flags	Metric	Ref	Use	Iface
192.168.1.0	0.0.0.0	255.255.255.0	U	2	0	0	wlan0
link-local	0.0.0.0	255.255.0.0	U	1000	0	0	wlan0
0.0.0.0	192.168.1.0	0.0.0.0	UG	0	0	0	wlan0

The route command can add to the table using the add option. With the add option, you can specify a host (-host) or a network (-net) as the destination. If no option is used, the route command assumes that you are configuring the host issuing the command. The most common uses for the route command are to add the default gateway for a host, for a host that has lost its routing table, or if the gateway address has changed. For example, to add a gateway with a specific IP address, you could use the following:

```
matthew@seymour:~$ sudo route add default gw 149.112.50.65
```

Note that you could use a hostname rather than an IP address if desired. Another common use is to add the network to the routing table right after using the ifconfig

18

command to configure the interface. Assuming that the 208.59.243.0 entry from the previous examples was missing, replace it using the following command:

matthew@seymour:~$ **sudo route add -net 208.59.243.0 netmask 255.255.255.0 dev eth0**

You also can use route to configure a specific host for a direct (point-to-point) connection. For example, suppose that you have a home network of two computers. One of the computers has a modem through which it connects to your business network. You typically work at the other computer. You can use the route command to establish a connection through specific hosts using the following command:

matthew@seymour:~$ **sudo route add -host 198.135.62.25 gw 149.112.50.65**

The preceding example makes the computer with the modem the gateway for the computer you are using. This type of command line is useful if you have a gateway or firewall connected to the Internet. There are many additional uses for the route command, such as manipulating the default packet size. See the man page for those uses.

/bin/netstat

The netstat command is used to display the status of your network. It has several parameters that can display as much or as little information as you prefer. The services are listed by *sockets* (application-to-application connections between two computers). You can use netstat to display the information in Table 18.2.

TABLE 18.2   netstat Options

Option	Output
-g	Displays the multicast groups configured
-i	Displays the interfaces configured by ifconfig
-s	Lists a summary of activity for each protocol
-v	Gives verbose output, listing both active and inactive sockets
-c	Updates output every second (good for testing and troubleshooting)
-e	Gives verbose output for active connections only
-C	Displays information from the route cache and is good for looking at past connections

Several other options are available for this command, but they are used less often. As with the route command, the man page can give you details about all options and parameters.

Network Configuration Files

As previously stated, five network configuration files can be modified to make changes to basic network interaction of your system:

▶ /etc/hosts—A listing of addresses, hostnames, and aliases

▶ /etc/services—Network service and port connections

▶ `/etc/nsswitch.conf`–Linux network information service configuration

▶ `/etc/resolv.conf`–*Domain Name Service (DNS)* domain (search) settings

▶ `/etc/host.conf`–Network information search order (by default, `/etc/hosts` and then DNS)

After these files are modified, the changes are active. As with most configuration files, you can add comments with a hash mark (#) preceding the comment. All these files have man pages, where you can find more information.

Adding Hosts to `/etc/hosts`

The `/etc/hosts` file is a map of IP to hostnames. If you are not using DNS or another naming service and you are connected to a large network, this file can get quite large and can be a real headache to manage. A small `/etc/hosts` file can look something like this:

```
127.0.0.1        localhost
127.0.1.1        optimus


# The following lines are desirable for IPv6 capable hosts
::1     ip6-localhost ip6-loopback
fe00::0 ip6-localnet
ff00::0 ip6-mcastprefix
ff02::1 ip6-allnodes
ff02::2 ip6-allrouters
ff02::3 ip6-allhosts
```

The first entry is for the loopback entry. The second is for the name of the machine. If no naming service is in use on the network, the only host that myhost recognizes by name is yourhost. (IP addresses on the network can still be used.)

Service Settings in `/etc/services`

The `/etc/services` file maps port numbers to services. The first few lines look similar to this. (The `/etc/services` file can be quite long, more than 500 lines.)

```
# Each line describes one service, and is of the form:
#
# service-name port/protocol [aliases ...]   [# comment]

tcpmux     1/tcp              # TCP port service multiplexer
tcpmux     1/udp              # TCP port service multiplexer
rje        5/tcp              # Remote Job Entry
rje        5/udp              # Remote Job Entry
echo       7/tcp
echo       7/udp
discard    9/tcp      sink null
discard    9/udp      sink null
systat     11/tcp     users
```

Typically, there are two entries for each service because most services can use either TCP or UDP for their transmissions. Usually after /etc/services is initially configured, you do not need to change it.

Using /etc/nsswitch.conf After Changing Naming Services

This file was initially developed by Sun Microsystems to specify the order in which services are accessed on the system. A number of services are listed in the /etc/nsswitch. conf file, but the most commonly modified entry is the hosts entry. A portion of the file can look like this:

```
passwd:         compat
group:          compat
shadow:         compat

hosts:          files dns mdns
networks:       files

protocols:      db files
services:       db files
ethers:         db files
rpc:            db files

netgroup:       nis
```

This tells services that they should consult standard UNIX/Linux files for passwd, shadow, and group (/etc/passwd, /etc/shadow, /etc/group, respectively) lookups. For host lookups, the system checks /etc/hosts; if there is no entry, it checks DNS. The commented hosts entry lists the possible values for hosts. Edit this file only if your naming service has changed.

Setting a Name Server with /etc/resolv.conf

/etc/resolv.conf is used by DNS, the Domain Name Service. The following is an example of resolv.conf:

```
nameserver 192.172.3.8
nameserver 192.172.3.9
search mydomain.com
```

This sets the nameservers and the order of domains for DNS to use. The contents of this file are set automatically if you use DHCP (see the "Dynamic Host Configuration Protocol" section later in this chapter).

Starting with 12.04, there was a pretty big change in how Ubuntu uses this file. Management of resolv.conf has been turned over to a program called resolvconf, which works with DHCP, with a Network Manager plug-in, and with `/etc/network/interfaces` to automatically generate a list of nameservers and domains to list in `/etc/resolv.conf`. What this means is that any manual changes made here are eventually overwritten and lost.

If you have a static IP configuration, you should now list each of your static IP interfaces as `dns-nameservers`, `dns-search` and `dns-domain` entries in `/etc/network/interfaces`.

You can override the configuration for `resolvconf` or add entries to it in the following files in `/etc/resolvconf/resolv.conf.d/` directory:

▶ `base`–This file is used when no other data can be found.

▶ `head`–This file is used as the header for `resolv.conf`, and you can use it to ensure a specific DNS server is always the first one on the list used.

▶ `original`–This file is a backup copy of your original `resolv.conf` file from the time when the `resolvconf` program was installed.

▶ `tail`–This file is used as a tail, appended to the end of the auto-generated `resolv.conf` file.

The format in these files is the same as the traditional format for `/etc/resolv.conf`. Splitting things this way gives more granular control while also allowing for DHCP auto-configuration.

Setting DNS Search Order with `/etc/host.conf`

The `/etc/host.conf` file lists the order in which your machine searches for hostname resolution. The following is the default `/etc/host.conf` file:

```
order hosts, bind
```

In this example, the host checks the `/etc/hosts` file first and then performs a DNS lookup. A couple more options control how the name service is used. The only reason to modify this file is if you use NIS for your name service or you want one of the optional services. The `nospoof` option can be a good option for system security. It compares a standard DNS lookup to a reverse lookup (host-to-IP then IP-to-host) and fails if the two don't match. The drawback is that often when proxy services are used, the lookup fails, so you want to use this with caution.

Using Graphical Configuration Tools

Ubuntu has made some big improvements to how desktop users may configure networking using graphical configuration tools. For most people, all you need to know is contained in Chapter 1, "Installing Ubuntu and Post-Installation Configuration," in the section about Network Manager. For others, you may configure your network connections by right-clicking the networking icon on your top panel and choosing Edit Connections

18

from the menu, as shown in Figure 18.1. From the Network Connections window that opens, you may select from various types of connections to configure, including Wired, Wireless, Mobile Broadband, VPN, and DSL, as shown in Figure 18.2. By default, each is set to autoconfigure, and most users never need to change the settings available here. If you do need to, just choose the appropriate tab and click the Add button; you can then configure and fine-tune settings as needed, such as in the wireless connection example in Figure 18.3.

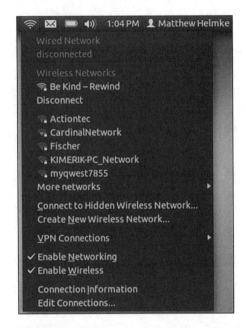

FIGURE 18.1   Use `nm-connection-editor` to configure your network devices.

FIGURE 18.2   Choose the connection type to configure from the tabs in Network Connections.

FIGURE 18.3   Assign a static IP address to a network interface.

Dynamic Host Configuration Protocol

As its name implies, *Dynamic Host Configuration Protocol (DHCP)* configures hosts for connection to your network. DHCP enables a network administrator to configure all TCP/IP parameters for each host as he connects to the network after activation of a NIC. These parameters include automatically assigning an IP address to a NIC, setting name server entries in `/etc/resolv.conf`, and configuring default routing and gateway information for a host. This section first describes how to use DHCP to obtain IP address assignment for your NIC and then how to quickly set up and start a DHCP server using Ubuntu.

> **NOTE**
>
> You can learn more about DHCP by reading RFC 2131, "Dynamic Host Configuration Protocol," at www.ietf.org/rfc/rfc2131.txt.

How DHCP Works

DHCP provides persistent storage of network parameters by holding identifying information for each network client that might connect to the network. The three most common pairs of identifying information are as follows:

▶ **Network subnet/host address**—Used by hosts to connect to the network at will

▶ **Subnet/hostname**—Enables the specified host to connect to the subnet

▶ **Subnet/hardware address**—Enables a specific client to connect to the network after getting the hostname from DHCP

DHCP also allocates to the client's temporary or permanent network (IP) addresses. When a temporary assignment, known as a *lease*, elapses, the client can request to have the lease extended, or, if the address is no longer needed, the client can relinquish the address. For hosts that will be permanently connected to a network with adequate addresses available, DHCP allocates infinite leases.

DHCP offers your network some advantages. First, it shifts responsibility for assigning IP addresses from the network administrator (who can accidentally assign duplicate IP addresses) to the DHCP server. Second, DHCP makes better use of limited IP addresses. If a user is away from the office for whatever reason, the user's host can release its IP address for use by other hosts.

Like most things in life, DHCP is not perfect. Servers cannot be configured through DHCP alone because DNS does not know what addresses that DHCP assigns to a host. This means that DNS lookups are not possible on machines configured through DHCP alone; therefore, services cannot be provided. However, DHCP can make assignments based on DNS entries when using subnet/hostname or subnet/hardware address identifiers.

> **NOTE**
>
> The problem of using DHCP to configure servers using registered hostnames is being addressed by Dynamic DNS which, when fully developed, will enable DHCP to register IP addresses with DNS. This will enable you, for example, to register a domain name (such as matthewhelmke.com) and be able to easily access that domain's web server without needing to use static IP addressing of a specific host. The largest hurdle to overcome is the security implication of enabling each host connecting to the system to update DNS. A few companies, such as Dyn.com (www.dyndns.org/), are already offering Dynamic DNS services and have clients for Linux.

Activating DHCP at Installation and Boot Time

Ubuntu automatically defaults your network interfaces to using DHCP because it is the simplest way of setting up a network interface. With *dynamic*, or DHCP-assigned IP addressing schemes for your NIC, the broadcast address is set at 255.255.255.255 because dhclient, the DHCP client used for IP configuration, is initially unaware of where the DHCP server is located, so the request must travel every network until a server replies.

You can find the instruction to use DHCP for your NIC /etc/network/interfaces, with a line that says dhcp.

Other settings specific to obtaining DHCP settings are saved in the file named dhclient. conf under the /etc/dhcp3/dhclient.conf directory and are documented in the dhclient.conf man page. More than 100 options are also documented in the dhcpoptions man page.

However, using DHCP is not that complicated. If you want to use DHCP and know that there is a server on your network, you can quickly configure your NIC by using the dhclient, as follows:

```
matthew@seymour:~$ sudo dhclient
Internet Systems Consortium DHCP Client V3.1.3
Copyright 2004-2009 Internet Systems Consortium.
All rights reserved.
For info, please visit https://www.isc.org/software/dhcp/

Listening on LPF/eth0/00:90:f5:8e:52:b5
Sending on   LPF/eth0/00:90:f5:8e:52:b5
Listening on LPF/virbr0/ee:1a:62:7e:e2:a2
Sending on   LPF/virbr0/ee:1a:62:7e:e2:a2
Listening on LPF/wlan0/00:16:ea:d4:58:88
Sending on   LPF/wlan0/00:16:ea:d4:58:88
Sending on   Socket/fallback
DHCPDISCOVER on eth0 to 255.255.255.255 port 67 interval 7
DHCPDISCOVER on wlan0 to 255.255.255.255 port 67 interval 3
DHCPOFFER of 192.168.1.106 from 192.168.1.1
DHCPREQUEST of 192.168.1.106 on wlan0 to 255.255.255.255 port 67
DHCPACK of 192.168.1.106 from 192.168.1.1
bound to 192.168.1.106 -renewal in 35959 seconds.
```

In this example, the first Ethernet device, eth0, has been assigned an IP address of 192.168.1.106 from a DHCP server at 192.168.1.1. The renewal will take place in 35959 seconds, or about 10 hours. (Cool tip: Google converts this for you if you search for 35959 seconds in hours.)

DHCP Software Installation and Configuration

Installation of the DHCP client and server is fairly straightforward, mainly because Ubuntu already includes dhclient in a default installation but also because installing software is easy using synaptic or apt-get.

DHCP dhclient

DHCP is automatically enabled when you install Ubuntu, so you do not need to worry about having to enable it. The DHCP client, dhclient, sends a broadcast message that the DHCP server replies to with networking information for your host. After it has this, you're done.

You can, however, fine-tune how dhclient works and where and how it obtains or looks for DHCP information. You probably will not need to take this additional effort; but if you do, you can create and edit a file named dhclient.conf and save it in the /etc directory with your settings.

18

CAUTION

You should not just go ahead and overwrite your `dhclient.conf` with any old file because doing so could lead you to painful networking problems. Instead, copy the file like this:

```
matthew@seymour:~$ sudo cp /etc/dhcp3/dhclient.conf/
➥etc/dhcp3/dhclient.conf.backup
```

That way, if anything goes wrong, you can then use the backup to restore the original settings by copying it back to its original location in place of the modified file.

A few of the `dhclient.conf` options include the following:

▶ `timeout time ;`—How long to wait before giving up trying. (The default is 60 seconds.)

▶ `retry time ;`—How long to wait before retrying. (The default is 5 minutes.)

▶ `select-timeout time ;`—How long to wait before selecting a DHCP offer. (The default is 0 seconds.)

▶ `reboot time ;`—How long to wait before trying to get a previously set IP. (The default is 10 seconds.)

▶ `renew date ;`—When to renew an IP lease, where `date` is in the form of *weekday year/month/day hour:minute:second*, such as in `3 2010/7/7 22:01:01` for Wednesday, July 7, 2010, at 10:01 p.m.

See the `dhclient.conf` man page for more information on additional settings.

DHCP Server

Again, the easiest way to install the DHCP server on your computer is to use either `synaptic` or `apt-get` to retrieve the `dhcp3-server` package. If you are so inclined, you can go to the *Internet Software Consortium (ISC)* website and download and build the source code yourself (www.isc.org/). However, we recommend you stay with the package in the Ubuntu repositories because it will be easy to update if there are security updates.

If you decide to install from a source downloaded from the ISC website, the installation is straightforward. Just unpack your `tar` file, run `./configure` from the root of the source directory, run `make`, and finally, if there are no errors, run `make install`. This puts all the files used by the DHCP daemon in the correct places. If you have the disk space, it is best to leave the source files in place until you are sure that DHCP is running correctly; otherwise, you can delete the source tree.

NOTE

For whichever installation method you choose, be sure that a file called `/etc/dhcp3/` `dhcpd.leases` is created. The file can be empty, but it does need to exist for `dhcpd` to start properly.

Using DHCP to Configure Network Hosts

Configuring your network with DHCP can look difficult but is actually easy if your needs are simple. The server configuration can take a bit more work if your network is more complex and depending on how much you want DHCP to do.

Configuring the server takes some thought and a little bit of work. Luckily, the work involves editing only a single configuration file, `/etc/dhcp3/dhcpd.conf`. To start the server at boot time, use the `service` or `ntsysv` commands.

The `/etc/dhcp3/dhcpd.conf` file contains all the information needed to run `dhcpd`. Ubuntu includes a sample `dhcpd.conf` in `/usr/share/doc/dhcp*/dhcpd.conf.sample`. The DHCP server source files also contain a sample `dhcpd.conf` file.

You can think of the `/etc/dhcp3/dhcpd.conf` file at as a three-part file. The first part contains configurations for DHCP itself. The configurations include the following:

▶ **Setting the domain name**—`option domain-name "example.org"`

▶ **Setting DNS servers**—`option domain-name-servers ns1.example.org, ns2.example.org` (IP addresses can be substituted.)

▶ **Setting the default and maximum lease times**—`default-lease-time 3600` and `max-lease-time 14400`

Other settings in the first part include whether the server is the primary (authoritative) server and what type of logging DHCP should use. These settings are considered defaults, and you can override them by the subnet and host portion of the configuration in more complex situations.

> **NOTE**
>
> The `dhcpd.conf` file requires semicolons (`;`) after each command statement. If your configuration file has errors or runs improperly, check for this.

The next part of the `dhcpd.conf` deals with the different subnets that your DHCP server serves; this section is quite straightforward. Each subnet is defined separately and can look like this:

```
subnet 10.5.5.0 netmask 255.255.255.224 {
 range 10.5.5.26 10.5.5.30;
 option domain-name-servers ns1.internal.example.org;
 option domain-name "internal.example.org";
 option routers 10.5.5.1;
 option broadcast-address 10.5.5.31;
 default-lease-time 600;
 max-lease-time 7200;
}
```

This defines the IP addressing for the `10.5.5.0` subnet. It defines the IP address ranging from `10.5.5.26` through `10.5.5.30` to be dynamically assigned to hosts that reside on that subnet. This example shows that you can set any TCP/IP option from the subnet portion of the configuration file. It shows which DNS server the subnet will connect to, which can be good for DNS server load balancing, or which can be used to limit the hosts that can be reached through DNS. It defines the domain name, so you can have more than one domain on your network. It can also change the default and maximum lease time.

If you want your server to ignore a specific subnet, you can do so as follows:

```
subnet 10.152.187.0 netmask 255.255.255.0 {
}
```

This defines no options for the `10.152.187.0` subnet; therefore, the DHCP server ignores it.

The last part of your `dhcp.conf` is for defining hosts. This can be good if you want a computer on your network to have a specific IP address or other information specific to that host. The key to completing the host section is to know the hardware address of the host. As you learned in the "Hardware Devices for Networking" section, earlier in this chapter, the hardware address is used to differentiate the host for configuration. You can obtain your hardware address by using the `ifconfig` command as described previously. The hardware address is on the `eth0` line labeled `Hwaddr`.

```
host hopper {
   hardware ethernet 08:00:07:26:c0:a5;
   fixed-address hopper.matthewhelmke.com;
}
```

This example takes the host with the hardware address `08:00:07:26:c0:a5` and does a DNS lookup to assign the IP address for hopper.matthewhelmke.com to the host.

DHCP can also define and configure booting for diskless clients like this:

```
host bumblebee {
   hardware ethernet 0:0:c0:5d:bd:95;
   filename "vmunix.bumblebee";
   server-name "kernigan.matthewhelmke.com";
}
```

The diskless host bumblebee gets its boot information from server `kernigan.` `matthewhelmke.com` and uses `vmunix.bumblebee` kernel. All other TCP/IP configuration can also be included.

> **CAUTION**
>
> Remember, to avoid problems, only one DHCP server should be configured on a local network. Your DHCP might not work correctly on a LAN with hosts running outdated legacy operating systems. Often, Windows NT servers have the Windows DHCP server installed by default. Because there is no configuration file for NT to sort through, that DHCP server configures your host before the Linux server if both machines are on the same LAN.

Check your NT servers for this situation and disable DHCP on the NT server; afterward, your other DHCP-enabled hosts should configure correctly. Also check to make sure that there are no conflicts if you use a cable or DSL modem, *wireless access point (WAP)*, or other intelligent router on your LAN that can provide DHCP.

Other Uses for DHCP

A whole host of options can be used in `dhcpd.conf`: Entire books are dedicated to DHCP. The most comprehensive book is *The DHCP Handbook*, available at www.dhcp-handbook .com/. You can define NIS domains, configure NetBIOS, set subnet masks, and define time servers or many other types of servers (to name a few of the DHCP options you can use). The preceding example gets your DHCP server and client up and running.

The DHCP server distribution contains an example of the `dhcpd.conf` file that you can use as a template for your network. The file shows a basic configuration that can get you started with explanations for the options used.

Wireless Networking

Linux has had support for wireless networking since the first standards were developed in the early 1990s. With computers getting smaller and smaller, the uses for wireless networking increased; meanwhile, the transmission speeds are increasing all the time. There are several ways to create a wireless network. The following sections introduce you to several Linux commands you can use to initialize, configure, and manage wireless networking on your Ubuntu system.

Support for Wireless Networking in Ubuntu

The Linux kernel that ships with Ubuntu provides extensive support for wireless networking. Related wireless tools for configuring, managing, or displaying information about a wireless connection include the following:

▶ `iwconfig`–Sets the network name, encryption, transmission rate, and other features of a wireless network interface

▶ `iwlist`–Displays information about a wireless interface, such as rate, power level, or frequency used

▶ `iwpriv`–Sets optional features, such as roaming, of a wireless network interface

▶ `iwspy`–Shows wireless statistics of a number of nodes

Support varies for wireless devices, but most modern (that is, post-2005) wireless devices should work with Ubuntu. In general, Linux wireless device software (usually in the form of a kernel module) support the creation of an Ethernet device that can be managed by traditional interface tools such as `ifconfig`—with wireless features of the device managed by the various wireless software tools.

18

For example, when a wireless networking device is first recognized and initialized for use, the driver most likely reports a new device:

```
zd1211rw 5-4:1.0: firmware version 4725

zd1211rw 5-4:1.0: zd1211b chip 050d:705c v4810 \
high 00-17-3f AL2230_RF pa0 G—ns

zd1211rw 5-4:1.0: eth2

usbcore: registered new interface driver zd1211rw
```

This output (from the `dmesg` command) shows that the `eth2` device has been reported. If DHCP is in use, the device should automatically join the nearest wireless subnet and be automatically assigned an IP address. If not, the next step is to use a wireless tool such as `iwconfig` to set various parameters of the wireless device. The `iwconfig` command, along with the device name (`eth2` in this example), shows the status:

```
matthew@seymour:~$ iwconfig eth2
eth2      IEEE 802.11b/g  ESSID:"SKY35120"  Nickname:"zd1211"
          Mode:Managed  Frequency:2.462 GHz  \
Access Point: 00:18:4D:06:8E:2A
          Bit Rate=24 Mb/s
          Encryption key:0EFD-C1AF-5C8D-B2C6-7A89-3790-07A7-AC64-0AB5\
-C36E-D1E9-A230-1DB9-D227-2EB6-D6C8   Security mode:open
          Link Quality=100/100  Signal level=82/100
          Rx invalid nwid:0  Rx invalid crypt:0  Rx invalid frag:0
          Tx excessive retries:0  Invalid misc:0   Missed beacon:0
```

This example shows a 24Mbps connection to a network named SKY35120. To change a parameter, such as the transmission rate, use a command-line option with the `iwconfig` command like this:

```
matthew@seymour:~$ sudo iwconfig eth2 rate 11M
```

Other options supported by the `iwconfig` command include `essid`, used to set the NIC to connect to a specific network by name; `mode`, used to enable the NIC to automatically retrieve settings from an access point or connect to another wireless host; and `freq`, to set a frequency to use for communication. Additional options include `channel`, `frag`, `enc` (for encryption), `power`, and `txpower`. Details and examples of these options are in the `iwconfig` man page.

You can then use the `ifconfig` command or perhaps a graphical Ubuntu tool to set the device networking parameters, and the interface will work as on a hardwired LAN. One handy output of the `iwconfig` command is the link quality output, which you can use in shell scripts or other graphical utilities for signal-monitoring purposes.

Advantages of Wireless Networking

Advantages of wireless networking are its mobility and potential range. If you have a large enough antenna network, your network can stretch many miles. This would be an expensive network, but one that would easily break out of the brick-and-mortar confines of the office.

Wireless networking is also a great advantage to college campuses, eliminating the need to tear through walls to install cabling as more and more students expect to have a network connection in their dorm rooms. Wireless networking cards are very reasonable in price and can easily be issued to each student as required.

Home networkers can also benefit from wireless networking. It is a potential solution for those who cannot make wired network modifications to their homes. In addition, wireless networking removes the unsightly wires running along baseboards and ceilings that are required to connect computers in different rooms. With a wireless home network, you are not even confined to inside the house. Depending on the transmit power of your router, you can sit out in your backyard and watch clouds drifting by as you type away.

Choosing the right types of wireless devices is an important decision. The next sections discuss some of the basic differences between current protocols used for wireless networking.

Choosing from Among Available Wireless Protocols

The *Institute of Electrical and Electronics Engineers (IEEE)* started to look seriously at wireless networking in 1990. This is when the 802.11 standard was first introduced by the Wireless Local Area Networks Standards Working Group. The group based the standard roughly around the architecture used in cellular phone networks. The wireless network is controlled by a base station, which can be just a transmitter attached to the network or, more commonly these days, a router.

Larger networks can use more than one base station. Networks with more than one base station are usually referred to as *distribution systems*. You can use a distribution system to increase coverage area and support roaming of wireless hosts. You can also use external omnidirectional antennas to increase coverage area, or if required, you can use point-to-point or directional antennas to connect distant computers or networks. Right now, the least expensive wireless Linux networks are built using devices (such as access points or NICs) supporting 802.11b, although the faster 802.11g devices tend to get more shelf space. Devices are available marketed as N or Pre-N, meaning that they implement a draft standard, while the IEEE carry on debating the full N standard. Significantly more power throughput and range are promised by hardware that supports N, but this specification has yet to be formally agreed on and so implementations are not necessarily standard.

An early standard, 802.11a, offers greater transmission rates than 802.11b, and a number of 802.11a wireless NICs are available. (Some products provide up to 72Mbps, but do not work with 802.11b devices.) Wireless networking devices based on 802.11g, which has the speed improvement of 802.11a and is compatible with 802.11b, are common. Other wireless protocols include Bluetooth, which provides up to 720Kbps data transfers.

Bluetooth is intended for short-range device communications (such as for a printer) and supports a typical range of only 10 meters. Bluetooth is unlike IrDA, which requires line of sight (devices that are aimed at each other). Bluetooth use conflicts with 802.11 networks because it also uses the 2.4GHz band. You can find out more at www.bluetooth.com/.

The 802.11 standard specifies that wireless devices use a frequency range of 2400MHz to 2483.5MHz. This is the standard used in North America and Europe. In Japan, however, wireless networks are limited to a frequency range of 2471MHz to 2479MHz because of Japanese regulations. Within these ranges, each network is given up to 79 nonoverlapping frequency channels to use. This reduces the chance of two closely located wireless networks using the same channel at the same time. It also allows for channel hopping, which can be used for security.

Beyond the Network and onto the Internet

Ubuntu supports Internet connections and the use of Internet resources in many different ways. You will find a wealth of Internet-related software included with this book's version of Ubuntu, and you can download hundreds of additional free utilities from a variety of sources. To use them, you must have a working Internet connection.

In this section, you learn how to set up an Internet connection in Ubuntu using a modem and *Point-to-Point Protocol (PPP)* as well as other connection methods, including *digital subscriber line (DSL)* and cable modem services. Just a few years ago, getting a dial-up connection working was difficult—hence, an entire chapter of this book was devoted to it. Today, as long as you have a hardware modem, dial-up configuration is simple. The Ubuntu developers and the wider Linux community have made great progress in making connectivity easier.

Although many experienced Linux users continue to use manual scripts to establish their Internet connectivity, new users and experienced system administrators alike will find Ubuntu's graphical network configuration interface much easier to use. You learn how to use the Internet Connection Wizard in this chapter and how to configure Ubuntu to provide dial-in PPP support. The chapter also describes how to use Roaring Penguin's DSL utilities to manage connectivity through a cable modem connection.

Common Configuration Information

Although Ubuntu enables great flexibility in configuring Internet connections, that flexibility comes at the price of an increase in complexity. To configure Internet connectivity in Ubuntu, you must know more about the details of the connection process than you can learn from the information typically provided by your Internet service provider (ISP). In this section, you learn what to ask about and how to use the information.

Some ISPs are unaware of Linux or unwilling to support its use with their service. Fortunately, that attitude is rapidly changing, and the majority of ISPs offer services using standard protocols that are compatible with Linux, even if they (or their technical support people) aren't aware that their own ISPs are Linux friendly. You just need to press a little for the information you require.

If you are one of the few remaining people using a dial-up modem account (referred to in Linux as *PPP* for the Point-to-Point Protocol it uses), your ISP will provide your computer with a static or dynamic *Internet Protocol (IP)* address. A dynamic IP address changes each time you dial in, whereas a static IP address remains the same. The ISP also might automatically provide your computer with the names of the *Domain Name Service (DNS)* servers. You need to know the telephone number that your computer will dial in to for making the connection; your ISP supplies that number, too. You also need a working modem and need to know the device name of the modem (usually /dev/modem).

> **NOTE**
>
> Most IP addresses are dynamically assigned by ISPs; ISPs have a pool of addresses, and you get whatever address is available. From the ISP's viewpoint, a small number of addresses can serve a large number of people because not everyone will be online at the same time. For most Internet services, a dynamic IP works well because it is the ISP's job to route that information to you, and it sits in the middle—between you and the service you want to use. But a dynamic IP address changes, and if someone needs to find you at the same address (if you run a website or a file transfer site, for example), an IP that changes every time you log on does not work well. For that, you need a static IP. Because your ISP cannot reuse that IP with its other customers, it will likely charge you more for a static IP than for a dynamic IP. Average consumers do not need the benefit of a static IP and so are happy paying less for a dynamically assigned IP. Also, the DNS information can be provided automatically by the ISP by DHCP.

If you are using DSL access or a cable modem, you might have a dynamic IP provided through DHCP, or you might be assigned a static IP. You might automatically be provided with the names of the DNS servers if you use DHCP, or you might have to set up DNS manually (in which case, you have to know the IP addresses of the DNS servers).

In all cases, you have to know your username, your password, and for the configuration of other services, the names of the mail servers and the news server. You can obtain this information from your ISP if you specifically ask for it.

> **NOTE**
>
> The information in this book helps you understand and avoid many connection issues, but you might experience connection problems. Keep the telephone number of the technical help service for your ISP on hand in case you cannot establish a connection. But be aware that few ISPs offer Linux support, and you might need to seek help from a Linux-savvy friend or a Linux user group if your special circumstances cannot be handled from the knowledge you gain from this book. Of course, the best place to look is on the Internet.

Configuring Digital Subscriber Line Access

Ubuntu also supports the use of a *digital subscriber line (DSL)* service. Although it refers to the different types of DSL available as *xDSL* (which includes ADSL, IDSL, SDSL, and other flavors of DSL service), you can configure all of them using the Internet Connection Wizard. DSL service generally provides 256Kbps to 24Mbps transfer speeds and transmits data over copper telephone lines from a central office to individual subscriber sites (such as your home). Many DSL services (technically, cable rather than DSL) provide asymmetric speeds with download speeds greater than upload speeds.

> **NOTE**
>
> DSL service is an "always-on" type of Internet service, although you can turn off the connection under Ubuntu using the network configuration tool found under System, Administration, Network. An always-on connection exposes your computer to malicious abuse from crackers who trawl the Internet attempting to gain access to other computer systems. In addition to the capability to turn off such connections, Ubuntu is preconfigured to not listen on any network ports, which means that any attempts to gain access to your computer fail because Ubuntu rejects the request. This is the Ubuntu equivalent to surrounding your computer with a 12-foot steel fence.

A DSL connection requires that you have an Ethernet NIC (sometimes a USB interface that is not easily supported in Linux) in your computer or notebook. Many users also configure a gateway, firewall, or other computer with at least two NICs to share a connection with a LAN. We looked at the hardware and protocol issues earlier in this chapter. Advanced configuration of a firewall or router, other than what was addressed during your initial installation of Ubuntu, is beyond the scope of this book.

Understanding PPP over Ethernet

Establishing a DSL connection with an ISP providing a static IP address is easy. Unfortunately, many DSL providers use a type of PPP protocol named *Point-to-Point Protocol over Ethernet (PPPoE)* that provides dynamic IP address assignment and authentication by encapsulating PPP information inside Ethernet frames. Roaring Penguin's rp-pppoe clients are available from the Roaring Penguin site (https://www.roaringpenguin.com/files/download/rp-pppoe-3.11.tar.gz), and these clients make the difficult-to-configure PPPoE connection much easier to deal with. You can download and install newer versions. (See the Roaring Penguin link in the "References" section at the end of this chapter.)

> **NOTE**
>
> When ISPs originally started to roll out ADSL services, they often provided the ADSL modems. Today, however, in much of the world these modems are optional, which is a good thing because many people choose to purchase a router with an built-in modem to create a dedicated connection. In the United States, these devices are rare, but you can usually replace the supplied modem with an aftermarket modem if you want to spend the money. Either way, using a router can save many headaches and enables you to easily connect more than one computer to an Internet connection. Note that if you are using a cable connection, they usually come with an Ethernet cable, in which case you just need a router (which is pretty much how all Internet access works in the United States because combination modem/router devices are rare in the United States). Check with your ISP before buying to ensure that whatever router you do end up with can be supported by them. You might find that your ISP even supplies a router as part of the package.

Configuring a PPPoE Connection Manually

You should only need to use these steps if you are using a modem supplied by your ISP, and not a router. The basic steps involved in manually setting up a DSL connection using Ubuntu involve connecting the proper hardware and then running a simple configuration script if you use rp-pppoe from Roaring Penguin.

First, connect your DSL modem to your telephone line, and then plug in your Ethernet cable from the modem to your computer's NIC. If you plan to share your DSL connection with the rest of your LAN, you need at least two network cards: designated eth0 (for your LAN) and eth1 (for the DSL connection).

The following example assumes that you have more than one computer and will share your DSL connection on a LAN.

First, log in as root, and ensure that your first eth0 device is enabled and up (perhaps using the ifconfig command). Next, bring up the other interface, but assign a null IP address like this:

```
matthew@seymour:~$ sudo ifconfig eth1 0.0.0.0 up
```

Now use the adsl-setup command to set up your system, as follows:

```
matthew@seymour:~$ sudo /sbin/adsl-setup
```

You are presented with a text script and asked to enter your username and the Ethernet interface used for the connection (such as eth1). You are then asked to use "on-demand" service or have the connection stay up all the time (until brought down by the root operator). You can also set a timeout in seconds, if desired. You are then asked to enter the IP addresses of your ISP's DNS servers if you haven't configured the system's /etc/resolv.conf file.

After that, you are prompted to enter your password two times and must choose the type of firewall and IP masquerading to use. (You learned about IP masquerading in the "Using IP Masquerading in Ubuntu" section, earlier in this chapter.) The actual configuration is done automatically. Using a firewall is essential today, so choose this option unless you intend to craft your own set of firewall rules (a discussion of which is beyond the scope of this book). After you have chosen your firewall and IP masquerading setup, you are asked to confirm, save, and implement your settings. You are also given a choice to allow users to manage the connection, a handy option for home users.

Changes are made to your system's /etc/sysconfig/network-scripts/ifcfg-ppp0, /etc/resolv.conf, /etc/ppp/pap-secrets, and /etc/ppp/chap-secrets files.

After configuration has finished, use the adsl-start command to start a connection and DSL session, like this:

```
matthew@seymour:~$ sudo /sbin/adsl-start
```

The DSL connection should be nearly instantaneous, but if problems occur, check to make sure that your DSL modem is communicating with the phone company's central office by

18

examining the status LEDs on the modem. Because this varies from modem to modem, consult your modem user's manual.

Make sure all cables are properly attached, that your interfaces are properly configured and that you have entered the correct information to the setup script.

If IP masquerading is enabled, other computers on your LAN on the same subnet address (such as `192.168.0.xxx`) can use the Internet but must have the same `/etc/resolv.conf` name server entries and a routing entry with the DSL-connected computer as a gateway. For example, if the host computer with the DSL connection has an IP address of `192.168.0.1`, and other computers on your LAN use addresses in the `192.168.0.xxx` range, use the `route` command on each computer like this:

```
matthew@seymour:~$ sudo route add default gw 192.168.0.1
```

Note that you can also use a hostname instead if each computer has an `/etc/hosts` file with hostname and IP address entries for your LAN. To stop your connection, use the `adsl-stop` command:

```
matthew@seymour:~$ sudo /sbin/adsl-stop
```

Configuring Dial-Up Internet Access

Most ISPs provide dial-up connections supporting PPP because it is a fast and efficient protocol for using TCP/IP over serial lines. PPP is designed for two-way networking; TCP/IP provides the transport protocol for data. One hurdle faced by new Ubuntu users is how to set up PPP and connect to the Internet. It is not necessary to understand the details of the PPP protocol to use it, and setting up a PPP connection is easy. You can configure the PPP connections manually using the command line or graphically during an X session using Ubuntu's Network Configuration Tool. Each approach produces the same results.

PPP uses several components on your system. The first is a daemon called `pppd`, which controls the use of PPP. The second is a driver called the *high-level data link control (HDLC)*, which controls the flow of information between two machines. A third component of PPP is a routine called *chat* that dials the other end of the connection for you when you want it to. Although PPP has many "tunable" parameters, the default settings work well for most people.

Ubuntu includes some useful utilities to get your dial-up connection up and running. In this section, we look at two options that will have you on the Internet in no time.

The first way is to configure a connection using `pppconfig`, a command-line utility to help you to configure specific dial-up connection settings.

Enter the following command:

```
matthew@seymour:~$ sudo pppconfig
```

Before you connect for the first time, you need to add yourself to both the `dip` and `dialout` groups by using these commands:

```
matthew@seymour:~$ sudo adduser YOURNAMEHERE dip
matthew@seymour:~$ sudo adduser YOURNAMEHERE dialout
```

After you have done this, it is just a simple matter of issuing the `pon` command to connect and the `poff` command to disconnect. You can create as many different profiles as you need and can launch specific ones by using the command `pon profilename`, again using the `poff` command to disconnect.

> **CAUTION**
>
> Many software modems will not work with Linux because the manufacturers will not release programming information about them or provide Linux drivers. An external serial port modem or ISA bus modem almost always work; USB and PCI modems are still problematic. It is suggested that you do a thorough Google search using your modem's name and model number to see how others have solved problems with that particular modem. Links to software modem compatibility sites appear at the end of this chapter.

Troubleshooting Connection Problems

The Linux Documentation Project at www.tldp.org/ offers many in-depth resources for configuring and troubleshooting these connections. Google is also an invaluable tool for dealing with specific questions about these connections. For many other useful references, see the "References" section at the end of this chapter.

Here are a few troubleshooting tips culled from many years of experience:

▶ If your modem connects and then hangs up, you are probably using the wrong password or dialing the wrong number. If the password and phone number are correct, it is likely an authentication protocol problem.

▶ If you get connected but cannot reach websites, it is likely a domain name resolver problem, meaning that DNS is not working. If it worked yesterday and you haven't "adjusted" the associated files, it is probably a problem at the ISP's end. Call and ask.

▶ Always make certain that everything is plugged in. Check again (and again).

▶ If the modem works in Windows but not in Linux no matter what you do, it is probably a software modem no matter what it said on the box.

▶ If everything just stops working (and you do not see smoke), it is probably a glitch at the ISP or the telephone company. Take a break and give them some time to fix it.

▶ Never configure a network connection when you have had too little sleep or too much caffeine; you will just have to redo it tomorrow.

18

RELATED UBUNTU AND LINUX COMMANDS

You use these commands when managing network connectivity in your Ubuntu system:

- ▶ `dhclient`—Automatically acquire and then set IP info for a NIC
- ▶ `ethereal`—GNOME graphical network scanner
- ▶ `ufw`—Ubuntu's basic firewalling tool
- ▶ `ifconfig`—Displays and manages Linux networking devices
- ▶ `iwconfig`—Displays and sets wireless network device parameters
- ▶ `route`—Displays and manages Linux kernel routing table
- ▶ `ssh`—The OpenSSH remote-login client and preferred replacement for telnet
- ▶ `nm-connection-editor`—Ubuntu's GUI for configuring network connections

References

- ▶ **https://help.ubuntu.com/14.04/serverguide/networking.html**—Official networking help for Ubuntu.

- ▶ **www.ietf.org/rfc.html**—Go here to search for, or get a list of, *Requests For Comments (RFC)*.

- ▶ **www.oth.net/dyndns.html**—A list of Dynamic DNS service providers.

- ▶ **www.isc.org/products/DHCP/**—The official siter for DHCP.

- ▶ **www.ieee.org**—The *Institute of Electrical and Electronics Engineers (IEEE)* website.

- ▶ Joe Casad, *Sams Teach Yourself TCP/IP Network Administration in 21 Days*, Sams Publishing, ISBN: 0-672-31250-6.

- ▶ Craig Hunt and Gigi Estabrook, *TCP/IP Network Administration*, O'Reilly Publishing, ISBN: 1-56592-322-7.

- ▶ Frank J. Derfler, Frank Derfler, and Jeff Koch, *Practical Networking*, Que Publishing, ISBN: 0-7897-2252-6.

- ▶ Steve Litt, *Samba Unleashed*, Sams Publishing, ISBN: 0-672-31862-8.

- ▶ Ralph Droms and Ted Lemon, *The DHCP Handbook*, Sams Publishing, ISBN: 0-672-32327-3.

# CHAPTER 19

Remote Access with SSH, Telnet, and VNC

Controlling your system remotely is one of the cooler things you can do with Ubuntu: With just a bit of configuration, you can connect from any Linux box to another computer in a variety of ways. If you just want to check something quickly or if you have limited bandwidth, you have the option of using only the command line, but you can also connect directly to the X server and get full graphical control.

Understanding the selection of tools available is largely a history lesson. For example, Telnet was an earlier way of connecting to another computer through the command line, but that has since been superseded by *Secure Shell (SSH)*. That is not to say that you should ignore Telnet; you need to know how to use it so you have it as a fallback. However, SSH is preferred because it is more secure. We cover both in this chapter.

Setting Up a Telnet Server

Telnet is an older service. The client is part of the default installation, but is not activated by default. The server is not part of the default installation. This is because everything Telnet transmits and receives is in plain text, including passwords and other sensitive information. Telnet is generally not a good choice for communication. However, you might want to install Telnet for certain situations, such as connecting to a piece of equipment that doesn't have SSH available, such as embedded systems where having a small OS footprint is important and more secure methods of communication are not available. In addition, sometimes Telnet is the quickest and easiest way to test newly installed services during configuration, such as a Postfix mail server.

You might also want to install Telnet to learn about it and test it, simply because you might run across moments in the real world where no other option exists.

If you decide to install Telnet, use Synaptic or apt to install `telnetd`, which installs the server.

Start by configuring your firewall to allow connections through port 23. If this port is blocked, you cannot use Telnet. See Chapter 20, "Securing Your Machines," for help doing this.

After making any needed configuration adjustments to your firewall, type `telnet` *your IP* to test to confirm both the client and server are installed and working by connecting from your terminal using the client back to the server running on your own computer. You are prompted to enter your username and password. The whole conversation should look something like this:

```
matthew@seymour:~$ telnet 192.168.1.102
Trying 192.168.1.102...
Connected to 192.168.1.102 (192.168.1.102)
Escape character is "^]".

Welcome to babbage
Ubuntu 12.04 LTS

* All access is logged *

login: matthew
Password:
Last login: Sun Jul  4 10:08:34 2012 from seymour
matthew@babbage~$
```

TIP

The server responds with `Welcome to babbage`, `Ubuntu 12.04 LTS`, which is a customized message. Your machine will respond similarly. This might not be secure: Giving away version numbers is often not a smart move on a machine that might be accessed from outside of a secure network as it can narrow down the options for an attacker to use. In fact, even saying `Ubuntu` might be questionable for the same reason. For those instances where you want to take an extra step in obscuring your information, you can edit the `issue` and `issue.net` files in your `/etc` directory to change the message displayed.

To use Telnet to connect to a different computer, use that computer's IP address on the network instead of using your own. You can use Telnet on local networks and across the Internet to connect to any computer running the server on an open port.

Telnet uses port 23, but you can use it with other ports by adding the port to the IP address, as in this example where we use it to connect to port 110 to test a POP3 connection/server:

```
matthew@seymour:~$ telnet 192.168.1.102 110.
```

Telnet Versus SSH

Although Telnet is worth keeping around as a fail-safe, last-resort option, SSH is superior in nearly every way. Telnet is fast but also unsecure. As stated earlier, it sends all your text, including your password, in plain text that can be read by anyone with the right tools. SSH, on the other hand, encrypts all your communication and so is more resource intensive but secure—even a government security agency sniffing your packets for some reason would still have a hard time cracking the encryption.

Andy Green, posting to the `fedora-list` mailing list, summed up the Telnet situation perfectly when he said, "As Telnet is universally acknowledged to encourage evil, the service `telnetd` is not enabled by default." It is worthwhile taking the hint: Use Telnet as a last resort only.

Setting Up an SSH Server

If not installed already, you can install the OpenSSH server by adding the `openssh-server` package. As you might have guessed, `sshd` is the name for the SSH server daemon.

Start by configuring your firewall to allow connections through port 22. If this port is blocked, you cannot use SSH. See Chapter 20, "Securing Your Machines," for help doing this.

Two different versions of SSH exist, SSH1 and SSH2. The latter is newer and more secure, comes with more features, and is the default in Ubuntu. Support for SSH1 clients is best left disabled so that older clients cannot connect. This is done by default in the `/etc/ssh/sshd_config` file on this line:

```
Protocol 2
```

If you have no other option and absolutely have to allow an older client to connect, add a new line:

```
Protocol 1
```

SSH Tools

To the surprise of many, OpenSSH actually is comprised of a suite of tools. We have already seen `ssh`, the Secure Shell command that connects to other machines, and `sshd`, the SSH server daemon that accepts incoming SSH connections. However, there is also `sftp`, a replacement for `ftp`, `scp`, and `rcp`.

You should already be familiar with the `ftp` command because it is the lowest common denominator system for handling FTP file transfers. Like Telnet, though, `ftp` is unsecure: It sends your data in plain text across the network, and anyone can sniff your packets to pick out a username and password. The SSH replacement, `sftp`, puts FTP traffic over an SSH link, thus securing it.

The `rcp` command might be new to you, largely because it is not used much anymore. Back in its day, `rcp` was the primary way of copying a single file to another server. As with `ftp`, `scp` replaces `rcp` by simply channeling the data over a secure SSH connection. The difference between `sftp` and `scp` is that the former enables you to queue and copy many files simultaneously, whereas the latter is usually used to just send one, although `scp` can be used with the `-r` option to send an entire directory at once. See the man page for details.

19

Using `scp` to Copy Individual Files Between Machines

The most basic use of the `scp` command is to copy a file from your current machine to a remote machine. You can do that with the following command:

```
matthew@seymour:~$ scp test.txt 192.168.1.102:
```

The first parameter is the name of the file you want to send, and the second is the server to which you want to send it. Note that there is a colon (`:`) at the end of the IP address. This is where you can specify an exact location for the file to be copied. If you have nothing after the colon, as in the previous example, `scp` copies the file to your `/home` directory. As with SSH, `scp` prompts you for your password before copying takes place.

You can rewrite the previous command so that you copy `test.txt` from the local machine and save it as `newtest.txt` on the server:

```
matthew@seymour:~$ scp test.txt 192.168.1.102:newtest.txt
```

Alternatively, if there is a directory where you want the file to be saved, you can specify it like this:

```
matthew@seymour:~$ scp test.txt 192.168.1.102:subdir/stuff/newtest.txt
```

The three commands so far have all assumed that your username on your local machine is the same as your username on the remote machine. If this is not the case, you need to specify your username before the remote address, as follows:

```
matthew@seymour:~$ scp test.txt usernamenewtest.txt
```

You can use `scp` to copy remote files locally, simply by specifying the remote file as the source and the current directory (`.`) as the destination:

```
matthew@seymour:~$ scp 192.168.1.102:remote.txt.
```

If you want to copy files from one remote machine to another remote machine using `scp`, the best method is to first `ssh` to one of the remote machines and then use `scp` from that location.

Using `sftp` to Copy Many Files Between Machines

`sftp` is a mix between `ftp` and `scp`. Connecting to the server uses the same syntax as `scp`—you can just specify an IP address to connect using your current username, or you can specify a username using *username@ipaddress. You can optionally add a colon and a directory, as with* `scp`. After you are connected, the commands are the same as `ftp`: `cd`, `put`, `mput`, `get`, `quit`, and so on.

In one of the `scp` examples, we copied a remote file locally. You can do the same thing with `sftp` with the following conversation:

```
matthew@seymour:~$ sftp 192.168.1.102
Connecting to 192.168.1.102...
matthew@192.168.1.102's password:
sftp> get remote.txt
```

```
Fetching /home/matthew/remote.txt to remote.txt
/home/matthew/remote.txt      100%  23   0.0KB/s    00:00
sftp> quit
matthew@seymour:~$
```

Although FTP remains prominent because of the number of systems that do not have support for SSH, SFTP is gaining in popularity. Apart from the fact that it secures all communications between client and server, SFTP is popular because the initial connection between the client and server is made over port 22 through the sshd daemon. Someone using SFTP connects to the standard sshd daemon, verifies himself, and then is handed over to the SFTP server. The advantage to this is that it reduces the attack vectors because the SFTP server cannot be contacted directly and so cannot be attacked as long as the sshd daemon is secure.

Using ssh-keygen to Enable Key-Based Logins

There is a weak link in the SSH system, and, inevitably, it lies with users. No matter what lengths system administrators go to in training users to be careful with their passwords, monitors around the world have Post-it notes attached to them with pAssw0rd written on them. Sure, it has a mix of letters and numbers, but it can be cracked in less than a second by any brute-force method. *Brute-forcing* is the method of trying every password possibility, starting with likely words (such as *password* and variants, or *god*) and then just trying random letters (for example, *a, aa, ab, ac*, and so on).

Even very strong passwords are no more than about 16 characters; such passwords take a long time to brute-force but can still be cracked. The solution is to use key-based logins, which generate a unique, 1024-bit private and public key pair for your machine. These keys take even the fastest computers a lifetime to crack, and you can back them up with a password to stop others from using them.

Creating an SSH key is done through the ssh-keygen command, like this:

```
matthew@seymour:~$ ssh-keygen -t dsa
```

Press Enter when it prompts you where to save your key, and enter a passphrase when it asks you to. This passphrase is just a password used to protect the key. You can leave it blank if you want to, but doing so would allow other people to use your account to connect to remote machines if they manage to log in as you.

After the key is generated, change the directory to .ssh (cd ~/.ssh), which is a hidden directory where your key is stored and also where it keeps a list of safe SSH hosts. Assuming you use the default options, here you see the files id_dsa and id_dsa.pub. The first is your private key, and you should never give it out. The second is your public key, which is safe for distribution. You need to copy the public key to each server you want to connect to via key-based SSH.

Using scp, you can copy the public key over to your server, like this:

```
matthew@seymour:~$ scp id_dsa.pub 192.186.1.102:
```

This places id_dsa.pub in your /home directory (for an account that uses the same username as your local account) on 192.186.1.102. The next step is to ssh into

192.186.1.102 normally and set up that key as an authorized key. So, you can `ssh` in as yourself:

```
matthew@seymour:~$ ssh 192.168.1.102
```

After logging in normally, type this:

```
matthew@babbage:~$ cat id_dsa.pub >> .ssh/authorized_keys
matthew@babbage:~$ chmod 400 .ssh/authorized_keys
```

The `touch` command creates the `authorized_keys` file (if it does not exist already); then you use `cat` to append the contents of `id_dsa.pub` to the list of already authorized keys. Finally, `chmod` is used to make `authorized_keys` read-only.

With that done, you can type `exit` to disconnect from the remote machine and return to your local machine. Then you can try running `ssh` again. If you are prompted for your passphrase, you have successfully configured key-based authentication.

That is the current machine secured, but what about every other machine? It is still possible to log in from another machine using only a password, which means your remote machine is still vulnerable.

The solution to this is to edit the `/etc/ssh/sshd_config` file. This requires super user privileges. Look for the `PasswordAuthentication` line and make sure it reads `no` (and that it is not commented out with a #). Save the file, and run `kill -HUP 'cat /var/run/sshd.pid'` to have `sshd` reread its configuration files. With that done, `sshd` accepts only connections from clients with authorized keys, which stops crackers from brute-forcing their way in.

TIP

For extra security, you are strongly encouraged to set `PermitRootLogin` to no in /etc/ssh/sshd_config. When this is set, it becomes impossible to `ssh` into your machine using the root account—you must connect with a normal user account and then use `su` or `sudo` to switch to root. This is advantageous because most brute-force attempts take place on the root account because it is the only account that is guaranteed to exist on a server.

Also, even if a cracker knows your user account, she has to guess both your user password and your root password to take control of your system.

Of course, if you don't have a root account enabled on your box, this isn't an issue because it is already impossible to log in directly as root. Hooray for slightly more secure defaults in Ubuntu.

Virtual Network Computing

Everything we have looked at so far has been about remote access using the command line, with no mention so far of how to bring up a *graphical user interface (GUI)*. There are several ways of doing this in Ubuntu, some of which are listed in the "Reference" section later in this chapter. Here we discuss the most popular and the most preferred by the Ubuntu community, which is also the best supported by the developers: *Virtual Network Computing (VNC)*.

VNC is a system for controlling a computer remotely and sharing desktops over a network using a graphical interface. It was created at the Olivetti & Oracle Research Lab, which was acquired by AT&T in 1999 and closed down in 2001. Since then, several of the members of the development team got together to create a free and open-source version of the code (using the GPL), and from that base many different versions have appeared. VNC is widespread in the Linux world and, to a lesser extent, in the Windows world. Its main advantage is its widespread nature: Nearly all Linux distros bundle VNC, and clients are available for a wide selection of platforms.

Start by configuring your firewall to allow connections through port 5900. If this port is blocked, you cannot use VNC.

To set up VNC on your Ubuntu computer to allow others to access your desktop, you only need to tell Ubuntu who should be allowed to connect to your session by searching the Dash for and opening Desktop Sharing. By default, your desktop is not shared. Check Allow Other Users to View Your Desktop to share it. Most likely, you also want to check Allow Other Users to Control Your Desktop; otherwise, people can see what you are doing but not interact with the desktop (which is not very helpful). If you are using this as a remote way to connect to your own desktop or one that is running unattended when you will need access, uncheck You Must Confirm Each Access to This Machine. If you don't do this, when you try to connect from your remote location, Ubuntu pops up a message box on the local machine asking Should This Person Be Allowed to Connect? Because you are not there to click Yes, the connection fails. If you want to let someone else remotely connect to your system, keep this box enabled so that you know when people are connecting. You should always enter a password, no matter who it is that will connect. The options suggested are shown in Figure 19.1.

To access a computer that is running VNC from your Ubuntu desktop, search the Dash for and run the Remmina Remote Desktop Client. The program starts by searching the local network for shared desktops. If any are found, they are listed. In Figure 19.2, Heather's computer is shown.

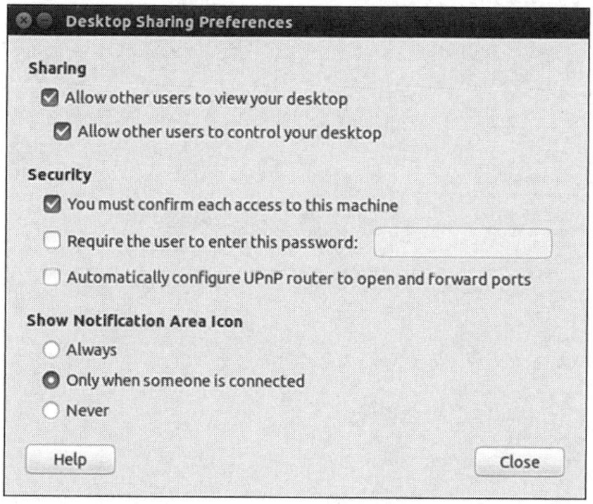

FIGURE 19.1   Desktop Sharing Preferences.

From the screen in Figure 19.2, select an entry and select the Open the connection icon at the top left, in the bar under the title bar with the window controls for close, minimize, and expand to full screen. If you have not yet entered any computers, then select the Create a new connection icon, just next to the first one, to enter the details for a computer you have already set up somewhere to be accessed using VNC as in Figure 19.3.

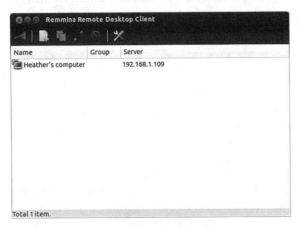

FIGURE 19.2   Remote Desktop Viewer.

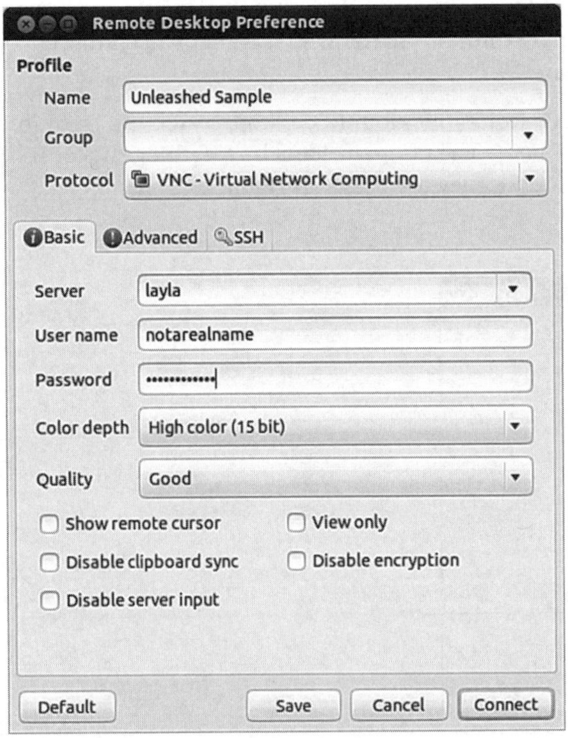

FIGURE 19.3   Enter details for the machine to which you want to connect.

When you have finished, close the window in which you are viewing the remote desktop.

VNC should not be considered secure over the Internet or on untrusted internal networks.

References

- ▶ www.telnet.org—Telnet's home page.

- ▶ https://help.ubuntu.com/community/SSH—The Ubuntu community documentation for SSH.

- ▶ www.openssh.com—The home page of the OpenSSH implementation of SSH that Ubuntu uses. It is run by the same team as OpenBSD, a secure BSD-based operating system.

- ▶ https://help.ubuntu.com/community/VNC—The Ubuntu community documentation for VNC.

- ▶ www.realvnc.com—The home page of the team that made VNC at AT&T's Cambridge Research Laboratory. It has since started RealVNC Ltd., a company dedicated to developing and supporting VNC.

- ▶ www.tightvnc.com—Here you can find an alternative to VNC called TightVNC that has several key advances over the stock VNC release. The most important feature is that TightVNC can use SSH for encryption, guaranteeing security.

- ▶ https://help.ubuntu.com/community/FreeNX—The Ubuntu community documentation for FreeNX.

- ▶ www.nomachine.com/—Another alternative to VNC is in the pipeline, called NX. The free implementation, FreeNX, is under heavy development at the time of writing but promises to work much faster than VNC.

19

Securing Your Machines

No computer with a connection to the Internet is 100 percent safe. If this information does not concern you, it should. Although there is no way to guarantee the ability to stop patient, creative, and serious crackers who are intent on getting into your computer or network, there are ways to make it harder for them and to warn you when they do. This chapter discusses all aspects of securing your Linux machines. You might have wondered why we did not spread this information around the book wherever it was appropriate, but the reason is simple: If you ever have a security problem with Linux, you know you can turn to this page and start reading without having to search or try to remember where you saw a tip. Everything you need is here in this one chapter, and we strongly advise you read it from start to finish.

BUILT-IN PROTECTION IN THE KERNEL

A number of networking and low-level protective services are built in to the Linux kernel. These services can be enabled, disabled, or displayed using the `sysctl` command, or by echoing a value (usually a `1` or a `0` to turn a service on or off) to a kernel process file under the `/proc` directory. See the discussion of setting a variable with `echo` in Chapter 11, "Command-Line Master Class Part 1," or the man pages for `sysctl` and `echo` for more.

Understanding Computer Attacks

There are many ways in which computer attacks can be divided for classification. Perhaps the easiest dichotomy is to separate attacks as *internal*, which are computer attacks done by someone with access to a computer on the local network, and *external*, which are attacks by someone with access to a computer through the Internet. This might sound like a trivial separation to make, but it is actually important: Unless you routinely hire talented computer crackers or allow visitors to plug computers into your network, the worst internal attack you are likely to encounter is from a disgruntled employee.

HACKER VERSUS CRACKER

In earlier days, there was a distinction made between the words *hacker* and *cracker*. A hacker was someone who used technology to innovate in new or unusual ways, whereas a cracker was someone who used technology to attack another's computers and cause harm. In the original definition, hackers did good or cool things and crackers did bad things.

This distinction was lost on the general public, so the term hacker has now regretfully come to mean the same thing as cracker for most people. However, we recognize the distinction and use the term cracker to mean a malicious person using a computer to cause problems for others. In your real-world conversations, realize that most people do not make a distinction, and so be prepared to define your terms if you call yourself a hacker.

Although you should never ignore the internal threat, you should arguably be more concerned with the outside world. The big bad Internet is a security vortex. Machines connected directly to the outside world can be attacked by people across the world, and invariably are, even only a few minutes after having been connected.

This situation is not a result of malicious users lying in wait for your IP address to do something interesting. Instead, canny virus writers have created worms that exploit a vulnerability, take control of a machine, and then spread it to other machines around them. As a result, most attacks today are the result of these autocracking tools; there are only a handful of true clever crackers around, and, to be frank, if one of them ever actually targets you seriously, it will take a mammoth effort to repel the cracker, regardless of which operating system you run.

Autocracking scripts also come in another flavor: prewritten code that exploits a vulnerability and gives its users special privileges on the hacked machine. These scripts are rarely used by their creators; instead, they are posted online and downloaded by wannabe hackers, who then use them to attack vulnerable machines.

So, the external category is itself made up of worms, serious day job crackers, and wannabe crackers (usually called *script kiddies*). Combined they will assault your Internet-facing servers, and it is your job to make sure your boxes stay up, happily ignoring the firefight around them.

On the internal front, things are somewhat more difficult. Users who sit inside your firewall are already past your primary source of defense and, worse, they might even have physical access to your machines. Anyone with malicious intent and physical access to a machine is nearly impossible to stop unless they are simply inept. The situation is only slightly better if they don't have physical access but do have access to your internal network.

Regardless of the source of the attack, you can follow a five-step checklist to help secure your box:

1. **Assess your vulnerability.** Decide which machines can be attacked, which services they are running, and who has access to them.

2. **Configure the server for maximum security.** Install only what you need, run only what you must, and configure a local firewall.

3. **Secure physical access to the server.**

4. **Create worst-case-scenario policies.**

5. **Keep up-to-date with security news.**

Each of these is covered in the following sections, and each is as important as the others.

Assessing Your Vulnerability

It is a common mistake for people to assume that switching on a firewall makes them safe. This is not the case and, in fact, has never been the case. Each system has distinct security needs, and taking the time to customize its security layout will give you maximum security and the best performance.

The following list summarizes the most common mistakes:

▶ **Installing every package**—Do you plan to use the machine as a DNS server? If not, why have BIND installed? Go through and ensure that you have only the software you need.

▶ **Enabling unused services**—Do you want to administer the machine remotely? Do you want people to upload files? If not, turn off SSH and FTP because they just add needless attack vectors. This goes for many other services.

▶ **Disabling the local firewall on the grounds that you already have a firewall at the perimeter**—In security, depth is crucial: The more layers someone has to hack through, the higher the likelihood the cracker will give up or get caught.

▶ **Letting your machine give out more information than it needs to**—Many machines are configured to give out software names and version numbers by default, which is just giving crackers a helping hand.

▶ **Placing your server in an unlocked room**—If you do, you might as well just turn it off now and save the worry. The exception to this is if all the employees at your company are happy and trustworthy. But why take the risk?

▶ **Plugging your machine into a wireless network**—Unless you need wireless, avoid it, particularly if your machine is a server. Never plug a server into a wireless network because it is just too fraught with security problems.

After you have ruled out these potential issues, you are onto the real problem: Which attack vectors are open on your server? In Internet terms, this comes down to which services are Internet-facing and which ports they are running on.

Two tools are often used to determine your vulnerabilities: Nmap and Nessus. The nmap package is available in the Ubuntu software repositories. If you want Nessus, you will have to download it from their website at http://www.tenable.com/products/nessus.

Nessus scans your machine, queries the services running, checks their version numbers against its list of vulnerabilities, and reports problems.

Although Nessus sounds clever, it does not work well in many modern distributions (Ubuntu included) because of the way patches are made available to software. For example, if you're running Apache 2.2.21 and a bug is found that's fixed in 2.2.22, Ubuntu backports that patch to 2.2.21. This is done because the new release probably also includes new features that might break your code, so the Ubuntu team takes only what is necessary and copies it into your version. As a result, Nessus sees the version 2.2.21 and thinks it is vulnerable to a bug that has in fact been backported.

The better solution is to use Nmap, which scans your machine and reports on any open TCP/IP ports it finds. Any service you have installed that responds to Nmap's query is pointed out, which enables you to ensure that you have locked everything down as much as possible.

Nmap is available to install from the Ubuntu software repositories. Although you can use Nmap from a command line, it is easier to use with the front end—at least until you become proficient. To run the front end, open a terminal and run `nmapfe`. If you want to enable all Nmap's options, you must have administrator privileges and run `sudo nmapfe`.

When you run Nmap (click the Scan button), it tests every port on your machine and checks whether it responds. If a port does respond, Nmap queries it for version information and then prints its results onscreen.

The output lists the port numbers, service name (what usually occupies that port), and version number for every open port on your system. Hopefully, the information Nmap shows you will not be a surprise. If there is something open that you do not recognize, it could be that a cracker placed a back door on your system to allow easy access, so you should check into it further.

Use the output from Nmap to help you find and eliminate unwanted services. The fewer services that are open to the outside world, the more secure you are. Only use Nmap on systems that you own. It is impolite to scan other people's servers, and you may also be accused of doing so in preparation for illegal activity.

Protecting Your Machine

After you have disabled all the unneeded services on your system, what remains is a core set of connections and programs that you want to keep. However, you are not finished yet: You need to clamp down your wireless network, lock your server physically, and put scanning procedures in place (such as Tripwire and promiscuous mode network monitors).

Securing a Wireless Network

Because wireless networking has some unique security issues, those issues deserve a separate discussion.

Wireless networking, although convenient, can be very unsecure by its very nature because transmitted data (even encrypted data) can be received by remote devices. Those devices could be in the same room; in the house, apartment, or building next door; or even several blocks away. You must use extra care to protect the actual frequency used by your network. Great progress has been made in the past couple of years, but the possibility of a security breach is increased when the attacker is in the area and knows the frequency on which to listen. It should also be noted that the encryption method used by more wireless NICs is weaker than other forms of encryption (such as SSH), and you should not consider it as part of your security plan.

> **TIP**
>
> Always use OpenSSH-related tools, such as `ssh` or `sftp`, to conduct business on your wireless LAN. Passwords are not transmitted as plain text, and your sessions are encrypted. See Chapter 19, "Remote Access with SSH, Telnet, and VNC," to see how to connect to remote systems using `ssh`.

The better the physical security is around your network, the more secure it will be. (This applies to wired networks as well.) Keep wireless transmitters (routers, switches, and so on) as close to the center of your building as possible. Note or monitor the range of transmitted signals to determine whether your network is open to mobile network sniffing—now a geek sport known as *war driving*. Wireshark is an example of a program that is useful for analyzing wireless traffic (as well as all network activity). An occasional walk around your building not only gives you a break from sitting at your desk, but can also give you a chance to notice any people or equipment that should not be in the area.

Keep in mind that it takes only a single rogue wireless access point hooked up to a legitimate network hub to open access to your entire system. These access points can be smaller than a pack of cigarettes, so the only way to spot them is to scan for them with another wireless device.

Passwords and Physical Security

The next step toward better security is to use secure passwords on your network and ensure that users use them as well. For somewhat more physical security, you can force the use of a password with the GRUB bootloader, remove bootable devices such as floppy and CD-ROM drives, or configure a network-booting server for Ubuntu.

Also keep in mind that some studies show that as many as 90 percent of network break-ins are done by current or former employees. If a person no longer requires access to your network, lock out access or, even better, remove the account immediately. A good security policy also dictates that any data associated with the account first be backed up

20

and retained for a set period of time to ensure against loss of important data. If you are able to, remove the terminated employee from the system before the employee leaves the building.

Finally, be aware of physical security. If a potential attacker can get physical access to your system, getting full access becomes trivial. Keep all servers in a locked room and ensure that only authorized personnel are given access to clients. Laptops and other mobile devices should be configured with only what is needed and any truly sensitive data should be kept on machines that are physically secured. When machines containing any sensitive data must be used outside of a secure environment, you should use hard drive encryption, such as is available when installing Ubuntu.

Something that you may find useful for laptops and other mobile devices is Prey. Prey has a basic version that is open source, free software that will help you track down a missing device, provided it was installed on the device before it was lost. There is also a paid version with a few more features. You can learn about Prey from their website at http://preyproject.com/.

Configuring and Using Tripwire

Tripwire is a security tool that checks the integrity of normal system binaries and reports any changes to syslog or by email. Tripwire is a good tool for ensuring that your binaries have not been replaced by Trojan horse programs. *Trojan horses* are malicious programs inadvertently installed because of identical filenames to distributed (expected) programs, and they can wreak havoc on a breached system.

There are two versions of Tripwire, an open-source version and a commercial product. The free version of Tripwire is available in the Ubuntu repositories. You can find out about the differences at www.tripwire.org.

To initialize Tripwire, use its -init option, like this:

```
matthew@seymour~:$ sudo tripwire -init
Please enter your local passphrase:
Parsing policy file: /etc/tripwire/tw.pol
Generating the database...
*** Processing Unix File System ***
....
Wrote database file: /var/lib/tripwire/shuttle2.twd
The database was successfully generated.
```

Note that not all the output is shown here. After Tripwire has created its database (which is a snapshot of your file system), it uses this baseline along with the encrypted configuration and policy settings under the /etc/tripwire directory to monitor the status of your system. You should then start Tripwire in its integrity checking mode, using a desired option. (See the tripwire manual page for details.) For example, you can have Tripwire check your system and then generate a report at the command line, like this:

```
matthew@seymour~:$ sudo tripwire -m c
```

No output is shown here, but a report is displayed in this example. The output could be redirected to a file, but a report is saved as /var/lib/tripwire/report/hostname-YYYYMMDD-HHMMSS.twr (in other words, using your host's name, the year, the month, the day, the hour, the minute, and the seconds). This report can be read using the twprint utility, like this:

```
matthew@seymour~:$ sudo twprint—print-report -r \
/var/lib/tripwire/report/shuttle2-20020919-181049.twr | less
```

Other options, such as emailing the report, are supported by Tripwire, which should be run as a scheduled task by your system's scheduling table, /etc/crontab, on off-hours. (It can be resource intensive on less powerful computers.) The Tripwire software package also includes a twadmin utility you can use to fine-tune or change settings or policies or to perform other administrative duties.

Plan to spend some time reading documentation if you want to use Tripwire. It is powerful but not simple. We recommend starting with the man pages and www.tripwire.com.

Devices

Do not ever advertise that you have set a NIC to promiscuous mode. Promiscuous mode (which can be set on an interface by using ifconfig's promisc option) is good for monitoring traffic across the network and can often enable you to monitor the actions of someone who might have broken into your network. The tcpdump command also sets a designated interface to promiscuous mode while the program runs; unfortunately, the ifconfig command does not report this fact while tcpdump is running!

Remember to use the right tool for the right job. Although you can use a network bridge to connect your network to the Internet, it would not be a good option. Bridges have almost become obsolete because they forward any packet that comes their way, which is not good when a bridge is connected to the Internet. A router enables you to filter which packets are relayed.

Viruses

In the right hands, Linux is every bit as vulnerable to viruses as Windows is. That might come as a surprise to you, particularly if you made the switch to Linux on the basis of its security record. However, the difference between Windows and Linux is that it is much easier to secure against viruses on Linux. Indeed, as long as you are smart and diligent, you need never worry about them. Here is why:

▶ Linux never puts the current directory in your executable path, so typing ls runs /bin/ls rather than any program named ls in the current directory.

▶ A nonroot user can infect only the files that user has write access to, which is usually only the files in the user's home directory. This is one of the most important reasons for never using sudo when you don't need to.

20

▶ Linux forces you to manually mark files as executable, so you can't accidentally run a file called `myfile.txt.exe` thinking it is just a text file.

▶ By having more than one common web browser and email client, Linux has strength through diversity: Virus writers cannot target one platform and hit 90 percent of the users.

Despite all that, Linux is susceptible to being a carrier for viruses. If you run a mail server, your Linux box can send virus-infected mails on to Windows boxes. The Linux-based server would be fine, but the Windows client would be taken down by the virus.

In this situation, consider a virus scanner for your machine. You have several to choose from, both free and commercial. The most popular free suite is Clam AV (www.clamav.net), but Central Command, BitDefender, F-Secure, Kaspersky, McAfee, and others all compete to provide commercial solutions. Look around for the best deal before you commit.

Configuring Your Firewall

Always use a hardware-based or software-based firewall on computers connected to the Internet. Ubuntu has a firewall application installed by default named *Uncomplicated Firewall (UFW)*. This tool enables you to implement selective or restrictive policies regarding access to your computer or LAN.

UFW is run from the terminal, and you must have administrative privileges to use it. Commands are given like this:

matthew@seymour~:$ **sudo ufw status**

The most useful commands are listed in Table 20.1. For others, the UFW man page. Many are described in greater detail after the table.

By default, the UFW or firewall is disabled. To enable the firewall, you run the following command:

matthew@seymour~:$ **sudo ufw enable**

To disable, replace `enable` with `disable`.

TABLE 20.1   Useful Commands for UFW

Command	Actions Performed
`Usage: sudo ufw COMMAND`	
`enable`	Enables the firewall
`disable`	Disables the firewall
`reload`	Reloads the firewall to ensure changes are applied
`default allow|deny|reject`	Sets default policy
`logging on|off`	Toggles logging (can also be used to set the level of logging, see manual)
`allow ARGS`	Adds allow rule

`deny ARGS`	Adds deny rule
`reject ARGS`	Adds reject rule
`limit ARGS`	Adds limit rule
`delete RULE`	Deletes rule
`status shows`	Firewall status
`status numbered`	Shows firewall status as numbered list of rules
`Usage: ufw COMMAND`	
`status verbose`	Shows verbose firewall status
`show REPORT`	Shows firewall report
`-version`	Displays version information

Next, you want to enable firewall logging. Much like the `enable` command, you run the following command:

`matthew@seymour~:$ `**`sudo ufw logging on`**

To enable specific ports on the firewall you can run the `ufw` command along with the port number to open. For example, if you want to allow port 80 (HTTP) incoming connections to your Ubuntu server you enter the following:

`matthew@seymour~:$ `**`sudo ufw allow 80`**

To remove the firewall rule allowing port 80 connections, run the following command:

`matthew@seymour~:$ `**`sudo ufw delete allow 80`**

Many services are already defined in `ufw`. This means you don't have to remember the standard ports those services use, and you can allow, deny, or delete using the service name, like this:

`matthew@seymour~:$ `**`sudo ufw allow ssh`**

You can also allow incoming connections from particular IP addresses. For example, if you want to let 192.168.0.1 to connect to your server, you enter the following:

`matthew@seymour~:$ `**`sudo ufw allow from 192.168.0.1`**

To remove the firewall rule allowing the previous IP address to connect, run the following command:

`matthew@seymour~:$ `**`sudo ufw delete allow from 192.168.0.1`**

There is a graphical interface that you can install from the Ubuntu repositories to manage UFW called *GUFW*. The same details apply, but the interface is easier and does not require you to remember as much, as you can see in Figure 20.1 where we have a rule to allow traffic in on port 22 (for the SSH service) and incoming traffic on port 5900 if it uses TCP (for the VNC service).

If you click Add, you can easily add rules for preconfigured services, as shown in Figure 20.2, or you can configure your own rules from the Simple and Advanced tabs.

20

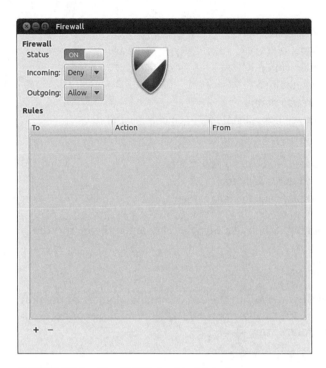

FIGURE 20.1   The GUFW graphical interface.

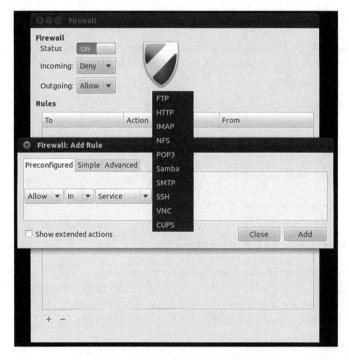

FIGURE 20.2   GUFW preconfigured service options.

UFW is based on `iptables`, which are tables used to configure the Linux kernel's built-in firewall. UFW simplifies the user tasks and syntax, but is really just using `iptables`. You probably won't need to know this on your Ubuntu machine, but for completeness and to help you if you use a different Linux distribution in the future, Table 20.2 lists simple, basic commands as a brief introduction to `iptables`, just to whet your appetite.

In the table, you will see words in all-caps like ACCEPT and DROP, which are policies to be set for things called chains. Chains are descriptions of specific types of network access, such as you can see below as INPUT, FORWARD, and OUTPUT. And other interactions in a network. You can, for example, define the default policy as DROP, which means to reject, and then ALLOW specific types of traffic to go through the firewall. `iptables` is quite complex and incredibly powerful.

TABLE 20.2   Useful Commands for iptables

Command	Actions Performed
Usage: COMMAND	
sudo iptables -L	Lists currently set firewall rules
sudo iptables -L -vn	Lists currently set firewall rules, but with more detail
sudo iptables -F	Deletes all currently set firewall rules
sudo iptables -P INPUT DROP	Drops all incoming traffic
sudo iptables -P FORWARD ACCEPT	Accepts all forwarded traffic
sudo iptables -P OUTPUT DROP	Drops all outgoing traffic
sudo iptables -A INPUT -s 8.8.8.8 -j DROP	Drops all traffic from a specific IP (the example is a Google DNS server, you probably don't want to block that one...)

You can block or allow traffic based on IP address, NIC, port, network, and more. You can set `iptables` to log all actions or just specific actions. You can even use it to configure NAT routers. For more, see the man pages for `iptables` and its IPv6 cousin, `ip6tables`.

AppArmor

AppArmor is a *mandatory access control (MAC)* system. It is less complicated than the better known SELinux (www.nsa.gov/research/selinux/), a MAC created by the U.S. *National Security Agency (NSA)*. AppArmor is designed to limit what specific programs can do by restricting them to the use of predetermined resources and only those resources. This is done via profiles, which are loaded into the kernel at boot. It can be run in complain mode, where information is logged about unsecure practices but no action is taken, or in enforce mode, where policies and limits are active.

This is a brief introduction to AppArmor. For a fuller introduction, check the links listed in the "References" section at the end of this chapter.

20

By default, AppArmor does little. You can install some extra profiles from the Ubuntu repositories by installing the `apparmor-profiles` package. These run in complain mode and log issues in `/var/log/messages`.

To unleash the power of AppArmor, you need to edit or create text files in `/etc/apparmor.d`. Profiles are named for the application they restrict, including the full path to the application in the filesystem. For example, the file `sbin.rsyslogd`, shown here, restricts the system logging daemon:

```
# Last Modified: Sun Sep 25 08:58:35 2011


#include <tunables/global>
# Debugging the syslogger can be difficult if it can't write to the file# that the
kernel is logging denials to. In these cases, you can do the# following:# watch -n 1
'dmesg | tail -5'
/usr/sbin/rsyslogd {  #include <abstractions/base>  #include <abstractions/
nameservice>
  capability sys_tty_config,  capability dac_override,  capability dac_read_search,
capability setuid,  capability setgid,  capability sys_nice,  capability syslog,
  # rsyslog configuration  /etc/rsyslog.conf r,  /etc/rsyslog.d/ r,  /etc/
rsyslog.d/** r,  /{,var/}run/rsyslogd.pid rwk,  /var/spool/rsyslog/ r,  /var/spool/
rsyslog/** rwk,
  /usr/lib{,32,64}/rsyslog/*.so mr,
  /dev/tty*                   rw,  /dev/xconsole                   rw,  @{PROC}/
kmsg            r,
  /dev/log                  wl,  /var/lib/*/dev/log                  wl,  /var/spool/
postfix/dev/log     wl,
  # 'r' is needed when using imfile  /var/log/**                   rw,
  # Add these for mysql support  #/etc/mysql/my.cnf r,  #/{,var/}run/mysqld/mysqld.
sock rw,
  # Add thes for postgresql support  ##include <abstractions/openssl>  ##include
<abstractions/ssl_certs>  #/{,var/}run/postgresql/.s.PGSQL.*[0-9] rw,
  # Site-specific additions and overrides. See local/README for details.  #include
<local/usr.sbin.rsyslogd>}
```

Even without knowing the syntax, you can see from this file that profiles are simple text files that support the use of comments, that absolute paths and globbing (pattern matching for filenames) are supported, that specific capabilities are allowed or disallowed, and what locations and programs in the filesystem may be accessed or used.

Each access rule specifies specific permissions from this list:

```
r    - read
w    - write
ux   - unconstrained execute
Ux   - unconstrained execute - scrub the environment
px   - discrete profile execute
Px   - discrete profile execute - scrub the environment
```

```
ix   - inherit execute
m    - allow PROT_EXEC with mmap(2) calls
l    - link
```

These permissions are listed at the end of lines.

Genprof is a program that helps you generate or update a profile. You supply the name of the executable (or the path, if it is not already in the path) and may optionally supply the path to the profiles, as well:

```
matthew@seymour~:$ sudo genprof google-chrome
```

You will be asked to start the program and use it for a bit. After it is complete, you are given an opportunity to choose whether access to each function should be allowed or denied. The program then writes a text file in /etc/apparmor.d using the name of the program and its path (in this case, opt.google.chrome.google-chrome, which I installed directly from Google [www.google.com/chrome?platform=linux], so no premade AppArmor profile exists on my system). You may then edit the text file as desired, which you must do if you want to change from complain to enforce mode.

After you have a set of profiles that cover what you need, these are the commands you will use most often:

```
start:
matthew@seymour~:$ sudo service apparmor start
```

```
stop:
matthew@seymour~:$ sudo service apparmor stop
```

```
reload:
matthew@seymour~:$ sudo service apparmor reload (or restart)
```

```
show status:
matthew@seymour~:$ sudo service apparmor status
```

We have just scratched the surface of AppArmor, but hopefully we have given you enough information to have whetted your appetite to do some further reading.

Forming a Disaster Recovery Plan

No one likes planning for the worst, which is why two-thirds of people do not have wills. It is a scary thing to have your systems hacked: One or more criminals has broken through your carefully laid blocks and caused untold damage to the machine. Your boss, if you have one, wants a full report of what happened and why, and your users want their email when they sit down at their desks in the morning. What to do?

20

If you ever do get hacked, nothing will take the stress away entirely. However, if you take the time to prepare a proper response in advance, you should at least avoid premature aging. Here are some tips to get you started:

▶ **Do not just pull the network cable out**—This acts as an alert that the cracker has been detected, which rules out any opportunities for security experts to monitor for that cracker returning and actually catching him.

▶ **Only inform the people who need to know**—Your boss and other IT people are at the top of the list; other employees are not. Keep in mind that it could be one of the employees behind the attack, and this tips them off.

▶ **If the machine is not required and you do not want to trace the attack, you can safely remove it from the network**—However, do not switch it off because some backdoors are enabled only when the system is rebooted.

▶ **Take a copy of all the log files on the system and store them somewhere else**—These might have been tampered with, but they might contain nuggets of information.

▶ **Check the /etc/passwd file and look for users you do not recognize**—Change all the passwords on the system and remove bad users.

▶ **Check the output of ps aux for unusual programs running**—Also check to see whether any `cron` jobs are set to run.

▶ **Look in /var/www and see whether any web pages are there that should not be.**

▶ **Check the contents of the .bash_history files in the /home directories of your users.** Are there any recent commands for your primary user?

▶ **If you have worked with external security companies previously, call them in for a fresh audit**—Hand over all the logs you have and explain the situation. They will be able to extract all the information from the logs that is possible.

▶ **Start collating backup tapes from previous weeks and months**—Your system might have been hacked long before you noticed, so you might need to roll back the system more than once to find out when the attack actually succeeded.

▶ **Download and install Rootkit Hunter from www.rootkit.nl/projects/rootkit _hunter.html**—This searches for (and removes) the types of files that bad guys leave behind for their return.

Keep your disaster recovery plan somewhere safe; saving it as a file on the machine in question is a *very* bad move.

References

▶ **https://help.ubuntu.com/community/InstallingSecurityTools**—Ubuntu community documentation of and suggestions for various security tools.

▶ **https://nmap.org**—The official site for Nmap.

▶ **www.tripwire.org**—Information and download links for the open-source version of Tripwire.

▶ **www.ubuntu.com/usn**—The official Ubuntu security notices list; well worth keeping an eye on.

▶ **https://help.ubuntu.com/community/UFW**—Ubuntu community documentation for UFW.

▶ **https://wiki.ubuntu.com/UncomplicatedFirewall**—Ubuntu documentation for UFW.

▶ **http://wiki.apparmor.net/**—The official documentation for AppArmor.

▶ **https://help.ubuntu.com/community/AppArmor**—Ubuntu community documentation for AppArmor.

▶ **https://wiki.ubuntu.com/Security/Features**—An Ubuntu wiki page outlining and describing security features, Ubuntu, and configuration.

20

Performance Tuning

Squeezing extra performance out of your hardware might sound like a pointless task given how cheap commodity upgrades are today. To a certain degree that is true; for most of us, it is cheaper to buy a new computer than to spend hours fighting to get a 5 percent speed boost. But what if the speed boost were 20 percent? How about if it were 50 percent?

The amount of benefit you can get by optimizing your system varies depending on what kinds of tasks you are running, but there is something for everyone. Over the next few pages we look at quick ways to optimize the Apache web server, both the KDE and GNOME desktop systems, both MySQL and PostgreSQL database servers, and more.

Before we start, you need to understand that *optimization* is not an absolute term: If we optimize a system, we have improved its performance, but it is still possible it could further be increased. We are not interested in getting 99.999 percent performance out of a system because optimization suffers from the law of diminishing returns—the basic changes make the biggest differences, but after that it takes increasing amounts of work to obtain decreasing speed improvements.

Hard Disk

Many Linux users love to tinker under the hood to increase the performance of their computers, and Linux gives you some great tools to do that. Whereas stability-loving nurturers generally tell us, "Don't fix what's not broken," experiment-loving hot-rodders often say, "Fix it until it breaks." In this section, you learn about many of the commands used to tune, or "tweak," your file system.

Before you undertake any under-the-hood work with Linux, however, keep a few points in mind. First, perform a benchmark on your system before you begin. Linux does not offer a well-developed benchmarking application, and availability of what exists changes rapidly. You can search online for the most up-to-date information for benchmarking applications for Linux. If you are a system administrator, you might choose to create your own bench-marking tests. Second, tweak only one thing at a time so you can tell what works, what does not work, and what breaks things. Some of these tweaks might not work or might lock up your machine, but if you are only implementing them one at a time, you will find it much easier to reverse a change that caused a problem.

Always have a working boot disc handy, such as the live Ubuntu CD or DVD. Remember that you are personally assuming all risks for attempting any of these tweaks. If you don't understand what you are doing or are not confident in your ability to revert any changes discussed here, do not attempt any of the suggestions in this chapter. The default settings in Ubuntu work very well for most people and really don't need adjusting; just as most people can use and enjoy their car just as it is. However, some people love taking their cars apart and building hot rods; they enjoy tweaking and breaking and fixing them. This chapter is for that sort of person. If you don't think you can fix it, don't risk breaking it.

Using the BIOS and Kernel to Tune the Disk Drives

One method of tuning involves adjusting the settings in your BIOS. Because the BIOS is not Linux and every BIOS seems different, always read your motherboard manual for better possible settings and make certain that all the drives are detected correctly by the BIOS. Change only one setting at a time.

Linux provides a limited means to interact with BIOS settings during the boot process (mostly overriding them). In this section, you learn about those commands.

Other options are in the following list and are more fully outlined in the BOOTPROMPT HOWTO and the kernel documentation. These commands can be used to force the IDE controllers and drives to be optimally configured. However, YMMV (your mileage may vary) because these do not work for everyone.

- **idex=dma**—This forces DMA support to be turned on for the primary IDE bus, where x=0, or the secondary bus, where x=1.

- **idex=autotune**—This command attempts to tune the interface for optimal performance.

- **hdx=ide-scsi**—This command enables SCSI emulation of an IDE drive. This is required for some CD-RW drives to work properly in write mode, and it might provide some performance improvements for regular CD-R drives, as well.

- **idebus=xx**—This can be any number from 20 to 66; autodetection is attempted, but this can set it manually if dmesg says that it isn't autodetected correctly or if you have it set in the BIOS to a different value (overclocked). Most PCI controllers are happy with 33.

- **pci=biosirq**—Some motherboards might cause Linux to generate an error message saying that you should use this. Look in dmesg for it; if you do not see it, you don't need to use it.

These options can be entered into `/etc/lilo.conf` or `/boot/grub/grub.conf` or GRUB2's `/boot/grub/grub.cfg` in the same way as other options are appended.

The `hdparm` **Command**

The `hdparm` utility can be used by root to set and tune the settings for IDE hard drives. You would do this to tune the drives for optimal performance. After previously requiring a kernel patch and installation of associated support programs, the `hdparm` program is now included with Ubuntu. You should only experiment with the file systems mounted read-only because some settings can damage some file systems when used improperly. The `hdparm` command also works with CD-ROM drives and some SCSI drives.

The general format of the command is this:

```
matthew@seymour:~$ hdparm command device
```

The following command runs a hard disk test:

```
matthew@seymour:~$ hdparm -tT /dev/hda
```

You must replace `/dev/hda` with the location of your hard disk. `hdparm` then runs two tests: cached reads and buffered disk reads. A good IDE hard disk should be getting 400MBps to 500MBps for the first test, and 20MBps to 30MBps for the second. Note your scores and then try this command:

```
matthew@seymour:~$ hdparm -m16 -d1 -u1 -c1 /dev/hda
```

That enables various performance-enhancing settings. Now try executing the original command again. If your scores increase from the previous measurement, you should run this command:

```
matthew@seymour:~$ hdparm -m16 -d1 -u1 -c1 -k1 /dev/hda
```

The extra parameter tells `hdparm` to write the settings to disk so that they will be used each time you boot, ensuring optimal disk performance in the future.

The man entry for `hdparm` is extensive and contains useful detailed information, but because the kernel configuration selected by Ubuntu already attempts to optimize the drives, it might be that little can be gained through tweaking. Because not all hardware combinations can be anticipated by Ubuntu or by Linux, and performance gains are always useful, you're encouraged to try.

TIP

You can use the `hdparm` command to produce a disk transfer speed result with

```
matthew@seymour:~$ hdparm -tT device
```

Be aware, however, that although the resulting numbers appear quantitative, they are subject to several technical qualifications beyond the scope of what is discussed and explained in this chapter. Simply put, do not accept values generated by `hdparm` as absolute numbers, but only as a relative measure of performance.

File System Tuning

Never content to leave things alone, Linux provides several tools to adjust and customize the file system settings. The belief is that hardware manufacturers and distribution creators tend to select conservative settings that will work well all the time, leaving some of the potential of your system leashed—that's why you have chosen *Ubuntu Unleashed* to help you.

The Linux file system designers have done an excellent job of selecting default values used for file system creation, and any version of the Linux kernel after 2.6.x contains code for the IDE subsystem that significantly improves *I/O (input/output)* transfer speeds over older versions, obviating much of the need for special tweaking of the file system and drive parameters if you use IDE disks. Although these values work well for most users, some server applications of Linux benefit from file system tuning. As always, observe and benchmark your changes.

SYNCHRONIZING THE FILE SYSTEM WITH SYNC

Because Linux uses buffers when writing to devices, the write will not occur until the buffer is full, until the kernel tells it to, or if you tell it to by using the `sync` command. Traditionally, the command is given twice, as in the following:

```
matthew@seymour:~$ sync ; sync
```

To do it twice is overkill. Still, it can be helpful before the unmounting of certain types of media with slow write speeds (such as some USB hard drives or PCMCIA storage media), but only because it delays the user from attempting to remove the media too soon, not because two syncs are better than one.

The `tune2fs` Command

With `tune2fs`, you can adjust the tunable file system parameters on an `ext2` or `ext3` file system. A few performance-related items of note are as follows:

▶ To disable file system checking, the `-c 0` option sets the maximal mount count to zero.

▶ The interval between forced checks can be adjusted with the `-i` option.

▶ The `-m` option sets the reserved blocks percentage with a lower value, freeing more space at the expense of `fsck` having less space to write any recovered files.

▶ Decrease the number of superblocks to save space with the `-O sparse_super` option. (Modern file systems use this by default.) Always run `e2fsck` after you change this value.

▶ More space can be freed with the `-r` option that sets the number of reserved (for root) blocks.

Note that most of these uses of `tune2fs` free up space on the drive at the expense of the capability of `fsck` to recover data. Unless you really need the space and can deal with the consequences, just accept the defaults; large drives are now relatively inexpensive.

The `e2fsck` Command

This utility checks an `ext2/ext3` file system. Some useful arguments taken from `man e2fsck` are as follows:

▶ -c—Checks for bad blocks and then marks them as bad

▶ -f—Forces checking on a clean file system

▶ -v—Verbose mode

The `badblocks` Command

Although not a performance-tuning program per se, the utility `badblocks` checks an (preferably) unmounted partition for bad blocks. It is not recommended that you run this command by itself, but rather allow it to be called by `fsck`. It should be used directly only if you specify the block size accurately; don't guess or assume anything.

The options available for `badblocks` are detailed in the man page. They allow for very low-level manipulation of the file system that is useful for data recovery by file system experts or for file system hacking, but they are beyond the scope of this chapter and the average user.

Disabling File Access Time

Whenever Linux reads a file, it changes the last access time (known as the *atime*). This is also true for your web server: If you are getting hit by 50 requests a second, your hard disk will be updating the atime 50 times a second. Do you really need to know the last time a file was accessed? If not, you can disable the atime setting for a directory by typing this:

```
matthew@seymour:~$ chattr -R +A /path/to/directory
```

The `chattr` command changes file system attributes, of which "don't update atime" is one. To set that attribute, use `+A` and specify `-R` so that it is recursively set. `/path/to/directory` gets changed, and so do all the files and subdirectories it contains.

Kernel

As the Linux kernel developed over time, developers sought a way to fine-tune some of the kernel parameters. Before `sysctl`, those parameters had to be changed in the kernel configuration, and then the kernel had to be recompiled.

The `sysctl` command can change some parameters of a running kernel. It does this through the `/proc` file system, which is a "virtual window" into the running kernel. Although it might appear that a group of directories and files exist under `/proc`, that is only a representation of parts of the kernel. When you're the root user (or using the `sudo` command), you can read values from and write values to those "files," referred to as *variables*. You can display a list of the variables as shown in the following. (An abbreviated list is presented because roughly 250 items, or more, exist in the full list.)

```
matthew@seymour:~$ sysctl -A
net.ipv4.tcp_max_syn_backlog = 1024
net.ipv4.tcp_rfc1337 = 0
net.ipv4.tcp_stdurg = 0
net.ipv4.tcp_abort_on_overflow = 0
net.ipv4.tcp_tw_recycle = 0
net.ipv4.tcp_syncookies = 0
net.ipv4.tcp_fin_timeout = 60
net.ipv4.tcp_retries2 = 15
net.ipv4.tcp_retries1 = 3
net.ipv4.tcp_keepalive_intvl = 75
net.ipv4.tcp_keepalive_probes = 9
net.ipv4.tcp_keepalive_time = 7200
net.ipv4.ipfrag_time = 30
```

The items shown are networking parameters, and tweaking these values is beyond the scope of this book. If you want to change a value, however, you use the -w parameter:

```
matthew@seymour:~$ sysctl -w net.ipv4.tcp_retries 2=20
```

This increases the value of that particular kernel parameter.

If you find that a particular setting is useful, you can enter it into the /etc/sysctl.conf file. The format is as follows, using the earlier example:

```
net.ipv4.tcp_retries 2=20
```

Of more interest to kernel hackers than regular users, sysctl is a potentially powerful tool that continues to be developed and documented.

TIP

The kernel does a good job of balancing performance for graphical systems, so there's not a great deal you can do to tweak your desktop to run faster.

Both GNOME and KDE are "heavyweight" desktop systems: They are all-inclusive, all-singing, and all-dancing environments that do far more than browse your file system. The drawback is that their size makes them run slow on older systems. On the flip side, Ubuntu has others available in the repositories like the Xfce and LXDE desktops, which are a great deal slimmer and faster than the other two. If you find GNOME and KDE are struggling just to open a file browser, Xfce or LXDE are likely for you.

Apache

Despite being the most popular web server on the Internet, Apache is by no means the fastest. Part of the "problem" is that Apache has been written to follow every applicable standard to the letter, so much of its development work has been geared toward standards compliancy rather than just serving web pages quickly. However, with a little tweaking you can convert an inexpensive middle-of-the-road server into something capable of surviving the Slashdot Effect (or "being Slashdotted").

> **NOTE**
>
> Slashdot.org is a popular geek news website that spawned the Slashdot Effect—the result of thousands of geeks descending on an unsuspecting website simultaneously. Although Slashdot is still popular, other sites are newer and have gained great momentum and popularity (we're looking at you, Reddit!). We are not trying to ignore the new sites, but rather honor the original. We freely acknowledge that many other wonderful sources of the effect exist.

The first target for your tuning should be the `apache2.conf` file in `/etc/apache2`, as well as the other files in `/etc/apache2`. The more modules you have loaded, the more load Apache is placing on your server. Take a look through the LoadModule list and comment out (start the line with a #) the ones you do not want. Some of these modules can be uninstalled entirely through the Add or Remove Packages dialog.

As a rough guide, you almost certainly need `mod_mime` and `mod_dir`, and probably also `mod_log_config`. The default Apache configuration in Ubuntu is quite generic, so unless you are willing to sacrifice some functionality you might also need `mod_negotiation` (a speed killer if there ever was one) and `mod_access` (a notorious problem). Both of those modules can and should work with little or no performance decrease, but all too often they get abused and just slow things down.

Whatever you do, when you are disabling modules you should ensure that you leave either `mod_deflate` or `mod_gzip` enabled, depending on your Apache version. Your bottleneck is almost certainly going to be your bandwidth rather than your processing power, and having one of these two compressing your content usually turns 10KB of HTML into 3KB for supported browsers (most of them).

Next, ensure keepalives are turned off. Yes, you read that right: Turn keepalives *off*. This adds some latency to people viewing your site because they cannot download multiple files through the same connection. However, it reduces the number of simultaneous open connections and so allows more people to connect.

If you are serving content that does not change, you can take the extreme step of enabling MMAP support. This allows Apache to serve pages directly from RAM without bothering to check whether they have changed, which works wonders for your performance. However, the downside is that when you do change your pages you need to restart Apache. Look for the `EnableMMAP` directive; it is probably commented out and set to off, so you will need to remove the comment and set it to on.

Finally, if speed is your greatest concern, you should do all you can to ensure that your content is static: Avoid PHP if you can, avoid databases if you can, and so on. If you know you are going to get hit by a rush of visitors, use plain HTML so that Apache is limited only by your bandwidth for how fast it can serve pages.

TIP

Some people, when questioned about optimizing Apache, recommend you tweak the `HARD_SERVER_LIMIT` in the Apache source code and recompile. Although we agree that compiling your own Apache source code is a great way to get a measurable speed boost if you know what you are doing, you should need to change this directive only if you are hosting a huge site.

The default value, `256`, is enough to handle the Slashdot Effect, and if you can handle that, then you can handle most things.

MySQL

Tuning your MySQL server for increased performance is exceptionally easy to do, largely because you can see huge speed increases simply by getting your queries right. However, you can tune various things in the server itself to help it cope with higher loads as long as your system has enough RAM.

The key is understanding its buffers. There are buffers and caches for all sorts of things, and finding out how full they are is crucial to maximizing performance. MySQL performs best when it is making full use of its buffers, which in turn places a heavy demand on system RAM. Unless you have 4GB RAM or more in your machine, you do not have enough capacity to set very high values for all your buffers; you need to pick and choose.

Measuring Key Buffer Usage

When you add indexes to your data, it enables MySQL to find data faster. However, ideally you want to have these indexes stored in RAM for maximum speed, and the variable `key_buffer_size` defines how much RAM MySQL can allocate for index key caching. If MySQL cannot store its indexes in RAM, you will experience serious performance problems. Fortunately, most databases have relatively small key buffer requirements, but you should measure your usage to see what work needs to be done.

To do this, log in to MySQL and type `SHOW STATUS LIKE '%key_read%';` that returns all the status fields that describe the hit rate of your key buffer. You should get two rows back: `Key_reads` and `Key_read_requests`, which are the number of keys being read from disk and the number of keys being read from the key buffer. From these two numbers you can calculate the percentage of requests being filled from RAM and from disk, using this simple equation:

```
100 - ((Key_reads / Key_read_requests) &infin; 100)
```

That is, you divide `Key_reads` by `Key_read_requests`, multiply the result by 100, and then subtract the result from 100. For example, if you have `Key_reads` of 1000 and `Key_read_requests` of 100000, you divide 1000 by 100000 to get 0.01; then you multiply that by 100 to get 1.0, and subtract that from 100 to get 99. That number is the percentage of key reads being served from RAM, which means 99 percent of your keys are served from RAM.

Most people should be looking to get more than 95 percent served from RAM, although the primary exception is if you update or delete rows very often—MySQL can't cache what keeps changing. If your site is largely read-only, this should be around 98 percent. Lower figures mean you might need to bump up the size of your key buffer.

If you are seeing problems, the next step is to check how much of your current key buffer is being used. Use the SHOW VARIABLES command and look up the value of the key_buffer_size variable. It is probably something like 8388600, which is 8 million bytes, or 8MB. Now, use the SHOW STATUS command and look up the value of Key_blocks_used.

You can determine how much of your key buffer is being used by multiplying Key_blocks_used by 1024, dividing by key_buffer_size, and multiplying by 100. For example, if Key_blocks_used is 8000, multiply that by 1024 to get 8192000; then divide that by your key_buffer_size (8388600) to get 0.97656, and finally multiply that by 100 to get 97.656. Thus, almost 98 percent of your key buffer is being used.

Now, the important part: You have ascertained that you are reading lots of keys from disk, and you also know that the reason for reading from disk is almost certainly because you do not have enough RAM allocated to the key buffer. A general rule is to allocate as much RAM to the key buffer as you can, up to a maximum of 25 percent of system RAM—128MB on a 512MB system is about the ideal for systems that read heavily from keys. Beyond that, you will actually see drastic performance decreases because the system has to use virtual memory for the key buffer.

Open /etc/my.cnf in your text editor and look for the line that contains key_buffer_size. If you do not have one, you need to create a new one. It should be under the line [mysqld]. When you set the new value, do not just pick some arbitrarily high number. Try doubling what is there right now (or try 16MB if there's no line already); then see how it goes. To set 16MB as the key buffer size, you need a line like this:

```
[mysqld]
set-variable = key_buffer_size=16M
datadir=/var/lib/mysql
```

Restart your MySQL server with service mysqld restart and then go back into MySQL and run SHOW VARIABLES again to see the key_buffer_size. It should be 16773120 if you have set it to 16M. Now, because MySQL just got reset, all its values for key hits and the like will also have been reset. You need to let it run for a while so that you can assess how much has changed. If you have a test system you can run, this is the time to run it.

After your database has been accessed with normal usage for a short while (if you get frequent accesses, this might be only a few minutes), recalculate how much of the key buffer is being used. If you get another high score, double the size again, restart, and retest. You should keep repeating this until your key buffer usage is below 50 percent or you find you don't have enough RAM to increase the buffer further. Remember that you should *never* allocate more than 25 percent of system RAM to the key buffer.

Using the Query Cache

Newer versions of MySQL allow you to cache the results of queries so that, if new queries come in that use the same SQL, the result can be served from RAM. In some ways the query cache is quite intelligent: If, for example, part of the result changes due to another query, the cached results are thrown away and recalculated next time. However, in other ways it is very simple. For example, it uses cached results only if the new query is exactly the same as a cached query, even down to the capitalization of the SQL.

The query cache works well in most scenarios. If your site has an equal mix of reading and writing, the query cache does its best but is not optimal. If your site is mostly reading with few writes, more queries are cached (and for longer), thus improving overall performance.

First, you need to find out whether you have the query cache enabled. To do this, use SHOW VARIABLES and look up the value of have_query_cache. All being well, you should get YES back, meaning that the query cache is enabled. Next, look for the value of query_cache_size and query_cache_limit. The first is how much RAM in bytes is allocated to the query cache, and the second is the maximum result size that should be cached. A good starting set of values for these two is 8388608 (8MB) and 1048576 (1MB).

Next, type SHOW STATUS LIKE 'qcache%'; to see all the status information about the query cache. You should get output like this:

```
mysql> SHOW STATUS LIKE 'qcache%';
+-------------------------+--------+
| Variable_name           | Value  |
+-------------------------+--------+
| Qcache_free_blocks      | 1      |
| Qcache_free_memory      | 169544 |
| Qcache_hits             | 698    |
| Qcache_inserts          | 38     |
| Qcache_lowmem_prunes    | 20     |
| Qcache_not_cached       | 0      |
| Qcache_queries_in_cache | 18     |
| Qcache_total_blocks     | 57     |
+-------------------------+--------+
8 rows in set (0.00 sec)
```

From that, we can see that only 18 queries are in the cache (Qcache_queries_in_cache); we have 169544 bytes of memory free in the cache (Qcache_free_memory), 698 queries have been read from the cache (Qcache_hits), 38 queries have been inserted into the cache (Qcache_inserts), but 20 of them were removed due to lack of memory (Qcache_lowmem_prunes), giving the 18 from before. Qcache_not_cached is 0, which means 0 queries were not cached—MySQL is caching them all.

From that, we can calculate how many total queries came in—it is the sum of Qcache_hits, Qcache_inserts, and Qcache_not_cached, which is 736. We can also calculate how well the query cache is being used by dividing Qcache_hits by that number and multiplying by 100. In this case, 94.84 percent of all queries are being served from the query cache, which is a great number.

In our example, we can see that many queries have been trimmed because there is not enough memory in the query cache. This can be changed by editing your `/etc/my.cnf` file and adding a line like this one, somewhere in the `[mysqld]` section:

```
set-variable = query_cache_size=32M.
```

An 8MB query cache should be enough for most people, but larger sites might need 16MB or even 32MB if you are storing a particularly large amount of data. Very few sites will need to go beyond a 32MB query cache, but keep an eye on the `Qcache_lowmem_prunes` value to ensure you have enough RAM allocated.

Using the query cache does not incur much of a performance hit. When MySQL calculates the result of a query normally, it throws it away when the connection closes. With the query cache, it skips the throwing away, and so there is no extra work being done. If your site does have many updates and deletes, be sure to check whether you get any speed boost at all from the query cache.

Miscellaneous Tweaks

If you have tuned your key buffer and optimized your query cache and yet still find your site struggling, you can make a handful of smaller changes that will add some more speed.

When reading from tables, MySQL has to open the file that stores the table data. How many files it keeps open at a time is defined by the `table_cache` setting, which is set to 64 by default. You can increase this setting if you have more than 64 tables, but be aware that Ubuntu imposes limits on MySQL about how many files it can have open at a time. Going beyond 256 is not recommended unless you have a particularly database-heavy site and know exactly what you are doing.

The other thing you can tweak is the size of the read buffer, which is controlled by `read_buffer_size` and `read_buffer_rnd_size`. Both of these are allocated per connection, which means you should be very careful to have large numbers. Whatever you choose, `read_buffer_rnd_size` should be three to four times the size of `read_buffer_size`, so if `read_buffer_size` is 1MB (suitable for very large databases), `read_buffer_rnd_size` should be 4MB.

Query Optimization

The biggest speed-ups can be seen by reprogramming your SQL statements so they are more efficient. If you follow these tips, your server will thank you:

▶ Select as little data as possible. Rather than SELECT *, select only the fields you need.

▶ If you need only a few rows, use LIMIT to select the number you need.

▶ Declare fields as NOT NULL when creating tables to save space and increase speed.

▶ Provide default values for fields and use them where you can.

▶ Be very careful with table joins because they are the easiest way to write inefficient queries.

▶ If you must use joins, be sure you join on fields that are indexed. They should also preferably be integer fields because these are faster than strings for comparisons.

▶ Find and fix slow queries. Add `log-long-format` and `log-slow-queries = /var/log/slow-queries.log` to your `/etc/my.cnf` file, under `[mysqld]`, and MySQL tells you the queries that took a long time to complete.

▶ Use `OPTIMIZE TABLE tablename` to defragment tables and refresh the indexes.

References

▶ www.coker.com.au/bonnie++/—The home page of bonnie, a disk benchmarking tool. It also contains a link to RAID benchmarking utilities and Postal, a benchmarking utility for SMTP servers.

▶ www.phoronix-test-suite.com/—The Phoronix Test Suite was created by a website that does automated performance testing and comparisons and is a quality benchmarking software to consider.

▶ http://httpd.apache.org/current/misc/perf-tuning.html—The official Apache guide to tuning your web server.

▶ http://dev.mysql.com/doc/refman/5.7/en/optimization.html—Learn how to optimize your MySQL server direct from the source, the MySQL manual.

▶ One particular MySQL optimization book will really help you get more from your system if you run a large site: *High Performance MySQL*, by Jeremy Zawodny and Derek Balling (O'Reilly), ISBN: 0-596-00306-4.

CHAPTER 22

Kernel and Module Management

A kernel is a complex piece of software that manages the processes and process interactions that take place within an operating system. As a user, you rarely, if ever, interact directly with it. Instead, you work with the applications that the kernel manages.

The Linux kernel is Linux. It is the result of years of cooperative (and sometimes contentious) work by numerous people around the world. There is only one common kernel source tree, but each major Linux distribution massages and patches its version slightly to add features, performance, or options. Each Linux distribution, including Ubuntu, comes with its own precompiled kernel as well as the kernel source code, providing you with absolute authority over the Linux operating system. This chapter covers the kernel and what it does for us and for the operating system.

In this chapter, you also learn how to obtain the kernel sources and how and when to patch the kernel. This chapter leads you through an expert's tour of the kernel architecture and teaches you essential steps in kernel configuration, how to build and install modules, and how to compile drivers in Ubuntu. This chapter also teaches you important aspects of working with GRUB2, the default Ubuntu boot loader. Finally, the chapter's troubleshooting information will help you understand what to do when something goes wrong with your Linux kernel installation or compilation process. As disconcerting as these problems can seem, this chapter shows you some easy fixes for many kernel problems.

Almost all users find that a precompiled Ubuntu kernel suits their needs (and there are several to choose from). At some point, you might need to recompile the kernel to support a specific piece of hardware or add a new feature to the operating system, although the Ubuntu kernel team works very hard to backport or enable any feature possible (as a module), so it is highly unlikely you will ever have a need to do this. They are also approachable and will gladly discuss specific needs and features. Sometimes features are not enabled just because no one has ever asked for or needed them. Occasionally, things are not enabled because of a conflict with another feature. The Ubuntu Kernel Team can help you discover what is going on in those cases (but don't abuse their kindness and availability, they already work quite hard and for long hours).

Really, the main reason today for people compiling their own kernel is because they want to learn to be a kernel developer. If you have heard horror stories about the difficulties of recompiling the Linux kernel, you can relax; this chapter gives you all the information you need to understand how to painlessly work through the process if you are interested in learning a new skill. This is a complex and detail-oriented task, but it is within the grasp of most technical users, even if it is completely unnecessary.

CAUTION

Building and using a custom kernel will make it difficult to get support for your system. Although it is a learning experience to compile your own kernel, you will not be allowed to file bugs in Ubuntu on the custom-built kernel (if you do, they will be rejected without further explanation) and if you have a commercial support contract with Ubuntu/Canonical, this will void the contract.

The Linux Kernel

The Linux kernel is the management part of the operating system that many people call *Linux*. Although many think of the entire distribution as Linux, the only piece that can correctly be called Linux is the kernel. Ubuntu, like many Linux distributions, includes a kernel packaged with add-on software that interacts with the kernel so that the user can interface with the system in a meaningful manner.

The system utilities and user programs enable computers to become valuable tools to a user.

THE FIRST LINUX KERNEL

In 1991, Linus Torvalds released version 0.99 of the Linux kernel as the result of his desire for a powerful, UNIX-like operating system for his Intel 80386 personal computer. Linus wrote the initial code necessary to create what is now known as the Linux kernel and combined it with Richard Stallman's GNU tools. Indeed, because many of the Linux basic system tools come from the GNU Project, many people refer to the operating system as *GNU/Linux*. Since then, Linux has benefited from thousands of contributors adding their talents and time to the Linux project. Linus still maintains the kernel, deciding what will and will not make it into the kernel as official releases, known to many as the *vanilla* or *Linus* Linux kernel.

The Linux Source Tree

The source code for the Linux kernel is kept in a group of directories called the *kernel source tree*. The structure of the kernel source tree is important because the process of compiling (building) the kernel is automated; it is controlled by scripts interpreted by the `make` application. These scripts, known as *makefiles*, expect to find the pieces of the kernel code in specific places; if they don't find them, they will not work. You learn how to use `make` to compile a kernel later in this chapter.

It is not necessary for the Linux kernel source code to be installed on your system for the system to run or for you to accomplish typical tasks such as email, web browsing, or word processing. It is necessary that the kernel sources be installed, however, if you want to compile a new kernel. In the next section, you learn how to install the kernel source files and how to set up the special symbolic link required. That link is `/usr/src/linux-4.1.3`, and it is how you will refer to the directory of the kernel source tree as we examine the contents of the kernel source tree.

> **NOTE**
>
> The pace of change in the Linux kernel has accelerated, much like the rest of our lives. In this chapter, we chose to use the version numbers for a recent LTS release of Ubuntu. The version numbers on your system may be different, but the processes and concepts will remain the same.

The `/usr/src/linux-4.1.3` directory contains the `.config` and the `Makefile` files among others. The `.config` file is the configuration of your Linux kernel as it was compiled. There is no `.config` file by default; you must select one from the `/configs` subdirectory. There, you will find configuration files for each flavor of the kernel Ubuntu provides; simply copy the one appropriate for your system to the default directory and rename it `.config`.

We have already discussed the contents of the `/configs` subdirectory, so let's examine the other directories found under `/usr/src/linux-4.1.3`. The most useful for us is the Documentation directory. In it and its subdirectories, you will find almost all the documentation concerning every part of the kernel. The file `00-INDEX` (each `Documentation` subdirectory also contains a `00-INDEX` file, as well) contains a list of the files in the main directory and a brief explanation of what they are. Many files are written solely for kernel programmers and application writers, but a few are useful to the intermediate or advanced Linux user when attempting to learn about kernel and device driver issues. Some of the more interesting and useful documents are as follows:

▶ `devices.txt`—A list of all possible Linux devices that are represented in the `/dev` directory, giving major and minor numbers and a short description. If you have ever gotten an error message that mentions `char-major-xxx`, this file is where that list is kept.

▶ `ide.txt`—If your system uses IDE hard drives, this file discusses how the kernel interacts with them and lists the various kernel commands that you can use to solve IDE-related hardware problems, manually set data transfer modes, and otherwise manually manage your IDE drives. Most of this management is automatic, but if you want to understand how the kernel interacts with IDE devices, this file explains it.

▶ `initrd.txt`—This file provides much more in-depth knowledge of initial RAM disks, giving details on the loopback file system used to create and mount them and explaining how the kernel interacts with them.

▶ `kernel-parameters.txt`—This file is a list of most of the arguments that you can pass at boot time to configure kernel or hardware settings, but it does not appear too useful at first glance because it is just a list. However, knowing that a parameter exists and might relate to something you are looking for can assist you in tracking down more information because now you have terms to enter into an Internet search engine such as Google.

▶ `sysrq.txt`—If you have ever wondered what that key on your keyboard marked SysRq is used for, this file has the answer. Briefly, it is a key combination hardwired into the kernel that can help you recover from a system lockup. Ubuntu disables this function by default for security reasons. You can reenable it at a root prompt by entering the command # `echo "1" > /proc/sys/kernel/sysrq`, and disable it by echoing a value of 0 rather than 1.

In the other directories found in `Documentation`, you find similar text files that deal with the kernel modules for CD-ROM drivers, file system drivers, game port and joystick drivers, video drivers (not graphics card drivers; those belong to X11R6 and not to the kernel), network drivers, and all the other drivers and systems found in the Linux operating system. Again, these documents are usually written for programmers, but they can also provide useful information to the intermediate and advanced Linux user.

The directory named `scripts` contains many of the scripts that `make` uses. It really does not contain anything of interest to anyone who is not a programmer or a kernel developer (also known as a *kernel hacker*).

After a kernel is built, all the compiled files wind up in the `arch` directory and its subdirectories. Although you can manually move them to their final location, you learn later in this chapter how the `make` scripts will do it for you. In the early days of Linux, this post-compilation file relocation was all done by hand; you should be grateful for `make`.

NOTE

The `make` utility is a complex program. You can find complete documentation on the structure of `make` files, as well as the arguments that it can accept, at www.gnu.org/software/make/manual/make.html.

The remaining directories in `/usr/src/linux-4.1.3` contain the source code for the kernel and the kernel drivers. When you install the kernel sources, these files are placed there automatically. When you patch kernel sources, these files are altered automatically. When you compile the kernel, these files are accessed automatically. Although you never need to touch the source code files, they can be useful. The kernel source files are nothing more than text files with special formatting, which means that you can look at them and read the programmer comments. Sometimes, a programmer writes an application but cannot (or often does not) write the documentation. The comments the programmer puts in the source code are often the only documentation that exists for the code.

Small testing programs are even "hidden" in the comments of some of the code, along with comments and references to other information. Because the source code is written in a language that can be read as easily—almost—as English, a nonprogrammer might be able to get an idea of what the application or driver is actually doing (see Chapter 38, "Using Programming Tools for Ubuntu" for an idea of how that could happen). This information might be of use to an intermediate to advanced Linux user when the user is confronted by kernel- and driver-related problems.

> **NOTE**
>
> The interaction and control of hardware is handled by a small piece of the kernel called a *device driver*. The driver tells the computer how to interact with a modem, a SCSI card, a keyboard, a mouse, and so on in response to a user prompt. Without the device driver, the kernel does not know how to interact with the associated device.

Types of Kernels

In the early days of Linux, kernels were a single block of code containing all the instructions for the processor, the motherboard, and the other hardware. If you changed hardware, you were required to recompile the kernel code to include what you needed and discard what you did not. Including extra, unneeded code carried a penalty because the kernel became larger and occupied more memory. On older systems that had only 4MB to 8MB of memory, wasting precious memory for unnecessary code was considered unacceptable. Kernel compiling was something of a "black art" as early Linux users attempted to wring the most performance from their computers. These kernels compiled as a single block of code are called *monolithic kernels*.

As the kernel code grew larger and the number of devices that could be added to a computer increased, the requirement to recompile became onerous. A new method of building the kernel was developed to make the task of compiling easier. The part of the kernel's source code that composed the code for the device drivers could be optionally compiled as a module that could be loaded and unloaded into the kernel as required. This is known as the *modular* approach to building the kernel. Now, all the kernel code could be compiled at once, with most of the code compiled into these modules. Only the required modules would be loaded; the kernel could be kept smaller, and adding hardware was much simpler.

The typical Ubuntu kernel has some drivers compiled as part of the kernel itself (called *inline drivers*) and others compiled as modules. Only device drivers compiled inline are available to the kernel during the boot process; modular drivers are available only after the system has been booted.

> **NOTE**
>
> As a common example, drivers for SCSI disk drives must be available to the kernel if you intend to boot from SCSI disks. If the kernel is not compiled with those drivers inline, the system does not boot because it cannot access the disks.
>
> A way around this problem for modular kernels is to use an initial RAM disk (`initrd`), discussed later in the "Creating an Initial RAM Disk Image" section. The `initrd` loads a small kernel and the appropriate device driver, which then can access the device to load the actual kernel you want to run.

Some code can be only one or the other (for technical reasons unimportant to the average user), but most code can be compiled either as modular or inline. Depending on the application, some system administrators prefer one way over the other, but with fast modern processors and abundant system memory, the performance differences are of little concern to all but the most ardent Linux hackers.

When compiling a kernel, the step in which you make the selection of modular or inline is part of the `make config` step detailed later in this chapter. Unless you have a specific reason to do otherwise, select the modular option when given a choice. Because you will be managing kernels more frequently than compiling kernels, the process of managing modules is addressed in the next section.

Managing Modules

When using a modular kernel, special tools are required to manage the modules. Modules must be loaded and unloaded, and it would be nice if that were done as automatically as possible. We also need to be able to pass necessary parameters to modules when we load them, things such as memory addresses and interrupts. (That information varies from module to module, so you need to look at the documentation for your modules to determine what, if any, information needs to be passed to it.) This section covers the tools provided to manage modules and then look at a few examples of using them.

Linux provides the following module management tools for our use. All these commands (and `modprobe.conf`) have man pages:

- ► `lsmod`—This command lists the loaded modules. It is useful to pipe this through the `less` command because the listing is usually more than one page long.

- ► `insmod`—This command loads the specified module into the running kernel. If a module name is given without a full path, the default location for the running kernel, `/lib/modules/*/`, is searched. Several options are offered for this command; the most useful is `-f`, which forces the module to be loaded.

- ► `rmmod`—This command unloads (removes) the specified module from the running kernel. More than one module at a time can be specified.

- ► `modprobe`—A more sophisticated version of `insmod` and `rmmod`, it uses the dependency file created by `depmod` and automatically handles loading, or with the `-r` option, removing modules. There is no force option, however. A useful option to `modprobe` is

-t, which causes modprobe to cycle through a set of drivers until it finds one that matches your system. If you are unsure of what module will work for your network card, use this command:

```
matthew@seymour:~$ sudo modprobe -t net
```

The term net is used because that is the name of the directory (/lib/modules/*/kernel/ net) where all the network drivers are kept. It tries each one in turn until it loads one successfully.

▶ **modinfo**—This queries a module's object file and provides a list of the module name, author, license, and any other information that is there. It often is not very useful.

▶ **depmod**—This program creates a dependency file for kernel modules. Some modules need to have other modules loaded first; that is, they "depend" on the other modules. (A lot of the kernel code is like this because it eliminates redundancy in the code base.) During the boot process, one of the startup files contains the command depmod -a, and it is run every time you boot to re-create the file /lib/modules/*/ modules.dep. If you make changes to the file /etc/modprobe.conf, run depmod -a manually. The depmod command, its list of dependencies, and the /etc/modprobe. conf file enable kernel modules to be automatically loaded as needed.

▶ **/etc/modprobe.conf**—This is not a command, but a file that controls how modprobe and depmod behave; it contains kernel module variables. Although the command syntax can be quite complex, most actual needs are simple. The most common use is to alias a module and then pass it some parameters. For example, in the following code, we alias a device name (from devices.txt) to a more descriptive word and then pass some information to an associated module. The i2c-dev device is used to read the CPU temperature and fan speed on our system. These lines for /etc/ modprobe.conf were suggested for our use by the program's documentation. We added them with a text editor:

```
alias char-major-89 i2c-dev
options eeprom ignore=2,0x50,2,0x51,2,0x52
```

A partial listing of lsmod is shown here, piped through the less command, enabling us to view it a page at a time:

```
matthew@seymour:~$ sudo lsmod | less
Module          Size    Used by
parport_pc      19392   1
Module          Size    Used by
parport_pc      19392   1
lp              8236    0
joydev          17377   0
parport         29640   2 parport_pc,lp
autofs4         10624   0
sunrpc          101064  1
```

The list is actually much longer, but here we see that the input module is being used by the `joydev` (joystick device) module, but the joystick module is not being used. This computer has a joystick port that was autodetected, but no joystick is connected. A scanner module is also loaded, but because the USB scanner is unplugged, the module is not being used. You use the `lsmod` command to determine whether a module was loaded and what other modules were using it. If you examine the full list, you will see modules for all the devices attached to your computer.

To remove a module, `joydev` in this example, use the following:

```
matthew@seymour:~$ sudo rmmod joydev
```

or

```
matthew@seymour:~$ sudo modprobe -r joydev
```

The output of `lsmod` now shows that it is no longer loaded. If we were to remove `input`, as well, we could then use `modprobe` to load both `input` and `joydev` (one depends on the other, remember) with a simple command, as follows:

```
matthew@seymour:~$ sudo modprobe joydev
```

If Ubuntu balks at loading a module (because it was compiled using a different kernel version from what you are currently running; for example, the NVIDIA graphics card module), you could force it to load like this:

```
matthew@seymour:~$ sudo insmod -f nvidia
```

You ignore the complaints (error messages) in this case if the kernel generates any.

When to Recompile

Ubuntu systems use a modified version of the plain-vanilla Linux kernel (a modified version is referred to as a *patched kernel*) with additional drivers and other special features compiled into it.

Ubuntu has quite an intensive testing period for all distribution kernels and regularly distributes updated versions. The supplied Ubuntu kernel is compiled with as many modules as possible to provide as much flexibility as possible. A running kernel can be further tuned with the `sysctl` program, which enables direct access to a running kernel and permits some kernel parameters to be changed. As a result of this extensive testing, configurability, and modularity, the precompiled Ubuntu kernel does everything most users need it to do. Most users only need to recompile the kernel to do the following:

▶ Accommodate an esoteric piece of new hardware

▶ Conduct a system update when Ubuntu has not yet provided precompiled kernels

▶ Experiment with the system capabilities

Ubuntu supplies precompiled versions of the kernel for 32- and 64-bit processors. For each architecture, they compile a generic kernel that works well for most uses, a server kernel that is optimized for server use, a preempt kernel designed for use in low latency servers, and an `rt` kernel for times when instant response is more important than balanced use (such as in professional audio/visual recording and editing). There is also a special kernel, called *virtual*, available for use in virtual machines. These are all available from the Ubuntu software repositories.

Also available are a series of packages called `linux-backports-modules-`, each with a specific set of kernel modules backported from newer mainline kernels into current version Ubuntu kernels. If you need an updated driver for a piece of hardware, look at the backported modules first.

Kernel Versions

The Linux kernel is in a constant state of development. As new features are added, bugs are fixed, and new technology is incorporated into the code base, it becomes necessary to provide stable releases of the kernel for use in a production environment. It is also important to have separate releases that contain the newest code for developers to test. To keep track of the kernels, version numbers are assigned to them. Programmers enjoy using sequential version numbers that have abstract meaning. Is version 8 twice as advanced as version 4 of the same application? Is version 1 of one application less developed than version 3 of another? The version numbers cannot be used for this kind of qualitative or quantitative comparison. It is entirely possible that higher version numbers can have fewer features and more bugs than older versions. The numbers exist solely to differentiate and organize sequential revisions of software.

For the latest stable version of the kernel at the time of writing, for example, the kernel version number from the Linux developers is 4.1.3. As this is being written, Ubuntu plans to ship 15.10 with either a 4.1 kernel with Ubuntu-specific patches applied. It will receive consistent updates throughout the release's life cycle.

The kernel version can be broken down into four sections:

▶ **Major version**—This is the major version number, now at 4.

▶ **Minor version**—This is the minor version number, now at 1 (again, version in most recent Ubuntu LTS release).

▶ **Sublevel number**—This number indicates the current iteration of the kernel; here it is number 3.

▶ **Extraversion level**—This is the number representing a collection of patches and additions made to the kernel by the Ubuntu engineers to make the kernel work for them (and you). Each collection is numbered, and the number is indicated here in the kernel name. There is not one in our preceding example. In the example below, it is 0.

Type `uname -r` at the command prompt to display your current kernel version, shown here with example output:

```
matthew@seymour:~$ uname -r4.1.3.0-generic
```

Obtaining the Kernel Sources

The Linux kernel has always been freely available to anyone who wants it. If you just want to recompile the existing kernel, install the `linux-source` package from the Ubuntu repositories. To get the very latest vanilla version, which is the commonly used term for the kernel version direct from the main kernel developers and which has not yet been patched or changed by any distribution-specific kernel team, open an FTP connection to ftp.kernel.org using your favorite FTP client and log in as anonymous. The latest stable kernel when this section was first written was 4.1.3, so we use it in the following examples.

Because you are interested in the 4.1 kernel, change directories to `/pub/linux/kernel/v4.1`.

> **NOTE**
>
> The ftp.kernel.org site receives more than its share of requests for download. It is considered a courtesy to use a mirror site to reduce the traffic that ftp.kernel.org bears. The website www.kernel.org/mirrors/ has a list of all mirrors around the world. Find one close to your geographic location and substitute that address for ftp.kernel.org.

A number of different entries are on the FTP archive site for each kernel version, but because you are interested only in the full kernel, it is necessary to get the full package of source code (for example, `linux-4.1.3.bz2`).

The `.bz2` extension is applied by the `bzip2` utility, which has better compression than `gzip`.

After it is downloaded, move the package to a directory other than `/usr/src` and unpack it. The `bzip2` unpack command is `tar -xjvf linux-4.1.3.tar.bz2`. After it is unpacked, the package creates a new directory, `linux-4.1.3`. Copy it to `/usr/src` or move it there. Then, create a symbolic link of `linux-4.1` to `linux-4.1.3`. (Otherwise, some scripts will not work.) Here is how to create the symbolic link:

```
matthew@seymour:~$ sudo rm /usr/src/linux-4.1
matthew@seymour:~$ sudo ln -s /usr/src/linux-4.1.3 /usr/src/linux-4.1
```

By creating a symbolic link to `/usr/src/linux-4.1`, it is possible to allow multiple kernel versions to be compiled and tailored for different functions: You just change the symbolic link to the kernel directory you want to work on.

> **CAUTION**
>
> The correct symbolic link is critical to the operation of `make`. Always have the symbolic link point to the version of the kernel sources you are working with.

Patching the Kernel

It is possible to patch a kernel to the newest Linux kernel version as opposed to downloading the entire source code. This choice can be beneficial for those who are not using a high-speed broadband connection. Whether you are patching existing sources or downloading the full source, the end results are identical.

Patching the kernel is not a mindless task. It requires the user to retrieve all patches from the current version to the version the user wants to upgrade to. For example, if you are currently running 4.1.1 (and have those sources) and want to upgrade to 4.1.3, you must retrieve the 4.1.2 and 4.1.3 patch sets, and so on. After you download these patches, you must apply them in succession to upgrade to 4.1.3. This is more tedious than download-ing the entire source, but it's useful for those who keep up with kernel hacking and want to perform incremental upgrades to keep their Linux kernel as up-to-date as possible.

To patch up to several versions in a single operation, you can use the patch-kernel script located in the kernel source directory for the kernel version you currently use. This script applies all necessary version patches to bring your kernel up to the latest version.

The format for using the patch-kernel script looks like this:

```
patch-kernel source_dir patch_dir stopversion
```

The source directory defaults to /usr/src/linux if none is given, and the patch_dir defaults to the current working directory if one is not supplied.

For example, assume that you have a 4.1.1 kernel code tree that needs to be patched to the 4.1.3 version. The 4.1.2 and 4.1.3 patch files have been downloaded from ftp.kernel .org and are placed in the /patch directory in the source tree. You issue the following com-mand in the /usr/src/linux-4.1 directory:

```
matthew@seymour:~$ sudo scripts/patch-kernel /usr/src/linux-4.1.1 /usr/src/
linux-4.1.1/patch
```

Each successive patch file is applied, eventually creating a 4.1.3 code tree. If any errors occur during this operation, files named xxx# or xxx.rej are created, where xxx is the version of the patch that failed. You have to resolve these failed patches manually by examining the errors and looking at the source code and the patch. An inexperienced per-son will not have any success with this because you need to understand C programming and kernel programming to know what is broken and how to fix it. Because this was a stock 4.1.1 code tree, the patches were all successfully applied without errors. If you are attempting to apply a nonstandard third-party patch, the patch might fail.

When you have successfully patched the kernel, you are ready to begin compiling this code tree as if you started with a fresh, stock 4.1.3 kernel tree.

USING THE PATCH COMMAND

If you have a special, nonstandard patch to apply—such as a third-party patch for a commercial product, for example—you can use the patch command rather than the special patch-kernel script that is normally used for kernel source updates. Here are some quick steps and an alternative method of creating patched code and leaving the original code alone:

1. Create a directory in your home directory and name it something meaningful, like `mylinux`.

2. Copy the pristine Linux source code there with the following:

   ```
   cp -ravd /usr/src/linux-4.1/* ~/mylinux
   ```

3. Copy the patch file to that same directory as follows:

   ```
   cp patch_filename ~/mylinux
   ```

4. Change to the ~/mylinux directory with this command:

   ```
   cd ~/mylinux
   ```

5. Apply the patch like this:

   ```
   -patch -p1 < patch_filename > mypatch.log 2>&1
   ```

   (This last bit of code saves the message output to a file so that you can look at it later.)

6. If the patch applies successfully, you are done and have not endangered any of the pristine source code. If the newly patched code does not work, you do not have to reinstall the original, pristine source code.

7. Copy your new code to `/usr/src` and make that special symbolic link described elsewhere in the chapter.

Compiling the Kernel

If you want to update the kernel from new source code you have downloaded, or you have applied a patch to add new functionality or hardware support, you must compile and install a new kernel to actually use that new functionality. Compiling the kernel involves translating the kernel's contents from human-readable code to binary form. Installing the kernel involves putting all the compiled files where they belong in `/boot` and `/lib` and making changes to the boot loader.

The process of compiling the kernel is almost completely automated by the make utility like the process of installing. By providing the necessary arguments and following the steps covered next, you can recompile and install a custom kernel for your use.

Here are the steps to compile and configure the kernel:

1. Do not delete your current kernel, so that you will have a backup that you can use to boot if there is a problem with the one you compile.

2. Apply all patches, if any, so that you have the features you desire. See the previous section for details.

3. Back up the `.config` file, if it exists, so that you can recover from the inevitable mistake. Use the following `cp` command:

```
matthew@seymour:~$ sudo cp .config .config.bak
```

> **NOTE**
>
> If you are recompiling the Ubuntu default kernel, the `/usr/src/linux-4.1/configs` directory contains several versions of configuration files for different purposes.
>
> Ubuntu provides a full set of `.config` files in the subdirectory `configs`, all named for the type of system they were compiled for. If you want to use one of these default configurations as the basis for a custom kernel, just copy the appropriate file to `/usr/src/linux-3.4` and rename it `.config`.

4. Run the `make mrproper` directive to prepare the kernel source tree, cleaning out any old files or binaries.

5. Restore the `.config` file that the command `make mrproper` deleted and edit the makefile to change the EXTRAVERSION number.

> **NOTE**
>
> If you want to keep any current version of the kernel that was compiled with the same code tree, manually edit the makefile with your favorite text editor and add some unique string to the EXTRAVERSION variable.
>
> You can use any description you prefer.

6. Modify the kernel configuration file using `make config`, `make menuconfig`, or `make xconfig`; we recommend the last one.

7. Run `make dep` to create the code dependencies used later in the compilation process.

> **TIP**
>
> If you have a multiprocessor machine, you can use both processors to speed the make process by inserting `-jx` after the `make` command, where as a rule of thumb, x is one more than the number of processors you have. You might try a larger number and even try this on a single processor machine (we have used `-j8` successfully on an SMP machine); it will only load up your CPU. For example:
>
> ```
> matthew@seymour:~$ sudo make -j3 bzImage
> ```
>
> All the `make` processes except `make dep` work well with this method of parallel compiling.

8. Run `make clean` to prepare the sources for the actual compilation of the kernel.

9. Run `make bzImage` to create a binary image of the kernel.

> **NOTE**
>
> Several choices of directives exist; the most common ones are the following:
>
> ▶ `zImage`—This directive compiles the kernel, creating an uncompressed file called `zImage`.
>
> ▶ `bzImage`—This directive creates a compressed kernel image necessary for some systems that require the kernel image to be under a certain size for the BIOS to be able to parse them; otherwise, the new kernel will not boot. It is the most commonly used choice. However, the Ubuntu kernel compiled with `bzImage` is still too large to fit on a floppy, so a smaller version with some modules and features removed is used for the boot floppies. Ubuntu recommends that you boot from the rescue CD-ROM.
>
> ▶ `bzDisk`—This directive does the same thing as `bzImage`, but it copies the new kernel image to a floppy disk for testing purposes. This is helpful for testing new kernels without writing kernel files to your hard drive. Make sure that you have a floppy disk in the drive because you will not be prompted for one.

10. Run `make modules` to compile any modules your new kernel needs.

11. Run `make modules_install` to install the modules in `/lib/modules` and create dependency files.

12. Run `make install` to automatically copy the kernel to `/boot`, create any other files it needs, and modify the boot loader to boot the new kernel by default.

13. Using your favorite text editor, verify the changes made to `/etc/lilo.conf` or `/boot/grub/grub.conf`; fix if necessary and rerun `/sbin/lilo` if needed.

14. Reboot and test the new kernel.

15. Repeat the process if necessary, choosing a configuration interface.

Over time, the process for configuring the Linux kernel has changed. Originally, you configured the kernel by responding to a series of prompts for each configuration parameter; this is the `make config` utility described shortly. Although you can still configure Linux this way, most users find this type of configuration confusing and inconvenient; moving back through the prompts to correct errors, for instance, is impossible.

The `make config` utility is a command-line tool. The utility presents a question about kernel configuration options. The user responds with a Y, N, M, or ?. (It is not case sensitive.) Choosing M configures the option to be compiled as a module. A response of ? displays context help for that specific options, if available. (If you choose ? and no help is available, you can turn to the vast Internet resources to find information.) We recommend that you avoid the `make config` utility.

If you prefer to use a command-line interface, you can use `make menuconfig` to configure the Linux kernel. `menuconfig` provides a graphical wrapper around a text interface. Although it is not as raw as `make config`, `menuconfig` is not a fancy graphical interface either; you cannot use a mouse but must navigate through it using keyboard commands.

The same information presented in `make config` is presented by `make menuconfig`, but it looks a little nicer. Now, at least you can move back and forth in the selection process if you change your mind or make a mistake.

In `make menuconfig`, you use the arrow keys to move the selector up and down and the spacebar to toggle a selection. The Tab key moves the focus at the bottom of the screen to either Select, Exit, or Help.

If a graphical desktop is not available, `menuconfig` is the best you can do. However, both `menuconfig` and `xconfig` (see the following explanation of each) offer an improvement over editing the `.config` file directly. If you want to configure the kernel through a true graphical interface—with mouse support and clickable buttons—`make xconfig` is the best configuration utility option. To use this utility, you must have the X Window System running. The application `xconfig` is really nothing but a Tcl/Tk graphics `widget set` providing borders, menus, dialog boxes, and the like. Its interface is used to wrap around data files that are parsed at execution time.

After loading this utility, you use it by clicking each of the buttons that list the configu-ration options. Each button you click opens another window that has the detail con-figuration options for that subsection. Three buttons are at the bottom of each window: Main Menu, Next, and Prev(ious). Clicking the Main Menu button closes the current window and displays the main window. Clicking Next takes you to the next configuration section. When configuring a kernel from scratch, click the button labeled Code Maturity Level Options and then continue to click the Next button in each subsection window to proceed through all the kernel configuration choices. When you have selected all options, the main menu is again displayed. The buttons on the lower right of the main menu are for saving and loading configurations. Their functions are self-explanatory. If you just want to have a look, go exploring! Nothing will be changed if you elect not to save it.

If you are upgrading kernels from a previous release, it is not necessary to go through the entire configuration from scratch. Instead, you can use the directive `make oldconfig`; it uses the same text interface that `make config` uses, and it is noninteractive. It just prompts for changes for any new code.

Using `xconfig` to Configure the Kernel

For simplicity's sake, during this brisk walkthrough, this discussion assumes that you are using `make xconfig` and that prior to this point you have completed the first five steps in the kernel compilation checklist shown previously.

As you learned in the preceding section, you configure the kernel using `make xconfig` by making choices in several configuration subsection windows. Each subsection window contains specific kernel options. With hundreds of choices, the kernel is daunting to configure. We cannot really offer you detailed descriptions of which options to choose because our configuration will not match your own system and setup.

Table 22.1 provides a brief description of each subsection's options so that you can get an idea of what you might encounter. We recommend that you copy your kernel's `.config` file to `/usr/src/linux-4.1` and run `make xconfig` from there. Explore all the options. So long as you do not save the file, absolutely nothing is changed on your system.

TABLE 22.1   Some Kernel Subsections for Configuration

Name	Description
Code maturity level options	Enables development code to be compiled into the kernel even if it has been marked as obsolete or as testing code only. This option should be used only by kernel developers or testers because of the possible unusable state of the code during development.
General setup	This section contains several different options covering how the kernel talks to the BIOS, whether it should support PCI or PCMCIA, whether it should use APM or ACPI, and what kind of Linux binary formats will be supported. Contains several options for supporting kernel structures necessary to run binaries compiled for other systems directly without recompiling the program.
Loadable module support	Determines whether the kernel enables drivers and other nonessential code to be compiled as loadable modules that can be loaded and unloaded at runtime. This option keeps the basic kernel small so that it can run and respond more quickly; in that regard, choosing this option is generally a good idea.
Processor type and features	Several options dealing with the architecture that will be running the kernel.
Power management options	Options dealing with ACPI and APM power management features.
Bus options	Configuration options for the PCMCIA bus found in laptops and PCI hotplug devices.
Memory Technology Devices	Options for supporting flash memory devices, such as (MTD) EEPROMS. Generally, these devices are used in embedded systems.
Parallel port support	Several options for configuring how the kernel will support parallel port communications.
Plug-and-play configuration	Options for supporting *plug-and-play (PnP)* PCI, ISA, and PnP BIOS support. Generally, it is a good idea to support PnP for PCI and ISA devices.
Block devices	Section dealing with devices that communicate with the kernel in blocks of characters instead of streams. This includes IDE and ATAPI devices connected via parallel ports, as well as enabling network devices to communicate as block devices.
ATA/IDE/MFM/RLL support	Large collection of options to configure the kernel to communicate using different types of data communication protocols to talk to mass storage devices, such as hard drives. Note that this section does not cover SCSI.
SCSI device support	Options for configuring the kernel to support Small Computer Systems Interface (SCSI). This subsection covers drivers for specific cards, chipsets, and tunable parameters for the SCSI protocol.

Old CD-ROM drivers	Configuration options to support obscure, older CD-ROM devices that do not conform to the SCSI or IDE standards. These are typically older CD-ROM drivers that are usually a proprietary type of SCSI (not SCSI, not IDE).
Multidevice support (RAID and LVM)	Options for enabling the kernel to support RAID devices in software emulation and the different levels of RAID. Also contains options for support of a logical volume manager.
Fusion MPT device support	Configures support for LSI's Logic Fusion Message Passing Technology. This technology is for high-performance SCSI and LAN interfaces.
IEEE1394 (firewire) support	Experimental support for FireWire devices.
I2O device support	Options for supporting the Intelligent Input/Output architecture. This architecture enables the hardware driver to be split from the operating system driver, thus enabling a multitude of hardware devices to be compatible with an operating system in one implementation.
Networking support	Several options for the configuration of networking in the kernel. The options are for the types of supported protocols and configurable options of those protocols.
Amateur radio support	Options for configuring support of devices that support the Ax25 protocol.
IrDA (infrared) support	Options for configuring support of the infrared Data Association suite of protocols and devices that use these protocols.
Bluetooth support	Support for the Bluetooth wireless protocol. Includes options to support the Bluetooth protocols and hardware devices.
ISDN subsystem	Options to support Integrated Services Digital Networks (ISDN) protocols and devices. ISDN is a method of connection to a large area network digitally over conditioned telephone lines, largely found to connect users to ISPs.
Telephony support	Support for devices that enable the use of regular telephone lines to support Voice over Internet Protocol (VoIP) applications. This section does not handle the configuration of modems.
Input device support	Options for configuring Universal *Serial Bus (USB)* human *interface devices (HID)* such as keyboards, mice, and joysticks.
Character devices	Configuration options for devices that communicate to the server in sequential characters. This is a large subsection containing the drivers for several motherboard chipsets.
Multimedia devices	Drivers for hardware implementations of video and sound devices such as video capture boards, TV cards, and AM/FM radio adapter cards.
Graphics support	Configures VGA text console, video mode selection, and support for frame buffer cards.

22

Sound	Large subsection to configure supported sound card drivers and chipset support for the kernel.
USB support	USB configuration options. Includes configuration for USB devices and vendor-specific versions of USB.
File system	Configuration options for supported file system types.
Additional device driver support	A section for third-party patches.
Profiling support	Profiling kernel behavior to aid in debugging and development.
Kernel hacking	This section determines whether the kernel will contain advanced debugging options. Most users will not want to include this option in their production kernels because it increases the kernel size and slows performance by adding extra routines.
Security options	Determines whether NSA Security *Enhanced Linux (SELinux)* is enabled.
Cryptographic options	Support for cryptography hardware (Ubuntu patches not found in the vanilla kernel sources).
Library routines	Contains `zlib` compression support.

After you select all the options you want, you can save the configuration file and continue with step 7 in the kernel compiling checklist shown earlier.

Creating an Initial RAM Disk Image

If you require special device drivers to be loaded to mount the root file system (for SCSI drives, network cards, or exotic file systems, for example), you must create an initial RAM disk image named `/boot/initrd.img`. For most users, it is not necessary to create this file, but if you are not certain, it really does not hurt. To create an `initrd.img` file, use the shell script `/sbin/mkinitrd`.

The format for the command is the following, where *file_name* is the name of the image file you want to create:

```
/sbin/mkinitrd file_name kernel_version
```

`mkinitrd` looks at `/etc/fstab`, `/etc/modprobe.conf`, and `/etc/ raidtab` to obtain the information it needs to determine which modules should be loaded during boot. For our system, we use the following:

```
matthew@seymour:~$ sudo mkinitrd initrd-4.1.3.img 3.4.6-1
```

When Something Goes Wrong

Several things might go wrong during a kernel compile and install, and several clues point to the true problem. You see error messages printed to the screen, and some error messages are printed to the file `/var/log/messages`, which you can examine with a text editor. If you have followed the directions for patching the kernel, you need to examine a special error log, as well. Do not worry about most errors because many problems are easily fixed with some research on your part. Some errors may be unfixable, however, depending on your skill level and the availability of technical information.

Errors During Compile

Although it is rare that the kernel will not compile, there is always a chance that something has slipped though the regression testing. Let's take a look at an example of a problem that might crop up during the compile.

It is possible that the kernel compile crashes and does not complete successfully, especially if you attempt to use experimental patches, add untested features, or build newer and perhaps unstable modules on an older system.

At this juncture, you have two options:

▶ Fix the errors and recompile.

▶ Remove the offending module or option and wait for the errors to be fixed by the kernel team.

Most users will be unable to fix some errors because of the complexity of the kernel code, although you should not rule out this option. It is possible that someone else discovered the same error during testing of the kernel and developed a patch for the problem: Check the Linux kernel mailing list archive. If the problem is not mentioned there, a search on Google might turn up something.

The second option, removing the code, is the easiest and is what most people do in cases in which the offending code is not required. In the case of the NTFS module failing, it is almost expected because NTFS support is still considered experimental and subject to errors. This is primarily because the code for the file system is reverse-engineered instead of implemented via documented standards. Read-only support has gotten better in recent kernels; write support is still experimental.

Finally, should you want to take on the task of trying to fix the problem yourself, this is a great opportunity to get involved with the Linux kernel and make a contribution that could help many others.

If you are knowledgeable about coding and kernel matters, you might want to look in the `Maintainers` file in the `/usr/src/linux-4.1/` directory of the kernel source and find the maintainer of the code. The recommended course of action is to contact the maintainer to see if the maintainer is aware of the problems you are having. If nothing has been documented for the specific error, submitting the error to the kernel mailing list is an option. The guidelines for doing this are in the README file in the base directory of the kernel source under the section IF SOMETHING GOES WRONG.

Runtime Errors, Boot Loader Problems, and Kernel Oops

Runtime errors occur as the kernel is loading. Error messages are displayed on the screen or written to the `/var/log/messages` file. Boot loader problems display messages to the screen; no log file is produced. Kernel oops are errors in a running kernel, and error messages are written to the `/var/log/messages` file.

Excellent documentation on the Internet exists for troubleshooting just about every type of error that GRUB2 or the kernel could give during boot. The best way to find this documentation is to go to your favorite search engine and type in the keywords of the error you received. Adjust the keywords you use as you focus your search.

If you have GRUB problems, the GRUB manual is online at www.gnu.org/software/grub/manual/, and further information is available at https://help.ubuntu.com/community/Grub2.

> **TIP**
>
> For best results, go to www.google.com/linux to find all things Linux on the Internet. Google has specifically created a Linux area of its database, which should allow faster access to information on Linux than any other search engine.

References

- ▶ **www.kernel.org/**—Linux Kernel Archives. The source of all development discussion for the Linux kernel.

- ▶ **www.gnu.org/**—Free Software Foundation. Source of manuals and software for programs used throughout the kernel compilation process. Tools such as `make` and `gcc` have their official documentation here.

- ▶ **https://wiki.ubuntu.com/Kernel**—The starting point for anything you want to know about both Ubuntu and its use of the Linux kernel.

- ▶ **https://wiki.ubuntu.com/Kernel/FAQ**—The Ubuntu Kernel Team answers the most commonly asked questions about Ubuntu's use of Linux kernels.

- ▶ **www.tldp.org/**—The Linux Documentation Project. The Mecca of all Linux documentation. Excellent source of HOWTO documentation, as well as FAQs and online books, all about Linux.

- ▶ **www.minix.org/**—The unofficial minix website. It contains a selection of links to information about minix and a link to the actual homepage. Although minix is still copyrighted, the owner has granted unlimited rights to everyone. See for yourself the OS used to develop Linux.

# CHAPTER 23

Sharing Files and Printers

In the early days of computing, file and printer sharing was pretty much impossible because of the lack of good networking standards and interoperability. If you wanted to use a printer connected to another computer, you had to save the file to a floppy disk and walk to the other computer. Sometimes people do the same thing today using a USB thumb drive or by emailing the file. However, there are better ways.

Both file and printer sharing are important because it is not unusual for someone to own more than one computer. Whether you want to share photographs among various computers or have a central repository available for collaboration, file sharing is an important part of the information age. Alongside this is the need to be able to share printers; after all, people do not want to have to plug and unplug a computer to a printer just so they can print out a quick letter.

Whatever your reasons for needing to share files and printers across a network, you find out how to do both in this chapter. This chapter shows you how you can share files using the popular UNIX NFS protocol and the more Windows-friendly Samba system. You also find out how to configure network-attached printers with interfaces such as JetDirect. The chapter covers both graphical and command-line tools, so you should find something to suit the way you work.

> **CAUTION**
>
> By default, Ubuntu ships with all its network ports blocked. That is, it does not listen to any requests on any network ports when it is first installed. To configure the firewall, use *Uncomplicated Firewall (UFW)* as described in Chapter 20, "Securing Your Machines."

Using the Network File System

Network File System (NFS) is the protocol developed by Sun Microsystems that enables computers to use a remote file system as if it were a real part of the local machine. A common use of NFS is to allow users' /home directories to appear on every local machine they use, thus eliminating the need to have physical home directories. This opens up hot desking and other flexible working arrangements, especially because no matter where the users are, their /home directories follow them around.

Another popular use for NFS is to share binary files between similar computers. If you have a new version of a package that you want all machines to have, you have to upgrade only on the NFS server, and all hosts running the same version of Ubuntu have the same upgraded package.

Installing and Starting or Stopping NFS

NFS is not installed by default on Ubuntu, so you need to install the nfs-kernel-server package. NFS itself consists of several programs that work together. One is portmap, which maps NFS requests to the correct daemon. Two others are nfsd, which is the NFS daemon, and mountd, which controls the mounting and unmounting of file systems.

Ubuntu automatically adds NFS to the system startup scripts, so it will always be available after you have configured it. To check this, use the command sudo /etc/init.d/nfs-kernel-server status and you see that the service is running. If you need to manually start the NFS server, use the following command:

```
matthew@seymour:~$ sudo /etc/init.d/nfs-kernel-server start
 * Exporting directories for NFS kernel daemon:   [ OK ]
Starting NFS kernel daemon:                       [ OK ]
```

In this example, NFS has been started. Use stop to stop the service or restart to restart the service. This approach to controlling NFS proves handy, especially after configuration changes have been made. See the next section on how to configure NFS support on your Ubuntu system.

NFS Server Configuration

You can configure the NFS server by editing the /etc/exports file. This file is similar to the /etc/fstab file in that it is used to set the permissions for the file systems being exported. The entries look like this:

```
/file/system yourhost(options) *.yourdomain.com(options) 192.168.0.0/24(options)
```

This shows three common clients to which to share /file/system. The first, yourhost, shares /file/system to just one host. The second, .yourdomain.com, uses the asterisk (*) as a wildcard to enable all hosts in yourdomain.com to access /file/system. The third share enables all hosts of the Class C network, 192.168.0.0, to access /file/share. For security, it is best not to use shares such as the last two across the Internet, because all data will be readable by any network the data passes by.

Table 23.1 shows some common options.

TABLE 23.1   `/etc/fstab` Options

Option	Purpose
rw	Gives read and write access
ro	Gives read-only access
async	Writes data when the server, not the client, feels the need
sync	Writes data as it is received

The following is an example of an `/etc/exports` file:

```
# /etc/exports: the access control list for filesystems which may be exported
#               to NFS clients.  See exports(5).
/home/matthew 192.168.0.0/24(rw,no_root_squash)
```

This file exports (makes available) `/home/matthew` to any host in `192.168.0.*` and allows users to read from and write to `/home/matthew`.

After you have finished with the `/etc/exports` file, the following command exports all the file systems in the `/etc/exports` file to a list named `xtab` under the `/var/lib` `/nfs` directory, which is used as a guide for mounting when a remote computer asks for a directory to be exported:

```
matthew@seymour:~$ sudo exportfs -a
```

The `-r` option stands for re-export and tells the command to reread the entire `/etc/` `exports` file and (re)mount all the entries. You can also use the `exportfs` command to export specific files temporarily. Here's an example using `exportfs` to export a file system:

```
matthew@seymour:~$ /usr/sbin/exportfs -o async yourhost:/usr/tmp
```

This command exports `/usr/tmp` to `yourhost` with the `async` option.

Be sure to restart the NFS server after making any changes to `/etc/exports`. If you prefer, you can use Ubuntu's `shares-admin` graphical client to set up NFS from the GUI. Search for *personal file* sharing in the Dash to start. Fill in the required information and off you go. You still need to install some packages on Ubuntu for this to work, the same ones mentioned earlier in this chapter in the Installing and Starting or Stopping NFS section and below in NFS Client Configuration.

NFS Client Configuration

To configure your host as an NFS client (to acquire remote files or directories), you need to ensure that you have the `nfs-common` package installed, to be able to access NFS shares. After you've installed this, edit the `/etc/fstab` file as you would to mount any local file system. However, instead of using a device name to be mounted (such as `/dev/sda1`), enter the remote hostname and the desired file system to be imported. For example, one entry might look like this:

```
# Device           Mount Point  Type  Options     Freq Pass
yourhost:/home/share /export/share  none   nfs   0    0
```

> **NOTE**
>
> If you use `autofs` on your system, you need to use proper `autofs` entries for your remote NFS mounts. See the Section 5 man page for `autofs` by entering `man 5 autofs` at the command line.

You can also use the `mount` command, as root, to quickly attach a remote directory to a local file system by using a remote host's name and exported directory. For example:

```
matthew@seymour:~$ sudo mount -t nfs 192.168.2.67:/music /music
```

After you press Enter, the entire remote directory appears on your file system. You can verify the imported file system using the `df` command, as follows:

```
matthew@seymour:~$ df
Filesystem           1k-blocks      Used Available Use% Mounted on
/dev/hda2             18714368   9642600   8121124  55% /
/dev/hda1                46636     13247     30981  30% /boot
none                    120016         0    120016   0% /dev/shm
192.168.2.67:/music  36875376  20895920  14106280  60% /music
```

Make sure that the desired mount point exists before using the `mount` command. When finished using the directory (perhaps for copying backups), you can use the `umount` command to remove the remote file system. Note that if you specify the root directory (/) as a mount point, you cannot unmount the NFS directory until you reboot (because Linux complains that the file system is in use).

Putting Samba to Work

Samba uses the *Session Message Block (SMB)* protocol to enable the Windows operating system (or any operating system) to access Linux files. Using Samba, you can make your Ubuntu machine look just like a Windows computer to other Windows computers on your network. You do not need to install Windows on your PC.

Samba is a complex program. Although Samba is complex, setting it up and using it does not have to be difficult. There are many options, which account for some of Samba's complexity. Depending on what you want, Samba's use can be as easy or as difficult as you would like it to be.

Fortunately, Ubuntu includes a very easy way to access files on a Windows network share by default. To start, search for Network in the Dash and open it. If there are other computers on the network with shared files using Windows or Samba, you will see a Windows Network icon that, when double-clicked, shows you all Windows domains or workgroups found on your network. Just double-click any computer icon there to access shares and files.

To share from your Ubuntu desktop, right-click a folder you own while using the file browser, most likely one in your `/home/username` directory, and select Local Network Share. You are given a chance to confirm your desire to share the folder and give it a name. Sharing gives others the permission to view, but not necessarily to create or delete files, although those permissions are also available from this menu. If you do not have the Windows sharing service already installed on your computer, Ubuntu prompts you for permission to install it.

> **NOTE**
>
> Most Ubuntu users will not need the information contained in the rest of this section because installing the sharing service also takes care of the configuration and, as a result, everything should just work.

For greater configurability and control, follow these instructions:

1. Install Samba and the GUI configuration application by installing these packages: `samba`, `samba-common`, `system-config-samba`, `python-glade2`, `gksu`.

2. From the Dash, search for `samba` and open it.

3. In the Samba configuration application, open Preferences > Server Settings. Here you will configure basic settings like setting Workgroup to the name of your Windows Workgroup name on your network and giving a description of your computer to be seen by others on the network. You can change the computer's network security options for Samba here as well, but the default settings are good.

4. Next, also in the Samba configuration application, open Preferences > Samba Users. Click Add User. You need to enter the details for a) the user on this Ubuntu machine who will be given privileges to use Samba to view files on other network computers and b) a Windows username that will be used when accessing this Ubuntu machine's files from a Windows machine on the network and c) a password that will be required with the Windows username when accessing files on this Ubuntu computer from a Windows machine.

5. Restart Samba from the terminal to finish: `sudo restart smbd && sudo restart nmbd`.

You can share a folder from the Samba configuration application, set directory, name, read/write permissions, and access users.

For even greater configurability, read through the editable configuration file at `/etc/samba/smb.conf`. It is well commented and clear and explained in greater detail below.

To learn more about Samba, see https://www.samba.org. This section delves into the basics of configuring Samba, and you should first read how to manually configure Samba to get an understanding of how the software works.

When you install Samba, it is a good idea to also install the `samba-doc` and `samba-doc-pdf` packages because they contain extensive documentation in text, PDF, and HTML format. After you install it, you can find this documentation in `/usr/share/doc/samba*/doc`. If you install Samba using your Ubuntu disc, you can find a large amount of documentation in the directory tree starting at `/usr/share/doc/samba-doc` or `/usr/share/doc/samba-doc-pdf` in several formats, including PDF, HTML, and text, among others. Altogether, almost 3MB of documentation is included with the source code.

After installing Samba, you can either create the file `/etc/samba/smb.conf` or use the `smb.conf` file supplied with Samba, which is located by default under the `/etc/samba` directory with Ubuntu. You can find nearly a dozen sample configuration files under the `/usr/share/doc/samba*/examples` directory.

NOTE

Depending on your needs, `smb.conf` can be a simple file of fewer than 20 lines or a huge file spanning many pages of text. If your needs are complex, I suggest you browse through The Official Samba HOWTO and Reference Guide, or TOSHARG. You can find this helpful guide at http://samba.org/samba/docs/man/Samba4-HOWTO/.

Manually Configuring Samba with `/etc/samba/smb.conf`

The `/etc/samba/smb.conf` file is broken into sections. Each section is a description of the resource shared (share) and should be titled appropriately. The three special sections are as follows:

▶ `[global]`—Establishes the global configuration settings (defined in detail in the `smb.conf` man page and Samba documentation, found under the `/usr/share/doc/samba/docs` directory)

▶ `[homes]`—Shares users' `/home` directories and specifies directory paths and permissions

▶ `[printers]`—Handles printing by defining shared printers and printer access

Each section in your `/etc/samba/smb.conf` configuration file should be named for the resource being shared. For example, if the resource `/usr/local/programs` is being shared, you could call the section `[programs]`. When Windows sees the share, it is called by whatever you name the section (`programs` in this example). The easiest and fastest way to set up this share is with the following example from `smb.conf`:

```
[programs]
path = /usr/local/programs
writeable = true
```

This bit shares the `/usr/local/programs` directory with any valid user who asks for it and makes that directory writeable. It is the most basic share because it sets no limits on the directory.

Here are some parameters you can set in the sections:

▶ Requiring a user to enter a password before accessing a shared directory

▶ Limiting the hosts allowed to access the shared directory

▶ Altering permissions users are allowed to have on the directory

▶ Limiting the time of day during which the directory is accessible

The possibilities are almost endless. Any parameters set in the individual sections override the parameters set in the [global] section. The following section adds a few restrictions to the [programs] section:

```
[programs]
path = /usr/local/programs
writeable = true
valid users = mhelmke
browseable = yes
create mode = 0700
```

> **NOTE**
>
> You can spell it as `writeable` or `writable`; either variant will work. Both spellings are used in this chapter.

The valid users entry limits userid to just mhelmke. All other users can browse the directory because of the browseable = yes entry, but only mhelmke can write to the directory. Any files created by ahudson in the directory give ahudson full permissions, but no one else will have access to the file. This is the same as setting permissions with the chmod command. Again, there are numerous options, so you can be as creative as you want when developing sections.

Setting Global Samba Behavior with the [global] Section

The [global] section set parameters establishes configuration settings for all of Samba. If a given parameter is not specifically set in another section, Samba uses the default setting in the [global] section. The [global] section also sets the general security configuration for Samba. The [global] section is the only section that does not require the name in brackets.

Samba assumes that anything before the first bracketed section not labeled [global] is part of the global configuration. (Using bracketed headings in /etc/samba/smb.conf makes your configuration file more readable.) The following sections discuss common Samba settings to share directories and printers. You will then see how to test your Samba configuration.

Sharing Home Directories Using the [homes] Section

The [homes] section shares out Ubuntu /home directories for the users. The /home directory is shared automatically when a user's Windows computer connects to the Linux server holding the /home directory. The one problem with using the default configuration is that the users see all the configuration files (such as .profile and others with a leading period in the filename) that they normally wouldn't see when logging on through Linux. One quick way to avoid this is to include a path option in the [homes] section. To use this solution, any users who require a Samba share of their /home directory need a separate "home directory" to act as their Windows /home directory.

This setting specifies that the directory named share under each user's directory is the shared Samba directory. The corresponding manual smb.conf setting to provide a separate "home directory" looks like this:

```
[homes]
        comment = Home Directories
        path = /home/%u/share
        valid users = %S
        read only = No
        create mask = 0664
        directory mask = 0775
        browseable = No
```

If you have a default [homes] section, the share shows up in the user's Network Neighborhood as the user's name. When the user connects, Samba scans the existing sections in smb.conf for a specific instance of the user's /home directory. If there is not one, Samba looks up the username in /etc/passwd. If the correct username and password have been given, the home directory listed in /etc/passwd is shared out at the user's /home directory. Typically, the [homes] section looks like this. (The browseable = no entry prevents other users from being able to browse your /home directory and is a good security practice.)

```
[homes]
browseable = no
writable = yes
```

This example shares out the /home directory and makes it writeable to the user. Here's how you specify a separate Windows /home directory for each user:

```
[homes]
browseable = no
writable = yes
path = /path/to/windows/directories
```

Sharing Printers by Editing the [printers] Section

The [printers] section works much like the [homes] section but defines shared printers for use on your network. If the section exists, users have access to any printer listed in your Ubuntu /etc/printcap file.

Like the [homes] section, when a print request is received, all the sections are scanned for the printer. If no share is found (with careful naming, there should not be unless you create a section for a specific printer), the /etc/printcap file is scanned for the printer name that is then used to send the print request.

For printing to work properly, you must correctly set up printing services on your Ubuntu computer. A typical [printers] section looks like this:

```
[printers]
comment = Ubuntu Printers
```

```
browseable = no
printable = yes
path = /var/spool/samba
```

The `/var/spool/samba` is a spool path set just for Samba printing.

Testing Samba with the `testparm` Command

After you have created your `/etc/smb.conf` file, you can check it for correctness by using the `testparm` command. This command parses through your `/etc/smb.conf` file and checks for any syntax errors. If none are found, your configuration file will probably work correctly. It does not, however, guarantee that the services specified in the file will work. It is merely making sure that the file is correctly written.

As with all configuration files, if you are modifying an existing, working file, it is always prudent to copy the working file to a different location and modify that file. Then, you can check the file with the `testparm` utility. The command syntax is as follows:

```
matthew@seymour:~$ sudo testparm /path/to/smb.conf.back-up
Load smb config files from smb.conf.back-up
Processing section "[homes]"
Processing section "[printers]"
Loaded services file OK.
```

This output shows that the Samba configuration file is correct, and as long as all the services are running correctly on your Ubuntu machine, Samba should be working correctly. Now copy your old `smb.conf` file to a new location, put the new one in its place, and restart Samba with the command `sudo smbd restart`. Your new or modified Samba configuration should now be in place.

Starting, Stopping, and Restarting the `smbd` Daemon

After your `smb.conf` file is correctly configured, you might want to start, stop, or restart your Samba server daemon. You can do this with the `/usr/sbin/smbd` command, which (with no options) starts the Samba server with all the defaults. The most common option you will change in this command is the location of the `smb.conf` file; you change this option if you don't want to use the default location `/etc/smb/smb.conf`. The `-s` option enables you to change the `smb.conf` file Samba uses; this option is also useful for testing whether a new `smb.conf` file actually works. Another useful option is the `-l` option, which specifies the log file Samba uses to store information.

To start, stop, or restart Samba from the command line, use this, replacing `start` with either `stop` or `restart` as appropriate:

```
matthew@seymour:~$ sudo  start smbd
```

Using the `smbstatus` Command

The `smbstatus` command reports on the current status of your Samba connections. The syntax is as follows:

```
/usr/bin/smbstatus [options]
```

Table 23.2 shows some of the available options.

TABLE 23.2   `smbstatus` Options

Option	Result
-b	Brief output
-d	Verbose output
-s /path/to /config	Used if the configuration file used at startup is not the standard one
-u username	Shows the status of a specific user's connection
-p	Lists current `smb` processes, which can prove useful in scripts

Connecting with the `smbclient` Command

The `smbclient` command allows users on other Linux hosts to access your `smb` shares. You cannot mount the share on your host, but you can use it in a way that is similar to an FTP client. Several options can be used with the `smbclient` command. The most frequently used is `-I` followed by the IP address of the computer to which you are connecting. The `smbclient` command does not require root access to run:

```
matthew@seymour:~$ smbclient -I 10.10.10.20 -Uusername%password
```

This gives you the following prompt:

```
smb: <current directory on share>
```

From here, the commands are almost identical to the standard UNIX/Linux FTP commands. Note that you can omit a password on the `smbclient` command line. You are then prompted to enter the Samba share password.

Mounting Samba Shares

There are two ways to mount Samba shares to your Linux host. Mounting a share is the same as mounting an available media partition or remote NFS directory except that the Samba share is accessed using SMB. The first method uses the standard Linux `mount` command:

```
matthew@seymour:~$ sudo mount -t smbfs //10.10.10.20/homes /mount/point -o
username=heather,dmask=777,\ fmask=777
```

> **NOTE**
>
> You can substitute the IP address for hostname if your name service is running or the host is in your `/etc/hosts` file.

The preceding command mounts `heather`'s `/home` directory on your host and gives all users full permissions to the mount. The permissions are equal to the permissions on the `chmod` command.

The second method produces the same results using the smbmount command, as follows:

```
matthew@seymour:~$ sudo smbmount //10.10.10.20/homes /mount/point -o
username=heather,dmask-777,\ fmask=777
```

To unmount the share, use the following standard command:

```
matthew@seymour:~$ sudo umount /mount/point
```

You can also use these mount commands to mount true Windows client shares to your Ubuntu host. Using Samba, you can configure your server to provide any service Windows can serve, and no one but you will ever know.

Network and Remote Printing with Ubuntu

Chapter 1, "Installing Ubuntu and Post-Installation Configuration," discusses how to set up and configure local printers and the associated print services. This section covers configuring printers for sharing and access across a network.

Offices all over the world benefit from using print servers and shared printers. It is a simple thing to do and can bring real productivity benefits, even in small settings.

Creating Network Printers

Setting up remote printing service involves configuring a print server and then creating a remote printer entry on one or more computers on your network. This section introduces a quick method of enabling printing from one Linux workstation to another Linux computer on a LAN. You also learn about SMB printing using Samba and its utilities. Finally, this section discusses how to configure network-attached printers and use them to print single or multiple documents.

Enabling Network Printing on a LAN

If the computer with an attached printer is using Ubuntu and you want to set up the system for print serving, use the system-config-printer client to create a new printer, which is available in the menu at System, Administration, Printing.

First, install any printers you have to the server as discussed in Chapter 1, "Installing Ubuntu and Post-Installation Configuration." (Click Add and wait a moment, and it is likely the printer will be detected automatically; it is probably easy enough that you don't have to look up what is written in the other chapter.)

Next, open Server, Settings and enable Publish Shared Printers Connected to This System. Click OK. Right-click any printer's icon and select Share. That's it. Most users will not need the information in the rest of this section, even to enable access to *Common UNIX Printing System (CUPS)* via the web interface.

To enable sharing manually, edit your /etc/cups/cupsd.conf file. Look for the section that begins with <Location /> and modify it so that it reads as follows:

```
<Location />
Order Deny,Allow
```

```
Deny From All
Allow From 127.0.0.1
Allow From 192.168.0.*
</Location>
```

This tells CUPS to share your printers across the network `192.168.0.*`, for example. Make sure to change this to match your own network settings.

Next you need to look in the same file for the section that starts:

```
Listen localhost:631
```

Modify it to show this:

```
Listen 631
```

This tells CUPS to listen on port 631 for any printer requests.

Session Message Block Printing

Printing to an SMB printer requires Samba, along with its utilities such as the `smbclient` and associated `smbprint` printing filter. You can use the Samba software included with Ubuntu to print to a shared printer on a Windows network or set up a printer attached to your system as an SMB printer. This section describes how to create a local printer entry to print to a remote shared printer using SMB.

You usually set up an SMB or shared printer under Windows operating systems through configuration settings using the Control Panel's Network device. After enabling print sharing, reboot the computer. In the My Computer, Printers folder, right-click the name or icon of the printer you want to share and select Sharing from the pop-up menu. Set the Shared As item and then enter a descriptive shared name, such as **HP2100**, and a password.

You must enter a shared name and password to configure the printer when running Linux. You also need to know the printer's workgroup name, IP address, and printer name and have the username and password on hand. To find this information, select Start, Settings, Printers, and then right-click the shared printer's listing in the Printers window. Select Properties from the pop-up window.

You can use CUPS to configure Samba to use your printers by editing the `smb.conf` file.

In the `[global]` section enter the following lines, if they are not already there:

```
...
load printers = yes
printing = cups
printcap name = cups
```

This tells Samba to use CUPS to provide printing services. Next you need to create a new section in the `smb.conf` file at the end of the file, as follows:

```
[printers]
comment = Use this for All Printers
path = /var/spool/samba
```

```
browseable = no
public = yes
guest ok = yes
writable = no
printable = yes
printer admin = root, andrew
```

This publishes your printers to the network and allows others to connect to them via Windows clients.

Make sure you restart the Samba service using the command shown earlier to make Samba pick up the changes to the configuration file.

Using the Common UNIX Printing System GUI

You can use CUPS to create printer queues, get print server information, and manage queues by launching a browser (such as Firefox) and browsing to http://localhost:631. CUPS provides a web-based administration interface, as shown in Figure 23.1.

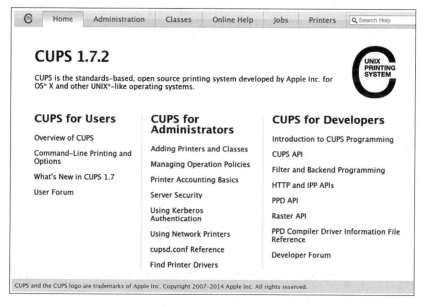

FIGURE 23.1   Use the web-based CUPS administrative interface to configure and manage printing.

If you click the Administration tab in the browser page, you can start configuring your printers, as shown in Figure 23.2.

Creating a CUPS Printer Entry

This section provides a short example of creating a Linux printer entry using CUPS's web-based interface. Use the CUPS interface to create a printer and device queue type (such as local, remote, serial port, or Internet); then you enter a device *uniform resource identifier (URI)*, such as `lpd://192.168.2.35/lp`, which represents the IP address of a remote UNIX print server and the name of the remote print queue on the server. You also need to specify the model or make of printer and its driver. A Printers page link enables you to print a test page, stop the printing service, manage the local print queue, modify the printer entry, or add another printer.

In the Admin page, click the Add Printer button and then enter the username and password of someone on this computer who has `sudo` privileges. You may then select from detected local printers, discovered network printers, or the type of printer for which you may want to enter details manually.

FIGURE 23.2   Select the Administration tab to perform printer administration with CUPS.

CUPS offers many additional features and after it is installed, configured, and running, provides transparent traditional UNIX printing support for Ubuntu.

> **NOTE**
>
> To learn more about CUPS and to get a basic overview of the system, browse to www.cups.org/.

Avoiding Printer Support Problems

Troubleshooting printer problems can prove frustrating, especially if you find that your new printer is not working properly with Linux. Keep in mind, however, that nearly all printers on the market today work with Linux. However, some vendors have higher batting averages in the game of supporting Linux. If you care to see a scorecard, browse to www.linuxprinting.org/vendors.html.

All-in-One (Print/Fax/Scan) Devices

Problematic printers, or printing devices that might or might not work with Ubuntu, include multifunction (or *all-in-one*) printers that combine scanning, faxing, and printing services. You should research any planned purchase and avoid any vendor unwilling to support Linux with drivers or development information.

One shining star in the field of Linux support for multifunction printers is the HP support of the HP OfficeJet Linux driver project at http://hpoj.sourceforge.net/. Printing and scanning are supported on many models, with fax support in development.

Using USB and Legacy Printers

Other problems can arise because of a lack of a printer's *Universal Serial Bus (USB)* vendor and device ID information—a problem shared by some USB scanners under Linux. For information about USB printer support, check with the Linux printing folks (at the URL in the start of this section) or with the Linux USB project at www.linux-usb.org/.

Although many newer printers require a USB port, excellent support still exists for legacy parallel-port (IEEE-1284) printers with Linux, enabling sites to continue to use older hardware. You can take advantage of Linux workarounds to set up printing even if the host computer does not have a traditional parallel printer port or if you want to use a newer USB printer on an older computer.

For example, to host a parallel-port-based printer on a USB-only computer, attach the printer to the computer using an inexpensive USB-to-parallel converter. USB-to-parallel converters typically provide a Centronics connector; one end of that connector is plugged in to the older printer, and the other end is plugged in to a USB connector. The USB connector is then plugged in to your hub, desktop, or notebook USB port. You can use an add-on PCI card to add USB support for printing (and other devices) if the legacy computer does not have a built-in USB port. Most PCI USB interface cards add at least two ports, and you can chain devices via a hub.

RELATED UBUNTU AND LINUX COMMANDS

The following commands can help you manage printing services:

- ▶ `accept`—Controls print job access to the CUPS server via the command line
- ▶ `cancel`—Cancels a print job from the command line
- ▶ `disable`—Control printing from the command line
- ▶ `enable`—Controls CUPS printers
- ▶ `lp`—Sends a specified file to the printer and allows control of the print service
- ▶ `lpc`—Displays the status of printers and print service at the console
- ▶ `lpq`—Views print queues (pending print jobs) at the console
- ▶ `lprm`—Removes print jobs from the print queue via the command line
- ▶ `lpstat`—Displays printer and server status

References

▶ **https://help.ubuntu.com/community/SettingUpNFSHowTo**—Ubuntu community documentation for setting up NFS

▶ **https://help.ubuntu.com/community/Samba**—Ubuntu community documentation for setting up Samba

▶ **www.samba.org/**—Base entry point for getting more information about Samba and using the SMB protocol with Linux, UNIX, Mac OS X, and other operating systems

▶ **www.cups.org/**—A comprehensive repository of CUPS software and information

▶ **www.pwg.org/ipp/**—Home page for the Internet Printing Protocol standards

# CHAPTER 24

Apache Web Server Management

This chapter covers the configuration and management of the Apache web server and includes an overview of some of the major components of the server and discussions of text-based and graphical server configuration. In this chapter, you learn how to start, stop, and restart Apache using the command line. The chapter begins with some introductory information and then shows you how to install, configure, and use Apache.

About the Apache Web Server

Apache is the most widely used web server on the Internet today.

The name *Apache* appeared during the early development of the software because it was "a patchy" server, made up of patches for the freely available source code of the NCSA HTTPd web server. For a while after the NCSA HTTPd project was discontinued, a number of people wrote a variety of patches for the code, to either fix bugs or add features they wanted. A lot of this code was floating around and people were freely sharing it, but it was completely unmanaged.

After a while, Brian Behlendorf and Cliff Skolnick set up a centralized repository of these patches, and the Apache project was born. The project is still composed of a small core group of programmers, but anyone is welcome to submit patches to the group for possible inclusion in the code.

There has been a surge of interest in the Apache project over the past several years, partially buoyed by a new interest in open source on the part of enterprise-level information services. It's also due in part to crippling security flaws found in Microsoft's *Internet Information Services (IIS)*; the existence of malicious web task exploits; and operating system and networking vulnerabilities to the now-infamous Code Red, Blaster, and Nimda worms. IBM made an early commitment to support and use Apache as the basis for its web offerings and has dedicated substantial resources to the project because it makes more sense to use an established, proven web server.

In mid-1999, the Apache Software Foundation was incorporated as a nonprofit company. A board of directors, who are elected on an annual basis by the ASF members, oversees the company. This company provides a foundation for several open-source software development projects, including the Apache Web Server project.

TIP

You can find an overview of Apache in its FAQs at https://wiki.apache.org/httpd/FAQ. In addition to extensive online documentation, you'll find the complete documentation for Apache in the HTML directory of your Apache server. If you have Apache running on your system, you can access this documentation by looking at http://localhost/manual/index.html.

To determine the precise version of Apache included with your system, use:

```
matthew@seymour:~$ apache2 -v
```

Installing the Apache Server

Install the `apache2` package from the Ubuntu software repositories. Updated packages usually contain important bug and security fixes. When an updated version is released, install it as quickly as possible to keep your system secure.

NOTE

Check the Apache site for security reports. Browse to http://httpd.apache.org/security_report.html for links to security vulnerabilities for Apache 2.0, 2.2, and 2.4. Subscribe to a support list or browse through up-to-date archives of all Apache mailing lists at http://httpd.apache.org/mail/ (for various articles) or http://httpd.apache.org/lists.html (for comprehensive and organized archives).

CAUTION

You should be wary of installing experimental packages, and never install them on production servers (that is, servers used in "real life"). Very carefully test the packages beforehand on a host that is not connected to a network!

For more information about installing software from the Ubuntu repositories, see Chapter 9, "Managing Software."

> **NOTE**
>
> If you are upgrading to a newer version of Apache, APT does not write over your current configuration files.

Starting and Stopping Apache

At this point, you have installed your Apache server with its default configuration. Ubuntu provides a default home page at `/var/www/html/index.html` as a test.

You can start Apache from the command line of a text-based console or X terminal window, and you must have root permission to do so. How you will do so depends on the release version of Ubuntu that you are running. For Ubuntu 16.04 and later, we use systemd commands. For earlier Ubuntu releases like 12.04 and 14.04 that used Upstart, we use Upstart commands. Some prefer to use apache2ctl commands, which work across most distributions.

Action	systemd	Upstart	apache2ctl
Start	`sudo systemctl start apache2.service`	`sudo start apache2`	`sudo apache2ctl start`
Stop	`sudo systemctl stop apache2.service`	`sudo stop apache2`	`sudo apache2ctl stop`

The server daemon, `apache2`, recognizes several command-line options you can use to set some defaults, such as specifying where `apache2` reads its configuration directives. The Apache `apache2` executable also understands other options that enable you to selectively use parts of its configuration file, specify a different location of the actual server and supporting files, use a different configuration file (perhaps for testing), and save startup errors to a specific log. The `-v` option causes Apache to print its development version and quit. The `-V` option shows all the settings that were in effect when the server was compiled.

The `-h` option prints the following usage information for the server:

```
matthew@seymour:~$ apache2 -h
Usage: apache2 [-D name] [-d directory] [-f file]
               [-C "directive"] [-c "directive"]
               [-k start|restart|graceful|stop]
               [-v] [-V] [-h] [-l] [-L] [-t]
Options:
  -D name            : define a name for use in <IfDefine name> directives
  -d directory       : specify an alternate initial ServerRoot
  -f file            : specify an alternate ServerConfigFile
  -C "directive"     : process directive before reading config files
  -c "directive"     : process directive after reading config files
  -e level           : show startup errors of level (see LogLevel)
  -E file            : log startup errors to file
  -v                 : show version number
```

```
-V                   : show compile settings
-h                   : list available command line options (this page)
-l                   : list compiled in modules
-L                   : list available configuration directives
-t -D DUMP_VHOSTS : show parsed settings (currently only vhost settings)
-t                   : run syntax check for config files
```

Other options include listing Apache's *static modules*, or special, built-in independent parts of the server, along with options that can be used with the modules. These options are called *configuration directives* and are commands that control how a static module works. Note that Apache also includes a large number of *dynamic modules*, or software portions of the server that can be optionally loaded and used while the server is running.

The -t option is used to check your configuration files. It's a good idea to run this check before restarting your server, especially if you've made changes to your configuration files. Such tests are important because a configuration file error can result in your server shutting down when you try to restart it. There is a bug in the internal username settings for apache2 in Ubuntu that gives you this error if you enter the following:

```
matthew@seymour:~$ sudo apache2 -t
apache2: bad user name ${APACHE_RUN_USER}
```

If this happens to you, enter the command this way to force the command to use the expected username settings and you will get the proper output:

```
matthew@seymour:~$ sudo APACHE_RUN_USER=www-data APACHE_RUN_GROUP=www-data apache2 -t
```

Runtime Server Configuration Settings

At this point, the Apache server will run, but perhaps you want to change a behavior, such as the default location of your website's files. This section covers the basics of configuring the server to work the way you want it to work.

Runtime configurations are stored in just one file—apache2.conf, which is under the /etc/apache2 directory. You can use this configuration file to control the default behavior of Apache, such as the web server's base configuration directory (/etc/apache2), the name of the server's PID file (/var/run/apache2.pid), or its response timeout (300 seconds). Apache reads the data from the configuration file when started (or restarted).

Runtime Configuration Directives

You perform runtime configuration of your server with configuration directives, which are commands that set options for the apache2 daemon. The directives are used to tell the server about various options you want to enable, such as the location of files important to the server configuration and operation. Apache supports nearly 300 configuration directives using the following syntax:

```
directive option option...
```

Each directive is specified on a single line. See the following sections for some directive examples and how to use them. Some directives only set a value such as a filename, whereas others enable you to specify various options. Some special directives, called *sections*, look like HTML tags. Section directives are surrounded by angle brackets, such as `<Directory>`. Sections usually enclose a group of directives that apply only to the directory specified in the section:

```
<Directory somedir/in/your/tree>
  directive option option
  directive option option
</Directory>
```

All sections are closed with a matching section tag that looks like this: `</Directory>`. Note that section tags, like any other directives, are specified one per line.

> **TIP**
>
> Apache is configured with an alias that lets you view the documentation installed in / usr/share/doc using your web browser at localhost/manual. After installing and starting Apache, you can find an index of directives at http://localhost/manual/mod/directives.html.

Editing apache2.conf

Most of the default settings in the config file are okay to keep, particularly if you've installed the server in a default location and aren't doing anything unusual on your server. The file includes clear comments describing most of the settings. In general, if you do not understand what a particular directive is for, leave it set to the default value.

The following sections describe some of the configuration file settings you *might* want to change concerning operation of your server.

ServerRoot

The `ServerRoot` directive sets the absolute path to your server directory. This directive tells the server where to find all the resources and configuration files. Many of these resources are specified in the configuration files relative to the `ServerRoot` directory.

Your `ServerRoot` directive should be set to `/etc/apache2` if you installed the Ubuntu package or `/usr/local/apache` (or whatever directory you chose when you compiled Apache) if you installed from the source. This is commented out in the file, but `apache2 -v` shows that this default has been compiled into the package.

Listen

The `Listen` directive is actually in a file called `ports.conf` that is included from `apache2.conf` and indicates on which port you want your server to run. By default, this is set to 80, which is the standard HTTP port number. You might want to run your server on another port—for example, when running a test server that you don't want people to find by accident. Do not confuse this with real security! See the "File System Authentication and Access Control" section for more information about how to secure parts of your web server.

User **and** Group

The User and Group directives should be set to the UID and GID the server will use to process requests.

In Ubuntu, set these configurations to a user with few or no privileges. In this case, they're set to user www-data and group www-data—a user defined specifically to run Apache. If you want to use a different UID or GID, be aware that the server will run with the permissions of the user and group set here. That means in the event of a security breach, whether on the server or (more likely) in your own CGI programs, those programs will run with the assigned UID. If the server runs as root or some other privileged user, someone can exploit the security holes and do nasty things to your site. Always think in terms of the specified user running a command such as rm -rf / because that would wipe all files from your system. That should convince you that leaving apache as a user with no privileges is probably a good thing.

Instead of specifying the User and Group directives using names, you can specify them using the UID and GID numbers. If you use numbers, be sure that the numbers you specify correspond to the user and group you want and that they're preceded by the pound (#) symbol.

Here's how these directives look if specified by name:

```
User apache
Group apache
```

Here's the same specification by UID and GID:

```
User #48
Group #48
```

TIP

If you find a user on your system (other than root) with a UID and GID of 0, your system has been compromised by a malicious user.

ServerAdmin

The ServerAdmin directive should be set to the address of the webmaster managing the server. This address should be a valid email address or alias, such as webmaster@matthe whelmke.com, because this address is returned to a visitor when a problem occurs on the server.

ServerName

The ServerName directive sets the hostname the server will return. Set it to a fully *qualified domain name (FQDN)*. For example, set it to www.your.domain rather than simply www. This is particularly important if this machine will be accessible from the Internet rather than just on your local network.

You do not need to set this unless you want a name other than the machine's canonical name returned. If this value isn't set, the server will figure out the name by itself and set it to its canonical name. However, you might want the server to return a friendlier address, such as www.your.domain. Whatever you do, ServerName should be a real *Domain Name Service (DNS)* name for your network. If you're administering your own DNS, remember to add an alias for your host. If someone else manages the DNS for you, ask that person to set this name for you.

DocumentRoot

Set this directive to the absolute path of your document tree, which is the top directory from which Apache will serve files. By default, it's set to /var/www/. If you built the source code yourself, DocumentRoot is set to /usr/local/apache/htdocs (if you did not choose another directory when you compiled Apache).

UserDir

The UserDir directive disables or enables and defines the directory (relative to a local user's /home directory) where that user can put public HTML documents. It is relative because each user has her own HTML directory. This setting is disabled by default but can be enabled to store user web content under any directory.

The default setting for this directive, if enabled, is public_html. Each user can create a directory called public_html under her /home directory, and HTML documents placed in that directory are available as

http://*servername*/~username

where

username

is the username of the particular user.

DirectoryIndex

The DirectoryIndex directive indicates which file should be served as the index for a directory, such as which file should be served if the URL

http://servername/_SomeDirectory/ is requested.

It is often useful to put a list of files here so that if index.html (the default value) isn't found, another file can be served instead. The most useful application of this is to have a CGI program run as the default action in a directory. If you have users who make their web pages on Windows, you might want to add index.htm as well. In that case, the directive looks like DirectoryIndex index.html index.cgi index.htm.

Apache Multiprocessing Modules

Apache version 2.0 and later now uses a new internal architecture supporting *multiprocessing modules (MPMs)*. These modules are used by the server for a variety of tasks, such as network and process management, and are compiled into Apache. MPMs enable

Apache to work much better on a wider variety of computer platforms, and they can help improve server stability, compatibility, and scalability.

Apache can use only one MPM at any time. These modules are different from the base set included with Apache (see the "Apache Modules" section later in this chapter) but are used to implement settings, limits, or other server actions. Each module in turn supports numerous additional settings, called *directives*, which further refine server operation.

The internal MPM modules relevant for Linux include the following:

▶ **mpm_common**—A set of 20 directives common to all MPM modules

▶ **prefork**—A nonthreaded, preforking web server that works similar to earlier (1.3) versions of Apache

▶ **worker**—Provides a hybrid multiprocess multithreaded server

MPM enables Apache to be used on equipment with fewer resources yet still handle massive numbers of hits and provide stable service. The `worker` module provides directives to control how many simultaneous connections your server can handle.

> **NOTE**
>
> Other MPMs are available for Apache related to other platforms, such as `mpm_netware` for NetWare hosts and `mpm_winnt` for NT platforms. An MPM named `perchild`, which provides user ID assignment to selected daemon processes, is under development. For more information, browse to the Apache Software Foundation's home page at www.apache.org.

Using `.htaccess` **Configuration Files**

Apache also supports special configuration files, known as `.htaccess` files. Almost any directive that appears in `apache2.conf` can appear in an `.htaccess` file. This file, specified in the `AccessFileName` directive in `apache2.conf` sets configurations on a per-directory (usually in a user directory) basis. As the system administrator, you can specify both the name of this file and which of the server configurations can be overridden by the contents of this file. This is especially useful for sites in which there are multiple content providers and you want to control what these people can do with their space.

To limit which server configurations the `.htaccess` files can override, use the `AllowOverride` directive. `AllowOverride` can be set globally or per directory. For example, in your `apache2.conf` file, you could use the following:

```
# Each directory to which Apache has access can be configured with respect
# to which services and features are allowed and/or disabled in that
# directory (and its subdirectories).
#
# First, we configure the "default" to be a very restrictive set of
# permissions.
#
<Directory />
```

```
        Options FollowSymLinks
        AllowOverride None
</Directory>
```

Options **Directives**

To configure which configuration options are available to Apache by default, you must use the Options directive. Options can be None; All; or any combination of Indexes, Includes, FollowSymLinks, ExecCGI, and MultiViews. MultiViews are not included in All and must be specified explicitly. These options are explained in Table 24.1.

TABLE 24.1   Switches Used by the Options Directive

Switch	Description
None	None of the available options are enabled for this directory.
Indexes	In the absence of an index.html file or another DirectoryIndex file, a listing of the files in the directory is generated as an HTML page for display to the user.
Includes	Server-side includes (SSIs) are permitted in this directory. This can also be written as IncludesNoExec if you want to allow includes but don't want to allow the exec option in them. For security reasons, this is usually a good idea in directories over which you don't have complete control, such as UserDir directories.
FollowSymLinks	Allows access to directories that are symbolically linked to a document directory. You should never set this globally for the whole server and only rarely for individual directories. This option is a potential security risk because it allows web users to escape from the document directory and could potentially allow them access to portions of your file system where you really don't want people poking around.
ExecCGI	CGI programs are permitted in this directory, even if it is not a directory defined in the ScriptAlias directive.
MultiViews	This is part of the mod_negotiation module. When a client requests a document that can't be found, the server tries to figure out which document best suits the client's requirements. See http://localhost/manuals/mod/_mod_negotiation.html for your local copy of the Apache documentation.

NOTE

These directives also affect all subdirectories of the specified directory.

AllowOverrides **Directives**

The AllowOverrides directives specify which configuration options .htaccess files can override. You can set this directive individually for each directory. For example, you can have different standards about what can be overridden in the main document `root` and in `UserDir` directories.

This capability is particularly useful for user directories, where the user does not have access to the main server configuration files.

`AllowOverrides` can be set to `All` or any combination of `Options`, `FileInfo`, `AuthConfig`, and `Limit`. These options are explained in Table 24.2.

TABLE 24.2   Switches Used by the `AllowOverrides` Directive

Switch	Description
Options	The `.htaccess` file can add options not listed in the `Options` directive for this directory.
FileInfo	The `.htaccess` file can include directives for modifying document type information.
AuthConfig	The `.htaccess` file might contain authorization directives.
Limit	The `.htaccess` file might contain `allow`, `deny`, and `order` directives.

File System Authentication and Access Control

You're likely to include material on your website that isn't supposed to be available to the public. You must be able to lock out this material from public access and provide designated users with the means to unlock the material. Apache provides two methods for accomplishing this type of access: authentication and authorization. You can use different criteria to control access to sections of your website, including checking the client's IP address or hostname, or requiring a username and password. This section briefly covers some of these methods.

> **CAUTION**
>
> Allowing individual users to put web content on your server poses several important security risks. If you're operating a web server on the Internet rather than on a private network, read the WWW Security FAQ at www.w3.org/Security/Faq/www-security-faq.html

Restricting Access with `Require`

One of the simplest ways to limit access to website material is to restrict access to a specific group of users, based on IP addresses or hostnames. Apache uses the `Require` directive to accomplish this. Here are some examples with comments, that could be placed within the apache2.conf file.

```
<RequireAll>
  Require all granted                    #permit all to access
  Require not ip 10.252.46.163           #except from this ip address
  Require not host horriblepeople.com #and also not from this domain
  Require not host gov                   #and finally, not from any .gov
</RequireAll>
```

There are many options beyond `RequireAll`, including `RequireAny`, and `RequireNone` along with a detailed set of options for each. For more, see https://httpd.apache.org/docs/2.4/howto/access.html.

Authentication

Authentication is the process of ensuring that visitors really are who they claim to be. You can configure Apache to allow access to specific areas of web content only to clients who can authenticate their identity. There are several methods of authentication in Apache; Basic Authentication is the most common (and the method discussed in this chapter).

Under Basic Authentication, Apache requires a user to supply a username and a password to access the protected resources. Apache then verifies that the user is allowed to access the resource in question. If the username is acceptable, Apache verifies the password. If the password also checks out, the user is authorized and Apache serves the request.

HTTP is a stateless protocol; each request sent to the server and each response is handled individually, and not in an intelligent fashion. Therefore, the authentication information must be included with each request. That means each request to a password-protected area is larger and therefore somewhat slower. To avoid unnecessary system use and delays, protect only those areas of your website that absolutely need protection.

To use Basic Authentication, you need a file that lists which users are allowed to access the resources. This file is composed of a plain text list containing name and password pairs. It looks very much like the `/etc/passwd` user file of your Linux system.

> **CAUTION**
>
> Do not use `/etc/passwd` as a user list for authentication. When you're using Basic Authentication, passwords and usernames are sent as base64-encoded text from the client to the server (which is just as readable as plain text). The username and password are included in each request that is sent to the server. So, anyone who might be snooping on Net traffic would be able to get this information!

To create a user file for Apache, use the `htpasswd` command. This is included with the Apache package. Running `htpasswd` without any options produces the following output:

```
Usage:
        htpasswd [-cmdps] passwordfile username
        htpasswd -b[cmdps] passwordfile username password

        htpasswd -n[mdps] username
        htpasswd -nb[mdps] username password
 -c  Create a new file.
 -n  Don't update file; display results on stdout.
 -m  Force MD5 encryption of the password.
 -d  Force CRYPT encryption of the password (default).
 -p  Do not encrypt the password (plaintext).
```

```
-s  Force SHA encryption of the password.
-b  Use the password from the command line rather than prompting for it.
-D  Delete the specified user.
```
On Windows, TPF and NetWare systems the '-m' flag is used by default.
On all other systems, the '-p' flag will probably not work.

As you can see, it is not a difficult command to use. For example, to create a new user file named gnulixusers with a user named wsb, you need to do something like this:

matthew@seymour:~$ **sudo htpasswd -c gnulixusers wsb**

You are then prompted for a password for the user. To add more users, repeat the same procedure, only omitting the -c flag.

You can also create user group files. The format of these files is similar to that of /etc /groups. On each line, enter the group name, followed by a colon (:), and then list all users, with each user separated by spaces. For example, an entry in a user group file might look like this:

gnulixusers: wsb pgj jp ajje nadia rkr hak

Now that you know how to create a user file, it's time to look at how Apache might use this to protect web resources.

To point Apache to the user file, use the AuthUserFile directive. AuthUserFile takes the file path to the user file as its parameter. If the file path is not absolute—that is, beginning with a /—it is assumed that the path is relative to the ServerRoot. Using the AuthGroupFile directive, you can specify a group file in the same manner.

Next, use the AuthType directive to set the type of authentication to be used for this resource. Here, the type is set to Basic.

Now you need to decide to which realm the resource will belong. Realms are used to group different resources that will share the same users for authorization. A realm can consist of just about any string. The realm is shown in the Authentication dialog box on the user's web browser. Therefore, you should set the realm string to something informative. The realm is defined with the AuthName directive.

Finally, state which type of user is authorized to use the resource. You do this with the require directive. The three ways to use this directive are as follows:

▶ If you specify valid-user as an option, any user in the user file is allowed to access the resource (that is, provided she also enters the correct password).

▶ You can specify a list of users who are allowed access with the users option.

▶ You can specify a list of groups with the group option. Entries in the group list, as well as the user list, are separated by a space.

Returning to the `server-status` example you saw earlier, instead of letting users access the `server-status` resource based on hostname, you can require the users to be authenticated to access the resource. You can do so with the following entry in the configuration file:

```
<Location /server-status>
    SetHandler server-status
    AuthType Basic
    AuthName "Server status"
    AuthUserFile "gnulixusers"
    Require valid-user
</Location>
```

Final Words on Access Control

If you have host-based as well as user-based access protection on a resource, the default behavior of Apache is to require the requester to satisfy both controls. But assume that you want to mix host-based and user-based protection and allow access to a resource if either method succeeds. You can do so using the `satisfy` directive. You can set the `satisfy` directive to `All` (this is the default) or `Any`. When set to `All`, all access control methods must be satisfied before the resource is served. If `satisfy` is set to `Any`, the resource is served if any access condition is met.

Here's another access control example, again using the previous `server-status` example. This time, you combine access methods so all users from the `Gnulix` domain are allowed access and those from outside the domain must identify themselves before gaining access. You can do so with the following:

```
<Location /server-status>
    SetHandler server-status
    Order deny,allow
    Deny from all
    Allow from gnulix.org
    AuthType Basic
    AuthName "Server status"
    AuthUserFile "gnulixusers"
    Require valid-user
    Satisfy Any
</Location>
```

There are more ways to protect material on your web server, but the methods discussed here should get you started and will probably be more than adequate for most circumstances. Look to Apache's online documentation for more examples of how to secure areas of your site.

Apache Modules

The Apache core does relatively little; Apache gains its functionality from modules. Each module solves a well-defined problem by adding necessary features. By adding or removing modules to supply the functionality you want Apache to have, you can tailor Apache server to suit your exact needs.

A number of core modules are included with the basic Apache server. Many more are available from other developers. The Apache Module Registry is a repository for add-on modules for Apache; you can find it at http://modules.apache.org/. The modules are stored in the `/usr/lib/apache2/modules` directory.

Each module adds new directives that you can use in your configuration files. As you might guess, there are far too many extra commands, switches, and options to describe them all in this chapter. The following sections briefly describe a subset of those modules available with Ubuntu's Apache installation.

To enable a module, use this command:

```
matthew@seymour:~$ sudo a2enmod module_name
```

To disable a module, use this:

```
matthew@seymour:~$ sudo a2dismod module_name
```

Note that these want the actual name of the module, not the filename; for example, `mod_version.so` is the filename, but `version` is the name of the module. You have to know the name of the module to use either command, but in most cases it is as simple as the difference in this example. Also, after you run either command, you need to restart `apache2` to activate the new configuration.

mod_access

`mod_access` controls access to areas on your web server based on IP addresses, hostnames, or environment variables. For example, you might want to allow anyone from within your own domain to access certain areas of your web. See the "File System Authentication and Access Control" section for more information.

mod_alias

`mod_alias` manipulates the URLs of incoming HTTP requests, such as redirecting a client request to another URL. It also can map a part of the file system into your web hierarchy. For example, the following fetches contents from the `/home/wsb/graphics` directory for any URL that starts with `/images/`:

```
Alias /images/ /home/wsb/graphics/
```

This is done without the client knowing anything about it. If you use a redirection, the client is instructed to go to another URL to find the requested content. You can accomplish more advanced URL manipulation with `mod_rewrite`.

mod_asis

mod_asis is used to specify, in fine detail, all the information to be included in a response. This completely bypasses any headers Apache might have otherwise added to the response. All files with an .asis extension are sent straight to the client without any changes.

As a short example of the use of mod_asis, assume you've moved content from one location to another on your site. Now you must inform people who try to access this resource that it has moved, as well as automatically redirect them to the new location. To provide this information and redirection, you can add the following code to a file with a .asis extension:

```
Status: 301 No more old stuff!
Location: http://gnulix.org/newstuff/
Content-type: text/html

<HTML>
 <HEAD>
  <TITLE>We've moved...</TITLE>
 </HEAD>
 <BODY>
   <P>We've moved the old stuff and now you'll find it at:</P>
   <A HREF="http://gnulix.org/newstuff/">New stuff</A>!.
 </BODY>
</HTML>
```

mod_auth

mod_auth uses a simple user authentication scheme, referred to as Basic Authentication, which is based on storing usernames and encrypted passwords in a text file. This file looks very much like UNIX's /etc/passwd file and is created with the htpasswd command. See the "File System Authentication and Access Control" section earlier in this chapter for more information about this subject.

mod_auth_anon

The mod_auth_anon module provides anonymous authentication similar to that of anonymous FTP. The module enables you to define user IDs of those who are to be handled as guest users. When such a user tries to log on, he is prompted to enter his email address as his password. You can have Apache check the password to ensure that it's a (more or less) proper email address. Basically, it ensures that the password contains an @ character and at least one . character.

mod_auth_dbm

mod_auth_dbm uses Berkeley DB files instead of text for user authentication files.

mod_auth_digest

An extension of the basic mod_auth module, instead of sending the user information in plain text, mod_auth_digest is sent via the *message digest 5 (MD5)* authentication process. This authentication scheme is defined in RFC 2617, "HTTP Authentication: Basic and Digest Access Authentication." Compared to using Basic Authentication, this is a much more secure way of sending user data over the Internet. Unfortunately, not all web browsers support this authentication scheme.

To create password files for use with mod_auth_dbm, you must use the htdigest utility. It has more or less the same functionality as the htpasswd utility. See the man page of htdigest for further information.

mod_autoindex

The mod_autoindex module dynamically creates a file list for directory indexing. The list is rendered in a user-friendly manner similar to those lists provided by FTP's built-in ls command.

mod_cgi

mod_cgi allows execution of CGI programs on your server. CGI programs are executable files residing in the /var/www/cgi-bin directory and are used to dynamically generate data (usually HTML) for the remote browser when requested.

mod_dir **and** mod_env

The mod_dir module is used to determine which files are returned automatically when a user tries to access a directory. The default is index.html. If you have users who create web pages on Windows systems, you should also include index.htm, like this:

```
DirectoryIndex index.html index.htm
```

mod_env controls how environment variables are passed to CGI and SSI scripts.

mod_expires

mod_expires is used to add an expiration date to content on your site by adding an Expires header to the HTTP response. Web browsers or cache servers won't cache expired content.

mod_headers

mod_headers is used to manipulate the HTTP headers of your server's responses. You can replace, add, merge, or delete headers as you see fit. The module supplies a Header directive for this. Ordering of the Header directive is important. A set followed by an unset for the same HTTP header removes the header altogether. You can place Header directives almost anywhere within your configuration files. These directives are processed in the following order:

1. Core server

2. Virtual host

3. `<Directory>` and `.htaccess` files
   `<Location>`
   `<Files>`

mod_include

`mod_include` enables the use of server-side includes on your server, which were quite popular before PHP took over this part of the market.

mod_info **and** mod_log_config

`mod_info` provides comprehensive information about your server's configuration. For example, it displays all the installed modules, as well as all the directives used in its configuration files.

`mod_log_config` defines how your log files should look. See the "Logging" section for further information about this subject.

mod_mime **and** mod_mime_magic

The `mod_mime` module tries to determine the MIME type of files from their extensions.

The `mod_mime_magic` module tries to determine the MIME type of files by examining portions of their content.

mod_negotiation

Using the `mod_negotiation` module, you can select one of several document versions that best suits the client's capabilities. There are several options to select which criteria to use in the negotiation process. You can, for example, choose among different languages, graphics file formats, and compression methods.

mod_proxy

`mod_proxy` implements proxy and caching capabilities for an Apache server. It can proxy and cache FTP, CONNECT, HTTP/0.9, and HTTP/1.0 requests. This is not an ideal solution for sites that have a large number of users and therefore have high proxy and cache requirements. However, it is more than adequate for a small number of users.

mod_rewrite

`mod_rewrite` is the Swiss army knife of URL manipulation. It enables you to perform any imaginable manipulation of URLs using powerful regular expressions. It provides rewrites, redirection, proxying, and so on. There is little that you cannot accomplish using this module.

> **TIP**
>
> If you have Apache installed and running, see http://localhost/manual/misc/rewriteguide.
> html for a cookbook that gives you an in-depth explanation of the `mod_rewrite` module's
> capabilities.

mod_setenvif

`mod_setenvif` allows manipulation of environment variables. Using small snippets of text-matching code known as *regular expressions,* you can conditionally change the content of environment variables. The order in which `SetEnvIf` directives appear in the configuration files is important. Each `SetEnvIf` directive can reset an earlier `SetEnvIf` directive when used on the same environment variable. Be sure to keep that in mind when using the directives from this module.

mod_speling

`mod_speling` is used to enable correction of minor typos in URLs. If no file matches the requested URL, this module builds a list of the files in the requested directory and extracts those files that are the closest matches. It tries to correct only one spelling mistake.

mod_status

You can use `mod_status` to create a web page containing a plethora of information about a running Apache server. The page contains information about the internal status as well as statistics about the running Apache processes. This can be a great aid when you're trying to configure your server for maximum performance. It's also a good indicator of when something's amiss with your Apache server.

mod_ssl

`mod_ssl` provides Secure Sockets Layer (versions 2 and 3) and Transport Layer Security (version 1) support for Apache. At least 30 directives exist that deal with options for encryption and client authorization and that can be used with this module. This mod requires that you also install openssl and generate or buy a certificate. This is covered later in the chapter in the HTTPS section.

mod_unique_id

`mod_unique_id` generates a unique request identifier for every incoming request. This ID is put into the `UNIQUE_ID` environment variable.

mod_userdir

The `mod_userdir` module enables mapping of a subdirectory in each user's `/home` directory into your web tree. The module provides several ways to accomplish this.

mod_usertrack

mod_usertrack is used to generate a cookie for each user session. This can be used to track the user's click stream within your web tree. You must enable a custom log that logs this cookie into a log file.

mod_vhost_alias

mod_vhost_alias supports dynamically configured mass virtual hosting, which is useful for *Internet service providers (ISPs)* with many virtual hosts. However, for the average user, Apache's ordinary virtual hosting support should be more than sufficient.

There are two ways to host virtual hosts on an Apache server. You can have one IP address with multiple CNAMEs, or you can have multiple IP addresses with one name per address. Apache has different sets of directives to handle each of these options. (You learn more about virtual hosting in Apache in the next section of this chapter.)

Again, the available options and features for Apache modules are too numerous to describe completely in this chapter. You can find complete information about the Apache modules in the online documentation for the server included with Ubuntu or at the Apache Project's website.

Virtual Hosting

One of the more popular services to provide with a web server is to host a virtual domain. Also known as a *virtual host*, a virtual domain is a complete website with its own domain name, as if it was a standalone machine, but it's hosted on the same machine as other websites. Apache implements this capability in a simple way with directives in the apache2.conf configuration file.

Apache now can dynamically host virtual servers by using the mod_vhost_alias module you read about in the preceding section of the chapter. The module is primarily intended for ISPs and similar large sites that host a large number of virtual sites. This module is for more advanced users and, as such, it is outside the scope of this introductory chapter. Instead, this section concentrates on the traditional ways of hosting virtual servers.

Address-Based Virtual Hosts

After you've configured your Linux machine with multiple IP addresses, setting up Apache to serve them as different websites is simple. You need only put a VirtualHost directive in your apache2.conf file for each of the addresses you want to make an independent website:

```
<VirtualHost 212.85.67.67>
   ServerName gnulix.org
   DocumentRoot /home/virtual/gnulix/public_html
   TransferLog /home/virtual/gnulix/logs/access_log
   ErrorLog /home/virtual/gnulix/logs/error_log
</VirtualHost>
```

Use the IP address, rather than the hostname, in the `VirtualHost` tag.

You can specify any configuration directives within the `<VirtualHost>` tags. For example, you might want to set `AllowOverrides` directives differently for virtual hosts than you do for your main server. Any directives that aren't specified default to the settings for the main server.

Name-Based Virtual Hosts

Name-based virtual hosts enable you to run more than one host on the same IP address. You must add the names to your DNS as CNAMEs of the machine in question. When an HTTP client (web browser) requests a document from your server, it sends with the request a variable indicating the server name from which it's requesting the document. Based on this variable, the server determines from which of the virtual hosts it should serve content.

Name-based virtual hosts require just one step more than IP address-based virtual hosts. You must first indicate which IP address has the multiple DNS names on it. This is done with the `NameVirtualHost` directive:

```
NameVirtualHost 212.85.67.67
```

You must then have a section for each name on that address, setting the configuration for that name. As with IP-based virtual hosts, you need to set only those configurations that must be different for the host. You must set the `ServerName` directive because it is the only thing that distinguishes one host from another:

```
<VirtualHost 212.85.67.67>
  ServerName bugserver.gnulix.org
  ServerAlias bugserver
  DocumentRoot /home/bugserver/htdocs
  ScriptAlias /home/bugserver/cgi-bin
  TransferLog /home/bugserver/logs/access_log
</VirtualHost>

<VirtualHost 212.85.67.67>
  ServerName pts.gnulix.org
  ServerAlias pts
  DocumentRoot /home/pts/htdocs
  ScriptAlias /home/pts/cgi-bin
  TransferLog /home/pts/logs/access_log
  ErrorLog /home/pts/logs/error_log
</VirtualHost>
```

TIP

If you are hosting websites on an intranet or internal network, users will likely use the shortened name of the machine rather than the FQDN. For example, users might type http://bugserver/index.html in their browser location field rather than http://bugserver

.gnulix.org/index.html. In that case, Apache would not recognize that those two addresses should go to the same virtual host. You could get around this by setting up `VirtualHost` directives for both `bugserver` and `bugserver.gnulix.org`, but the easy way around it is to use the `ServerAlias` directive, which lists all valid aliases for the machine:

```
ServerAlias bugserver
```

For more information about `VirtualHost`, refer to the help system on http://localhost/_
manual.

Logging

Apache provides logging for just about any web access information you might be interested in. Logging can help with the following:

▶ System resource management, by tracking usage

▶ Intrusion detection, by documenting bad HTTP requests

▶ Diagnostics, by recording errors in processing requests

Two standard log files are generated when you run your Apache server: `access_log` and `error_log`. They are found under the `/var/log/apache2` directory. (Others include the SSL logs `ssl_access_log`, `ssl_error_log` and `ssl_request_log`.) All logs except for the `error_log` (by default, this is just the `access_log`) are generated in a format specified by the `CustomLog` and `LogFormat` directives. These directives appear in your `apache2.conf` file.

A new log format can be defined with the `LogFormat` directive:

```
LogFormat "%h %l %u %t \"%r\" %>s %b" common
```

The common log format is a good starting place for creating your own custom log formats. Note that most of the available log analysis tools assume you're using the common log format or the combined log format, both of which are defined in the default configuration files.

The following variables are available for `LogFormat` statements:

▶ **%a**—Remote IP address.

▶ **%A**—Local IP address.

▶ **%b**—Bytes sent, excluding HTTP headers. This is shown in Apache's *Combined Log Format (CLF)*. For a request without any data content, a - is shown instead of 0.

▶ **%B**—Bytes sent, excluding HTTP headers.

▶ **%{VARIABLE}e**—The contents of the environment variable VARIABLE.

▶ **%f**—The filename of the output log.

▶ **%h**—Remote host.

▶ **%H**—Request protocol.

▶ **%{HEADER}i**—The contents of HEADER; header lines in the request sent to the server.

▶ **%l**—Remote log name (from identd, if supplied).

▶ **%m**—Request method.

▶ **%{NOTE}n**—The contents of note NOTE from another module.

▶ **%{HEADER}o**—The contents of HEADER; header lines in the reply.

▶ **%p**—The canonical port of the server serving the request.

▶ **%P**—The PID of the child that serviced the request.

▶ **%q**—The contents of the query string, prepended with a ? character. If there's no query string, this evaluates to an empty string.

▶ **%r**—The first line of request.

▶ **%s**—Status. For requests that were internally redirected, this is the status of the original request (%>s for the last).

▶ **%t**—The time, in common log time format.

▶ **%{format}t**—The time, in the form given by format.

▶ **%T**—The seconds taken to serve the request.

▶ **%u**—Remote user from auth; this might be bogus if the return status (%s) is 401.

▶ **%U**—The URL path requested.

▶ **%V**—The server name according to the UseCanonicalName directive.

▶ **%v**—The canonical ServerName of the server serving the request.

You can put a conditional in front of each variable to determine whether the variable is displayed. If the variable isn't displayed, - is displayed instead. These conditionals are in the form of a list of numeric return values. For example, %!401u displays the value of REMOTE_USER unless the return code is 401.

You can then specify the location and format of a log file using the CustomLog directive:

```
CustomLog logs/access_log common
```

If it is not specified as an absolute path, the location of the log file is assumed to be relative to the ServerRoot.

HTTPS

The mod_ssl module listed above gives Apache2 the ability to encrypt communications using openssl. What this means is that your website can be accessed using https:// instead of just http:// and all communications to and from the site will be encrypted. The module is included in the main `apache2-common` package, so if you installed that from the Ubuntu repositories when you installed Apache, you don't have to install additional `apache` packages.

Enter this to enable the module:

```
matthew@seymour:~$ sudo a2enmod ssl
```

This includes a default HTTPS configuration file, found in `/etc/apache2/sites-available` `/default-ssl`. For HTTPS to work, a certificate and a key are required. The default configuration includes a certificate and key generated by the ssl-cert package, and they are adequate for testing. However, for real use you should either generate a self-signed certificate and key (adequate for internal use or for personal sites) or buy a certificate from a certified CA authority (necessary if you want anyone to trust your site for commercial ventures).

To configure Apache2 for HTTPS using the default configuration for testing, use this command:

```
matthew@seymour:~$ sudo a2enmsite default-ssl
```

And restart Apache2.

You can now access web pages on your server using https://. This is adequate for testing, but not for anything else.

Next we will create a self-signed certificate and key, which is a step in the right direction.

To generate a key for the certificate, use this command:

```
matthew@seymour:~$ openssl genrsa -des3 -out server.key 2048
```

This will generate a basic key using Triple-DES and 2048-bit encryption. See the man page for `openssl` for more information about possible settings.

To generate a Certificate Signing Request (CSR), use this command:

```
matthew@seymour:~$ openssl req -new -key server.key -out server.csr
```

You will be asked for some information to complete the request.

To generate a self-signed certificate, use this command:

```
matthew@seymour:~$ openssl x509 -req -days 365 -in server.csr -signkey server.key
-out server.crt
```

This will create a certificate that is valid for 365 days. Certificates, even from vendors, have expiration dates. Certificates should be renewed regularly to make your site visitors feel comfortable that they are dealing with who they think they are dealing with.

To copy the certificate to its proper location, use this command:

```
matthew@seymour:~$ cp server.crt /etc/ssl/certs/
```

To copy the key to its proper location, use this command:

```
matthew@seymour:~$ cp server.key /etc/ssl/private/
```

Next we will edit the default-ssl file, /etc/apache2/sites-available/default-ssl, to change the values of these lines to what I show here. This tells Apache2 to use SSL and where to find the proper certificate and key files.

```
SSLEngine on
SSLCertificateFile /etc/ssl/certs/server.crt
SSLCertificateKeyFile /etc/ssl/private/server.key
```

To configure Apache2 for HTTPS using the edited default configuration with the self-signed certificate and key file, use this command:

```
matthew@seymour:~$ sudo a2enmsite default-ssl
```

And restart Apache2.

During the restart you will be asked to input the certificate's key password. Enter it when requested. You now have a server that is secure and good for internal use, but not for a customer-facing production environment.

The best thing to do, if you are going to host a professional site, is to use a certified CA authority. Every CA has their preferred method, so you should read their requirements before you start. The basic process is usually like this:

1. Create a private and public encryption key pair.

2. Create a certificate based on the public key.

3. Create a certificate request with information about your server and the company hosting it.

4. Send your certificate request and public key along with proof of your company's identity and payment to the CA.

5. They verify the request and your identity and send back a certificate like the self-signed one we created, but signed by the CA.

6. You install that certificate on your server and configure Apache2 to use it.

The CA-signed certificate provides advantages. First, browsers are built with data about most CA authorities and will automatically recognize a signature from one of them on your certificate most of the time. A self-signed certificate will cause the browser to display a rather scary looking (to a non-technical person) warning and require the user to bypass it before viewing your site. In addition, when the CA issues the signed certificate they are guaranteeing the identity of the organization providing the web pages.

To learn more about certificates and keys, including installation of keys and certificates you pay for, see http://tldp.org/HOWTO/SSL-Certificates-HOWTO/index.html.

References

▶ **http://news.netcraft.com/archives/web_server_survey.html**—A statistical graph of web server usage by millions of servers. The research points out that Apache is by far the most widely used server for Internet sites.

▶ **https://httpd.apache.org/**—The Apache HTTP Server Project website where you can find extensive documentation and information about Apache.

24

CHAPTER 25

Nginx Web Server Management

This chapter covers the configuration and management of the Nginx web server and includes an overview of some of the major components of the server and discussions of server configuration. In this chapter, you learn how to start, stop, and restart Nginx using the command line. The chapter begins with some introductory information and then shows you how to install, configure, and use Nginx.

About the Nginx Web Server

Pronounced "engine-x," this is a lightweight and extremely fast web server. It is free and open source. Some well-known websites such as GitHub, Netflix, and WordPress.com use Nginx because it is stable and fast under high-traffic conditions while using fewer resources. It is not as configurable as Apache, but for specific use cases it is an excellent option and is quite easy to set up and use.

NEWS

The W3Techs website, which tracks trends on the web, posted an article in July 2013 titled "Nginx just became the most used web server among the top 1000 websites." They summarized the article this way: "34.9% of the top 1000 web sites rely on Nginx. That makes it the most trusted web server on high traffic sites, just ahead of Apache."

Source: http://w3techs.com/blog/entry/nginx_just _became_the_most_used_web_server_among_the _top_1000_websites

The original design of Nginx was created to allow higher numbers of concurrent website requests. Larger websites often have tens of thousands of clients connected simultaneously, each one making HTTP requests that must be responded to. The designers of Nginx heard this problem described as C10K and decided they could write a web server that would be capable of serving at least 10,000 clients simultaneously.

THE C10K PROBLEM

The canonical website for learning more about this problem is www.kegel.com/c10k .html. The article linked here is from the early 2000s and describes ideas for configuring operating systems and writing code to solve the problem of serving at least 10,000 simultaneous clients from a web server. Today, this problem is even more common, and with the continuing maturity of Nginx, lighttpd, and other web servers, many of the largest, highest traffic sites have switched away from Apache.

Newer versions of the Apache and other modern web servers rely on a concept of threads. *Threads* are kind of like lightweight processes. This deserves some explanation. A process is a specific instance of a computer program running. The process contains both the machine code (the binary, or the compiled version of the program that the computer processor can understand and obey—this is either precompiled as in C or C++ programs or may be the output of a just-in-time compilation as happens with languages like Python or Perl) as well as the current activity of that program, such as the calculations it is performing or the data it stores in memory on which it is operating. Serving an HTTP page by running a complete process each time would be bad because the server's resources would be quickly used up if the site was even moderately popular. Process after process would be started and would fight for attention. A thread is the ordered control of a program: First, do this; then, do that; finally, do this other thing. One process may control many threads. This is good for resource management. By using threads instead of processes, a larger number of client requests can be served using less system resources than a process-based server.

Most web servers have traditionally been either process based or thread based. There are also examples of hybrid models, where many multithread processes are used. Process-based servers are great because they are stable and the crash of one process does not affect other processes. However, they cannot handle as many clients because the creation and destruction of all of those processes creates a lot of processor overhead and requires a large amount of memory. Thread-based servers are great because requests can share memory, making them more efficient and thereby able to serve more requests more quickly. However, a crash in one thread could bring the entire server down.

What makes Nginx different is that it uses an event-driven architecture to handle requests. Instead of starting a new process or a new thread for each request, in an event-driven architecture, the flow of the program is controlled by events, some form of message sent from another process or thread. Here, you have a process that runs as a "listener" or "event detector" that waits for a request to come in to the server. When the request arrives, instead of a new process starting, the "listener" sends a message to a different part of the server called an "event handler," which then performs a task. The simplified outcome of serving web pages this way is that less processor time and less memory are needed. There are some significant difficulties inherent in using this method, not the least of which can be greater code complexity, which can make fixing bugs, adding features, and understanding code as a newcomer (or even a returning veteran of the same codebase, but who has been away from it for a little while) more difficult.

Nginx is designed to scale well from one small, low-powered server up to large networks involving many servers.

For configuration, Nginx uses a system of virtual hosts, similar to Apache, using a similar set of configuration files. The differences are semantic and not terribly difficult. You can create URL rewrites in Nginx using a rather different syntax. In addition, there is nothing similar to Apache's rewrite conditions. Occasional blog posts and web tutorials exist to give some workarounds that will handle some of the more common forms, but if this is something you do often, you might not want to use Nginx.

One missing file that many people use and love in Apache is `.htaccess`. There is nothing similar in Nginx, so if you need the ability to make changes to rewrites or configurations without restarting the server, you are out of luck. This is probably the primary reason that you don't see shared hosting offering Nginx.

Finally, another well-documented option is to use both Apache and Nginx together, where Apache handles any and all dynamic requests and Nginx handles all static requests. This is faster and lighter than using Apache alone but comes with the burden of added complexity and the increased potential for problems that brings.

Installing the Nginx Server

You can install Nginx through APT or build it yourself from source code. The Nginx source builds on just about any UNIX-like operating system and on Win32.

If you are about to install a new version of Nginx, shut down the old server. Even if it's unlikely that the old server will interfere with the installation procedure, shutting it down ensures that there will be no problems. If you do not know how to stop Nginx, see the "Starting and Stopping Nginx" section later in this chapter.

Installing from the Ubuntu Repositories

You can install the `nginx` package from the Ubuntu software repositories. Updated packages usually contain important bug and security fixes. When an updated version is released, install it as quickly as possible to keep your system secure.

For more information about installing software from the Ubuntu repositories, see Chapter 9, "Managing Software."

Building the Source Yourself

You can download the source directly from http://wiki.nginx.org/Install.

After you have the `tar` file, you must open it in a temporary directory, such as `/tmp`. Opening this `tar` file creates a directory called `nginx_version_number`, where `version_number` is the version you have downloaded (for example, `nginx_1.4.4`).

> **TIP**
>
> As with many software packages distributed in source code form for Linux and other UNIX-like operating systems, extracting the source code results in a directory that contains a README and an INSTALL file. Be sure to peruse the INSTALL file before attempting to build and install the software.

Using ./configure to Build Nginx

To build Nginx, run the ./configure script in the directory just created. Use this command:

```
matthew@seymour:~$ ./configure
```

This generates the makefile that is used to compile the server code.

Next, run make to compile the server code.

```
matthew@seymour:~$ make
```

After the compilation is complete, install the server. This may only be done using admin privileges.

```
matthew@seymour:~$ sudo make install
```

> **TIP**
>
> It is strongly recommended that you use Ubuntu's version of Nginx until you really know what happens at system startup. No "uninstall" option is available when installing Nginx from source! For the remainder of this chapter, we assume you have installed Nginx this way. If you install from source, you should check the Nginx documentation as there may be differences from what we describe here.

Configuring the Nginx Server

You can now configure the server. Nginx is most commonly run using Virtual Hosts, like what most people do with Apache these days. The process is similar, with mainly syntax differences.

If you install using the package manager, all configuration files for Nginx are located in /etc/nginx. The primary configuration file is /etc/nginx/nginx.conf. Here is an example of that file:

```
user www-data;
worker_processes  1;

# error_log  /var/log/nginx/error.log;
```

```
events {
    worker_connections  1024;
}

http {
    include        /etc/nginx/mime.types;
    default_type  application/octet-stream;

    access_log  /var/log/nginx/access.log;

    sendfile          on;

    tcp_nopush        on;
    #tcp_nodelay      on;

    #keepalive_timeout  0;
    keepalive_timeout  65;

    gzip  on;

    include /etc/nginx/sites-enabled/*;
}
```

The `nginx.conf` file contains these parts:

▶ **user**—Sets the system user that will be used to run Nginx. This is `www-data` by default. You can add a group to this setting by inserting a second entry, which in our example would read: `user www-data www-data;`

▶ **worker processes**—Allows you to set how many processes Nginx may spawn on your server. The default value of 1 is fine for most users, although some recommend setting this as high as 4. You can experiment, but do so carefully.

▶ **error_log**—This is commented out in our example. You can set the location for an error log by removing the # that marks the line as a comment that should not be processed by Nginx, then adjusting the listed directory location, if you don't want to use the default log location.

▶ **events** and **worker_connections**—This setting adjusts how many concurrent connections Nginx will allow per process. It may be helpful to think of it this way: `worker_connections` times `worker_processes` will give you the maximum number of clients that may connect to your server concurrently. Memory plays a factor in whether your server can actually serve all the permitted connections you configure, so if you aren't sure whether your server has enough memory to go higher, leave both settings at their defaults and you should be fine.

▶ **http**—This section contains the base settings for http access:

▶ Leave the `include` and `default_type` lines alone, unless you enjoy trying to figure out why content is not being displayed or you know you must adjust which types of content are permitted.

▶ Feel free to adjust the location of the `access_log`, which records all attempts to connect to your server, or comment out the line to disable it.

▶ `sendfile` is used when you permit Nginx to ignore the contents of the file it is sending, such as when serving larger files that do not require a multiple request and confirmation system when being served, thereby freeing system resources for items that do require Nginx to watch over. It is recommended that you leave this setting on unless you know why you are turning it off, as it saves resources when serving things like graphics.

▶ `tcp_nopush` sends HTTP response headers in one packet, and this is actually a pretty good thing, but experimenting with it is okay.

▶ `tcp_nodelay` is for use with items that do not require a response, but most general web use does demand responses, so this is often best commented out, although trying it to see if it makes a difference in your circumstance is okay.

▶ The `keepalive_timeout` sets the number of seconds that Nginx will keep a connection open when a request is made. The default is to keep this connection open for over a minute, which seems a bit odd since you have a limited number of connections available and keeping a connection alive prevents another requester from using that slot again until the time-out occurs. Setting this to a low number like 2 or 3 seconds seems to permit more people to connect in a minute than would be able to do so otherwise. If you are serving a website with little traffic, the setting won't matter. If you have a lot of traffic, a lower number is generally a good idea.

▶ `gzip` allows the use of on-the-fly gzip compression, which can make data transfers a bit faster.

▶ `include` defines files that are located outside of the `nginx.conf` file that are to be read by Nginx and used for its configuration. You can include multiple files, just create a new line for each. Listed in our example is a directive to include everything listed in a directory that is generally used for Virtual Hosts, as described in the Virtual Hosting section. You could instead place a `server` variable here and define it (as we will in the Virtual Hosts section), instead of the `include`, but if you have multiple sites, configuring how Nginx works for each site individually can be useful, especially if you have one site that has a lot of traffic and another that has little.

Whenever you make a change to the `nginx.conf` file, you must restart Nginx to reload the configuration into Nginx for the changes to take effect, like this:

```
matthew@seymour:~$ sudo service nginx restart
```

Some prefer to stop and start it, perhaps doing the configuration work in between. This is quite common as Nginx in the past had a habit of not performing restarts perfectly. In my experience, bad resets are rare, however this method prevents any doubt:

```
matthew@seymour:~$ sudo service nginx stop
matthew@seymour:~$ sudo service nginx start
```

Virtual Hosting

One of the more popular services to provide with a web server is to host a virtual domain. Also known as a *virtual host*, a virtual domain is a complete website with its own domain name, as if it was a standalone machine, but it's hosted on the same machine as other websites.

Nginx implements this capability in a simple way: just create a configuration file for your virtual host, name it for that host, and place it in `/etc/nginx/sites-enabled`. We prefer to place our files in `/etc/nginx/sites-available` and then create a symlink in `sites-enabled`, but that is not a requirement. Doing so does allow you to disable one out of several sites by simply deleting the symlink and reloading the configuration or restarting Nginx while preserving the complete configuration for the site, so we recommend you give it a try.

You can place the actual files for your website wherever you like. The configuration files for Nginx will tell the web server where to find them. We like to create them in the main website creator/maintainer's directory, but others prefer `/var/www` and still others opt for a different location. Choose a location you like and make a note of it. You will need it shortly.

Here is an example file for a virtual host, which we will call yourdomain.com. Name the file *yourdomain.com* and place it in `sites-enabled` or `sites-available`, as described above. This file includes comments that will help you fill in your specific details:

```
#this first server module is just a rewrite directive - it is not required, and you
#can make the rewrite go the other way, to force NOT using www
server {
  listen   80;                      #sets the HTTP port from which the website is
served
  server_name  www.yourdomain.com;  #names the server using the www prefix

  #if a server request is made without www, this next line will rewrite it
  rewrite ^/(.*) http://yourdomain.com/$1 permanent;
  }


#this second server module tells Nginx where to find the files when requested
server {
  listen   80;                      #sets the HTTP port from which the website is
served
  server_name  yourdomain.com;      #names the server being configured
  location / {                      #sets the location of the files being served
    root  /home/<yourusername>/public_html/yourdomain.com/; #top directory for the
site
    index index.html;
  }
}
```

25

Earlier in this section we mentioned that you may place the files for your website wherever you like. The root line in the file just created is where you will place this information. Here we use <yourusername>'s personal home folder, and place within it a directory called `public_html` specifically created for placing website files. Since our example anticipates serving multiple websites with this one server, it goes further and creates a directory for our example website, *yourdomain.com*.

At this point, everything should work for simple HTML sites. To add additional domains, repeat these steps for each domain being served.

Setting Up PHP

If you have CGI or other script content, such as a website written in PHP like WordPress or Drupal, you have more work to do. While the ability to serve PHP is available by default in Nginx (it didn't use to be), it still requires additional setup. This section will add the ability to serve PHP content to our existing Nginx server. As a result, there are some PHP-specific parts to this process. They should be obvious.

First, we need to make sure PHP is installed on the server. There are many ways to do this. For this example, we will use PHP-FPM, which you can learn more about at http://php-fpm.org.

To do this, install the following packages: `php5-cli`, `php5-cgi`, `psmisc`, `spawn-fcgi`, and `php5-fpm`.

Edit the file `/etc/php5/fpm/pool.d/www.conf` to make php-fpm use a unix socket instead of a TCP/IP connection by finding this line:

```
listen = 127.0.0.1:9000
```

and replacing it with:

```
listen = /tmp/php5-fpm.sock
```

This is where you need to check the requirements of whatever PHP-based application you intend to install and use. Some require other PHP extensions in addition. You may also need a database. We will skip this step as the details differ for each application, but this is when you would likely want to take care of these details, although you can probably make them up later. If all you want to do is serve PHP scripts that you have written or run them on your server, you are probably fine not worrying about this and moving on.

Next, you need to edit either `/etc/nginx/nginx.conf` or the file for your virtual host, like `/etc/nginx/sites-enabled/yourdomain.com` from our earlier example, to include information that Nginx needs to know how to deal with PHP content. Editing either will work, the difference is that editing the virtual host file will only affect that website while editing `nginx.conf` will affect everything on your server.

Here is an example of an edited *server* module in one of these files. Note what is moved and what is added from the previous example:

```
server {
  listen    80;                    #sets the HTTP port from which the website is
served
  server_name  www.yourdomain.com;  #names the server using the www prefix

  #if a server request is made without www, this next line will rewrite it
  rewrite ^/(.*) http://yourdomain.com/$1 permanent;
  }


#this second server module tells Nginx where to find the files when requested
server {
  listen    80;                    #sets the HTTP port from which the website is
served
  server_name  yourdomain.com;       #names the server being configured
  root  /home/<yourusername>/public_html/yourdomain.com/; #top directory for the
site
  index index.html index.php;
  client_max_body_size 1G;
  fastcgi_buffers 64 4K;
  location / {                      #sets the location of the files being served
    try_files $uri =404;
    include fastcgi_params;
    fastcgi_split_path_info ^(.+\.php)(/.+)$;
    fastcgi_pass unix:/tmp/php5-fpm.sock;
    fastcgi_param SCRIPT_FILENAME $document_root$fastcgi_script_name;
    }
  }
```

Restart Nginx and you are all set. See http://wiki.nginx.org/PHPFcgiExample for more details.

Adding and Configuring Modules

This topic is bigger than can or should be covered in this book, where we only intend to introduce and help you acquire a basic competence with a wide range of technologies and features available in/with/for Ubuntu. In this chapter, we have only set up a basic server. This will serve the needs of most people, but there are tons of other settings available for you to use and many other configuration options for core modules and even optional modules you can add to your server.

Adding additional modules is something that must be done when Nginx is compiled, so if you need something that is not included by default in the package from the Ubuntu repositories, you will have to read the official documentation, download Nginx from the website, and compile it yourself. The best way to start is to immerse yourself in the official module documentation at http://nginx.org/en/docs/.

To configure an enabled module, whether a default module or an optional one, start at the same documentation, find the module you want to configure in the list, and click its entry to learn about the various options. Even the Core module that we configured in our `nginx.conf` example has a ton of extra options. You may not need any of them, but you may find something useful.

HTTPS

Nginx comes with the ability to encrypt communications using `openssl`. What this means is that your website can be accessed using https:// instead of just http:// and all communications to and from the site will be encrypted.

For HTTPS to work, a certificate and a key are required. You should either generate a self-signed certificate and key (adequate for internal use or for personal sites) or buy a certificate from a certified CA authority (necessary if you want anyone to trust your site for commercial ventures).

To generate a key for the certificate, use this command:

```
matthew@seymour:~$ openssl genrsa -des3 -out server.key 2048
```

This will generate a basic key using Triple-DES and 2048-bit encryption. See the man page for `openssl` for more information about possible settings.

To generate a Certificate Signing Request (CSR), use this command:

```
matthew@seymour:~$ openssl req -new -key server.key -out server.csr
```

You will be asked for some information to complete the request.

To generate a self-signed certificate, use this command:

```
matthew@seymour:~$ openssl x509 -req -days 365 -in server.csr -signkey server.key -out server.crt
```

This will create a certificate that is valid for 365 days. Certificates, even from vendors, have expiration dates. Certificates should be renewed regularly to make your site visitors feel comfortable that they are dealing with who they think they are dealing with.

To copy the certificate to its proper location, use this command:

```
matthew@seymour:~$ cp server.crt /etc/nginx/ssl/
```

To copy the key to its proper location, use this command:

```
matthew@seymour:~$ cp server.key /etc/nginx/ssl/
```

Next, we must modify our Nginx configuration to use the server certificate and key files. This is done in the *server* module of the config file. Here is our earlier example, with the additions we need in **bold**.

```
server {
  listen    80;                    #sets the HTTP port from which the website is served

  listen  443 ssl;

  server_name  www.yourdomain.com;  #names the server using the www prefix

  ssl_certificate /etc/nginx/ssl/server.crt
  ssl_certificate /etc/nginx/ssl/server.key

  #if a server request is made without www, this next line will rewrite it
  rewrite ^/(.*) http://yourdomain.com/$1 permanent;
  }
```

You can now access web pages on your server using https://. This is adequate for testing and internal use, but not for anything else.

The best thing to do, if you are going to host a professional site, is to use a certified CA authority. Every CA has their preferred method, so you should read their requirements before you start. The basic process is usually like this:

1. Create a private and public encryption key pair.

2. Create a certificate based on the public key.

3. Create a certificate request with information about your server and the company hosting it.

4. Send your certificate request and public key along with proof of your company's identity and payment to the CA.

5. They verify the request and your identity and send back a certificate like the self-signed one we created, but signed by the CA.

6. You install that certificate on your server and configure Apache2 to use it.

The CA-signed certificate provides advantages. First, browsers are built with data about most CA authorities and will automatically recognize a signature from one of them on your certificate most of the time. A self-signed certificate will cause the browser to display a rather scary looking (to a non-technical person) warning and require the user to bypass it before viewing your site. In addition, when the CA issues the signed certificate they are guaranteeing the identity of the organization providing the web pages.

To learn more about certificates and keys, including installation of keys and certificates you pay for, see http://tldp.org/HOWTO/SSL-Certificates-HOWTO/index.html.

References

▶ **http://nginx.org/en/docs/**—The Nginx wiki website where you can find extensive documentation and information about Nginx, including installation instructions, downloads, and tips for configuration and use.

CHAPTER 26
Other HTTP Servers

To determine the best web server for your use, consider the needs of the website you manage. Does it need heavy security (for e-commerce), multimedia (music, video, and pictures), or the capability to download files easily? How much are you willing to spend for the software? Do you need software that is easy to maintain and troubleshoot or that includes tech support? The answers to these questions might steer you to something other than what's covered in Chapter 24, "Apache Web Server Management" or Chapter 25, "Nginx Web Server Management."

lighttpd

lighttpd, or "lighty" is a speedy open-source lightweight server. Like Nginx, lighttpd is designed for high-performance and low resource use. YouTube, Wikipedia, and others are using lighttpd for its scalability and quickness. Also like Nginx, lighttpd uses an event-driven architecture.

One thing that sets lighttpd apart from Nginx is that while Nginx natively handles static content incredibly well, it can also require a bit more work to get it functioning as a server for CGI content, such as websites built with PHP. Obviously, because the main WordPress site that they host themselves uses Nginx and is built with PHP, this is not an insurmountable task with Nginx (and web tutorials abound). With lighttpd, this feature is built in, making it quicker to install, configure, and use if this is the sort of site you intend to host.

Configuring lighttpd is again done using a system of configuration files. The syntax is a bit different from either Apache or Nginx, but to anyone familiar with using either, lighttpd will be easy to understand and use.

Rewrite rules are available for lighttpd, and you can do them using conditionals and regular expressions. However, the syntax for doing this is different and takes a little time to study and use effectively.

lighttpd has a nice website with professional documentation available. Reading through it should give you a good sense of whether lighttpd is suitable for a specific site.

Yaws

Yaws stands for *Yet Another Web Server*. It is written in the Erlang programming language, which is enough to make it unique and interesting for many people. Erlang is primarily designed for and used to build scalable real-time systems that require high availability. It is often found in telephony applications, instant messaging, commerce, and banking, and it's designed to support concurrency and fault tolerance. Yaws was written from the ground up to be scalable and multithreaded. Like newer versions of Apache, Yaws uses threads, in this case one thread per request, to serve content. What makes Yaws an interesting alternative is how the underlying language deals with concurrent processes. Because it uses Erlang, Yaws should be significantly faster, even using the same base method for serving content.

Yaws is configured using one configuration file. Virtual servers are the standard, and the syntax of the file is familiar enough that most simple configurations should be quick and easy to set up.

Rewrites are possible in Yaws, but not in the same manner as with Apache. Here is where a major weakness comes in: The documentation available from the Yaws website at the time of this writing was quite sparse, and much of it is outdated (this is acknowledged by the site with a disclaimer). The official site links to a user's blog from 2009 to give information for setting up Yaws to work with WordPress permalinks. This is not unlike past experiences with Nginx, which has greatly improved its official documentation; but be warned, unless you have simple needs, you might get to spend a lot of time trying things out, adjusting, and playing to get your site up and running. On the positive side, if you are looking for a fun experiment, perhaps as a student running a server just to learn rather than to host vital content, Yaws could be exactly what you want. Who knows, because it is an open-source project, you might find yourself studying Erlang and contributing either code or documentation.

Cherokee

The distinguishing feature of Cherokee among the crowd that claims both speed and lightness is its ease of configuration. Cherokee supports all the big features, like virtual hosts, CGI, load balancing, and so on. It also includes a graphical interface for configuration, which makes it unique among all the options in this chapter. The claim is that you can configure Cherokee without ever editing a configuration file.

Setting up Cherokee is as easy as installing it on your system and then opening the Cherokee admin interface by issuing the `cherokee-admin-launcher` command as root. The downside is that this assumes you are running a graphical user interface on the same system as your web server, which is something that most Linux admins do not do. However, fear not. It is possible to use this interface remotely from a system with a web browser and terminal access via `ssh` using the remote system's IP address and a specific port (which is configurable).

The other features of Cherokee are comparable to lighttpd and Nginx. If you like what they offer, but want to use a GUI for your administration tasks, Cherokee is worth a closer look. The end user documentation available from their site is excellent and should get you up and running easily.

Jetty

If you are hosting a personal WordPress site or a few static HTML pages, Jetty is not what you need. Jetty is an Eclipse Foundation project that is written in Java. The Eclipse Foundation exists to provide open-source development tools, software frameworks, and more to anyone who wants to use them. Jetty is a web server *and* client. It is a `javax.servlet` container. It supports Web Sockets and many other integrations. All of Jetty's components are open source and freely available, even for commercial use and distribution. Jetty powers frameworks such as Google Web Toolkit (code.google.com/webtoolkit/) and Yahoo!'s Hadoop (developer.yahoo.com/hadoop/). It works with Apache Maven (http://maven.apache.org) to provide a way to run a web application locally while in development.

Jetty isn't really a standalone web server in the traditional sense, but rather creates a way to use Java code for web applications. Jetty is complex enough to warrant a book of its own. If you are developing web applications using Java and want a highly configurable network of connectors and handlers at your disposal (and you know what that phrase means), Jetty is a pretty good choice. Jetty components are simple, Plain Old Java *Objects* (POJOs). Jetty has an API that makes using it in Java easy. As the website says, "Jetty provides an HTTP server and Servlet container capable of serving static and dynamic content either from a standalone or embedded instantiations." If you need it, it is great. If you don't, it will be overkill.

thttpd

thttpd is a very light, decidedly not flashy or feature-filled web server. It has not been abandoned, but does not seem to be updated frequently. It is included here for one main reason: It has an interesting feature that makes it unique. First, we give you a general description of the web server.

thttpd is small and simple. It claims to have only slightly more than is necessary to support HTTP 1.1. No bells. No whistles. The positive side is that simple code generally has fewer stability issues, has fewer security and performance problems, and uses less memory. Your Virtual hosts can be easily configured in thttpd using a familiar format. Getting CGI-type content to run is more complicated than with any of the other servers in this chapter as it is not supported out of the box.

Here is the really interesting part: thttpd has a throttling feature that lets you set maximum byte rates on URLs or URL groups. You can limit the speed or use of your site's bandwidth according to the URL being requested by the client. You could use this to host media files and allow them to be accessed while assuring you have plenty of bandwidth available for other users to access your static HTML pages.

thttpd does not appear to have been updated since sometime in 2005, so it might not be suitable for use on a production server, although there is some evidence that it was once used on a few well-known websites. It seems the world has moved on. However, the throttle-by-requested-URL is an interesting idea making it worthy of a mention here.

Apache Tomcat

Apache Tomcat is a common and frequently used open-source Java servlet container that implements Oracle's Java Servlet and JavaServer Pages (JSP) specifications. By doing so, Tomcat provides the means to run Java code in a web server environment. Java programmers love it because they can write web applications in a language they already know. Tomcat can be used as a standalone pure-Java web server, but is often used in conjunction with the regular Apache or another general purpose web server. In those instances, Tomcat serves requests from the other web server.

References

▶ **www.lighttpd.net**—The main website for lighttpd.

▶ **http://yaws.hyber.org**—The main website for Yaws.

▶ **www.cherokee-project.com**—The main website for Cherokee.

▶ **http://eclipse.org/jetty/**—The main website for Jetty.

▶ **www.acme.com/software/thttpd/**—The main website for thttpd.

▶ **http://tomcat.apache.org**—The main website for Apache Tomcat.

# CHAPTER 27

Remote File Serving with FTP

*F*ile Transfer Protocol (FTP) was once considered the primary method used to transfer files over a network from computer to computer. FTP is still heavily used today, although many graphical FTP clients now supplement the original text-based interface command. As computers have evolved, so has FTP, and Ubuntu includes many ways with which to use a graphical interface to transfer files over FTP.

This chapter contains an overview of the available FTP software included with Ubuntu, along with some details concerning initial setup, configuration, and use of FTP-specific clients. Ubuntu also includes an FTP server software package named vsftpd, the Very Secure FTP Daemon, and a number of associated programs you can use to serve and transfer files with the FTP protocol.

Choosing an FTP Server

FTP uses a client/server model. As a client, FTP accesses a server, and as a server, FTP provides access to files or storage. Just about every computer platform available has software written to enable a computer to act as an FTP server, but Ubuntu provides the average user with the capability to do this without paying hefty licensing fees and without regard for client usage limitations.

There are two types of FTP servers and access: anonymous and standard. A *standard* FTP server requires an account name and password from anyone trying to access the server. *Anonymous* servers allow anyone to connect to the server to retrieve files. Anonymous servers provide the most flexibility, but they can also present a security risk. Fortunately, as you will read in this chapter, Ubuntu is set up to use proper file and directory permissions and common-sense default configuration, such as disallowing root to perform an FTP login.

> **NOTE**
>
> Many Linux users now use OpenSSH and its suite of clients, such as the `sftp` command, for a more secure solution when transferring files. The OpenSSH suite provides the `sshd` daemon and enables encrypted remote logins. (See Chapter 19, "Remote Access with SSH, Telnet, and VNC," for more information.)

Choosing an Authenticated or Anonymous Server

When you are preparing to set up your FTP server, you must first make the decision to install either the authenticated or anonymous service. *Authenticated* service requires the entry of a valid username and password for access. As previously mentioned, *anonymous* service allows the use of the username `anonymous` and an email address as a password for access.

Authenticated FTP servers are used to provide some measure of secure data transfer for remote users but will require maintenance of user accounts given that usernames and passwords are used. Anonymous FTP servers are used when user authentication is not needed or necessary and can be helpful in providing an easily accessible platform for customer support or public distribution of documents, software, or other data.

If you use an anonymous FTP server in your home or business Linux system, it is vital that you properly install and configure it to retain a relatively secure environment. Generally, sites that host anonymous FTP servers place them outside the firewall on a dedicated machine. The dedicated machine contains only the FTP server and should not contain data that cannot be restored quickly. This dedicated-machine setup prevents malicious users who compromise the server from obtaining critical or sensitive data. For an additional, but by no means more secure setup, the FTP portion of the file system can be mounted read-only from a separate hard drive partition or volume, or mounted from read-only media, such as CD-ROM, DVD, or other optical storage.

Ubuntu FTP Server Packages

The Very Secure `vsftpd` server is licensed under the GNU GPL. The server can be used for personal or business purposes and is the FTP server covered in the remainder of this chapter.

Other FTP Servers

One alternative server is NcFTPd, available from www.ncftp.com. This server provides its own optimized daemon. In addition, NcFTPd has the capability to cache directory listings of the FTP server in memory, thereby increasing the speed at which users can obtain a list of available files and directories. Although NcFTPd has many advantages over some other FTP servers, NcFTPd is not GPL-licensed software, and its licensing fees vary according to the maximum number of simultaneous server connections ($199 for 51 or more concurrent users and $129 for up to 50 concurrent users, but free to education institutions with a compliant domain name).

> **NOTE**
>
> Do not confuse the `ncftp` client with `ncftpd`. The `ncftp` package included with Ubuntu is the client software, a replacement for `ftp`, and includes the `ncftpget` and `ncftpput` commands for transferring files via the command line or by using a remote file uniform resource locator (URL) address. `ncftpd` is the FTP server, which can be downloaded from www.ncftpd.com.

Another FTP server package for Linux is ProFTPD, licensed under the GNU GPL. This server works well with most Linux distributions and has been used by a number of Linux sites, including ftp.kernel.org and ftp.sourceforge.net. ProFTPD is actively maintained and updated for bug fixes and security enhancements. Its developers recommend that you use the latest release (1.3.3e at the time of this writing) to avoid exposure to exploits and vulnerabilities. Browse to www.proftpd.org to download a copy.

Yet another FTP server package is `Bsdftpd-ssl`, which is based on the BSD `ftpd` (and distributed under the BSD license). `Bsdftpd-ssl` offers simultaneous standard and secure access using security extensions; secure access requires a special client. For more details, browse to http://bsdftpd-ssl.sc.ru.

Previously, this book covered an FTP server called `wu-ftp`. We had some concerns about it, such as the fact that when testing it to update this chapter, we discovered it runs as root by default and therefore presents a significant security risk. For that reason, and the fact that the package seems to be abandoned and no longer maintained by its authors, we are not covering it in this edition.

Finally, another alternative is to use Apache (and HTTP) for serving files. Using a web server to provide data downloads can reduce the need to monitor and maintain a separate software service (or directories) on your server. This approach to serving files also reduces system resource requirements and gives remote users a bit more flexibility when downloading (such as enabling them to download multiple files at once). See Chapter 24, "Apache Web Server Management," for more information about using Apache.

Installing FTP Software

As part of the standard installation, the client software for FTP is already installed. You can verify that some FTP-related software is installed on your system by using `dpkg`, `grep`, and `sort` commands in this query:

```
matthew@seymour:~$ dpkg --get-selections | grep ftp | sort
ftp                     install
lftp                    install
```

27

The preceding output is from a fresh installation of Ubuntu 11.10, and what you see are basic FTP clients. These allow you to use FTP to connect to other computers to interact with remote files. You need an FTP server to allow other systems to interact with files on your computer. This chapter covers one FTP server application, `vsftpd`.

If `vsftpd` is not installed, install the package `vsftpd` from the Ubuntu repositories. For more information about installing packages, see Chapter 9, "Managing Software."

NOTE

If you host an FTP server connected to the Internet, make it a habit to always install security updates and bug fixes for your server software.

The FTP User

Instead of files being uploaded or managed by a current user when anonymous connections are made to your FTP server, an FTP user is created when `vsftp` is installed. This user is not a normal user per se, but a name for anonymous FTP users. The FTP user entry in `/etc/passwd` looks like this:

```
ftp:x:116:124:ftp daemon,,,:/srv/ftp:/bin/false
```

The numbers differ on each system because they depend on the number of configured users on the system, but the rest of the information is the same.

NOTE

The FTP user, as discussed here, applies to anonymous FTP configurations and server setup. Our FTP user is configured to use `/srv/ftp` as the default directory. Other Linux distributions may use a different default directory, such as `/usr/local/ftp`, for FTP files and anonymous users.

This entry follows the standard `/etc/passwd` entry: username, password, user ID, group ID, comment field, home directory, and shell. To learn more about `/etc/password`, see the section "Configuring Your Firewall" in Chapter 20, "Securing Your Machines."

Each of the items in this entry is separated by colons. In the preceding example, you can see that the Ubuntu system hosting the server uses shadowed password (indicated by the *X* in the traditional password field). The shadow password system is important because it adds an additional level of security to Ubuntu; the shadow password system is normally installed during the Ubuntu installation.

The FTP server software uses this user account to assign permissions to users connecting to the server. By using a default shell of `/bin/false` for anonymous FTP users versus `/bin/bash` or some other standard, interactive shell, an anonymous FTP user will be unable to log in as a regular user. `/bin/false` is not a shell, but a program usually assigned to an account that has been locked. As root inspection of the /etc/shadow file shows (see Listing 27.1), it is not possible to log in to this account, denoted by the * as the password.

LISTING 27.1   Shadow Password File ftp User Entry

```
# cat /etc/shadow
bin:*:11899:0:99999:7:::
daemon:*:11899:0:99999:7:::
adm:*:11899:0:99999:7:::
lp:*:11899:0:99999:7:::
...
ftp:*:12276:0:99999:7:::
...
```

The shadow file (only a portion of which is shown in Listing 26.1) contains additional information not found in the standard /etc/passwd file, such as account expiration, password expiration, whether the account is locked, and the encrypted password. The * in the password field indicates that the account is not a standard login account; thus, it does not have a password.

Although shadow passwords are in use on the system, passwords are not transmitted in a secure manner when using FTP. Because FTP was written before the necessity of encryption and security, it does not provide the mechanics necessary to send encrypted passwords. Account information is sent in plain text on FTP servers; anyone with enough technical knowledge and a network sniffer can find the password for the account you connect to on the server. Many sites use an anonymous-only FTP server specifically to prevent normal account passwords from being transmitted over the Internet.

27

QUICK-AND-DIRTY FTP SERVICE

Conscientious Linux administrators take the time to carefully install, set up, and configure a production FTP server before offering public service or opening up for business on the Internet. However, you can set up a server very quickly on a secure LAN by completing a few simple steps:

1. Ensure that the FTP server package is installed, networking is enabled, and firewall rules on the server allow FTP access. See Chapter 18, "Networking," to learn about firewalling.

2. If anonymous access to server files is desired, create and populate the /srv/ftp/public directory. Do this by mounting or copying your content, such as directories and files, under this directory. You don't want to use symlinks, however, because a clever anonymous user could easily use that against you to access other parts of your file system. If you are new to this, copy your content into the directory.

3. Edit and then save the appropriate configuration file (such as /etc.vsftpd.conf for vsftpd) to enable access.

4. You must then start or restart the FTP server like this: sudo service vsftpd restart.

You can use the service to start, stop, restart, and query the `vsftpd` server. You must have root permission to use the `vsftpd` script to control the server, but any user can query the server (to see whether it is running and to see its process ID number) using the `status` keyword, like this:

```
matthew@seymour:~$ sudo service vsftpd status
```

You can also use a shorter version just for finding the status of the FTP daemon, as follows:

```
matthew@seymour:~$ status vsftpd
```

Administrator permissions are not required to use the `status` command, so we do not need to use `sudo`.

Configuring the Very Secure FTP Server

The Very Secure FTP server offers simplicity, security, and speed. It has been used by a number of sites, such as ftp.debian.org, ftp.gnu.org, rpmfind.net, and ftp.gimp.org. Note that despite its name, the Very Secure FTP server does not enable use of encrypted usernames or passwords.

Its main configuration file is `vsftpd.conf`, which resides under the `/etc` directory. The server has a number of features and default policies, but you can override these by changing the installed configuration file.

By default, anonymous logins are disabled. Users are not allowed to download or upload files, create new directories, or delete or rename files. The configuration file installed by Ubuntu allows local users (that is, users with a login and shell account) to log in and then access their `/home` directory. This configuration presents potential security risks because usernames and passwords are passed without encryption over a network. The best policy is to deny your users access to the server from their user accounts. To change these and other settings, edit the well-commented config file at `/etc/vsftp.conf`. For example, to change these two settings, edit the following lines:

```
# Allow anonymous FTP? (Disabled by default)
anonymous_enable=NO
#
# Uncomment this to allow local users to log in.
local_enable=YES
```

If you want to allow anonymous use of your FTP server, change NO to YES in the first couplet. As you can see in the second couplet, in Ubuntu 10.10, the local user setting was changed by Ubuntu from the default setting that did not allow local users to log in. We suggest commenting the line back out by placing a # at the front if you are going to run an anonymous FTP server. The default settings here work great if you are only allowing one user FTP access on the back end of a web server, for example, which is becoming the more common use for FTP, at least until we can convince the world to move to using SSH. See the "Telnet Versus SSH" section in Chapter 19, "Remote Access with SSH, Telnet, and VNC," and replace *Telnet* with *FTP* for an idea about why this would be a good move.

Controlling Anonymous Access

Toggling anonymous access features for your FTP server is done by editing the `vsftpd. conf` file and changing related entries to `YES` or `NO` in the file. Settings to control how the server works for anonymous logins include the following:

▶ `anonymous_enable`—Disabled by default. Use a setting of `YES` and then restart the server to turn on anonymous access.

▶ `anon_mkdir_write_enable`—Allows or disallows creating of new directories.

▶ `anon_other_write_enable`—Allows or disallows deleting or renaming of files and directories.

▶ `anon_upload_enable`—Controls whether anonymous users can upload files (also depends on the global `write_enable` setting). This is a potential security and liability hazard and should rarely be used; if enabled, consistently monitor any designated upload directory.

▶ `anon_world_readable_only`—Allows only anonymous users to download files with world-readable (444) permission.

After making any changes to your FTP server configuration file, make sure to restart the server; this forces `vsftpd` to reread its settings.

Other `vsftpd` Server Configuration Files

You can edit `vsftpd.conf` to enable, disable, and configure many features and settings of the `vsftpd` server, such as user access, filtering of bogus passwords, and access logging. Some features might require the creation and configuration of other files, such as the following:

▶ `/etc/vsftpd.user_list`—Used by the `userlist_enable` and the `userlist_deny` options; the file contains a list of usernames to be denied access to the server.

▶ `/etc/vsftpd.chroot_list`—Used by the `chroot_list_enable` and `chroot_local_ user` options, this file contains a list of users who are either allowed or denied access to a home directory. An alternative file can be specified by using the `chroot_list_ file` option.

▶ `/etc/vsftpd.banned_emails`—A list of anonymous password entries used to deny access if the `deny_email_enable` setting is enabled. An alternative file can be specified by using the `banned_email` option.

▶ `/var/log/vsftpd.log`—Data transfer information is captured to this file if logging is enabled using the `xferlog_enable` setting.

27

> **TIP**
>
> Whenever you're editing the FTP server files, make a backup file first. Also, it is always a good idea to comment out (using a pound sign, #, at the beginning of a line) what is changed instead of deleting or overwriting entries. Follow these comments with a brief description explaining why the change was made. This leaves a nice audit trail of what was done, by whom, when, and why. If you have any problems with the configuration, these comments and details can help you troubleshoot and return to valid entries if necessary. You can use the `dpkg` command or other Linux tools (such as `mc`) to extract a fresh copy of a configuration file from the software's package archive. Be aware, however, that the extracted version replaces the current version and overwrites your configuration changes.

Default `vsftpd` Behaviors

The contents of a file named `.message` (if it exists in the current directory) are displayed when a user enters the directory. This feature is enabled in the configuration file. FTP users are not allowed to perform recursive directory listings, which helps reduce bandwidth.

Other default settings are that specific user login controls are not set, but you can configure the controls to deny access to one or more users.

The data transfer rate for anonymous client access is unlimited, but you can set a maximum rate (in bytes per second) by using the `anon_max_rate` setting in `vsftpd.conf`. This can be useful for throttling bandwidth use during periods of heavy access, but waiting until heavy use occurs to change the setting could cause problems because you would kill any current connections when you restart the FTP server daemon. If you anticipate heavy FTP usage, change this setting before it happens or during a scheduled maintenance cycle. Another default is that remote clients will be logged out after five minutes of idle activity or a stalled data transfer. You can set idle and stalled connection timeouts by uncommenting `idle_session_timeout` and setting the time in seconds before idle sessions are disconnected.

Other settings that might be important for managing your system's resources (networking bandwidth or memory) when offering FTP access include the following:

- ▶ `dirlist_enable`—Toggles directory listings on or off.

- ▶ `dirmessage_enable`—Toggles display of a message when the user enters a directory. A related setting is `ls_recurse_enable`, which you can use to disallow recursive directory listings.

- ▶ `download_enable`—Toggles downloading on or off.

- ▶ `max_clients`—Sets a limit on the maximum number of connections.

- ▶ `max_per_ip`—Sets a limit on the number of connections from the same IP address.

Using the `ftphosts` File to Allow or Deny FTP Server Connection

You can create a file in `/etc` called `ftphosts` to allow or deny specific users or addresses from connecting to the FTP server. The format of the file is the word `allow` or `deny`, optionally followed by a username, followed by an IP or a DNS address:

```
allow username address
deny username address
```

Listing 27.2 shows a sample configuration of this file.

LISTING 27.2   `ftphosts` Configuration File for Allowing or Denying Users

```
# Example host access file
#
# Everything after a '#' is treated as comment,
# empty lines are ignored
allow fatima 208.164.186.1 208.164.186.2 208.164.186.4
deny richard 208.164.186.5
allow jane ubuntuforums.org
deny john naughtysite.net
allow ahmed 192.168.101.*
allow ahmed *.ubuntu.com
allow ahmed *.matthewhelmke.net
deny anonymous 201.*
```

The `*` is a wildcard that matches any combination of that address. For example, `allow ahmed *.matthewhelmke.net` allows the user `ahmed` to log in to the FTP server from any address that contains the domain name `matthewhelmke.net`. Similarly, the anonymous user is not allowed to access the FTP if the user is coming from a 201 public Class C IP address. You should set the permissions on this file to `600`.

Changes made to your system's FTP server configuration files only become active after you restart `inetd` because configuration files are only parsed at startup. To restart `inetd` as root, issue the command `/etc/init.d/inetutils-inetd restart`. This makes a call to the same shell script that is called at system startup and shutdown for any runlevel to start or stop the `inet` daemon. `inetd` should report its status as follows:

```
matthew@seymour:~$ sudo /etc/init.d/inetutils-inetd restart
Stopping internet superserver inetd:                              [  OK  ]
Starting internet superserver inetd:                             [  OK  ]
```

After it is restarted, the FTP server is accessible to all incoming requests.

27

References

▶ www.cert.org/—Computer Emergency Response Team.

▶ www.openssh.com/—The OpenSSH home page and source for the latest version of OpenSSH and its component clients, such as sftp.

▶ http://vsftpd.beasts.org/—Home page for the vsftd FTP server.

▶ https://help.ubuntu.com/community/FtpServer—Ubuntu community documentation for setting up and using an FTP server.

▶ https://help.ubuntu.com/14.04/serverguide/ftp-server.html—Official Ubuntu documentation for setting up and using vsftp.

# CHAPTER 28

Handling Email

Email is still the dominant form of communication over the Internet. It is fast, free, and easy to use. However, much of what goes on behind the scenes is extremely complicated and would appear scary to anyone who does not know much about how email is handled. Ubuntu comes equipped with a number of powerful applications that will help you build anything from a small email server, right through to large servers able to handle thousands of messages.

This chapter shows you how to configure Ubuntu to act as an email server. We look at the options available in Ubuntu and examine the pros and cons of each one. You also learn how mail is handled in Linux and, to a lesser extent, in UNIX.

How Email Is Sent and Received

Email is transmitted as plain text across networks around the world using the *Simple Mail Transfer Protocol (SMTP)*. As the name implies, the protocol itself is fairly basic, and it has been extended to add further authentication and error reporting/messaging to satisfy the growing demands of modern email. *Mail transfer agents (MTAs)* work in the background transferring email from server to server, allowing emails to be sent all over the world. You might have come across such MTA software such as Sendmail, Postfix, Fetchmail, Exim, or Qmail.

SMTP allows each computer that the email passes through to forward it in the right direction to the final destination. When you consider the millions of email servers across the world, you have to marvel at how simple it all seems.

Here is a simplified example of how email is successfully processed and sent to its destination:

1. matthew@seymourcray.net composes and sends an email message to heather@gracehopper.net.

2. The MTA at seymourcray.net receives Matthew's email message and queues it for delivery behind any other messages that are also waiting to go out.

3. The MTA at seymourcray.net contacts the MTA at gracehopper.net on port 24. After gracehopper.net acknowledges the connection, the MTA at seymourcray.net sends the mail message. After gracehopper.net accepts and acknowledges receipt of the message, the connection is closed.

4. The MTA at gracehopper.net places the mail message into Heather's incoming mailbox; Heather is notified that she has new mail the next time she logs on.

However, several things can go wrong during this process. Here are a few examples:

▶ What if Heather does not exist at gracehopper.net? In this case, the MTA at gracehopper.net rejects the email and notifies the MTA at seymourcray.net of what the problem is. The MTA at seymourcray.net then generates an email message and sends it to matthew@seymourcray.net, informing him that no Heather exists at gracehopper.net (or perhaps just silently discards the message and gives the sender no indication of the problem, depending on how the email server is configured).

▶ What happens if gracehopper.net doesn't respond to seymourcray.net's connection attempts? (Perhaps the server is down for maintenance.) The MTA at seymourcray.net notifies the sender that the initial delivery attempt has failed. Further attempts will be made at intervals decided by the server administrator until the deadline is reached, and the sender will be notified that the mail is undeliverable.

The Mail Transport Agent

Several MTAs are available for Ubuntu, each with its pros and cons. Normally they are hidden under the skin of Ubuntu, silently moving mail between servers all over the world with need for little or no maintenance. Some MTAs are extremely powerful, being able to cope with hundreds of thousands of messages each day, whereas some are geared more toward smaller installations. Other MTAs are perhaps not as powerful but are packed full with features. In the next section, we take a look at some of the more popular MTAs available for Ubuntu.

Sendmail

Sendmail handles the overwhelming majority of emails transmitted over the Internet today. It is extremely popular across the Linux/UNIX/BSD world and is well supported. A commercial version is available that has a GUI interface for ease of configuration.

As well as being popular, Sendmail is particularly powerful compared to some of the other MTAs. However, it is not without its downsides, and you will find that other MTAs can handle more email per second in a larger environment. The other issue with Sendmail is that it can be extremely complicated to set it up exactly as you want it. A few books are available specifically for Sendmail, but the most popular one has more than a thousand pages, reflecting the complex nature of the Sendmail configuration.

We can be thankful, however, that the default configuration for Sendmail works fine for most basic installations out of the box, making further configurations unnecessary. Even if you want to use it as a basic email server, you only need to do some minor tweaks. The level of complexity associated with Sendmail often leads to system administrators replacing it with one of the other alternatives that is easier to configure.

Postfix

Postfix has its origins as the IBM Secure Mailer but was released to the community by IBM. Compared to Sendmail, it is much easier to administer and has a number of speed advantages. Postfix offers a pain-free replacement for Sendmail, and you are able to literally replace Sendmail with Postfix without the system breaking a sweat. In fact, the applications that rely on Sendmail automatically use Postfix instead and carry on working correctly (because Postfix uses a Sendmail wrapper, which deceives other programs into thinking that Postfix is Sendmail). This wrapper, or more correctly interface, makes switching to Postfix extremely easy if you are already running Sendmail. Postfix also happens to be the MTA of choice for Ubuntu, so it is this one that we spend more time on later in this chapter.

For enhanced security, many Postfix processes used to use the `chroot` facility (which restricts access to only specific parts of the file system) for improved security, and there are no `setuid` components in Postfix. In Ubuntu, a `chroot` configuration is *no longer used* and is, in fact, discouraged by the Postfix author. You can manually reconfigure Postfix to a `chroot` configuration, but that is no longer supported by Ubuntu.

If you are starting from scratch, Postfix is considered a better choice than Sendmail.

Qmail and Exim

Qmail is a direct competitor to Postfix but is not provided with Ubuntu. Qmail is designed to be easier to use than Sendmail, as well as faster and more secure. However, Qmail is not a drop-in replacement for Sendmail, so migrating an existing Sendmail installation to Qmail is not quite as simple as migrating from Sendmail to Postfix. Qmail is relatively easy to administer, and it integrates with a number of software add-ons, including web mail systems and POP3 servers. Qmail is available from www.qmail.org/.

Exim is yet another MTA, and it is available at www.exim.org/. Exim is considered faster and more secure than Sendmail or Postfix but is much different to configure than either of those. Exim and Qmail use the `maildir` format rather than `mbox`, so both are considered "NFS safe" (see the following sidebar).

MDIR VERSUS MAILBOX

Qmail also introduced `maildir`, which is an alternative to the standard UNIX method of storing incoming mail. `maildir` is a more versatile system of handling incoming email, but it requires your email clients to be reconfigured, and it is not compatible with the traditional UNIX way of storing incoming mail. You will need to use mail programs that recognize the `maildir` format. (The modern programs do.)

The traditional `mbox` format keeps all mail assigned to a folder concatenated as a single file and maintains an index of individual emails. With `maildir`, each mail folder has three subfolders: `/cur`, `/new`, and `/tmp`. Each email is kept in a separate, unique file. If you are running a mail server for a large number of people, you should select a file system that can efficiently handle a large number of small files.

`mbox` does offer one major disadvantage. While you are accessing the monolithic `mbox` file that contains all your email, suppose that some type of corruption occurs, either to the file itself or to the index. Recovery from this problem can prove difficult. The `mbox` files are especially prone to problems if the files are being accessed over a network and can result in file corruption; one should avoid accessing `mbox` mail mounted over NFS, the *Network File System*, because file corruption can occur.

Depending on how you access your mail, `maildir` does permit the simultaneous access of `maildir` files by multiple applications; `mbox` does not.

The choice of a *mail user agent (MUA)*, or email client, also affects your choice of mail directory format. For example, the `pine` program does not cache any directory information and must reread the mail directory any time it accesses it. If you are using `pine`, `maildir` is a poor choice. More-advanced email clients perform caching, so `maildir` might be a good choice, although the email client cache can get out of synchronization. It seems that no perfect choice exists.

Ubuntu provides you with mail alternatives that have both strong and weak points. Be aware of the differences among the alternatives and frequently reevaluate your selection to make certain that it is the best one for your circumstances.

Choosing an MTA

Other MTAs are available for use with Ubuntu, but those discussed in the previous sections are the most popular. Which one should you choose? That depends on what you need to do. Postfix's main strengths are that it scales well and can handle large volumes of email at high speeds, not to mention that it is much easier to configure than the more cryptic Sendmail. However, you may find that there are specific things that you need that only Sendmail can provide. It is easy to switch between MTAs when you need to.

The Mail Delivery Agent

SMTP is a server-to-server protocol that was designed to deliver mail to systems that are always connected to the Internet. Dial-up systems connect only at the user's command; they connect for specific operations, and are frequently disconnected. To accommodate this difference, many mail systems also include a *mail delivery agent (MDA)*. The MDA transfers mail to systems without permanent Internet connections. The MDA is similar to an MTA (see the following note), but does not handle deliveries between systems and does not provide an interface to the user.

NOTE

Procmail or Spamassassin are examples of MDAs; both provide filtering services to the MDA while they store messages locally and then make them available to the MUA or email client for reading by the user.

The MDA uses the *Post Office Protocol version 3 (POP3)* or *Internet Message Access Protocol (IMAP)* for this process. In a manner similar to a post office box at the post office, POP3 and IMAP implement a "store and forward" process that alleviates the need to maintain a local mail server if all you want to do is read your mail. For example, dial-up Internet users can intermittently connect to their ISP's mail server to retrieve mail using Fetchmail—the MDA recommended by Ubuntu (see the section "Using Fetchmail to Retrieve Mail" later in this chapter).

The Mail User Agent

The *mail user agent (MUA)* is another necessary part of the email system. The MUA is a mail client, or mail reader, that enables the user to read and compose email and provides the user interface. (It is the email application itself that most users are familiar with as "email.") Some popular UNIX command-line MUAs are elm, pine, and mutt. Ubuntu also provides modern GUI MUAs: Evolution, Thunderbird, Mozilla Mail, Balsa, Sylpheed, and KMail. For comparison, common non-UNIX MUAs are Microsoft Outlook, Outlook Express, Pegasus Mail, and Apple Inc.'s Mail.

The Microsoft Windows and Macintosh MUAs often include some MTA functionality; UNIX does not. For example, Microsoft Outlook can connect to your Internet provider's mail server to send messages. On the other hand, UNIX MUAs generally rely on an external MTA such as Sendmail. This might seem like a needlessly complicated way to do things, and it is if used to connect a single user to her ISP. For any other situation, however, using an external MTA allows you much greater flexibility because you can use any number of external programs to handle and process your email functions and customize the service. Having the process handled by different applications gives you great control over how you provide email service to users on your network, as well as to individual and *small office/home office (SOHO)* users.

For example, you could do the following:

▶ Use Evolution to read and compose mail

▶ Use Sendmail to send your mail

▶ Use xbiff to notify you when you have new mail

▶ Use Fetchmail to retrieve your mail from a remote mail server

▶ Use Procmail to automatically sort your incoming mail based on sender, subject, or many other variables

▶ Use Spamassassin to eliminate the unwanted messages before you read them

Basic Postfix Configuration and Operation

Because Postfix is the Ubuntu-recommended MTA, the following sections provide a brief explanation and examples for configuring and operating your email system. As mentioned earlier, however, Postfix is an extremely complex program with many configuration options. Therefore, this chapter only covers some of the basics.

Postfix is not installed by default. To use it, install the `postfix` package from the Ubuntu software repositories. During installation, you are asked a series of questions to help configure Postfix immediately. Research the settings for your situation before you start; some are merely preferential, but others are based on your hardware, network, and use case. You are asked the following:

```
General type of mail configuration: Internet Site

System mail name: mail.matthewhelmke.com
Root and postmaster mail recipient: <admin_user_name>
Other destinations for mail: mail.example.com, example.com, localhost.example.com,
➥localhost
Force synchronous updates on mail queue?: No
Local networks: 127.0.0.0/8

Mailbox size limit (bytes): 0
Local address extension character: +
Internet protocols to use: all
```

If you make a mistake and answer a configuration question incorrectly, you can go back through the process again by entering the following command from the command line:

```
matthew@seymour:~$ sudo dpkg-reconfigure postfix
```

Postfix configuration is maintained in files in the `/etc/postfix` directory with much of the configuration being handled by the file `main.cf`. You don't have to use the preceding command to change these settings; you may do so by editing the appropriate files. The syntax of the configuration file, `main.cf`, is fairly easy to read (see the following example):

```
# See /usr/share/postfix/main.cf.dist for a commented, more complete version
# Debian specific:  Specifying a file name will cause the first
# line of that file to be used as the name.  The Debian default
# is /etc/mailname.
#myorigin = /etc/mailname

smtpd_banner = $myhostname ESMTP $mail_name (Ubuntu)
biff = no

# appending .domain is the MUA's job.
append_dot_mydomain = no
```

```
# Uncomment the next line to generate "delayed mail" warnings
#delay_warning_time = 4h

# TLS parameters
smtpd_tls_cert_file=/etc/ssl/certs/ssl-cert-snakeoil.pem
smtpd_tls_key_file=/etc/ssl/private/ssl-cert-snakeoil.key
smtpd_use_tls=yes
smtpd_tls_session_cache_database = btree:${queue_directory}/smtpd_scache
smtp_tls_session_cache_database = btree:${queue_directory}/smtp_scache

# See /usr/share/doc/postfix/TLS_README.gz in the postfix-doc package for
# information on enabling SSL in the smtp client.

myhostname = optimus
alias_maps = hash:/etc/aliases
alias_database = hash:/etc/aliases
mydestination = optimus, localhost.localdomain, , localhost
relayhost =
mynetworks = 127.0.0.0/8
mailbox_size_limit = 0
recipient_delimiter = +
inet_interfaces = all
```

A useful command for configuring Postfix is `postconf`. It enables you to display and change many configuration settings without editing and saving configuration files. The command's syntax is rather complex, but once learned it becomes a faster way to quickly adjust settings.

If you type the command by itself, it outputs a list of all configuration parameters. This can be quite long, so we recommend either sorting using a pipe and `grep` or sending the output to a file. See Chapter 11, "Command-Line Master Class Part 1," for more on how to do this. This example shows the command piped into `grep` with a search for `hostname`:

```
matthew@seymour:~$ postconf | grep hostname
invalid_hostname_reject_code = 501
lmtp_lhlo_name = $myhostname
lmtp_tls_verify_cert_match = hostname
local_transport = local:$myhostname
milter_macro_daemon_name = $myhostname
myhostname = ubuntu
smtp_helo_name = $myhostname
smtp_tls_verify_cert_match = hostname
smtpd_banner = $myhostname ESMTP $mail_name (Ubuntu)
smtpd_proxy_ehlo = $myhostname
unknown_helo_hostname_tempfail_action = $reject_tempfail_action
unknown_hostname_reject_code = 450
```

To show the default parameter settings instead of the current settings, use this:

```
matthew@seymour:~$ postconf -d
```

Use this to discover which parameters have been changed from their defaults and display the current settings:

```
matthew@seymour:~$ postconf -n
```

Setting a parameter requires root privileges. For example, to set the `myhostname` parameter, use the following:

```
matthew@seymour:~$ sudo postconf -e "myhostname=mail.matthewhelmke.com"
myhostname=mail.matthewhelmke.com
```

This works with the parameters listed in the Postfix `main.cf` file:

```
matthew@seymour:~$ sudo postconf -e "smtp_sasl_auth_enable = yes"
myhostname=othername.matthewhelmke.com
```

As you can see, `postconf` is quite convenient. You can learn more about `postconf` from the man page.

You start, stop, and restart Postfix using this command, using the appropriate one of those three action words:

```
matthew@seymour:~$ sudo /etc/init.d/postfix start
```

Complicated email server setup is beyond the scope of this book; consider *Postfix: The Definitive Guide,* by Kyle Dent, for more information. This is a great reference and rather unusual because it is a complete and useful reference in only 250 pages or so. However, if you want to know something specific about Postfix, this is the book to read.

However, the following five sections address some commonly used advanced options. For more information on Postfix, as well as other MTAs, see the "References" section at the end of this chapter.

Configuring Masquerading

Sometimes you might want to have Postfix masquerade as a host other than the actual hostname of your system. Such a situation could occur if you have a dial-up connection to the Internet and your ISP handles all your mail for you. In this case, you want Postfix to masquerade as the domain name of your ISP. For example, the following strips any messages that come from `matthew.gracehopper.net` to just `gracehopper.net`:

```
masquerade_domains = gracehopper.net
```

Using Smart Hosts

If you do not have a full-time connection to the Internet, you will probably want to have Postfix send your messages to your ISP's mail server and let it handle delivery for you. Without a full-time Internet connection, you could find it difficult to deliver messages to some locations (such as some underdeveloped areas of the world where email services are unreliable and sporadic). In those situations, you can configure Postfix to function as a smart host by passing email on to another sender instead of attempting to deliver the email directly. You can use a line such as the following in the `main.cf` file to enable a smart host:

```
relayhost = mail.isp.net
```

This line causes Postfix to pass any mail it receives to the server `mail.isp.net` rather than attempt to deliver it directly. Smart hosting will not work for you if your ISP blocks any mail relaying. Some ISPs block relaying because it is frequently used to disseminate spam.

Setting Message Delivery Intervals

As mentioned earlier, Postfix typically attempts to deliver messages as soon as it receives them, and again at regular intervals after that. If you have only periodic connections to the Internet, as with a dial-up connection, you likely would prefer Sendmail to hold all messages in the queue and attempt to deliver them whenever you connect to your ISP.

As dial-up connections have become the exception rather than the rule and are now quite rare, Ubuntu does not configure them by default and does not include the `pppd` daemon in the default installation. If you need this, install `pppd` from the Ubuntu software repositories. You can then configure Postfix to hold messages for later delivery by adding the following line to `/etc/ppp/peers/ppp0`:

```
/usr/sbin/sendmail -q
```

This line causes Postifix to automatically send all mail when connecting to your ISP.

However, Postfix still attempts to send mail regardless of whether the computer is on or off line, meaning that your computer may dial out just to send email. To disable this, you need to enter the following line into `mail.cf`:

```
defer_transports = smtp
```

This stops any unwanted telephone calls from being placed!

> **TIP**
>
> If you use networking over a modem, there is a configuration file for `pppd` called `ppp0`, which is located in `/etc/ppp/peers`. Any commands in this file automatically run each time the PPP daemon is started. You can add the line `sendmail -q` to this file to have your mail queue automatically processed each time you dial up your Internet connection.

28

Mail Relaying

By default, Postfix will not relay mail that did not originate from the local domain. This means that if a Postfix installation running at `gracehopper.net` receives mail intended for `seymourcray.net`, and that mail did not originate from `gracehopper.net`, the mail will be rejected and will not be relayed. If you want to allow selected domains to relay through you, add an entry for the domain to the `main.cf` file like this:

```
mynetworks = 192.168.2.0/24, 10.0.0.2/24, 127.0.0.0/8
```

The IP address needs to be specified in *classless inter-domain routing (CIDR)* format. For a handy calculator, head on over to www.subnet-calculator.com/cidr.php. You must restart Postfix for this change to take effect.

CAUTION

You need a good reason to relay mail; otherwise, do not do it. Allowing all domains to relay through you will make you a magnet for spammers who will use your mail server to send spam. This can lead to your site being blacklisted by many other sites, which then will not accept any mail from you or your site's users—even if the mail is legitimate!

Forwarding Email with Aliases

Aliases allow you to have an infinite number of valid recipient addresses on your system, and you don't have to worry about creating accounts or other support files for each address. For example, most systems have "postmaster" defined as a valid recipient but do not have an actual login account named postmaster. Aliases are configured in the file `/etc/aliases`. Here is an example of an alias entry:

```
postmaster: root
```

This entry forwards any mail received for postmaster to the root user. By default, almost all the aliases listed in the `/etc/aliases` file forward to root.

CAUTION

Reading email as root is a security hazard; a malicious email message can exploit an email client and cause it to execute arbitrary code as the user running the client. To avoid this danger, you can forward all of root's mail to another account and read it from there. You can choose one of two ways for doing this.

You can add an entry to the `/etc/aliases` file that sends root's mail to a different account. For example, `root: foobar` would forward all mail intended for root to the account foobar.

The other way is to create a file named `.forward` in root's home directory that contains the address that the mail should forward to.

Any time you make a change to the /etc/aliases file, you must rebuild the aliases database before that change will take effect. Use the following command to do this:

matthew@seymour:~$ **sudo newaliases**

Using Fetchmail to Retrieve Mail

SMTP is designed to work with systems that have a full-time connection to the Internet. What if you are on a dial-up account? What if you have another system store your email for you and then you log in to pick it up once in a while? (Most users who are not setting up servers will be in this situation.) In this case, you cannot easily receive email using SMTP, and you need to use a protocol, such as POP3 or IMAP, instead.

> **NOTE**
>
> Remember when we said that some mail clients can include some MTA functionality? You can configure Microsoft Outlook and Outlook Express to use SMTP, and if you use a dial-up connection, they offer to start the connection and then use SMTP to send your mail, so a type of MTA functionality is included in those mail clients.

Unfortunately, many MUAs do not know anything about POP3 or IMAP. To eliminate that problem, you can use a program called Fetchmail to contact mail servers using POP3 or IMAP, download mail off the servers, and then inject those messages into the local MTA just as if they had come from a standard SMTP server. The following sections explain how to install, configure, and use the Fetchmail program.

Installing Fetchmail

Similar to other packages, you can install Fetchmail using either synaptic or apt-get.

You can get the latest version of Fetchmail at www.catb.org/~esr/fetchmail.

Configuring Fetchmail

After you have installed Fetchmail, you must create the file .fetchmailrc in your home directory, which provides the configuration for the Fetchmail program.

You can create and subsequently edit the .fetchmailrc file by using any text editor. The configuration file is straightforward and quite easy to create; the following sections explain the manual method for creating and editing the file. The information presented in the following sections does not discuss all the options available in the .fetchmailrc file, but covers the most common ones needed to get a basic Fetchmail installation up and running. You must use a text editor to create the file to include entries like the ones shown as examples—modified for your personal information, of course. For advanced configuration, see the man page for Fetchmail. The man page is well written and documents all the configuration options in detail.

28

CAUTION

The `.fetchmailrc` file is divided into three sections: global options, mail server options, and user options. It is important that these sections appear in the order listed. Do not add options to the wrong section. Putting options in the wrong place is one of the most common problems that new users make with Fetchmail configuration files.

Configuring Global Options

The first section of `.fetchmailrc` contains the global options. These options affect all the mail servers and user accounts that you list later in the configuration file. You can override some of these global options with local configuration options, as you learn later in this section. Here is an example of the options that might appear in the global section of the `.fetchmailrc` file:

```
set daemon 600
set postmaster foobar
set logfile ./.fetchmail.log
```

The first line in this example tells Fetchmail that it should start in daemon mode and check the mail servers for new mail every 600 seconds, or 10 minutes. Daemon mode means that after Fetchmail starts, it moves itself into the background and continues running. Without this line, Fetchmail checks for mail once when it started and then terminates and never checks again.

The second option tells Fetchmail to use the local account `foobar` as a last-resort address. In other words, any email that it receives and cannot deliver to a specified account should be sent to foobar.

The third line tells Fetchmail to log its activity to the file `./.fetchmail.log`. Alternatively, you can use the line `set syslog`—in which case, Fetchmail logs through the syslog facility.

Configuring Mail Server Options

The second section of the `.fetchmailrc` file contains information on each of the mail servers that should be checked for new mail. Here is an example of what the mail section might look like:

```
poll mail.samplenet.org
proto pop3
no dns
```

The first line tells Fetchmail that it should check the mail server `mail.samplenet.org` at each poll interval that was set in the global options section (which was 600 seconds in our example). Alternatively, the first line can begin with skip. If a mail server line begins with skip, it will not be polled as the poll interval, but will only be polled when it is specifically specified on the Fetchmail command line.

The second line specifies the protocol that should be used when contacting the mail server. In this case, we are using POP3. Other legal options are IMAP, *Authenticated Post Office Protocol (APOP)*, and *Kerberized Post Office Protocol (KPOP)*. You can also use AUTO here, in which case Fetchmail attempts to automatically determine the correct protocol to use with the mail server.

The third line tells Fetchmail that it should not attempt to do a *Dynamic Name Server (DNS)* lookup. You probably want to include this option if you are running over a dial-up connection.

Configuring User Accounts

The third and final section of .fetchmailrc contains information about the user account on the server specified in the previous section. Here is an example:

```
user foobar
pass secretword
fetchall
no flush
```

The first line, of course, simply specifies the username that is used to log in to the email server, and the second line specifies the password for that user. Many security-conscious people cringe at the thought of putting clear-text passwords in a configuration file, and they should if it is group or world readable. The only protection for this information is to make certain that the file is readable only by the owner; that is, with file permissions of 600.

The third line tells Fetchmail that it should fetch all messages from the server, even if they have already been read.

The fourth line tells Fetchmail that it should delete the messages from the mail server after it has completed downloading them. This is the default, so we would not really have to specify this option. If you want to delete the messages from the server after downloading them, use the option flush.

The configuration options you just inserted configured the entire .fetchmailrc file to look like this:

```
set daemon 600
set postmaster foobar
set logfile ./.fetchmail.log

poll mail.samplenet.org
proto pop3
no dns

user foobar
pass secretword
fetchall
flush
```

28

This file tells Fetchmail to do the following:

▶ Check the POP3 server `mail.samplenet.org` for new mail every 600 seconds.

▶ Log in using the username foobar and the password secretword.

▶ Download all messages off the server.

▶ Delete the messages from the server after it has finished downloading them.

▶ Send any mail it receives that cannot be delivered to a local user to the account `foobar`.

As mentioned earlier, many more options can be included in the `.fetchmailrc` file than are listed here. However, the options offered in this section will get you up and running with a basic configuration.

For additional flexibility, you can define multiple `.fetchmailrc` files to retrieve mail from different remote mail servers while using the same Linux user account. For example, you can define settings for your most often used account and save them in the default `.fetchmailrc` file. Mail can then quickly be retrieved like this:

```
matthew@seymour:~$ fetchmail -a
1 message for matthew at mail.matthewhelmke.com (1108 octets).
reading message 1 of 1 (1108 octets) . flushed
```

By using Fetchmail's `-f` option, you can specify an alternative resource file and then easily retrieve mail from another server, as follows:

```
matthew@seymour:~$ fetchmail -f .myothermailrc
2 messages for matthew at matthew.helmke.com (5407 octets).
reading message 1 of 2 (3440 octets) ... flushed
reading message 2 of 2 (1967 octets) . flushed
You have new mail in /var/spool/mail/matthew
```

By using the `-d` option, along with a time interval (in seconds), you can use Fetchmail in its daemon, or background mode. The command launches as a background process and retrieves mail from a designated remote server at a specified interval. For more-advanced options, see the Fetchmail man page, which is well written and documents all options in detail.

CAUTION

Because the `.fetchmailrc` file contains your mail server password, it should be readable only by you. This means that it should be owned by you and should have permissions no greater than `600`. Fetchmail complains and refuses to start if the `.fetchmailrc` file has permissions greater than this.

Choosing a Mail Delivery Agent

Because of the modular nature of mail handling, it is possible to use multiple applications to process mail and accomplish more than simply deliver it. Getting mail from the storage area and displaying it to the user is the purpose of the MDA. MDA functionality can be found in some of the mail clients (MUAs), which can cause some confusion to those still unfamiliar with the concept of UNIX mail. As an example, the Procmail MDA provides filtering based on rulesets; KMail and Evolution, both MUAs, provide filtering, but the MUAs pine, mutt, and Balsa do not. Some MDAs perform simple sorting, and other MDAs are designed to eliminate unwanted emails, such as spam and viruses.

You would choose an MDA based on what you want to do with your mail. We look at five MDAs that offer functions you might find useful in your particular situation. If you have simple needs (just organizing mail by rules), one of the MUAs that offers filtering might be better for your needs. Ubuntu provides the Evolution MUA as the default selection (and it contains some MDA functionality as previously noted), so try that first and see whether it meets your needs. If not, investigate one of the following MDAs provided by Ubuntu.

Unless otherwise noted, all the MDA software is provided in the Ubuntu repositories. Chapter 9, "Managing Software," details the general installation of any software.

Procmail

As a tool for advanced users, the Procmail application acts as a filter for email, as it is retrieved from a mail server. It uses rulesets (known as *recipes*) as it reads each email message. No default configuration is provided; you must manually create a ~/.procmail file for each user, or users can create their own.

There is no system-wide default configuration file. The creation of the rulesets is not trivial and requires an understanding of the use of regular expressions that is beyond the scope of this chapter. Ubuntu does provide three examples of the files in /usr/share /doc/procmail/examples, as well as a fully commented example in the /usr/share/doc /procmail directory, which also contains a README and FAQ. You can find details for the rulesets in the man page for Procmail and in the man pages for procmailrc, procmailsc, and procmailex, which contain examples of Procmail recipes.

Spamassassin

If you have used email for any length of time, you have likely been subjected to *spam*, unwanted email sent to thousands of people at the same time. Ubuntu provides an MDA named *Spamassassin* to assist you in reducing and eliminating unwanted emails. Easily integrated with Procmail and Sendmail, it can be configured for both system-wide and individual use. It uses a combination of rule sets and blacklists (Internet domains known to mail spam).

Enabling Spamassassin is simple. You must first have installed and configured Procmail. The README file in /usr/share/doc/spamassassin provides details on configuring the .procmail file to process mail through Spamassassin. Spamassassin tags probable spam with a unique header; you can then have Procmail filter the mail in any manner you choose. One interesting use of Spamassasin is to use it to tag email received at special email accounts established solely for the purpose of attracting spam. This information is then shared with the Spamassassin site where these "spam trap"–generated hits help the authors fine-tune the rulesets.

Squirrelmail

Perhaps you do not want to read your mail in an MUA. If you use your web browser often, it might make sense to read and send your mail via a web interface, such as the one used by Gmail, Hotmail, or Yahoo! Mail. Ubuntu provides Squirrelmail for just that purpose. Squirrelmail is written in PHP and supports IMAP and SMTP. It supports MIME attachments and an address book and folders for segregating email.

You must configure your web server to work with PHP 4. You can find detailed installation instructions in `/usr/share/doc/squirrelmail/INSTALL`. After you configure Squirrelmail, point your web browser to the default install location, www.yourdomain .com/squirelmail/, to read and send email.

Virus Scanners

Although the currently held belief is that Linux is immune to email viruses targeted at Microsoft Outlook users, it certainly makes no sense for UNIX mail servers to permit infected email to be sent through them. Although Ubuntu does not provide a virus scanner by default, some of the more popular scanners are available in the Ubuntu repositories. Take a look at ClamAV as the most popular example.

Autoresponders

Autoresponders automatically generate replies to received messages; they are commonly used to notify others that the recipient is out of the office. Mercifully, Ubuntu does not include one by default, but you can find and install an autoresponder like `vacation` or `gnarwl` from the Ubuntu software repositories. If you are subscribed to a mailing list, be aware that automatic responses from your account can be very annoying to others on the list. Please unsubscribe from mail lists before you leave the office with your autoresponder activated.

Alternatives to Microsoft Exchange Server

One of the last areas in which a Microsoft product has yet to be usurped by open-source software is a replacement for Microsoft Exchange Server. Many businesses use Microsoft Outlook and Microsoft Exchange Server to access email and to provide calendaring, notes, file sharing, and other collaborative functions. General industry complaints about Exchange Server center around scalability, administration (backup and restore in particular), and licensing fees.

A "drop-in" alternative needs to have compatibility with Microsoft Outlook because it is intended to replace Exchange Server in an environment in which there are Microsoft desktops in existence using Outlook. A "work-alike" alternative provides similar features to Exchange Server but does not offer compatibility with the Microsoft Outlook client itself; the latter is typical of many of the open-source alternatives.

Several "drop-in" alternatives exist, none of which are fully open source because some type of proprietary connector is needed to provide the services to Microsoft Outlook clients (or provide Exchange services to the Linux Evolution client). For Outlook compatibility, the key seems to be the realization of a full, open implementation of *MAPI*, the Microsoft *Messaging Application Program Interface*. That goal is going to be difficult to achieve because MAPI is a poorly documented Microsoft protocol. For Linux-only solutions, the missing ingredient for many alternatives is a usable group calendaring/ scheduling system similar in function to that provided by Exchange Server/Outlook.

Of course, independent applications for these functions abound in the open-source world, but one characteristic of "groupware" is its central administration; another is that all components can share information.

The following sections examine several of the available servers, beginning with Microsoft Exchange Server itself and moving toward those applications that have increasing incompatibility with it. None of these servers are provided with Ubuntu.

Microsoft Exchange Server/Outlook Client

Exchange Server and Outlook seem to be the industry benchmark because of their widespread deployment. They offer a proprietary server providing email, contacts, scheduling, public folders, task lists, journaling, and notes using Microsoft Outlook as the client and MAPI as the API. If you consider what Microsoft Exchange offers as the "full" set of features, no other replacement offers 100 percent of the features exactly as provided by Microsoft Exchange Server—even those considered drop-in replacements. The home page for the Microsoft Exchange server is www.microsoft.com/exchange/.

CommuniGate Pro

CommuniGate Pro is a proprietary, drop-in alternative to Microsoft Exchange Server, providing email, webmail, *Lightweight Directory Access Protocol (LDAP)* directories, a web server, file server, contacts, calendaring (third party), Voice over IP (VoIP), and a list server. The CommuniGate Pro MAPI Connector provides access to the server from Microsoft Outlook and other MAPI-enabled clients. The home page for this server is www.stalker.com/.

Oracle Beehive

Oracle Beehive is probably the closest that you will get to an Exchange replacement. It enables you to collaborate with instant messaging, email, file sharing (workspaces), calendaring, and other tools. Beehive is available for Linux platforms, and its home page is www.oracle.com/us/products/middleware/beehive/index.html.

28

Bynari

Bynari provides a proprietary group of servers to act as a drop-in replacement for Microsoft Exchange Server for email, calendaring, public folders, scheduling, address book, webmail, and contacts. Although it runs on Linux, it offers no Linux clients, although you can use it with Evolution and Thunderbird, and the connector provides services to Microsoft Outlook only. The home page is www.bynari.net/.

Open-Xchange

Open-Xchange has a great pedigree, having been owned and developed by Novell/SUSE until being spun off by itself into its own company. Working with open standards, it provides a number of collaboration options and is firmly based on Linux. It can work with a wide variety of protocols, making it one of the best connected suites available. You can get the open-source version at www.open-xchange.com.

Horde

Horde is a PHP-based application framework. When combined with an HTTP server (Apache, Microsoft IIS, Netscape) and MySQL database, IMP/Horde offers modules that provide webmail, contact manager, calendar, CVS viewer, file manager, time tracking, email filter rules manager, notes, tasks, chat, newsgroups, forms, bug tracking, FAQ repository, and presentations. The home page is www.horde.org/.

References

▶ **www.sendmail.org/**—The Sendmail home page. Here you can find configuration information and FAQs regarding the Sendmail MTA.

▶ **www.postfix.org/**—The Postfix home page. If you are using the Postfix MTA, you can find documentation and sample configurations at this site.

▶ **help.ubuntu.com/community/Postfix**—Ubuntu community documentation for Postfix.

▶ **www.qmail.org/**—The home page for the Qmail MTA. It contains documentation and links to other resources on Qmail.

▶ **https://help.ubuntu.com/community/ClamAV**—Ubuntu community documentation for ClamAV.

▶ **www.rfc-editor.org/**—A repository of *Request For Comments (RFCs)*, which define the technical "rules" of modern computer usage.

▶ **www.procmail.org/**—The Procmail home page.

▶ *Sendmail* (O'Reilly Publishing) by Brian Costales, Claus Assmann, George Jansen, and Gregory Neil Shapiro, ISBN: 0-596-51029-2—The de facto standard guide for everything Sendmail. It is loaded with more than 1,000 pages, which gives you an idea of how complicated Sendmail really is.

▶ *Postfix* (Sams Publishing) by Richard Blum, ISBN: 0-672-32114-9—An excellent book from Sams Publishing that covers the Postfix MTA.

▶ *Postfix: The Definitive Guide* (O'Reilly Publishing) by Kyle D. Dent, ISBN: 0-596-00212-2—Another excellent resource for Postfix.

▶ *Running Qmail* (Sams Publishing) by Richard Blum, ISBN: 0-672-31945-4—This is similar to the Postfix book from Sams Publishing except that it covers the Qmail MTA.

28

CHAPTER 29

Proxying, Reverse Proxying, and Virtual Private Networks (VPN)

You can never have enough of two things in this world: time and bandwidth. Ubuntu comes with a proxy server—Squid—that enables you to cache web traffic on your server so that websites load faster and users consume less bandwidth. Sometimes proxy servers are recommended for security and privacy, but a virtual private network (VPN) is an even better option if security and privacy are your main concerns. The last section of the chapter is about VPNs. Both proxy servers and VPNs have the interesting side effect that when they are in use, everything that your computer connects to—say a website—assumes the IP address of the proxy or VPN server is your IP address.

What Is a Proxy Server?

A *proxy server* lies between client machines—the desktops in your company—and the Internet. As clients request websites, they do not connect directly to the Web and send the HTTP request. Instead, they connect to the local proxy server. The proxy then forwards their requests on to the Web, retrieves the result, and hands it back to the client. At its simplest, a proxy server really is just an extra layer between client and server, so why bother?

The three main reasons for deploying a proxy server are as follows:

▶ **Content control**—You want to prevent access to certain types of content.

▶ **Speed**—You want to cache common sites to make the most of your bandwidth.

▶ **Security**—You want to monitor what people are doing.

Squid accomplishes these things and more.

Installing Squid

You can easily install Squid as usual from the Ubuntu software repositories, where it is called `squid3`. After Squid is installed, it is automatically enabled for each boot. You can check this by running `ps aux | grep squid` when the machine boots. If you see nothing there, run `sudo start squid`.

Configuring Clients

Before you configure your new Squid server, set up the local web browser to use it for its web access. Doing so enables you to test your rules as you are working with the configuration file.

To configure Firefox, while Firefox is running in the foreground select Preferences from the Edit menu from the top panel of the Ubuntu desktop. From the dialog that appears, select the Advanced settings using the icon in the top row, and within Advanced, select the Network tab. Then click the Settings button next to Configure how Firefox connects to the Internet and select the Manual Proxy Configuration option. Check the box beneath it labeled Use the Same Proxy for All Protocols. Enter `127.0.0.1` in the HTTP Proxy box and `3128` as the port number. See Figure 29.1 for how this should look. If you are configuring a remote client, specify the IP address of the Squid server rather than 127.0.0.1.

FIGURE 29.1   Setting up Firefox to use 127.0.0.1 routes all its web requests through Squid.

You can similarly configure other web browsers such as Google Chrome, Opera, and so on. The difference is the labels used and menu locations for the options, so you might have to do a little digging to discover where this may be adjusted in a specific browser's settings.

Access Control Lists

The main Squid configuration file is /etc/squid3/squid.conf, and the default Ubuntu configuration file is full of comments to help guide you. The default configuration file allows full access to the local machine but denies the rest of your network. This is a secure place to start; we recommend you try all the rules on yourself (localhost) before rolling them out to other machines.

Before you start, open two terminal windows. In the first, change to the directory /var/log/squid3 and run this command:

matthew@seymour:~$ **sudo tail -f access.log cache.log**

That reads the last few lines from both files and (thanks to the -f flag) follows them so that any changes appear in there. This allows you to watch what Squid is doing as people access it. We refer to this window as the "log window," so keep it open. In the other window (again, with sudo), bring up the file /etc/squid/squid.conf in your favorite editor. We refer to this window as the "config editor," and you should keep it open, too.

To get started, search for the string acl all; this brings you to the access control section, which is where most of the work needs to be done. You can configure a lot elsewhere, but unless you have unusual requirements, you can leave the defaults in place.

> **NOTE**
>
> The default port for Squid is 3128, but you can change that by editing the http_port line. Alternatively, you can have Squid listen on multiple ports by having multiple http_port lines; 80, 8000, and 8080 are all popular ports for proxy servers.

The acl lines make up your *access control lists (ACLs)*. The first 16 or so define the minimum recommended configuration that set up ports to listen to, and so on. You can safely ignore these. If you scroll down further (past another short block of comments), you come to the http_access lines, which are combined with the acl lines to dictate who can do what. You can (and should) mix and match acl and http_access lines to keep your configuration file easy to read.

Just below the first block of http_access lines is a comment like # INSERT YOUR OWN RULE(S) HERE TO ALLOW ACCESS FROM YOUR CLIENTS. This is just what we are going to do. First, though, scroll just a few lines further; you should see the following two lines (they are not necessarily next to each other in the actual file):

```
http_access allow localhost
http_access deny all
```

These lines are self-explanatory: The first says, "Allow HTTP access to the local computer, but deny everyone else." This is the default rule, as mentioned earlier. Leave that in place for now and run `service squid` start to start the server with the default settings. If you have not yet configured the local web browser to use your Squid server, do so now so that you can test the default rules.

In your web browser (Firefox is assumed from here on because it is the default in a standard Ubuntu install, but it makes little difference), go to the URL www.ubuntulinux.org. You should see it appear as normal in the browser, but in the log window you should see a lot of messages scroll by as Squid downloads the site for you and stores it in its cache. This is all allowed because the default configuration allows access to the `localhost`.

Go back to the config editor window and add this before the last two `http_access` lines:

```
http_access deny localhost
```

So, the last three lines should look like this:

```
http_access deny localhost
http_access allow localhost
http_access deny all
```

Save the file and quit your editor. Then, run this command:

```
matthew@seymour:~$ kill -SIGHUP 'cat /var/run/squid.pid'
```

That looks for the *process ID (PID)* of the `squid` daemon and then sends the `SIGHUP` signal to it, which forces it to reread its configuration file while running. You should see a string of messages in the log window as Squid rereads its configuration files. If you now go back to Firefox and enter a new URL, you should see the Squid error page informing you that you do not have access to the requested site.

The reason you are now blocked from the proxy is because Squid reads its ACL lines in sequence, from top to bottom. If it finds a line that conclusively allows or denies a request, it stops reading and takes the appropriate action. So, in the previous lines, `localhost` is being denied in the first line and then allowed in the second. When Squid sees `localhost` asking for a site, it reads the `deny` line first and immediately sends the error page; it does not even get to the `allow` line. Having a `deny all` line at the bottom is highly recommended so that only those you explicitly allow are able to use the proxy.

Go back to editing the configuration file and remove the `deny localhost` and `allow localhost` lines. This leaves only `deny all`, which blocks everyone (including the `localhost`) from accessing the proxy. Now you are going to add some conditional `allow` statements. You want to allow `localhost` only if it fits certain criteria.

Defining access criteria is done with the `acl` lines, so above the `deny all` line, add this:

```
acl newssites dstdomain news.bbc.co.uk slashdot.org
http_access allow newssites
```

The first line defines an access category called `newssites`, which contains a list of domains (`dstdomain`). The domains are `news.bbc.co.uk` and `slashdot.org`, so the full line reads, "Create a new access category called newssites that should filter on domain, and contain the two domains listed." It does *not* say whether access should be granted or denied to that category; that comes in the next line. The line `http_access allow newssites` means, "Allow access to the category newssites with no further restrictions." It is not limited to `localhost`, which means that applies to every computer connecting to the proxy server.

Save the configuration file and rerun the `kill -SIGHUP` line from before to restart Squid; then go back to Firefox and try loading www.ubuntu.com. You should see the same error as before because that was not in your `newssites` category. Now try http://news.bbc.co.uk, and it should work. However, if you try www.slashdot.org, it will *not* work, and you might also have noticed that the images did not appear on the BBC News website either. The problem here is that specifying slashdot.org as the website is specific: It means that http://slashdot.org will work, whereas www.slashdot.org will not. The BBC News site stores its images on the site http://newsimg.bbc.co.uk, which is why they do not appear.

Go back to the configuration file and edit the `newssites` ACL to this:

```
acl newssites dstdomain .bbc.co.uk .slashdot.org
```

Putting the period in front of the domains (and in the BBC's case, taking the news off, too) means that Squid will allow any subdomain of the site to work, which is usually what you want. If you want even more vagueness, you can just specify `.com` to match `*.com` addresses.

Moving on, you can also use time conditions for sites. For example, if you want to allow access to the news sites in the evenings, you can set up a time category using this line:

```
acl freetime time MTWHFAS 18:00-23:59
```

This time, the category is called `freetime` and the condition is `time`, which means we need to specify what time the category should contain. The seven characters following that are the days of the week: Monday, Tuesday, Wednesday, tHursday, Friday, sAturday, and Sunday. Thursday and Saturday use capital *H* and *A* so they do not clash with Tuesday and Sunday.

With that category defined, you can change the `http_access` line to include it, like this:

```
http_access allow newssites freetime
```

For Squid to allow access now, it must match both conditions—the request must be for either `*.bbc.co.uk` or `slashdot.org`, and during the time specified. If either condition does not match, the line is not matched and Squid continues looking for other matching rules beneath it. The times you specify here are inclusive on both sides, which means users in the `freetime` category are able to surf from 18:00:00 until 23:59:59.

You can add as many rules as you like, although you should be careful to try to order them so that they make sense. Keep in mind that all conditions in a line must be matched for the line to be matched. Here is a more complex example:

▶ You want a category `newssites` that contains serious websites people need for their work.

▶ You want a category `playsites` that contains websites people do not need for their work.

▶ You want a category `worktime` that stretches from 09:00 to 18:00.

▶ You want a category `freetime` that stretches from 18:00 to 20:00, when the office closes.

▶ You want people to be able to access the news sites, but not the play sites, during working hours.

▶ You want people to be able to access both the news sites and the play sites during the free time hours.

To do that, you need the following rules:

```
acl newssites dstdomain .bbc.co.uk .slashdot.org
acl playsites dstdomain .tomshardware.com ubuntulinux.org
acl worktime time MTWHF 9:00-18:00
acl freetime time MTWHF 18:00-20:00
http_access allow newssites worktime
http_access allow newssites freetime
http_access allow playsites freetime
```

> **NOTE**
>
> The letter *D* is equivalent to MTWHF, meaning "all the days of the working week."

Notice that there are two `http_access` lines for the `newssites` category: one for `worktime` and one for `freetime`. This is because all the conditions must be matched for a line to be matched. Alternatively, you can write this:

```
http_access allow newssites worktime freetime
```

However, if you do that and someone visits http://news.bbc.co.uk at 2:30 p.m. (14:30) on a Tuesday, Squid works like this:

▶ Is the site in the `newssites` category? Yes, continue.

▶ Is the time within the `worktime` category? Yes, continue.

▶ Is the time within the `freetime` category? No; do not match rule and continue searching for rules.

It is because of this that two lines are needed for the `worktime` category.

One particularly powerful way to filter requests is with the `url_regex` ACL line. This enables you to specify a regular expression that is checked against each request: If the expression matches the request, the condition matches.

For example, if you want to stop people downloading Windows executable files, you use this line:

```
acl noexes url_regex -i exe$
```

The dollar sign (\$) means "end of URL," which means it would match www.somesite .com/virus.exe but not www.executable.com/innocent.html. The `-i` part means "not case sensitive," so the rule matches .exe, .Exe, .EXE, and so on. You can use the caret sign (^) for "start of URL."

For example, you could stop some pornography sites using this ACL:

```
acl noporn url_regex -i sex
```

Do not forget to run the `kill -SIGHUP` command each time you make changes to Squid; otherwise, it does not reread your changes. You can have Squid check your configuration files for errors by running `squid -k parse as root`. If you see no errors, it means your configuration is fine.

> **NOTE**
>
> It is critical that you run the command `kill -SIGHUP` and provide it the PID of your Squid daemon each time you change the configuration; without this, Squid does not reread its configuration files.

Specifying Client IP Addresses

The configuration options so far have been basic, and you can use many more to enhance the proxying system you want.

After you are past deciding which rules work for you locally, it is time to spread them out to other machines. You do so by specifying IP ranges that should be allowed or disallowed access, and you enter these into Squid using more ACL lines.

If you want to, you can specify all the IP addresses on your network, one per line. However, for networks of more than about 20 people or using *Dynamic Host Control Protocol (DHCP)*, that is more work than necessary. A better solution is to use *classless interdomain routing (CIDR)* notation, which enables you to specify addresses like this:

```
192.0.0.0/8
192.168.0.0/16
192.168.0.0/24
```

Each line has an IP address, followed by a slash and then a number. That last number defines the range of addresses you want covered and refers to the number of bits in an IP address. An IP address is a 32-bit number, but we are used to seeing it in dotted-quad notation: A.B.C.D. Each of those quads can be between 0 and 255 (although in practice some of these are reserved for special purposes), and each is stored as an 8-bit number.

The first line in the previous code covers IP addresses starting from 192.0.0.0; the /8 part means that the first 8 bits (the first quad, 192) is fixed and the rest is flexible. So, Squid treats that as addresses 192.0.0.0, 192.0.0.1, through to 192.0.0.255, then 192.0.1.0, 192.0.1.1, all the way through to 192.255.255.255.

The second line uses /16, which means Squid allows IP addresses from 192.168.0.0 to 192.168.255.255. The last line has /24, which allows from 192.168.0.0 to 192.168.0.255.

These addresses are placed into Squid using the src ACL line, as follows:

```
acl internal_network src 10.0.0.0/24
```

That line creates a category of addresses from 10.0.0.0 to 10.0.0.255. You can combine multiple address groups together, like this:

```
acl internal_network src 10.0.0.0/24 10.0.3.0/24 10.0.5.0/24 192.168.0.1
```

That example allows 10.0.0.0 through 10.0.0.255, then 10.0.3.0 through 10.0.3.255, and finally the single address 192.168.0.1.

Keep in mind that if you are using the local machine and you have the web browser configured to use the proxy at 127.0.0.1, the client IP address will be 127.0.0.1, too. So, make sure you have rules in place for localhost.

As with other ACL lines, you need to enable them with appropriate http_access allow and http_access deny lines.

Sample Configurations

To help you fully understand how Squid access control works, and to give you a head start developing your own rules, the following are some ACL lines you can try. Each line is preceded with one or more comment lines (starting with a #) explaining what it does:

```
# include the domains news.bbc.co.uk and slashdot.org
# and not newsimg.bbc.co.uk or www.slashdot.org.
acl newssites dstdomain news.bbc.co.uk slashdot.org

# include any subdomains or bbc.co.uk or slashdot.org
acl newssites dstdomain .bbc.co.uk .slashdot.org

# only include sites located in Canada
acl canadasites dstdomain .ca

# only include working hours
acl workhours time MTWHF 9:00-18:00
```

```
# only include lunchtimes
acl lunchtimes time MTWHF 13:00-14:00

# only include weekends
acl weekends time AS 00:00-23:59

# include URLs ending in ".zip". Note: the \ is important,
# because "." has a special meaning otherwise
acl zipfiles url_regex -i \.zip$

# include URLs starting with https
acl httpsurls url_regex -i ^https

# include all URLs that match "Hotmail""
url_regex hotmail url_regex -i hotmail

# include three specific IP addresses
acl directors src 10.0.0.14 10.0.0.28 10.0.0.31

# include all IPs from 192.168.0.0 to 192.168.0.255
acl internal src 192.168.0.0/24

# include all IPs from 192.168.0.0 to 192.168.0.255
# and all IPs from 10.0.0.0 to 10.255.255.255
acl internal src 192.168.0.0/24 10.0.0.0/8
```

When you have your ACL lines in place, you can put together appropriate `http_access` lines. For example, you might want to use a multilayered access system so that certain users (for example, company directors) have full access, whereas others are filtered. For example:

```
http_access allow directors
http_access deny hotmail
http_access deny zipfiles
http_access allow internal lunchtimes
http_access deny all
```

Because Squid matches those in order, directors will have full, unfiltered access to the Web. If the client IP address is not in the directors list, the two deny lines are processed so that the user cannot download zip files or read online mail at Hotmail. After blocking those two types of requests, the allow rule on line four allows internal users to access the Web, as long as they do so only at lunchtime. The last line (which is highly recommended) blocks all other users from the proxy.

Virtual Private Networks (VPN)

A *virtual private network*, or *VPN* as they are more commonly called, creates a way for networks that are otherwise isolated or inaccessible to communicate with one another. This is often used by businesses at an enterprise level to keep internal business networks secure while allowing workers to access the internal network from a remote location, such as when an executive is traveling and needs to use a laptop to download and reply to email using an internal business server. The VPN keeps all traffic out except that traffic which originates within the network itself or traffic that attempts to connect from the outside using a VPN connection with proper access credentials. This sounds similar to remote access standards already in place in Unix, Linux, and Ubuntu, but using a VPN takes security to a new level.

There are other types of VPNs in use as well. Not only can one be used to allow remote access to secure internal networks, but they can also be used to allow two networks to connect to one another using a different network in the middle, for example two networks that each use IPv6 could connect to one another over an IPv4 network using a VPN connection. This is much less common, so we concentrate on the first scenario of a remote user connecting to a secure, internal network. You might be asking how this is different than using a proxy server, as it seems that the VPN is somehow working as an intermediary or bridge between the remote user and the secure system. It is a little more complicated than that. When a proxy server is in use, it is another layer between the two ends of a connection, an intermediary. When a VPN is in use, it provides direct access between the two ends, but via an encrypted tunnel; it is analogous to running a cable directly from one end system to the other, effectively making the remote computer an actual part of the system to which it is connecting. From this moment, the remote system tunnels all of its network traffic through the main system.

Where proxies generally work via web browser and secure all traffic that passes through the browser, a VPN tunnels all traffic. When using a VPN, the remote computer no longer perceives itself as connected first to the Internet, then to the secure system, but rather it perceives itself as if it is connected directly to the secure system and the VPN is its router. The difference is illustrated in Figure 29.2.

Some use an Internet router as a metaphor to help explain how a VPN works. In this analogy, the remote computer connects directly to the VPN, which uses the Internet to connect it to its ultimate host computer, the secure network.

So, why do we care? The differences between proxy servers and a VPN make the most difference when it comes time for implementation. Which will best serve your needs? Here are some facts to help you decide:

▶ Proxy servers are usually cheaper and easier to set up. VPNs generally cost more and are more difficult to set up, but after they're set up they're easy to use and are more secure.

▶ A single proxy server can service hundreds or thousands of users, but usually a VPN is designed for one connection that is specific to one remote computer and a secure host (yes, exceptions exist, they are beyond the scope of this introductory material).

▶ Each piece of software that uses a proxy must be set up separately. Web browsers are the most common way to use a proxy server, but others can also be configured to use one. When a VPN is up and running, all Internet software on the computer automatically uses it without additional configuration.

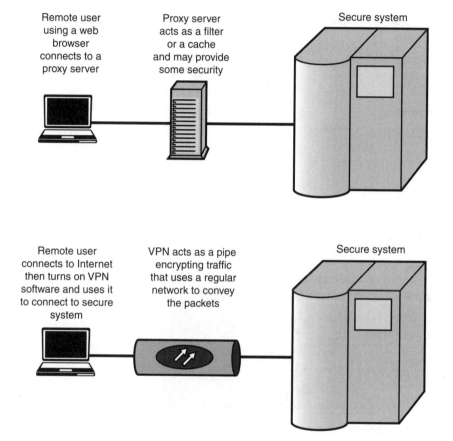

FIGURE 29.2   Comparing a proxy connection to a VPN connection.

Setting Up a VPN Client

The easy part of using a VPN is also the most commonly needed part. It is generally companies that set up VPN servers and then provide access to their secure networks to company employees or clients who use a VPN client installed on their local system, such as a laptop.

Most VPN servers run a protocol that is easily used on Ubuntu, especially from the type of GUI-based system that a typical user who is using Unity would have. You need to check with the administrator of the VPN network to which you intend to connect to find out which VPN client you will use and also to get your credentials so that you may connect.

We use the default Network-Manager, which is installed by default with Unity and is the default way to manage all Internet connections in a typical Ubuntu installation, to manage our VPN client connection.

Install the VPN client software needed for the specific type of VPN server in use by the network to which you will connect. The following table will help you to find what you need.

If you need to use	Install this
Cisco Concentrator	`network-manager-vpnc`
Cisco OpenConnect	`network-manager-openconnect`
OpenVPN	`network-manager-openvpn`
PPTP (Microsoft VPN)	`network-manager-pptp`
strongSwan (for some IPSec VPNs)	`network-manager-strongswan`

Restart Network-Manager to make it aware of the new package(s):

```
matthew@seymour:~$ sudo restart network-manager
```

Click the Network icon in the top panel of the Unity screen. Hover over VPN Connections and select Configure VPN, as shown in Figure 29.3.

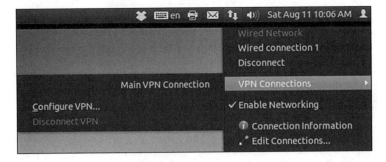

FIGURE 29.3   Network-Manager makes configuring a VPN client easy.

Click Add to create a new VPN connection.

Choose your VPN connection type from the list. If you aren't certain of your connection type, try the one you think is correct; if it doesn't work, come back and edit the connection to try another type.

Click Create.

Enter the information about your VPN connection. You need to enter things like the gateway IP address of the server, your account username and password, perhaps a group name and group password, and where to find the certificate authority (CA) file. In some cases, you might need to click the Advanced button to enter other details such as the encryption method, NAT traversal, and more. When you have your information entered, click Save.

To begin using this VPN connection, use the same menu as in Figure 29.3, but this time select your VPN connection from the list, shown as Main VPN Connection in our example.

Setting Up a VPN Server

We use OpenVPN to set up a simple server. Advanced configuration can become quite complex, but it is easy to get started if you only require a basic server.

Install `openvpn` from the Ubuntu software repositories.

The next several steps create a public key infrastructure (PKI) for your OpenVPN.

Set up the certificate authority to generate your own certificates and keys.

```
matthew@seymour:~$ sudo mkdir /etc/openvpn/easy-rsa
matthew@seymour:~$ sudo cp -r /usr/share/doc/openvpn/examples/easy-rsa/2.0/*
/etc/openvpn/easy-rsa/
```

Enter your specific details by editing `/etc/openvpn/easy-rsa/vars` and adjusting the following:

```
export KEY_COUNTRY="us"
export KEY_PROVINCE="IA"
export KEY_CITY="Iowa City"
export KEY_ORG="Your Company"
export KEY_EMAIL="yourContact@yourEmailDomain.com"
```

Generate your certificate authority and key:

```
matthew@seymour:~$ cd /etc/openvpn/easy-rsa
matthew@seymour:~$ sudo source vars
matthew@seymour:~$ sudo ./clean-all
matthew@seymour:~$ sudo ./build-ca
matthew@seymour:~$ sudo cp -r /usr/share/doc/openvpn/examples/easy-rsa/2.0/*
/etc/openvpn/easy-rsa/
```

Generate a certificate and private key for the server. Replace *yourservername* with the name of your server:

```
matthew@seymour:~$  sudo ./buid-key-server yourservername
```

Build the Diffie Hellman parameters:

```
matthew@seymour:~$  sudo ./build-dh
```

Copy the certificates and keys. Replace *yourservername* with the name of your server.

```
matthew@seymour:~$ cd keys/
matthew@seymour:~$ sudo cp yourservername.crt yourservername.key ca.crt dh1024.pem
/etc/openvpn/
```

You must create a different certificate for each client using this method. This is because the larger, proprietary VPN vendors distribute their certificates with their server and client software, but you are creating your own. Do this on the server machine for each client, replacing `clientname` with the name of each client system.

```
matthew@seymour:~$ cd /etc/openvpn/easy-rsa/
matthew@seymour:~$ source vars
matthew@seymour:~$ ./build-key clientname
```

Now, copy the following files you just generated to the client for which it was generated. Repeat as needed for each client replacing `clientname` with the name of each client system.

```
/etc/openvpn/ca.crt
/etc/openvpn/easy-rsa/keys/clientname.crt
/etc/openvpn/easy-rsa/keys/clientname.key
```

Remove the files from the server after they are installed on the client.

Many sample configuration files are included with OpenVPN in `/usr/share/doc/openvpn/examples/sample-config-files/`. You can read through them if you have more complex needs than our simple setup. For our setup, we only need the most basic configuration files. Copy and unpack this file:

```
matthew@seymour:~$ sudo cp /usr/share/doc/openvpn/examples/sample-config-files/
server.conf.gz /etc/openvpn
matthew@seymour:~$ sudo gzip -d /etc/openvpn/server.conf.gz
```

Edit /etc/openvpn/server.conf to point to and use the certificates and keys you created earlier by changing or adding these lines. Replace `yourservername` with the name of your server. Leave all the other default settings in place.

```
ca ca.crt
cert yourservername.crt
key yourservername.key
dh dh1024.pem
```

Start your server:

```
matthew@seymour:~$ sudo /etc/init.d/openvpn start
```

OpenVPN should create a new networking interface on your computer called `tun0`. To make sure the interface is created, enter:

```
matthew@seymour:~$ sudo ifconfig tun0
```

To use your new VPN server with the client described in the previous section, select OpenVPN as the VPN type, enter `yourservername` from this section as the Gateway, set Type to Certificates (TLS), point User Certificate to use the client certificate you created and moved to the client machine, CA Certificate to use the credential authority certificate you created and moved to the client machine, and Private Key to use the private key file you created and moved to the client machine.

References

► www.squid-cache.org/—The home page of the Squid web proxy cache.

► www.deckle.co.za/squid-users-guide/—The home page of *Squid: A User's Guide*, a free online book about Squid.

► https://help.ubuntu.com/community/Squid—Ubuntu community documentation for setting up Squid.

► There are two excellent books on the topic of web caching. The first is *Squid: The Definitive Guide* (O'Reilly) by Duane Wessels, ISBN: 0-596-00162-2. The second is *Web Caching* (O'Reilly) also by Duane Wessels, ISBN: 1-56592-536-X. Of the two, the former is more practical and covers the Squid server in depth. The latter is more theoretical, discussing how caching is implemented. Wessels is one of the leading developers on Squid, so both books are of impeccable technical accuracy.

► https://help.ubuntu.com/14.04/serverguide/openvpn.html—Official Ubuntu server documentation for setting up OpenVPN.

29

CHAPTER 30

Administering Relational Database Services

This chapter is an introduction to MySQL and PostgreSQL, two database systems that are available in the Ubuntu repositories. In this chapter, you learn what these systems do, how the two programs compare, and how to consider their advantages and disadvantages. This information can help you choose and deploy which one to use for your organization's database needs.

SIMILAR TO MYSQL

In April 2009, Oracle announced it was buying Sun Microsystems, who owned MySQL. The deal was completed in January 2010. In the short term this really hasn't had any effect, but the database world is watching to see what will happen with MySQL, and at least two groups have forked the code to ensure that the database stays free and open source while still in active development. These groups have released and are working on MariaDB (https://mariadb.org/), Drizzle (http://www.drizzle.org), and Percona Server (http://www.percona.com/software/percona-server). Although no one really knows yet what will happen, we suggest keeping an eye on these projects and other potential replacements for MySQL should the worst fears be realized and Oracle decides that the free MySQL is too much of a competitor to their paid database offerings and kills or weakens the project. It is interesting to note that some pretty big Linux distributions and organizations have already switched away from MySQL, such as Fedora, OpenSUSE, and Wikipedia (all are now using MariaDB). The good news is that anything you learn about MySQL from this chapter is likely to apply perfectly to the other options mentioned.

The *database administrator (DBA)* for an organization has several responsibilities, which vary according to the size and operations of the organization, supporting staff, and so on.

Depending on the particular organization's structure, if you are the organization's DBA, your responsibilities might include the following:

▶ **Installing and maintaining database servers**—You might install and maintain the database software. Maintenance can involve installing patches as well as upgrading the software at the appropriate times. As DBA, you need to have root access to your system and know how to manage software (see Chapter 9, "Managing Software"). You also need to be aware of kernel, file system, and other security issues.

▶ **Installing and maintaining database clients**—The database client is the program used to access the database (you learn more about that later in this chapter, in the section "Database Clients"), either locally or remotely over a network. Your responsibilities might include installing and maintaining these client programs on users' systems. This chapter discusses how to install and work with the clients from both the Linux command line and through its graphical interface database tools.

▶ **Managing accounts and users**—Account and user management include adding and deleting users from the database, assigning and administering passwords, and so on. In this chapter, you find out how to grant and revoke user privileges and passwords for MySQL and PostgreSQL.

▶ **Ensuring database security**—To ensure database security, you need to be concerned with things like access control, which ensures that only authorized people can access the database, and permissions, which ensure that people who can access the database cannot do things they should not do. In this chapter, you learn how to manage *Secure Shell (SSH)*, web, and local *graphical user interface (GUI)* client access to the database. Planning and overseeing the regular backup of an organization's database and restoring data from those backups is another critical component of securing the database.

▶ **Ensuring data integrity**—Of all the information stored on a server's hard disk storage, chances are the information in the database is the most critical. Ensuring data integrity involves planning for multiple-user access and ensuring that changes are not lost or duplicated when more than one user is making changes to the database at the same time.

A Brief Review of Database Basics

Database services under Linux that use the software discussed in this chapter are based on a *client/server* model. Database clients are often used to input data and to query or display query results from the server. You can use the command line or a graphical client to access a running server. Databases generally come in two forms: flat file and relational. A *flat file* database can be as simple as a text file with a space, tab, or some other character delimiting different parts of the information. One example of a simple flat file database is the /etc/passwd file. Another example is a simple address book that might look something like this:

```
Doe~John~505 Some Street~Anytown~NY~12345~555-555-1212
```

You can use standard UNIX tools such as `grep`, `awk`, and `perl` to search for and extract information from this primitive database. Although this might work well for a small database such as an address book that only one person uses, flat file databases of this type have several limitations:

▶ **They do not scale well**—Flat file databases cannot perform random access on data. They can only perform sequential access. This means they have to scan each line in the file, one by one, to look for specific information. As the size of the database grows, access times increase, and performance decreases.

▶ **Flat file databases are unsuitable for multiuser environments**—Depending on how the database is set up, it either enables only one user to access it at a time or allows two users to make changes simultaneously, and the changes could end up overwriting each other, which results in data loss.

These limitations obviously make the flat file database unsuitable for any kind of serious work in even a small business—much less in an enterprise environment. Relational databases, or *relational database management systems (RDBMSs)* to give them their full name, are good at finding the relationships between individual pieces of data. An RDBMS stores data in tables with fields much like those in spreadsheets, making the data searchable and sortable. RDBMSs are the focus of this chapter.

NOSQL

There is an exception to what was just said. A fairly new category of databases is now in use, usually referred to as *NoSQL* in casual conversation. Unlike typical flat file databases, NoSQL databases are a form of structured storage that is suitable for large- and high-traffic uses. These databases have been written and put into use in places where flat files are unsuitable but where relational databases are slower than desired. It is important to note that although NoSQL databases work great when scalability and speed are desirable, you cannot be certain with all NoSQL databases that data is replicated and available instantly across a large installation. It generally is, but there is no guarantee of up-to-the-moment data. This is okay for some applications (web search) but would be disastrous for others (like a financial institution).

There are many forms of NoSQL databases, each with different intents and applications. Some are created and used by big names you might recognize, such as Google's BigTable and Apache's Cassandra. Ubuntu uses Apache's CouchDB for several applications. Other common ones include MongoDB and Berkeley DB. For this chapter, we concentrate on the more traditional relational databases that are used for most applications, but we urge you to keep an eye on what is happening in the NoSQL world. For more information about NoSQL databases, see Chapter 31, "NoSQL Databases."

30

Oracle, DB2, Microsoft SQL Server, and the freely available PostgreSQL and MySQL are all examples of RDBMSs. The following sections discuss how relational databases work and provide a closer look at some of the basic processes involved in administering and using databases. You also learn about SQL, the standard language used to store, retrieve, and manipulate database data.

How Relational Databases Work

An RDBMS stores data in tables, which you can visualize as spreadsheets. Each column in the table is a field; for example, a column might contain a name or an address. Each row in the table is an individual record. The table itself has a name you use to refer to that table when you want to get data out of it or put data into it. Figure 30.1 shows an example of a simple relational database that stores name and address information.

In the example shown in Figure 30.1, the database contains only a single table. Most RDBMS setups are much more complex than this, with a single database containing multiple tables. Figure 30.2 shows an example of a database named `sample_database` that contains two tables.

last_name	first_name	address	city	state	zip	phone
Doe	John	501 Somestreet	Anytown	NY	55011	555-555-1212
Doe	Jane	501 Somestreet	Anytown	NY	55011	555-555-1212
Palmer	John	205 Anystreet	Sometown	NY	55055	123-456-7890
Johnson	Robert	100 Easystreet	Easytown	CT	12345	111-222-3333

FIGURE 30.1   In this visualization of how an RDBMS stores data, the database stores four records (rows) that include name and address information, divided into seven fields (columns) of data.

phonebook

last_name	first_name	phone
Doe	John	555-555-1212
Doe	Jane	555-555-1212
Palmer	John	555-123-4567
Johnson	Richard	555-111-4321

cd_collection

id	title	artist	year	rating
1	Mindbomb	The The	1989	4
2	For All You've Done	Hillsong	2004	
3	Trouser Jazz	Mr Scruff	2002	5
4	Natural Elements	Acoustic Alchemy	1988	3
5	Combat Rock	The Clash	1982	4
6	Life for Rent	Dido	2003	5
7	Adiemus 4	Karl Jenkins	2000	4
8	The Two Towers	Howard Shore	2002	5

FIGURE 30.2   A single database can contain two tables—in this case, phonebook and cd_collection.

In the `sample_database` example, the `phonebook` table contains four records (rows) and each record hold three fields (columns) of data. The `cd_collection` table holds eight records, divided into five fields of data.

If you are thinking that there is no logical relationship between the `phonebook` table and the `cd_collection` table in the `sample_database` example, you are correct. In a relational database, users can store multiple tables of data in a single database, even if the data in one table is unrelated to the data in others.

For example, suppose you run a small company that sells widgets and you have a computerized database of customers. In addition to storing each customer's name, address, and phone number, you want to be able to look up outstanding order and invoice information for any of your customers. You could use three related tables in an RDBMS to store and organize customer data for just those purposes. Figure 30.3 shows an example of such a database.

customers

cid	last_name	first_name	shipping_address
1	Doe	John	505 Somestreet
2	Doe	Jane	505 Somestreet
3	Palmer	John	200 Anystreet
4	Johnson	Richard	1000 Another Street

orders

cid	order_num	stock_num	priority	shipped	date
1	1002	100,252,342	3	Y	8/31/01
1	1221	200,352	1	N	10/2/01
3	1223	200,121	2	Y	10/2/01
2	1225	221,152	1	N	10/3/01

overdue

cid	order_num	days_overdue	action
1	1002	32	sent letter

FIGURE 30.3   You can use three related tables to track customers, orders, and outstanding invoices.

In the example in Figure 30.3, we have added a customer ID field to each customer record. This field holds a customer ID number that is the unique piece of information that can be used to link all other information for each customer to track orders and invoices. Each customer is given an ID unique to him; two customers might have the same data in their name fields, but their ID field values will never be the same. The Customer ID field data in the Orders and Overdue tables replaces the Last Name, First Name, and Shipping Address field information from the `Customers` table. Now, when you want to run a search for any customer's order and invoice data, you can search based on one key rather than multiple keys. You get more accurate results in faster, easier-to-conduct data searches.

30

Now that you have an idea of how data is stored in an RDBMS and how the RDBMS structure enables you to work with that data, you are ready to learn how to input and output data from the database. This is where SQL comes in.

Understanding SQL Basics

SQL (pronounced "S-Q-L" or "sequel" depending on who is talking) is a database query language understood by virtually all RDBMSs available today. You use SQL statements to get data into and retrieve data from a database. As with statements in any language, SQL statements have a defined structure that determines their meanings and functions.

As a DBA, you should understand the basics of SQL, even if you will not be doing any of the actual programming yourself. Fortunately, SQL is similar to standard English, so learning the basics is simple.

Creating Tables

As mentioned previously, an RDBMS stores data in tables that look similar to spreadsheets. Of course, before you can store any data in a database, you need to create the necessary tables and columns to store the data. You do this by using the CREATE statement.

For example, the cd_collection table from Figure 30.2 has five columns, or fields: id, title, artist, year, and rating.

SQL provides several column types for data that define what kind of data will be stored in the column. Some of the available types are INT, FLOAT, CHAR, and VARCHAR. Both CHAR and VARCHAR hold text strings, with the difference being that CHAR holds a fixed-length string, whereas VARCHAR holds a variable-length string.

There are also special column types, such as DATE, that only take data in a date format, and ENUMS (enumerations), which can be used to specify that only certain values are allowed. If, for example, you want to record the genre of your CDs, you could use an ENUM column that accepts only the values POP, ROCK, EASY_LISTENING, and so on. You learn more about ENUM later in this chapter.

Looking at the cd_collection table, you can see that three of the columns hold numeric data and the other two hold string data. In addition, the character strings are of variable length. Based on this information, you can discern that the best type to use for the text columns is type VARCHAR, and the best type to use for the others is INT. You should notice something else about the cd_collection table: One of the CDs is missing a rating, perhaps because we have not listened to it yet. This value, therefore, is optional; it starts empty and can be filled in later.

You are now ready to create a table. As mentioned earlier, you do this by using the CREATE statement, which uses the following syntax:

```
CREATE TABLE table_name (column_name column type(parameters) options, ...);
```

You should know the following about the CREATE statement:

▶ **SQL commands are not case sensitive**—For example, `CREATE TABLE`, `create table`, and `Create Table` are all valid.

▶ **Whitespace is generally ignored**—This means you should use it to make your SQL commands clearer.

The following example shows how to create the table for the `cd_collection` database:

```
CREATE TABLE cd_collection
(
id INT NOT NULL,
title VARCHAR(50) NOT NULL,
artist VARCHAR(50) NOT NULL,
year VARCHAR(50) NOT NULL,
rating VARCHAR(50) NULL
);
```

Notice that the statement terminates with a semicolon (;). This is how SQL knows you are finished with all the entries in the statement. In some cases, you can omit the semicolon, and we point out these cases when they arise.

TIP

SQL has a number of reserved keywords that cannot be used in table names or field names. For example, if you keep track of CDs, you want to take with you on vacation, you would not be able to use the field name `select` because that is a reserved keyword. Instead, you should either choose a different name (`selected?`) or just prefix the field name with an `f`, such as `fselect`.

Inserting Data into Tables

After you create the tables, you can put data into them. You can insert data manually with the `INSERT` statement, which uses the following syntax:

```
INSERT INTO table_name VALUES('value1', 'value2', 'value3', ...);
```

This statement inserts `value1`, `value2`, and so on into the table `table_name`. The values that are inserted constitute one row, or *record*, in the database. Unless specified otherwise, values are inserted in the order in which the columns are listed in the database table. If, for some reason, you want to insert values in a different order (or if you want to insert only a few values and they are not in sequential order), you can specify which columns you want the data to go in by using the following syntax:

```
INSERT INTO table_name (column1,column4) VALUES('value1', 'value2');
```

You can also fill multiple rows with a single INSERT statement, using syntax such as the following:

```
INSERT INTO table_name VALUES('value1', 'value2'),('value3', 'value4');
```

In this statement, value1 and value2 are inserted into the first row, and value3 and value4 are inserted into the second row.

The following example shows how you insert the Nevermind entry into the cd_collection table:

```
INSERT INTO cd_collection VALUES(9, 'Nevermind', 'Nirvana', '1991', NULL);
```

MySQL requires the NULL value for the last column (rating) if you do not want to include a rating. PostgreSQL, in contrast, lets you get away with just omitting the last column. Of course, if you had columns in the middle that were null, you would need to explicitly state NULL in the INSERT statement.

Normally, INSERT statements are coded into a front-end program, so users adding data to the database do not have to worry about the SQL statements involved.

Retrieving Data from a Database

Of course, the main reason for storing data in a database is so you can later look up, sort, and generate reports on that data. Basic data retrieval is done with the SELECT statement, which has the following syntax:

```
SELECT column1, column2, column3 FROM table_name WHERE search_criteria;
```

The first two parts of the statement—the SELECT and FROM parts—are required. The WHERE portion of the statement is optional. If it is omitted, all rows in the table table_name are returned.

The column1, column2, column3 syntax indicates the name of the columns you want to see. If you want to see all columns, you can also use the wildcard * to show all the columns that match the search criteria. For example, the following statement displays all columns from the cd_collection table:

```
SELECT * FROM cd_collection;
```

If you want to see only the titles of all the CDs in the table, you use a statement such as the following:

```
SELECT title FROM cd_collection;
```

To select the title and year of a CD, you use the following:

```
SELECT title, year FROM cd_collection;
```

If you want something a little fancier, you can use SQL to print the CD title followed by the year in parentheses, as is the convention. Both MySQL and PostgreSQL provide string concatenation functions to handle problems such as this. However, the syntax is different in the two systems.

In MySQL, you can use the CONCAT() function to combine the title and year columns into one output column, along with parentheses. The following statement is an example:

```
SELECT CONCAT(title,"(",year, ")") AS TitleYear FROM cd_collection;
```

That statement lists both the title and year under one column that has the label TitleYear. Note that there are two strings in the CONCAT() function along with the fields; these add whitespace and the parentheses.

In PostgreSQL, the string concatenation function is simply a double pipe (||). The following command is the PostgreSQL equivalent of the preceding MySQL command:

```
SELECT (genus||'' ('||species||')') AS TitleYear FROM cd_collection;
```

Note that the parentheses are optional, but they make the statement easier to read. Once again, the strings in the middle and at the end (note the space between the quotes) are used to insert spacing and parentheses between the title and year.

Of course, more often than not, you do not want a list of every single row in the database. Rather, you only want to find rows that match certain characteristics. For this, you add the WHERE statement to the SELECT statement. For example, suppose you want to find all the CDs in the cd_collection table that have a rating of 5. You would use a statement like the following:

```
SELECT * FROM cd_collection WHERE rating = 5;
```

Using the table from Figure 30.2, you can see that this query would return the rows for *Trouser Jazz*, *Life for Rent*, and *The Two Towers*. This is a simple query, and SQL is capable of handling queries much more complex than this. You can write complex queries using logical AND and logical OR statements. For example, suppose you want to refine the query so it lists only those CDs that were not released in 2003. You use a query like the following:

```
SELECT * FROM cd_collection WHERE rating = 5 AND year != 2003;
```

In SQL, != means "is not equal to." So, once again looking at the table from Figure 30.2, you can see that this query returns the rows for *Trouser Jazz* and *The Two Towers* but does not return the row for *Life for Rent* because it was released in 2003.

So, what if you want to list all the CDs that have a rating of 3 or 4 except those released in the year 2000? This time, you combine logical AND and logical OR statements:

```
SELECT * FROM cd_collection WHERE rating = 3 OR rating = 4 AND year != 2000;
```

This query returns entries for *Mind Bomb*, *Natural Elements*, and *Combat Rock*. However, it does not return entries for *Adiemus 4* because it was released in 2000.

30

> **TIP**
>
> One of the most common errors among new database programmers is confusing logical AND and logical OR. For example, in everyday speech, you might say, "Find me all CDs released in 2003 and 2004." At first glance, you might think that if you fed this statement to the database in SQL format, it would return the rows for *For All You've Done* and *Life for Rent*. In fact, it would return no rows at all. This is because the database interprets the statement as "Find all rows in which the CD was released in 2003 and was released in 2004." It is, of course, impossible for the same CD to be released twice without requiring a new ISBN and therefore a new database entry, so this statement would never return any rows, no matter how many CDs were stored in the table. The correct way to form this statement is with an OR statement instead of an AND statement.

SQL is capable of far more than is demonstrated here. But as mentioned earlier, this section is not intended to teach you all there is to know about SQL programming; rather, it teaches you the basics so you can be a more effective DBA.

Choosing a Database: MySQL Versus PostgreSQL

If you are just starting out and learning about using a database with Linux, the first logical step is to research which database will best serve your needs. Many database software packages are available for Linux; some are free, and others cost hundreds of thousands of dollars. Expensive commercial databases, such as Oracle, are beyond the scope of this book. Instead, this chapter focuses on two freely available databases: MySQL and PostgreSQL.

Both of these databases are quite capable, and either one could probably serve your needs. However, each database has a unique set of features and capabilities that might serve your needs better or make developing database applications easier for you.

Speed

Until recently, the speed choice was simple: If the speed of performing queries was paramount to your application, you used MySQL. MySQL has a reputation for being an extremely fast database. Until recently, PostgreSQL was quite slow by comparison.

Newer versions of PostgreSQL have improved in terms of speed (when it comes to disk access, sorting, and so on). In certain situations, such as periods of heavy simultaneous access, PostgreSQL can be significantly faster than MySQL, as you will see in the next section. However, MySQL is still plenty fast when compared to many other databases.

Data Locking

To prevent data corruption, a database needs to put a lock on data while it is being accessed. As long as the lock is on, no other process can access the data until the first process has released the lock. This means that any other processes trying to access the data have to wait until the current process completes. The next process in line then locks the data until it is finished, and the remaining processes have to wait their turn, and so on.

Of course, operations on a database generally complete quickly, so in environments with a small number of users simultaneously accessing the database, the locks are usually of such short duration that they do not cause any significant delays. However, in environments in which many people are accessing the database simultaneously, locking can create performance problems as people wait their turn to access the database.

Older versions of MySQL lock data at the table level, which can be considered a bottleneck for updates during periods of heavy access. This means that when someone writes a row of data in the table, the entire table is locked so no one else can enter data. If your table has 500,000 rows (or records) in it, all 500,000 rows are locked any time one row is accessed. Once again, in environments with a relatively small number of simultaneous users, this doesn't cause serious performance problems because most operations complete so quickly that the lock time is extremely short. However, in environments in which many people are accessing the data simultaneously, MySQL's table-level locking can be a significant performance bottleneck.

PostgreSQL, in contrast, locks data at the row level. In PostgreSQL, only the row currently being accessed is locked. Other users can access the rest of the table. This row-level locking significantly reduces the performance effect of locking in environments that have a large number of simultaneous users. Therefore, as a general rule, PostgreSQL is better suited for high-load environments than MySQL.

The MySQL release bundled with Ubuntu gives you the choice of using tables with table-level or row-level locking. In MySQL terminology, MyISAM tables use table-level locking and InnoDB tables use row-level locking.

> **NOTE**
>
> MySQL's data locking methods are discussed in more depth at www.mysql.com/doc/en/Internal_locking.html.
>
> You can find more information on PostgreSQL's locking at www.postgresql.org/docs/9.1/static/sql-lock.html.

ACID Compliance in Transaction Processing to Protect Data Integrity

Another way MySQL and PostgreSQL differ is in the amount of protection they provide for keeping data from becoming corrupted. The acronym ACID is commonly used to describe several aspects of data protection:

► **Atomicity**—This means that several database operations are treated as an indivisible (atomic) unit, often called a *transaction*. In a transaction, either all unit operations are carried out or none of them are. In other words, if any operation in the atomic unit fails, the entire atomic unit is canceled.

► **Consistency**—Ensures that no transaction can cause the database to be left in an inconsistent state. Inconsistent states can be caused by database client crashes, network failures, and similar situations. Consistency ensures that, in such a situation, any transaction or partially completed transaction that would cause the database to be left in an inconsistent state is *rolled back*, or undone.

▶ **Isolation**—Ensures that multiple transactions operating on the same data are completely isolated from each other. This prevents data corruption if two users try to write to the same record at the same time. The way isolation is handled can generally be configured by the database programmer. One way that isolation can be handled is through locking, as discussed previously.

▶ **Durability**—Ensures that, after a transaction has been committed to the database, it cannot be lost in the event of a system crash, network failure, or other problem. This is usually accomplished through transaction logs. Durability means, for example, that if the server crashes, the database can examine the logs when it comes back up and it can commit any transactions that were not yet complete into the database.

PostgreSQL is ACID compliant, but again MySQL gives you the choice of using ACID-compliant tables or not. MyISAM tables are not ACID compliant, whereas InnoDB tables are. Note that ACID compliancy is no easy task: All the extra precautions incur a performance overhead.

SQL Subqueries

Subqueries enable you to combine several operations into one atomic unit, and they enable those operations to access each other's data. By using SQL subqueries, you can perform some extremely complex operations on a database. In addition, using SQL subqueries eliminates the potential problem of data changing between two operations as a result of another user performing some operation on the same set of data. Both PostgreSQL and MySQL have support for subqueries in this release of Ubuntu, but this was not true in earlier releases.

Procedural Languages and Triggers

A *procedural language* is an external programming language that you can use to write functions and procedures. With a procedural language, you can do things that aren't supported by simple SQL. A *trigger* enables you to define an event that invokes the external function or procedure you have written. For example, you can use a trigger to cause an exception if an INSERT statement containing an unexpected or out-of-range value for a column is given.

For example, in the CD tracking database, you could use a trigger to cause an exception if a user enters data that does not make sense. PostgreSQL has a procedural language called PL/pgSQL. Although MySQL has support for a limited number of built-in procedures and triggers, it does not have any procedural language. It does have a feature called *stored procedures* that is similar, but it doesn't do quite the same thing.

Configuring MySQL

A free and stable version of MySQL is included with Ubuntu. MySQL is also available from www.mysql.com. The software is available in source code, binary, and APT format for Linux. See Chapter 9, "Managing Software," for the details on adding (or removing) software.

After you have MySQL installed, you need to initialize the grant tables or permissions to access any or all databases and tables and column data within a database. You can do this by issuing `mysql_install_db` as root. This command initializes the grant tables and creates a MySQL root user.

> **CAUTION**
>
> The MySQL data directory needs to be owned by the user that owns the MySQL process, most likely `mysql` (you might need to change the directory's owner using the `chown` command). In addition, only this user should have any permissions on this directory. (In other words, the permissions should be set to `700` by using `chmod`.) Setting up the data directory any other way creates a security hole.

Running `mysql_install_db` should generate output similar to the following:

```
matthew@seymour:~$ sudo mysql_install_db
Preparing db table
Preparing host table
Preparing user table
Preparing func table
Preparing tables_priv table
Preparing columns_priv table
Installing all prepared tables
020916 17:39:05 /usr/libexec/mysqld: Shutdown Complete
...
```

The command prepares MySQL for use on the system and reports helpful information. The next step is to set the password for the MySQL root user, which is discussed in the following section.

> **CAUTION**
>
> By default, the MySQL root user is created with no password. This is one of the first things you must change because the MySQL root user has access to all aspects of the database. The following section explains how to change the password of the user.

Setting a Password for the MySQL Root User

To set a password for the root MySQL user, you need to connect to the MySQL server as the root MySQL user; you can use the command `mysql -u root` to do so. This command connects you to the server with the MySQL client. When you have the MySQL command prompt, issue a command like the following to set a password for the root user:

```
mysql> SET PASSWORD FOR root = PASSWORD("secretword");
```

secretword should be replaced by whatever you want to be the password for the root user. You can use this same command with other usernames to set or change passwords for other database users.

30

After you enter a password, you can exit the MySQL client by typing `exit` at the command prompt.

Creating a Database in MySQL

In MySQL you create a database by using the CREATE DATABASE statement. To create a database, you connect to the server by typing `mysql -u root -p` and pressing Enter. After you do so, you are connected to the database as the MySQL root user and prompted for a password. After you enter the password, you are placed at the MySQL command prompt. Then you use the CREATE DATABASE command. For example, the following commands create a database called `animals`:

```
matthew@seymour:~$ mysql -u root -p
Enter password:
Welcome to the MySQL monitor. Commands end with ; or \g.
Your MySQL connection id is 1 to server version: 3.23.58

Type 'help;' or '\h' for help. Type '\c' to clear the buffer.

mysql> CREATE DATABASE animals;
Query OK, 1 row affected (0.00 sec)
mysql>
```

Another way to create a database is to use the `mysqladmin` command, as the root user, with the `create` keyword and the name of a new database. For example, to create a new database named reptiles, you use a command line like this:

```
matthew@seymour:~$ sudo mysqladmin -u root -p create reptiles
Granting and Revoking Privileges in MySQL
```

You probably want to grant yourself some privileges, and eventually you will probably want to grant privileges to other users. Privileges, also known as *rights*, are granted and revoked on four levels:

- ▶ **Global level**—These rights allow access to any database on a server.
- ▶ **Database level**—These rights allow access to all tables in a database.
- ▶ **Table level**—These rights allow access to all columns within a table in a database.
- ▶ **Column level**—These rights allow access to a single column within a database's table.

> **NOTE**
>
> Listing all the available privileges is beyond the scope of this chapter. See the MySQL documentation for more information.

To add a user account, you connect to the database by typing `mysql -u root -p` and pressing Enter. You are then connected as the root user and prompted for a password.

(You did set a password for the root user, as instructed in the last section, right?) After you enter the root password, you are placed at the MySQL command prompt.

To grant privileges to a user, you use the GRANT statement, which has the following syntax:

```
grant what_to_grant ON where_to_grant TO user_name IDENTIFIED BY 'password';
```

The first option, what_to_grant, is the privileges you are granting to the user. You specify these privileges with keywords. For example, the ALL keyword is used to grant global-, database-, table-, and column-level rights for a specified user.

The second option, where_to_grant, specifies the resources on which the privileges should be granted. The third option, user_name, is the username to which you want to grant the privileges. Finally, the fourth option, *password*, is a password that should be assigned to this user. If this is an existing user who already has a password and you are modifying permissions, you can omit the IDENTIFIED BY portion of the statement.

For example, to grant all privileges on a database named sampledata to a user named foobar, you could use the following command:

```
GRANT ALL ON animals.* TO foobar IDENTIFIED BY 'secretword';
```

The user foobar can now connect to the database sampledata by using the password secretword, and foobar has all privileges on the database, including the ability to create and destroy tables. For example, the user foobar can now log in to the server (by using the current hostname—shuttle2, in this example) and access the database like this:

```
matthew@seymour:~$  mysql -h shuttle2 -u foobar -p animals
Enter password:
Welcome to the MySQL monitor. Commands end with ; or \g.
Your MySQL connection id is 43 to server version: 3.23.58

Type 'help;' or '\h' for help. Type '\c' to clear the buffer.

mysql>
```

> **NOTE**
>
> See the section "The MySQL Command-Line Client" for additional command-line options.

Later, if you need to revoke privileges from foobar, you can use the REVOKE statement. For example, the following statement revokes all privileges from the user foobar:

```
REVOKE ALL ON animals FROM foobar;
```

Advanced database administration, privileges, and security are complex topics that are beyond the scope of this book. See the "References" section at the end of this chapter for links to online documentation. You can also check out Luke Welling's and Laura Thompson's book, *PHP and MySQL Web Development* from Sams Publishing (ISBN: 0-672-32919-6).

Configuring PostgreSQL

If you do not want to use the version of PostgreSQL bundled with Ubuntu, the latest PostgreSQL binary files and source are available at www.postgresql.org. The PostgreSQL packages are distributed as several files. At a minimum, you want the postgresql package. You should see the README file in the FTP directory ftp://ftp.postgresql.org/pub/ to determine whether you need any other packages.

If you are installing from the Ubuntu package files, a necessary postgres user account (that is, an account with the name of the user running the server on your system) is created for you automatically:

```
matthew@seymour:~$ fgrep postgres /etc/passwd
postgres:x:26:26:PostgreSQL Server:/var/lib/postgresql:/bin/bash
```

Otherwise, you need to create a user called postgres during the installation. This user should not have login privileges because only root should be able to use su to become this user, and no one will ever log in directly as the user. (See Chapter 13, "Managing Users," for more information on how to add users to an Ubuntu system.) After you have added the user, you can install each of the PostgreSQL packages you downloaded using the standard dpkg -i command for a default installation.

Initializing the Data Directory in PostgreSQL

Installation initializes the database and sets the permissions on the data directory to their correct values.

> **CAUTION**
>
> The initdb program sets the permissions on the data directory to 700. You should not change these permissions to anything else to avoid creating a security hole.

You can start the postmaster program with the following command (make sure you are still the user postgres):

```
matthew@seymour:~$ postmaster -D /usr/local/pgsql/data &
```

If you have decided to use a directory other than /usr/local/pgsql/data as the data directory, you should replace the directory in the postmaster command line with whatever directory you are using.

> **TIP**
>
> By default, Ubuntu makes the PostgreSQL data directory /var/lib/pgsql/data. This is not a very good place to store the data, however, because most people do not have the necessary space in the /var partition for any kind of serious data storage. Note that if you do change the data directory to something else (such as /usr/local/pgsql/data, as in the examples in this section), you need to edit the PostgreSQL startup file (named postgres) located in /etc/init.d to reflect the change.

Creating a Database in PostgreSQL

Creating a database in PostgreSQL is straightforward, but it must be performed by a user who has permissions to create databases in PostgreSQL—for example, initially the user named `postgres`. You can then simply issue the following command from the shell prompt (not the PSQL client prompt, but a normal shell prompt):

```
matthew@seymour:~# su - postgres
-bash-2.05b$ createdb database
```

where *database* is the name of the database you want to create.

The `createdb` program is actually a wrapper that makes it easier to create databases without having to log in and use `psql`. However, you can also create databases from within `psql` with the `CREATE DATABASE` statement. Here is an example:

```
CREATE DATABASE database;
```

You need to create at least one database before you can start the `psql` client program. You should create this database while you're logged in as the user `postgres`. To log in as this user, you need to use `su` to become root and then use `su` to become the user `postgres`. To connect to the new database, you start the `psql` client program with the name of the new database as a command-line argument, like this:

```
matthew@seymour:~$ psql sampledata
```

If you don't specify the name of a database when you invoke `psql`, the command attempts to connect to a database that has the same name as the user as which you invoke `psql` (that is, the default database).

Creating Database Users in PostgreSQL

To create a database user, you use `su` to become the user `postgres` from the Linux root account. You can then use the PostgreSQL `createuser` command to quickly create a user who is allowed to access databases or create new database users, as follows:

```
matthew@seymour:~$ createuser heather
Shall the new user be allowed to create databases? (y/n) y
Shall the new user be allowed to create more new users? (y/n) y
CREATE USER
```

In this example, the new user named `phudson` is created and allowed to create new databases and database users. (Carefully consider who is allowed to create new databases or additional users.)

You can also use the PostgreSQL command-line client to create a new user by typing `psql` along with name of the database and then use the `CREATE USER` command to create a new user. Here is an example:

```
CREATE USER foobar ;
```

CAUTION

PostgreSQL allows you to omit the `WITH PASSWORD` portion of the statement. However, doing so causes the user to be created with no password. This is a security hole, so you should always use the `WITH PASSWORD` option when creating users.

NOTE

When you are finished working in the `psql` command-line client, you can type `\q` to get out of it and return to the shell prompt.

Deleting Database Users in PostgreSQL

To delete a database user, you use the `dropuser` command, along with the user's name, and the user's access is removed from the default database, like this:

```
matthew@seymour:~$ dropuser msmith
DROP USER
```

You can also log in to your database by using `psql` and then use the `DROP USER` commands. Here is an example:

```
matthew@seymour:~$ psql demodb
Welcome to psql, the PostgreSQL interactive terminal.

Type: \copyright for distribution terms
 \h for help with SQL commands
 \? for help on internal slash commands
 \g or terminate with semicolon to execute query
 \q to quit

demodb=# DROP USER msmith ;
DROP USER
demodb=# \q
```

Granting and Revoking Privileges in PostgreSQL

As in MySQL, granting and revoking privileges in PostgreSQL is done with the `GRANT` and `REVOKE` statements. The syntax is the same as in MySQL except that PostgreSQL doesn't use the `IDENTIFIED BY` portion of the statement because with PostgreSQL, passwords are assigned when you create the user with the `CREATE USER` statement, as discussed previously. Here is the syntax of the `GRANT` statement:

```
GRANT what_to_grant ON where_to_grant TO user_name;
```

The following command, for example, grants all privileges to the user `foobar` on the database `sampledata`:

```
GRANT ALL ON sampledata TO foobar;
```

To revoke privileges, you use the REVOKE statement. Here is an example:

```
REVOKE ALL ON sampledata FROM foobar;
```

This command removes all privileges from the user foobar on the database sampledata.

Advanced administration and user configuration are complex topics. This section cannot begin to cover all the aspects of PostgreSQL administration or of privileges and users. For more information about administering PostgreSQL, see the PostgreSQL documentation or consult a book on PostgreSQL, such as *PostgreSQL* (Sams Publishing) by Korry Douglas.

Database Clients

Both MySQL and PostgreSQL use a client/server system for accessing databases. In the simplest terms, the database server handles the requests that come into the database, and the database client handles getting the requests to the server as well as getting the output from the server to the user.

Users never interact directly with the database server even if it happens to be located on the same machine they are using. All requests to the database server are handled by a database client, which might or might not be running on the same machine as the database server.

Both MySQL and PostgreSQL have command-line clients. A command-line client is a primitive way of interfacing with a database and generally isn't used by end users. As a DBA, however, you use the command-line client to test new queries interactively without having to write front-end programs for that purpose. In later sections of this chapter, you discover a bit about the MySQL graphical client and the web-based database administration interfaces available for both MySQL and PostgreSQL.

The following sections examine two common methods of accessing a remote database, a method of local access to a database server, and the concept of web access to a database.

> **NOTE**
>
> You should consider access and permission issues when setting up a database. Should users be able to create and destroy databases? Or should they only be able to use existing databases? Will users be able to add records to the database and modify existing records? Or should users be limited to read-only access to the database? And what about the rest of the world? Will the general public need to have any kind of access to your database through the Internet? As DBA, you must determine the answers to these questions.

30

SSH Access to a Database

Two types of remote database access scenarios are briefly discussed in this section. In the first scenario, the user directly logs in to the database server through *Secure Shell (SSH)* (to take advantage of the security benefits of encrypted sessions) and then starts a program on the server to access the database. In this case, shown in Figure 30.4, the database client is running on the database server itself.

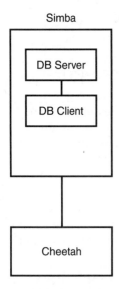

FIGURE 30.4   The user logs in to the database server located on host `simba` from the workstation (host `cheetah`). The database client is running on `simba`.

In the other scenario, shown in Figure 30.5, the user logs in to a remote host through SSH and starts a program on it to access the database, but the database is actually running on a different system. Three systems are now involved: the user's workstation, the remote host running the database client, and the remote host running the database server.

The important thing to note in Figure 30.5 is the middleman system `leopard`. Although the client is no longer running on the database server itself, it isn't running on the user's local workstation, either.

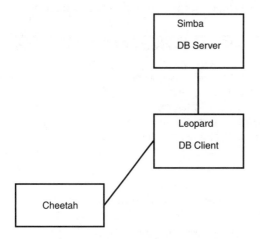

FIGURE 30.5   The user logs in to the remote host `leopard` from the workstation (host `cheetah`) and starts a database client on `leopard`. The client on `leopard` then connects to the database server running on host `simba`. The database client is running on `leopard`.

Local GUI Client Access to a Database

A user can log in to the database server by using a graphical client (which could be running on Windows, Macintosh, or a UNIX workstation). The graphical client then connects to the database server. In this case, the client is running on the user's workstation. Figure 30.6 shows an example.

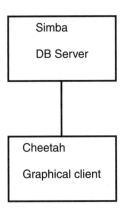

FIGURE 30.6   The user starts a GUI database program on the user's workstation (hostname `cheetah`). This program, which is the database client, then connects to the database server running on the host `simba`.

Web Access to a Database

This section looks at two basic examples of web access to the database server. In the first example, a user accesses the database through a form located on the World Wide Web. At first glance, it might appear that the client is running on the user's workstation. Of course, in reality it is not; the client is actually running on the web server. The web browser on the user's workstation simply provides a way for each user to enter the data that the user wants to send to the database and a way for the results sent from the database to be displayed to the user. The software that actually handles sending the request to the database is running on the web server in the form of a CGI script; a Java servlet; or embedded scripting such as the PHP or Sun Microsystems, Inc.'s JavaServer Pages (JSP).

Often, the terms *client* and *front end* are used interchangeably when speaking of database structures. However, Figure 30.7 shows an example of a form of access in which the client and the front end are not the same thing at all. In this example, the front end is the form displayed in the user's web browser. In such cases, the client is referred to as *middleware*.

30

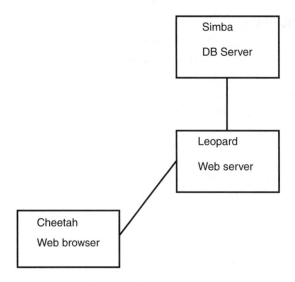

FIGURE 30.7   The user accesses the database through the World Wide Web. The front end is the user's web browser, the client is running on `leopard`, and the server is running on `simba`.

In another possible web access scenario, it could be said that the client is a two-piece application in which part of it is running on the user's workstation and the other part is running on the web server. For example, the database programmer can use JavaScript in the web form to ensure that the user has entered a valid query. In this case, the user's query is partially processed on the user's own workstation and partially on the web server. Error checking is done on the user's own workstation, which helps reduce the load on the server and also helps reduce network traffic because the query is checked for errors before being sent across the network to the server.

The MySQL Command-Line Client

The MySQL command-line client is `mysql`, and it has the following syntax:

```
mysql [options] [database]
```

Some of the available options for `mysql` are discussed in Table 30.1. `database` is optional, and if given, it should be the name of the database to which you want to connect.

TABLE 30.1   Command-Line Options to Use When Invoking `mysql`

Option	Action
-h hostname	Connects to the remote host `hostname` (if the database server isn't located on the local system).
-u username	Connects to the database as the user `username`.
-p	Prompts for a password. This option is required if the user you are connecting as needs a password to access the database. Note that this is a lowercase *p*.
-P n	Specifies `n` as the number of the port that the client should connect to. Note that this is an uppercase *P*.
-?	Displays a help message.

More options are available than are listed in Table 30.1, but these are the most common options. See the man page for `mysql` for more information on the available options.

CAUTION

Although `mysql` allows you to specify the password on the command line after the `-p` option, and thus allows you to avoid having to type the password at the prompt, you should never invoke the client this way. Doing so causes your password to display in the process list, and the process list can be accessed by any user on the system. This is a major security hole, so never give your password on the `mysql` command line.

You can access the MySQL server without specifying a database to use. After you log in, you use the `help` command to get a list of available commands, like this:

```
mysql> help

MySQL commands:
Note that all text commands must be first on line and end with ';'
help   (\h) Display this help.
?      (\?) Synonym for 'help'.
clear  (\c) Clear command.
connect (\r) Reconnect to the server. Optional arguments are db and host.
edit   (\e) Edit command with $EDITOR.
ego    (\G) Send command to mysql server, display result vertically.
exit   (\q) Exit mysql. Same as quit.
go     (\g) Send command to mysql server.
nopager (\n) Disable pager, print to stdout.
notee  (\t) Don't write into outfile.
pager  (\P) Set PAGER [to_pager]. Print the query results via PAGER.
print  (\p) Print current command.
quit   (\q) Quit mysql.
rehash (\#) Rebuild completion hash.
source (\.) Execute a SQL script file. Takes a file name as an argument.
```

```
status (\s) Get status information from the server.
tee (\T) Set outfile [to_outfile]. Append everything into given outfile.
use (\u) Use another database. Takes database name as argument.
```

You can then access a database by using the `use` command and the name of a database that has been created (such as `animals`) and that you are authorized to connect to, as follows:

```
mysql> use animals
Database changed
mysql>
```

The PostgreSQL Command-Line Client

You invoke the PostgreSQL command-line client with the command `psql`. Like `mysql`, you can invoke `psql` with the name of the database to which you would like to connect. Also like `mysql`, `psql` can take several options. These options are listed in Table 30.2.

TABLE 30.2   Command-Line Options to Use When Invoking `psql`

Option	Action
-h hostname	Connects to the remote host `hostname` (if the database server isn't located on the local system).
-p n	Specifies `n` as the number of the port that the client should connect to. Note that this is a lowercase *p*.
-U username	Connects to the database as the user `username`.
-W	Prompts for a password after connecting to the database. In PostgreSQL 7 and later, password prompting is automatic if the server requests a password after a connection has been established.
-?	Displays a help message.

Several more options are available in addition to those listed in Table 30.2. See the `psql` man page for details on all the available options.

Graphical Clients

If you prefer to interact with a database by using a graphical database client than with the command-line clients discussed in the previous section, you are in luck: A few options are available.

MySQL has an official graphical client called *MySQLGUI*. MySQLGUI is available in both source and binary formats from the MySQL website at www.mysql.com.

Postgresql has *pgAdmin*, which comes with the `postgres` package on Ubuntu.

Web-based administration interfaces are also available for MySQL and PostgreSQL. phpMyAdmin and phpPgAdmin are two such products. Both of these products are based on the PHP-embedded scripting language and therefore require you to have PHP installed. Of course, you also need to have a web server installed.

RELATED UBUNTU AND DATABASE COMMANDS

The following commands are useful for creating and manipulating databases in Ubuntu:

- ▶ `createdb`—Creates a new PostgreSQL database
- ▶ `createuser`—Creates a new PostgreSQL user account
- ▶ `dropdb`—Deletes a PostgreSQL database
- ▶ `dropuser`—Deletes a PostgreSQL user account
- ▶ `mysql`—Interactively queries the mysqld server
- ▶ `mysqladmin`—Administers the mysqld server
- ▶ `mysqldump`—Dumps or backs up MySQL data or tables
- ▶ `psql`—Accesses PostgreSQL via an interactive terminal

References

- ▶ **www.mysql.com**—This is the official website of the MySQL database server. Here you can find the latest versions as well as up-to-date information and online documentation for MySQL. You can also purchase support contracts here. You might want to look into this if you will be using MySQL in a corporate setting. (Many corporations balk at the idea of using software for which the company has no support contract in place.)

- ▶ **http://drizzle.org/**—The home page for Drizzle.

- ▶ **http://mariadb.org**—The home page for MariaDB.

- ▶ **www.postgresql.org**—The official website of the PostgreSQL database server.

30

NoSQL Databases

If you read Chapter 30, "Administering Relational Database Services," you have already read a brief description of the databases in this chapter. *NoSQL* is a broad term covering a large number of database styles. There are some similarities, but each of these databases was developed for a specific purpose. That means that they are not necessarily interchangeable, although it might be possible to force one to serve a task for which it is not designed. That is rarely a good idea. Also, although there has been a lot of press and hype about NoSQL over the past few years, NoSQL will not and should not be considered as a replacement for relational databases. Rather, this is a new set of databases designed to excel in specific situations, especially in large-scale, high-traffic-volume applications. If you have a need for storing and interacting with specific types of data as is described in one of the following sections, only then do we recommend using a database listed in that section.

NOT ONE SIZE FITS ALL

"It's not a one size fits all anymore. One will use multiple technologies. If I were a CTO, I'd want to use NoSQL for scalable high performance operational data access, lots of reads and writes at high speed and [for] semi real-time and low latency for end users. And you need another for reporting and BI. These [NoSQL] technologies are not optimal for that. In general, a classic data warehouse is a good solution for those things."

—Dwight Merriman, CEO of MongoDB, at OSCON 2011, as quoted in an article from ZDNet at www.zdnet.com/article/mongodb-chief-it-will-be-mixed-sql-nosql-world/.

There are different definitions and even some controversy over what NoSQL means. Does it mean that the database does not use SQL for interactions? Perhaps, but that is not absolute. Does it mean, as some now suggest, "not only SQL?" Maybe. That is certainly a broader and more accurate description, although it is also a bit misleading as it seems to include all the relational databases that use SQL. Here is a well-known secret: There is no consistent definition of the term. With that said, here is a reasonably accurate set of features that the databases that are generally labeled NoSQL share:

▶ They store structured data (organized in a way that is defined and identifiable).

▶ They do not store data relationally (no tables with rows and columns and relationships between tables).

That's about it.

The advantages to using a NoSQL option instead of a relational database are as follows:

▶ NoSQL databases are designed for really large sets of data and can often handle more than any relational database.

▶ NoSQL databases are designed to scale as needed. That is, instead of buying a bigger database server to handle increased load as you would with a relational model, you can add additional database hosts easily and spread the database out across them. This is designed to work with commodity hardware and transparently.

▶ Commodity hardware is much cheaper than dedicated, professional relational database server hardware, making NoSQL a cheaper option in many cases.

▶ Data models with NoSQL are much more relaxed. Some would call this a disadvantage, but it is included in the advantages list because there are some types of data models that may change frequently. In a relational system, data model changes require taking the database off line to modify the structure. Often, NoSQL databases have very little or even no data model restrictions and can allow quick and dirty changes.

The disadvantages to using a NoSQL database are these:

▶ Support is not as readily available. Most of the NoSQL databases are relatively small open-source projects, which is something that should please most readers of this book. However, this also means that, unlike most enterprise-focused relational databases, there is probably not any enterprise support available for businesses. This will frighten many managers.

▶ Most NoSQL projects are fairly new. This also means that they are untested in large enterprises and businesses. It can also mean that it takes longer to set up because of the learning curve; known solutions can be implemented more quickly.

▶ NoSQL is not always ACID (*atomicity, consistency, isolation, durability*) compliant. Instead of guaranteeing that every data transaction is instantly and properly recorded, that only one interaction may occur with a piece of data at any given time, and only the current version is available to the end user, NoSQL databases often work on a system of replication of data across multiple hosts that each get updated eventually. This may happen quickly, but there is no guarantee that at a given moment you will retrieve the most up-to-date data. This matters when dealing with financial transactions but might not be a concern with web search results where "close enough" might be all that is wanted or necessary.

▶ There is no particular advantage to NoSQL unless you have data that is large enough to benefit from it or your project fits neatly into a specific use case.

▶ It isn't difficult to migrate to NoSQL from traditional relational databases if the need arises. You know Donald Knuth's saying that "premature optimization is the root of all evil." It might be wiser to design your site or application using known technology and then migrate later if the need arises.

One facet that is sometimes described as an advantage and at other times as a disadvantage relates to administration. Relational databases often require trained staff to administer them. The positive side is that qualified *database administrators (DBAs)* are plentiful, if expensive. NoSQL databases are designed to be created and, at least in theory, require little to no further maintenance. Some pundits claim cost savings; others claim that DBAs will still be needed, but for different tasks, and that there are very few people who are trained and available to perform those tasks because of this perspective and the newness of the database style.

NOW, A QUICK WAFFLE ON THE NAME

Google and others seem to like the name "NewSQL" more than "NoSQL." Some only apply "NewSQL" to a certain group of databases that are somehow different than "NoSQL" databases. While "NoSQL" is much more common to hear, "NewSQL" is the latest buzzword in the database world. Here is one description why:

"NewSQL" is our shorthand for the various new scalable/high performance SQL database vendors. We have previously referred to these products as 'ScalableSQL' to differentiate them from the incumbent relational database products. Since this implies horizontal scalability, which is not necessarily a feature of all the products, we adopted the term 'NewSQL' in the new report.

"And to clarify, like NoSQL, NewSQL is not to be taken too literally: the new thing about the NewSQL vendors is the vendor, not the SQL."

The 451 Group's Matt Aslett, as recorded at http://blogs.the451group.com/information_management/2011/04/06/what-we-talk-about-when-we-talk-about-newsql/.

An interesting development in the NoSQL world is that specifications are being created for a new database query language called UnQL (pronounced "uncle"), which stands for *Unstructured Query Language*. This is being developed as a joint project by two developers: Richard Hipp, the creator of SQLite; and Damien Katz, the creator of CouchDB. They expect more to join them soon. In a nutshell, the language contains some familiar commands, such as SELECT, INSERT, UPDATE, and DELETE. However, it is different from SQL because these commands do not work on tables, but rather on collections of unordered sets of objects that are described using *JavaScript Object Notation (JSON)*. You can learn more about UnQL from the first product we have seen that uses it at www.unqlite.org.

The sections that follow group databases by similarities between them, choosing one standout feature as the name of the section. Because NoSQL databases are still fairly new, it is unclear which, if any, will become a long-term standard. For that reason, this chapter gives high-level coverage of a larger number of options rather than deep coverage of a couple of primary options.

Key/Value Stores

Key/value stores are listed first because they are the simplest of the NoSQL databases, at least in the sense of interactions. You have a piece of data of any type; this is your value. You give it a name of some sort; this is your key. Any time you need that specific piece of data, you ask for it using the key. Values might be bits of text, binaries, pretty much anything, and the data type does not need to be defined in advance, or often at all. The database never needs to know what the value object is, just that it is stored using the given key. These databases have no schema. The contents might be vastly different from one another in type, size, domain, and so on. It is the client, the application that uses the database, that is required to know about the value (what it is and the context in which it can be used). The database merely stores it using a key, knows the key/value pair, and serves the value when requested using its key.

Key/value stores are great for things like contents of a website shopping cart, user preference lists, a post in a social media site. Think of things that are not vital, things that might be useful but that will not cause problems if lost. You would not want to use this for credit card information, personal identification, health records, and such. You would want it for high-traffic sites that need to make sure that a local user has quick and accurate access to the information, but where the information can take time to replicate to other database nodes or which might not require replication across nodes at all, where there is heavy access to the database itself, but where users are not necessarily using the same data concurrently.

Berkeley DB

Berkeley DB was originally created at the University of California, Berkeley, to create a disk hash table that worked better than an existing solution while also helping the university clean up its free UNIX version called BSD by removing code inherited from AT&T. Several years later, Netscape asked the developers to add some desired features to make Berkeley DB more useful to them. This resulted in spinning off Berkeley DB from the university to a company founded for this purpose called Sleepycat Software, which headed development for many years. As of the purchase of Sleepycat Software in 2006, Berkeley DB is now owned by Oracle.

Although it is listed under key/value stores, this is not the only way to interact with a Berkeley DB database. Support also exists for using SQL and Java. Interaction is accomplished using an *application programming interface (API)*. Berkeley DB is very fast and very small. As a result, it can be found running on large-scale systems and embedded within applications and even running on mobile devices.

Berkeley DB is easily the most mature database mentioned in this chapter and is most notable for its use within many well-known software projects including Subversion, Postfix, and OpenLDAP. It was even included as a data storage backend for MySQL prior to MySQL 5.1.

Cassandra

Cassandra was developed by Facebook for their Inbox searching feature. It was released open source when Facebook turned it over to Apache in 2008. Cassandra is a key/value store that runs on a flexible cluster of nodes and is also a wide column store, like HBase discussed later in the "Wide Column Store" section. Nodes may be added and removed from the cluster. Data is replicated across multiple nodes of the cluster. There is no central node, access to data exists from any node; if the node receiving the request does not house the specific data requested, it still services the request by retrieving and sending the data. The main goal of Cassandra is fast retrieval of data with fault tolerance being handled through replication across nodes and speed adjustments via adding additional nodes to create more access points.

One interesting feature is that Cassandra may be tuned to adjust the trade-off between speed of transactions and consistency of data. When data is stored, it is initially stored in memory and gets sent to disk only when specific criteria are met. This makes interaction very quick. In fact, not all data stored in Cassandra is designed to persist over time, and data might not get written to disk at all. This means that not all readers or seekers of data may find a specific piece, but in cases like Facebook's need to store Inbox search data that only has limited time value (like search results, that could be different tomorrow or even ten minutes from now), this might not matter at all. In these cases, both access speed and convenience are more important.

Cassandra is being used by Facebook, Twitter, Reddit, and many others.

Memcached and MemcacheDB

Memcached stores data requested on a system in RAM for a specific period of time to make retrieving that data faster if it is requested again. The time that data persists can be based on a specific setting, memory needs, and other criteria. The goal is to reduce the number of times that data stores must be accessed. Data that is accessed often is held in memory, from where it is much more quickly retrieved. This can alleviate problems such as a page on a blog that has suddenly become popular as a result of the URL being posted on a social networking site. The spike in traffic could be kept manageable because the content of the blog post is being held in memory instead of being requested over and over from the database.

MemcacheDB is an implementation of the Memcached API that uses a key/value format based on Berkeley DB. However, where Memcached is designed as a cache solution to speed up data access from memory, MemcacheDB is designed as a persistent storage engine. Because it uses the same API protocol as Memcached, it is an easy way to add data persistence where caching is already in place with Memcached.

Memcached is used by sites like Twitter, Reddit, YouTube, and Facebook, and it is also supported and often used by websites based on content management systems like Drupal and WordPress.

Redis

Initially released in 2009, Redis is intended for applications where performance and flexibility are more important than persistence and absolute data integrity. It is an open-source key/value store written in C. Keys can contain strings, hashes, lists, sets, and stored sets. Redis works in RAM for speed, occasionally dumping to disk. Because actions are performed in memory, they are done faster. Operations include appending to a string, incrementing a hash value, pushing to a list, set computations, and more. Redis is also designed so that master-slave replication is easy to set up.

Riak

Riak is a fault tolerant, distributed database designed for scalability and use in the cloud. It is masterless, meaning there should be no single point of failure. It is designed for speed, simplicity, and stability. Riak is based on a paper by Amazon describing *Dynamo*, which is an internal, proprietary system owned by Amazon. The Riak Wiki describes the database in one place as "the most boring database you'll ever run in production. No sharding required, just horizontal scaling and straightforward capacity planning. The same operational tasks apply to small clusters and large clusters. More machines does not mean more ops."

Document Stores

Document stores are designed to store data that is already structured in some form of notation like JSON or XML. They typically focus on one specific type of notation and are intended to allow entire objects, including arrays and hashes, to be stored and retrieved at once.

Many times document stores are implemented as a layer between an application and a relational database to hold the output of certain types of queries. For example, it might be convenient to aggregate information that is typically requested together such as a set of user preferences or name and address information and store it as one object. Requesting and retrieving only one object that is already formatted in an object notation like JSON is faster than making many database queries, and it supplies preformatted data for the client application that can be used to both style output and display specific data at the same time.

Data that is stored and served this way does not have to fit database-specific formatting requirements in a NoSQL database. There are no tables to relate, and data may be larger or smaller and include more or less information. This is generally called *semistructured data*. Listings 31.1 and 31.2 are a quick snippet of two sets of user preferences in JSON—one that includes many user-set preferences and one that includes only one. The client application could be created to assume a set of default preferences that will be used unless specifically overridden by this file.

LISTING 31.1   Sandra's Preferences

```
{"userpreferences": {
    "displayName": "Don'tHitOnMe",
    "gender":"DoNotDisplay",
    "siteTheme":"Springtime",
    "postsDisplayed":"25",
    "keepLoggedIn":"True"
    }
}
```

LISTING 31.2   Matthew's Preferences

```
{"userpreferences": {
    "siteTheme":"TieDye",
    }
}
```

CouchDB

CouchDB began in 2005 as a self-funded personal project of Damien Katz. In 2008, it was given to Apache, where development continues. The goal of CouchDB is to provide a database useful for serving web applications. The emphasis is on scalability and fault tolerance while using commodity hardware (*Couch* is an acronym for *cluster of unreliable commodity hardware*). This is not an easy task, but when done successfully it lowers costs.

CouchDB uses a RESTful HTTP API that is designed from the beginning to be used on and for the Web. All stored items have a unique uniform resource identifier (URI), and full create, read, update, and delete (CRUD) functions are available directly using standard HTTP calls, making CouchDB very easy to integrate into web applications. These calls can be made from a browser or from a command line using a tool like cURL, which is available on many typical server platforms, including Ubuntu.

A nice feature of CouchDB is that it is designed with the ability to include ACID compliance, unlike many NoSQL options. This makes it possible to use CouchDB with more consistency-sensitive data.

CouchDB is written in Erlang, which is a language designed for concurrency. That makes CouchDB even better suited for use in a concurrent distributed system. CouchDB is designed to store JSON document objects.

CouchDB is used by several software and web applications, including many Facebook games and applications, internal use at the BBC, and Ubuntu One, Canonical's cloud storage.

MongoDB

MongoDB is similar to CouchDB in that both are designed as document stores for JSON objects and, like Cassandra, is designed for replication and high-availability. It is created and supported by a company called 10gen and is newer, with its first public release in 2009. A unique feature for this open-source database is that the developer offers commercial, enterprise-class support, training, and consulting. This has made adoption of MongoDB much faster than is typical for NoSQL products.

MongoDB supports *sharding*, which automatically partitions data across servers for increased performance and scalability. This produces a form of load and data balancing and also offers a way to add nodes simply. Sharding is also intended to support an automatic failover system where node data is replicated, allowing no single point of failure.

In addition, MongoDB includes support for indexing in a manner that is more extensive and powerful than most NoSQL solutions.

MARKETING HYPE OR GREAT DESIGN?

MongoDB wasn't designed in a lab. We built MongoDB from our own experiences building large-scale, high-availability, robust systems. We didn't start from scratch, we really tried to figure out what was broken, and tackle that. So the way I think about MongoDB is that if you take MySQL, and change the data model from relational to document based, you get a lot of great features: embedded docs for speed, manageability, agile development with schema-less databases, easier horizontal scalability because joins aren't as important. There are lots of things that work great in relational databases: indexes, dynamic queries, and updates, to name a few; and we haven't changed much there. For example, the way you design your indexes in MongoDB should be exactly the way you do it in MySql or Oracle; you just have the option of indexing an embedded field.

—Eliot Horowitz, 10gen CTO and co-founder

Obviously, the people behind MongoDB are good at marketing. At the same time, if you listen closely to the crowd, you don't hear many negative comments about MongoDB, and they have an impressive list of users including Craigslist, Shutterfly, SourceForge, the *New York Times*, and GitHub. They have quickly garnered great respect and are constantly spreading use.

BaseX

BaseX was started by Christian Grün at the University of Knostanz in 2005 and was subsequently released using a BSD license in 2007. It is a simple, lightweight database that does not support a lot of features, but which could be just right for specific applications. Rather than using JSON like CouchDB and MongoDB, BaseX is designed to store document objects in XML. It supports standard XML tools like XPath and Xquery and also includes a lightweight GUI.

BaseX creates indexes, supports W3C recommendations and standards, ACID-safe transactions, large documents, and various APIs like REST/JAX-RX and XML:DB. Although not as sexy or well known as other options in this section, perhaps because of the newness and popularity of JSON over XML, BaseX is respected and used by many universities and enterprises.

Wide Column Stores

Wide column stores are often referred to as big table stores, after one of the best-known examples, Google's BigTable. Typically, a relational database reads data from tables using rows. Data is then sorted to find only those contents of a row that are needed. Wide column stores change the system by reading data from tables in columns, selecting the attributes first before reading in data. This is more efficient for input and output read-only queries. This means that wide column stores tend to be very efficient for databases that are mostly used for reading stored data, especially from very large data sets.

Wide column stores use something like tables, with a defined schema for each table. Unlike relational databases, wide column stores do not record relationships between tables. These are not relational databases, but are more like maps that show where data exists across multiple dimensions. They are designed for scalability and as distributed systems.

Two examples of wide column stores are discussed here. One more, Cassandra, was discussed earlier in this chapter and fits into both this category and the earlier key/value stores category.

BigTable

BigTable is a proprietary Google product that is only used by Google. It is designed to work with Google's MapReduce framework, which was created to process huge data sets across large clusters of computing nodes.

BigTable stores the massive sets of data used by many Google programs like Google Reader, My Search History, Google Earth, YouTube, and Gmail. BigTable is not available for use outside of Google.

The papers that describe Google's design for both BigTable and MapReduce are listed in the "References" section of this chapter.

HBase

HBase is the database used by Hadoop. Hadoop is the Apache Project's free software application for processing huge amounts of data across large clusters of compute nodes in a cluster. Hadoop is modeled in part after the information in Google's MapReduce and Google File System papers. HBase is to BigTable what Hadoop is to MapReduce.

The main feature of HBase is its ability to host very large tables, on the scale of billions of rows across millions of columns. It is designed to host them on commodity hardware. HBase provides a RESTful web service interface that supports many formats and encodings and is optimized for real-time queries.

Numerous companies are using Hadoop, including some very big names like Amazon, eBay, Facebook, IBM, LinkedIn, Rackspace, and Yahoo!

Graph Stores

Graph stores, or graph databases, literally store data as a graph. What that means is the data is represented as a series of nodes and how they relate to each other. In the simplest case, a graph with only one node, all that need be recorded is the record and its properties. The properties list can be as short as one or as long as a few million (perhaps more).

Rather than allow that awkwardness to grow, most will start creating new nodes sooner, each node having its own properties and also explicit relationships that tie each node to other nodes. It is the relationships that organize the nodes, and the structure is therefore flexible. A graph can look like a list or a map or a tree or something else entirely.

Graph databases are queried using traversals. A traversal begins at defined starting nodes and follows through related nodes to answer questions such as, "What classes are my friends taking that I am not enrolled in?" or, "If server X has a network connection problem, what web services will be disrupted?" In a graph database, an index is just a special type of traversal, usually something commonly used such as finding specific nodes or relationships according to a property they share.

Graph stores are not terribly common, but are beloved by those who promote them. There is less differentiation between the options available in this category, at least when compared to the differentiation between the other categories of NoSQL databases in this chapter.

Neo4j

Neo4j is the graph store that most people have heard of in the NoSQL world. It has both a free version and a commercial version. Language bindings exist for Java, Python, and Ruby. It is scalable up to graphs of several billion nodes/relationships/properties on a single machine and can be scaled across multiple machines. It can be deployed on a standalone server or as a small-footprint database coexisting on the same machine with other software.

OrientDB

OrientDB is a free database, released under the Apache 2.0 license. It uses a different indexing algorithm called MVRB-Tree, which it claims is significantly faster. You might remember an older relational database called Orient ODBMS. OrientDB is related and can be used with a subset of SQL, but it is a complete rewrite using a document/graph database foundation.

HyperGraphDB

HyperGraphDB is another free option that uses the LGPL. It is designed primarily for use with the semantic web, knowledge management, and artificial intelligence projects. In mathematics, the definition of a hypergraph is an extension to the standard graph, allowing an edge to point to more than two nodes. According to the HyperGraphDB website, "HyperGraphDB extends this even further by allowing edges to point to other edges as well and making every node or edge carry an arbitrary value as payload." HyperGraphDB seems to be focused on the academic side of things, so students might be especially interested in it because HyperGraphDB appears to be trying out some new research ideas.

FlockDB

FlockDB is used by Twitter to store social graphs, such as who follows whom, and for some secondary indices. It is free and open source, using the Apache 2.0 license. It is simpler than other graph databases as it seems to try to solve fewer problems, being designed for one primary use. FlockDB is designed for online, low-latency, high-throughput environments such as websites like Twitter; even then, it's only for storing specific types of data.

References

- ▶ www.oracle.com/us/products/database/berkeley-db/index.html—The main Berkeley DB website.

- ▶ http://cassandra.apache.org/—The main website for Cassandra.

- ▶ www.memcached.org/—The main website for Memcached.

- ▶ http://memcachedb.org/—The main website for MemcacheDB.

- ▶ http://redis.io/—The main website for Redis.

- ▶ http://basho.com/products/riak-s2/—The main website for Riak.

- ▶ http://couchdb.apache.org/—The main website for CouchDB.

- ▶ http://mongodb.org/—The main website for MongoDB.

- ▶ http://basex.org/—The main website for BaseX.

- ▶ http://research.google.com/archive/bigtable.html—The paper describing BigTable.

- ▶ http://research.google.com/archive/mapreduce.html—The paper describing MapReduce.

- ▶ http://hadoop.apache.org/—The main website for Hadoop.

- ▶ http://hbase.apache.org/—The main website for Hbase, the Hadoop database.

- ▶ http://research.google.com/archive/gfs.html—The paper describing Google File System.

- ▶ http://neo4j.org/—The main website for Neo4j.

- ▶ http://orientdb.org/—The main website for OrientDB.

- ▶ http://www.hypergraphdb.org/—The main website for HyperGraphDB.

- ▶ https://github.com/twitter/flockdb—The main website for FlockDB.

Lightweight Directory Access Protocol (LDAP)

The *Lightweight Directory Access Protocol* (*LDAP*, pronounced ell-dap) is one of those technologies that, although hidden, forms part of the core infrastructure in enterprise computing. Its job is simple: It stores information about users. However, its power comes from the fact that it can be linked into dozens of other services. LDAP can power login authentication, public key distribution, email routing, and address verification; more recently, it has formed the core of the push toward single sign-on technology.

TIP

Most people find the concept of LDAP easier to grasp when they think of it as a highly specialized form of database server. Behind the scenes, Ubuntu uses a database for storing all its LDAP information; however, LDAP does not offer anything as straightforward as SQL for data manipulation.

OpenLDAP uses Sleepycat Software's Berkeley DB (BDB), and sticking with that default is highly recommended. However, alternatives exist if you have specific needs.

This chapter looks at a relatively basic installation of an LDAP server, including how to host a companywide directory service that contains the names and email addresses of employees. LDAP is a client/server system, meaning that an LDAP server hosts the data and an LDAP client queries it. Ubuntu comes with OpenLDAP as its LDAP server, along with several LDAP-enabled email clients, including Evolution and Mozilla Thunderbird. This chapter covers all three of these applications.

Because LDAP data is usually available over the Internet—or at least your local network—it is imperative that you make every effort to secure your server. This chapter gives specific instruction on password con-figuration for OpenLDAP, and we recommend you follow the instructions closely.

Configuring the Server

If you have been using LDAP for years, you will be aware of its immense power and flexibility. But if you are just trying LDAP for the first time, it will seem like the most broken component you could imagine. LDAP has specific configuration requirements, is vastly lacking in graphical tools, and has a large number of acronyms to remember. On the bright side, all the hard work you put in is worth it because when it works LDAP improves your networking experience immensely. You should read the entire chapter and understand it before you start. Then, read the README file in `/etc/ldap/schema` before you do anything.

The first step in configuring your LDAP server is to install the client and server applications. Install the `slapd` and `ldap-utils` packages from the Ubuntu repositories. Doing so also installs three other packages: `odbcinst`, `odbcinstdebian2`, and `unixodbc`.

By default, Ubuntu configures `slapd` with the minimum options necessary to run the daemon. We are going to configure everything from that bare-bones installation up to where it will be useful.

Now you need to know the fully qualified domain name (FQDN) of your server. In a moment, you will begin to write/modify some configuration files, and this will be a vital part of that process. The example uses matthewhelmke.com. Whenever you see this, change it to your FQDN.

From the FQDN you acquire your domain component, which is the name of your domain as stored in DNS. This is abbreviated as dc. LDAP considers each part of a domain name (separated by a dot) to be domain components. In the example, there are two dc items: `matthewhelmke` and `com`.

OpenLDAP now uses a separate directory containing the `cn=config` *Directory Information Tree (DIT)* to configure the `slapd` daemon dynamically. This enables you to modify schema definitions, indexes, and so on without stopping and restarting the service, as was required in earlier versions. You need two files for this configuration: a back end that has only a minimal configuration and a front end that uses a traditional format that is compatible with and accessed by external programs using established standards.

Creating Your Schema

Start by loading some premade schema files. This makes configuration faster and easier by preloading some settings. If you are building an enterprise server, read the official OpenLDAP documentation and start from scratch so that you know precisely what everything on your server is doing and why. For the example, load these three files into the directory using these commands:

```
matthew@seymour:~$ sudo ldapadd -Y EXTERNAL -H ldapi:/// -f /etc/ldap/schema/
➥cosine.ldif
matthew@seymour:~$ sudo ldapadd -Y EXTERNAL -H ldapi:/// -f /etc/ldap/schema/
➥nis.ldif
```

matthew@seymour:~$ **sudo ldapadd -Y EXTERNAL -H ldapi:/// -f /etc/ldap/schema/**
➥**inetorgperson.ldif**

Next, create a file called `backend.matthewhelmke.com.ldif` with these contents:

```
# Load dynamic backend modules
dn: cn=module,cn=config
objectClass: olcModuleList
cn: module
olcModulepath: /usr/lib/ldap
olcModuleload: back_hdb


# Database settings
dn: olcDatabase=hdb,cn=config
objectClass: olcDatabaseConfig
objectClass: olcHdbConfig
olcDatabase: {1}hdb
olcSuffix: dc=matthewhelmke,dc=com
olcDbDirectory: /var/lib/ldap
olcRootDN: cn=admin,dc=matthewhelmke,dc=com
olcRootPW: changeMEtoSOMETHINGbetter
olcDbConfig: set_cachesize 0 2097152 0
olcDbConfig: set_lk_max_objects 1500
olcDbConfig: set_lk_max_locks 1500
olcDbConfig: set_lk_max_lockers 1500
olcDbIndex: objectClass eq
olcLastMod: TRUE
olcDbCheckpoint: 512 30
olcAccess: to attrs=userPassword by dn="cn=admin,dc=matthewhelmke,dc=com" write by
anonymous auth by self write by * none
olcAccess: to attrs=shadowLastChange by self write by * read
olcAccess: to dn.base="" by * read
olcAccess: to * by dn="cn=admin,dc=matthewhelmke,dc=com" write by * read
```

Make sure you change all instances of `matthewhelmke` and `com` to fit your FQDN and change the entry for `olcRootPW` to a more secure password of your choosing. Then, add the new file to the directory (I am assuming you are entering this command from the directory where the file was created):

matthew@seymour:~$ **sudo ldapadd -Y EXTERNAL -H ldapi:/// -f backend.example.**
com.ldif

Populating Your Directory

The back end is ready. Now you need to populate the front-end directory to make this useful. Create another file called `frontend.matthewhelmke.com.ldif` with the following contents:

```
# Create top-level object in domain
dn: dc=matthewhelmke,dc=com
```

```
objectClass: top
objectClass: dcObject
objectclass: organization
o: Example Organization
dc: Example
description: LDAP Example

# Admin user.
dn: cn=admin,dc=matthewhelmke,dc=com
objectClass: simpleSecurityObject
objectClass: organizationalRole
cn: admin
description: LDAP administrator
userPassword: changeMEtoSOMETHINGbetter

dn: ou=people,dc=example,dc=com
objectClass: organizationalUnit
ou: people

dn: ou=groups,dc=matthewhelmke,dc=com
objectClass: organizationalUnit
ou: groups

dn: uid=john,ou=people,dc=matthewhelmke,dc=com
objectClass: inetOrgPerson
objectClass: posixAccount
objectClass: shadowAccount
uid: matthew
sn: Helmke
givenName: Matthew
cn: Matthew Helmke
displayName: Matthew Helmke
uidNumber: 1000
gidNumber: 10000
userPassword: changeMEtoSOMETHINGbetter
gecos: Matthew Helmke
loginShell: /bin/bash
homeDirectory: /home/matthew
shadowExpire: -1
shadowFlag: 0
shadowWarning: 7
shadowMin: 8
shadowMax: 999999
shadowLastChange: 10877
mail: matthew@matthewhelmke.com
postalCode: 85711
l: Tucson
```

```
o: Example
mobile: +1 (520) xxx-xxxx
homePhone: +1 (520) xxx-xxxx
title: System Administrator
postalAddress: I'm not putting it in the book.
initials: MH

dn: cn=example,ou=groups,dc=example,dc=com
objectClass: posixGroup
cn: example
gidNumber: 10000
```

Remember to change the details to fit your information. Then add this to the LDAP directory:

matthew@seymour:~$ **sudo ldapadd -x -D cn=admin,dc=example,dc=com -W -f frontend.example.com.ldif**

To check that your content has been added to the LDAP directory correctly, you can use ldapsearch, as follows:

matthew@seymour:~$ **ldapsearch -xLLL -b "dc=example,dc=com" uid=john sn givenName cn**

```
dn: uid=matthew,ou=people,dc=matthewhelmke,dc=com
cn: Matthew Helmke
sn: Helmke
givenName: Matthew
```

In this example, dn stands for distinguished name, uid refers to user identification, ou tells the organizational unit, dc represents domain component, cn is common name, sn is the family or surname, and many cultures know givenName as your first name.

When you use LDAP, you can organize your data in many ways. You can use a number of currently existing schemas, such as in the previous example using the LDIF files you loaded at the start, or you can write your own. The /etc/ldap/schemas directory has many fine examples in the files with a .schema suffix and a few that have been converted to *LDAP Data Interchange Format (LDIF)*. To be used, the file must be in the LDIF (or when used as a file suffix, .ldif). You can convert one of the example schemas or create your own schema.

Configuring Clients

Although Ubuntu comes with a selection of email clients, there is not enough room here to cover them all. So, we discuss the two most frequently used clients: Evolution, the default; and Thunderbird. Both are powerful messaging solutions and so both work well with LDAP. Of the two, Thunderbird seems to be the easier to configure. We have had various problems with Evolution in the past in situations where Thunderbird has worked the first time.

Evolution

To configure Evolution for LDAP, click the arrow next to the New button and select Address Book. A new screen appears; its first option prompts you for the type of address book to create. Select On LDAP Servers.

For Name, just enter `Address book`, and for Server, enter the IP address of your LDAP server (or `127.0.0.1` if you are working on the server), as shown in Figure 32.1. Leave the port as `389`, which is the default for `slapd`. Switch to the Details tab and set Search Base to be the entire DN for your address book (for example, `ou=People,dc=matthewhelmke,dc=com`). Set Search Scope to be Sub so that Evolution performs a comprehensive search. To finish, click Add Address Book.

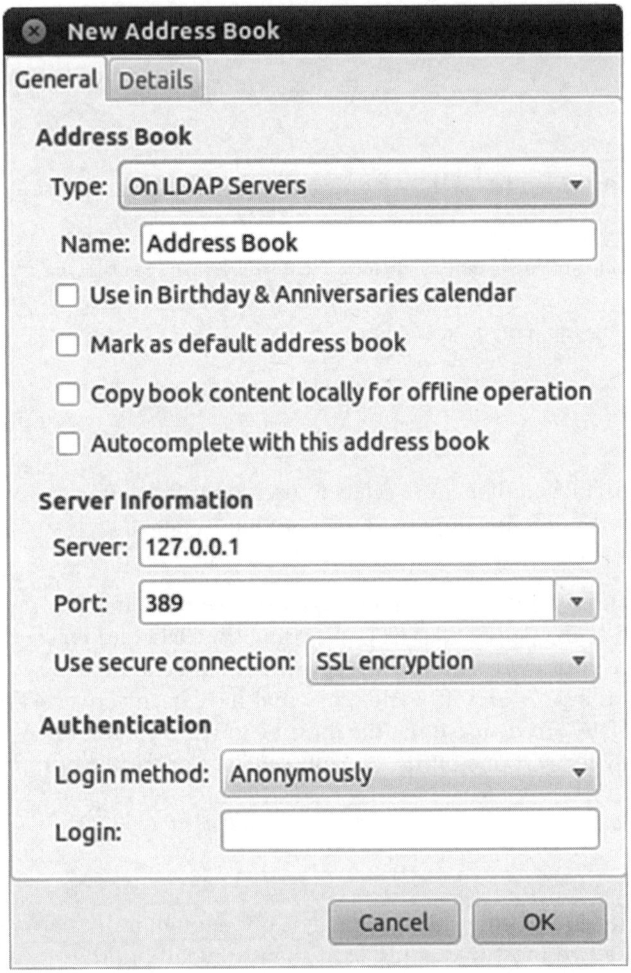

FIGURE 32.1   Configuring Evolution to use LDAP for addresses is easy for anonymous connections.

Thunderbird

Thunderbird is a little easier to configure than Evolution and tends to work better, particularly with entries that have multiple CNs. To enable it, go to the Edit menu, click Preferences, and then select Composition from the tabs along the top.

From the Addressing subtab, check the Directory Server box and click the Edit Directories button to its right. From the dialog box that appears, click Add to add a new directory. You can give it any name you want because this is merely for display purposes. As shown in Figure 32.2, set the Hostname field to be the IP address of your LDAP server (or 127.0.0.1 if you are working on the server). Set the Base DN to be the DN for your address book (for instance, ou=People,dc=matthewhelmke,dc=com) and leave the port number as 389. Click OK three times to get back to the main interface.

FIGURE 32.2   Thunderbird's options are buried deeper than Evolution's, but it does allow you to download the LDAP directory for offline use.

Administration

After you have your LDAP server and clients set up, they require little maintenance until something changes externally. Specifically, if someone in your directory changes jobs, changes her phone number, gets married (changing her last name [surname]), quits, or so forth, you need to be able to update your directory to reflect the change.

You installed some useful utilities with the ldap-utils package earlier. Here are what they do. Each one requires administration privileges, so use sudo.

▶ **ldapsearch**—Opens a connection to an LDAP server and searches its directory for requested information

▶ **ldapmodify**—Opens a connection to an LDAP server and allows you to add or modify entries

▶ **ldapadd**—Opens a connection to an LDAP server and allows you to add an entry

▶ **ldapdelete**—Opens a connection to an LDAP server and allows you to delete one or more entries

None of these are simple to use, but all come with moderate amounts of documentation in their man pages.

A much smarter option is to use phpLDAPadmin, which is an LDAP administration tool that enables you to add and modify entries entirely through your web browser. The program is available in the Ubuntu software repositories as `phpldapadmin`.

Starting, stopping, or restarting the `slapd` daemon is done in the usual way for system daemons (that do not yet have Upstart methods written for them):

```
sudo /etc/init.d/slapd start/stop/restart
```

References

▶ **www.openldap.org**—The home page of the OpenLDAP project where you can download the latest version of the software and meet other users.

▶ **http://ldap.perl.org/**—The home of the Perl library for interacting with LDAP provides comprehensive documentation to get you started.

▶ **https://help.ubuntu.com/lts/serverguide/openldap-server.html**—Official Ubuntu Server documentation for OpenLDAP.

▶ **http://phpldapadmin.sourceforge.net/**—The official documentation for phpLDAPadmin.

▶ The definitive book on LDAP is *LDAP System Administration* (O'Reilly) by Gerald Carter, ISBN: 1-56592-491-6. It is an absolute must for the bookshelf of any Linux LDAP administrator. For more general reading, try *LDAP Directories Explained* (Addison-Wesley) by Brian Arkills, ISBN: 0-201-78792-X. It has a much stronger focus on the Microsoft Active Directory LDAP implementation, however.

# CHAPTER 33

Linux Terminal Server Project (LTSP)

The *Linux Terminal Server Project* (LTSP) is an add-on package for Linux that enables you to run multiple thin clients, low-powered terminals, from one main server. A *thin client* is a small, energy-efficient, and generally lower-powered system designed to be used in conjunction with a more powerful server. The thin client has limited processing power and speed and limited storage, making it very inexpensive. All it is used for is receiving input from a device such as a keyboard or mouse, communicating with a server, and displaying output to a screen.

Processing of information and the actual running of programs are offloaded to the server, meaning the server does all the hard work and is the only system in the network that has strong requirements for processor power and speed, memory, storage, and so on. Thin clients are also generally smaller in size and quieter, which also make them more convenient to use when space and noise are potential issues. Those of us who have been around longer or who have worked in enterprise environments will see an immediate relationship to big metal servers and dumb client terminals, and it is reasonable to think of an LTSP setup this way. In our case, the server isn't as big or as powerful, and the thin clients aren't as dumb and weak, but the idea is the same.

Thin clients are great in places such as classrooms and computer labs where strict control and strong security are desirable, where money for a room of full-powered systems might not be available, and where installing and maintaining core software on one server is preferable to doing so on many systems. For this reason, Edubuntu, a community-led official subproject of Ubuntu, is designed for easy LTSP installation and configuration. We focus on using LTSP with standard Ubuntu, but if you want to use LTSP in an education-specific context, or if you just want an additional perspective and more information about LTSP, Edubuntu is worth a closer look. Other common places you are likely to find thin clients in use are libraries for catalog access and searches and in some airports that make courtesy terminals for checking email available for travelers.

Links to several thin client hardware sources are included in the "References" section of this chapter, although they are included to inform and should not be taken as endorsements. (We don't own and have not used equipment from every company listed and can't make any honest recommendations about them.) In addition to those mentioned, you are sure to find others. In fact, computers that often make excellent thin clients are not advertised as such. You can look for compact format systems that use an ARM, VIA, or maybe an Intel Atom processor, for example, and are likely to find they make wonderful thin clients. You can even recycle older hardware that would otherwise be bound for the trashcan and make it useful again as a thin client.

Now that you have a sense of why you might use LTSP and how the network is created, it is a good time to fill you in on some of the details of what LTSP is, what it is not, and how it is designed to work. Armed with this knowledge, you will be able to find documentation to help you decide what you can afford to buy, how you want to configure it, and even whether this is a configuration that is applicable and useful to your situation.

LTSP is add-on software for Linux that creates a server that can be used to boot client computers over a network. It allows client computers to access and run applications on the server while the client remains responsible for input and display and the server handles processing data and storage. This allows many inexpensive hardware clients to be used to do things that would normally be beyond the capability of the hardware and streamlines administration by placing all the configuration and software on one server. The biggest limitations result from server and networking hardware (for example, switch or hub, 1GB versus 100MB ports, high-end server and storage or less-expensive just-adequate equipment).

Requirements

Our minimum recommended specifications for thin clients are a processor running at 400MHz with 128MB RAM and the ability to boot via PXE (a common network boot protocol). Nearly any system sold today and advertised as a thin client exceeds these requirements by a wide margin. We list them here in case you want to try to reuse old hardware that is otherwise obsolete. Server and other hardware recommendations are listed in the "Installation" section.

Let's start by looking at several wiring schemes to show appropriate methods of using LTSP. The first one, shown in Figure 33.1, is the default install without an Internet connection and is the simplest way to use LTSP.

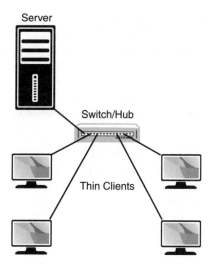

Server

Switch/Hub

Thin Clients

FIGURE 33.1   A default LTSP install without an Internet connection.

From the diagram alone, you can see the main pieces of hardware needed: a server, a switch/hub, and a number of thin clients. The switch/hub is the first piece of hardware we discuss.

For simplicity, we only show four thin clients in each example, but this is not an actual limit. The number of thin clients is limited by your switch/hub and even an inexpensive hub supports four connections, although it is common for quality enterprise-grade switches to have 48 or more ports. A switch is generally faster and more expensive than a hub and is often preferable for reasons beyond the scope of this chapter, but they both serve the same basic purpose, and either can work in an LTSP setting. They are used to control traffic on a network and make sure that communication happens between computers as it is intended.

Ideally, you want a piece of hardware here that supports a GB connection between the server and a switch, with at least 100MB connections between the thin clients and the switch, and enough unused communication ports to make future expansion easy without requiring the addition of another switch or hub and layer of complexity. If money is an issue and ideal performance isn't vital, an inexpensive hub that only had 100MB ports all around and just enough ports to connect everything will certainly work. If you are connecting more than 10 clients to the server, a gigabyte connection to the server is strongly recommended. Life is full of trade-offs, and money supplies are not limitless, so use your best judgment and buy the best you can afford.

For the server, recommended specifications depend greatly on the intended use. If everyone will be using the same program on each client, you do not need as much memory and processor speed as you would if everyone is doing different things at the same time. You can easily run LTSP server on a repurposed old machine you have sitting around with 512MB RAM, a 1GHz Celeron processor, and a decent, working hard drive, and it will work, but we don't really recommend that if you are going to have more than a couple of clients doing anything beyond simple and identical tasks.

Our minimum recommendation is the same as the current recommendation for a minimum Ubuntu desktop installation: a 1GHz x 86 processor, 1GB RAM, and a 15GB hard drive. At least a 100MB Ethernet card is vital. Ideally, you would bump each category up to the highest level you can afford and expect better performance as a result. Our minimum-if-you-want-a-great-experience recommendation is a current-issue fast-as-you-can-afford multicore 64-bit processor, 4GB RAM, at least two fast hard drives in a RAID array for performance and data backup, and at least one and perhaps two gigabyte Ethernet cards.

Most of the time you use LTSP you will want the network to be connected to the Internet. There are two main ways to do this. Figure 33.2 shows the network with an Internet connection via an Internet router connected to the switch/hub. This is a common method and works well.

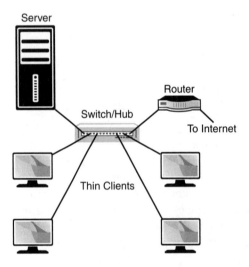

FIGURE 33.2   A typical LTSP install with an Internet connection via an Internet router.

Another common method is to connect the server directly to the Internet router as in Figure 33.3. This has the benefit of enabling you to easily configure and use the server as a gateway to control thin client access to the Internet. To do this, the server must have two network cards, and we again recommend that the one used to connect to the switch is a 1GB card; all the thin client traffic has to travel between the switch and server over that one connection, so a 1GB card will cause fewer bottlenecks than if you have multiple clients connecting to a switch at 100MB trying to share a single 100MB connection to a server. The card from the server to the Internet router should be adequate for the Internet connection available, but there is no reason to put anything faster in there. If you have only a 100MB connection with your Internet service provider, using a 1GB card will not give any particular benefit.

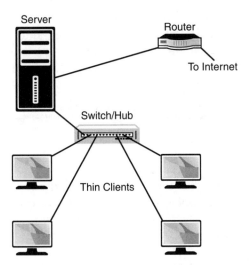

FIGURE 33.3   Using a server with two Ethernet cards as a portal to the Internet.

Installation

After you decide how you want to set up your network and connect all the hardware, you can get to the task of installing the software. In Ubuntu, the LTSP software is available for installation in two ways. If you are repurposing a server that already has a current release of Ubuntu installed on it, you install the ltsp-server-standalone and openssh-server packages from the Ubuntu repositories and run the following to set up the environment:

```
matthew@seymour:~$ sudo ltsp-build-client
```

If your server is a 64-bit system and your thin clients use a different processor architecture, you want to run that command with the --arch option, as follows:

```
matthew@seymour:~$ sudo ltsp-build-client --arch i386
```

Most people will be installing from scratch and not reusing a system with Ubuntu already installed. This is still quite easy. You must download the alternative install CD from the Ubuntu website at http://releases.ubuntu.com/. From here, find the release version of Ubuntu you want to use for the server. Some of you will want the current release (at this writing, 15.10), and others will want to use an LTS release like 14.04 LTS. Click the release version you want to use and then find the link for the alternative install CD for your server's processor architecture, either 32-bit or the 64-bit. Download it and burn the image to a CD as discussed in Chapter 1, "Installing Ubuntu and Post-Installation Configuration."

Make sure all your thin clients are connected and set to boot from network using PXE but turned off. Then boot the server using the alternative CD, press F4 for the Modes menu, and choose Install an LTSP Server. A regular Ubuntu installation begins. Near the end of the installation a message appears that lets you know the thin client system is being built on the server. You are notified that it is being compressed into an image, and when the process is complete you reboot your server, removing the CD at the appropriate moment in the process.

After the server has rebooted and is running, you may turn on your thin clients and they boot from the network using the image on the server. Thin clients can run any programs installed on the server.

Using LTSP

When you boot a thin client in an LTSP network, it retrieves the boot image from the LTSP server and uses it to create the environment to be displayed to the user. The process includes using *Dynamic Host Control Protocol (DHCP)* to request from and assign to the client an IP address on the network. The process then downloads the kernel and initial RAM disk from the server and then downloads the LTSP configuration and mounts the server-hosted file system. It uses chroot to use this file system as the client's own root file system and then finishes the boot using the instructions in that file system. This is a highly configurable process. By default, the client boots to a login screen using the *LTSP Display Manager (LDM)* in place of GDM that is used by Ubuntu, KDM that is used by Kubuntu, or others. User accounts are used to limit or control access, and the LDM initializes the details for communication between the server and client, including launching the desktop, mounting storage devices and /home directories, and creating menu items. The entire desktop is run on the server and displayed on the client.

By default, LTSP uses inherent abilities in Linux but has configured them to work together smoothly. You may modify details to suit your needs. For example, communication between an application server and a client is done by tunneling an X11 session over ssh, making the sharing of a graphical desktop easy and using a standard method while also being a secure method of communicating user credentials.

One really useful feature in LTSP is that you are not limited to using only one server in a network. If your network of thin clients grows to a point where your current server is being taxed, there is an easy way to configure and add a second or multiple servers to the network to share the load. In this case, the server that a thin client uses to boot is not necessarily the same server that a user will log in to. When you add servers, one server is chosen to be the primary server and controls thin client boots, data storage, and runs additional services. Additional, secondary servers can be much simpler because all they do is host desktop sessions and will be configured to use the central services from the primary server for everything else. In a multiple-server network, authentication of users is something that you need to think through and configure because it becomes a little more complex. There are many ways to do this, including the obvious choice: LDAP.

Creating and maintaining an LTSP network is very useful in specific situations and can be a cost-effective way of using administrator time while providing useful functionality to end users. Although the foundation sounds simple in this introductory chapter, it can be a complex task worthy of an entire book. Our intent with this chapter is to give enough information for you to determine whether LTSP is a technology that suits your needs and is deserving of a closer look. To that end, we offer several useful links in the following section and suggest them as your next step.

References

▶ www.ltsp.org/—The official upstream LTSP website.

▶ https://help.ubuntu.com/community/UbuntuLTSP—The Ubuntu community documentation page, which is easily the best resource for LTSP because it includes an organized and up-to-date set of links to information on any aspect you should need.

▶ https://help.ubuntu.com/community/UbuntuLTSP/Tour—This gives an overview of the differences between a traditional LTSP installation and the Ubuntu community modifications to the process for ease of installation, software updates, and security.

▶ https://help.ubuntu.com/community/UbuntuLTSP/ThinClientHowtoNAT/—If you use the network design in Figure 33.3, this tells you how to configure your server so that your thin clients have access to the Internet.

A sampling of companies advertising thin clients:

▶ www.artecgroup.com/thincan

▶ http://www.chippc.com/products/

▶ http://www.devonit.com/thin-client-solutions

▶ www.disklessworkstations.com/

▶ www.lucidatech.com/

▶ http://www.dell.com/us/business/p/cloud-client-computing?~ck=bt#!tabId=8886AFAC

Virtualization on Ubuntu

Virtualization is an important topic today, but it isn't a difficult one to understand, at least conceptually. We cover two distinct use cases in this chapter: server virtualization and virtualization on the desktop. Most of the options covered in this chapter work for either use case. In the sections that follow, this chapter points out specific moments that are focused solely on one use case. There are several scenarios, both large and small, that are helpful to illustrate the potential of virtualization and to give the idea some definition.

For starters, imagine a large corporation or business that processes huge amounts of data. That corporation has many dedicated computers to assist with the task. In the past, they might have used mainframes, single computers capable of performing multiple tasks concurrently while dealing with large data sets and multiple, concurrent users. Today, the same company might use a server farm, a network of smaller computers that is extensible and which can have specific servers in the network dedicated to precise tasks.

The problem is that some of these servers do not get used to their capacity. Take, for example, a payroll server that might get extensive use at certain times, but which might sit nearly idle at other times. That seems like a waste of resources.

What if a systems administrator could pool the resources of all these machines and then dole those resources out as they are needed? She can by using virtualization.

At other times, there is a need for servers that do not exist and which will not be needed in the long term. A statistics department might have a one-time need for extra processing power for a big project. It would take a long time to set up a dedicated server, and it is hard to justify the effort for a one-time task.

What if a system administrator could easily create and destroy servers for a specific task, making them appear, completely configured, as needed and then making them disappear when the need no longer exists, freeing up the physical resources for other uses? He can by using virtualization.

Networks of physical servers can be created using virtualization where the physical resources of each server are pooled together and then passed out as designated by an administrator. It is as if, instead of having 10 servers, each with 4 processors, 8GB of RAM, and 100GB of physical disk storage, you now have one huge resource pool with 40 processors, 80GB of RAM, and 1TB of disk space. Virtual machines can then use these resources.

A *virtual machine (VM)* is a computer that operates on top of a virtualization layer, often called a hypervisor. It isn't real in the sense that it runs on defined, discrete physical resources, but it does all of the same tasks as a "real" computer. The virtualization layer on which the VM runs defines a set of virtual interfaces for the VM, which appear to VM's operating system as if they were real network cards, memory, hard drives, and so on. In a sense, virtualization fools the guest operating system in the VM into thinking it is running on specific physical equipment that is emulated by the virtualization software while the virtualization software takes care of the details of interacting with the actual hardware, which may even change without affecting the VM. This is called *hardware emulation*, sometimes abbreviated to emulation.

Virtual machines are flexible; their allocated resources may be changed, in some cases without any downtime. A VM can be created quickly, as needed, and then removed when it is no longer needed, to make the resources it was using once again available to the pool. Servers that are vital but generally use few resources that can be created using far fewer resources than one of the physical servers in the pool. Others that are needed for larger tasks might be able to take advantage of the resources of many physical servers in the pool.

It is possible for VMs to be created and then have their image saved, so that instead of starting with operating system installation each time a VM is created, the VM starts up with a full operating system and installed programs all configured to work together for a desired task. One neat trick is to run a set of servers locally and then add compute resources from a cloud computing pool such as Amazon's EC2, Ubuntu Enterprise Cloud (using Eucalyptus), Ubuntu Cloud Infrastructure (using OpenStack), or OpenStack to start up VMs on their network as needed, using them while paying for the time they are running and then deleting them (see Chapter 35, "Ubuntu in the Cloud"). This saves a lot of time and money.

Some readers might think, "That sounds great, but I run only one machine, and it is my desktop (or laptop)." Virtualization might be useful to you, as well. Have you ever wanted to test out a different operating system than the one you are using? Perhaps you found that you have a need to run a specific program that only runs on Windows, but you have Ubuntu installed on your system. Maybe you want to run the latest development version of Ubuntu to help with testing, but you don't want to use it as your main system operating system. You might want to try out another distribution of Linux or even BSD. In the past, doing these things might involve partitioning your hard drive and installing both operating systems side by side. That worked, but you couldn't easily move data from one to the other, and you couldn't run both operating systems at the same time. Wouldn't it be great if you could run another operating system as a guest on your same machine? You can with virtualization.

There is a trade-off with virtualization, depending on the software used. Some virtualization software runs as an additional layer on top of another operating system. This is great if you want to test something while running on your local desktop machine, but it can add some unwanted and sometimes unacceptable delays when creating a new server. Other virtualization software runs on or near "bare metal," meaning that the virtualization software is either a part of the operating system kernel or runs as the operating system and there are no other software layers between it and the physical resources being used/managed. This method is faster but not as convenient on the desktop, at least for users who are not as technically advanced.

Virtualization is not new. For example, IBM had useful virtualization running on its mainframes in the 1960s. What has created the recent buzz is that the technology became available to perform the task on much less-expensive x86 hardware.

In November 2005, Intel released its first processors that supported an extension called VT-x, which allows virtualization software access to the processor and other hardware. Before this, virtualization on any x86 platform was slow because it required difficult software workarounds and massaging to get it working. VT-x is available on many of Intel's processors, but not necessarily all of them as it is one of the ways that Intel differentiates the processors to segment their marketing across various price points. Also, with some motherboards, the extension is not enabled by default but must be enabled in the BIOS before it becomes available.

Following closely behind is AMD, who in May 2006 released virtualization extensions for their processors. Called AMD-V, these extensions are available on many of AMD's processors, but not on all AMD processors, as this is a higher-end feature.

A related topic deserves a quick mention here. In the cloud, the idea of "containers" has become quite popular. If you are interested in virtualization for use in cloud computing, read the coverage of containers in Chapter 35, "Ubuntu in the Cloud," before you make any decisions.

KVM

The *Kernel-based Virtual Machine (KVM)* is a part of the Linux kernel. KVM does not perform hardware emulation, but only provides the lower-level tasks. It needs a second layer to run in user space. This is much faster than running the entire virtualization process in user space, on top of another operating system. KVM is designed for use on processors that have either the VT-x or AMD-V extension enabled. Managing VMs with KVM in Ubuntu is accomplished using libvirt and QEMU. You can check whether a system has the extensions enabled by installing and running the `kvm-ok` package. It is a simple command-line tool that exits with output `0` if the system is suitable or non-`0` if not.

Start by installing the following packages from the Ubuntu software repositories: `qemu-kvm`, `libvirt-bin`, `virtinst`, and `bridge-utils`:

▶ **qemu-kvm** is the necessary user-space component of KVM.

▶ **libvirt-bin** is a binary of a C toolkit to interact with the virtualization capabilities of Linux and currently supports not only KVM, but also XEN, VirtualBox, and more.

▶ **virtinst** is a set of command-line tools for creating VMs.

▶ **bridge-utils** is a set of utilities for configuring Ethernet connections in Linux.

You might want to add `virt-viewer`, which provides a nice GUI and VNC interface to VMs, and `virt-manager`, which provides a nice GUI for managing VMs. If installed, you can find both in the Dash listing of applications.

Log out and back in so that the automatic addition of your user to the `libvirtd` group is certain to be made effective.

By default, any operating system you install as a guest using KVM has access to network services but is not visible to other machines on the network. It is able to download software updates and browse the Web, for example, but it cannot run as a server accessible by other systems. By default, VMs receive an IP address in the 10.0.2.0/24 range and hosts are reachable from within a VM using 10.0.2.2. This should be adequate for simple uses such as testing other operating systems, copying files back and forth using `scp`, or making *virtual private network (VPN)* connections from a host to a guest.

BRIDGED NETWORKING

If you want to change the network settings to enable the use of a VM as an outside-accessible server, you need bridged networking. This enables VMs to use a physical interface to connect to the outside network, making them appear to the rest of the network as any other typical server. Note that to do this you must not use the default Network Manager to control the hardware being bridged. Also this works only with wired, not wireless hardware. See Chapter 18, "Networking," if you need help understanding the concepts used here.

To start, install `libcap2-bin`. Next, you need to grant QEMU the ability to administer networking by setting `cap_net_admin`. If you have a 64-bit system, use the following:

matthew@seymour:~$ **sudo setcap cap_net_admin=ei /usr/bin/qemu-system-x86_64**

And if you have a 32-bit system, use this:

matthew@seymour:~$ **sudo setcap cap_net_admin=ei /usr/bin/qemu**

Then create a bridge interface called `br0` in `/etc/network/interfaces` by adding these lines to use DHCP or your network settings if you want to configure it yourself:

```
auto br0
iface br0 inet dhcp
        bridge_ports eth0
```

```
        bridge_stp off
    bridge_fd 0
    bridge_maxwait 0
```

Restart networking by entering this:

matthew@seymour:~$ **sudo /etc/init.d/networking restart**

Finally, you need to create guest VMs that use this bridged network. Manually define your guest OS to use the new br0 interface, as you usually would in that operating system.

There are several ways to create VMs for use with KVM. One way is vmbuilder. This is a Python script that is best for servers on which you intend to run Ubuntu JeOS, a specialized, very light Ubuntu server variant that includes a tuned kernel with only the base elements necessary to run as a virtual server, especially under KVM and VMware. Install python-vm-builder to get the package. You run vmbuilder from the command line with two necessary parameters: the virtualization software and the distribution you will run. However, there are literally tons of useful options and customizations available. Here is an example that builds a VM for KVM from the 15.10 (WilyWerewolf) release of Ubuntu using the virtual flavor (for example, JeOS) in an i386 architecture while overwriting any previous edition of the VM, instructing libvirt to inform the local virtualization environment to add the resulting VM to the list of available virtual machines, give the new VM a specific IP address, the hostname lovelace, and to use the br0 bridge interface. Phew! That's a lot in one command.

matthew@seymour:~$ **sudo vmbuilder kvm ubuntu --suite wily --flavour virtual --arch**
➥**i386 -o --libvirt qemu:///system --ip 192.168.0.100 --hostname lov elace**
➥**--bridge br0**

You can learn more from the help file:

matthew@seymour:~$ **vmbuilder kvm ubuntu --help**

Because vmbuilder is so specialized, here we focus on using the tools from virtinst as they are more likely to appeal to a general audience. However, if you are looking to create server VMs to run on a KVM or VMware installation, you definitely want to explore vmbuilder more fully. However, you might not need to do so. A set of official, prebuilt and Ubuntu-supported VM images are available for download at http://cloud-images .ubuntu.com. These are the exact images that Ubuntu uses in EC2.

> **NOTE**
>
> One of the Ubuntu Server developers, Dustin Kirkland, has a blog post outlining a method for preseeding Ubuntu Server installations, making the process even faster. You can read it at http://blog.dustinkirkland.com/2011/03/ubuntu-server-quick-install-no.html

---

virtinst consists of several tools. Here we focus on two: virt-install, to provision new virtual machines; and virt-clone, to clone existing virtual machines.

You can do similar things with `virt-install` as was done earlier with `vmbuilder`. The major difference are the options available and that `virt-install` can also make desktop images that include a GUI, accessible using VNC. See Chapter 19, "Remote Access with SSH, Telnet, and VNC," for a discussion of VNC.

Here is an example:

```
matthew@seymour:~$ sudo virt-install -n hopper -r 512 --disk
↳path=/var/lib/libvirt/images/hopper.img,size=20 -c /dev/cdrom --accelerate --
↳connect=qemu:///system --vnc --noautoconsole -v
```

The preceding example includes the following options:

▶ `-n hopper` defines the name of the new VM.

▶ `-r 512` specifies the amount of memory the virtual machine will be allotted, in megabytes.

▶ `--disk path=...` is the path to the virtual disk. It can be a file, a partition, or a logical volume. Here we create a 20GB file named `hopper.img` in `/var/lib/libvirt/images`.

▶ `-c /dev/cdrom` is the path to the host's CD-ROM device. You can also use an ISO file.

▶ `--accelerate` enables use of the kernel's acceleration.

▶ `--connect` defines the hypervisor to use.

▶ `--vnc` exports the guest using a VNC virtual console.

▶ `--noautoconsole` prevents automatic connecting to the virtual machine's console.

▶ `-v` creates a fully virtualized guest.

To copy a virtual machine, use `virt-clone`:

```
matthew@seymour:~$ sudo virt-clone -o hopper -n knuth -f /var/lib/libvirt/images/
↳knuth.img –connect=qemu:///system
```

The preceding example includes the following options:

▶ `-o hopper` defines the name of the origin or source VM.

▶ `-n knuth` defines the name of the new VM.

▶ `-f` defines the path to the file, partition, or logical volume that the new VM will use.

▶ `--connect` defines the hypervisor to use.

To start a virtual machine, use the following:

```
matthew@seymour:~$ virsh -c qemu:///system start hopper
```

To stop a virtual machine, use this:

```
matthew@seymour:~$ virsh -c qemu:///system shutdown hopper
```

After a VM is installed and running, you can connect to it using the configured IP address and a utility like `ssh`. You can also use a GUI with the following:

```
matthew@seymour:~$ virt-viewer -c qemu:///system hopper
```

You may use a GUI to manage your VMs by connecting to the following:

```
matthew@seymour:~$ virt-manager -c qemu:///system
```

If you are interested in an easy way to use KVM to test Ubuntu development versions, see Chapter 41, "Helping with Ubuntu Testing and QA," and the discussion of Test Drive, which automates this entire process, including the downloading of specific Ubuntu ISO files.

VirtualBox

VirtualBox is much easier to use than KVM, especially if all you want to do is run a second operating system on top of Ubuntu. It was created by innotek GmbH, purchased by Sun Microsystems, and is now owned and developed by Oracle after their purchase of Sun. VirtualBox is installed on top of another operating system, so it isn't ideal for processing intensive activity where every processor cycle counts. However, for testing or for running another operating system because you need specific applications, it is great. VirtualBox runs on top of most UNIX-type operating systems such as Linux, BSD, and Mac OS X (as well as on Windows).

There is a version of VirtualBox in the Ubuntu software repositories, but in general downloading the one from the VirtualBox website is a better idea. Go to www.virtualbox.org/wiki/Downloads. From there, you can download a version for any operating system you are likely to use, including on the Linux page an Ubuntu DEB file that installs using the *Advanced Packing Tool (APT)*, so package management isn't a problem. However, this also gives you easy access to download the extension pack, which isn't available in the Ubuntu repositories, so you can get it installed quickly and easily. The extension pack adds a few nice, but proprietary, features that cannot be made available under the GPL used for the main program, such the ability to connect to the USB port of a host computer from a guest VM in VirtualBox. After you've installed it, start VirtualBox at the command line using the following:

```
matthew@seymour:~$ virtualbox
```

If you want to be able to close your terminal and keep VirtualBox running, run VirtualBox in the background by putting an ampersand (&) after the command, like this:

```
matthew@seymour:~$ virtualbox &
```

Either way, when you are done, just close the GUI program and VirtualBox shuts down. When you run either, the GUI appears (Figure 34.1).

FIGURE 34.1   Oracle VM VirtualBox Manager.

From here you can create a new VM by selecting New at the top left. Change the settings on any currently installed VM by selecting Settings. Start any installed VM by selecting Start. Delete any VM by selecting Discard. You can see details of the currently selected VM using Details at the upper right or your saved snapshots of existing VMs using Snapshots. Everything is configurable from the GUI. VirtualBox is easy and intuitive to use, even for a complete novice.

From the GUI, you can clone a machine, export it, and import it on another machine running VirtualBox. A command-line interface is available for scripting, focused on VM management activities. You can run VirtualBox headless and access it using *Remote Display Protocol (RDP)*. These activities are beyond the scope of this book but can make VirtualBox a little more interesting to someone who wants to run VMs remotely (although most who are going to go through the trouble would probably go ahead and use KVM and connect to a VM using VNC).

VMware

VMware is an enterprise-focused virtualization platform. The company offers a limited-feature version that runs on the desktop for free and also sells a full-featured version. It runs well, is easy to use, and has better features than VirtualBox. It also requires buying a new license each year, and the license isn't cheap. Their enterprise server offerings are considered by many to be the most powerful and well-featured in the business. The VMware software runs on bare metal; it is the operating system that gets installed on all the servers in a VMware installation. Then, all the resources are controlled from one central location. VMs can be moved while running from one physical machine to another in the system with no loss of usability and no downtime. This can even be done automatically based on administrator-set criteria, such as bandwidth, available memory, or processor load. It is also quite expensive to license. VMware is primarily designed for use by large corporations in enterprise environments. It deserves a mention here but is not really targeted toward the same audience as this book.

Xen

Xen is a well-known open-source virtualization platform. It is in widespread use by researchers, hobbyists, developers, and others. Web hosting companies that offer virtual servers often use Xen. Generally, Xen installs on bare metal, like VMware. It can be installed on top of another operating system in a host/guest arrangement. However, in 2008, Ubuntu made a decision not to support Xen. Instead, the Ubuntu community has focused its efforts on KVM. This is not a value statement that one is better than the other, but only that KVM seemed to be a better fit for the needs of an Ubuntu developer community that did not have the resources to give quality support to two similar virtualization platforms. It does appear possible to run Xen on Ubuntu, but there are no guarantees. For this reason, many choose to use one of the Linux distributions that use Xen as their primary virtualization platform, such as SUSE, Red Hat, or CentOS, if Xen is preferred. At the time this book was being written, rumors began to surface that Ubuntu will once again support Xen in the near future, but no solid news was yet available.

References

- ▶ www.linux-kvm.org—The main page for KVM.
- ▶ www.virtualbox.org—The main page for VirtualBox.
- ▶ www.vmware.com—The main page for VMware.
- ▶ http://www.xenproject.org/—The main page for Xen.

CHAPTER 35

Ubuntu in the Cloud

Cloud computing enables you to build large, flexible systems for on-demand processing of data. When your requirements are low, you use few resources. As the need arises, your processes scale to use multiple systems with optimized performance according to the requirements of the moment. This is an efficient way to use hardware and minimize waste.

To accomplish this feat of computer engineering, a special network is set up using on-demand virtual systems that consume resources only as needed and release those resources for use by others when they are not in use. Virtualization is the technology that enables this concept. This may be accomplished locally using third-party virtualization platforms such as VMware, VirtualBox, Parallels, and others (see Chapter 34, "Virtualization on Ubuntu"). Ubuntu has another option to offer, the Ubuntu Cloud, which moves virtualization into the cloud and is the main focus of this chapter. Beyond being an outstanding cloud hosting platform, Ubuntu Server is being developed with a strong intent to make it an outstanding cloud guest. Look for the term *Ubuntu cloud guest* to become more popular as time goes by.

SYSADMIN VERSUS DEVOPS

The traditional title for someone who keeps systems up and running is *systems administrator*, or *sysadmin* (sometimes called *ops*, for *operations*). The traditional title for someone who creates the software that runs on those systems is software developer. Over the past few years, a new title has emerged, *DevOps*. DevOps combine many of the talents and responsibilities of sysadmins and developers, but often with a cloud computing environment focus and some specific refinements. They aren't purely one or the other and often don't fit neatly into other existing categories like engineer, but they do combine many of the skills of all of these while adding to it a QA-like focus on making sure that new features do not break anything that was working previously. DevOps are the ones who develop large applications to run on cloud resources while simplifying the orchestration of those resources with automation and configuration management. This chapter is not only for DevOps, but the chapter describes the sorts of tools and environments that these folks are likely to love.

Ubuntu Cloud is a stack of applications from Canonical that are included in the Ubuntu Server Edition. These applications make it easy to install and configure an Ubuntu-based cloud. The software is free and open source, but Canonical offers paid technical support.

INSTALL INSTRUCTIONS

Install instructions change regularly and the most up-to-date version is always on the provider's site. Instead, in this chapter we provide a high-level view to help you understand how a cloud can be set up and work, why you should care, who the big players are, and where to look for the next steps.

Why a Cloud?

Businesses and enterprises have built computer networks for years. There are many reasons, but usually networks are built because specific computation or data processing tasks are made easier and faster using more than one computer. The size of the network generally depends on the tasks that need to be done. Building a network usually entails taking a detailed survey of needs, analyzing those requirements, and gathering together the necessary hardware and software to fulfill those needs now, perhaps with a little room for growth if money permits.

Cloud computing is designed to make that easier by providing resources such as computing power and storage as services on the Internet in a way that is easy to access remotely, available on demand, simple to provision and scale, and highly dynamic. In the ideal case, this saves both time and money.

Some of the greatest benefits are the ease with which new resources may be added to a cloud, the fault tolerance inherent in the built-in redundancy of a large pool of servers, and the payment schedules that charge for resources only when they are used. There is also a great benefit in abstracting the complexity out of the process; clients perform the tasks they want to perform, and the cloud computing platform takes care of the details of adding resources as needed without the end user being aware of the process. *Virtual machines (VMs)* are created, configured, and used when needed and destroyed immediately after they are no longer needed, freeing up system resources for other purposes. These VMs can be created to suit a wide range of needs.

Hardware, storage, networks, and software are abstracted as services instead of being manually built and configured. They are then accessed locally on demand when the additional resources are required. Sometimes these service model abstractions are referred to as *software as a service (SaaS)*, *platform as a service (PaaS)*, and *infrastructure as a service (IaaS)*.

Software as a Service (SaaS)

SaaS is sometimes referred to as *on-demand software*. In this service model, it is the software application and its related data that are moved to the cloud. Access is generally through a web browser, although a thin client and server style configuration are not uncommon. Someone else takes care of everything else. This is kind of like renting a hotel room— everything is provided and set up for you and you just enjoy and use it for a specific need. Some examples of this include email hosts like Yahoo! Mail, services like Google Docs, web games, and customer relationship management (CRM) software.

Platform as a Service (PaaS)

PaaS takes things a step further. In this service model, an entire computing platform is provided in the cloud. This typically includes the operating system, programming language interpreters or execution environments, databases, web servers, and so on. They are accessed directly for computing platform maintenance using provider portals, application programming interfaces (APIs), software development kits (SDKs), or services like SSH. Then, what is built on the platform is accessed by the end user the same way it would be accessed if it were running on a locally owned and operated piece of hardware or hardware that's running in a large datacenter. Someone else takes care of everything else, but they take care of less than they do with SaaS, which means that you take care of more. This scenario is more like an apartment—you rent the space and decorate and configure it as you like within structured guidelines. Some examples of this include the Google App Engine, raw compute nodes used to scale services, and social application platforms like Facebook.

Infrastructure as a Service (IaaS)

IaaS goes even further. In this service model, you are transitioning your entire server to the cloud. Your provider offers computers, most like virtual ones, on which you can install any operating system (perhaps within a set menu they allow) and you can configure it as you like. Someone else takes care of the physical machines and networks, and you take care of all the rest. This is like buying a condominium—you own it and can do whatever you want inside it, but someone else takes care of the grounds and landscaping.

Metal as a Service (MaaS)

Generally, the only other step available from here is traditional server building, where you are responsible for the physical machine and everything on it. However, Ubuntu has added another service to the list, *Metal as a Service (MaaS)*, which is designed to bring the language of the cloud to physical servers. Their goal is to make it as easy to set up the physical hardware, to deploy your app or service, and to scale up or down dynamically as it is in the cloud. It is installed on the physical hardware and then managed using one web interface to manage all the various machines. There is a section later in this chapter dedicated to this topic.

Before You Do Anything

You don't have to create your own cloud infrastructure, but you can. You can also deploy Ubuntu Cloud to providers like Rackspace or HP. Before you do anything, you need to carefully consider what your needs are and decide what sort of service(s) you need. Do you just want to run a web application on someone else's already-set-up server, or do you want to set up a system for scalable computing where additional Hadoop nodes can be added and removed at will when big jobs start and end? Only you know the answer. When you have it figured out, you can seek your solution and can think about how you can use Ubuntu to set it up. This chapter describes many options, but you are the one who is in control. That is a powerful, and sometimes overwhelming, position. Thought and planning prevent painful mistakes and repeated engineering.

Deploy/Install Basics: Public, Private, or Hybrid?

There are two ways to deploy Ubuntu in the cloud: on a private cloud or on a public cloud. Both have benefits and drawbacks. This section presents the things you need to consider when choosing. We also look at a way to mix the two, which is called a *hybrid cloud*.

A *public cloud* is built on a cloud provider's systems. This means your local hardware requirements are minimal, your startup costs are low, deployment is quick, and growth is easy. This can be incredibly useful for testing, and has gained the stability and reputation for also being a great idea for production. The drawback to working this way is that you do not physically control the hardware on which your cloud is running. For many this is a benefit, but this might not be suitable for high security needs. Although you alone control the software and processes on your public cloud, there might be some worry about who has access to the machines. Although a cloud provider would not last long in business if its data centers and machines were not secure, some applications and data are so sensitive you cannot afford to allow *any* outside risk. Legal constraints, such as from the Sarbanes-Oxley Act, sometimes force IT policy decisions in an organization and make the public option impossible.

A *private cloud* is created on hardware you own and control. This requires a large upfront commitment, but you have the security of running everything behind a company firewall and with complete knowledge of who is able to physically access your machines and who is listening on the network.

One thing to consider is the possibility of starting your Ubuntu Cloud as a private cloud and then creating interfaces from there to public services, creating a hybrid cloud. Perhaps you prefer to keep some of your data and services stored on the private cloud, but you have other data that is less sensitive and want to use some services and applications on a public cloud. This is an avenue worth exploring if your company has a mixture of "must be secured and held in-house" and "we still want to keep it away from prying eyes, but if something happens it won't be catastrophic" needs. The big issue with this method is moving data between public and private servers; if you have large amounts of data that may move between the two, this can be prohibitive. As always, do your due diligence.

Ubuntu Cloud and OpenStack

OpenStack is an Apache-licensed cloud computing platform. It was founded as a collaboration between NASA and Rackspace. After less than a year, it boasted a worldwide community of developers. Adoption has been swift, and already many large corporations, universities, and institutions are using OpenStack for cloud computing. Ubuntu and OpenStack have worked closely together for a long time, have similar release schedules, and Ubuntu is the reference operating system for OpenStack.

OpenStack is not a service provider. They don't operate systems or data centers. OpenStack is open-source software for building public and private and hybrid clouds. There are many companies who have implemented and use OpenStack, which is a good thing. This means that if you develop your cloud deployment and it works on one company's servers, if they are using OpenStack, you can move that deployment to another company's servers with little or even no changes, if the second company is also running OpenStack. In fact, it is easy enough to create your deployment across several different providers, using cloud servers from multiple companies concurrently according to your needs.

For a current list of cloud providers offering OpenStack to customers for cloud deployments, see http://www.openstack.org/marketplace/public-clouds/. You will find big names like HP and Rackspace along with many you have not yet heard of who may be just a suitable or perhaps even better for your needs.

Many cloud providers offer free trials that give users a certain amount of usage for a limited amount of time. This can be handy for testing out the capabilities of different providers while testing out deployments of components of your system.

One interesting option while you are exploring and learning about cloud computing is DevStack, from http://devstack.org, which is a shell script with documentation that builds complete OpenStack development environments. This is not an option designed for production environments, but it can be very useful for getting started and testing the capabilities of cloud computing. The program and the documentation are maintained by a community of developers rather than one company, again emphasizing the portability aspect.

If what you read in this chapter interests you, the combination of a free trial period and DevStack may provide you with an easy way to try out what you are learning.

OpenStack uses a set of APIs for its services that are compatible with the Amazon EC2/S3 APIs. Client tools written for those can also be used with OpenStack. OpenStack has several main service families, each described in the following subsections.

OpenStack is in active development. Newer releases may have details that differ from what is recorded in this chapter. Check the official OpenStack website, listed in the "Resources," section of this chapter, for current details.

Compute Infrastructure (Nova)

Nova manages the compute resources, networking, and scaling for the OpenStack cloud. By itself, it does not perform any virtualization tasks, but rather it uses `libvirt` APIs to interact with supported hypervisors and is the management component of the system. Nova has an Amazon EC2-compatible RESTful API.

Nova consists of several components:

▶ `nova-api`—The API server provides an interface to enable outside systems to interact with the cloud infrastructure.

▶ `rabbit-mq`—The message queue server performs asynchronous calls to communicate with other Nova components, such as the scheduler or the network controller.

▶ `Qpid`—Like `rabbit-mq`, this is a message queue server and has similar functions. Research both to see which is the best fit for your situation.

▶ `nova-compute`—The compute nodes' host instances. They carry out operations based on requests received by the message queue. Instances are deployed on available compute nodes based on a scheduling algorithm managed by the scheduler.

▶ `nova-network`—The network controller allocates IP addresses, configures VLANs, configures networks, and implements security groups for compute nodes. It is expected that this will eventually be replaced by Neutron, when Neutron is ready.

▶ `nova-volume`—The volume worker manage *Logical Volume Manager (LVM)*–based storage volumes. They create and delete volumes, attach and detach volumes from instances, and provide persistent storage for use by instances.

▶ `nova-scheduler`—The scheduler uses an adjustable algorithm to determine which compute, network, or storage volume servers should be used from an available pool of resources. Schedules can be configured based on server loads, availability zones, or random chance.

Storage Infrastructure (Swift)

Swift is an object store. It is scalable up to multiple petabytes and billions of objects. It is elastic. It has built-in redundancy and failover. Swift is designed to store a very large number of objects distributed across a commodity hardware.

Networking Service (Neutron)

Neutron provides "networking as a service" between interface devices (e.g., vNICs) managed by other Openstack services (e.g., nova).

Identity Service (Keystone)

Keystone is the identity service used for authentication (authN) and high-level authorization (authZ). It supports token-based authN and user-service authorization.

Imaging Service (Glance)

Glance is a lookup and retrieval system for VM images. It can use one of three back ends: OpenStack Object Store, S3 storage, or S3 Storage using the OpenStack Object Store as an intermediary.

Dashboard (Horizon)

Horizon is the standard implementation of OpenStack's Dashboard, which provides a web-based user interface to OpenStack services including Nova, Swift, Neutron, Keystone, etc.

Learning More

OpenStack has many more features not discussed here. Some include OpenStack Heat, from https://wiki.openstack.org/wiki/Heat, for orchestration and management of infrastructure and applications within an OpenStack cloud and OpenStack Ironic, from https://wiki.openstack.org/wiki/Ironic, which is a bare metal provisioning program. See https://wiki.openstack.org/wiki/Programs for a current list of official Open Stack programs.

Juju

Juju has been described as APT for the cloud. As you learned from Chapter 9, "Managing Software," APT does an amazing job of installing, configuring, and starting complicated software stacks and services, but only as long as all of that happens on only one system. Juju extends this ability across multiple machines. Often, Linux servers are set up for similar tasks. Multiple physical machines may be deployed with similar configurations to work with one another in a network, perhaps for load distribution or redundancy to prevent downtime in the event of one failing or being overloaded. Systems administrators are masters at creating and orchestrating these networks. However, doing so traditionally requires setting up each machine individually, configuring its software settings and so on.

Tools have appeared over the years to help with this great task, such as Chef and Puppet; see Chapter 36, "Managing Sets of Servers," for a little more about these. Juju works to do for servers what package managers do for individual systems. It enables you to deploy services quickly and easily across multiple servers, simplifying the configuration process, and is particularly designed with cloud servers in mind. As with Chef's recipes, those services are deployed using formulas that standardize communication, for example, and which may have been written by different people.

What makes Juju different from Chef and Puppet is that the Juju formulas, called *charms*, encapsulate services, defining all the ways that services need to expose or consume configuration data to or from other services. This can be done many ways in the Juju charm, including via shell scripts or using Chef itself in solo mode. Also, Juju orchestrates provisioning by tracking its available resources (such as EC2, Eucalyptus, or OpenStack machines) and adding or removing them as appropriate.

Juju is pretty cool, but it hasn't seen much serious adoption outside of Canonical, especially now that the OpenStack tools are growing in number and scope. However, it does have some unique features and it definitely is worth your consideration.

Getting Started

Start by installing Juju on a server:

```
matthew@wolfram~$: sudo apt-get install juju
```

> **NOTE**
>
> The release of Juju 2.0 is imminent as this chapter is being revised, but some command syntax and details are still changing and it is not yet ready. This chapter currently introduces Juju 1.25. See the Juju website listed in this chapter's "Resources" section for the most current version and technical details.

Next, you must bootstrap the system, configuring it to use either a cloud resource, like Amazon Web Services or EC2 or your local environment (if you are using a local machine for development and testing). The specific information you enter here will differ, but the initial command is always the same:

```
matthew@wolfram~$: juju bootstrap
```

The first time this is run, it creates a file, `~/.juju/environments/yaml`, which looks something like the following:

```
default: sample
environments:
  sample:
    type: ec2
    control-bucket: juju-faefb490d69a41f0a3616a4808e0766b
    admin-secret: 81a1e7429e6847c4941fda7591246594
    default-series: precise
    juju-origin: ppa
    ssl-hostname-verification: true
```

The preceding sample was taken directly from the official Juju documentation. Yours will look different in some places and also needs to be adjusted appropriately with your settings. For example, if you are using Amazon AWS, you will probably want to add lines to this file with your AWS access key and secret key so that Juju can access and use your Amazon AWS account. Because the typical Juju user is a DevOps or SysAdmin type who has been doing this sort of thing manually for a while, we will gloss over this step and move on.

Bootstrapping takes a few minutes. If you want to check on the status of your Juju deployment, enter

```
matthew@wolfram~$: juju status
```

You see something similar to the following (again from the official Juju docs):

```
machines:
  0:
    agent-state: running
```

```
      dns-name: ec2-50-16-107-102.compute-1.amazonaws.com
      instance-id: i-130c9168
      instance-state: running
services:
```

When the status shows the deployment up and running, it is a good idea to start a debug log session. This is not required but makes troubleshooting much easier, should it be needed.

matthew@wolfram~$: **juju debug-log**

Now comes the fun part, deploying service units. We chose a simple one for our sample: deploying a WordPress blog on our server with all needed services. This is done using *charms*, which are prepackaged installation and configuration details for specific services. Here's how it works:

matthew@wolfram~$: **juju deploy mysql**
matthew@wolfram~$: **juju deploy wordpress**

Now, your services are deployed, but they are not yet connected with each other. We do this by adding relations, in this case:

matthew@wolfram~$: **juju add-relation wordpress mysql**

Now, if you check your status as shown earlier, you see something like this:

```
machines:
  0:
    agent-state: running
    dns-name: localhost
    instance-id: local
    instance-state: running
services:
  mysql:
    charm: cs:precise/mysql-3
    relations:
      db:
      - wordpress
    units:
      mysql/0:
        agent-state: started
        machine: 2
        public-address: 192.168.122.165
  wordpress:
    charm: cs:precise/wordpress-3
    exposed: false
    relations:
```

```
   db:
    - mysql
  units:
    wordpress/0:
      agent-state: started
      machine: 1
      public-address: 192.168.122.166
```

Now, expose your WordPress service to the world so that you can connect with it from outside the server:

```
matthew@wolfram~$: juju expose wordpress
```

And as simple as that, your install is ready. Using the public-address shown earlier in the status message, open 192.168.122.166 in your browser, and you should go to your WordPress configuration page.

What happens if you get your WordPress blog set up and running and then it suddenly gets popular? In a traditional setting, you would need to reinstall on heftier equipment and migrate the database over. Not here. Instead you just add units:

```
matthew@wolfram~$: juju add-unit wordpress
```

This creates a new WordPress instance, joins the relation with the existing WordPress instance, discovers in that configuration that it is related to a specific MySQL database, and also relates this one. That's it. One command and you are done!

When a Juju-created environment is no longer needed, there is only one command to issue:

```
matthew@wolfram~$: juju destroy-environment
```

Beware, this command also destroys all service data, so if you are doing something that is important long-term, make sure you extract your data first.

Charms

Charms define how services are to be deployed and integrated and how they react to events. Juju orchestrates all of this based on the instructions in charms. Charms are created using plain text metadata files. These files, with the extension .yaml, describe the details needed for deployment. These are the supported fields in a charm:

- ▶ **name**—The name of the charm.
- ▶ **summary**—A one-line description.
- ▶ **maintainer**—This must include an email address for the main point of contact.
- ▶ **description**—A long description of the charm and its features.
- ▶ **provides**—Relations that are made available from this charm.

▶ **requires**—Relations that must already exist for this charm to work.

▶ **peers**—Relations that work together with this charm.

This sounds complicated, and it is. But with a little study, anyone who knows enough about a service can write a charm for it. Here are example charms for the two services we deployed earlier. First, MySQL:

```
name: mysql
summary: "A pretty popular database"
maintainer: "Juju Charmers <juju@lists.ubuntu.com>"

provides:
  db: mysql
```

And WordPress:

```
name: wordpress
summary: "A pretty popular blog engine"
maintainer: "Juju Charmers <juju@lists.ubuntu.com>"
provides:
  url:
    interface: http

requires:
  db:
   interface: mysql
```

Probably the most confusing part of a charm to most newcomers are the relations. The preceding examples might help clear those up a little bit. As you can see, there are subfields used with relations that define how the relation will work. Here is a list of available subfields for relations:

▶ **interface**—The type of relation, such as http or mysql. Services will only be permitted to use interfaces listed here to interact with other services.

▶ **limit**—The maximum number of relations of this kind that will be established to other services.

▶ **optional**—Denotes whether the relation is required. A value of *false* means it is not optional.

▶ **scope**—Controls which units of related-to services can be communicated with via this relation, whether global or container. Container means restricted to units deployed in the same container, specifically subordinate services.

There is also a way to notify a service unit about changes happening in its lifecycle or the larger distributed environment. Called *hooks*, these are executable files that can query the environment, make desired changes on the local machine, and change relation settings. Hooks are implemented by placing the executable file in the hooks directory of the charm directory. Juju executes the hook based on its filename, when the corresponding event occurs. Hooks are optional. For example, a hook titled *install* would run just once during the service unit's life, when it was first set up, and it might check whether package dependencies are met. Hooks with titles like *start* or *stop* might run when the service is begun or ended. There are possibilities for creating hooks for relations, opening and closing ports, and more.

There are many charms already written and available from the Ubuntu Juju Charm Browser (the link is listed in Resources). You can quickly deploy a Jenkins build integration server or slave, a Hadoop database or node, a MediaWiki instance, a Minecraft game server, and tons more using already-written and -available charms. This is probably how most readers will interact with charms.

If you want to try your hand at writing and creating charms for services, you can. Much more detail is available at https://juju.ubuntu.com/docs/write-charm.html to help you learn the process, the semantics, and how to get your charm included in the Charm Store.

Juju has a charm feature called bundles. A bundle is a set of services with a specific configuration and all corresponding relations in a convenient package that can deploy the services in one single step.

The Juju GUI

Juju has a GUI available, as in Figure 35.1. You must first deploy a charm for the Juju GUI, and then you access it using a local URL. The charm is new and may change slightly, so rather than print the details, we are choosing to send you to the Charm Browser so you can learn about it directly from the developers. See: http://jujucharms.com/charms/precise/juju-gui.

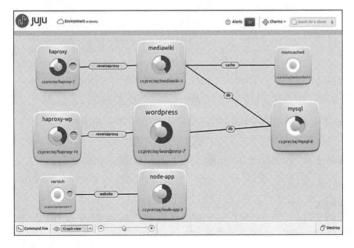

FIGURE 35.1   The Juju GUI.

Juju Quickstart

A recent addition to Juju is the `quickstart` command, which helps you get started by walking you through an installation, taking away much of the pain of the manual process. Quickstart helps you enter the configuration information needed to set up local clouds or with providers using OpenStack, Windows Azure, and Amazon EC2. It even installs the Juju GUI for you. Quickstart works with and can deploy Juju charm bundles. If the environment is not already bootstrapped, Quickstart will bring up the environment, install the GUI, and then deploy the bundle.

Juju on Mac OS X and Windows

It is possible to use a Juju client on your Mac or Windows machine to manage your Ubuntu servers. See: https://juju.ubuntu.com/install/ to download the client.

Mojo: Continuous Delivery for Juju

Mojo helps you with configuration and tools to verify the success of Juju deployments. It is made by Canonical. It gives you a structured means of having an entirely repeatable deployment process, specifically going from an entirely empty environment with no VMs running to VMs with the services deployed on them, relations established between each, and a fully working service. More information is available at https://mojo.canonical.com/.

Snappy Ubuntu Core

Snappy Ubuntu Core is minimalistic Ubuntu installation with transactional updates. This is a bare-bones server image with the same libraries as regular Ubuntu. However, applications are installed in a new way. The idea is that applications are deployed in an encapsulated way, as Snap packages, such that a change to one application cannot affect any other applications. This provides more predictable behavior and stronger security. Application updates come as "delta updates," meaning only the changes are downloaded and installed, leading to smaller downloads and faster upgrades. See Chapter 9, "Managing Software," to learn how to use Snap packages; Chapter 39, "Opportunistic Development," for information about creating Snap packages of existing software; and www.ubuntu.com/cloud/snappy for more.

Ubuntu Metal as a Service (MaaS)

Juju exists to deploy workloads to the cloud. Ubuntu Metal as a Service is built as a first step to deploy that cloud, when you are creating the cloud on hardware you own or that you have bare-metal configuration control over. Ubuntu Metal as a Service is a collection of best practices for deploying Ubuntu servers from Ubuntu servers. It is designed to assist with deployments to cloud servers numbering in the dozens, hundreds, or even thousands. You install Ubuntu MaaS directly to bare metal on one server and from there all other bare-metal servers are provisioned and set up; an entire data center could be implemented quickly and easily. After it's deployed, MaaS provides automatic federation and integrated management, monitoring, and logging. You can add physical equipment, remove it, repurpose it within your cloud, and more. You can do this dynamically, scaling up or down and managing resources as needed. It is powerful and very cool.

This is all done from the standard Ubuntu Server install CD, which you can download as described in Chapter 1, "Installing Ubuntu and Post-Installation Configuration," except you want the server version instead of the regular version of Ubuntu. At the time of this writing, the Ubuntu community is still creating documentation for Metal as a Service (the link is given below in Resources), so if this interests you, take a look at their page.

Landscape

Landscape is an enterprise-focused systems management and monitoring tool that is available from Canonical. It can monitor Ubuntu Cloud servers like the ones discussed in this chapter. Landscape can be deployed locally on your cloud or used as part of a paid service from Canonical called *Ubuntu Advantage*. Landscape is described further in Chapter 36, "Managing Sets of Servers."

References

- ▶ **http://www.ubuntu.com/cloud**—The official Ubuntu introduction to cloud computing.

- ▶ **www.linux-kvm.org/page/Main_Page**—The main page for KVM, the Kernel-based Virtual Machine.

- ▶ **www.openstack.org**—The official website for OpenStack.

- ▶ **https://landscape.canonical.com**—Canonical's Landscape is a commercial management tool for Ubuntu Cloud and Amazon EC2 instances.

- ▶ **http://juju.ubuntu.com**—The official Ubuntu documentation for Juju.

- ▶ **http://jujucharms.com/**—The official Ubuntu Juju Charm Browser.

- ▶ **http://conjure-up.io**—The official site for Conjure Up, which is an easy way to deploy big software stacks to the cloud using Juju.

- ▶ **http://maas.io/**—The official Ubuntu documentation Ubuntu and MAAS.

# CHAPTER 36

Managing Sets of Servers

This chapter provides a quick introduction to some tools that might be useful, especially for people who manage large numbers of servers. The tools here are designed for system administrators and developers—people who are responsible for keeping more than one or two servers up and running, managing their configurations, and so on. Systems have grown to the point that managing each one individually is becoming unwieldy at times and so tools have been created that decrease some of the stress and complexity by reducing the job to managing the software that in turn manages all of the servers. Okay, any system administrator or developer will tell you that this is a bit of an oversimplification, but it is close.

Because this is such a complex task, one on which many thick books are written, we just provide a quick overview of some of the options you should consider and then leave you the task of further research. Some of these options have entire books just to themselves, but if you are someone who needs to manage sets of servers, you will want to do it right. Do your research. This chapter helps you get started with a quick description of some of the things that are being used on Ubuntu to assist with this task.

Juju

One entry that would fit well into this chapter, juju, is instead covered in Chapter 35, "Ubuntu in the Cloud," because it is so closely tied with Ubuntu's cloud server. It includes for free many of the features of other software's paid enterprise versions and is well worth a look.
This chapter became quite short when we moved the information on Juju to Chapter 35, "Ubuntu in the Cloud."

Puppet

Puppet is a configuration management tool written in Ruby. It is designed to make it easier to deploy servers and scale applications across a network and does so using a custom declarative language. It has both open-source and commercial (closed-source) versions.

Puppet does four basic things. First, it provides a place for you define the desired state for your infrastructure's configuration. Second, Puppet simulates changes before enforcing them. Third, Puppet enforces the desired state automatically, making corrections for drifting configurations. Finally, Puppet gives you a report on the differences between the actual and desired states before you make any changes.

A site called Puppet Forge (listed in Resources) provides access to downloadable *modules*, which are bits of Puppet code for automating tasks, such as setting up a specific type of server. Instructions there are also available for creating and sharing your own modules.

Much of the power of Puppet is made available in its for-payment Enterprise version, which also includes a nice GUI. The open-source version will work with Amazon EC2 for provisioning, will manage configurations for operating systems and applications, lets you use Puppet modules from Puppet Forge, and has community support via the Web. If you need anything more than this, either find a different product or pay for it to use Puppet's enterprise version, which has a good reputation for maturity and usefulness.

Puppet Labs, the company that develops Puppet, recently bought Cloudsmith (http://www.cloudsmith.com/), a company that makes developer tools based on Puppet. This development is sure to make Puppet an even stronger contender in the market.

Chef

Chef is a configuration management tool, also written in Ruby. It uses a services-oriented architecture to help automate tasks. For Chef, you write recipes that describe how you want your server or a specific server software to be configured, such as an HTTP server or database server. The recipes describe each resource, such as services that should be running or packages that should be installed, and the state in which each should be found. It then makes sure that configuration is maintained or updated across all servers being managed.

Chef is open source. However, to really use it you must pay for a hosted version (called Hosted) or a standalone version (called Private) that you can install inside your corporate firewall with a service contract. Downloading the source code and getting it up and running is not a trivial task, and support for the open-source version (called Open Source) without a service contract is limited. That said, like Puppet, Chef is mature and well respected and worth your time if you need what it offers.

CFEngine

CFEngine is probably the oldest option for automating infrastructure. It is written in C, so it might be a little faster than the other options. It manages server builds, deployment, and management, and it performs some very useful audits and reports. Some really big names are known to use CFEngine, such as AT&T, IBM, Pixar, and Qualcomm.

CFEngine has open-source and enterprise versions. The differences are a little less extreme than with some of the other options, but again, the enterprise version has all the flashy chrome and a few really useful features that make it worth the expenditure for most users who need or want the added benefits they offer.

Ansible

Ansible is an orchestration engine. It does configuration management, application deployment, and more. It is a proprietary product that runs on Linux and is receiving a bit of buzz lately. It claims easy use and the ability to manage devices without having to install special software on those devices.

Landscape

Landscape is an enterprise-focused systems management and monitoring tool that is available from Canonical. It is a part of the Ubuntu Advantage program (http://www.canonical.com/services), which is a paid service. You can run landscape as a hosted service from Canonical's Ubuntu Advantage, or you can install it locally. It can monitor both local servers as well as cloud servers, such as are discussed in Chapter 35, "Ubuntu in the Cloud."

References

- ▶ www.puppetlabs.com—The official website for Puppet.

- ▶ http://forge.puppetlabs.com/—The official website for Puppet Forge.

- ▶ https://www.chef.io/chef/—The official website for Chef.

- ▶ http://cfengine.com/—The official website for CFEngine.

- ▶ http://www.ansibleworks.com/—The official website for Ansible.

- ▶ http://www.ubuntu.com/management—The official website for Landscape and Ubuntu Advantage.

- ▶ http://help.ubuntu.com/14.04/serverguide/index.html—The official Ubuntu server guide.

CHAPTER 37

Name Serving with the Domain Name System (DNS)

Humans enjoy naming things. We name our kids, our pets, and we often name inanimate objects as well. Cars, boats, and computers are not immune. This is especially true of networked computers. Remembering names is easier for most of us than remembering numbers. When we must remember numbers, we can; I can still remember the phone number of the house I lived in when I was a kid. However, when we can use a name instead, we tend to prefer to do so; today I can't remember my daughter's cell phone number, because it is programmed into my phone and I just select her picture in the directory to call her.

If you are working in a data center, especially one with a large number of servers networked together, you won't easily remember the IP addresses of each system. Besides, it is fun to pick a theme and name everything on the network using that theme: varieties of apples, characters from your favorite science fiction or fantasy world, brands of guitars you wish you owned. "Hey, Liz, can you go check on sontaran for me? It isn't responding to my ping requests." Is so much more fun to say and easy to communicate than "...can you check on the server at IP 192.168.2.46..."

Mnemonic devices like these are useful, but they then must map the names we give to the numbers the systems actually use. Mapping is just matching, connecting the words with the numbers in a way that allows a human to request http://google.com and get the information stored at http://74.125.224.72/.

The Domain Name System (DNS) converts human-readable names given to networked machines to the IP addresses that machines use. See Chapter 18, "Networking," for more on IP addresses. DNS works in both directions, taking names and giving IP addresses or taking IP addresses and giving names.

When you set up a DNS Server using the Bind 9 DNS server software we discuss in this chapter you gain the power to set the name/IP details for domains you own, either internal on your network or internet domain names you have purchased through a registrar like Namecheap.com or GoDaddy. But, these registrars run DNS servers and allow you to perform this setup through their lovely web GUIs. Why would anyone want to do this themselves? There are several possible reasons:

▶ You have an internal network, a local area network that is not accessible from outside that network, also called a LAN. Your internal network assigns and uses private IP addresses, but you want to make things easier for your LAN users by assigning names to the various systems. These domain names will not be assigned by a domain name registrar because they are internal-only; they won't include top-level domains like .com or .net at the end of them and will only be use-able within the network.

▶ You want to improve performance by caching. Most DNS queries are shared by a large number of computers. If those individual computers don't have to each connect to the internet and get their domain names resolved by your internet service provider's DNS server (or another public DNS server), but can instead get that information from a server on the local network, it could speed things up. This isn't an issue for most of us, but for large networks, it can be a huge benefit.

▶ You want to ban access to a harmful domain. Maybe an email came in to your company's employees with a link to a specific website that is distributing viruses and you want to prevent naïve internal network users from accessing that website. You can change the IP that is served for this domain name so that it instead forwards users to an HTML page you write up describing the problem. Your change only affects computers on your internal network, so this is not something that will make people outside your company angry or that they will even know is happening.

▶ You run a local network at home. You want to make your life a little easier when it comes time to login to each and perform updates, so you want to give names to each computer and allow access to each computer using a pet name for each instead of the IP address on your network.

No doubt we could come up with other examples. To be honest, most of us will not need to set up or run a DNS server, but you are the type of person who reads books like Ubuntu Unleashed and you like to tinker with technology. It is likely that most people reading this just want to play something new and have some fun. This chapter will get you started.

Understanding Domain Names

Simply put, a domain name is a string of characters that is used to represent an IP address. Domain names are intended to be easier to remember than strings of numbers. Generally, they are set up as a set of letters separated by dots. Each of these sets of letters is called a label. The label on the far right denotes the widest group, or top-level domain (TLD). Each label to the left is a subdomain of the one to the right of it. Here is an example: `news.google.com`.

Here we see three labels.

▶ The top level refers to the top-level domain, in this case com. Other top-level domains include the original set of `com`, `edu`, `gov`, `mil`, `net`, and `org`. Others include country-code TLDs such as `uk` or `in`, sponsored TLDs like the Société Internationale de Télécommunications Aéronautiques owned `aero`, and geographic TLDs like `asia`. Others also exist. All are controlled by a group called ICANN, the Internet Corporation for Assigned Names and Numbers, with whom domain names must be registered to work on the internet (see: www.icann.org). The TLD generally defines, with varying firmness, the content permitted on subdomains; some TLDs are far more controlled than others.

▶ The first subdomain, in this case `google`, is called the root zone. The root zone is required to create a fully qualified domain name (FQDN), which is the combination of the root zone and the TLD. When you register a domain name with a registrar, so you can put a website on the internet, you register a root zone for a TLD, as in `matthewhelmke.com` or `matthewhelmke.net`. The complete FQDN is required for DNS to work across the internet.

▶ After the first subdomain, others may be created, such as `news` in our example. These are optional. Some standard ones are `www`, `mail`, and `ftp`, which each denote specific uses for defined subdomains. They are not required, but if you are to host more than one thing using a FQDN, then you must define and use subdomains. Subdomains are defined in a DNS server in the same manner as TLDs.

When a full set consisting of TLD and all needed subdomains are put together, this is called a host name. On a local network, this could be a single word. On the internet, it requires at least a TLD and root zone and often includes at least one other subdomain, as in www.icann.org. Another way to define a host name is any domain name that is associated with one or more IP addresses. The "or more" is often used when load balancing between one or more machines. You can have DNS cycle from one IP address to another each time the hostname is requested.

DNS Servers

DNS servers receive requests or queries and respond by resolving that query and returning the information mapped to it, if it exists. There is not one canonical DNS server for the entire internet. Instead, when a domain is registered, that registration is listed on a series of ICANN-run servers scattered around the world. Contained in that registration is information about where the authoritative DNS information is stored for that domain. This is usually, but not necessarily, a DNS server or set of DNS servers operated by the domain name registrar.

DNS requests work in a hierarchical fashion. Here is an example:

▶ A full request comes in to your internet service provider's DNS server. If it knows the information, it responds.

▶ If it recognized the root name, but not a subdomain, it will submit a request itself to a known server with information about that root name and, if successful, it will return the information it receives.

▶ If it cannot find any cached information about the host name, it will contact an ICANN server using the TLD. The ICANN server can then respond with the information it has, which at a minimum will be the registered IP that correlates to the host-name, if it exists.

This hierarchy is why some DNS requests take longer than others; sometimes the search involves multiple DNS servers across a wider and wider set of data. It also means that if one server goes down, this is not catastrophic; instead, the information can be searched for and found elsewhere.

DNS Records

All of these are placed in a zone file, which is discussed further in Setting Up a DNS Server with BIND. There are several ways to define the IP/hostname. Some of these DNS records are optional. Many can have multiple entries. The most critical and commonly used ones are listed here, but there are many more available, and many more options available that what is listed here. See https://en.wikipedia.org/wiki/List_of_DNS_record_types for more information.

A

The A record maps a hostname to a 32-bit IPv4 address, as in this example:

```
example.com IN A 192.0.2.0
```

The hostname comes first. IN indicates internet. A indicates that this is an A record. The IPv4 address address comes last.

AAAA

The AAAA record maps a hostname to a 128-bit IPv6 address, as in this example:

```
example.com AAAA 2001:db8::/32
```

The hostname comes first. The four As next, using four because 128-bit IPv6 addresses are four times larger than 32-bit IPv4 addresses. See Chapter 18, "Networking," for more about IPv4 and IPv6 addresses. Finally, the IPv6 address.

CNAME

This maps one or more aliases to the canonical name of a machine. The aliased domain receives all the subdomains and DNS records of the original, canonical name it is matched with. For example, if you have a machine named weirdname.example.com that is set up to be an email server, but you want to use a different URL, you can set up an alias so it also uses mail.example.com, as in this example:

```
mail.example.com CNAME weirdname.example.com
```

The alias comes first. CNAME indicates this is being mapped to the canonical name that comes next. The server that has an A record is listed last. CNAME records never point to IP addresses, only to other domain names that are already defined using A or AAAA records.

One neat trick is that you can create CNAME records for every subdomain on a machine that is running multiple services, such as `ftp.example.com`, `www.example.com`, and `mail .example.com` and have every one of them point to the same A or AAAA record for the server with the name `example.com`. That A or AAAA record points to the IP address, so if you ever need to change the IP address, such as when you move your server or establish a new server, you only have to change the IP record in one place.

MX

An MX record maps a domain name to a list of mail servers for that domain. MX comes from "mail exchange." If you do not use a domain for email, this record is not needed. Here is an example record:

```
example.com. 14400 IN MX 0 mail.example.com.
```

First off, notice the important dots after the two domain names. These are vital because omitting them will cause email to be misrouted.

The example says that any email coming in to an address @example.com (leftmost field) should be routed to the server at example.com (rightmost field). The DNS A or AAAA record for mail.example.com or a CNAME record sets the IP address of that mailserver. 14400 defines in seconds how often to update the DNS entry in any other server that has cached this record; 14400 is 4 hours and is standard. MX defines this as a mail exchange record.

The zero indicates preference. This is because you can list more than one MX server. Smaller numbers are preferred over larger numbers. Setting multiple servers to the same value means that a random server with that value is to be used. If there is only one, use 0. A multiple server MX record looks like this:

```
example.com. 14400 IN MX 10 mail.example.com.
example.com. 14400 IN MX 20 mail2.example.com.
```

NS

An NS records maps a domain name to a list of DNS servers that are authoritative for that domain. It is most used at domain name registrars and tells any query that comes in to the domain name registrar where to look for the complete DNS record.

37

For example, a request from an ICANN server would look first at the domain name registrar, which would then look wherever it says in the NS record, if the complete DNS is not hosted here. Here is an example:

```
example.com. IN NS ns1.domainregistrationcompany.com.
```

The domain comes first, again with a dot at the end. This is followed by IN for internet and NS for name server. At the end, the name server is listed, again with a dot at the end.

SOA

A start of authority or SOA record specifies the DNS server that provides authoritative information about a domain, the email of the domain administrator, the domain serial number, and configuration for timers related to refreshing the zone. This is a vital part of the zone file. Here is an example:

```
; name TTL class rr Nameserver email-address
example.com. 14400 IN SOA ns.mydomainnameserver.com. root.ns.mydomainnameserver.com. (
2013080600 ; serial number
86000 ; refresh rate in seconds
7200 ; update retry in seconds
3600000 ; expiration in seconds
600 ; minimum in seconds )
```

In this file, the semicolon denotes the beginning of a comment, so everything after it is ignored by the system and is intended only for the human reading the file. The first line reminds us how to format the next line. Everything else in the file is contained in the parentheses, the first of which must be on the first line.

We are using example.com as our domain in the example. Remember the dot at the end.

14400 is the TTL or time in seconds that we are allowing the record to be cached by other servers before they have to submit a query again. If set to 0, it is not permitted to be cached at all.

IN is the class or type of the record, in this case, "internet." No other options are in use any more.

SOA denotes this is a start of authority record.

Our example uses ns.mydomainnameserver.com as the sample domain of our DNS server. Replace this with your DNS server's domain. Remember the dot at the end.

The email of the domain name administrator is a little confusing, because we expect an @ symbol and none exists. In the example above, root.ns.mydomainnameserver.com means root@ns.mydomainnameserver.com. Replace this with the email address for your admin, using a dot instead of the @ symbol. Remember the dot at the end.

The serial number is a revision numbering system. It is changed every time the file is changed. Convention is to use YYYYMMDDnn where YYYY is year, MM is month,

DD is day, and nn is an extra number to allow you to increment when multiple edits and saves occur in one day. For example, 2013080600 is the first edit on the 6th of August in 2013.

The refresh rate sets the time in seconds when the slave DNS server will refresh from the master DNS server.

The retry rate sets how long to wait after a failed refresh before making another attempt.

The expiration sets how long to keep a zone file cached.

Minimum is the default time that slave servers should cache the zone file. If your DNS changes frequently, you want to set this to a low number, like 12 hours or so. If infrequently, then every 1 to 5 days is a good balance between keeping updated and keeping requests served quickly.

TXT

You may put any text you like in a TXT record. It is most used to implement the Sender Policy Framework (SPF), which is an email validation system designed to help detect and prevent email spam by detecting email spoofing. Spoofing is where email is sent out to look like it originates in one location, but actually originated somewhere else. SPF records must indicate the version identifier for SPF and a default mechanism. Here is an example of SPF info in a TXT record:

```
example.com. TXT "v=spf1 -all"
```

This indicates to use SFP version 1 and that no servers at this domain send email. If your server does not send email, use this to prevent email/web hosting companies from blocking your domain if someone tries to send email pretending to come from your domain.

If your server sends email, you would do something like this:

```
example.com. TXT "v=spf1 mx -all"
```

The difference is that "mx" has been added to indicate that any servers tied to this domain may send email.

Many more variations of SPF records are available. Itemize what you have and then read the specification at www.openspf.org/SPF_Record_Syntax to learn what you need to write.

Setting Up a DNS Server with BIND

The Berkeley Internet Name Domain (BIND) software has been foundational to the internet since the 1980s. The original BIND was created at the University of California, Berkeley using grant funding. It was released as free and open source with the BSD (Berkeley Software Distribution) version of UNIX and was quickly adopted as the standard software for DNS. Internet Systems Consortium now maintains BIND and provides updates and documentation on their site at www.isc.org.

When you create NS records for your domains with your domain name registrar, pointing at ns1.domainregistrationcompany.com or whatever domain they give you, you are most

37

likely pointing to a server running BIND, although other options exist. In this section, we will install and set up a very basic DNS server using BIND.

Start by installing `bind9` from the Ubuntu software repositories.

Next, use your favorite text editor to open /etc/bind/named.conf.local, which is a configuration file set up with default settings. This is where we must declare the zones we are setting up and associating with our domain. Zones are domain names that are referenced in the DNS server. Leave all the default text in the file and add this to the end of the file, after replacing example.com with your domain name:

```
# This is the zone definition.
zone "example.com" {
        type master;
        file "/etc/bind/zones/example.com.db";
        };
```

Save the file and exit.

Next, open the configuration options file at /etc/bind/named.conf.options and modify the section titled *forwarders*, by replacing 8.8.8.8 in our example with the IP address of your provider's DNS server:

```
forwarders {
      8.8.8.8;
};
```

Save the file and exit.

Now we must create a zone definition file. First, create a directory to hold it:

matthew@seymour:~$ **sudo mkdir /etc/bind/zones**

Then, create a new file, but replace *example.com* with your domain:

matthew@seymour:~$ **sudo touch /etc/bind/zones/example.com.db**

This zone definition file will contain all of the addresses and machine names that we are hosting. This is where you enter all of the DNS records discussed in the previous section of the book. Each record gets its own line. For human readability, it is nice to put an empty line between each and start each record with a comment, using // to begin comment lines. In this example, replace example.com with your domain, ns with the domain for your DNS server, and enter whatever other records you wish to enter, modifying as the comments note here:

```
example.com. 14400 IN SOA ns.example.com. admin.ns.example.com. (
2013080600   ; serial number
86000        ; refresh rate in seconds
7200         ; update retry in seconds
3600000      ; expiration in seconds
600          ; minimum in seconds )
```

```
// Replace the following lines as necessary:
// example.com = your domain name
// ns1 = your DNS server name
// mta = your mail server name
example.com.      IN      NS              ns1.example.com.
example.com.      IN      MX      10      mta.example.com.

// Replace the IP address with your IP addresses.
www              IN      A       192.168.0.2
mta              IN      A       192.168.0.3
ns1              IN      A       192.168.0.1
```

Now, restart BIND:

```
matthew@seymour:~$ sudo service bind9 restart
```

You can also use start, stop, and so on as with other services. You should be all set. To test your DNS server, edit /etc/resolv.conf (make a backup of the original!) and replace the contents with the following, replacing example.com with your domain name and 192.168.1.1 with the address of your new DNS server:

```
search example.com
nameserver 192.168.1.1
```

Then, test your DNS using `ping` to see what it returns for example.com:

```
matthew@seymour:~$ dig example.com
```

Besides the `ping` utility just mentioned, `dig`, is an excellent tool for reviewing DNS records. You may also find `nslookup` and `whois` useful. Also, `named-checkzone` is included with BIND9 and may be useful to you.

References

▶ www.bind9.net—A website with tons of useful information about both DNS and Bind.

▶ **DNS and BIND** by Cricket Liu and Paul Albitz is the canonical guide to understanding both of these technologies.

Using Programming Tools for Ubuntu

If you're looking to learn C or C++ programming or Java programming, this part of the book isn't the right place to start. Unlike Perl, Python, PHP, or even C#, it takes more than a little dabbling to produce something productive with languages like these, so this chapter is primarily focused on the tools Ubuntu offers you as a programmer.

Whether you're looking to compile your own code or someone else's, the *GNU Compiler Collection* (gcc) is there to help. It understands C, C++, Fortran, Pascal, and dozens of other popular languages, which means you can try your hand at whatever interests you. Ubuntu also ships with hundreds of libraries you can link to, from the GUI toolkits behind GNOME and KDE to XML parsing and game coding. Some use C, others C++, and still others offer support for both, meaning you can choose what you're most comfortable with.

WHY USE C OR C++?

Every language has its benefits and its shortcomings. Some languages make life easier for the programmer, but at the expense of runtime. Languages such as Perl and Python and even Java make it hard for the user to guarantee that memory is fetched sequentially or that it fits in cache, due to things such as checks on the bounds on each access. They are useful languages, but they run slower than languages that are harder for the programmer, but faster at runtime like C or Fortran.

For some programs, such as short shell scripts or a quick one-liner in Perl to search text in a file, the difference in the runtime speed is negligible. On a desktop computer, it might not matter that your music player is written in

Python, and if it seems slow, then buying a newer, faster desktop system might be an acceptable solution.

There are some applications, however, where the time needed to run your program can make a big difference. For example, using a slow-to-run language to perform calculations on scientific data, especially if you are doing it on *High-Performance Computing (HPC)* resources like a supercomputing cluster is foolish; to take advantage of the platform, it is both time- and cost-effective to use the fastest language available to you, like C.

This idea was reinforced in a 2011 conversation between Matthew Helmke and Dan Stanzione, then deputy director of the Texas Advanced Computing Center at the University of Texas at Austin. Stanzione said that HPC computing resources are expensive, so it is often wiser to spend grant money to hire a good C programmer for a year than it is to run a bioinformatics program written in Perl or Python on an HPC system. As he put it, "If your computer costs $2,000, the programmer's time is the dominant cost, and that is what drives software development. If your computer costs $100 million or more, then having a programmer spend an extra month, or year, or decade working on software optimization is well worth it. Toughen up and write in C."

Programming with Linux

C is the programming language most frequently associated with UNIX-like operating systems such as Linux or BSD. Since the 1970s, the bulk of the UNIX operating system and its applications have been written in C. Because the C language doesn't directly rely on any specific hardware architecture, UNIX was one of the first portable operating systems. In other words, the majority of the code that makes up UNIX doesn't know and doesn't care which computer it is actually running on. Machine-specific features are isolated in a few modules within the UNIX kernel, which makes it easy for you to modify them when you are porting to different hardware architectures.

Because it is so important to UNIX and Linux, we will use C as our example here. Much of what is discussed will apply to other languages, perhaps with slight variations for language-specific features.

C is a *compiled* language, which means that your C source code is first analyzed by the *preprocessor* and then translated into assembly language before it's translated into machine instructions that are appropriate to the target CPU. An assembler then creates a binary, or *object*, file from the machine instructions. Finally, the object file is linked to any required external software support by the *linker*. A C program is stored in a text file that ends with a .c extension and always contains at least one routine, or function, such as main(), unless the file is an *include* file (with a .h extension, also known as a *header* file) containing shared variable definitions or other data or declarations. *Functions* are the commands that perform each step of the task that the C program was written to accomplish.

> **NOTE**
>
> The Linux kernel is mostly written in C, which is why Linux works with so many different CPUs. To learn more about building the Linux kernel from source, see Chapter 22, "Kernel and Module Management."

C++ is an object-oriented extension to C. Because C++ is a superset of C, C++ compilers compile C programs correctly, and it is possible to write non-object-oriented code in C++. The reverse is not true: C compilers cannot compile C++ code.

C++ extends the capabilities of C by providing the necessary features for object-oriented design and code. C++ also provides some features, such as the capability to associate functions with data structures that do not require the use of class-based object-oriented techniques. For these reasons, the C++ language enables existing UNIX programs to migrate toward the adoption of object orientation over time.

Support for C++ programming is provided by `gcc`, which you run with the name `g++` when you are compiling C++ code.

Using the C Programming Project Management Tools Provided with Ubuntu

Ubuntu is replete with tools that make your life as a C/C++ programmer easier. There are tools to create programs (editors), compile programs (`gcc`), create libraries (`ar`), control the source (Git, Mercurial, Subversion), automate builds (`make`), debug programs (`gdb` and `ddd`), and determine where inefficiencies lie (`gprof`).

The following sections introduce some of the programming and project management tools included with Ubuntu. If you have some previous UNIX experience, you will be familiar with most of these programs because they are traditional complements to a programmer's suite of software.

Building Programs with `make`

You use the `make` command to automatically build and install a C program, and for that use it is an easy tool. If you want to create your own automated builds, however, you need to learn the special syntax that `make` uses; the following sections walk you through a basic `make` setup.

Using Makefiles

The `make` command automatically builds and updates applications by using a makefile. A *makefile* is a text file that contains instructions about which options to pass on to the compiler preprocessor, the compiler, the assembler, and the linker. The makefile also specifies, among other things, which source code files have to be compiled (and the compiler command line) for a particular code module and which code modules are needed to build the program—a mechanism called *dependency checking*.

The beauty of the `make` command is its flexibility. You can use `make` with a simple makefile, or you can write complex makefiles that contain numerous macros, rules, or commands that work in a single directory or traverse your file system recursively to build programs, update your system, and even function as document management systems. The `make` command works with nearly any program, including text processing systems such as TeX.

You could use make to compile, build, and install a software package, using a simple command like this:

```
matthew@seymour:~$ sudo make install
```

You can use the default makefile (usually called Makefile, with a capital *M*), or you can use make's -f option to specify any makefile, such as MyMakeFile, like this:

```
matthew@seymour:~$ sudo make -f MyMakeFile
```

Other options might be available, depending on the contents of your makefile. You might have a source file named hi.c and just run make hi, where make figures out what to do automatically to build the final executable. See make's built-in rules with make -p.

Using Macros and Makefile Targets

Using make with macros can make a program portable. Macros allow users of other operating systems to easily configure a program build by specifying local values, such as the names and locations, or *pathnames*, of any required software tools. In the following example, macros define the name of the compiler (CC), the installer program (INS), where the program should be installed (INSDIR), where the linker should look for required libraries (LIBDIR), the names of required libraries (LIBS), a source code file (SRC), the intermediate object code file (OBJS), and the name of the final program (PROG):

```
# a sample makefile for a skeleton program
CC= gcc
INS= install
INSDIR = /usr/local/bin
LIBDIR= -L/usr/X11R6/lib
LIBS= -lXm -lSM -lICE -lXt -lX11
SRC= skel.c
OBJS= skel.o
PROG= skel

skel:   ${OBJS}
        ${CC} -o ${PROG} ${SRC} ${LIBDIR} ${LIBS}

install: ${PROG}
        ${INS} -g root -o root ${PROG} ${INSDIR}
```

> **NOTE**
>
> The indented lines in the previous example are indented with tabs, not spaces. This is important to remember! It is difficult for a person to see the difference, but make can tell. If make reports confusing errors when you first start building programs under Linux, check your project's makefile for the use of tabs and other proper formatting.

Using the makefile from the preceding example, you can build a program like this:

```
matthew@seymour:~$ sudo make
```

To build a specified component of a makefile, you can use a target definition on the command line. To build just the program, you use make with the skel target, like this:

```
matthew@seymour:~$ sudo make skel
```

If you make any changes to any element of a target object, such as a source code file, make rebuilds the target automatically. This feature is part of the convenience of using make to manage a development project. To build and install a program in one step, you can specify the target of install like this:

```
matthew@seymour:~$ sudo make install
```

Larger software projects might have a number of traditional targets in the makefile, such as the following:

- ▶ **test**—To run specific tests on the final software
- ▶ **man**—To process an include or a troff document with the man macros
- ▶ **clean**—To delete any remaining object files
- ▶ **archive**—To clean up, archive, and compress the entire source code tree
- ▶ **bugreport**—To automatically collect and then mail a copy of the build or error logs

Large applications can require hundreds of source code files. Compiling and linking these applications can be a complex and error-prone task. The make utility helps you organize the process of building the executable form of a complex application from many source files.

Using the autoconf Utility to Configure Code

The make command is only one of several programming automation utilities included with Ubuntu. There are others, such as pmake (which causes a parallel make); imake (which is a dependency-driven makefile generator that is used for building X11 clients); automake; and one of the newer tools, autoconf, which builds shell scripts that can be used to configure program source code packages.

Building many software packages for Linux that are distributed in source form requires the use of GNU's autoconf utility. This program builds an executable shell script named configure that, when executed, automatically examines and tailors a client's build from source according to software resources, or *dependencies* (such as programming tools, libraries, and associated utilities) that are installed on the target host (your Linux system).

Many Linux commands and graphical clients for X downloaded in source code form include configure scripts. To configure the source package, build the software, and then install the new program, the `root` user might use the script like this (after uncompressing the source and navigating into the resulting build directory):

```
matthew@seymour:~$ ./configure ; make ; sudo make install
```

The `autoconf` program uses a file named `configure.in` that contains a basic *ruleset*, or set of macros. The `configure.in` file is created with the `autoscan` command. Building a properly executing `configure` script also requires a template for the makefile, named `Makefile.in`. Although creating the dependency-checking `configure` script can be done manually, you can easily overcome any complex dependencies by using a graphical project development tool such as KDE's KDevelop or GNOME's Glade. (See the "Graphical Development Tools" section, later in this chapter, for more information.)

Debugging Tools

Debugging is both a science and an art. Sometimes, the simplest tool—the code listing—is the best debugging tool. At other times, however, you need to use other debugging tools. Three of these tools are `splint`, `gprof`, and `gdb`.

Using `splint` to Check Source Code

The `splint` command is similar to the traditional UNIX `lint` command: It statically examines source code for possible problems, and it also has many additional features. Even if your C code meets the standards for C and compiles cleanly, it might still contain errors. `splint` performs many types of checks and can provide extensive error information. For example, this simple program might compile cleanly and even run:

```
matthew@seymour:~$ gcc -o tux tux.c
matthew@seymour:~$ ./tux
```

But the `splint` command might point out some serious problems with the source:

```
matthew@seymour:~$ splint tux.c
Splint 3.1.2 -- 29 Apr 2009

tux.c: (in function main)
tux.c:2:19: Return value (type int) ignored: putchar(t[++j] -...
  Result returned by function call is not used. If this is intended, can cast
  result to (void) to eliminate message. (Use -retvalint to inhibit warning)
Finished checking -- 1 code warning
```

You can use the splint command's `-strict` option, like this, to get a more verbose report:

```
matthew@seymour:~$ splint -strict tux.c
```

gcc also supports diagnostics through the use of extensive warnings (through the `-Wall` and `-pedantic` options):

```
matthew@seymour:~$ gcc -Wall tux.c
tux.c:1: warning: return type defaults to 'int'
```

```
tux.c: In function 'main':
tux.c:2: warning: implicit declaration of function 'putchar'
```

Using `gprof` **to Track Function Time**

You use the `gprof` (profile) command to study how a program is spending its time. If a program is compiled and linked with `-p` as a flag, a `mon.out` file is created when it executes, with data on how often each function is called and how much time is spent in each function. `gprof` parses and displays this data. An analysis of the output generated by `gprof` helps you determine where performance bottlenecks occur. Using an optimizing compiler can speed up a program, but taking the time to use `gprof`'s analysis and revising bottleneck functions significantly improves program performance.

Doing Symbolic Debugging with `gdb`

The `gdb` tool is a symbolic debugger. When you compile a program with the `-g` flag, the symbol tables are retained, and you can use a symbolic debugger to track program bugs. The basic technique is to invoke `gdb` after a *core dump* (a file containing a snapshot of the memory used by a program that has crashed) and get a stack trace. The stack trace indicates the source line where the core dump occurred and the functions that were called to reach that line. Often, this is enough to identify a problem. It isn't the limit of `gdb`, though.

`gdb` also provides an environment for debugging programs interactively. Invoking `gdb` with a program enables you to set breakpoints, examine the values of variables, and monitor variables. If you suspect a problem near a line of code, you can set a breakpoint at that line and run `gdb`. When the line is reached, execution is interrupted. You can check variable values, examine the stack trace, and observe the program's environment. You can single-step through the program to check values. You can resume execution at any point. By using breakpoints, you can discover many bugs in code.

A graphical X Window interface to `gdb` is called the *Data Display Debugger*, or `ddd`.

Using the GNU C Compiler

If you elected to install the development tools package when you installed Ubuntu (or perhaps later on, using `synaptic`), you should have the *GNU C compiler* (`gcc`). Many different options are available for the GNU C compiler, and many of them are similar to those of the C and C++ compilers that are available on other UNIX systems. Look at the man page or information file for `gcc` for a full list of options and descriptions.

NOTE

The GNU C compiler is a part of the GNU Compiler Collection, which also includes compilers for several other languages.

When you build a C program using `gcc`, the compilation process takes place in several steps:

1. First, the C preprocessor parses the file. To do so, it sequentially reads the lines, includes header files, and performs macro replacement.

2. The compiler parses the modified code to determine whether the correct syntax is used. In the process, it builds a symbol table and creates an intermediate object format. Most symbols have specific memory addresses assigned, although symbols defined in other modules, such as external variables, do not.

3. The last compilation stage, linking, ties together different files and libraries and then links the files by resolving the symbols that had not previously been resolved.

> **NOTE**
>
> Most C programs compile with a C++ compiler if you follow strict ANSI rules. For example, you can compile the standard `hello.c` program (everyone's first program) with the GNU C++ compiler. Typically, you name the file something like `hello.cc`, `hello.C`, `hello.c++`, or `hello.cxx`. The GNU C++ compiler accepts any of these names.

Graphical Development Tools

Here we will branch out into information that more obviously applies to other languages. For example, Java is in widespread use and you can develop in Java from Ubuntu.

Ubuntu has a number of graphical prototyping and development environments available. If you want to build client software for KDE or GNOME, you might find the KDevelop, Qt Designer, and Glade programs extremely helpful. You can use each of these programs to build graphical frameworks for interactive windowing clients, and you can use each of them to automatically generate the necessary skeleton of code needed to support a custom interface for your program. If you want to program in Java using your favorite Integrated Development Environment (IDE) or a language with a standard Software Development Kit (SDK), you can do that, too.

Using the KDevelop Client

You can launch the KDevelop client (shown in Figure 38.1) from the application's menu, or from the command line of a terminal window, like this:

```
matthew@seymour:~$ kdevelop &
```

After you press Enter, the KDevelop Setup Wizard runs, and you are taken through several short wizard dialogs that set up and ensure a stable build environment. You must then run `kdevelop` again (either from the command line or by clicking its menu item under the desktop panel's Programming menu). You then see the main KDevelop window and can start your project by selecting KDevelop's Project menu and clicking the New menu item.

You can begin building your project by stepping through the wizard dialogs. When you click the Create button, KDevelop automatically generates all the files that are normally found in a KDE client source directory (including the `configure` script, which checks dependencies and builds the client's makefile). To test your client, you can either first click the Build menu's Make menu item (or press F8) or just click the Execute menu item (or press F9), and the client is built automatically. You can use KDevelop to create KDE clients, plug-ins for the `Konqueror` browser, KDE `kicker` panel applets, KDE desktop themes, Qt library-based clients, and even programs for GNOME.

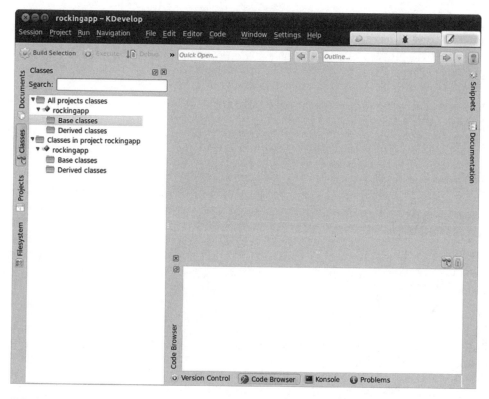

FIGURE 38.1   KDE's Kdevelop is a rapid prototyping and client-building tool for use with Linux.

The Glade Client for Developing in GNOME

If you prefer to use GNOME and its development tools, the Glade GTK+ GUI builder can help you save time and effort when building a basic skeleton for a program. You launch Glade from the desktop panel's Programming menu.

When you launch Glade, a directory named `Projects` is created in your home directory, and you see a main window, along with two floating Palette and Properties windows (see Figure 38.2, which shows a basic GNOME client with a calendar widget added to its main window). You can use Glade's File menu to save the blank project and then start building your client by clicking and adding user interface elements from the Palette window. For example, you can first click the Palette window's Gnome button and then click to create your new client's main window. A window with a menu and a toolbar appears—the basic framework for a new GNOME client.

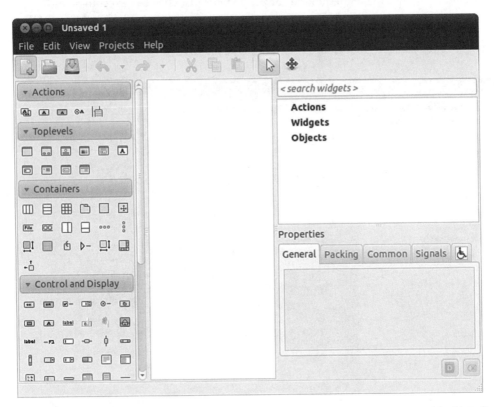

FIGURE 38.2   You can use the GNOME Glade client to build and preview a graphical interface for a custom GNOME program.

Use an IDE or SDK

Integrated development environments (IDE) and software development kits (SDK) have become extremely popular. While some still prefer to write and edit software using a standard text editor, like nano or vi (covered in Chapter 12, "Command-Line Master Class Part 2"), many programmers prefer using a tool that is more powerful. The first of these started out as a text editor, but as more and more features were added, it evolved into something more. This is Emacs, and it is also covered in Chapter 12. By adding tools and features to make the programmer's life easier, Emacs unintentionally became the template for modern IDEs.

Some IDEs support multiple languages, like Emacs does. Others focus on only one language. Most include not only programming language specific features like code highlighting, to help you read and browse code more quickly and efficiently, but also contain a compiler and debugger and even build automation tools. If you read through the details earlier in this chapter of using `make` with C, you can understand the value added.

So, what is the downside? Well, you can't run a typical IDE on a server because you need a graphical interface, so if you are working on code that will run on a server that only has a command line or text interface available to you, you want to make sure you are comfortable with traditional methods. That doesn't mean you can't use a local desktop machine for development using an IDE and then push your code out to the server. It just means you should cover your bases, just in case.

The most commonly used IDEs seem to also be used most frequently by Java developers. We will use three of them as examples in this chapter. Each should be downloaded directly from the provider as this will ensure you install the most current and standard version.

Oracle, which owns Java, provides an IDE for Java called Oracle JDeveloper. It is most commonly used in enterprise settings, where a team of developers work together using a standard tool. It is the least popular of the three mentioned here. You can learn more about it from http://www.oracle.com/technetwork/developer-tools/jdev/overview/index .html.

NetBeans is an extremely popular IDE that works with multiple languages. It is now owned by Oracle, but was started by student programmers who were looking to create more useful tools for their needs. Others asked to contribute code and soon it developed into a commercial program with plugins to extend its capabilities, many contributed by a large supporting community. Sun Microsystems, who developed and owned Java, bought NetBeans and released it under an open source license. When Oracle acquired Sun, it also acquired NetBeans; due to its popularity, it is worth a look. You can learn about and download NetBeans from https://netbeans.org/.

Eclipse was originally created by IBM, but has been spun off to a foundation created just for it. The Eclipse Foundation is non-profit and exists to coordinate efforts of volunteers and companies that contribute time, money, and code to this open source project. Like NetBeans, Eclipse is very widely used and popular. It supports multiple languages and there are many plugins available to extend its capabilities.

An SDK is a set of software development tools that are focused not only on one language, but something narrower like one software package or framework, such as the Android development SDK described in Chapter 43, "Beginning Mobile Development for Android." SDKs are provided by companies that want to encourage outsiders to write programs that run on the company's product, such as their platform (like a game system from Nintendo or Sega) or operating system (like Android or iOS). Many open source enthusiasts will not participate in writing code for these platforms, so SDKs are less popular in this environment than they are on Windows and other platforms. Also, depending on the software license used to release the SDK, the potential uses of the code produced using the SDK can be limited and not everyone is comfortable with those limitations. However, many SDKs are in use and if you want to write code for a project that releases an SDK, they generally contain useful code examples, tools, and documentation to make the task much easier. Do your homework and make a choice that you are comfortable with.

Ubuntu has an SDK for developers who are interested in writing apps to run on Ubuntu. More information will be available from the website at https://developer.ubuntu.com/en/apps/.

References

▶ www.cprogramming.com—A useful website for learning C and C++.

▶ http://gcc.gnu.org/—The main website for gcc, the GNU Compiler Collection.

▶ www.gnu.org/software/autoconf/autoconf.html—More information about the GNU Project's autoconf utility and how to build portable software projects.

▶ http://www.qt.io/—The main Qt website.

▶ http://glade.gnome.org—Home page for the Glade GNOME developer's tool.

▶ www.kdevelop.org—Site that hosts the KDevelop Project's latest versions of the KDE graphical development environment, KDevelop.

▶ *The C Programming Language*, by Brian W. Kernighan and Dennis M. Ritchie (Prentice Hall), ISBN: 0-13-110362-8.

▶ *The Annotated C++ Reference Manual*, by Margaret A. Ellis and Bjarne Stroustrup (ANSI Base Document), ISBN: 0-201-51459-1.

▶ *Programming in ANSI C*, by Stephen G. Kochan (Sams Publishing), ISBN: 0-672-30339-6.

▶ *Sams Teach Yourself C in 21 Days*, by Peter Aitken and Bradley Jones (Sams Publishing), ISBN: 0-672-32448-2.

▶ *Sams Teach Yourself C++ for Linux in 21 Days*, by Jesse Liberty and David B. Horvath (Sams Publishing), ISBN: 0-672-31895-4.

▶ *C How to Program* and *C++ How to Program*, both by Harvey M. Deitel and Paul J. Deitel (Deitel Associates), ISBNs: 0-132-99044-X and 0-132-66236-1.

CHAPTER **39**

Opportunistic Development

There are some among us who love to write program code. Others are able to write code but do not particularly enjoy doing so. Most of this section of the book (Part V, "Programming Linux") is dedicated to the first group—those who love to code and want to know how to get started using their favorite tools in Ubuntu. However, it also applies to those of us who just want to scratch a specific itch by coding up a quick program to do something useful and make it available to other Ubuntu users, but who are not interested in learning how to become a package maintainer, upload to the official software repositories, and so on. We call this process *opportunistic development*, where an end user codes up a quick solution to a problem. This is in direct contrast to systematic development with professional planning, requirements gathering, design, processes, and procedures. We have a couple of links in the "References" section if serious, sustained development and helping with official packaging is your ultimate goal; but to get started, let's look at a ways to help scratch that itch—to get something written and then make it available to others quickly and easily. We start with information about version control systems, then move on to a short survey of some initiatives in the Ubuntu community to whet your appetite and help you know where to look to get connected and get started if you want to do further work to make your program available to others.

Version Control Systems

It was difficult to decide whether to include this information in this chapter. On one hand, someone who only wants to scratch an itch quickly may not be interested in setting up a version control system. On the other hand, they are not difficult to set up, especially when used with the assistance of a code hosting site like the ones discussed in each section, and they are immensely valuable if code is to have a life outside of your system.

Although you can use `make` to manage a small software project (see Chapter 38, "Using Programming Tools for Ubuntu"), larger software projects require document management, source code controls, security, and revision tracking as the source code goes through a series of changes during its development. Version control systems provide utilities for this kind of large software project management. Changes to files placed in version control are tracked. Files can be checked out by one developer, changed in their local environment, and tested before those changes are saved in the version control system. Changes that are later discovered to be unwanted can be found and removed from the tracked files. Various version control systems manage projects differently; some use a central repository, others a distributed format where any and every copy could become the master copy.

The next few sections introduce the three most commonly used version control systems at the moment. You have certainly heard of others, and new ones crop up every few years. Each has its strengths and benefits. At the end of the chapter, in the "References" section, is a list of resources for learning more aboutGit, Bazaar, Subversion, and Mercurial to further your knowledge after you peruse this chapter's short and basic introduction to each.

> **NOTE**
>
> Subversion and Mercurial are still in heavy use, but most developers today have switched to Git and Bazaar for new projects. Keep that in mind as you read the next few sections.

Managing Software Projects with Git

Git was initially created by Linux kernel creator Linus Torvalds and was first released in 2005 to host all development files for the Linux kernel. It is now actively developed by a large team of developers led by Junio Hamano and is widely used by many other open-source projects.

Git works without a central repository and works from a different perspective than other version control systems while accomplishing the same goals. Every directory that is tracked by Git acts as an individual repository with full history and source changes for whatever is contained in it. There is no need for central tracking. Source code control is done from the command line, as shown in the following examples. You first need to install Git from the Ubuntu software repositories, where it is called `git`.

To create a new repository, access the top-level directory for the project and enter the following:

```
matthew@seymour:~$ git init
```

To check out code from an existing central repository, you must first tell Git where that repository is:

```
matthew@seymour:~$ git remote add origin git://path_to_repository/directory/proj.git
```

Then you can pull the code from that repository to your local one:

```
matthew@seymour:~$ git pull git://path_to_repository/directory/proj.git
```

To add new files to the repository, use the following:

```
matthew@seymour:~$ git add file_or_dir_name
```

To delete files from the repository, use this:

```
matthew@seymour:~$ git rm file_or_dir_name
```

To check in code after you have made changes, use the -m flag to add a note, which is a good idea so that others will know what the commit contains:

```
matthew@seymour:~$ git commit -m 'This fixes bug 204982.'
```

In Git, a commit does not change the remote files, it only commits the change to your local copy. If you want others to see your changes, you must push the changes to them:

```
matthew@seymour:~$ git push git://path_to_repository/directory/proj.git
```

Many open-source projects that use Git host their code using GitHub. You can find it at http://github.com.

Managing Software Projects with Bazaar

Bazaar was created by Canonical and first released in 2007 to host all development files for Ubuntu and other projects. It is actively developed and widely used, not only by Canonical and Ubuntu developers, but also by many other open-source projects. Launchpad, covered later in this chapter, uses Bazaar.

Bazaar supports working with or without a central repository. Then, changes are tracked over any and all files you check out, including multiple versions of files. Source code control is done from the command line, as shown in the following examples. You first need to install Bazaar from the Ubuntu software repositories, where it is called bzr.

There are two ways to create a new repository. If you are starting with an empty directory, use the following:

```
matthew@seymour:~$ bzr init your_project_name
```

If you are creating a repository for an existing project, enter the top-level directory for the project and enter the following:

```
matthew@seymour:~$ bzr init
matthew@seymour:~$ bzr add .
```

To check out code from an existing central repository, use this:

```
matthew@seymour:~$ bzr checkout your_project_name
```

39

To check your changes before you check them in, you can use `bzr diff` or `bzr cdiff`. They do the same thing, but `bzr cdiff` does so with colored output:

```
matthew@seymour:~$ bzr cdiff
```

To check in code after you have made changes, use the `-m` flag to add a note, which is a good idea so that others know what the `commit` contains:

```
matthew@seymour:~$ bzr commit -m "This fixes bug 204982."
```

In Bazaar, a `commit` does not change the remote files, it only commits the change to your local copy. If you want others to see your changes, you must `push` the changes to them:

```
matthew@seymour:~$ bzr push sftp://path.to.main/repository
```

To update the source code in your local repository from the main repository to make sure you have all the latest changes to the code from other developers, use the following:

```
matthew@seymour:~$ bzr pull
```

Many open-source projects that use Bazaar host their code using Launchpad, which receives more press later in this chapter as it is where Ubuntu development takes place. You can find it at http://launchpad.net.

Managing Software Projects with Subversion

Subversion was first created in 2000 as a replacement for an older version control system called the *Concurrent Versioning System (CVS)*. At that time, CVS was 10 years old, and although it served its purpose well, it lacked some features that developers wanted. It is actively developed and widely used.

In Subversion, you check out a file from a repository in which code is stored in a client/server fashion. Then, changes are tracked over any and all files you check out, including multiple versions of files. You can use Subversion to backtrack or branch off versions of documents inside the scope of a project. It can also be used to prevent or resolve conflicting entries or changes made to source code files by multiple developers. Source code control with Subversion is done from the command line, as shown in the following examples. You first need to install Subversion from the Ubuntu software repositories, where it is called `subversion`.

You can create a new repository as follows:

```
matthew@seymour:~$ svnadmin create /path/to/your_svn_repo_name
```

To add a new project to the repository, first enter the top directory of the code that is going to be placed into the repository. Then, create three subdirectories: `branches`, `tags`, and `trunk`. Move all of your files into `trunk` and enter the following:

```
matthew@seymour:~$ svn import project file:///your_svn_repo_name/your_project -m
➥"First Import"
```

To check out code from an existing central repository, use this:

```
matthew@seymour:~$ svn checkout file:///your_svn_repo_name/your_project/trunk
➥your_project
```

To check in code after you have made changes, use the `-m` flag to add a note, which is a good idea so that others know what the `commit` contains:

```
matthew@seymour:~$ svn commit -m "This fixes bug 204982."
```

To update the source code in your local repository from the main repository to make sure you have all the latest changes to the code from other developers, use this:

```
matthew@seymour:~$ svn update
```

To add new files to the repository, use the following:

```
matthew@seymour:~$ svn add file_or_dir_name
```

To delete files from the repository, use this:

```
matthew@seymour:~$ svn delete file_or_dir_name
```

Many open-source projects that use Subversion host their code using SourceForge, which also works with Git and Mercurial. Like the other code-hosting sites discussed in the following sections, SourceForge is a great place to find open-source software projects that might be useful to you or to which you might want to contribute through participation. You can find it at http://sourceforge.net.

Managing Software Projects with Mercurial

The Linux kernel used to be hosted using a version control system and code-hosting service that was free to use, but it wasn't open source. This was often a source of tension among free software advocates within the Linux community. Then, that service announced it was moving to a for-payment plan and gave some time for transition. Out of that decision, two new version control systems were birthed. Mercurial is one of them, and Git is the other. Both were initially written to host the code for the Linux kernel. Git, as it was originally written by the main kernel developer himself, Linus Torvalds (in just 2 weeks), won out. However, the wider open-source development community was the ultimate winner as two interesting and useful version control systems were birthed.

Mercurial was created by and development is still led by one developer: Matt Mackall. It uses a distributed architecture and is designed to be fast, even when working with large codebases. Its commands are similar to Subversion, which makes transition and initial use quick and easy. One interesting feature is that Mercurial is extensible; extensions may be installed from the project's wiki or written by users to change how things work or to add features without changing the original code. Source code control is done from the command line, as shown in the following examples. You first need to install Mercurial from the Ubuntu software repositories, where it is called `mercurial`.

39

> **NOTE**
>
> The chemical symbol for mercury is Hg. This is why Mercurial commands use `hg`.

To create a new repository, create an empty project directory:

```
matthew@seymour:~$ hg init your_project_name
```

Then add your files to the directory. `cd` into the directory if you are not already in it, and enter the following:

```
matthew@seymour:~$ hg add
```

To check in code the first time or after you have made changes, use the `-m` flag to add a note, which is a good idea so that others know what the `commit` contains:

```
matthew@seymour:~$ hg commit -m 'First commit.'
```

In Mercurial, a `commit` does not change the remote files, it only commits the change to your local copy. If you want others to see your changes, you must `push` the changes to them:

```
matthew@seymour:~$ hg push
```

To update the source code in your local repository from the main repository to make sure you have all the latest changes to the code from other developers, use this:

```
matthew@seymour:~$ hg update
```

Many open-source projects that use Mercurial host their code using Bitbucket. You can find it at http://bitbucket.org.

Introduction to Opportunistic Development

You have an idea for a program that will save time by automating a repetitive task. You plan for it to have a pretty GUI, and you think there are probably others out there who would like to use the tool after it is written. The problem is that you work full time, have a family, and already have a ton of side projects that do not get enough attention. You are either not able or not willing to sit down and study how Ubuntu packages programs to get them into the official software repositories. (If you are, see the links in the "References" section.)

It used to be that you had one simple choice at this juncture: Write the program and put it on a website for others to find—and hope that maybe someone would find it useful, make a DEB package, and upload it into either the Debian or Ubuntu repositories. That is no longer the only option if your goal is simply to write your tool and make the software available to Ubuntu users. Now, you need to be technically proficient at writing whatever code you want to write, and you need to be able to understand complex systems, but Ubuntu is lowering the complexity for getting that code written and making it available to the wider community. This enables developers who want only to scratch that one itch to do so without reading tons of documentation about tools they expect to use rarely or only once.

Launchpad

To get started, you need to sign up for an account on Launchpad (see Figure 39.1). Launchpad is an infrastructure created to simplify communication, collaboration, and processes within software development. It was developed and is supported by Canonical, the company that supports the Ubuntu community, but it is used by many software projects, including several that are not a part of the Ubuntu community.

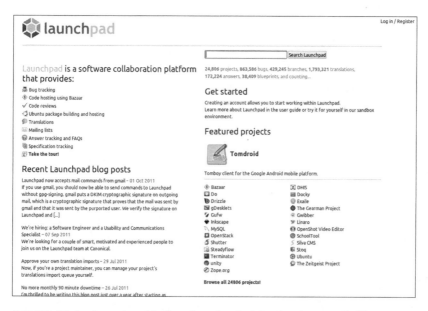

FIGURE 39.1   Launchpad is the place to start for development in Ubuntu.

Launchpad is where most Ubuntu development takes place, although some has moved to Git. It integrates Bazaar, the version control system introduced earlier, to make keeping track of changes to software code much simpler and permit those changes to be reverted when necessary while tracking who is performing the actions. Launchpad also incorporates Soyuz, which is a distribution and archive management software that handles the automatic package builds within Launchpad.

For developers using Launchpad, this means that the process became a bit simpler. They can concentrate on writing and editing their code and let Launchpad deal with keeping track of the changes and creating their packages. This is useful for active developers who write and maintain big projects that need source code version control and so on. It also hosts bug reporting and tracking, mailing lists, software interface translation, and much more. Most of this is beyond the scope of this chapter but of great interest to the serious developer.

What is of interest to us is that registered Launchpad users can create a *personal package archive (PPA)*. This is a much simpler way to make programs available. Anyone with a PPA can upload source code to be built in to packages. Those packages will then be made available in an apt repository that may be added to any Ubuntu user's list of source repositories and downloaded or removed using any of the standard package management tools in Ubuntu, such as `apt`, Ubuntu Software Center, and Synaptic. Instructions are included on the web page for each Launchpad PPA, describing how to add that repository, making this an easy method to share software that may be added and removed by even the most nontechnical end user. Figure 39.2 shows the PPA for the stable version of Google Chromium.

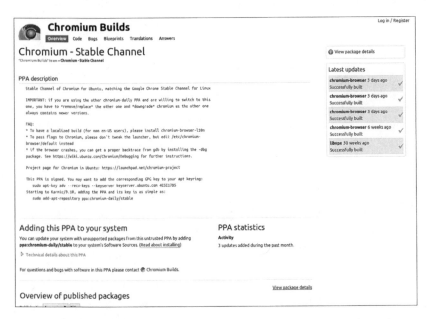

FIGURE 39.2   A Launchpad PPA for the stable version of Google Chromium.

Ubuntu Make

Ubuntu Make is a command-line tool that sets up your system for development use quickly and easily. It allows you to download the latest version of popular developer tools and their dependencies, enable multi-arch, and more. Install `ubuntu-make` to get started. Then, run commands like this to install tools:

```
matthew@seymour:~$ umake android
```

In this example, you will be prompted to accept the install path and Google license, and then Ubuntu Make will download and install Android Studio and the latest SDK, configure everything, and if you are running on a 64-bit platform, even add a Unity launcher icon.

See https://wiki.ubuntu.com/ubuntu-make to learn more about the packages available and get started.

Creating Snap Packages

One of the more exciting opportunities for developers is the new snap package format. Along with the basic installation and other details given in Chapter 9, "Managing Software," snap packaging also allows single packaged application to be used across multiple Linux distributions. Although snap packages are not expected to replace traditional packaging formats like DEBs, which we cover in Chapter 40, "Helping with Ubuntu Development," it is reasonable to expect snaps to find wide use for applications provided by third-party vendors like Mozilla, who are already committed to using it for their Firefox web browser, and for applications intended for use on devices like phones, routers, switches, and the new category of IoT (internet of things) devices (see https://en.wikipedia.org/wiki/Internet_of_things). For desktop applications, snap packaging enables the developer to submit free or even for-payment apps for review and inclusion in the Ubuntu Software application (see Chapter 9, "Managing Software").

The tool used to create snap packages is Snapcraft, available from http://snapcraft.io/. Snapcraft is designed to take your already-created application and bundle it with any and all dependencies for easy installation and updating.

Another helpful community project related to snap packaging is Snappy Playpen at https://github.com/ubuntu/snappy-playpen, which exists to share knowledge and best practices about snap packaging while helping test the packages that community members and others create.

Bikeshed and Other Tools

Bikeshed was started by Dustin Kirkland in September 2010 as a project to package a series of tools he wrote to scratch some personal itches that he had as an Ubuntu developer working on Canonical's Ubuntu Server Team or that he thought would be useful to others. Every good developer, systems administrator, and DevOps guru eventually writes scripts to perform specific tasks they find useful. This project began when Dustin gathered his scripts together and made them accessible to the world. The wider Ubuntu community is invited to give suggestions or submit patches to make them better. The project describes itself as "a collection of random useful tools and utilities that either do not quite fit anywhere else, or have not yet been accepted by a more appropriate project. Think of this package as an 'orphanage,' where tools live until they are adopted by loving, accepting parents." The slogan for Bikeshed on the Launchpad project page is "While others debate where some tool should go, we put it in the Bikeshed."

To give credit where credit is due, much of the content in this section comes, with permission, from Dustin's blog at http://blog.dustinkirkland.com, from direct communication with him, or from the tool man pages. Dustin also wrote Byobu, a tool that is covered at the end of Chapter 12, "Command-Line Master Class Part 2," and which contains some of the tools that have graduated from Bikeshed.

39

The first set of tools in this section are available by installing the `bikeshed` package from the Ubuntu repositories. Bikeshed sometimes works as an incubator, housing specific tools until they are ready to stand alone as a separate package or until they are accepted into an existing package. All the tools run from the command line, and most have useful man pages. (Others are still being written.)

The current contents of Bikeshed are as follows:

▶ **apply-patch**—wraps the patch utility and makes it a little easier to use by automatically detecting the patch strip level.

▶ **bch**—determines the files that have been modified in the current Bazaar (`bzr`) tree, opens `debian/changelog` for editing, uses `dch`, and appends a `changelog` entry for the current list of modified files.

▶ **bzrp**—is the same as `bzr`, except that output is piped to a pager to make reading easier.

▶ **col1**—splits and prints a given column, where the column to print is the name of the script program you are running (`col1` to `col9`). `col2` to `col9` are symlinks to `col1`; their behavior simply changes based on the name called. For example, instead of using `awk '{print $5}'` you can use `col5`.

▶ **cloud-sandbox**—launches a cloud instance and connects directly to it using `ssh`, with the cloud system running isolated as what is generally called a *sandbox*.

▶ **dman**—remotely retrieves man pages from http://manpages.ubuntu.com but reads them on the local system. This is useful to read the man page for a utility you to not have installed on the local system.

▶ **pbget**—retrieves content uploaded to a pastebin by `pbput` or `pbputs`.

▶ **pbput**—uploads text files, binary files, or entire directory structures to a pastebin. It is similar to `pastebinit`, covered later, but adds support for binaries and only uses http://pastebin.com.

▶ **pbputs**—operates exactly like `pbput`, except the user is prompted for a passphrase for encrypting the content with `gpg` before uploading. `pbget` automatically prompts the user for the preshared passphrase when the file is requested.

▶ **release**—creates a release of a project for Ubuntu.

▶ **release-build**—takes project information for a `bzr` project in a Launchpad PPA that uses specific parameters and builds the project as an upstream project that can then be released to Ubuntu.

▶ **socks-prox**—establishes an encrypted connection for tunneling traffic through a `socks` proxy.

▶ **system-search**—performs a unified search through a set of system commands, packages, documentation, and files.

- ▶ `uquick`—performs a quick server installation.

- ▶ `what-provides`—determines which package provides a specific binary in your path.

- ▶ `wifi-status`—monitors a wireless interface for connection and associated information.

The contents of Bikeshed are expected to change over time. Some of these tools may graduate to standalone tools, merge into other existing packages, or get added to more official upstream packages. You can always check the Launchpad page to find a current list of Bikeshed's contents.

The rest of the tools in this section are not an actual part of Bikeshed but have either graduated from Bikeshed and been spun off as freestanding tools or were developed individually by Dustin or others in the Ubuntu community. All the tools run from the command line and have useful man pages.

Other useful tools that you can find in the Ubuntu repositories include the following:

- ▶ `pastebinit`—is a script to upload a file or the result of a command to the pastebin you want and gives you the URL in return. It was written by another Ubuntu developer, Stéphane Graber, and you can find it at https://launchpad.net/pastebinit or from the Ubuntu repositories. By default, it uses http://pastebin.com, but it is configurable to use others such as http://paste.ubuntu.com.

- ▶ `run-one`—runs no more than one unique instance of a command with a unique set of arguments. This is often useful with cronjobs, when you want no more than one copy running at a time, but where a cronjob has the potential to run long and finish after the next scheduled run. Also see: `run-one-constantly`, `run-one-until-failure`, and `run-one-until-success`.

- ▶ `run-this-one`—is exactly like `run-one`, except that it uses `pgrep` and `kill` to find and kill any running processes owned by the user and matching the target commands and arguments. It blocks while trying to kill matching processes until all matching processes are dead.

- ▶ `keep-one-running`—operates exactly like `run-one` except that it respawns `"COMMAND [ARGS]"` any time `COMMAND` exits (zero or nonzero).

- ▶ `ssh-import-id`—uses a secure connection to contact a public key server, https://launchpad.net by default, to retrieve one or more user's public keys and append them to the current user's `~/.ssh/authorized_keys` file.

- ▶ `bootmail`—is called by `cron` to send an email any time a system is rebooted. It reads a list of one or more comma-separated email addresses from `/etc/bootmail/recipients` and then loops over a list of whitespace-separated files in `/etc/bootmail/logs` to construct the email. This is useful to know when remote systems are rebooted.

- ▶ `purge-old-kernels`—looks for old kernels on your system and removes them. This is a part of the byobu package.

39

▶ `col1`—splits and prints a given column, where the column to print is the name of the script program you are running (`col1` to `col9`). `col2` to `col9` are symlinks to `col1`; their behavior simply changes based on the name called. For example, instead of using `awk '{print $5}'` you can use `col5`. This used to be in bikeshed but is not part of the byobu package.

▶ `wifi-status`—monitors a wireless interface for connection and associated information. This used to be in bikeshed but is not part of the byobu package.

References

▶ http://subversion.apache.org/—The main website for Subversion.

▶ http://bazaar.canonical.com/en/—The main website for Bazaar.

▶ http://www.mercurial-scm.org—The main website for Mercurial.

▶ http://git-scm.com/—The main website for Git.

▶ https://launchpad.net/—Launchpad is an open-source website that hosts code, tracks bugs, and helps developers and users collaborate and share.

▶ https://launchpad.net/ubuntu/+ppas—Personal package archives allow source code to be uploaded and built in to .deb packages and made available to others as an apt repository.

▶ http://www.pygtk.org/, based on http://www.gtk.org/—PyGTK is the toolkit most used by Ubuntu developers when creating GUI interfaces with GTK in Python, which is what Quickly is set to do in the ubuntu-application template.

▶ http://glade.gnome.org/—A user interface designer for GTK.

▶ www.freedesktop.org/wiki/Specifications/desktopcouch, http://couchdb.apache.org/ and https://launchpad.net/desktopcouch—Desktop Couch is a data storage format used by Ubuntu One and many desktop programs for easy integration data storage, replication from one computer to another, and synchronization into programs.

▶ http://projects.gnome.org/gedit/—gedit is the default text editor in the GNOME desktop environment.

▶ https://launchpad.net/bikeshed—The main page for Bikeshed.

▶ https://help.ubuntu.com/community/PowerUsersProgramming—Another Ubuntu community page filled with programming resources.

CHAPTER 40

Helping with Ubuntu Development

Where the previous chapter talked about developing to scratch your own itch, this chapter focuses on how to become a part of a larger team, specifically the group of talented men and women who develop and package software for Ubuntu as a whole. Ubuntu is made up of thousands of different components. These are written in several different programming languages. Every component is available as source code, which is gathered into source packages. Source packages also include other content, specifically metadata describing things like copyright and licensing information, required dependencies, and build instructions for compiling or assembling the software for use. These source packages are used to build binary .deb packages, which are then included in the Ubuntu software repositories and made available for quick and easy installation by users. There are ways for anyone interested and willing to do a bit of study to use their skills to help.

Every time a bug is found, it only gets fixed if someone helps out and spends the time exploring the program code to find and fix it. Then, the fix only becomes available to the wider community if someone takes the time to build a new package that includes the fix and then uploads that package to an appropriate location in the Ubuntu software repositories.

This chapter has several parts. Each builds upon the previous, at least if you want to have a full understanding of the process. If only one part of the process interests you, say a later one like packaging, that is okay. You will benefit from reading the previous sections of the chapter, even if you only end up focusing your work on later steps in the process. You can participate in any part of the process, provided you are willing to learn how to do so. This chapter gets you started, but it is not the end of your required study. The process here is accurate, but there are more interesting and intricate details not included. Software development, especially on a big project, is not something to be done lightly or flippantly. For that reason, patches and bug fixes are only accepted from people willing to put in the effort necessary to produce detailed work with the highest quality. If a person hasn't the time or isn't interested in learning the steps properly, his software will probably also reflect this and is therefore not really wanted. The Ubuntu community is really nice, but they are also really busy. They will make time to mentor new developers and packagers who do their homework and make quality efforts, but it isn't polite to waste their time with half-hearted attempts at getting the details correct.

Introduction to Ubuntu Development

Ubuntu development follows a six-month cycle. The process begins before and at a Ubuntu Developers' Summit (UDS) with planning and discussion. Here, the goal is to unify the efforts of all those who will be involved to make the best use of limited resources. Everyone gets together via remote online participation, and in live discussions they make decisions about the priorities for the upcoming or the current release. The UDS happens once every three months, once at the start of a development cycle and once in the middle of the same cycle.

When a new release is created, is given a new code name. The release is referred to using this code name, such as "Wily Werewolf," until its official release date, when it starts to be officially referred to using the release number, such as 16.04.

Some development begins by taking the newest versions of software from upstream software developers, either via Debian or directly from the specific application's source. Some will have modifications, or patches, added to the code. All these are made into Ubuntu packages.

Other development begins internally, as there are some packages that have been written entirely by Ubuntu developers, including both those paid by Canonical and those who are volunteers in the wider Ubuntu community doing so for personal or community benefit or just for fun. These packages receive the new features slated for the release and are then made into new Ubuntu packages.

Testing occurs throughout the cycle, starting as soon as the first new packages begin to be uploaded. As a result of testing, bugs are often found. Bugs are problems with the software, such as errors that occur when the program is run. Bug reports are made using Launchpad, which is the issue tracker and code hosting solution created by Canonical for Ubuntu. Bugs are read by developers and community members and triaged into categories based on their importance. Critical bugs must be fixed before final release. Important bugs should be fixed as soon as possible. Other bugs might be irritating, but they are not vital to the operation of the program or the overall Ubuntu system, and, because of limited resources, they might be put off until someone has the time to deal with them. Every time bugs are fixed a new package must be made for the software so that it can be again uploaded into a repository for testing and review.

Alpha releases are made. Beta releases are made. Testing and bug fixing continue. Some software might be found to include new bugs that make the software unsuitable for use, so the previous version of the software is used. This is called "rolling back" to the previous version.

Eventually, the release day arrives. Everything works. The Ubuntu community rejoices and takes a week or two off. Then, it is time for the next UDS.

Setting Up Your Development System

Before you can begin, you must set up your system so that it works seamlessly with the rest of the Ubuntu community. There is a standard set of packages to install. There are some standard steps you must perform.

Install Basic Packages and Configure

The Ubuntu development community has created a convenient package that installs everything you need to get started. Install `packaging-dev` from the Ubuntu software repositories, which includes

- ▶ `gnupg`, the GNU Privacy Guard, which includes the cryptographic tools you need to sign your packages when you upload them to Launchpad

- ▶ `pbuilder`, which creates reproducible builds of a package in a clean, isolated environment

- ▶ `bzr-builddeb`, which includes `bzr`; together these serve as your version control and package management systems

- ▶ `apt-file`, which helps you find the binary package that includes a needed file

Set Up GPG

Generate your GPG key so that you can sign packages. Packages must be signed before they will be accepted for upload into the Ubuntu software repositories. This allows for tracking who is creating software and minimizes the risk of malicious software acts.

```
matthew@seymour:~$ gpg --gen-key
```

You will be asked what kind of key you want to generate. You can safely choose the default settings. Create a passphrase when asked. When this is done, a message like this one will be returned:

```
pub    2048R/38E0C789 2012-08-25

       Key fingerprint = 6363 387F 7455 8929 E6E2  4619 4798 DFD9 38E0 C789

uid    Matthew Helmke <matthew@matthewhelmke.com>

sub    2048R/BDE097FF 2012-08-2
```

40

> **NOTE**
>
> I created this GPG key specifically for this book and it is not used anywhere else. You won't see it in use on Launchpad, for example, or for signing packages.

You need the key ID, which in this example is `38E0C789`. Use this below. Upload your key ID to a keyserver, replacing `keyID` with your key ID.

```
matthew@seymour:~$ gpg --send-keys keyID
```

Create Your SSH Key

Next, create an SSH key that enables you to connect securely to another computer for file transfer. This is used when you're uploading source files to Launchpad.

```
matthew@seymour:~$ ssh-keygen -t rsa
```

Choose the defaults and create a passphrase.

Set Up pbuilder

Finally, set up `pbuilder` so that you can build packages on your local machine. Replace `release` below with the name of the release for which you will develop; for example, the release being developed when this was written is quantal. You can do this for multiple releases at the same time, and not only for Ubuntu, but also for Debian releases like sid.

```
matthew@seymour:~$ pbuilder-dist release create
```

It takes some time for all the needed files to be downloaded and installed, but when they are, this step is complete.

Create a Launchpad Account

Launchpad was described in Chapter 39, "Opportunistic Development." If you have already signed up for an account, you can skip this step. If not, open https://help .launchpad.net/YourAccount/NewAccount and sign up. You can develop for yourself without a Launchpad account, as in Chapter 39, "Opportunistic Development," but to develop for Ubuntu, you must have an account.

Set Up Your Environment to Work with Launchpad

This involves several steps and builds upon the previous steps you just completed.

Upload your GPG Key to Launchpad

Find your GPG fingerprint. Replace `youremail` with the email address you used earlier to create your GPG key.

```
matthew@seymour:~$ gpg --fingerprint youremail
```

Something like this will be returned.

```
pub     2048R/38E0C789 2012-08-25

        Key fingerprint = 6363 387F 7455 8929 E6E2  4619 4798 DFD9 38E0 C789

uid                     Matthew Helmke <matthew@matthewhelmke.com>

sub     2048R/BDE097FF 2013-08-25
```

Open https://launchpad.net/~/+editpgpkeys and copy the entire set of numbers and letter to the right of `Key fingerprint =` into the text box on the web page. Click Import Key on the web page. This fingerprint is used by Launchpad to check the Ubuntu key server for the key that you uploaded earlier.

You will be sent an encrypted email asking you to confirm the key import. You need to use an email client that supports OpenPGP encryption and enter the passphrase you created when you created the key to read this email. If you do not have an email reader that supports OpenPGP, you can also perform this step at the command line by typing `gpg` and copying/pasting the text of the email into the terminal window before hitting Enter.

Follow the directions in the email to complete this step.

Upload Your SSH Key to Launchpad

Open https://launchpad.net/~/+editsshkeys. Also open ~/.ssh/id_rsa.pub in a text editor. The contents of this file are the public part of your SSH key, so it is safe to share it with Launchpad. Copy the contents of the file and paste them into the Add an SSH Key text box on the web page that says. Now click Import Public Key.

Configure Bazaar

Bazaar is covered in Chapter 39, "Opportunistic Development." Here, all you need to do is tell Bazaar you who are. This is a two-step process. The first step tells Bazaar which name and email address it should use when creating commit messages. Replace my name and email address with your information.

```
matthew@seymour:~$ bzr whoami "Matthew Helmke" <matthew@matthewhelmke.com>
```

This second step sets up Bazaar with your Launchpad ID so that the code you sign and upload is associated with your Launchpad account. Replace *yourLaunchpadID* with your Launchpad ID. If you can't remember your ID, see where https://launchpad.net/~ redirects you to. The part that is automatically added after the ~ is your Launchpad ID.

```
matthew@seymour:~$ bzr launchpad-login yourLaunchpadID
```

Configure Your Local Bash Shell

The Ubuntu packaging tools that run at the command line on your development machine need to be configured with your information as well, in the same way that they are

40

configured for Ubuntu's parent, Debian. Open ~/.bashrc in your favorite text editor and add the following lines at the end, changing them to use your information instead of mine.

```
matthew@seymour:~$ gpg --fingerprint youremail
```

Reload the Bash shell configuration file.

```
matthew@seymour:~$ export DEBFULLNAME="Matthew Helmke"
matthew@seymour:~$ export DEBEMAIL="matthew@matthewhelmke.com"
```

If you are using a shell other than the default, Bash, then you need to configure your shell similarly.

Developing Apps and Scopes

If you want to develop apps specific to Ubuntu or scopes, which are an Ubuntu-specific way of interacting with content and services, that fit smoothly into the Ubuntu UI, this section is for you. In an attempt to draw developers in, Ubuntu has created a software development kit (SDK) called Ubuntu SDK. It is an integrated development environment (IDE) that contains a large number of tools and widgets to set up and create projects quickly and much more easily than doing so from scratch. You will find the details at https://developer.ubuntu.com/en/start/, from which you can download the Ubuntu SDK and find instructions and a quick start guide to help you begin. I haven't seen this in wide use yet, as it is quite new, but it looks promising.

Fixing Bugs and Packaging

This section covers the process for fixing bugs and packaging your code. It does not cover the mechanics of reading program code and fixing it. Here, it is assumed that you know how to program in the language used in the software you are fixing.

From a high level, the process is easy to understand. Here are the steps:

1. Find a problem, a software bug.
2. Download the source code.
3. Fix the problem.
4. Test the fix on your local machine.
5. Commit the changes.
6. Request that your changes be merged into the main source.

Finding the problems to fix is something you learn with time and experience. The next section, "Finding Bugs to Fix with Harvest," can help you. Other places to look, if you aren't fixing an issue you discovered yourself, are in Ubuntu mailing lists, Launchpad bug reports, and in community gathering places like the Ubuntu Forums or AskUbuntu.

Before you do any work on a bug, do an extensive search to make sure it has not already been fixed and that someone else is not already working on the bug. You should obviously look in Launchpad in the section for the specific package. You can also check the upstream and/or Debian bug trackers for open and closed bugs and the upstream revision history or newer release(s). When you know of a bug you want to fix, download the source code from the Ubuntu software repositories. To start, find out which file contains the code you want to work on. The example uses an imaginary application, `matthewsapp`. In all the examples that follow, replace `matthewsapp` with the name of the program or application that you want to work on. We know that the `matthewsapp` binary is located at `/usr/bin/matthewsapp`. To find the Ubuntu package that contains `matthewsapp`, enter

```
matthew@seymour:~$ apt-file find /usr/bin/matthewsapp
```

This returns output something like this.

```
matthewsapp: /usr/bin/matthewsapp
```

You can also use apt-cache to learn the source package for a binary package. Sometimes, source packages have the same name as their resulting binary packages. Sometimes they do not. Here are two examples.

```
matthew@seymour:~$ apt-cache showsrc tomboy | grep ^Package:
Package: tomboy
```

```
matthew@seymour:~$ apt-cache showsrc python-vigra | grep ^Package:
Package: libvigraimpex
```

In the first example, the binary `tomboy` is in the `tomboy` package. In the second example, the binary `python-vigra` is in the `librigraimpex` package. When you know the package that contains the source code you need, get a copy of the source code itself. You do this in Ubuntu by branching the source package. Launchpad manages all the code for source packages and is the place from which you will download and create a local branch. You fix your bugs in the local branch and test them on your machine and then submit a merge proposal so that code from your branch can be examined and merged back into the main branch of the code, to then be used to build a new package of the code.

Create a local repository on your machine for the code. The following again uses `matthewsapp`, which you should replace with the name of the source package you need.

```
matthew@seymour:~$ bzr init-repo matthewsapp
```

Change to the newly created directory.

```
matthew@seymour:~$ cd matthewsapp
```

Create a new local branch. Name it something obvious. Many Ubuntu developers name the new target directory the same as the original, with .dev added at the end, like this.

```
matthew@seymour:~$ bzr branch ubuntu:matthewsapp matthewsapp.dev
```

40

After you have done this a few times with packages already in the Ubuntu repositories, you can read the official Ubuntu Packaging Guide to find out how to perform similar tasks with code from other Ubuntu releases, from Debian, or from an upstream tar file. For now, we concentrate on doing this the easy way to help you get started.

Create a patch that will include the fix for the bug.

```
matthew@seymour:~$ edit-patch 99-new-patch
```

This copies the packaging of the file to a new temporary directory. Edit the files with a text editor, or use a patch to do so in a temporary shell, like this.

```
matthew@seymour:~$ patch -p1 < ../bugfix.patch
```

You can exit the temporary shell by entering exit or using Control+D.

Build a test package using your patch to test your changes. Replace *release* with the name of the release, such as quantal. Replace *package* and *version* with the name and number of the package.

```
matthew@seymour:~$ bzr builddeb -- -S -us -uc
matthew@seymour:~$ pbuilder-dist release build ../package_version.dsc
```

When the build completes, install the package from ~/pbuilder/*release*_result/ and test to see if the bug is fixed.

```
matthew@seymour:~$ sudo dpkg -i package_version.deb
```

Test it. Get it running. Try to break it. If you are convinced the bug is fixed in the software, only then is it time to move on. Feel free to repeat this cycle as often as necessary until it is really fixed.

When your changes are complete, create a new entry in the debian/changelog file.

```
matthew@seymour:~$ dch -i
```

Boilerplate text for the changelog entry that includes the first and last lines with placeholder text for the middle is provided for you. Use a text editor to edit the middle line(s) and include in your entry a specific bug fix tag that indicates which Launchpad bug you are fixing. Make sure you include where in the code you made the change(s), what you changed, and where the discussion of the change occurred.

The format for this is quite strict and looks like this:

```
matthewsapp (0.9.2-1ubuntu3) quantal; urgency=low

  * debian/control: don't bacon the narwhals at midnight in line 35 as
discussed on launchpad (LP: #3263827)

 -- Matthew Helmke <matthew@matthewhelmke.com>  Sat, 25 Aug 2013 13:29:01 -0500
```

Commit the change locally.

```
matthew@seymour:~$ debcommit
```

Push the change to Launchpad. Replace items in italic with your information.

```
matthew@seymour:~$ bzr push lp:~yourLaunchpadID/ubuntu/release/package/branchname
matthew@seymour:~$ bzr lp-propose
```

The first command sends your code to Launchpad. The last command opens the Launchpad page of the merge proposal in your browser.

Finding Bugs to Fix with Harvest

For many, this is a great place to start because it helps you find ways to practice while also helping the community. Harvest is a to-do list for Ubuntu development. Some of the bugs listed in Harvest are things that have been fixed upstream but have not been incorporated yet into Ubuntu packaged versions. Others are small items that no one has yet had time to fix; these are called "bitesize" bugs in Ubuntu parlance.

The bitesize bugs are the perfect place for newcomers to help out. Some of these are as simple as fixing typos in displayed text that is somewhere in a program's code. Fixing simple bugs at first lets you focus on learning the system. This frees you from wondering whether it is your programming skill or your packaging if you run into problems. The Resources section includes a link to the Harvest web page to help you get started.

Masters of the Universe

Fixing bugs is not the only reason people get involved with Ubuntu development and packaging. The Masters of the Universe—or, as it is better known, the MOTU—is a team of volunteers that finds useful software from upstream developers and packages it for easy installation from the Ubuntu repositories. This means that end users will find more software available without having to go and find source code packages and learn how to package and install themselves. You can find packages created by the MOTU in the Universe and Multiverse repositories. You have probably been using their work without even knowing it.

Everyone here starts as a contributor. To earn the MOTU title, you work with the MOTU team, who you can easily get in touch with and who will answer your questions to help you through the process. Some are very active, hands-on, and others are busier and might only respond when you ask questions. There are tons of opportunities. The References section includes a link to the MOTU web page.

40

References

▶ https://uds.ubuntu.com—The main website for the Ubuntu Developers' Summit.

▶ http://developer.ubuntu.com/—The main website for Ubuntu development.

▶ http://developer.ubuntu.com/apps—Useful resources for developing apps for Ubuntu to be run on multiple device platforms. Included here and available for download is the Ubuntu SDK, loaded with tools to assist in this task.

▶ https://myapps.developer.ubuntu.com/dev/—An additional collection of resources for creating Ubuntu apps.

▶ http://developer.ubuntu.com/resources/—A great list of useful resources for Ubuntu development.

▶ http://packaging.ubuntu.com/—The main website for the Ubuntu Packaging Guide. This chapter would have been much more difficult to write without this guide, and the guide goes into far greater detail than this chapter. This packaging guide is also available directly from the Ubuntu software repositories in the `ubuntu-packaging-guide` package.

▶ http://harvest.ubuntu.com/—The main website for Harvest.

▶ https://wiki.ubuntu.com/UbuntuDevelopment/BugFixingInitiative—The main website for the Ubuntu community Bug Fixing Initiative.

▶ https://wiki.ubuntu.com/MOTU—The main website for the Ubuntu community Masters of the Universe (MOTU) team.

▶ http://daniel.holba.ch/blog/—Daniel Holbach works for Canonical. He organized the original MOTU team. His primary job today is making it easy and fun for people in the community to join in and participate with Ubuntu development. His blog is an excellent resource.

# CHAPTER 41

Helping with Ubuntu Testing and QA

There are many ways to help the Ubuntu community create, refine, and promote the operating system. Some are highly technical, like writing code or packaging programs to be included in the software repositories. Some are less technical, such as helping promote Ubuntu locally or through blogging interesting news items from the community. Somewhere in the middle, leaning toward the technical side, is a task that is wide open for greater community involvement.

This is a rather brief and intentionally vague chapter. Testing by volunteers is something that requires more than a casual interest if it is going to be helpful to the developers and not an annoyance. For that reason, this chapter covers the basics of how to get involved and some of the opportunities, but not the precise details. If you are interested, and after reading this chapter we hope you are, the next step is to visit the websites listed at the end of the chapter.

Community Teams

Two community teams would love to see volunteers who can follow directions, be careful and methodical, and who notice details. Both teams work to refine the distribution during the development cycle to help make Ubuntu the best it can be.

The Ubuntu QA Team looks directly at the overall quality of the distribution, trying out default programs and configurations and trying to break things. The goal is to find bugs during the development cycle and make clear reports about them, trying to get them fixed before end users ever know of their existence. The goal here is product improvement and quality control or assurance.

These are big tasks. Even with several Canonical employees working on these full time, it is nearly impossible to test every hardware configuration or use case. It is also impossible to guess what creative ways users will attempt to perform tasks that developers have designed to perform differently. Testing as many of these options as possible is key when the goal is to create a positive experience for as many people as possible. This is why volunteers are both welcome and actively recruited.

These are also exacting tasks. Testing and bug reporting (or fixing) requires careful attention so that problems are reported clearly with steps that can be repeated by developers. This enables them to find where problems lie and more easily fix them. Not everyone is well suited for this sort of thing, but those who are able to be clear and precise and who can follow the directions given in testing plans and procedures are worth their weight in gold. You might not receive public glory for testing, but you will receive honor from those working with you in testing if you can do the job well.

You will notice some crossover in the team descriptions that follow. That is because the teams work together closely. Although each has a main focus, each may perform similar tasks from time to time. Even the individual team's web pages link to the others and offer similar information to help coordinate and direct any interested volunteers to the tasks they feel most equipped to help with.

Ubuntu Testing Team

Members of the Ubuntu Testing Team are probably best known for their work during a release week, when they help validate all of the CD and DVD images. They also operate during the release cycle testing beta releases and release candidates. In addition, they test update packages for stable releases before the packages are pushed out to users. They do this by enabling a new software repository called -proposed and trying out the software there before it ends up in the -updates repository. In addition, they help developers by coordinating communications and actively seeking and connecting additional volunteers when specific testing needs are encountered.

To get started, you need a Launchpad account. Then join the Ubuntu Testing Team via the team's page in Launchpad at https://launchpad.net/~ubuntu-testing. It is also a good idea to subscribe to the team's email list at https://lists.ubuntu.com/mailman/listinfo/ubuntu-qa. When testers are needed, the Launchpad team list and the mailing list are the initial points of contact for those that are asked to help.

There are many ways to get involved in testing; each has varying requirements on time and technical skill. Some tasks are quick and easy, and others might be more involved. Some of the tests are general in nature, and others involve specific features, applications, and hardware. Some tests are automated and require specific test software to be downloaded and installed. Others are given as a list of instructions. Opportunities exist for many skill levels and most time schedules.

QA Team

The QA Team has a stronger focus on developing and using tools to automate the process. This enables people using the tools to run a large battery of tests against a code base very quickly while ensuring they are probing precisely what is needed. Much of their work is useful for hardware certification, logic testing, and bug discovery. They have developed an Ubuntu developer-focused suite of tools called `ubuntu-qa-tools`, a library called Mago for the *Linux Desktop Testing Project (LDTP)* to simplify testing of Ubuntu within the wider realm of Linux desktops, a framework called Checkbox that tests and sends test data directly to Launchpad, and more.

Bug Squad

One of the first places people become involved in Ubuntu testing is with Bug Squad. These volunteers are the initial point of contact for most bugs filed with Ubuntu. They read bug reports to see whether the bug seems legitimate (for example, that it isn't something like "Ubuntu doesn't work," but is rather specific and measurable), that it is filed against the appropriate software package, and that adequate information is included with each report for the developers to be able to figure out the problem. If the bug report meets the criteria, the Bug Squad determines which developer or team should be notified. Sometimes during the triage process they might ask reporters for more information. They attempt to determine the severity of the bug and might assign a priority setting to the report.

Test Drive

One specific tool used by both volunteers and developers that deserves a mention is Test Drive. When he wrote Test Drive, Dustin Kirkland was an Ubuntu developer on Canonical's Ubuntu Server team (he still develops for Ubuntu as a community member, but has moved on to another job). He was looking for an easy way to download and run the latest daily development snapshot of Ubuntu using a virtual machine such as KVM or VirtualBox. Like any good developer who doesn't want to repeat tasks unnecessarily, he wrote a tool to automate the process. While creating Test Drive, he made it configurable to use different virtual machines with different settings according to the user's taste. It can even download and run any ISO that may be accessed via a URL, which means it could be used to download and run images from other distributions during their development cycles.

Test Drive is written in a way that enables even a nontechnical Ubuntu user to consistently test Ubuntu development releases. Test Drive is available in the Ubuntu repositories as `testdrive`. It runs from the command line.

When you run the program, you are offered a menu:

```
matthew@seymour:~$ testdrive

Welcome to Testdrive!

   1. Ubuntu Desktop (saucy-amd64)
   2. Ubuntu Desktop (saucy-i386)
   3. Ubuntu Alternate (saucy-amd64)
   4. Ubuntu Alternate (saucy-i386)
   5. Ubuntu DVD (saucy-amd64)
   6. Ubuntu DVD (saucy-i386)
   7. Ubuntu Server (saucy-amd64)
   8. Ubuntu Server (saucy-i386)
   9. Other (prompt for ISO URL)

Select an image to testdrive [1]:
```

Type a number to download and run a specific ISO. As you can see, the preceding example is from the development cycle for Saucy Salamander, which eventually became Ubuntu 13.10.

The Test Drive configuration is stored in a simple text file and is easy to understand and edit (although many using Test Drive will never need to edit it). Test Drive looks several places for the testdriverc file, including the default location /etc/testdriverc and in the user's /home directory at /home/matthew/.testdriverc and /home/matthew/.config/testdrive/testdriverc

Here is an example:

```
# This is the global configuration file for the testdrive(1) utility.
[testdrive-common]

# CACHE is the directory to cache the ISOs and disk images
# Default: $HOME/.cache/testdrive
#CACHE = /path/to/your/cache

# CACHE_IMG and CACHE_ISO will default to $CACHE/img and $CACHE/iso, respectively.
# You can set them explicitly if you want (especially interesting if you are
# trying to run the image off /dev/shm. Make sure you have enough space there!!!
#CACHE_IMG = /dev/shm

# CLEAN_IMG will remove the just-generated image at the end of run. By default the
image
# is kept, unless nothing was changed (i.e., the disk image was created, but no
installation
# was actually tried).
# If running the image off /dev/shm, then *by default* the image will be removed
```

41

```
(memory is a
# restricted resource, and we should not over-allocate it)
#CLEAN_IMG = False


# VIRT is the type of hypervisor to use
# VIRT can be either 'kvm', 'virtualbox', or 'parallels'
VIRT = kvm
#VIRT = virtualbox
#VIRT = parallels


# MEM is the amount of memory in MB to give to the VM guest
# Default: 384
MEM = 384
#MEM = 512
#MEM = 1024


# SMP is the number of processors to give to the VM guest if
# running in KVM.
# Default is the number of CPUs in the host
#SMP = 1


# DISK_SIZE is the size of the disk image
# Note that this will be a sparse, qcow2 file, so it should not actually
# take that much space on the filesystem.
# Default: 6G
DISK_SIZE = 6G
#DISK_SIZE = 10G


# KVM_ARGS is a string of arbitrary KVM_ARGS to use when launching the VM
# See kvm(1) for a comprehensive list of arguments
KVM_ARGS = -usb -usbdevice tablet -net nic,model=virtio -net user -soundhw es1370 -
vga cirrus


# Uncomment the following line if you want to hardcode the Ubuntu release
# and arch; otherwise, TestDrive will try to determine it dynamically.
#r = maverick
#m = i386
u = rsync://cdimage.ubuntu.com/cdimage


# Section for TestDrive (Command-line) specific variables.
[testdrive]


# DISK_FILE is the full path to the disk image
# Default: $CACHE/$ISO.img
#DISK_FILE = /path/to/foo.img
```

```
# The following line determines the default Ubuntu Flavor used by TestDrive.
# Possible flavors are:
#
ubuntu/kubuntu/xubuntu/edubuntu/mythbuntu/ubuntustudio/lubuntu/cloud-server/
cloud-desktop
f = ubuntu

# Section for TestDrive GTK specific variables.
[testdrive-gtk]

# The following line determines the default Ubuntu Flavors used by
TestDrive GTK.
# Possible flavors are:
# ubuntu/kubuntu/xubuntu/edubuntu/mythbuntu/ubuntustudio/lubuntu
f = ubuntu, kubuntu, xubuntu
```

A GUI version of Test Drive is available in the Ubuntu repositories. It is called `testdrive-gtk`. The back-end software is the same, but the GUI version eliminates the need for new users to interact using the command line.

References

▶ http://www.ubuntu.com/info/testing—An invitation from the Ubuntu website to get involved in testing.

▶ http://community.ubuntu.com/contribute/quality/—The starting point for understanding and volunteering for QA Testing.

▶ https://wiki.ubuntu.com/BugSquad—The Ubuntu Bug Squad.

▶ https://launchpad.net/testdrive—The official location for downloading TestDrive and assisting with its development.

CHAPTER 42

Using Popular Programming Languages

Students and developers who pay attention to either computer programming history or current trends are already aware of a vast swath of possibilities that deserve some attention. The goal of this chapter is to introduce many different languages available for you to use, some that are old and some that are new.

This short chapter does not teach you how to use these languages, but rather exposes you to them, making you aware of their existence and giving just enough information about them to help you decide whether each one sounds interesting or useful to you and points to resources to help guide your next steps. The introductions include information for installing and getting started with each language on Ubuntu. Sometimes the version of the language included in the Ubuntu repositories is a little outdated or is a free (as in freedom) version instead of an official, proprietary version. If you discover you need something more up-to-the-minute current or a version not mentioned, check the "References" section to find links to more information for most languages.

The organization of this chapter was tricky. The original idea was to order the chapter by how well known a language is, but that is problematic. Older languages generally have better name recognition, even though newer ones might be more commonly used. How do we measure popularity and use it to enforce order on a list of programming languages? The people who use them tend to form strong emotional bonds with those they prefer, just as geeks do with text editors (Emacs versus vi), email programs (web based versus Thunderbird versus Mutt), and more important matters like comic book universes (Marvel versus DC). Ultimately, it seemed like an alphabetic order would be best. If your favorite language is not included in this edition, and you think it should be included in future editions, please email your suggestion and reasoning to the author at matthew@matthewwhelmke.com for consideration.

You will notice an interesting mix of old and new languages here. Some have asked why these languages are included, especially the older ones. They are included because they are still in use in the real world. There may not be many or even any new projects being created using some of these languages, but if you are attentive, you are likely to find each of these in use somewhere. A quote from The Register illustrates this beautifully, "The venerable PDP-11 minicomputer is still spry to this day, powering GE nuclear power-plant robots—and will do so for another 37 years. That's right: PDP-11 assembler coders are hard to find, but the nuclear industry is planning on keeping the 16-bit machines ticking over until 2050—long enough for a couple of generations of programmers to come and go." (from: http://www.theregister.co.uk/2013/06/19/nuke_plants_to_keep_pdp11_until_2050/). The PDP-11 came out in 1970 and has not been produced since the early 1990s. Programming languages, like programs, always seem to outlast their expected or intended lifespan. Who knows? Learning that old language that everyone laughs about may benefit you with a well-paying, unique job as well as help you to think about human-computer communication in a different way.

Ada

Ada is based on Pascal. It is named after Ada Lovelace (1815–1852), who wrote the first algorithm designed to be processed by a machine, specifically the mechanical computing device created by Charles Babbage.

The language is most known for its use in embedded systems, especially in the aeronautics and avionics realm. Ada is well known as a reliable and efficient real-time language. It is most commonly encountered in aircraft systems, air traffic control and railroad systems, and medical devices. It is also often used as a teaching language for computer science courses.

Language highlights include static typing, concurrency, synchronous message passing, protected objects, modularization, and exception handling. Ada is object oriented, has standard libraries for things like I/O and containers, good interfaces to other languages like C, and works well with distributed systems and numeric processing.

To use Ada on Ubuntu, you write programs in your favorite text editor. To compile, you need the package gnat, which is the *GNU Ada Compiler*. You may want to consider gnat-gps, which installs the Gnat Programming System, an *integrated development environment (IDE)* specifically for Ada and C programming.

Clojure

Clojure is a newer dialect of Lisp that runs on the *Java Virtual Machine (JVM)*. It is intended for general-purpose use. It encourages functional programming and is designed to make writing multithreaded applications easier. Because of the close integration with Java, Clojure applications can be packaged and deployed to JVM environments without adding complexity. It also provides easy access to Java frameworks, and Clojure's data structures all implement standard Java interfaces.

Closures are a common in programming, especially in functional programming languages, including Clojure. (The name is rumored to be a mash-up of *closure* and *Java*.) Typically, variables are designed to only work within a defined function. A closure is a way to bend that rule temporarily. A closure starts with a function and allows the value of one or more variables from that function to be available outside of that function while being maintained in the function. Another way to phrase that is to say a closure is a combination of a function and the variables that were in scope at the time that the function was defined; the function can refer to those variables even if they are no longer in scope when the function is called. When you are working in a programming language with first-class functions that can be passed around like variables, closures are a convenient way to provide encapsulation without using objects or classes. An example use of a closure is when a function is encapsulated completely within another function but is still able to read the state of a variable that exists in the containing function.

Clojure is unlike most languages in that you don't generally install Clojure itself; it's just a library that's loaded into the JVM. You don't interact with it directly, you use a build tool and editor/IDE integration instead (well, except for when you are interacting using the REPL—in any case, you never run a tool called "clojure" from the command line). That process is a bit beyond the short introduction of this chapter; however, you can get started quickly using one of these two methods:

▶ Install `clojure`. Among other things, this installs a REPL (read-eval-print loop, an interactive programming environment) that can be used by entering `clojure` at the command line. When you install this package, you get what you need for using Clojure in a JVM, but you need to set up your development environment to use Clojure. See the documentation from each environment for instructions. Note that the most popular, perhaps even the de facto, build tool for Clojure is Leiningen, which adds some really useful functionality, such as the ability to manage project dependencies, start a REPL easily, and even install Clojure itself. See https://github.com/technomancy/leiningen#readme for more.

▶ You can try Clojure in a live REPL using www.try-clojure.org.

COBOL

COBOL, *Common Business Oriented Language*, has been around since the 1960s and is one of the oldest programming languages, and is still the dominant language for (legacy) business applications. The majority of big business applications, such as payroll and accounting, were written in COBOL, and most programmers who knew it well have retired. A job market exists for younger programmers willing to learn it and willing to support older applications that are stable and trusted and still running all over the place. This is especially true if you are able to understand the business processes modeled in COBOL and can integrate it with modern technology, which isn't always an easy task.

COBOL's syntax was designed to mimic natural human language. Often a newcomer can read COBOL source code and have a pretty good idea of what it does, even if the reader has little to no programming experience. An interesting feature in early COBOL that is deprecated in more recent versions is self-modifying code, which had the potential to create some interesting situations. COBOL has always been a little controversial, as illustrated by the time that Edsger Dijkstra remarked that "the use of COBOL cripples the mind; its teaching should, therefore, be regarded as a criminal offense."

In a 2012 survey in ComputerWorld, 46% of the respondents said they are already noticing a Cobol programmer shortage, while 50% said the average age of their Cobol staff is 45 or older and 22% said the age is 55 or older (see: https://www.computerworld .com/s/article/9225099/Cobol_brain_drain_Survey_results). Organizations are trying to move away from COBOL, but it is still in extensive use.

To use COBOL on Ubuntu, you write programs in your favorite text editor. To compile, you need the package `open-cobol`, which actually translates the programs into C and compiles them using `gcc`.

D

The D language is a lot like C, but much newer. It has similar syntax. It also has static typing. However, it is much newer and has some differences that are designed for convenience, power, and continued efficiency. In D, you are able to write large amounts of code without redundantly specifying types. Static inference deduces types and other code properties. Also, memory management is automatic and you have built-in linear and associative arrays, slices, and ranges. D has new methods of dealing with concurrency, scaling, and internal integration of features in a way that the presence of one feature does not harm another, for example offering classic polymorphism, value semantics, functional style, contract programming, and more. Like C, D is compiled to native code.

We haven't really seen D in use in the "real world" yet, but it is receiving a lot of attention in the academic and research world. The buzz among programmers is that D is very promising and could become a successor to C, as it is intended to be.

To use D on Ubuntu, you write programs in your favorite text editor. To compile, you must first download and install a package from the D Programming Language website at http://dlang.org/download.html. There are instructions on that site.

Dart

Dart is a new language and open-source project headed up by Google. The goal is a suite of tools and libraries focused on scalable web application engineering. You write code in Dart and it is compiled to JavaScript, which means that what you write will already be able to run in every major web browser and on nearly all servers. Dart is class based and object oriented. The code is concise without being enigmatic. The syntax looks very familiar and is pretty easy to figure out if you have some experience with other major languages. Dart allows you to create and use types, but does not require it, and is designed to be modular and scalable with the ability to organize your code with functions, classes, libraries and so on. The compiler can weed extraneous libraries from your code, such as those you included but never used, during compilation to create a smaller application. It can even minify as it compiles to JavaScript.

To use Dart on Ubuntu, download it along with the editor and tools from the Dart website at www.dartlang.org.

Elixir

Elixir is a dynamic, functional language based on Erlang. It has an interactive mode and an executable mode. The main differences between Elixir and Erlang lie in the realm of convenience. Elixir has its own package management system, macros, and build tool. It is compatible with existing Erlang libraries. Its main use at the moment is for building scalable web-based applications.

To use Elixir on Ubuntu, install the package `elixir`.

Erlang

From the official website, "Erlang is a programming language used to build massively scalable soft real-time systems with requirements on high availability. Some of its uses are in telecoms, banking, e-commerce, computer telephony and instant messaging. Erlang's runtime system has built-in support for concurrency, distribution and fault tolerance." Erlang is a declarative, functional language that includes real-time garbage collection and hot-swapping of code. It is primarily designed for distributed applications used in essential applications that require extreme uptime.

Erlang's greatest strength is its ability to create a large number of concurrent processes, each with low overhead, and allow them to communicate with one another using an asynchronous message handling system. In addition, the Erlang developers have a philosophy of development that emphasizes keeping things running, meaning that future stable Erlang updates should not break running code. They like to test extensively and try to break as much as possible in testing to prevent breakage in production systems. One of the technical editors mentioned a neat feature while reading this chapter: Erlang's processes can communicate with each other even if they don't live on the same box. You have to explicitly allow this in your code, but the ability is built in to the language runtime and syntax and is not a third-party library.

To use Erlang on Ubuntu, you write programs in your favorite text editor. To compile, you need the package `erlang`, which installs the Erlang/OTP runtime, applications, sources, code examples and the Erlang editing mode for Emacs.

Forth

Forth first appeared in the 1970s. It is an interactive, procedural, imperative language with typeless data that runs as a shell. Sets of instructions can be saved and compiled as bytecode programs. It is a very small language by itself and is therefore very useful in boot loaders and embedded systems, and has even been used by NASA in space applications.

On the surface, Forth is a simple language, but it is highly extensible. In essence, a programmer creates a dictionary, beginning with the small set of predefined words. These are combined in new ways to extend the lexicon and create new things that may be done. This is powerful, but it is also dangerous. The lack of standards can lead to less-than-stellar programmers creating unclear sets of vocabulary that make it impossible for anyone else to maintain what they have written. However, thoughtful programmers who are disciplined and organized have created highly complex, yet maintainable, programs in Forth that have been used for decades across multiple platforms.

Perhaps Forth might be described as a language for experienced programmers who can handle total control over the CPU and want to build sophisticated systems running in extremely limited environments. If you are old enough to remember HP calculators and their "reverse Polish" notation, where the operator is placed after the operands, you will find Forth familiar.

To use Forth on Ubuntu, install the package `gforth`, which is the GNU implementation of a Forth programming environment.

Go

Go is an open-source project and language being developed by people at Google. It is an expressive language that aims for concise, clean code and efficient use of resources. It has concurrency mechanisms built in to take advantage of multiple core machines and networked machines. Go includes a unique type system designed for flexible and modular code, and it's a compiled language that also has garbage collection. It is advertised as "a fast, statically typed, compiled language that feels like a dynamically typed, interpreted language."

To use Go on Ubuntu, write your programs in your favorite text editor and install the `golang` compiler. Install the `golang-docs` package for technical documentation.

Fortran

Fortran was developed by IBM in the 1950s for engineering and scientific applications. Its popularity spread quickly in areas of science that are dominated by numeric computation. Today, many of those same Fortran programs are still maintained and in use in fields such as weather modeling and prediction, fluid dynamics, and segments of chemistry and physics. In a published article from 2010, Eugene Loh, an engineer at Oracle, called Fortran the most commonly used and perhaps the ideal language for high performance computing (http://queue.acm.org/detail.cfm?id=1820518).

Fortran is a terse language in which complex applications may be written with relatively few statements. It is a procedural language with object-oriented abilities. It excels at numeric computation and is often used as the language in which programs are written to test supercomputers for speed.

To use Fortran on Ubuntu, you write programs in your favorite text editor. To compile, you need the package `gfortran`, the GNU Fortran 95 compiler, which compiles Fortran

95 on platforms supported by the gcc compiler. It uses the `gcc` back end to generate optimized code.

Groovy

Groovy, like Clojure, is designed for the JVM. It was written to enable features like closures and dynamic typing from popular languages like Python and Ruby to be used by Java developers. It uses a Java-like syntax, making it familiar to those programmers. It can be compiled into standard Java bytecode and used within any Java project. It can also be used dynamically for scripting, templating, or writing unit tests.

To use Groovy on Ubuntu, you must first install a JVM. Then, you need the package `groovy`. You can then run Groovy code in a shell by entering `groovysh` at the command line, in an interactive console by entering `groovyConsole`, or run a specific Groovy script by entering the script file's name at the command line prefaced by `groovy`, like this:

```
matthew@seymour:~$ groovy scriptname.groovy
```

Haskell

Haskell is a purely functional programming language. It has built-in concurrency and parallelism and good support for integration with other languages. In that sense, it is similar to Erlang. From the beginning in 1990, it has been developed as an open-source project with strong community input and participation. Haskell uses lazy evaluation, meaning that the evaluation of an expression is put off until the last possible moment, until its value is required. This significantly speeds up runtime by avoiding unnecessary or repeated evaluation.

To use Haskell on Ubuntu, install `haskell-platform`, a suite of tools and libraries that contain the most important and best-supported components. It is meant to be a starting point for Haskell developers who are looking for libraries to use. To compile, you need the package `ghc`, which is the *Glorious Glasgow Haskell Compilation system (GHC)*, a compiler for Haskell.

Java

Java was created by Sun Microsystems, now owned by Oracle, as a write-once, run-anywhere language. Java programs are compiled to a bytecode that will run on any JVM. A *Java Virtual Machine (JVM)* must exist on a hardware platform for Java code to run, but no recompilation of the program itself is needed for it to run on different hardware platforms. Java is object oriented, and writing program instructions for a virtual machine is generally easier than doing so for a real machine. Java syntax is similar to C and C++ but is a bit simpler and has fewer low-level abilities. It is currently one of the most popular programming languages. Originally, Java technology was proprietary and licensed for use by Sun. In May 2007, several years before being bought by Oracle, Sun finished relicensing and releasing most Java technology under the GNU GPL. (There were parts they could not relicense because they did not own the copyright to the code.)

Java uses automatic garbage collection to remove objects from memory when they are no longer in use. This frees programmers from thinking about memory management. It includes a graphical user interface library called Swing.

Most Java development occurs in an IDE, several of which are available from the Ubuntu repositories. The most popular include Eclipse (www.eclipse.org) and NetBeans (www.netbeans.org). Each of these include plug-ins that help the programmer include and use libraries, compile to bytecode, and do many other tasks quickly and efficiently.

To program in Java on Ubuntu, you write programs in your favorite text editor or IDE. To compile, you need the package `default-jdk`, which installs the Java Development Kit appropriate for the hardware being used.

JavaScript

JavaScript is an object-oriented, functional programming language designed primarily for scripting. It supports closures, dynamic and weak typing, and has a syntax that is influenced by C and Java, even though it is unrelated to either (except for the circumstantial name similarity with Java). JavaScript was designed to be used by the Netscape web browser as a way to run short programs on web clients. The name is a result of a mid-1990s marketing agreement between Netscape and Sun to try to leverage the buzz about Java and make JavaScript the shiny, new programming language for the Web. You will occasionally see JavaScript referred to using its original name, EMCAScript. The JavaScript trademark is now owned by Oracle under a license from the technology creators, including Mozilla, the descendant of Netscape.

JavaScript is easily the most popular scripting language for the Web, widely used in programming web applications. Combined with HTML and CSS, it is used to create interesting, diverse, and powerful websites. JavaScript has spawned tons of extensions and development kits such as Node.js and JSP. It is commonly combined with other technologies like XML to create interactive websites using Ajax. Information is often passed using *JavaScript Object Notation*, or JSON, which is rapidly becoming the successor to XML. Whether people love JavaScript or hate it, it is universally acknowledged as a "must know" technology for programmers today.

To use JavaScript on Ubuntu, you write programs in your favorite text editor. Nothing special is needed. Put the script somewhere and open it with your web browser.

Lisp

Lisp is slightly younger than Fortran, making it not-quite the oldest language discussed in this chapter. It was first released in 1958. Clojure, discussed earlier, is a dialect of Lisp. Lisp is designed to process lists. Linked lists are the language's main data structure. It was originally created to be used as a practical mathematical notation for computer programs but became popular as a program for research in artificial intelligence.

There have been many versions of Lisp over the years, and many dialects. The most commonly used "regular Lisp" in use today is probably ANSI Common Lisp, of which there are also multiple implementations. To use ANSI Common Lisp on Ubuntu, install the package `clisp`. Type `clisp` from the command line to bring up a REPL (from which you may exit by entering `quit`).

Many Lisp programmers prefer to use Emacs as their editor, which was written in a Lisp dialect called elisp. Emacs includes many useful tools for Lisp and has other plug-ins available. From here it is easy to save code in files, compile it, and enable it to be run a programs rather than from the REPL interface.

Another interesting dialect of Lisp is Scheme, which is also available from the Ubuntu repositories, but is not covered in this chapter.

Lua

Lua is a scripting language created in Brazil in the 1990s. It is similar to and based on Scheme. It is a dynamically typed procedural language with memory management and garbage collection. It is small and often used for embedded applications. It can be compiled on any platform that has a C compiler. Lua is also extensible with a reputation for being simple without being simplistic. It was originally designed for extending applications but is frequently used for standalone and general-purpose needs.

To use Lua on Ubuntu, you write programs in your favorite text editor. To run them, you need the package `lua50`, which is the Lua interpreter. Run a program by entering `lua` *programName* at the command line.

Mono

Although Microsoft intended it for Windows, the Microsoft .NET platform has grown to encompass many other operating systems. No, this isn't a rare sign of Microsoft letting customers choose which OS is best for them. Instead, the spread of .NET is because of the Mono project, which is a free reimplementation of .NET available under the GPL license.

Because of the potential for patent complications, it took most distros a long time to incorporate Mono, but it's here now and works just fine. What's more, Mono supports both C# and Visual Basic .NET, as well as the complete .NET 1.0 and 1.1 Frameworks (and much of the 2.0 Framework, too), making it easy to learn and productive to use.

There were some fears that Mono might cease to exist. In early May 2011, Attachmate bought Novell along with its SUSE Linux distribution. Novell headed up the Mono project. One of the first things that Attachmate did after the acquisition was cancel the Mono project. Then they laid off all the Mono developers, about 30 people.

On May 16, 2011, the lead developer of Mono, Miguel de Icaza, announced on his blog the creation of a new company called Xamarin (http://xamarin.com). The new company was created to continue Mono development and to build Mono applications. Many, if not most, of the original developers working on Mono at Novell are now employed by Xamarin. On July 18, 2011, it was announced by SUSE that an intellectual property agreement and perpetual license had been extended to Xamarin to continue to use and develop Mono as a platform and products that use Mono.

No one knows what the future holds for Mono, but at least we know it has not yet been abandoned. Mono and a few programs written in Mono are installed by default in Ubuntu 12.04, but plans for 12.10 were uncertain when this chapter was finalized for this edition. It is certain that Mono will continue to be available from the Ubuntu repositories, but whether it will be installed by default is not. You can learn more about Mono from http://mono-project.com/. Either way, to compile your own programs in Mono on Ubuntu, you need to install the `mono-devel` package.

OCaml

Functional programming never really goes away. Sometimes the most elegant way to write something is not by using a class or a method or a framework. Sometimes, the most elegant implementation is simply a function. This is why Lisp endures and why newer languages like OCaml and Haskell appear. Well, we say "appear," but in reality OCaml is a modern dialect of a very old functional language called ML, which was developed in the early 1970s. OCaml is used primarily, but not exclusively, in the financial world, in programs for electronic trading, markets, and investments. It has an advanced type system and supports not only functional, but also imperative and object-oriented styles of programming. It includes a memory manager and incremental garbage collection.

To use OCaml on Ubuntu, you write programs in your favorite text editor. To run them, you need the package `ocaml`, which includes two compilers. `ocamlc` compiles to bytecode and `ocamlopt` compiles to native code.

Perl

This language has a digital-only chapter, found in previous editions of the book, at www.informit.com/title/0134268113.

Perl is a well-established programming language that has been around since the 1980s. It started as a Common Gateway Interface (CGI) language for web servers. Over time, people have used it for scripting, systems administration, network programming, and a ton of other things. You will find Perl everywhere being used in ways never dreamed of by its originators. It is an incredibly flexible and powerful language. The downside to that is that it is also a complex language that some joking describe as looking like a cat walked across your keyboard. If you know what you are doing with Perl, you can work magic. If you can't remember what you did and didn't document it, you will probably end up hating yourself along with anyone else who has to interact with your code. All joking aside, it is worth learning, even just a little.

Perl is installed by default and already in use on your system. To use Perl on Ubuntu, you write programs in your favorite text editor. Nothing special is needed. Put the script somewhere and run it from the command line, like this: `perl yourscriptname.pl`.

PHP

This language has a digital-only chapter, found in previous editions of the book, at www.informit.com/title/0134268113.

PHP is another well-established programming language originally created for web development, but which now sees use in many other roles. Often it is used for simple scripts on servers. PHP is kind of a cross between Java and Perl. It is quick and easy to learn and commonly found. PHP is another one worth learning, even if just a little.

PHP is installed by default and already in use on your system. To use PHP on Ubuntu, you write programs in your favorite text editor. Nothing special is needed. Put the script somewhere and run it from the command line, like this: `php yourscriptname.php`.

Python

This language has a digital-only chapter, found in previous editions of the book, at www.informit.com/title/0134268113.

Python is one of the easiest to read languages out there. It has been developed with the idea that there should be one obvious "right" way to do things. As a result, most people who use it believe that Python requires very few comments in the code, because the code is easy to read and understand. For the most part, they are right. Python is also a power, fast, easy to use and learn language that is worth learning, even if just a little.

Python is installed by default and already in use on your system. To use Python on Ubuntu, you write programs in your favorite text editor. Nothing special is needed. Put the script somewhere and run it from the command line, like this: `python yourscriptname.py`.

Ruby

In Ruby, everything is an object. Every object can be given its own properties and methods. You can use closures (called blocks in Ruby). You do not need to declare variables, and only single inheritance exists. Ruby includes garbage collection, exception handling, and can be extended by writing extensions in C. Ruby was heavily influenced in different ways by Lisp, Perl, Python, and Smalltalk and was originally designed for systems administration-type scripting.

Most Ruby programmers seem to prefer using Ruby in combination with a web application framework called Rails, making what is known as *Ruby on Rails*. This framework is strongly tied to the DRY philosophy: "Don't repeat yourself." Every piece of information is stored in a single, unambiguous place. Ruby on Rails runs on top of a web server like Apache or Nginx and is extensible using Ruby Gems (rubygems.org).

To use Ruby on Ubuntu, you write programs in your favorite text editor. To run them, you can install the interpreter package `ruby1.8` from the Ubuntu repositories. Because Ruby changes often, the official Ruby documentation recommends *not* using a distribution's package manager, but rather downloading the latest version directly from the Ruby website.

Rust

Rust is developed by Mozilla, the people behind the Firefox browser. It is advertised on www.rust-lang.org as

"...a curly-brace, block-structured expression language. It visually resembles the C language family, but differs significantly in syntactic and semantic details. Its design is oriented toward concerns of 'programming in the large', that is, of creating and maintaining boundaries—both abstract and operational—that preserve large-system integrity, availability and concurrency."

Rust is not yet available in the Ubuntu repositories, but as it is being developed and used by people at Mozilla, it is likely to be of interest to a few of this book's readers and deserves a quick mention here.

Scala

Scala takes its name from "scalable language." It is designed to grow with its users' needs. Scala runs on a JVM. It is suited for both functional and object-oriented programming. Scala programs are bytecode compatible with Java and you can call either language from the other. Support for the .NET Framework is also available. Scala syntax is much more succinct than Java. Programs are generally shorter to write. Like Ruby, in Scala everything is an object. Types are inferred and do not need to be made explicit. Like Clojure, it suits the desire that many have to perform functional programming on a JVM.

To use Scala on Ubuntu, you write programs in your favorite text editor. To compile, you need the package `scala`. To compile, use `scalac` *sourceFile* and to run using the interpreter, use `scala` *sourceFile*.

Scratch

Scratch is a programming language primarily designed for educators and children. It is from MIT and was created with the hope of making it easy to create fun interactive stories, animations, games, music, and art, all while teaching creative thinking, systematic reasoning skills, mathematical and computational ideas, and collaboration. Creations can be shared on the Web and then accessed from anywhere. Scratch has an online component, but development happens on a local machine.

To use Scratch on Ubuntu, install `scratch`. Then, check out the website at http://scratch .mit.edu to get started.

Vala

Vala is a very new language. It was designed to make the lives of the developers of GNOME easier by bringing features from modern languages into C for use in the GNOME desktop environment development. The syntax is very similar to C#. Vala is a compiled language, but instead of being complied directly to bytecode, Vala is compiled to C, which is then compiled with a C compiler for each specific platform.

In C, a programmer must manually manage reference in memory. In Vala, this is automated if the built-in reference types are used instead of plain pointers. Vala also uses the GNOME GObject system to provide reference counting. For the most part, usage of Vala is primarily by people working on GNOME, which makes sense because this is the reason Vala was developed. Time will tell whether it receives wider interest.

To use Vala on Ubuntu, you write programs in your favorite text editor. To compile, you need the package `valac`, which is the Vala Compiler. You then need to compile the output from that with a C compiler such as the GNU C Compiler described in Chapter 38, "Using Programming Tools for Ubuntu."

References

▶ www.adaic.org/—The main website for the Ada Information Clearinghouse, an excellent resource for learning Ada.

▶ http://clojure.org/—The main website for Clojure.

▶ www.cobol.com/—The main website for Cobol.

▶ http://dlang.org/—The main website for D.

▶ http://www.dartlang.org—The main website for Dart.

▶ http://elixir-lang.org/—The main website for Elixir.

▶ www.erlang.org/—The main website for Erlang.

▶ www.forth.org/—The main website for the Forth Interest Group, a great place to learn more about Forth.

▶ www.jwdt.com/~paysan/gforth.html—The main website for Gforth, the GNU project's implementation of Forth.

▶ http://gcc.gnu.org/fortran/—The main website for Gfortran.

▶ http://groovy.codehaus.org/—The main website for Groovy.

▶ http://haskell.org/—The main website for Haskell.

▶ www.java.com/—The main website for Java.

▶ www.w3schools.com/js/default.asp—The W3C Tutorial page for JavaScript. The site is also a great place to learn HTML and CSS.

▶ www.lisp.org/—The Association of Lisp Users web page.

▶ www.clisp.org/—The main website for GNU Cisp, an implementation of Common Lisp.

▶ www.lua.org/—The main website for Lua.

▶ www.perl.org/—The main website for Perl.

▶ http://php.net/—The main website for PHP.

▶ **www.python.org/**—The main website for Python.

▶ **www.ruby-lang.org/en/**—The main website for Ruby.

▶ **www.scala-lang.org/**—The main website for Scala.

▶ **http://live.gnome.org/Vala**—The main website for Vala.

▶ **http://scratch.mit.edu**—The main website for Scratch.

▶ **https://help.ubuntu.com/community/PowerUsersProgramming**—A wiki page about programming using Ubuntu as your development platform.

CHAPTER 43

Beginning Mobile Development for Android

So many Linux users have embraced not only smartphones, but specifically those based on Android. Android is owned by Google and based on the Linux kernel and is one of the best-selling platforms for smartphones and tablet computers. Android includes the operating system, middleware, and several key applications. Middleware and application examples include an integrated web browser based on WebKit, optimized graphics libraries, media support for most formats, and structured data storage with SQLite. It also includes software for hardware-dependent functions such as GSM, Bluetooth, 3G, Wi-Fi, camera, GPS, and more.

Most of the Android source code is freely available and licensed using the Apache License. Google operates an online app store called *Google Play* where anyone with an Android phone or tablet computer can download free and for-payment applications to extend the functionality of their devices. Other third-party sites exist for the same purpose, thereby creating many paths by which one may make one's software available to Android users.

This chapter helps you get started writing software for Android on your Ubuntu machine by describing how to find and set up the development tools you need. It discusses the basic details you need to know as you consider whether you want to develop programs for the Android platform, and if so, whether you want to try to get those programs uploaded to and made available via Google Play or a third-party site.

Introduction to Android

Before we get further into the details of development of software for Android, a more detailed introduction to the Android architecture seems appropriate. Our description starts with the hardware and builds layer upon layer from that foundation.

Hardware

Although it has been proved possible to run Android on other platforms, the main target platform is ARM. ARM processors are 32-bit *reduced instruction set computer (RISC)* processors. Like other RISC processors, they are designed for speed with the idea that a simpler set of processor instructions creates greater efficiency and throughput. ARM processors are also designed for low power usage, making them ideal for mobile and embedded devices. Indeed, ARM is the dominant processor in these markets.

Linux Kernel

The first layer of software to run in the Android stack is a customized Linux kernel. Most of the customizations take the form of feature enhancements or optimizations to help Android and Linux work together more efficiently. Originally, Google made a point of contributing code it developed, but some of the features were rejected by the mainline Linux kernel developers for inclusion in the standard Linux kernel. This meant that to keep its desired code customizations, Google had to create a fork of the Linux kernel, which is permissible due to the license under which the kernel is released. Chapter 22, "Kernel and Module Management," gives an introduction to the Linux kernel.

Libraries

On top of the kernel run a set of software libraries. These are used by the higher-level components of Android and are made available to developers to use when writing Android applications using the Android software development kit (SDK), which is discussed later in this chapter. These libraries include a version of the standard C library (`libc`), libraries for recording and playback of many popular media formats, graphics and web browser engines, font rendering, and more.

Android Runtime

Some of the higher-level components of Android in the Application Layer (described next) interact directly with the libraries just described. Other parts of the Application Layer interact with the libraries via the Android Runtime. Android software is primarily written in Java, using Google-developed and specific Java libraries. That software runs on the Android Runtime, comprised of some additional core libraries running on top of a special virtual machine called Dalvik. The core libraries provide most of the functionality of Java. Dalvik performs *just-in-time (JIT)* compilation and is optimized for mobile devices.

Application Framework

The Application Framework is a set of useful systems and services that top-level applications can call. These provide standardized means of accessing system information, using device hardware, creating notifications, and so on. They are the same set that are used by the core applications included in Android, so end-user-created applications can have the same look, feel, and interaction style as those provided by Android.

Applications

Android comes with a set of core applications. These include a web browser, programs for text messaging, managing contacts, a calendar, an email client, and more. As noted earlier, Android software is written in Java.

Installing Android Studio

Android provides a bundled integrated development environment (IDE) with software development kit, which is a set of tools to enable the creation of applications to run on Android. Android Studio has versions available for Linux, Mac OS X, and for Windows.

Install Android Studio

Download the latest version of Android Studio from the Android Developers website at http://developer.android.com/studio/index.html. For Ubuntu, you need the Linux version, which is made available as a ZIP file. Unpack the file in the location where you want the development kit to reside (for example, `/home/matthew`). Doing so creates a new directory called `android-studio`. Note where you put this directory; you will need the information later.

Navigate to the `android-studio/bin/` directory and run `studio.sh`.

```
matthew@seymour:~$ studio.sh
```

The first time you run Android Studio, a wizard will appear and walk you through the initial setup procedure and then download and install any basic components you need.

Install SDK Packages

The initial setup installs the basics, but to start developing you will want other tools, platforms, and packages. This is done within Android Studio (Figure 43.1) using the Android SDK Manager. From Android Studio (Figure 43.2) select **Configure** and then click **SDK Manager**.

FIGURE 43.1   The main Android Studio options appear when you start it.

FIGURE 43.2   You can configure Android Studio to suit your preferences as a developer.

In the Android SDK Manager, select and install the tools and other packages you want (Figure 43.3). You will want to include tools for any Android platform/release for which you want to develop. It is strongly suggested that you do not remove any of the files that were installed by default to ensure the best results.

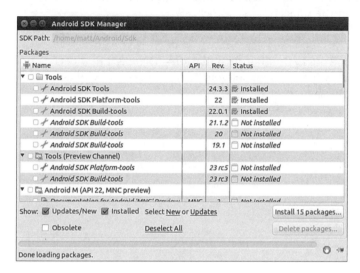

FIGURE 43.3   Use Android SDK Manager to find what you need and remove what you do not.

At a minimum, we suggest you install the following.

▶ From the **Tools** directory, **Android SDK Tools**.

▶ From the **Tools** directory, **Android SDK Platform Tools**.

▶ From the **Tools** directory, **Android SDK Build-tools** (the highest version listed).

▶ From the first **Android X.X** directory, which is the latest version listed, **SDK Platform**.

▶ From the first **Android X.X** folder, a system image for the emulator, such as **ARM EABI v7a System Image**.

▶ From the **Extras** directory, **Android Support Library**.

▶ From the **Extras** directory, **Google Play Services**.

Create Your First Application

Now you are ready to begin. Click **Start a new Android Studio Project** and use the wizard to enter the basic details of your new application.

References

▶ **http://developer.android.com/**—The main website for Android development. Most of this chapter could not exist if it were not for this site, which goes into much greater detail than this short introduction and is where this book's author learned most of what he knows on the subject.

▶ **http://developer.android.com/sdk/**—The main web page for Android Studio.

▶ **https://wiki.ubuntu.com/Touch/DualBootInstallation**—There is a new beta project being tested that may interest some of you. This provides a way to dual boot Ubuntu and Android on the same device.

CHAPTER 44

Developing for Ubuntu Mobile/Touch

Whҽn Ubuntu first announced the creation and release of their Unity interface, discussed in Chapter 3, "Working with Unity," and the idea that Unity was to be the interface of the future, many were skeptical. The idea that one interface could be used across a wide variety of devices seemed impossible. Today, Unity has matured and is quite usable on desktop computers and laptops. Not everyone realizes that it also works on touch screen devices like phones and tablets, and can even run on some TVs. Convergence is the word and the goal: one interface for all your computing, whether mobile, traditional, or something unusual like a television.

Now that the unification of the style, look, and feel of the interface has occurred, the next step in convergence that is needed is to deal with the issue of different forms of human-computer interaction. Traditionally, we interacted with a device using a keyboard. Then we added the mouse. Then notebook computing came along and brought touchpads with them. The newest devices use touchscreen technology. Right-clicking, left-clicking, hovering, and many other concepts are tied directly to the mouse or touchpad style of interacting with a computer. This is not how people use touchscreen devices.

Here is where this chapter comes in. Applications that are developed for touchscreen platforms can be adapted for traditional devices, just as traditional applications can be adapted for touchscreen platform use. But, what if applications were developed in a way that keeps both interaction styles in mind? This is the idea behind developing for Ubuntu Mobile, also called Ubuntu Touch. An app created to run on Unity on a touchscreen device can also be used on Unity on a traditional device using a mouse. Where you may slide your finger across a telephone screen, you can hold down a mouse button and move the mouse cursor in the same manner on a laptop screen to perform the same action. No more having to learn new methods of interacting every time you pick up a new type of device!

Developing in this manner is new. The process is still being adjusted as Ubuntu is learning what works well, what doesn't, and gets advice from groups like the Ubuntu Carrier Advisory Group (CAG). CAG is made up of representatives of and advisors from many of the world's largest mobile phone companies and was set up to help guide Ubuntu in creating a platform that they will find useful as well as one that users will love.

So, because this is new, what is written is this chapter is subject to probable and sometimes rapid change. Check the resources available in the Reference section if you discover something that seems different from what is expressed in this chapter (please send me a note at matthew@matthewhelmke.com so that I can be certain to include the adjustment when I update future editions).

Install the SDK

The Ubuntu Software Development Kit (SDK) includes a set of development tools to make the job of writing applications easier and faster. It isn't yet in the Ubuntu repositories. It is, however, in a Personal Package Archive (PPA), which are described in Chapter 39, "Opportunistic Development." It is stable and in active use by Ubuntu developers writing applications right now. It is also the default and recommended method, so let's use it.

First, we will add the PPA to our sources, like this:

```
matthew@seymour:~$ sudo add-apt-repository ppa:ubuntu-sdk-team/ppa
```

Update your local cache of what is available in the software repositories, so that the contents of this PPA are included:

```
matthew@seymour:~$ sudo apt-get update
```

Install the SDK:

```
matthew@seymour:~$ sudo apt-get install ubuntu-sdk
```

Create Your First Application

Writing apps for Ubuntu Mobile is done in the SDK. Launch the wizard from within the SDK menu at **File > New File or Project**. This will walk you through the process and is quite simple for even moderately experienced developers.

From here, read the official documentation listed under Resources. The processes and procedures are undergoing rapid development and change, making print versions of any documentation quickly obsolete.

References

▶ **http://developer.ubuntu.com/en/phone/**—The website for official documentation from Ubuntu about getting started as an Ubuntu developer for mobile.

▶ **http://www.ubuntu.com/phone**—The main web page for Ubuntu on phones.

▶ **http://www.ubuntu.com/tablet**—The main web page for Ubuntu on tablets.

▶ **http://www.ubuntu.com/tv**—The main web page for Ubuntu on televisions.

▶ **https://wiki.ubuntu.com/Touch/**—The main web page for Ubuntu Touch.

▶ **https://wiki.ubuntu.com/Touch/Emulator**—The main web page for the Ubuntu Touch Emulator, a tool to help with development for Touch while using a traditional device like a desktop or laptop.

44

Index

Symbols

C

E

F

M

P

Q

S